Computers in You

Roberta L. Baber
Fresno City College
&
Marilyn Wertheimer Meyer
Fresno City College

Computers in Your Future 98

Copyright ©1998 by Que® Education and Training

Library of Congress Catalog No.: 97-066688

ISBN: 1-57576-838-0

99 98   2

Interpretation of the printing code: the rightmost double-digit number is the year of the book's printing; the rightmost single-digit number, the number of the book's printing. For example, a printing code of 98-5 shows that the fifth printing of the book occurred in 1998.

Screens reproduced in this book were created using Collage Plus from Inner Media, Inc., Hollis, NH.

This book was produced digitally by Macmillan Computer Publishing and manufactured using computer-to-plate technology (a film-less process) by GAC/Shepard Poorman, Indianapolis, Indiana.

Publisher: Robert Linsky

Executive Editor: Kyle Lewis

Director of Product Marketing: Susan L. Kindel

Managing Editor: Caroline Roop

Editorial Assistant: Angie Denny

Cover Designer: Karen Ruggles

Cover Illustration: Michael McGurl

Book Designer: Gary Adair

Production Team: Daniela Raderstorf & Pamela Woolf

Developed by Kezia Endsley and Susan Pink

Copy edited by Jeannine Freudenberger and David F. Noble

Technical edit by Garrett Pease

Composed in *Stone Serif* and *MCPdigital* by Que Corporation

Dedication

To our families, for their love, patience, understanding, and inspiration.

Jim, Greg, Erin, and Matt—R. B.

Dan and Matt—M. M.

Brief Table of Contents

Detailed Table of Contents

Part IV   Computers Shaping Society and Your Future

Topical Sidebars

Preface

For our readers...

Computers in Your Future 98 carries forward Que Education and Training's pioneering effort to show how computers affect our daily lives and how they will continue to have an increasing impact on our future. The common-sense, real-world emphasis of the first edition is evident in this 1998 edition. The many student learning aids present in the first and second editions appear in this edition, changed only to reflect current developments in the world of computers and computing. Among the special features are the following:

➤ **Sidebars** address current events in the computer world. In many cases, these events affect your personal or business life. Some examples tell you how computers are used all over the world:

  ➤ Computers aid in scientific research, education, and law enforcement.

  ➤ The Year 2000 problem and its potential impact on businesses and consumers worldwide. Information Technology professionals are in such short supply that the U.S. government is taking aggressive steps to help solve the problem.

  ➤ Computers are used for timing and scoring at the Indy 500.

  ➤ Virtual reality and computers help people overcome all kinds of handicaps.

➤ **TechTalk** margin notes provide clear definitions of computer jargon.

➤ **BITS** margin notes offer interesting sidelights to the text.

To help students learn, the authors have provided this information in *byte*-sized portions called lessons. Each lesson deals with one topic in a clear, succinct presentation. Because these lessons are modular, they can be covered in any sequence.

Each lesson opens with an outline of the major topics in that lesson. For easy review, the bulleted learning objectives, immediately following the outline, list the important concepts covered in the lesson. Key terms appear in boldface in the text and are defined within the lesson; they are also listed at the end of the lesson and are defined again in the Glossary at the end of the book. The end-of-lesson material provides additional self-testing through matching, multiple-choice, completion, and review questions. In the past decade, many educators have voiced the concern that schools have overemphasized the mastery of basic facts to the neglect of thinking skills. To address this issue, *Computers in Your Future 98* also includes brief **Critical Thinking** projects in both the book and the *Test Bank*. **On-line Discovery** sections provide practice in using the World Wide Web to research Internet resources and answer relevant questions.

To give you an extended review and greater success in this course, the authors of this text have written a **Student Study Guide**. This supplement provides a chapter overview; lesson outlines; learning objectives; key terms; and a large number of true/false, multiple-choice, matching, completion, and critical thinking questions.

Que Education & Training created **Computers in Your Future 98 Interactive Edition** to provide students with a unique, discovery-based learning tool. The *Interactive Edition* includes interactive multimedia explorations of key textbook topics, seamless integration of the World Wide Web, personalized study guides, and electronic review exercises with e-mailable results.

For the Instructor...

Que Education & Training offers a dynamic and useful collection of teaching and learning resources for qualified adopters of *Computers in Your Future 98*.

Computers in Your Future 98 Annotated Instructor's Edition (1-58076-079-1)

Computers in Your Future 98 Annotated Instructor's Edition is chock full of teaching resources and includes a fully annotated version of the student text showing how and when to integrate the *Interactive Edition*, QuePresents, and www.ciyf98.com. The annotations include ideas for alternative lecture topics, tips on dealing with common student questions, and other useful information designed to help you in the classroom.

Computers in Your Future 98 Instructor's Manual (1-58076-080-5)

The *Instructor's Manual* provides chapter outlines with learning objectives and lesson outlines. The manual also gives the answers to all the end-of-lesson material in the student edition. For the novice teacher, as well as seasoned instructors looking for new ways to teach this course, the *Instructor's Manual* includes Teaching Tips, Projects and Activities, and Lecture Notes beyond those presented in the *Annotated Instructor's Edition*.

Computers in Your Future 98 QuePresents (1-58076-084-8)

QuePresents is a CD-ROM packed with a library of PowerPoint 97 presentations designed to enhance your classroom presentations. These presentations include a variety of materials used by the author team in their classrooms. QuePresents can be used as is or customized to meet the needs of your students.

QueTest by inQsit (1-58076-081-3)

The finest Web-based testing system available! QueTest by inQsit (developed by Ball State University) utilizes the World Wide Web and Web technologies to present questions, record answers, and return customized graded results. HTML can be directly integrated within the test modules so graphics, sound, videos, and links to additional Web/Internet resources may be added. An internal security system prevents unauthorized access to questions, answer keys, and student scores. QueTest comes with a vault of questions for *Computers in Your Future 98*. QueTest uses Smart Wizards to help you create your tests and has a variety of question types that can be selected at will or at random. QueTest supports proctored tests, transference of existing test questions, and test item analysis!

www.ciyf98.com

This Web site is an extraordinary and unique teaching and learning resource. We've moved beyond the usual publisher Web sites to create a truly useful place for you and your students to expand your horizons. ciyf98.com includes a Listserve, Chat room, Message Boards, TEQNews clipping service that provides customizable news for your classes, and the On-line Discovery Zone.

Computers in Your Future 98 Interactive Edition (1-58076-082-1)

An innovative discovery-based learning tool helps you blow the covers off the textbook by offering interactive multimedia explorations of key textbook topics, seamless integration of the World Wide Web, personalized study guides, and electronic review exercises with e-mailable results.

➤ Navigation is easy and intuitive because it's done through Internet Explorer or Netscape Navigator.

➤ QueLabs provide students with opportunities to experience many of the concepts covered in the text. Each Lab includes sound, video, interactive review questions, and a hands-on exercise for a complete learning experience.

➤ QueNotes allows students to build a personal study guide by cutting and pasting or adding their own materials.

➤ The end-of-chapter Review Exercises are now available electronically with the capability for your students to e-mail their results to you!

➤ "Whacked" World Wide Web sites are included so that students without live access to the Web have an opportunity to experience the Web's power.

For more information about Que E&T's extraordinary teaching and learning resources, please contact your local Macmillan Computer Publishing representative. To obtain the name of your representative, call 1-800-428-5331. You may also contact us on the Web at http://www.queet.com

Que Education & Training's Software Applications Series

Que Education & Training offers a variety of computer lab applications manuals to suit the needs of your students. Any of these manuals can be used in conjunction with *Computers in Your Future 98* or as stand-alone tutorials.

The *Quest* Custom Publishing Program...

Que E&T also offers custom publishing that is as easy as 1,2,3 through our Quest Custom Publishing Program. Please contact your local Macmillan Computer Publishing representative for more details. To obtain the name of your representative, call 1-800-428-5331. You may also contact us on the Web at http://www.queet.com

SERIES	Essentials	Complete	Learn	MOUS Essentials	SmartStarts
Applications	Windows 3.1/95/98	Windows 95/98	Windows 95/98	Windows 95/98	DOS/Windows 3.1/95/98
Level B = Beginning I= Intermediate A = Advanced	B, I, A for all Win 95 and higher	B - A	B	Proficient and Expert	B - I
Course Length	8-12 contact hours	Full semester	6-8 contact hours	8-12 contact hours	12-24 contact hours
Features	• 4 color (most first levels) • Project orientation teaches problem solving • Step-by-step approach and over-sized screenshots • End-of-chapter exercises combine skill assessment and application • All first level Office 97 books include Screen ID and Challenge exercises	• 4 color • Business problem orientation • Full integration of the World Wide Web • Cross-curricular projects	• 4 color • Screen shots show results of steps taken • Learn On-Demand software	• 4 color • Microsoft-approved for MOUS program • Included appendix on Certification process	• 2 color • Skills focus emphasizes practical knowledge • Material is organized around objectives • End-of-chapter exercises integrate material from earlier exercises
Learning Tools	• Why Would I Do This? • Jargon Watch • If You Have Problems • Inside Stuff • Running marginal glossary • Lesson objectives	• In Depth • Caution, Shortcuts • Finished project illustrates each lesson opener	• Completed screen shots at chapter opener • In Depth, Caution, and Shortcuts	• Why Would I Do This? • If You Have Problems • Inside Stuff • Required activities and MS Test Notes give students guidelines and tips for preparing for the certification exams	• Objectives and end-of-chapter summaries • Running marginal glossary • "Notes" • Running cases
Resources	• Instructor's Manual with data disks • Annotated Instructor's • Manuals (Office 97 apps only) • QueTest (Office 97 apps only) • Virtual Tutor CD-ROM	• Annotated Instructor's Editions • QueTest	• Annotated Instructor's Manual w/ data disk • QueTest • Learn On-Demand	• Annotated Instructor's Edition	• Instructor's Manual with data disk

About Que Education and Training...

We are the educational publishing imprint of Macmillan Computer Publishing, the world's leading computer book publisher. Macmillan Computer Publishing books have taught more than 20 million people how to be productive with their computers.

This expertise in producing high-quality computer books is evident in every Que Education and Training title. The same tried-and-true authoring and product development process that makes Macmillan Computer Publishing books best-sellers is used to ensure that every Que Education and Training textbook has the most accurate and up-to-date information. Experienced and respected college instructors write and review every manuscript to provide class-tested pedagogy. Every Que Education and Training book receives a thorough "tech edit;" quality assurance editors at Macmillan Computer Publishing check every keystroke and command in our books to guarantee that the instructions are clear and precise.

Above all, Macmillan Computer Publishing and, in turn, Que Education and Training have years of experience in meeting the learning demands of computer users in schools, homes, and businesses. This "real world" experience means that Que Education and Training textbooks help students understand how the skills they learn will be applied and why these skills are important.

Que Education and Training. Helping your students see the possibilities.

Acknowledgments

We, the authors, have discovered that a partnership is much more than the sum of its parts. We have come to appreciate each other's work, and the work of our hidden partners at Que Education and Training of Macmillan Publishing.

Que Education and Training is grateful for the assistance provided by the following reviewers of the first edition: Virginia T. Anderson, Ph.D., University of North Dakota; Greg Alexander, Davenport College; Bruce L. Black, Polk Community College; Kelly Black, California State University, Fresno; Frederick W. Bounds, DeKalb College; Robert M. Burris, Indiana University (IUPUI); Connie Campbell, Cincinnati State Technical and Community College; Mark Ciampa, Volunteer State Community College; James R. Daniels, St. Catherine College; Marvin Daugherty, Indiana VoTech College; Barbara B. Denison, Wright State University; Lynne Fairservice, Royal Melbourne Institute of Technology, Australia; Terry Fries, Jefferson Community College; John T. Gorgone, Bentley College; Jan Harris, Lewis and Clark Community College; Patricia Harris, Mesa Community College; Shirley Hudson, Southern Illinois University at Carbondale; Richard Lee Kerns, East Carolina University; Terry Kibiloski, Sullivan College; Ronald J. Kizior, Loyola University; Sim Kim Lau, University of Wollongong; Anthony Mann, Sinclair Community College; Donna Matherly, Tallahassee Community College; Anne Olsen, Wingate College; Pat Ormand, Utah Valley Community College; Sally Peterson, University of Wisconsin, Madison; Sylvia Clark Pulliam, Western Kentucky University; Dolores Pusins, Hillsborough Community College, Tampa; Cliff Ragsdale, Virginia Polytechnic Institute and State University; William Rayburn, Austin Peay State University; Dorothy Reiss, Manchester Community-Technical College; Linda Salchenberger, Loyola University, Chicago; Luann K. Stemler, Illinois State University; Dale Underwood, Lexington Community College; Karen Weil-Yates, Hagerstown Junior College; Melinda White, Santa Fe Community College, Gainesville, FL; Janice Willis, College of San Mateo; Judy Wright, Wayne State University; and Alan Wyatt, Discovery Computing Inc.

Que Education and Training is grateful also for the assistance provided by the following reviewers of the 98 edition: Michelle Bokoros, Manchester Community College; Mike Bozonie, Metropolitan State University; Wiliam F. Borowski, Trident Technical College; Sally Kurz, Coastline Community College; Dr. Jerome Lewis, University of South Carolina, Spartanburg; Dr.

Donna Matherly, Tallahassee Community College; Phillip Morrison, Aiken Technical College; Barbara B. Neequaye, Central Piedmont Community College; Femi Onabajo, Galveston College; Banks Peacock, Wayne Community College; Samantha Penrod, Purdue University, Calumet; Judith Scheeren, Westmoreland County Community College; Michael Shook, Embry-Riddle Aeronautical University; and Garrett Pease, Discovery Computing, for his technical review.

A hearty thank-you to the following individuals and firms for their help in gathering information about new and unusual uses of computers: Dr. Wayman Baker, National Oceanic and Atmospheric Administration (NOAA); C-CAD; Ty Cheatham, MicroServices; Chrysler Corporation; The CocaCola Company; Alice Curtin, AT&T Consumer Interactive Video Services; Frank DiGialleonardo, NOAA; Electronic Arts; Roger Frizzell, GTE; Art Graham, United States Auto Club; Indiana Pacers; Dean P. Inman, Ph.D., Oregon Research Institute, Virtual Reality Labs; Robert Kidwell, NOAA; Janis Lamar, TRW Information Services; Bisil "Bud" Littin, National Weather Service; Stephen Lord, National Meteorological Center; Andre F. Marion, President, Applied Biosystems Division of The Perkin Elmer Corporation; Steve Merritt, PianoDisc; Danielle Miller, The GLOBE Program; North Slope Borough School District; Ann Redelfs, San Diego SuperComputer Center; Hank Roden, The GLOBE Program; SEGA; Dr. Joseph Shaffer, National Weather Service, Severe Storm Watch Center; John Stackpole, National Meteorological Center; Julie Wright, EDS; Yamaha Corporation of America Keyboard Division.

About the Authors

Roberta L. Baber has more than 30 years of experience in the computer field. Currently, she is Professor and Department Chair of Information Systems at Fresno City College. She started her career as a programmer, systems analyst, and project leader in southern California. After working in the industry for 17 years, she relocated to central California and began teaching at the college level. She is married, with two children currently attending college.

Marilyn Wertheimer Meyer is Professor of Information Systems at Fresno City College. She holds a B.S. in quantitative analysis and an M.S. in applied computer systems from California State University Fresno. She also holds a CCP and is working on her doctorate. She has been a computer programmer/analyst for several years and has extensive teaching experience at both the university and community college levels. She has written a number of information systems instructor's manuals and two computer programming texts. She is currently Student Success Coordinator at Fresno City College.

PART I

The Basics

When you watch the news on television or read your newspaper, do you hear about computers and computer terms that you are not sure you understand? The basic terminology of computer technology has become common in the media. You won't be able to follow the discussion or even some conversations with your friends and colleagues if you don't know the meanings of this "computer talk."

CHAPTER 1
Understanding Computers

A silent invasion is occurring at a disconcertingly rapid pace. We share our schools, workplaces, and homes with electronic computer systems that change our very existence. Knowledge of these systems—and how they work—is essential to our future. This book will take you into that future with the self-assurance and confidence that only knowledge can give.

Chapter 1 gives you a basic understanding of computer systems and their sometimes mystifying terminology. You will see that this invasion poses a promise, not a threat, for all who learn to use the computer as a tool.

Lesson 1A introduces the concept of computer literacy and the input-processing-output-storage cycle. The lesson discusses basic computer terminology, known as "computerese," that you need in order to read and converse intelligently about computers.

Lesson 1B gives you the historical background necessary to understand how the computer industry has developed and what capabilities we can expect to see in future computers.

Computer Concepts and Computer Literacy

Outline

The Need for Computer Literacy
The Computer Defined
The Computer: Its Uses
The Five Elements of the Computing Process
    Hardware
    Software
        Programming Languages
        System and Application Software Packages
    Data
    People
    Procedures
The Computer: Its Advantages
Positive and Negative Effects

Learning Objectives

When you have finished reading this lesson, you will be able to

➤ Explain the need for computer literacy in tomorrow's computer society

➤ Explain what a computer is and how it processes data to produce information

➤ Discuss the characteristics of computers that explain why they are so widely used

➤ Distinguish the major types of computers and their principal uses

➤ Describe the major types of general-purpose application programs and provide examples of their uses

➤ Distinguish between data and information

➤ Explain how computers represent data (bits and bytes)

➤ Identify the main elements of a typical computing process

➤ Explain the relationship between computer professionals and other computer users

➤ Understand the computer's positive and negative effects on society

QUE Lab

➤ **Computer Fundamentals**

Today, did you stop for a red signal or buy something at a store? Did you watch a movie or a television program? Did you drive a car or ride a bus? All these activities, and thousands more, involve computers in some way. Computers of every size affect our lives. Supercomputers forecast weather and launch satellites. Embedded computer processor chips make "smart" devices such as a car that warns you of problems, or a microwave oven that warms your breakfast.

Courtesy of International Business Machines Corporation

Computers put banking at your fingertips anytime and anywhere. Would you choose a bank that didn't have automated teller machines (ATMs)? In addition, you no longer need to carry cash or checks all the time; you can buy many things—from groceries to gasoline to hamburgers—by using a debit card.

The newest university in the California State College and University system, at Monterey, has a bookless library. How do you do research? You use a computer.

Information from all over the world is available to anyone with a computer, a modem, a telephone line, and an Internet account. Students from kindergarten to graduate school are using computers to gather data. Networks and telecommunications give "looking it up" a new meaning.

Even political boundaries are challenged by computers. When you are "talking" on a network such as the Internet, you can communicate with people from around the world.

A revolution changes the way we do things and think about things, and computers have created a revolution. We have become dependent on computers—we expect them to be there for us. Computers are shaking up our world.

Courtesy of International Business Machines Corporation

Courtesy of Hewlett-Packard Company

Computers are part of our daily lives at home, at work, and at school.

Courtesy of International Business Machines Corporation

The Need for Computer Literacy

A major technological revolution has both positive and negative effects. Because the computer revolution is so new, many effects are still to be discovered. But there's one effect you can count on—the effect on you and your future. Because computers have moved into society so rapidly and so completely, you need basic computer skills just to pursue your career goals and function effectively in society. In short, you need **computer literacy**, sufficient computer knowledge to prepare you for working and living in a computerized society.

For many people, computer literacy means simply knowing which key to press. That knowledge is important, but it isn't enough. You need to understand some fundamental concepts about how computer systems are set up and how they work. To see this point, think about cars. Assume that you have learned to drive and you can get from point A to point B. If you want to maintain your car and drive with maximum safety, however, you must learn more. For example, does your car have an antilock braking system (ABS)? If so, in a sudden stop, the brake pedal normally vibrates. But some people do not know this fact. They think that something is wrong, and they release the brake pedal—resulting in crashes that could have been prevented. In the same way, lack of knowledge causes people to make mistakes using computers.

Distance Learning Goes the Distance

Kids watching TV may get bad press in some areas, but in the North Slope Borough School District (NSBSD) of Alaska, students watch TV for academic credit.

The North Slope Borough School District is the nation's largest school district. The borough, which has only 9,000 people, stretches across the northern coast of Alaska entirely above the Arctic Circle. About 650 miles across, the borough encompasses 88,000 square miles—about the size of Minnesota—and has approximately 2,000 students, 86 percent of whom are Inupiat Eskimos. The school district consists of ten schools: one school in each of the seven villages and three in the city of Barrow. Barrow (population 3,800) is the northernmost community in the United States and the largest city of the borough.

No roads connect these communities. Travel between the villages is by small aircraft; within the villages, snowmobiles and four-wheelers provide transportation.

Many of the village schools have fewer than 100 students (preschool through high school). The smallest village school has only 42 students and six staff members; the largest has 221 students and 21 staff members.

Until 1992, providing comprehensive education for the students of the borough was difficult because of the vast distances. But just before the 1992–1993 school year, the district implemented a video conferencing program called Distance Education Delivery.

Compressed video was phased into the existing satellite telecourse network. The system enables audio and video interaction between teachers and students and between schools. From the district's communications hub in Barrow, satellites link the seven outlying village schools with voice, data, and video communications. The three schools in Barrow are directly linked by fiber optics to the district's central office. Courses such as art and advanced math are taught over the satellite system.

"In village schools with few high school students, it is difficult to have the trained professional staff to teach all subjects," says Pat Aamodt, NSBSD superintendent (*Communication News*, February, 1993). "Because of its size, Barrow High School can employ teachers who have training in specialized subject matter. Through video conferencing, all of our students in the other seven villages have access to these instructors."

Martin Cary, coordinator of information and technology says, "We believe that our students will perform better if they can participate more actively with their instructors and classmates. Two-way video has also provided our curriculum developers with more course options" (*Communication News*, February, 1993).

According to the April 1994 issue of *Wired*, two studio cameras bring the instructor, text, and graphics into remote sites via full-time dedicated circuits. Instructors have two monitors—one to see themselves, the other to see the classrooms—shown one at a time. When a student in a classroom speaks, the camera turns toward the sound so that everyone can see who is talking.

continues

Courtesy of North Slope Borough School District

Homework assignments are faxed back and forth, and questions are handled by e-mail or telephone. Tests are sent by e-mail.

Acceptance of the system has been overwhelmingly positive. New applications for the technology are suggested by teachers, administrators, and the community (*Communication News*, February, 1993). More important, students of NSBSD are provided with excellent learning opportunities in spite of the distances that separate schools on Alaska's North Slope.

Courtesy of North Slope Borough School District

An added benefit to the system is that students gain a wider circle of friends because they are communicating with other students in remote classes. Martin Cary says

that the opportunity to socialize is a tremendous bonus for the students. "They exchange ideas and opinions over these distances. It's something they couldn't do before" (*Fortune*, December 28, 1992).

Families are pleased with this innovation, too. Instead of sending their children away from home to get an education, parents and grandparents can view and participate in their children's learning experiences.

Another benefit is the experience students gain in operating and maintaining the technology. A television production class is popular. One student, who began working in the studio to earn money, plans to study TV production in college. "Once you learn and get good at it, you crave it," she says (*School Happenings North Slope School District*).

In addition to the advanced and enrichment classes, courses in Inupiat languages and Alaska Studies are popular. In these courses, Inupiat Elders share traditional stories and skills. The Inupiat classes are called "a wonderful new feature in Distance Delivery course offerings" by the *1993–94 NSBSD Annual Report*.

NSBSD is also linked to the University of Alaska, various community colleges, and the Internet. With distance learning and computer networks in place, NSBSD is poised to enter the twenty-first century.

Lack of knowledge also causes some people to fear computers. We have even coined a term to describe this irrational fear: **cyberphobia**.

The purpose of this book is to teach you the fundamental concepts of computers and their uses. With this knowledge, you will be able to learn more rapidly how to use computers effectively—tomorrow's computers as well as today's. You will quickly recognize tasks that can benefit from computer applications. You will know how to make wise choices when you select computer equipment. You will know how to gauge the gravity of the computer's potentially negative effects, such as its threat to jobs and individual privacy. And most of all, you will be prepared for full citizenship in a society that requires computer literacy for the best jobs and careers.

This lesson introduces fundamental computer concepts. You learn what a computer is, what it does, and—to some extent—how it works.

Computers influence many of the activities in a typical day—from watching television to shopping to recreation.

Photographs courtesy of International Business Machines Corporation

The Computer Defined

To many people, the word *computer* suggests "computation," and that word means "math," which scares some people. But this connection is misleading. Computers are not calculators, although you can turn a computer into a calculator. In the simplest definition, a **computer** is an electronic device—a flexible machine that can manipulate data. Many of these manipulations have nothing to do with math. In addition to being used for such tasks as adding up your supermarket bill or getting $20 bills at an ATM, computers are used by writers, television producers, musicians, poets, graphics illustrators, and scholars of medieval history!

Why are computers so flexible that physicists and poets feel equally at home using them? A computer is **programmable**; that is, what the computer does depends on the program the computer is using. (A **program** is a list of instructions telling the computer what to do.) A computer's **hard-ware**—the machine and its components—is designed to be as flexible as possible. By using computer programs, called **software**, you transform this flexible hardware into a tool for a specific purpose.

No matter which program a computer is using, the machine itself performs only four basic operations. The most widely accepted definition of the computer includes the following operations:

➤ **Input**. A computer accepts data that is provided by means of an **input device**, such as a keyboard.

➤ **Processing**. A computer performs operations on the data to transform it in some way.

➤ **Output**. A computer produces output on a device, such as a printer or monitor, that shows the results of processing operations.

➤ **Storage**. A computer stores the results of processing operations for future use.

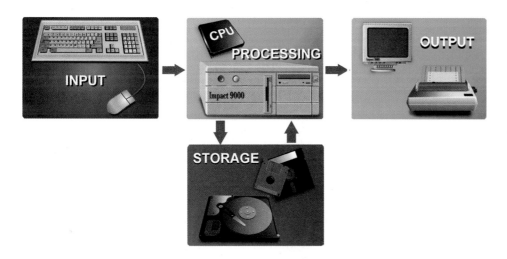

This definition is often referred to as the **IPOS cycle**. The four steps of the IPOS cycle—input, processing, output, storage—don't have to occur in a rigid I-P-O-S sequence. Under the direction of a program, a computer uses the steps of this process when needed and as often as needed.

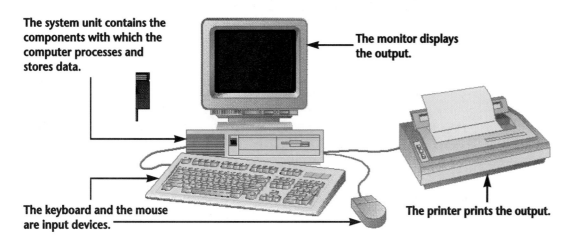

The system unit contains the components with which the computer processes and stores data.

The monitor displays the output.

The keyboard and the mouse are input devices.

The printer prints the output.

The use of a **personal computer**, a computer designed to meet an individual's computing needs, illustrates these four basic computer operations. You use the keyboard to input data. The computer's internal circuitry processes the data. You see the results (output) on the computer's **monitor** (the TV-like display), and you can print these results on the printer. You can also store the results on the computer's internal disk or on a removable disk.

The Computer: Its Uses

The purpose of the computer is to transform data into information. In this context, **data** means some kind of unorganized material that can be entered into the computer—a rough sketch that needs work, a first draft of an essay that needs revision or polishing, figures from a company's books, a list of names and addresses. What results from processing operations is **information**, data that has been made meaningful and useful.

For example, with the right software, you can use a computer to do your income taxes. You begin by inputting all the data concerning your wages, the amounts withheld from your paycheck, and the amounts of your exemptions and deductions. The computer processes this data and produces output that looks just like the forms used by the Internal Revenue Service (IRS). And what's the information? All the data that you have input has been processed to produce the form for the IRS and the key figure—the amount of your tax refund or the amount you owe. You can then print and store the results.

This capability to process data can be used in a variety of ways. People have come up with some very interesting uses:

➤ Today's dairy farmers are using computers to optimize feeding times, resulting in gains of up to 30 percent in milk output. Dairy farmers produce as much milk today as they did 30 years ago, but with fewer cows, lower costs, and less pollution.

➤ *The Federalist Papers* are some of America's most important historical documents, but some of the articles weren't signed. Who wrote them? Using computers to analyze the writing styles of James Madison, Patrick Henry, and other known authors of the *Papers*, scholars have been able to identify the authors of the unsigned texts.

➤ A psychologist keeps a computer in the counseling room. At the touch of a key, the psychologist can search through references on a computer disk for information relating to topics that come up during counseling sessions.

The Five Elements of the Computing Process

Computers consist of hardware, the physical parts of the computer, and software, the programs that tell the computer what to do. Processing data into information (the computing process) involves more elements than just hardware and software, though. And all these elements must be organized so that each works smoothly and efficiently with the others. During the **computing process**, computers integrate the use of five key elements:

➤ Hardware

➤ Software

➤ Data

➤ People

➤ Procedures

The computing process, in short, includes everything and everyone necessary for the computer to perform a useful task. The following sections show how each of these elements works in the process.

Hardware

The term *hardware* refers to the physical parts of the computer. Computer hardware is versatile—what it does depends on the computer program you use.

The key to the computer's versatility is **memory**. You can think of memory as a temporary workspace. The computer's processor uses this workspace as a scratch pad during processing.

Many people confuse memory with storage. Memory is temporary. When you turn off the computer, everything in memory is lost. Storage is usually permanent. On most computers, storage also has far greater capacity than memory.

Understanding the distinction between memory and storage is essential. Some programs keep their output in memory. You must transfer the information to a storage device, such as a disk drive, if you want to keep the information permanently. If you switch off the computer without **saving** this information (transferring it to storage), the information is lost. More than a few students have stayed up all night to finish a paper, only to lose all their work because they didn't understand this distinction.

The key to the computer's precision is the fact that it represents data digitally. Computers use binary digits, which are numbers using a base 2 number system rather than a decimal (or base 10) number system. A binary digit, commonly called a **bit**, has a value of either 0 (zero) or 1 (one). Eight bits are grouped together to represent a **character**—a letter, number, or special character. This group is called a **byte**. Many people use the terms *character* and *byte* to mean the same thing.

People talk about bytes when they talk about the capacity of computer memories and storage devices. Because one byte equals only one character, these devices must be capable of storing thousands, millions, or even billions of bytes. To describe these large capacities, the terms **kilobyte** (K), **megabyte** (M), and **gigabyte** (G) are used. A kilobyte equals approximately one thousand bytes, a megabyte equals approximately one million bytes, and a gigabyte equals approximately one billion bytes. (The actual number of bytes in a megabyte is slightly higher because computer storage amounts are actually measured in base 2 numbers.)

Software

Software is the set of instructions (also called a program) that guides the hardware through its job. The following sections explore additional aspects of software.

Programming Languages

Software programs must be written in **programming languages**. **Programmers**—people trained in the use of a programming language—write programs.

Before 1952, the only available programming language was **machine language**, now called a **low-level language**. A machine language is recognized by a given brand or design of computer processor. Machine language consists of nothing but the 0s and 1s with which the computer works. Machine language is difficult to learn, and early programs were few and short.

In 1952, a new low-level programming language called **assembly language** was introduced. In assembly language, programmers use short letter codes (such as RTJ) that stand for specific machine operations. A program called an **assembler** translates these codes into machine language so that the computer can carry out the instructions. Assembly language is easier than machine language, but by contemporary standards, assembly language is difficult to use. The programmer in assembly language must pay careful attention to how the machine works.

In the 1960s, high-level programming languages emerged. With a **high-level language**, the programmer uses simple English words and familiar mathematical expressions. The programmer is free to concentrate on the desired result—what the program is supposed to accomplish—rather than worry about the details of how the computer operates.

System and Application Software Packages

Today's complex computer programs, such as Microsoft Word (a word processing program), consist of many separate programs that are designed to run together. In recognition of this fact, people sometimes speak of **software packages**. When you buy Microsoft Word, you are actually buying a software package rather than a single program.

Based on the function of the package, software packages are divided into two categories: system software and application software. Computer literacy involves learning how to use both system software and one or more application programs.

Computers need **system software** to function. System software integrates the computer's hardware components and provides tools for day-to-day maintenance tasks, such as displaying a list of the files contained on a disk. MS-DOS, UNIX, Microsoft Windows 95, and System 7 are well-known examples of system software.

Application software turns the computer into a tool for a specific task, such as writing. Not all application programs will prove useful to you. Some application programs are **special-purpose programs**, which perform a specific task for a single profession. For example, safety managers use a program that prints records of occupation-related injuries and illnesses in a format required by a Federal regulatory bureau. If you aren't a safety manager, you won't find this application program interesting or useful.

Other application programs are called **general-purpose programs**. Millions of people use these programs for a variety of tasks. Commonly used general-purpose programs include the following:

> ➤ **Word processing**. More than 85 percent of the personal computers now in existence are equipped with a word processing program, which transforms the computer into a tool for creating, editing, proofing, printing, and storing text. Many of today's books originated in text typed into computers—including this one!

> ➤ **Desktop publishing**. In the past, newsletters and magazines were created through an expensive, tedious process called layout, in which someone cut and pasted photographs, borders, and text to create a pleasing design. With desktop publishing software and your computer, you can produce attractive results with a little special training. Community organizations everywhere are doing a better job of keeping in touch with their members, thanks to desktop publishing tools.

> ➤ **Electronic spreadsheet**. Businesses previously worked out budgets and made forecasts using accountant's paper and a calculator. Electronic spreadsheet programs enable you to type the headings and numbers into a computerized version of accountant's paper, but with a twist. You can hide formulas within the on-screen "paper." These formulas perform computations with the data. The payoff is that you can change any number and immediately see the effect of the change. People use electronic spreadsheets for many purposes, not just business-related ones. In California, for example, a forest ranger uses an electronic spreadsheet to analyze data concerning endangered animal populations.

> ➤ **Database**. A database program creates an electronic version of a card file—and the program gives you the tools you need to organize this file (for example, by alphabetizing it) and to retrieve information. An eighth-grade English teacher, for instance, could create a database of interesting uses of language—and retrieve examples for use in class discussions.

> ➤ **Telecommunications software**. Do you want access to computer resources available elsewhere? Telecommunications software transforms a computer into a terminal, which can connect to a multiuser computer system by means of the telephone. Commercial multiuser systems enable you to join discussion groups, exchange mail with other users, make plane and hotel reservations, and obtain free software for your computer.

High-Tech Computer Games

The video game story is one of increasing sophistication and realism. Each generation has built on the one before, with more detailed and naturalistic imagery, more dynamic action, more brilliant sound, and more convincing simulations.

In the same way, technological advances of computers have also affected games. Because the chips can manage more data, they can support richer audio and visual output. The color palette produces pictures of near-television quality; motion is more fluid. With CD-ROM-based machines, actual digitized soundtracks approach the quality of music CDs.

Companies have hired Hollywood script writers, animators, and video directors, as well as engineers and computer programmers from leading high-tech companies—even composers and musicians with successful backgrounds in the recording industry.

Some companies, looking ahead to a marriage of game technology and educational multimedia efforts, have coined the term *infotainment* to describe their products. (Educational multimedia software companies are calling their efforts *edutainment*.) Interactive television is potentially another area for joint efforts. Merger possibilities are endless.

The release of *Road Rash* in August 1994 marked the first integration of motion picture technology with video games and alternative rock music videos. This game integrates video footage of the bands and several of their music videos mixed with extensive motorcycle racing footage.

Another next-generation product, *Wing Commander III*, uses the conventions of film to tell a story. But the viewer and players become part of the action by interacting at key points in the plot, advancing and changing the course of events as they unfold.

Courtesy of Electronic Arts

The latest version *of FIFA International Soccer*, a sports game, is complete with crowd chants available in four languages, eleven different camera angles, and instant replays directed by the user. *John Madden Football* has also been rereleased for the next-generation platform.

From the sci-fi menu comes *Shock Wave: Invasion Earth 2019*. From the cockpit of a space aircraft, players fly over texture-mapped landscapes created from aerial photography. Players experience real video and radio broadcasts from other pilots as they fly combat missions around the world.

Courtesy of Electronic Arts

continues

Lesson 1A: Computer Concepts and Computer Literacy · 1-15

Escape from Monster Manor provides Halloween-type entertainment in a fast-paced action game featuring special effects.

Twisted: The Game Show lets a whole family interact with various game show formats, challenging the players' hand and eye coordination, manual dexterity, logic skills, and memory.

Preschoolers are not ignored. *Sesame Street: Numbers* brings Elmo, Bert, Ernie, and Big Bird to life. Children learn as they interact to solve math-based games and activate animations.

USA Today (June 28, 1994) reviewed a number of next-generation games showcased at the Summer Consumer Electronics Show in Chicago.

Virtua Racing (Sega) zips your race car through three race courses from four camera views. Other high-tech games that Sega is introducing include *Doom, Star Wars Arcade, Super Motocross, Super Afterburner,* and *Fahrenheit.* Golf and basketball games are also scheduled to be released.

In *The Lion King,* the player grows up from a cub into a full-sized lion. At one point, Simba gets caught in a wildebeest stampede, and the players experience wildebeests seemingly "leaping right over their heads."

Beavis and Butt-Head has the look and feel of the hit MTV show, according to *USA Today.* Others are *Mickey Mania: The Timeless Adventures of Mickey Mouse, Earthworm Jim, Ecco: The Tides of Time,* and *Ecco Jr. Urban Strike* allows the player to "make like Rambo."

New hardware introduced at the Chicago show includes a virtual guitar that chords while the player strums, two new virtual reality headsets, and a wireless mouse that straps to the user's index finger.

A far cry from solitaire, computer games now have something for everyone.

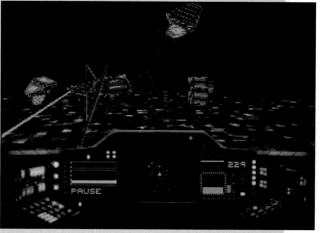

Courtesy of Electronic Arts

➤ **Graphics software**. Is there a public presentation in your future? If so, you need to learn how to use presentation graphics programs to create attractive charts and graphs that you can share with your audience.

➤ **Resource discovery software**. Currently, the latest wrinkle in application software is a set of tools for exploring the riches of the Internet, a global network of linked computer networks. Such tools as Archie, Gopher, and the World Wide Web help you find computer resources available on millions of publicly accessible computers throughout the globe.

BITS
Web browsers are software that search for key words or data in a collection of files. Netscape Navigator and Microsoft Internet Explorer are popular Web browsers.

TechTalk
The Information Superhighway is a proposed system of computer networks used to transmit information. The builders of the Information Superhighway are constantly working to improve the access, speed, quality, and amount of information transmitted. The Internet, which you learn about in this textbook, is a prototype for this *super*highway.

Data

Computers transform data into information. What's the difference between these two terms? *Data* is the raw material; *information* is processed data. Data is the input to the processing; information is the output.

A useful model to describe the relationship between data and information is called the **systems model**. It shows that data goes into a process and information is then output.

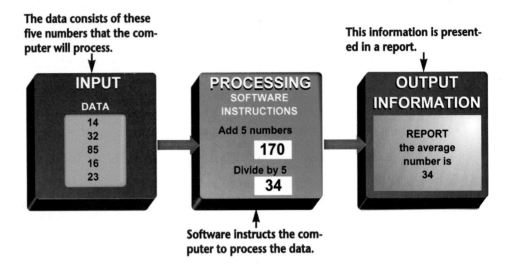

The data consists of these five numbers that the computer will process.

This information is presented in a report.

Software instructs the computer to process the data.

Several characteristics distinguish useful information from data. The purpose of information is to help people make well-informed decisions, but what makes information useful? Information must be relevant, timely, accurate, concise, and complete in order to be useful. Data must be accurate but doesn't need to be relevant, timely, or concise. Table 1A.1 describes these characteristics.

Table 1A.1	Characteristics of Useful Information
Relevant	Information applies to the current situation.
Timely	Information is up-to-date and available when it is needed.
Accurate	Data given to the computer and the output are correct in every detail.
Concise	Information is condensed into a usable length.
Complete	All important items are included.

People

You may be surprised to learn that people are part of the computing process. Some computers, such as the computer chip that controls an automobile engine, function without human intervention. But even these computers were designed by people and occasionally require maintenance by people. Most computers require people, who are called **users** (or sometimes **end users**).

Some users progress beyond the basics of computer literacy. They learn the advanced features of application programs. With this knowledge, these users can customize an application program for a specific task. These knowledgeable people are called **power users**.

Computer professionals have taken intermediate and advanced courses about computers. These people apply their professional training to improve the performance, ease of use, and efficiency of computer systems. One kind of computer professional is the programmer, who creates new computer programs. Excellent career opportunities exist for students interested in becoming computer professionals. Lesson 9A discusses computer professionals and computer careers.

Procedures

Procedures are the steps that you must follow to accomplish a specific computer-related task. Part of a user's computer literacy is knowing common procedures.

Chances are, you already know several computer procedures. For example, you have probably used an automated teller machine (ATM). Inside the ATM is a computer. In response to on-screen messages called **prompts**, you insert your card, enter your personal identification number (PIN), and tell the machine how much money you want. You also follow computer procedures when you program your VCR or set the coffee pot to brew your coffee at 7:00 A.M. In this course, you will become familiar with many more computer procedures.

The Computer: Its Advantages

No matter where computers are found or how they are applied, they're used for input, processing, output, and storage. But computers wouldn't be worth the trouble without the following characteristics:

A computer is a tool that people can use to write books, produce music, create illustrations, and communicate with other computer users.

➤ They are *fast*. Many of today's computers can perform hundreds of millions of processing operations in one second.

➤ They are *reliable*. Today's computers may run day in and day out for years without failure.

➤ They are *accurate*. The computer's physical processing circuits rarely make errors. Computers make errors, of course, but they are almost always due to faulty programs or incorrect data input.

➤ They can *store massive amounts of information*. Today's personal computers can be equipped with disks capable of storing more than one billion characters (letters or numbers). That capacity is enough to store the complete works of William Shakespeare, an unabridged English

TechTalk
GIGO stands for "garbage in, garbage out" and is used to indicate that humans are the source of most "computer errors."

dictionary, a 32-volume encyclopedia, a world atlas and almanac, dozens of computer programs, and all your written work from the third grade through graduate school—with room for more.

➤ They can *move information* very quickly from one place to another. Using an experimental connection that may soon play a role in the Information Superhighway, one computer can send the entire text of the *Encyclopedia Britannica* to another linked computer in less than one second.

People like to think of the computer as a useful tool. A computer-literate person knows that the computer is a tool for creating useful information that can be printed, communicated to others, and stored for future use.

Computers come in many sizes. **Supercomputers** are highly sophisticated computers that perform complex calculations very quickly; supercomputers are most often used for scientific research. **Mainframe computers** are large, expensive computers designed to meet a large organization's computing needs. **Minicomputers** are smaller than mainframes but still large enough to meet the computing needs of a medium-sized or small organization. Personal computers, or **microcomputers**, meet the computing needs of individuals. **Notebook computers** provide a personal computer's capabilities in a small, lightweight, portable package. All around us are **embedded computers**, special-purpose computers that perform control functions in such devices as microwave ovens, fuel-injection systems, and wristwatches.

Positive and Negative Effects

Computer literacy means learning fundamental computer concepts and application programs. Computer literacy means also recognizing both the positive and the negative consequences of computers in our society.

The positives are all around us. For example, a rescue squad has reduced its emergency response time by nearly 20 percent by using a custom-designed computer system that optimizes its operations. For some accident victims, the difference is literally a matter of life or death. Computers also ease your daily activities by brewing your coffee, printing your newspaper, and helping you write your letters and pay your bills.

But there are negatives too:

➤ Computers may pose a threat to personal privacy, because firms can so easily accumulate a detailed picture of an individual's buying habits.

➤ Computer manufacturing processes require the use of hazardous chemicals, which could endanger workers and pollute water supplies.

➤ Discarded computers are taking up too much room in our nation's landfills.

➤ Too much work at the computer can result in painful nerve injuries, such as carpal tunnel syndrome, the fastest growing type of occupational injury in the U.S.

➤ Computer failures do occur—and if they occur in a critical system, such as the air traffic control system, lives may be endangered.

➤ Computers may displace workers by automating tasks that people used to perform or by enabling fewer workers to perform tasks more efficiently. Displaced workers may find jobs that pay substantially less—if they can find jobs at all.

Like it or not, computers are part of our lives. A good grounding in computer concepts and applications can help you get the benefits and understand the negatives of the computer's massive penetration into society.

Lesson Summary

➤ Computers have changed the way we view our lives. Understanding the fundamental concepts of how computer systems are set up and how they work, as well as how to apply the computer to various tasks, contributes to computer literacy.

➤ Some people who are not computer literate have cyberphobia—a fear of computers.

➤ A computer is a tool that can manipulate data. You can use software (lists of instructions) to instruct computer hardware (the machine and its components) to do a variety of tasks that involve processing data.

➤ The cycle that the computer hardware and software follows is known as the IPOS cycle. Input is the data that goes into a process, supported by storage, where the input is converted into output.

➤ The computing process can be described in terms of five elements: hardware, software, data, people, and procedures.

➤ Hardware is the equipment—it includes storage and memory. Memory is temporary whereas storage is permanent.

➤ Hardware works with digital units. The digits are kept in binary form, with each binary digit (called a bit) being placed in either memory or storage.

➤ The characteristics of computers that give them their power are speed, reliability, accuracy, storage capacity, and the capability to move data quickly from one place to another.

➤ Hardware comes in various sizes, but the most common types are supercomputers, mainframes, minicomputers, microcomputers, and embedded microprocessors.

➤ Software, or programs, gives computers their flexibility. When a task is needed, the instructions for it are loaded into memory. When the task is completed, a different program can be loaded to do a different task.

➤ The basic language of the computer is machine language, but it is in binary form and extremely difficult to work with. Assembly languages were developed to simplify working with machine languages. High-level languages were developed to make programming available to most people.

➤ Software packages are of two types: system software, which works directly with the hardware to maintain the computer system; and application software, which accomplishes either a specific or a general task.

➤ General-purpose application software includes word processing, electronic spreadsheets, graphics, communications, and database programs.

➤ Data is input to the computer so that it can be transformed into information. To be useful, information must be relevant, timely, concise, accurate, and complete.

➤ People who use computers can be users (or end users), power users, or computer professionals. Whatever their role, people provide the direction for the hardware and software to process the data.

➤ Procedures are the steps that you take to have the computer do the necessary processing.

➤ Using computers has both positive and negative effects on our lives. Your goal is to take advantage of the positives and either reduce the negatives or deal with their results in the best way for you.

Lesson Review

Key Terms

application software	end user	microcomputer	resource discovery
assembler	general-purpose program	minicomputer	software
assembly language	gigabyte	monitor	saving
bit	graphics software	multimedia	software
byte	hardware	notebook computer	software package
character	high-level language	output	special-purpose program
computer	information	personal computer	storage
computer literacy	input	power user	supercomputer
computer professional	input device	procedure	system software
computing process	IPOS cycle	processing	systems model
cyberphobia	kilobyte	program	telecommunications soft-
data	low-level language	programmable	ware
database	machine language	programmer	user
desktop publishing	mainframe computer	programming language	word processing
electronic spreadsheet	megabyte	prompt	
embedded computer	memory		

Matching

In the blank next to each of the following terms or phrases, write the letter of the corresponding term or phrase.

_____	1. Usually represents a character	**a.** cyberphobia
_____	2. Permanent	**b.** hardware
_____	3. Also called programs	**c.** software
_____	4. Desktop publishing	**d.** microcomputer
_____	5. Fear of computers	**e.** byte
_____	6. Temporary storage	**f.** memory
_____	7. MS-DOS	**g.** storage
_____	8. Processed data	**h.** system software
_____	9. A computer and its components	**i.** general-purpose software
_____	10. Another name for a personal computer	**j.** information

Multiple Choice

Circle the letter of the correct choice for each of the following.

1. In the long run, what is the purpose of using computers?

   a. to produce reports

   b. to be able to get on the Internet

   c. to process data into information

   d. to be computer literate

2. What is computer literacy?

   a. the ability to understand the basic concepts of computers

   b. the ability to evaluate the positive and negative effects of computers

   c. the ability to use the computer as a tool to do appropriate tasks

   d. all of the above

3. Which of the following are the two parts of the computer system that must be present?

   a. hardware and software

   b. input and output

   c. keyboard and printer

   d. none of the above

4. Which cycle describes the computer's processing of data?

   a. processing cycle

   b. cyberphobia cycle

   c. hardware cycle

   d. IPOS cycle

5. The purpose of the computer is to process data into what?

    a. useful data

    b. information

    c. reports

    d. formulas

6. What are the five elements of computer processing?

    a. hardware, software, information, word processing, and spreadsheets

    b. hardware, programs, information, communications, and people

    c. hardware, software, data, people, and procedures

    d. input, processing, output, storage, and people

7. The difference between memory and storage is that _____ is temporary and _____ is permanent.

    a. storage, memory

    b. memory, storage

    c. disk, storage

    d. RAM, memory

8. Which of the following is not a characteristic of computers that makes them useful?

    a. They are fast.

    b. They can store massive amounts of data.

    c. They are concise.

    d. They are accurate.

9. How are software packages categorized?

    a. special purpose and word processing

    b. system software and application software

    c. hardware and software

    d. none of the above

10. What is the purpose of information?

    a. to process into data

    b. to be timely

    c. to help people make decisions

    d. all of the above

Completion

In the blank provided, write the correct answer for each of the following.

1. The irrational fear of computers is called _____.

2. A program is a list of _____ telling the hardware what to do.

3. The machine and its components are called _____.

4. Using memory to hold a program improves the _____ of the use of the computer.

5. A binary digit, commonly called a(n) _____ has a value of either zero or one.

6. When you discuss a computer's memory, a megabyte means a capacity of approximately one _____ bytes.

7. Computers designed to meet the computing needs of individuals are called _____.

8. A group of programs designed to work together to perform a task is called a software _____.

9. Application programs that can be used to do many related tasks are called _____ programs.

10. When information is a usable length, it is said to be _____.

Review

On a separate sheet of paper, answer the following questions.

1. What is the difference between hardware and software? Why do we need both?

2. Describe the IPOS cycle.

3. What are the five elements of the computing process?

4. What is the difference between memory and storage? Why do we need both?

5. Explain why computers are called digital devices.

6. List at least five sizes of computers and give an example of how each size could be used.

7. Why was the development of high-level languages important?

8. What is the difference between data and information? Why is information important?

9. List the characteristics of useful information.

10. What are the differences among end users, power users, and computer professionals?

Critical Thinking

On a separate sheet of paper, answer the following questions.

1. Describe the process of registering for a class in terms of the IPOS cycle.

2. Can cyberphobia affect you even if you don't suffer from it personally? If so, how? If not, why not?

3. What does becoming computer literate mean to you? How do you envision using the knowledge gained in this course?

4. Describe a negative consequence that computers could have on society. Suggest a way to correct this negative situation.

5. List three general-purpose application software packages and describe how you will be likely to use them in the next few years.

Further Discovery

Computer Science: An Overview, Fifth Edition. J. Glenn Brookshear (Redwood City, CA: Benjamin/Cummings, 1997).

How Computers Work. Ron White (Emeryville, CA: Ziff-Davis, 1995).

IBM Dictionary of Computing (New York: McGraw-Hill, 1994).

Que's Computer & Internet Dictionary, 6th Edition. Bryan Pfaffenberger (Indianapolis, IN: Que, 1995).

 ## On-line Discovery

You can access the Internet resources for the following questions by going to the Que Education and Training Web site at URL http://www.ciyf98.com/discovery. From this page, click the link for Lesson 1A and then click the link to the resource you want to access.

1. Because the Internet was originally created and used by computer experts, a lot of information about computers and computing has always been available on the Internet. Yahoo! is an Internet directory service that collects useful Internet resources—sort of a *Yellow Pages* for the Internet. Use the Yahoo! directory page on **Computers and Internet** (http://www.yahoo.com/Computers_and_Internet) to explore the many uses, forms, and suppliers of computers and computer-related services. Do you find anything that surprises you? What different types of computers can be found in these resources? After looking through many of these resources, name four different uses of computers that you discover, as well as four different types of businesses related to computers. How do these businesses differ?

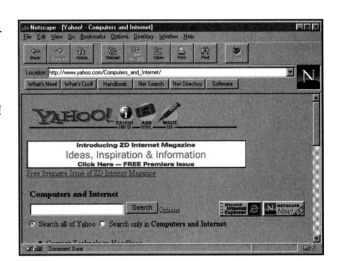

2. Computers seem to generate the use of jargon and many abbreviations. Although some of these words are eventually integrated into standard English, most of them remain a mystery to most people. Computing dictionaries, such as the **Free On-line Dictionary of Computing** (http://wfn-shop.princeton.edu/foldoc/) can help dispel some of the mystery. Take a look at this dictionary and try to learn at least four different computer-related terms or abbreviations.

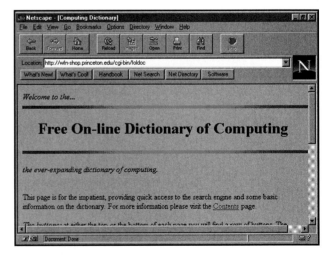

A note about On-line Discovery. The On-line Discovery section, found at the end of each lesson, gives you the opportunity to use the World Wide Web to explore in more detail some of the topics discussed in the lesson.

To be able to access the sites described in On-line Discovery, you will need access to the World Wide Web. You may have access in a number of different ways, depending on your particular setup. You may, for example, access the Web through a commercial online service such as America Online, CompuServe, or Prodigy. If you get access to the Internet through your college or university, or through a local Internet service provider, you probably have a direct connection to the Internet; in this case, you access the Web through a browser program such as Netscape Navigator, Microsoft Internet Explorer, or Mosaic. Finally, certain types of Internet accounts provide access to the Web through a text-only program called Lynx. If your account provides text-only access, you will be able to access the sites mentioned in On-line Discovery, but you might not be able to access all the information present; with text-only access, you will not be able to view graphics.

In the On-line Discovery sections, the addresses of all the Internet resources and home pages mentioned in the examples are provided. These addresses are in the form of URLs, or Uniform Resource Locators, which are sort of like street addresses of pages on the Internet.

The URL of the Que Education and Training home page, for example, is http://www.queet.com. You can enter this address into your Web browser to retrieve and view the Que Education and Training home page. The way in which you enter addresses and view documents will vary depending on the Web browser you are using. In Netscape Navigator, you simply click the button labeled Open, and in the box that appears, you type the address of the document you want to view.

Although the addresses of all the resources mentioned in the On-line Discovery sections are provided for you in the examples, you can also access all these addresses directly from the Que Education and Training Web page that has been set up for you, at URL http://www.ciyf98.com. If you enter this address into your Web browser, you can then follow links that will lead you to all the resources mentioned in On-line Discovery.

At the time of this book's publication, the Web sites used in the examples were accessible, but some sites may have been closed or moved to new locations. If you have any difficulty getting access to the World Wide Web or to any of the resources in On-line Discovery, you should ask your instructor for help.

The Historical Perspective

Outline

Learning Objectives

When you have finished reading this lesson, you will be able to

➤ Understand how computer technology has evolved

➤ Identify key people in the development of computers

➤ Explain the main differences among the generations of computers

➤ Discuss trends in the development of computers

In the final episode of *Star Trek: The Next Generation*, Captain Jean-Luc Picard finds himself moving among the past, the present, and the future. Jean-Luc discovers that his actions in these three time periods have interwoven to destroy history as we know it. Although this scenario is fictional, the lesson to be learned is valid. The past does, indeed, help determine both the present and the future. As you learn how and why people attempted to create early computers, you will appreciate all the more the important role that computers have today.

The First Computers

The idea of computing is as old as civilization itself—and maybe older. Computers are merely complex counting devices.

The first computing device could have been as simple as a set of stones used to represent bushels of wheat or herds of animals. Figuring the total number of animals in two combined herds or trading cattle for wheat could be represented with stones. When people followed a standard set of procedures to perform calculations with these stones, they created a digital counting device, the predecessor of a computer.

BITS
In 1947, a Japanese accountant using an abacus went head-to-head with an American army private who had the latest electromechanical calculator. The abacus won every match, except for the multiplication contest.

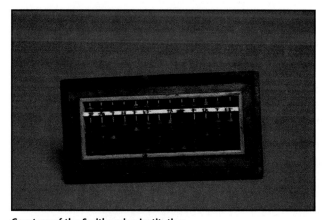
Courtesy of the Smithsonian Institution

In skilled hands, this Japanese abacus is an efficient calculator.

The abacus illustrates how these ancient computers worked. This computing device could be seen during a stroll through the marketplaces of ancient Beijing, and it is still used today. An abacus has a wooden frame holding wires on which beads are strung. To show a number, you pull down the beads so that each rod represents a digit. For example, you use four rods to represent the number 3,741. To solve a math problem, you simply follow a set of instructions telling you when and where to move the beads.

Another counting device, "Napier's bones," was invented at the beginning of the 1600s by John Napier, a Scottish mathematician. The "bones" were strips of ivory with numbers written on them. When the bones were arranged properly, the user could read the numbers in adjacent columns to find the answer to a multiplication operation.

Clockwork Calculators

If you can solve problems by following a set of simple rules (as you do with an abacus), you can produce a machine to calculate answers automatically. During the sixteenth through the nineteenth centuries, Europeans created several calculating machines that made use of existing technology, specifically clockwork gears and levers.

The first known automatic calculating machine was invented in France in 1642 by Blaise Pascal, who was only nineteen years old at the time. Pascal would later become one of Europe's great philosophers and mathematicians. He was the son of a tax commissioner and frequently worked in his father's office. The job must have bored Pascal, for he dreamed about a device that would save people like his father from the drudgery of doing sums over and over. Pascal's answer was the Pascaline, a mechanical calculator that worked with clockwork gears and levers. To add and subtract, the Pascaline rotated wheels to register values and used a lever to perform the carrying operation from one wheel to another.

BITS
Many important contributions to the development of computers have been made by young people—probably because they were not set in their ways and could see beyond the technology of their day.

Although the Pascaline was not accepted by businesses, Pascal was the first of many computing innovators who were ahead of their time. In recognition of Pascal's contribution to the computing field, a computer programming language has been named for him. This language, **Pascal**, is often used to teach programming to beginning computer science majors.

The next significant improvement in calculating devices was made in 1673 by Gottfried Wilhelm von Leibniz. Leibniz is best known for his work with Sir Isaac Newton in developing the branch of mathematics known as calculus. Leibniz invented a calculator that could add, subtract, multiply, and divide accurately. The calculator also performed a square root function, although not always accurately.

The first calculator with commercial prospects was known as the "arithmometer." It was developed by the Frenchman Charles Xavier Thomas (known as Charles of Colmar) and won a gold medal at the International Exhibition in London in 1862. The machine could add, subtract, multiply, divide, and calculate square roots with precision.

Leibniz's calculator, the "stepped reckoner," was never perfected enough to be marketed.

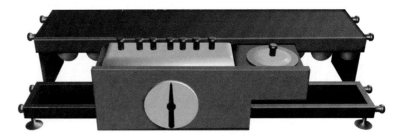

Representing Data: From Looms to Business Machines

As inventors worked to improve mechanical calculators, they needed a better way to input data than setting clockwork dials. The means for this better way had already been created, and in an unlikely place—the weaving rooms of France.

The Jacquard Loom

In the early nineteenth century, a French weaver named Joseph Marie Jacquard developed a loom that could be programmed. The loom used large cards with holes punched in them to control automatically the pattern that was woven into the material. The result was a thick, rich cloth with repetitive floral or geometric patterns. Before the invention of this loom, only the wealthy could afford cloth with elaborate patterns. An instant success, Jacquard patterns are still produced to this day.

The **punched cards** used in Jacquard's loom were adapted by others to serve as the primary form of computer input. Punched cards were used to enter both data and programs, until about twenty years ago.

Charles Babbage and the First Modern Computer Design

Charles Babbage, born and raised in England in the early 1800s, created the first modern computer design. While Babbage was working on his doctorate, he had to solve many complex formulas, and he could not solve these problems manually in a reasonable length of time. To solve the equations, Babbage began developing a steam-powered machine, which he called the **difference engine.**

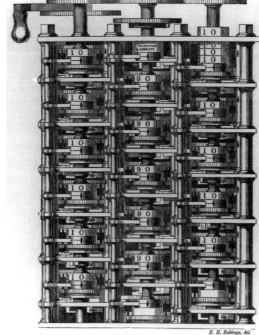

Impression from a woodcut of a small portion of Mr. Babbage's Difference Engine No. I, the property of Government, at present deposited in the Museum at South Kensington.

It was commenced 1823.
This portion put together 1833.
The construction abandoned 1842.
This plate was printed June, 1853.
This portion was in the Exhibition 1862.

Courtesy of Charles Babbage Institute, University of Minnesota

Later, Babbage turned to planning a far more ambitious device, the **analytical engine.** The machine was designed to use a form of punched card similar to Jacquard's punched cards for data input. This device would have been a full-fledged modern computer with a recognizable IPOS cycle (input, processing, output, and storage). Unfortunately, the technology of Babbage's time could not produce the parts required to complete the analytical engine.

In 1991, the London Science Museum built the difference engine using Babbage's plans, as shown in this woodcut. The machine worked perfectly.

Babbage worked on his plans for years with Augusta Ada Byron, the daughter of the famed poet Lord Byron and the Countess of Lovelace. Augusta Ada, a brilliant mathematician, contributed greatly to Babbage's plans and can be considered the world's first female computer scientist and the first computer programmer. A programming language called Ada is named in her honor.

TechTalk
A computer programmer writes the instructions that tell a computer what to do.

Photographs courtesy of Charles Babbage Institute, University of Minnesota

Augusta Ada Byron, the world's first computer programmer, provided valuable help to Charles Babbage, the "father of the computer."

But the end of Babbage's story isn't a happy one—he depleted much of his fortune trying to build the analytical engine. A working analytical engine was built from Babbage's plans in 1991, and it is currently on display at the Charles Babbage Institute in Minnesota. Charles Babbage has been recognized as "the father of the computer."

Hollerith and the Automated Census Bureau

The next major figure in the history of computing was Dr. Herman Hollerith, a statistician. The United States Constitution calls for a census of the population every ten years, as a means of determining representation in the U.S. House of Representatives. By the late nineteenth century, the hand-processing techniques were taking so long that the 1880 census results took more than seven years to tabulate. The need to automate the census became apparent.

Dr. Hollerith devised a plan to encode the answers to the census questions on punched cards. He also developed a punching device; an electronic, manually fed reader that could process fifty cards in a minute; and a sorting device. These innovations enabled the 1890 census to be completed in two and one-half years—a big improvement over the 1880 census.

When the census was completed, Hollerith decided to perfect his punched-card equipment and market it. He founded the Tabulating Machine Company in 1896 to continue his work.

Although the demand for his machines was great, Hollerith did not enjoy selling or providing service to his customers. In 1911, the Tabulating Machine Company merged with two other companies to form the Computing-Tabulating-Recording Company. Now Hollerith was free to concentrate on inventing better equipment.

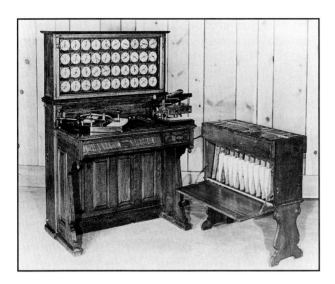

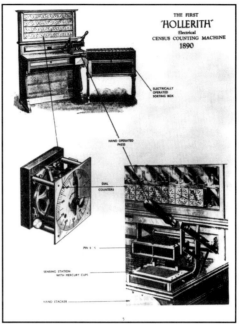

Hollerith's punched-card tabulating machines are the predecessors of today's business computers.

One of the partners, a marketing expert named Thomas Watson Sr., led the new company. Under his guidance, the company was extremely successful. In 1924, management decided that a new name would better indicate the progressive nature of the firm, so the Computing-Tabulating-Recording Company became International Business Machines Corporation (IBM).

Toward Modern Computing

The first electronic computers were complex machines that required large investments to build and use. The computer industry might never have developed without government support and funding. World War II provided a stimulus for governments to invest enough money in research to create powerful computers. The earliest computers, created during the war, were the exclusive possessions of government and military organizations. Only in the 1950s did businesses become producers and consumers of computers. And only in the 1960s did it become obvious that a huge market existed for these machines.

To describe the computer's technical progress since World War II, computer scientists speak of "computer generations." Each generation of technology has its own identifying characteristics. We're now using fourth-generation computer technology, and some experts say a fifth generation is already upon us.

Before the First Generation: Early Electronic Computers

In the late 1930s, the English mathematician Alan Turing wrote a paper describing all the capabilities and limitations of a hypothetical general-purpose computing machine that became known as the **Turing machine**.

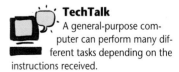

TechTalk
A general-purpose computer can perform many different tasks depending on the instructions received.

Turing also helped construct the British computer known as Robinson during World War II to decode German messages that had been encrypted by the German Enigma machine. In 1950, Turing published a paper entitled "Computing Machinery and Intelligence," in which he proposed the **Turing test** of artificial intelligence. Scientists still use this test as a standard. Stated simply, the Turing test requires that a computer be capable of holding a "conversation" (using keyboard and screen) with a person without the person's knowing that he or she is conversing with a computer.

TechTalk
A special-purpose computer is designed to perform one specialized task.

Professor John Atanasoff of Iowa State University has been credited with developing some of the concepts that led to the invention of the electronic computer. In 1939, he and a graduate student named Clifford Berry built an electronic calculating machine that could solve systems of equations. Known as the ABC (Atanasoff Berry Computer), it was the first special-purpose, electronic digital computer.

Soon after this, Dr. Howard Aiken of Harvard, who had read the notes of Augusta Ada Byron and wanted to construct an "analytical engine," approached IBM. Although IBM was doing very well selling punched-card equipment, the company was interested in opportunities to expand. Thomas Watson hired Aiken and allocated $1 million to undertake the venture. Aiken, along with a team of IBM engineers, completed the Mark I computer in 1944. The Mark I was partly electronic and partly mechanical. It was huge—8 feet high and 55 feet long—and slow, taking 3 to 5 seconds to perform a single multiplication operation. Today's $5 pocket calculators outperform the Mark I.

World War II created a need for the American military to calculate trajectories for missiles quickly. The military asked Dr. John Mauchly at the University of Pennsylvania to develop a machine for this purpose. Mauchly worked with a graduate student, J. Presper Eckert, to build the device. Eckert and Mauchly met with Atanasoff and Berry and used their work as a reference. Although commissioned by the military for use in the war, the ENIAC (Electronic Numeric Integrator and Calculator) was not completed until two months after the war ended.

ENIAC used 18,000 vacuum tubes, and it is said that the lights would dim in Philadelphia whenever ENIAC was turned on. ENIAC was 10 feet high, 10 feet wide, and 100 feet long!

Courtesy of International Business Machines Corporation

ENIAC could do five multiplication operations in a second, which was much faster than the Mark I. However, ENIAC was difficult to use because every time it was used to solve a new problem, the staff had to rewire it completely to enter the new instructions. At a chance meeting, Eckert discussed these problems with John von Neumann. (At the age of twenty, von Neumann was already known to be a brilliant mathematician. Born, raised, and educated in Hungary, von Neumann moved to America and became a professor of mathematics at Princeton University.) After this discussion, "the wheels started turning." The result was von Neumann's solution to the problems Eckert described: the stored-program concept.

With the **stored-program concept**, the computer's program is stored in internal memory with the data. One key advantage of this technique is that the computer can easily go back to a previous instruction and repeat it. Most of the interesting tasks that today's computers perform stem from repeating certain actions over and over. Since then, all computers that have been sold commercially (beginning with UNIVAC) have used the stored-program concept.

Courtesy of Richard Goldstein, RAND Corporation

John von Neumann, the "second father of the computer."

The First Generation (1951 to 1959)

Until 1951, electronic computers were the exclusive possessions of scientists, engineers, and the military. No one had tried to create an electronic digital computer for business purposes. Then ENIAC's creators, Mauchly and Eckert, formed a company to market a commercial version of their latest machine. Known as UNIVAC, this computer used IBM punched cards for input. Because the U.S. Census Bureau was already using IBM punched cards, it was a natural for the Bureau to purchase the first computer in 1951. Mauchly and Eckert's company became the UNIVAC division of Sperry-Rand Corporation (later known as UNISYS).

This UNIVAC I was a commercial version of the ENIAC.

Courtesy of Charles Babbage Institute, University of Minnesota

Vacuum tubes could multiply two ten-digit numbers forty times per second.

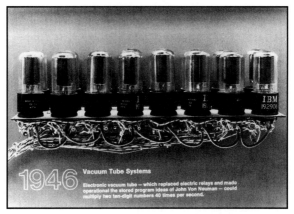

Courtesy of International Business Machines Corporation

The first generation of computers—usually dated from 1951 to 1959—used vacuum tubes. (You will find that dates for computer generations are not precise, varying from source to source. A change in generation has usually been the result of a major hardware innovation.) First-generation computers were large and slow, and they produced lots of heat. The vacuum tubes failed frequently, so first-generation computers were "down" (not working) much of the time. But they caught the public's imagination. In newspapers and magazines, journalists wrote of "electronic brains" that would change the world.

Noting that a market existed for business computers, IBM announced its first commercial computer, the IBM 701, in 1953. IBM made a total of 19 of these computers. At the time, industry leaders felt that 19 computers should be sufficient to take care of the computing needs of American business! Large, slow, and expensive, these first computers required special facilities and highly trained personnel.

First-generation computers were given instructions in machine language, which is composed entirely of the numbers 0 and 1. Machine language was designed in this manner because electronic computers use the binary number system. Because machine language is very difficult to work with, only a few specialists understood how to program these early computers.

Magnetic drums provided secondary storage for first-generation computers.

Courtesy of Charles Babbage Institute, University of Minnesota

All data and instructions came into the first-generation computers from punched cards. Computer secondary storage consisted of magnetic drums. It wasn't until 1957 that magnetic tape was introduced as a faster and more convenient secondary storage medium. A single tape could hold the contents of approximately 1,100 punched cards (about 21 pages of information).

The Second Generation (1959 to 1963)

First-generation computers were notoriously unreliable, largely because the vacuum tubes kept burning out. To keep the ENIAC running, for example, students with grocery carts full of tubes were on hand to change the dozens of tubes that would fail during an average session. But a 1948 invention, the transistor, was to change the way computers were built, leading to the second generation of modern computer technology. Unlike vacuum tubes, transistors are small, require very little power, and run cool. And they're much more reliable. Because second-generation computers were created with transistors instead of vacuum tubes, these computers were faster, smaller, and more reliable than first-generation computers.

In the second generation, memory was composed of small magnetic cores strung on wire within the computer. For secondary storage, magnetic disks were developed, although magnetic tape was still commonly used.

Second-generation computers were easier to program than first-generation computers. The reason was the development of high-level languages, which are much easier for people to understand and work with than assembly languages. Also, unlike assembly language, a high-level language is not machine specific; this makes it possible to use the same program on computers produced by different manufacturers.

Second-generation computers could communicate with each other over telephone lines, transmitting data from one location to another. Communication was fairly slow, but a new method of exchanging data and ideas was now available.

These second-generation computers had some problems. The input and output devices were so slow that the computer itself frequently sat idle, waiting for cards to be read or reports to be printed. Two different but equally important solutions solved this problem. Although both projects began during the second generation and used second-generation technology, neither was completed until well into the third generation.

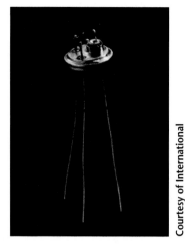

Courtesy of International Business Machines Corporation

The transistor was invented by John Bardeen, Walter Brattain, and William Shockley of Bell Telephone Laboratories.

TechTalk
When slow I/O devices caused the computer to be idle, the central processing unit (CPU) was said to be "I/O bound."

Magnetic core memory reduced calculation times.

Photographs courtesy of International Business Machines Corporation

Dr. Daniel Slotnick developed the first solution. Working with Burroughs Corporation, Slotnick was responsible for designing a computer for the U.S. Department of Defense. He decided to have this new computer address the problem of the machine's idle time waiting for input and output. The computer, known as ILLIAC IV, was completed in 1964. ILLIAC IV was unique in that it had four control units; thus, ILLIAC IV could perform input, output, and math operations at the same time. ILLIAC IV was acknowledged as the first supercomputer, and Slotnick was granted a patent for **parallel processing**. More commonly known as multiprocessing (because there are multiple central processing units), parallel processing has been used on all supercomputers and numerous mainframes since ILLIAC IV.

A group of professors and students at Massachusetts Institute of Technology developed the second solution. Through Project MAC, (Multiple Access Computer), they created a **multiprogramming** system that could concurrently process programs being run by different users. Because the computer could switch between programs, it did not have to sit idle waiting for input and output operations.

The Third Generation (1963 to 1975)

As with the first generation of computers, a device that ended the second generation was invented before the second generation began. In 1958, Jack St. Clair Kilby and Robert Noyce invented the first integrated circuit. **Integrated circuits** incorporate many transistors and electronic circuits on a single wafer or chip of silicon. (Integrated circuits are sometimes called chips because of the way they are made.)

TechTalk
Integrated circuits are also called semiconductors because they are formed by combining layers of materials that have varying capacities to conduct electricity. By etching patterns into these layered materials, the creators can include many transistors and other electronic components on one very small chip.

Integrated circuits are shown here with first-generation vacuum tubes and second-generation transistors.

Courtesy of International Business Machines Corporation

Amazing Grace

Admiral Grace Murray Hopper, Ph.D., was known as "Amazing Grace." She earned her nickname for her many achievements in business and academics.

During World War II, Grace Hopper enlisted in the Navy and was sent to Harvard to work on the first large-scale digital computer. She later wrote the first COBOL compiler and is often referred to as "the mother of COBOL."

Hopper traveled to computer conferences and colleges giving lectures about the data processing insights and computer concerns she acquired during her years in the profession. She wrote more than fifty papers and articles on software and programming languages and coauthored a college computer literacy textbook.

Courtesy of Virginia Anderson

One of the stories Hopper tells in a videotape recording of a lecture at the University of Maryland in February 1983 is a classic that has been told and retold. The story has to do with the origin of the words **bug** and **debug**. The word *bug*, as a fluke or problem, has been around a long time, but Dr. Hopper tells the story of the "first actual bug found" in her book *Understanding Computers* (West, 1984).

In the summer of 1945, scientists were working on the Mark II, one of the earliest computers. The Mark II had stopped for no apparent reason, and the programmers were trying to figure out what was wrong. They finally discovered that a moth was caught in one of the relays, causing the malfunction. They removed the bug and the computer worked fine. Since then, computer scientists have used the term *debugging* to refer to removing any type of error or malfunction from either a computer's hardware or software. (The original "bug" is taped to a page in a logbook on display at the Naval Weapons Museum in Dahlgren, Virginia.)

Dr. Hopper received 27 honorary doctorates, as well as awards from learned societies in both Europe and the United States. In fact, the Data Processing Management Association selected her as its first computer sciences "Man of the Year"!

Amazing Grace died in her sleep January 1, 1992.

Integrated circuit technology is responsible for the computer industry's technical progress. By the second generation, scientists knew that more powerful computers could be created by building more complex circuits. But because the circuits had to be wired by hand, these computers were too complex and expensive to build. Integrated circuit technology removed this barrier. The result was a computer that cost no more than first-generation computers but offered more memory and faster processing.

In 1962, a new company built a plant in what is now known as the "Silicon Valley," near San Jose, California. Digital Equipment Corporation (DEC) rocked the computer industry with the announcement of a revolutionary type of computer based on integrated circuits. The first commercially available **minicomputer** was introduced in 1965. The PDP-8 (Programmed Data Processor) could fit easily in the corner of a room and did not require the attention of a full-time computer operator. Most unusual, the computer could be accessed by users from different locations in the same building (the implementation of **time-sharing**, which was developed in second-generation computers). This minicomputer's price tag was about one-fourth the cost of a traditional mainframe. For the first time, smaller companies could afford computers.

Courtesy of Charles Babbage Institute, University of Minnesota

Some models of the DEC PDP-8 minicomputer were small enough to fit in the trunk of a car.

During this time, IBM secured domination of the mainframe market by releasing its 360 family of computers. The 360s were different sizes of mainframes based on the same machine language. This sharing of a single machine language enabled businesses to easily upgrade their computers without the usual costs of replacing peripheral equipment and modifying programs to run on new systems.

By 1967, so many different programming languages were in use that IBM decided to "unbundle" its systems. Before that time, buyers received language translators for all the languages that could run on the computer systems they purchased. Now buyers purchased only the translators they needed. The result was a competitive market for language translators and the beginning of the software industry.

Another significant development of this generation was the launching of the first telecommunications satellite. Communications stations on the earth could transmit and receive data to and from the satellites, enabling worldwide communications between computer systems.

The Fourth Generation (1975 to Today)

In the early 1970s, an Intel Corporation engineer, Dr. Ted Hoff, was given the task of designing an integrated circuit to power a digital watch. Previously, these circuits had to be redesigned every time a new model of the watch appeared. Hoff decided that he could avoid costly redesigns by creating a tiny computer on a chip. The result was the Intel 4004, the world's first **microprocessor**. A microprocessor chip holds *on a single chip* the entire control unit and arithmetic-logic unit of a computer.

The significance of the microprocessor cannot be overstated—it has changed the world. The techniques, called **very large scale integration** (**VLSI**), used to build microprocessors enable chip companies to mass-produce computer chips that contain hundreds of thousands, or even millions, of transistors.

The microprocessor's bright future wasn't clear in 1974, though. The company that had asked Intel to make the watch circuit wasn't impressed and never used it fully. Still, Intel persisted. The company's 8080 chip interested only computer hobbyists, but it had technical improvements that made it suitable for serious computing.

The large computer companies considered the **microcomputer** nothing but a toy, and the first microcomputers were aimed at computer hobbyists. The MITS Altair, marketed in 1975, was the first commercially available microcomputer. The Altair used Intel's 8080 chip. Calling the Altair a microcomputer may be dignifying it more than it deserves, however. It had no screen, no keyboard, and no capability to store programs or data! Third-party firms quickly developed these additional devices for the Altair.

During the late 1970s, many companies released microcomputer kits, but they were difficult to assemble. However, two young entrepreneurs, Steve Jobs and Steve Wozniak, dreamed of creating an "appliance computer." They wanted a microcomputer so simple that you could take it out of the box, plug it in, and use it, just as you use a toaster oven. Jobs and Wozniak set up shop in a garage after selling a Volkswagen for $1,300 to raise the needed capital. With the help of business expert Mike Markkula, they founded Apple Computer, Inc., in April 1977. Its first product, the Apple I, was a processor board intended for hobbyists, but the experience the company gained in building the Apple I led to the Apple II computer system.

Photographs courtesy of Apple Computer, Inc.

The two Steves—Steve Jobs (in the white sweater and red shirt) and Steve Wozniak—are holding the Apple I board.

Early Apple computers.

Courtesy of Apple Computer, Inc.

The Apple I.

Courtesy of International Business Machines Corporation

The IBM PC.

The Apple II was a huge success. With a keyboard, monitor, floppy disk drive, and operating system, the Apple II was a complete microcomputer system. Apple Computer, Inc., became one of the leading forces in the microcomputer market. The introduction of the first electronic spreadsheet software, VisiCalc, in 1979 helped convince the world that these little microcomputers were more than toys.

In 1980, IBM decided that the microcomputer market was too promising to ignore and contracted with Microsoft Corporation to write an operating system for a new microcomputer. The IBM Personal Computer (PC), with a microprocessor chip made by Intel Corporation and a Microsoft operating system, was released in 1981. Because Microsoft and Intel were independent contractors, they were free to place their products on the open market. As a result, many different manufacturers produced microcomputers that are now known as **IBM compatibles**.

Fourth-generation technology is still going strong. Efforts to pack even more transistors on one chip have led to such developments as Intel's Pentium Pro microprocessor. It contains 5.5 million transistors—a far cry from the 2,250 transistors found in the first Intel chip. Many experts believe that further miniaturization efforts will create billions of transistors on one chip.

Although high-level languages are still used extensively, very high-level languages appeared during the fourth generation. A very high-level language is really a way of writing instructions for a complex application program that has a large command set. Most new languages are based on a concept known as object-oriented programming (OOP), which encourages programmers to reuse code by maintaining libraries of code segments.

Another fourth-generation development is the spread of high-speed computer networking, which enables computers to communicate and share data. Within organizations, **local area networks** (**LANs**) connect several dozen or even several hundred computers within a limited geographic area (one building or several buildings near each other). **Wide area networks** (**WANs**) provide global connections for today's computers.

Computer Technology Today

Today's microcomputer is smaller, faster, cheaper, and more powerful than ENIAC. Microcomputers are available in desktop, laptop, notebook, and palmtop models. The Christmas season of 1994 was notable for the computer industry because for the first time, the sales of microcomputers exceeded the sales of television sets. It has been estimated that by 2010, microcomputers will be as common as television sets.

Because of microcomputers, individuals who are not computer profession- als are now the majority of users. To make computers more **user friendly** (easier to work with), companies developed graphical user interfaces. A **graphical user interface** (**GUI**) provides icons (pictures) and menus (lists of command choices) that users can select with a mouse. The first commercially marketed GUI, known as Finder, was introduced by Apple for the Macintosh in 1984. Microsoft has developed a similar GUI, known as Windows, that is popular on IBM-compatible microcomputers. In addition, most new applications include tutorials and extensive help for new users.

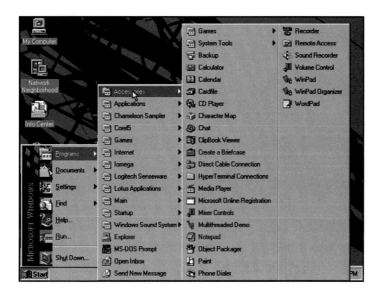

Graphical user interfaces, such as Microsoft Windows 95, enable new computer users to learn to use a personal computer quickly.

The microcomputer industry has been split between the Apple and IBM families of microcomputers since 1981. Historically, these two families could not use the same programs. This changed in 1991 when Apple, IBM, and Motorola entered into an agreement that has resulted in the develop- ment of microcomputers that can switch between a Macintosh mode and an IBM mode. Since 1992, all Apple Macintosh computers come equipped with the capability of reading IBM formatted floppy disks and executing programs written for IBM microcomputers. In late 1995, IBM released com- puters capable of reading Apple formatted floppy disks and running pro- grams written for Apple computers. In 1996, IBM purchased license rights to the Apple Macintosh operating system. It is a matter of time before the two families become one.

A Fifth Generation?

If there is a fifth generation, it's slow in coming; after all, the last one began in 1975. (Remember though, that dates are arbitrary, and we may soon learn that the fifth generation began in 1990!) Major changes are occurring in software as well as in hardware. According to experts, the trademark of the next generation will be **artificial intelligence** (**AI**). Computers that use artificial intelligence will have some attributes associated with human intelligence, such as the capabilities to decode and respond to natural lan- guage (a human language such as English), to reason and draw inferences, and to recognize patterns in sensory input.

Your Personal Translator

Sprechen zie Deutsch? If not, don't despair. A special kind of software is coming to the rescue, to help you communicate confidently with people in foreign lands, in their own languages.

In computers, the written word is the mainstay of communication. Whether we use e-mail, word processing documents, or desktop publishing files, we communicate with words. Words are usually fine when you are communicating with people in your own country, but the computer has an increasingly international reach. Communicating with colleagues in a foreign land, however, may be difficult. You can either learn the foreign language (or arrogantly insist that others learn yours), or you can find someone else to do the translation for you.

At this point, *machine-assisted translation* comes in handy. Several companies have developed software programs that take your original document and translate it into a foreign language. Traditionally, these translations were poor at best, but new improvements in artificial intelligence have made the process faster and more reliable. The programs must accomplish two tasks: analyze the words and analyze the context in which the words are used. If this analysis is not performed successfully, the translation loses quite a bit of accuracy.

One company making translation software is Intergraph Corporation. Its Transcend software is aimed at minimizing the complexity of language and therefore increasing the accuracy of translation. The software interprets the sentence structure of the original text and generates a translation by converting those structures into the rules of the target language.

Machine-assisted translation is a boon to people who need to communicate with others around the world, but this technique still has a long way to go. Most software (including Transcend) produces a *draft translation,* which means that it is simply a first-pass translation. This limitation is necessary because human languages contain many ambiguities that make them complex and hard to translate automatically. These ambiguities can be lexical (related to the grammatical properties of a word), syntactic (related to the context in which the word is used), or semantic (related to the meaning of the word). The

software must make "educated guesses" on how these ambiguities should be resolved.

Although the translated document is understandable, it still needs an experienced human translator to get it ready for widespread publication. Therefore, translation software is acceptable for casual or noncritical business communication but cannot be relied on for diplomatic, financial, legal, or commercial communication (such as advertising copy). It is interesting to note that machine-assisted translation is highly successful for technical documents because they avoid many of the ambiguities mentioned.

In the past, many people had all but given up on machine-assisted translation. But the current successes with machine-translation software increase the prospects for even more dramatic success in the future.

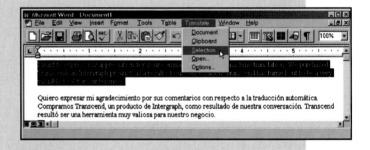

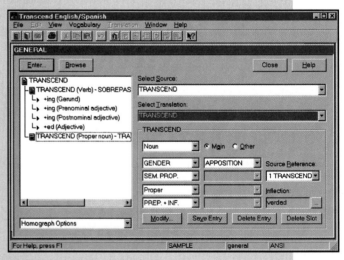

Courtesy of Intergraph Corporation

Table 1B.1	Four Stages, or Generations, of Computer Development		
Generation	Years	Circuitry	Characterized By
First	1951 to 1959	Vacuum tubes	Magnetic drum and magnetic tape; difficult to program; used machine language and assembly language
Second	1959 to 1963	Transistors	Magnetic cores and magnetic disk; used high-level languages and were easier to program
Third	1963 to 1975	Integrated circuit	Minicomputer accessible by multiple users from remote terminals
Fourth	1975 to present	VLSI and the microprocessor chip	Personal computer and user-friendly programs; very high-level language; object-oriented programming (OOP)

The human drive to learn required innovations in equipment. Past inventions made future innovations possible. Innovations, from graphics capabilities to parallel processing, have filtered down from the supercomputers to the mainframes. Minicomputers and microcomputers capable of parallel processing are being perfected even as you read this book. You can foresee the future of small computers by watching the developments in the larger machines.

Lesson Summary

➤ The history of calculating devices is important to undertanding the development of computers.

➤ Charles Babbage designed the first computer. He is known as the "father of the computer."

➤ Herman Hollerith used punched cards to automate the U.S. Census Bureau. He later became one of the founders of IBM.

➤ ENIAC was invented by Eckert and Mauchly for the U.S. Department of Defense during World War II.

➤ First-generation computers were large, slow, and based on vacuum tube technology. They were programmed using machine language and assembly language.

➤ Second-generation computers were based on transistors and used a magnetic core for primary storage, with magnetic tape and disk as secondary storage. These computers were programmed using high-level languages.

➤ Multiprogramming is the capability of a computer to switch between programs requested by different users and to execute the programs concurrently.

➤ Multiprocessing is possible on a computer system that has more than one central processing unit. Each processor can execute a program, enabling simultaneous processing of programs.

➤ The invention of the integrated circuit enabled smaller computers to be invented. The minicomputers that were developed in the late 1960s can fit in a corner of a room.

➤ Fourth-generation computers are very small, from microcomputers to notebook computers to palmtop computers.

Lesson Review

Key Terms

analytical engine	IBM compatible	parallel processing	user friendly
artificial intelligence	integrated circuit	Pascal	very large scale integration
bug	local area network (LAN)	punched card	(VLSI)
debug	microcomputer	stored-program concept	wide area network (WAN)
difference engine	microprocessor	time-sharing	
graphical user interface	minicomputer	Turing machine	
(GUI)	multiprogramming	Turing test	

Matching

In the blank next to each of the following terms or phrases, write the letter of the corresponding term or phrase.

_____ 1. Developed during the second generation of computers to make programs portable and easier to write

_____ 2. Founded IBM Corporation

_____ 3. Made computing affordable for small- and medium-sized businesses

_____ 4. Known as "the father of the computer"

_____ 5. Used as input to first- and second-generation computers

_____ 6. Programs for the first-generation computers were written in this

_____ 7. Founded Apple Corporation

_____ 8. A single chip containing the control and arithmetic-logic units of a computer

_____ 9. The main hardware component of first-generation computers

_____ 10. A chip that contains many transistors and electronic circuits

a. microprocessor

b. minicomputer

c. high-level language

d. machine language

e. Charles Babbage

f. vacuum tubes

g. punched cards

h. Jobs and Wozniak

i. Hollerith and Watson

j. integrated circuit

Multiple Choice

Circle the letter of the correct choice for each of the following.

1. Which calculating device was used in ancient times?
   a. arithmometer
   b. computer
   c. stepped reckoner
   d. abacus

2. What characterizes first-generation computers?
   a. vacuum tubes and magnetic drum
   b. magnetic tape and transistors
   c. minicomputers
   d. none of the above

3. Which of the following is *not* true of computers as we progress from one generation to the next?
   a. Computer size decreased.
   b. Computer cost decreased.
   c. Speed of processing increased.
   d. Memory/storage capacities decreased.

4. What are Steve Jobs and Steve Wozniak known for?
   a. the first IBM-compatible computer
   b. the first communications satellite
   c. the first Apple computer
   d. the stored-program concept

5. Which of the following is true about GUIs?
   a. They make computers easier to use for nonprofessionals.
   b. They use icons and menus that users can select with a mouse.
   c. They were first introduced for the Macintosh by Apple Computer, Inc.
   d. all of the above

6. What is Jon von Neumann credited with?
   a. designing the first electronic computer
   b. automating the U.S. Census Bureau
   c. the stored-program concept
   d. inventing the microprocessor

7. What invention enabled developers to create microcomputers?
   a. integrated circuit
   b. transistor
   c. vacuum tube
   d. magnetic disk

8. What is Admiral Grace Hopper known for developing?
   a. the microprocessor chip
   b. the COBOL language
   c. the stored-program concept
   d. multiprocessing

9. What type of system concurrently processes programs submitted by different users?
   a. multiprocessing
   b. microcomputer
   c. GUI
   d. multiprogramming

10. Multiprogramming was developed by students and professors at which school?
    a. Harvard
    b. MIT
    c. Cambridge
    d. University of Pennsylvania

Completion

In the blank provided, write the correct answer for each of the following.

1. Joseph Jacquard used _____ to give instructions to an automated loom.

2. High-level language was introduced during the _____ computer generation.

3. _____ was the first computer programmer.

4. _____ and _____ built the first special-purpose electronic digital computer.

5. Sending data from one computer to another using telephone lines started during the _____ generation.

6. The "Silicon Valley" is located in _____.

7. The software industry started when computer manufacturers _____ their systems and started selling language translators separately.

8. The _____ was the first commercially available microcomputer.

9. Computer programs that are easy to learn to work with are called _____.

10. A(n) _____ holds the control unit and arithmetic-logic unit of a computer.

Review

On a separate sheet of paper, answer the following questions.

1. What major innovation of the nineteenth century used ideas similar to the programmable loom to aid in the census taking? Explain in what way the innovation was similar.

2. What major hardware technology characterized each of the four generations of computers?

3. What have you observed regarding the size, cost, and processing speed of computers throughout the four generations?

4. What is a GUI? Why is it valuable? Name two companies responsible for developing the first GUIs.

5. Who was Lady Augusta Ada Byron?

6. What is Herman Hollerith remembered for?

7. What is the Turing test?

8. Explain the stored-program concept.

9. What are the two major families of microcomputers?

10. Why were Apple microcomputers on the market for so long before any compatibles appeared, even though IBM compatibles appeared almost immediately?

Critical Thinking

On a separate sheet of paper, answer the following questions.

1. Do you believe that the fifth generation of computers has already started? If not, why? If so, what innovation do you believe marked the beginning?

2. What problems do you think you would have encountered if you had been working for the U.S. Census Bureau at the time it purchased the first commercially available computer, UNIVAC?

3. In what way were computers that used the stored-program concept different from earlier computers that did not?

4. What might have been the immediate and long-range consequences if Babbage's difference engine and analytical engine had been successfully produced?

5. Provide two examples of how artificial intelligence might be used in the future to improve the quality of living for people.

Further Discovery

Computer: A History of the Information Machine. Martin Campbell-Kelly and William Aspray (New York: BasicBooks, 1996).

Engines of the Mind. Joel Shurkin (New York: W. W. Norton, 1996).

Landmarks in Digital Computing: A Smithsonian Pictorial History. Peggy Aldrich Kidwell and Paul E. Ceruzzi (Washington, DC: Smithsonian Institution Press, 1994).

On-line Discovery

You can access the Internet resources for the following questions by going to the Que Education and Training Web site at URL http://www.ciyf98.com/discovery. From this page, click the link for Lesson 1B and then click the link to the resource you want to access.

1. Michelle Hoyle, from the University of Regina in Canada, has made available through the World Wide Web a presentation that she gives on the history of computing. In **Computers: From the Past to the Present** (http://calypso.cs.uregina.ca/Lecture/default.html), she recounts some of the most important events in the development of computers and computing, many of which are discussed in this lesson. What do you think are the most important developments in the history of computing? If you were to write the history of computing fifty years from now, what kinds of developments do you think you might be recounting?

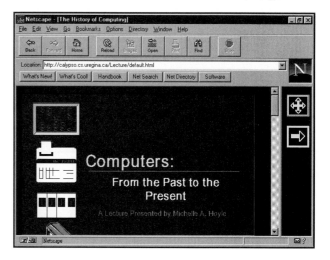

2. For a detailed time line of events in the history of computers, none is better than Ken Polsson's **Chronology of Events in the History of Microcomputers** (http://www.islandnet.com/~kpolsson /comphist.htm). See whether you can pick out certain themes in the events that make up computing history, including the impact of technological developments, the impact of entrepreneurship, and the impact of law and the courts.

CHAPTER 2

Computer Hardware

Imagine a computer. What do you think of? A box sitting on a desk and connected to a screen, a keyboard, and a printer? Do you know how the computer works?

Most people think of a computer as a microcomputer on a desk. But there are computers large enough to fill a room and small enough to fit in a briefcase.

Most people don't really understand the process of transforming raw data into usable information. Most don't understand what goes on inside the computer. Many people are confused by the need for storage and the different types of storage. Even more fail to understand that all computers, large and small, work in much the same way. When you finish this chapter, you will know how computers process and store data, and you will understand the similarities and differences among the sizes of computer systems.

Lesson 2A explains how the computer can process data and describes the different kinds of memory.

Lesson 2B discusses data, information, and ways to organize data so that it can be processed into information. Whether you are doing a statistical analysis of experiment results, running a trial balance of a ledger, or writing a new best-seller, you are having the computer process data.

Lesson 2C discusses computer input and output devices, such as keyboards, monitors, and printers.

Lesson 2D describes the different sizes of computers and explains some of their similarities and differences.

LESSON 2A

Processing and Memory

Outline

Processing
- Data Representation
- The Central Processing Unit
  - Compatibility
  - Data Bus
  - System Clock
  - Address Bus
  - CISC and RISC
  - Numeric Coprocessor
- New Processor Chips
  - Intel Chips
  - Motorola Chips
  - Digital Equipment Corporation Chips

Memory
- RAM (Random-Access Memory)
- Cache Memory
- ROM (Read-Only Memory)

The Motherboard

Learning Objectives

When you have finished reading this lesson, you will be able to

➤ Explain how computers represent data

➤ Compare the performances of commonly used microprocessors

➤ Explain the role played by the computer's internal memory

➤ Explain the different forms of memory

QUE Labs

➤ **Computer Fundamentals**

➤ **Input/Output Devices**

➤ **CPU**

➤ **Binary Logic**

For most users, what's inside the **system unit**—the big box that contains the processing circuitry and storage devices—is a mystery. Yet a little knowledge of what's inside that box is essential for computer literacy. It is important that you know enough about processing to make intelligent selections when buying a computer. This knowledge also comes in handy so that you can use application programs efficiently.

Processing

Computers represent data in digital form; computers treat everything, even text, numerically. The central processing unit (CPU) processes the data, and internal memory keeps program instructions and data readily available in an electronic scratch pad. This lesson examines what really happens inside the system unit.

Data Representation

Computers can operate in only two states: on and off. The on state is represented by 1; the off state, by 0. Computers work with data that has been encoded using nothing but the **binary digits** 0 and 1. These are the only digits in the binary, or base 2, number system used by computers.

Binary digits, also called **bits**, can be grouped to form letters, numbers, or special symbols. To represent the numbers 0 through 9 and the letters *a* through *z* and *A* through *Z*, computer designers have created coding systems consisting of several hundred standard codes. In one code, for instance, the binary number 01000001 stands for the letter *A*. An understanding of the way computers code data will help you understand how they operate.

There are two competing coding standards. Most supercomputers and mainframe computers use a code called Extended Binary Coded Decimal Interchange Code (**EBCDIC**). Almost all smaller computers, including minicomputers and personal computers, use the American Standard Code for Information Interchange (**ASCII**). As shown in Table 2A.1, the character representations differ. ANSI, a superset of ASCII, is the basis of the code used in Microsoft Windows.

Some application programs attach special meanings to certain ASCII codes. These codes are used for designated purposes, such as formatting (for example, boldface or italic). As a result, one program often cannot read data created in another program unless the receiving program has the capability to translate the other program's codes.

Sometimes you hear computer users ask for data in "plain ASCII." They mean data that contains nothing but the standard ASCII codes (with no special codes that application programs add). Almost any program can use data that contains nothing but the standard ASCII codes.

Originally, ASCII used a seven-bit system and EBCDIC used a six-bit system, but those systems didn't allow computers to represent enough characters. Today, both ASCII and EBCDIC use an eight-bit coding system. This eight-bit group is known as a **byte**, or a character. Most computers are designed to add a ninth bit to each character's code. This extra bit, a **parity bit**, provides a way to check for memory or data communication errors. These errors can occur if a computer transfers a character incorrectly. For example, a speck of dust or smoke on a disk can cause the computer to interpret a 0 as a 1, or vice versa.

Character	ASCII	EBCDIC	Character	ASCII	EBCDIC
A	01000001	11000001	S	01010011	11100010
B	01000010	11000010	T	01010100	11100011
C	01000011	11000011	U	01010101	11100100
D	01000100	11000100	V	01010110	11100101
E	01000101	11000101	W	01010111	11100110
F	01000110	11000110	X	01011000	11100111
G	01000111	11000111	Y	01011001	11101000
H	01001000	11001000	Z	01011010	11101001
I	01001001	11001001	0	00110000	11110000
J	01001010	11010001	1	00110001	11110001
K	01001011	11010010	2	00110010	11110010
L	01001100	11010011	3	00110011	11110011
M	01001101	11010100	4	00110100	11110100
N	01001110	11010101	5	00110101	11110101
O	01001111	11010110	6	00110110	11110110
P	01010000	11010111	7	00110111	11110111
Q	01010001	11011000	8	00111000	11111000
R	01010010	11011001	9	00111001	11111001

Table 2A.1   Some ASCII and EBCDIC Codes

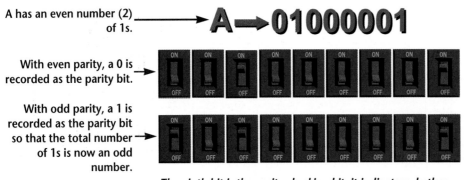

A has an even number (2) of 1s. A → 01000001

With even parity, a 0 is recorded as the parity bit.

With odd parity, a 1 is recorded as the parity bit so that the total number of 1s is now an odd number.

The ninth bit is the parity-checking bit; it indicates whether an odd number or an even number of 1s is transmitted.

C has an odd number (3) of 1s. C → 01000011

With even parity, a 1 is recorded as the parity bit so that the total number of 1s will be an even number.

With odd parity, a 0 is recorded as the parity bit.

Computers use odd parity or even parity. The computer counts the number of 1s in each byte and records a 1 or a 0 as the parity bit, whichever is necessary to equal an odd or an even number of 1s. (The word *parity* means "equality.") In **odd parity**, the computer sets a 1 bit if the sum of the other 1 bits is an even number. In **even parity**, the computer sets a 0 bit if the sum of the other 1 bits is an even number. The parity bit is extremely important when two computers exchange information. To interpret the incoming information properly, each computer needs to know whether the other computer is using even parity or odd parity.

The Central Processing Unit

No other single element of a computer determines its overall performance as much as the **central processing unit** (**CPU**). If you understand how CPUs are designed and know the kinds of CPUs available, you can quickly evaluate any computer's capabilities.

The CPU is composed of two parts:

> ➤ Control unit

> ➤ Arithmetic-logic unit

The **control unit** coordinates and controls all the other parts of the computer system. The control unit even oversees the operations of the input and output devices. The **arithmetic-logic unit** does the actual processing by performing mathematical operations and logical operations, such as making comparisons. In a **microprocessor**, the control unit and the arithmetic-logic unit are mounted on a single silicon chip.

Large computer systems, as well as newer workstations and network servers, frequently contain more than one central processing unit. Multiple CPUs enable the computer to execute more than one instruction, or process more than one program, at the same time. This capability is known as **multi-processing**.

TechTalk
A network server is a high-capacity, high-speed computer that controls all or some of the procedures on a network.

Here are some key points you should know about processors:

> ➤ Software must be written in accordance with a particular CPU's requirements. For this reason, programs written for one processor may not be compatible with a processor that is designed differently.

> ➤ Some CPUs process data much more quickly than others. You should learn how to evaluate a given processor's speed. To do this, you need to understand how the data bus width and system clock speed affect performance.

> ➤ The width of a CPU's address bus determines the maximum amount of memory it can use.

> ➤ The performance of most CPUs can be improved through the use of a coprocessor, a second processing chip that handles numeric or graphics computations.

The following sections explain these points and define important terms.

This PowerPC 601 silicon chip (lower right) is inserted on a main circuit board, which is housed inside a personal computer.

Courtesy of International Business Machines Corporation

Compatibility

Every processor has its own unique instruction set. An **instruction set** is a list of the specific instructions that tell the CPU what to do. The machine language designed for a specific CPU must be designed to work with the CPU's instruction set.

Because each processor has a unique instruction set, programs devised for one computer will not run on another (with two exceptions, discussed shortly). Programs must be written using instructions recognized by that

CPU. For example, a program written for the Apple Macintosh will not run on an IBM PC. A program that can run on a given computer is **compatible** with that computer's processor. Or you can say that a program is a **native application** for a given CPU design.

One exception to the rule that a program written for one brand of processor will not run on another involves a program called a **software emulator**, which can make one CPU "pretend" to be another. For example, the Apple Macintosh can emulate an IBM PC and run IBM PC programs. This emulation, though, brings a severe performance penalty. IBM PC programs run very slowly on a Macintosh. The second exception is to have programs written for a particular operating system and then have the operating system tailored to fit the CPU. One example of this approach is Windows NT.

Panda Project, Inc., entered the microcomputer market last year with a system that can run with different microprocessor chips. You just pull out a board with one type of microprocessor and plug in another board with a different type of microprocessor. Panda states that upgrading to new, faster microprocessors will be equally easy.

Microprocessor manufacturers must carefully consider compatibility when introducing new models. In particular, manufacturers must decide whether to make the new chip downwardly compatible with previous models. A **downwardly compatible** chip can run the programs designed to run with the earlier chip(s). To introduce a microprocessor that is not downwardly compatible with previous models is very risky. People may not buy a computer that cannot run the programs they already own. Manufacturers learned this lesson with early mainframe computers.

For this reason, the microprocessors used in today's personal computers are descendants of older microprocessor designs. Two brands predominate: Intel and Motorola (although Digital Equipment Corporation is also producing some impressive microprocessors). Intel microprocessors, including the Pentium chip, are downwardly compatible with chips dating all the way back to Ted Hoff's 4004, the world's first microprocessor. The Motorola 68040 series microprocessor is downwardly compatible with the 68000 (dating from the early 1980s), the 68020, and the 68030.

CPU performance is evaluated by the number of operations that the processor can carry out in one second. Today's fastest processors can carry out many millions of operations per second! A microprocessor's speed is determined by two major factors: bus width and clock speed.

Data Bus

The first element that determines a CPU's speed is its data bus width, measured in bits (8, 16, 32, or 64). **Bus width** is what people are talking about when they say, "That's a 16-bit computer" or "That's a 32-bit computer." The number of bits in the bus determines the number of bits that the computer can work with at a time; this number is the computer's **word** size. A 16-bit computer works with a 16-bit word, while a 32-bit computer works with a 32-bit word.

What does bus width mean? The control unit and arithmetic-logic unit—as well as all the components of the computer—are connected by a **bus**, which is a "highway" of parallel wires. The bus is a pathway for the electronic impulses that form bytes.

A **data bus** connects the CPU and memory and provides a pathway to the computer's peripherals. A microprocessor has both an internal data bus and an external data bus. Sometimes the internal data bus is wider than the external data bus. The internal data bus operates only within the microprocessor itself; the external bus regulates communication with the rest of the computer. For example, the CPU used in the original IBM PC had a 16-bit internal data bus and an 8-bit external data bus. The use of a narrower external bus enables designers to use inexpensive, existing peripherals, such as disk drives and memory chips. However, this design is a compromise that results in a substantial performance penalty.

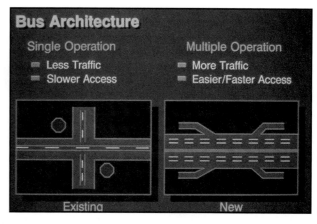

Courtesy of International Business Machines Corporation

Similar to a multilane highway, a wider computer bus enables more bits of data to travel simultaneously from one part of the computer system to another part.

There are two types of bus systems: open and closed. An **open bus system** has expansion slots on the motherboard. To add a new peripheral, a board must be plugged into an expansion slot, and the system must be instructed to accept the new device. A **closed bus system** comes with established ports into which cables attached to peripheral devices can be plugged.

System Clock

Bus width is not the only design factor that affects a computer's speed. The **system clock** regulates the CPU's processing functions by emitting a pulse at regular intervals. The **clock speed** is the number of times that the system clock pulses in one second. Clock speed is usually measured in millions of pulses, or cycles. One million cycles is a **megahertz**.

Clock speed alone is not an adequate gauge of a microprocessor's performance. A 32-bit chip can process data much more rapidly than a chip hobbled by a 16-bit external data bus, even if the clock speed is the same. The number of operations per clock tick, or cycle, also affects performance. Most computers perform one operation per cycle. The Pentium and Pentium Pro chips, however, use a superscalar architecture that permits more than one instruction to be executed each clock tick.

Courtesy of Digital Equipment Corporation

Perched on a sea of blue marbles, this Alpha chip from Digital Equipment Corporation is the highest-performance chip available. It operates at 275MHz and is used in all kinds of computers—from PCs to supercomputers.

Address Bus

Like a post office box at the post office, every storage location in the computer's memory has a unique address. The address for the location does not change, but the data stored there can change. (Again using the mailing address analogy, the street address for a house doesn't change even though different people may move in and out of the house.) The width of the CPU's **address bus**—a set of wires running from the CPU to the memory—determines the maximum number of storage locations.

CISC and RISC

Another aspect of microprocessor design that you should be aware of is the distinction between CISC and RISC. Each has advantages and disadvantages.

Differences in Buses

A bus is a thoroughfare for travel in the electronic city.

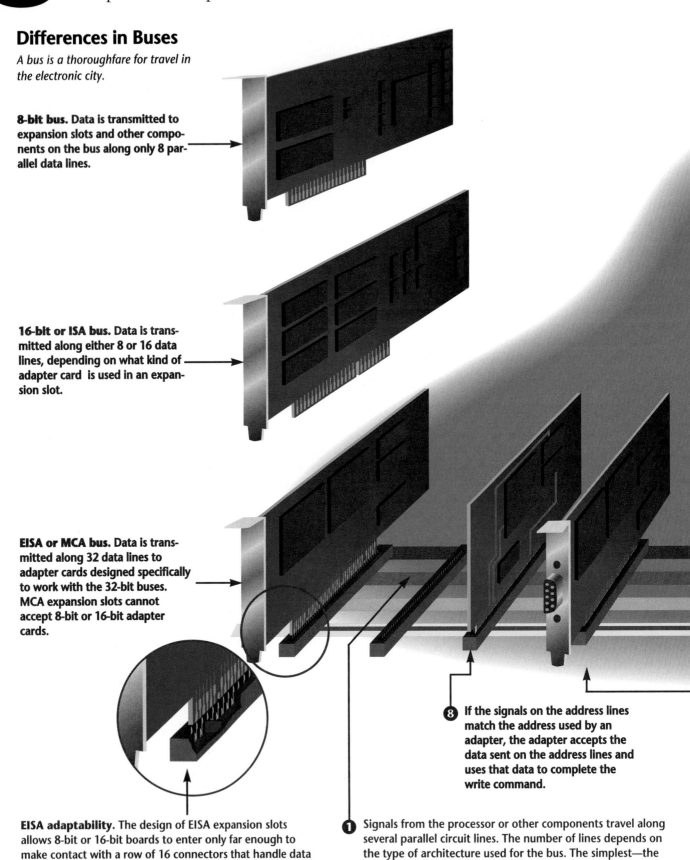

8-bit bus. Data is transmitted to expansion slots and other components on the bus along only 8 parallel data lines.

16-bit or ISA bus. Data is transmitted along either 8 or 16 data lines, depending on what kind of adapter card is used in an expansion slot.

EISA or MCA bus. Data is transmitted along 32 data lines to adapter cards designed specifically to work with the 32-bit buses. MCA expansion slots cannot accept 8-bit or 16-bit adapter cards.

8 If the signals on the address lines match the address used by an adapter, the adapter accepts the data sent on the address lines and uses that data to complete the write command.

EISA adaptability. The design of EISA expansion slots allows 8-bit or 16-bit boards to enter only far enough to make contact with a row of 16 connectors that handle data based on the ISA bus. But boards designed specifically for the EISA slot can enter farther and align their connectors with 32 special slot connections that handle data based on EISA specifications.

1 Signals from the processor or other components travel along several parallel circuit lines. The number of lines depends on the type of architecture used for the bus. The simplest—the 8-bit bus used in the original IBM PC—uses 62 lines to connect to adapter cards. Any signal sent to an adapter card is received by all adapter cards.

Data Traveling Along the Bus

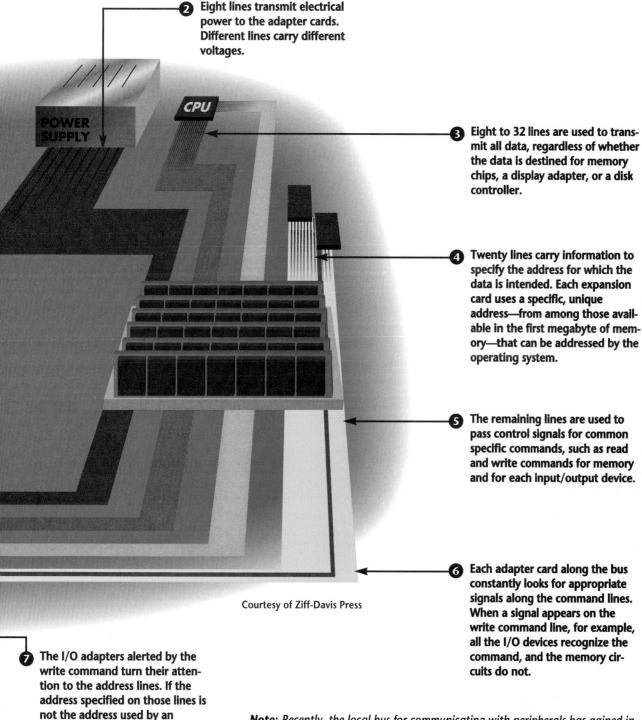

2 Eight lines transmit electrical power to the adapter cards. Different lines carry different voltages.

POWER SUPPLY

CPU

3 Eight to 32 lines are used to transmit all data, regardless of whether the data is destined for memory chips, a display adapter, or a disk controller.

4 Twenty lines carry information to specify the address for which the data is intended. Each expansion card uses a specific, unique address—from among those available in the first megabyte of memory—that can be addressed by the operating system.

5 The remaining lines are used to pass control signals for common specific commands, such as read and write commands for memory and for each input/output device.

6 Each adapter card along the bus constantly looks for appropriate signals along the command lines. When a signal appears on the write command line, for example, all the I/O devices recognize the command, and the memory circuits do not.

Courtesy of Ziff-Davis Press

7 The I/O adapters alerted by the write command turn their attention to the address lines. If the address specified on those lines is not the address used by an adapter, the adapter ignores the signals sent on the data lines.

Note: Recently, the local bus for communicating with peripherals has gained in popularity. The design overcomes the speed limitation imposed on all other bus designs. The original bus was designed to run at 8MHz, which was roughly twice as fast as the original IBM PC's 8088 processor. As processor speeds increased to 10MHz, 25MHz, 50MHz, and faster, the bus speed stayed at 8MHz. The local bus is designed to transmit 32 bits of data at the local speed of a PC's processor. Usually, a PC with a local bus limits that architecture to one or two slots, used for display adapters or disk controllers, where speed is most crucial. Slower conventional expansion slots are used to communicate with the serial and parallel ports and with the keyboard, where speed is not crucial.

CISC stands for **complex instruction set computer**. A CISC chip, such as the Motorola 68040 or the Intel Pentium, provides programmers with many instructions, and the processing circuitry includes many special-purpose circuits that carry out these instructions at high speed. Because the chip provides so many processing tools, CISC designs make the programmer's job easier. CISC chips, however, are complex and expensive to produce, and they run hot because they consume so much current.

RISC stands for **reduced instruction set computer**. A RISC chip offers a "bare bones" instruction set. For this reason, RISC chips are less complex, less expensive to produce, and more efficient in power usage. The drawback of the RISC design is that the computer must combine or repeat operations to complete many processing operations. (For example, you can eliminate multiplication circuitry by repeated addition.) RISC chips also place extra demands on programmers, who must consider how to get complex results by combining simple instructions. But careful tests show that this design results in faster processing than the CISC chips. An example of a RISC chip (with certain CISC compromises) is the PowerPC processor, which was developed jointly by Apple, IBM, and Motorola.

Computer designers argue about which design is best, but the marketplace will decide. Which will win—CISC or RISC? CISC chips are still in production because so many people use CISC software. (RISC chips can run CISC programs only under software emulation, which slows performance.) RISC chips, such as the PowerPC, may become popular if enough native applications become available.

Even so, the distinction between CISC and RISC may become meaningless. CISC manufacturers are employing many RISC design features that enable the chips to carry out more than one instruction at a time. These features include **superscalar architecture** (a design that enables the computer to process more than one instruction at a time), **pipelining** (a design that provides two or more processing pathways that can be used simultaneously), and **branch prediction** (a module that tries to predict the most effective way to route an instruction through the microprocessor). In the meantime, RISC manufacturers are finding that they must include some CISC design components to ensure compatibility.

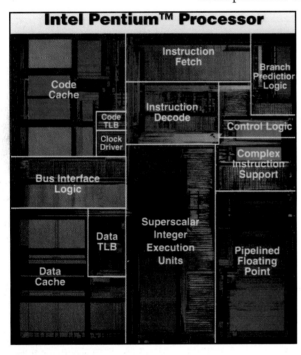

The two cache sections and the bus interface logic section on the Intel Pentium chip are part of the control unit. The other sections are part of the arithmetic-logic unit. The Pentium is a CISC chip, which operates at speeds up to 100MHz and is faster than many RISC chips.

Photographs courtesy of Intel Corporation

Numeric Coprocessor

For applications requiring intensive computation, such as spreadsheets, system performance can be enhanced by including a **numeric coprocessor**. Numeric coprocessors enable computers to perform mathematical operations faster. Until recently, numeric coprocessors were separate chips that could be added to a computer system as an option. Increasingly, numeric coprocessing circuitry is included in the microprocessor design.

All this information should help you understand some of the specifications of microprocessors. The distinctions among the Intel 486, Pentium, and Pentium Pro chips are much clearer when you understand the terminology. The 486DX chip operates at a maximum clock speed of 100 megahertz (the 486DX4-100) and has a 32-bit architecture (internal data bus, external data bus, and address bus.) The Pentium chip has a 32-bit internal data bus and address bus but also has a 64-bit external data bus. The Pentium Pro has clock speeds up to 200MHz. The recently announced P7 (a joint venture of Hewlett-Packard and Intel, slated for release in 1997) is expected to have speeds exceeding 250MHz.

New Processor Chips

More than anything else, the microprocessor determines the computer's overall performance. Learning about microprocessors can help you understand the differences in computer systems so that you can make rational buying decisions.

Remember, a microprocessor is designed to run at a certain clock speed. The clock speed is the rate at which the computer's tiny internal clock ticks a beat; the purpose of this mechanism is to synchronize internal data movements. As an example, the Pentium 75 runs at 75MHz. (One megahertz is one million clock ticks per second.)

Microprocessor chips produced by Intel, Motorola, and Digital Equipment Corporation (DEC) are primary movers in today's computer industry. And the industry has been moving quickly. The newest chip on the market today will probably be outdated next year!

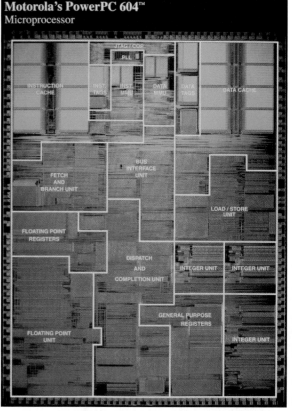

Courtesy of Apple Computers, Inc.

The PowerPC 604 microprocessor runs Macintosh System 7, MS-DOS, and Windows NT operating systems, among others.

Intel Chips

Most IBM and IBM-compatible microcomputers use microprocessor chips made by Intel. The 486 chips that were considered standard entry-level systems in the early and mid-1990s are now rarely seen. Today, the minimum configuration of most Intel machines includes some form of the Pentium chip.

The original Pentium chip, the hot new item of 1993-94 (maximum speed 200MHz) is in the twilight of its career. At a minimum, new computers will implement the Intel Pentium MMX with extensions to improve graphics and audio in multimedia applications written for it. This chip is available at 166, 200, and 233MHz. As newer, faster chips are released, on-line trade journals are becoming the best and most efficient way to keep up with changing industry standards.

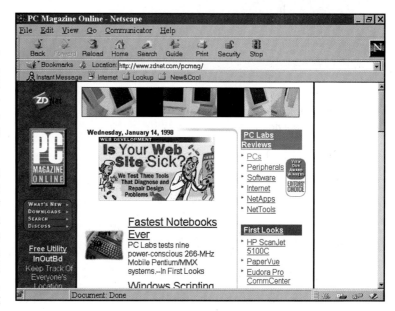

PC Magazine Online is an excellent source of information on the latest hardware.

The Pentium Pro (or 80686) Intel chip was originally announced at Comdex in November 1995. The Pentium Pro was the first of the Intel chips designed to be used in a multiprocessor system. Currently at the top of the line is the Pentium II, which essentially combines Pentium Pro

A schematic of the Pentium Pro chip.

Courtesy of Intel Corporation

The Pentium Pro chip.

architecture with MMX extensions. The Pentium II crams 7.5 million transistors onto the chip, compared to 5.5 million for the Pentium Pro and 4.5 million on the Pentium MMX. It was initially released, in May 1997, at 233, 266, and 300MHz. The beginning of 1998 brought a 333MHz version. This Pentium II is a substantial improvement over the first crop because it reduces the size of the circuitry from 0.33 microns to 0.25 microns. (By comparison, a human hair averages 75 microns.) The smaller size reduces the distance electrical signals need to travel. It also requires less power and, therefore, produces less heat. Before the end of 1998, 450MHz Pentium II's are likely with continued improvements through the end of the century.

Amazingly, still newer and faster chips are being designed. The P7 (786) chip is being developed by Intel in cooperation with Hewlett-Packard at a research facility in Sweden. The IntelP7/HPPA9000 is a 64-bit RISC chip that is scheduled for release in mid-1999. (The *PA* in the code stands for precision architecture.) Its anticipated 0.18 micron technology will allow it to carry at least 10 million transistors and run at speeds upward of 500MHz. The P7 should not impact individual users over the short term. It will initially be aimed at servers and high-end workstations. The second generation of P7 is already being planned for 2001 with a clock speed of 1GHz.

Motorola Chips

The Macintosh computer by Apple uses Motorola 68000 series microprocessors. The Motorola 68040 performs in a similar way to the Intel 486 chips. Introduced in 1989, this chip runs at 25MHz and uses a 32-bit word. The 68040V is a comparable chip that includes some energy-saving features and was designed specifically for the PowerBook laptop computer. The newer Motorola 68060, introduced in 1994, is quicker than the 68040, operating at 66MHz.

Power Macintoshes use PowerPC chips jointly designed by Motorola, IBM, and Apple Computer. In Power Macintoshes, the PowerPC runs software designed for 68000 series microprocessors by using emulation. The more powerful Power Macintoshes, such as the 7101 and 8101 models, can run Microsoft Windows software by using a different emulation program. However, there is a performance penalty when emulation is used.

The most widely used PowerPC chip is the 603e, which was designed specifically for use on laptops but works equally well on a desktop computer. The 603e is reasonably priced and is available in either 100MHz or 120MHz speed with a 32-bit word. The PowerPC 604, introduced in 1994, executes four instructions per cycle. With a speed of 133MHz, this is a fast, 32-bit processor. The PowerPC 620 appeared in 1995. This is the most ambitious PowerPC chip, offering full 64-bit processing capabilities and performing twice as fast as earlier PowerPC models. The 620 is designed primarily for technical and scientific workstations or for network servers.

Digital Equipment Corporation Chips

The Digital Equipment Corporation (DEC) Alpha micro-processor is a versatile RISC chip that has been used in super-minicomputers, mainframes, and supercomputers. The Alpha family of chips are all 64-bit processors that do not support 8- or 16-bit operations.

The new family of computers, based on the Alpha 21164 processor, is designed primarily for use in a client/server environment. The Digital AlphaServer 1000 with four 266MHz Alpha 21164 processors, for example, is priced beginning at $16,000 and can go as high as $250,000, depending on primary memory size and potential peripheral configuration. The Alpha 21164 has been acknowledged as the world's fastest—and first—billion instructions per second (BIPS) processor.

Memory

Computers use memory as a "scratch pad" to hold the programs and data in use by the CPU. Most computers have several types of memory: RAM, virtual memory, cache memory, and ROM. The following sections explain these terms.

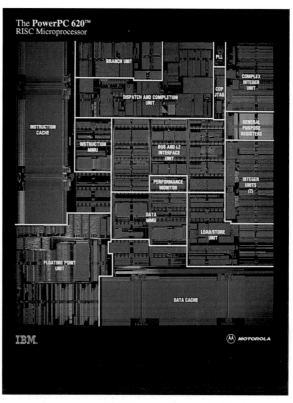

The PowerPC 620 chip.

RAM (Random-Access Memory)   *Volatile (temporary)*

No processor could function without high-speed memo-ry, where the processor can store the programs and data it is using. (When an advertisement states that a comput-er system has 4M of RAM, the ad is referring to high-speed memory.) Think of memory as a temporary scratch pad that the processor uses while carrying out its opera-tions. Storage devices, such as disk drives, store and retrieve data too slowly for this purpose.

Memory has many different names. It is called **random-access memory**—or just **RAM**—as well as **primary memory**. And sometimes, just to confuse things further, memory is called primary storage. This storage is in con-trast to storage devices that are referred to as secondary storage, such as disks.

Generally speaking, the more memory, the better. For today's Microsoft Windows and Macintosh applications, 8M of RAM is the absolute minimum, and 16M is much better. Many pro-grams run much more quickly with 16M, which is large enough to enable most of the program's instructions to be kept in memory. With 8M, the program must access instructions from secondary storage, which is much slower.

With most personal computers, the computer's motherboard is designed so that you can easily add more memory—you just add **memory chips**. Most memory chips are now mounted on boards, and all you need to do is to plug the board into a slot on the motherboard. Adding more memory chips may be necessary to run large or graphics-intensive applications.

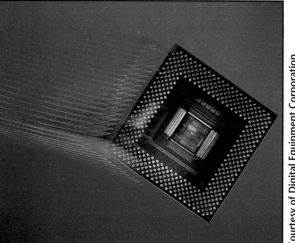

The DEC Alpha chip.

BITS
Whichever term is used for memory, the underlying point is the same. The pur-pose of memory is to keep data and program instructions close to the processing circuitry so that they're available for high-speed retrieval and modification.

The Microprocessor

The brain of the machine is the microprocessor. Note the presence of the control unit and the arithmetic-logic unit. Main memory is on separate ICs.

1 The prefetch unit, which queues instructions for processing, asks the bus interface unit to retrieve from memory the next instruction—in this example, a command to add two numbers. The goal of the prefetch unit is to make sure that the instruction decode unit won't have idle time while it waits for its next instructions.

2 At the same time, the segment and paging units convert the location of that instruction from a virtual address, which software understands, to a physical address (an actual location in memory), which the bus interface unit understands.

9 The control unit tells the bus interface unit to store the sum in RAM. The segment and paging units translate the virtual address specified by the control unit for that sum into a physical address, completing the instruction.

8 The arithmetic-logic unit, which is the microprocessor's calculator, produces the sum of the number that was just retrieved from RAM and the first number that had been stored in the internal registers.

7 The bus interface unit locates and retrieves the number stored at that address. The number travels back through the protection test unit to the execution unit, where it is stored in one of the chip's internal registers. The registers function as a combination scratch pad and working memory for the execution unit. A similar operation results in the second number also being fetched to the execution unit.

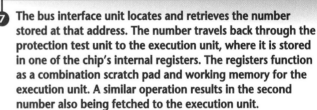

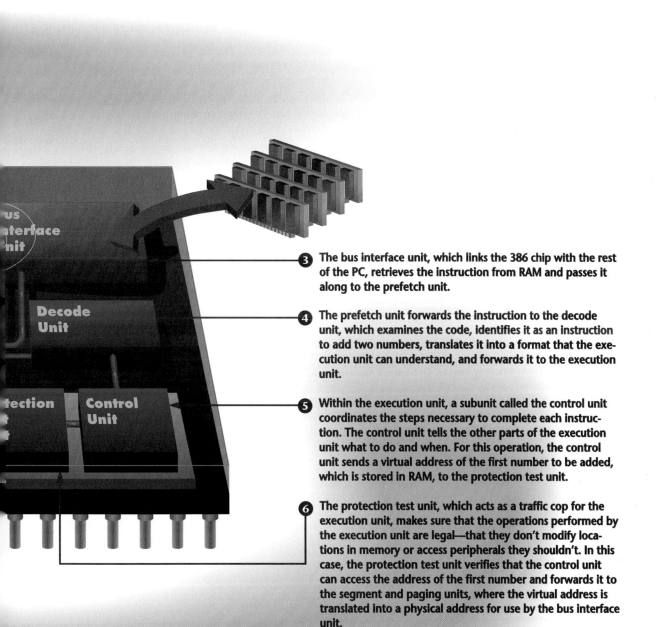

3 The bus interface unit, which links the 386 chip with the rest of the PC, retrieves the instruction from RAM and passes it along to the prefetch unit.

4 The prefetch unit forwards the instruction to the decode unit, which examines the code, identifies it as an instruction to add two numbers, translates it into a format that the execution unit can understand, and forwards it to the execution unit.

5 Within the execution unit, a subunit called the control unit coordinates the steps necessary to complete each instruction. The control unit tells the other parts of the execution unit what to do and when. For this operation, the control unit sends a virtual address of the first number to be added, which is stored in RAM, to the protection test unit.

6 The protection test unit, which acts as a traffic cop for the execution unit, makes sure that the operations performed by the execution unit are legal—that they don't modify locations in memory or access peripherals they shouldn't. In this case, the protection test unit verifies that the control unit can access the address of the first number and forwards it to the segment and paging units, where the virtual address is translated into a physical address for use by the bus interface unit.

Note: There are several types of 80386 microprocessors. Most are distinguished by the speed at which they run, usually expressed in megahertz. The higher the megahertz number, the faster the processor. There are also DX and SX versions of the 386. The DX communicates with RAM over a path that's 32 bits wide. The SX handles data internally, 32 bits at a time, just as the DX chip does, but the SX communicates with RAM only 16 bits at a time. The SX is easier and cheaper to incorporate into older PC designs, which is its only advantage.
Since the 386 was released, Intel has also created an 80486. It too manipulates data 32 bits at a time, but it includes two components that the 80386 does not. One is a built-in 8K RAM cache that works similarly to an external RAM cache to ensure that the processor is not forced to wait for the data it needs. The other component is a built-in math coprocessor, which is a set of instructions streamlined for handling complex math. The several types of Pentium chips use a similar basic processing architecture as the 386 and 486 types.

Larger computers have greater memory requirements because they usually run more than one program at a time. (The Cray-4 supercomputer comes standard with 256M of RAM; the DEC AXP/150 minicomputer has 128M of RAM standard.) This capability to run many programs submitted by different users is known as multiprogramming. In **multiprogramming**, memory is divided and then allocated to the programs being processed concurrently.

Some CPUs are designed to use **virtual memory** to run very large programs or two or more smaller programs, without running out of memory. Virtual memory systems divide large programs into smaller pieces and enable the computer to use free hard disk space as an extension of RAM. The computer will "swap" portions of the program between the hard drive and RAM as they are needed. Virtual memory can enable a computer with 4M of RAM to run a program that requires 6M.

Random-access memory is fast, but it has one drawback; it is **volatile**—which is a fancy way of saying that all the data disappears if the power fails. Nonvolatile media, such as disks, tapes, and CD-ROMs, are needed to store programs and data when the power is switched off. These types of media are discussed in Lesson 2B.

Cache Memory

When designing a computer, an engineer can include some options that make the machine run much faster. One of these options is cache memory. Storing instructions and data in cache memory can minimize the number of times that the computer needs to access secondary storage.

Cache memory (pronounced "cash" memory) is a specialized chip used with the computer's memory. Cache chips are faster and more expensive than regular RAM chips. The computer stores the most frequently used instructions and data in cache. Cache has a relatively small storage capacity but can significantly increase the system's speed.

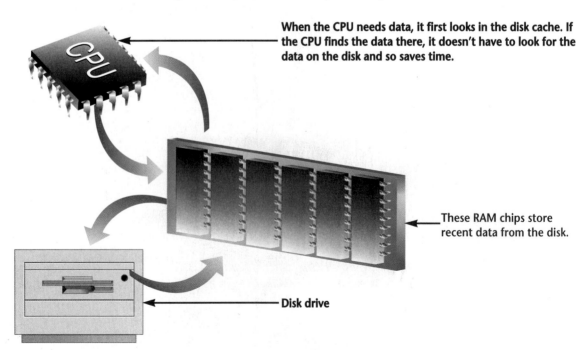

When the CPU needs data, it first looks in the disk cache. If the CPU finds the data there, it doesn't have to look for the data on the disk and so saves time.

These RAM chips store recent data from the disk.

Disk drive

ROM (Read-Only Memory) _non volatile_

If everything in RAM is erased when the power is turned off, how does the computer start again? The answer is **read-only memory (ROM)**. The instructions to start the computer are stored in read-only memory chips, which are not volatile. Read-only memory chips are manufactured with instructions stored permanently on them. The instructions to start the computer are on a special chip known as a **ROM BIOS (Basic Input/Output System) chip**.

Some ROM chips are manufactured with instructions that are appropriate for a specific end user. For example, NASA has different needs than a school has. These specially programmed ROM chips are **PROM (Programmable Read-Only Memory) chips**. Once the chip is programmed, the contents cannot be altered. Newer chips, **EPROM (Erasable PROM) chips**, can be removed from the computer, erased using a special device, and reprogrammed. The newest type of ROM chips, **EEPROM (Electrically Erasable PROM) chips**, can be altered electrically using special programs, without being removed from the computer.

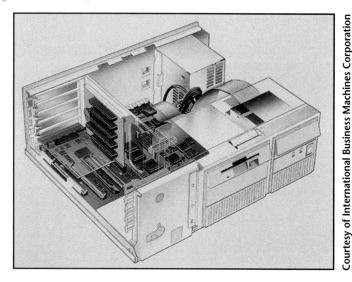

The IBM PS/2 77 mother-board houses microprocessor chips, such as Intel's 486DX2 and 486SX chips.

Courtesy of International Business Machines Corporation

The Motherboard

In a microcomputer, all the components previously discussed in this lesson are located on the **motherboard**, which is a large circuit board. (Some people prefer to use the term *mainboard*.)

In addition to housing the CPU, memory, and coprocessor chips, the motherboard also has expansion slots designed for expansion cards. An **expansion card**, also called an **adapter**, is a circuit board that provides additional capabilities for the computer. Expansion cards are available for many different purposes. One type of expansion card controls a monitor, another expansion card controls a mouse, and still another provides an internal fax modem.

An Intel motherboard.

Also found on the motherboard are one or more **ports**, which enable the computer to communicate with **peripheral devices**, such as printers, modems, and scanners. Most personal computers have **parallel ports** (commonly used for printers) and **serial ports** (commonly used for modems). A **modem** is an accessory that enables your computer to communicate with another computer through a telephone.

New motherboards developed by Intel for network servers have chip sets with built-in management features to help guard against system failure. These chip sets include sensors to detect errors and correct RAM, bus, and I/O failures. These new boards will increase system reliability without significantly increasing cost.

Courtesy of Intel Corporation

Lesson Summary

➤ Computers represent all data and instructions using the binary number system, which consists of 0s and 1s.

➤ Large computers use a data coding system called EBCDIC; smaller computers use the ASCII coding system.

➤ Eight bits, known as a byte, are used to represent any given letter or number.

➤ The computer adds a parity bit to each byte to help protect against errors.

➤ The central processing unit (CPU) is composed of a control unit and an arithmetic-logic unit. A microprocessor is a CPU on a single silicon chip.

➤ Computer programs are written to run on a specific processor. Most new processors are designed to be compatible with older processors so that existing programs can run on the new processor.

➤ A computer's performance, or speed, is determined by the size of the data bus and the address bus and by the speed of the system clock.

➤ Two types of microprocessor chips are in use today: CISC chips and RISC chips.

➤ Primary memory is composed of RAM, ROM, and cache chips. RAM and cache are volatile.

Lesson Review

Key Terms

adapter	complex instruction set	modem	random-access memory
address bus	computer (CISC)	motherboard	(RAM)
arithmetic-logic unit	control unit	multiprocessing	read-only
ASCII	data bus	multiprogramming	read-only memory (ROM)
binary digit	downwardly compatible	native application	reduced instruction set
bit	EBCDIC	numeric coprocessor	computer (RISC)
branch prediction	EEPROM (Electrically	odd parity	ROM BIOS chip
bus	Erasable PROM) chip	open bus system	serial port
bus width	EPROM (Erasable PROM)	parallel port	software emulator
byte	chip	parity bit	superscalar architecture
cache memory	even parity	peripheral device	system clock
central processing unit	expansion card	pipelining	system unit
(CPU)	instruction set	port	virtual memory
clock speed	megahertz	primary memory	volatile
closed bus system	memory chip	PROM (Programmable	word
compatible	microprocessor	Read-Only Memory) chip	

Matching

In the blank next to each of the following terms or phrases, write the letter of the corresponding term or phrase.

_____ **1.** A processor that works with a limited instruction set

_____ **2.** A 0 (zero) or a 1 (one)

_____ **3.** A volatile form of memory

_____ **4.** A technique to supplement RAM

a. cache memory

b. random-access memory

c. ROM BIOS

d. virtual memory

e. read-only memory

_____ **5.** A chip that holds many of the instructions needed to start the computer

_____ **6.** A collection of 0s and 1s that represents a letter, number, or special symbol

_____ **7.** A form of memory that is manufactured with instructions permanently stored on it

_____ **8.** A form of memory that holds frequently used data and instructions

_____ **9.** A processor that uses a large, complex set of instructions

_____ **10.** A unit of measurement for the number of clicks of the system clock in a second

f. byte

g. megahertz

h. RISC

i. CISC

j. bit

Multiple Choice

Circle the letter of the correct choice for each of the following.

1. Which of the following represents a computer code?

   a. WORM

   b. FAT

   c. EBCDIC

   d. EEPROM

2. What holds ROM, RAM, the CPU, and expansion cards?

   a. computer bus

   b. motherboard

   c. hard disk

   d. cache memory

3. Which of the following is *not* a determining factor of computer speed?

   a. number of disk drives

   b. internal data bus width

   c. clock speed

   d. external data bus width

4. Where are the instructions for starting the computer housed?

   a. read-only memory chips

   b. random-access memory

   c. hard disk

   d. CD-ROM

5. Which of the following is an example of volatile memory?

   a. ROM

   b. PROM

   c. EPROM

   d. RAM

6. Which of the following statements about a data bus is true?

   a. It is a form of secondary storage.

   b. It performs mathematical operations.

   c. It connects the CPU and memory.

   d. It can carry one byte of data.

7. Which of the following is *not* kept in primary memory?

    a. program instructions

    b. data

    c. the bus

    d. parts of the operating system

8. Software that can make one CPU pretend to be another is a(n) _____.

    a. virtual memory program

    b. emulator

    c. simulator

    d. word

9. The most popular coding systems use a(n) _____-bit byte.

    a. five

    b. six

    c. seven

    d. eight

10. When someone talks about the "memory" of a computer, that person is usually referring to _____.

    a. virtual memory

    b. cache memory

    c. random-access memory

    d. read-only memory

Completion

In the blank provided, write the correct answer for each of the following.

1. Data and instructions are stored in _____ during processing.

2. A(n) _____ is used to speed up mathematical operations in a computer.

3. It is important that new processors be _____ with older processors.

4. A(n) _____ represents a number, letter, or special symbol.

5. _____ is the data representation code used on most microcomputers.

6. The width of a computer's _____ determines how much memory can be accessed.

7. The _____ holds the instructions needed to start the computer.

8. The _____ is where all the mathematical and comparison operations are executed.

9. The _____ holds the memory, carries the bus lines, and contains expansion slots.

10. _____ is a technique that uses hard disk space to supplement memory.

Review

On a separate sheet of paper, answer the following questions.

1. Compare ROM and RAM with respect to their purpose and accessibility.

2. Briefly discuss the factors that determine the speed of a computer.

3. Why is the ROM BIOS chip so important to a computer?

4. Why is more than one coding method (ASCII and EBCDIC) used on computers?

5. How are the word size and the bus width on a computer related?

6. How does cache memory help programs execute faster?

7. How does cache memory differ from the rest of random-access memory?

8. What are the differences in ROM, PROM, EPROM, and EEPROM?

9. What is the purpose of a port in a computer system?

10. What is the difference between open and closed bus systems?

Critical Thinking

On a separate sheet of paper, answer the following questions.

1. Imagine the computer system of the year 2000. From the devices described in this lesson, select the type of memory the system will have.

2. Compare the way the components of a computer system function with the general way our brain accepts, processes, and outputs data.

3. Commonly, the ASCII code and the EBCDIC code use eight positions to represent different combinations of 1s and 0s. Each different grouping is associated with a unique character. Show how many characters could be represented if you used one, two, three, and four positions. Do you see a pattern?

4. Can you think of any advantages or disadvantages to having a computer system with only ROM, RAM, and a hard drive but no tape drive and no removable hard disks?

5. List some reasons why users might be reluctant to purchase a computer based on a new, fast processor that is not downwardly compatible.

Further Discovery

The Indispensable PC Hardware Book. Hans-Peter Messmer (Reading, MA: Addison-Wesley, 1996).

PC Magazine 1996 Computer Buyer's Guide. John Dvorak (Emeryville, CA: Ziff-Davis, 1996).

Winn L. Rosch Hardware Bible, Third Edition. Winn L. Rosch (Indianapolis, IN: Sams, 1994).

On-line Discovery

You can access the Internet resources for the following questions by going to the Que Education and Training Web site at URL http://www.ciyf98.com/discovery. From this page, click the link for Lesson 2A and then click the link to the resource you want to access.

1. ASCII is described as an 8-bit coding system that represents about 255 symbols or characters. However, the increasing need to represent the characters of many different languages and scripts has led to the development of Unicode, a 16-bit coding system. Unicode represents many thousands of characters, and it is still under development. Examine the **Unicode** Web site (http://www.stonehand.com/unicode.html). What kinds of languages and scripts are available with the Unicode system? What kinds of languages are not available? What are some of the issues being faced by Unicode designers?

2. The latest developments in processor technology are captured at the **CPU Information Center** (http://infopad.eecs.berkeley.edu/CIC). When you look at this site, what is the "state of the art" in computer processors? How fast are the processors under development? What other unique or distinctive features do the latest microprocessors sport?

LESSON 2B

How Computers Store Data

Outline

Storage Media
    Traditional Storage—Magnetic Tape
    Today's Preferred Storage—Magnetic Disk
        Floppy Disks and Disk Drives
        Hard Disks
        Hard Disk Interfaces
        Removable Storage
    The Storage of the Future—Optical Disk
Storing Data in Files
    Types of Files
    Naming Files
Organizing Files into Directories
Storage in Data Processing Applications
Types of Files in Data Processing Applications
File Organization in Data Processing Applications
    Sequential File Organization
    Direct (Random) File Organization
    Indexed Sequential File Organization

Learning Objectives

When you have finished reading this lesson, you will be able to

➤ Explain why storage is necessary

➤ Describe the different forms of storage

➤ Describe the advantages and disadvantages of commonly used storage devices

➤ Explain how computer files are organized on disk, tape, and CD-ROM

➤ List and describe several types of data files

➤ Describe how files are named

➤ List and describe five types of files in data processing applications

➤ List and discuss three ways that data is organized for computer retrieval

QUE Labs

➤ **Defragmentation**
➤ **File Management Systems**
➤ **Storage Devices**

Imagine going into your favorite video store, asking for a movie that you want to see, and being told that you will just have to look around because the employees don't know which movies the store has. If all of our data weren't stored in some logical manner, this scenario might be commonplace. Because of this kind of inquiry, however, we have developed manual filing systems that store records on index cards, in file folders, and on other media. To answer such a query would be equally difficult—even with computers—if we didn't have some organized method for storing all the data. Fortunately, computer storage methods can produce the answer in just a fraction of a minute. In this lesson, you learn how a computer stores data and what storage methods are used in data processing applications.

Storage Media

To understand how a computer stores data, you need to know about the storage media that computers use. In Lesson 2A, you learned that the computer translates into binary form all the data and instructions stored internally. You learned that letters, numbers, and special symbols are represented as groups of bits, based on EBCDIC or ASCII coding. Because a computer's memory (RAM) is volatile, you must save data by transferring it from memory to a storage device such as a disk. These storage devices, frequently called **secondary storage**, are not volatile. They can hold large amounts of data for as long as the user wants. This lesson explains how data is organized when it is saved to a storage device.

Secondary storage is very inexpensive compared to primary storage (memory). Most computers have a large amount of storage. However, storage devices do not transfer data as quickly as RAM does. When you finish working with an application, you save the results of your work on a secondary storage medium.

Traditional Storage—Magnetic Tape

Magnetic tape is one of the oldest forms of computer storage. First- and second-generation computers used magnetic tape for most of their storage needs. Today, magnetic tape is not used as often—the reasons why are discussed in this section.

Magnetic tape storage devices work in much the same way that a tape recorder works. Instead of *play* and *record*, the terms *read* and *write* are used. The magnetic tape used by a computer is very much like the tape used on an audio tape recorder. Most mainframe computers use reel-to-reel tapes, minicomputers use cartridges (similar to a VCR tape), and microcomputers use cassettes. Like the tape used in a tape recorder, computer tape can access what is stored on it only in the order in which the data was recorded (sequentially). This limited **sequential access**, which slows down data access, is such a significant disadvantage that tape is used primarily to back up data that is also stored on disk or that will not be needed frequently.

There are some good reasons to use magnetic tape, despite the disadvantages mentioned. Tapes can be recorded, erased, and reused many times, and they are inexpensive. Tapes are easily transported from one location to another, and tape drives can store large amounts of data quickly. Magnetic tape capacity is measured in bytes per inch (bpi), known as the tape density. Low-density tapes generally store 1,600 bpi, and high-density tapes can store 6,250 bpi. The newest tapes, called R-DATs, can store more than 14

TechTalk
A *gigabyte* is one billion characters; a *megabyte* is one million characters.

gigabytes on a single 90-meter tape. The speed, storage capability, and cost of tape are reasons why it is still frequently used as a backup medium.

Today's Preferred Storage—Magnetic Disk

Disk drives can store large amounts of data and have the capability to directly access a file or record. A **magnetic disk**, coupled with a disk drive that can store and retrieve data on the disk, is a **random-access storage medium**; that is, if you need the 157th item, the drive head can go directly to that item and read it. The disk drive's magnetic head is called a **read/write head**. When you insert a disk into the disk drive, the disk fits on a rod that rotates the disk. The read/write head reads the magnetic impulses. It can move laterally above the surface of the disk, just as you would move a phonograph's arm to locate a specific track on an LP record. A different read/write head is used for each surface of each platter in a disk pack. All the read/write heads are mounted on a single arm, so that each head reads the same track and sector on its platter at the same time. It is important to remember that disk drives are mechanical devices. Problems can occur, so backup copies of important programs and data are essential.

Before a disk can be used for storage, it must be prepared by means of a process called **formatting**. In this process, the disk drive's read/write head lays down a magnetic pattern on the disk's surface. This pattern enables the disk drive to store data in an organized manner. Formatting is one of the basic tasks handled by the computer's operating system.

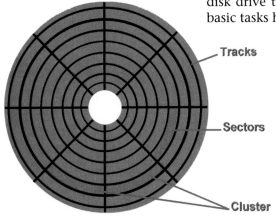

Tracks

Sectors

Cluster

Data is recorded on disk in concentric circular bands called **tracks**. The tracks on a disk are similar to the grooves on a phonograph record. Each track is divided into pie-shaped wedges called **sectors**. Two or more sectors combine to form a **cluster**.

Most computers maintain on the disk a table with the sector and track locations of data. This table, the **file allocation table** (**FAT**), enables the computer to locate data easily.

There are two popular types of magnetic disk: floppy disk and hard disk. Most of today's personal computers are equipped with both.

TechTalk
Most of the disks in common use today are double-sided disks. On these disks, the tracks with the same number are grouped as cylinders. For example, cylinder 39 consists of track 39 on side 1 and track 39 on side 2.

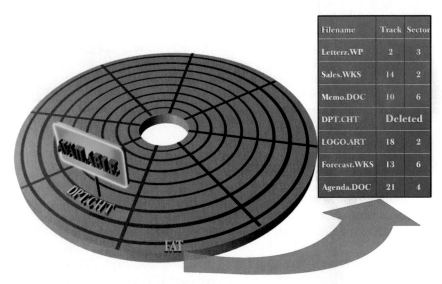

Filename	Track	Sector
Letterz.WP	2	3
Sales.WKS	14	2
Memo.DOC	10	6
DPT.CHT	Deleted	
LOGO.ART	18	2
Forecast.WKS	13	6
Agenda.DOC	21	4

The FAT.

Floppy Disks and Disk Drives

A **floppy disk** is a flexible circle of mylar plastic. The 3.5-inch version is encased in a hard plastic cover. The 5.25-inch version is encased in a square jacket that is harder than the disk itself but is still flexible. The 3.5-inch disk is a newer design than the 5.25-inch disk, which is rapidly disappearing.

Most personal computers are equipped with one or two **disk drives**. A disk drive can perform two operations: read and write. A *read* operation is similar to playing a CD-ROM. The drive "plays"

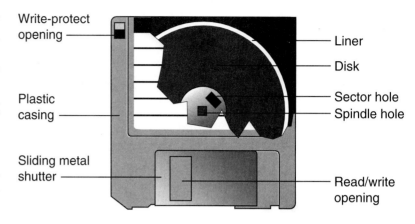

A 3.5-inch disk.

information from the disk and relays it to the processor. A *write* operation is similar to recording on a cassette tape. The drive records information on the disk. Unlike operating a cassette recorder, though, you don't have to push buttons; these actions occur under the direction of the program you are using. Disks contain a write-protection tab that you can open to protect data from being overwritten or deleted.

The amount of information that can be stored on a floppy disk is determined by the density of the magnetic particles on the disk's surface. **Double-density disks** store more than the single-density disks of a decade ago, but **high-density disks** are increasingly common today.

A double-density disk.

A high-density disk.

Amount of Data That Can Be Stored on a Floppy Disk		
	5.25-Inch Disk	*3.5-Inch Disk*
Double density	360K	720K (IBM)
		800K (Macintosh)
High density	1.2M	1.44M (IBM)
		1.4M (Macintosh)
Extra high density		2.88M

Disks are inexpensive, usually costing less than a dollar each. The storage capacity of floppy disks is relatively limited. In addition, because floppy disks spin only about 300 revolutions per minute, locating data (seek time), waiting for the disk to spin to the correct sector (rotational delay time), and transferring the data to primary memory (data transfer time) takes a comparatively long time. (The combination of seek time, rotational delay time, and transfer time is known as the **access time**.) For this reason, all new personal computer systems are equipped with hard disks, which have much more storage and operate considerably faster.

Hard Disks

A **hard disk** works similarly to a floppy disk, but the hard disk is made of rigid metallic **platters**, can hold much more data, and operates much faster. Most hard disks are permanently encased in the disk drive, although some drives use removable cartridges. Removable disks, generally known as **Bernoulli disks**, consist of a single platter encased in a plastic cartridge. A hard disk pack, which is usually found in a desktop computer (or larger), consists of several platters, with data encoded on both sides of each platter. All tracks and sectors in the same relative location on a disk pack form a **cylinder**. (For example, track 20 sector 2 on platter 1 and track 20 sector 2 on all the other platters in the disk pack form a cylinder.) Many small notebook computers use a hard card, which is a small disk mounted on an expansion card, rather than a full disk drive and pack.

Read/write head

Platters

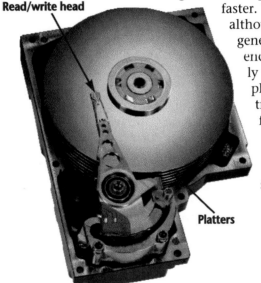

The portable Zip Drive uses a special 3.5-inch cartridge that holds 100M.

Courtesy of Iomega Corporation

TechTalk
A disk crash occurs when the read/write head makes contact with a hard disk. The read/write head will nick and scratch the disk so that data cannot be retrieved from it.

Hard disks spin so rapidly that the read/write head does not touch the surface of the disk. Serious damage can be caused if the read/write head encounters an obstacle, such as dust or a smoke particle causing the read/write head to bounce on the disk surface.

Why do hard disks perform so much better than floppy disks and floppy disk drives? There are several reasons:

➤ A single hard drive may have several platters, providing large data storage capacities.

➤ Most hard disks are permanently encased within the disk drive in a sealed environment free from dust and dirt. The disk can spin very rapidly, with the read/write head "floating" above the disk's surface.

➤ Hard disks spin at an average of 3,600 revolutions per minute, making data retrieval very fast.

Intense competition and technological innovation are driving hard disk prices down, even as storage capacities rise. Many personal computers have hard disks capable of storing a giga-byte—one billion characters—or more.

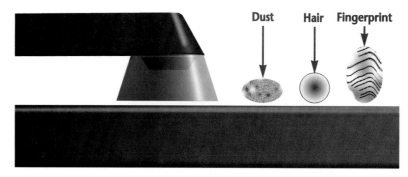

Hard drive recommendations will grow considerably in 1998. As the space required for software increases so will the size of the hard drives. Six gigabytes is a good estimate to consider. It provides enough room to grow over the next few years. It may seem like a lot, but many PC enthusiasts will tell you that you can never have enough space.

Larger computer systems are beginning to use a new type of hard disk storage. A **RAID (Redundant Array of Inexpensive Disks)** can be composed of more than one hundred 5.25-inch disks with a controller mounted in a single box. RAID storage first appeared on the market in 1993. A RAID can send data simultaneously over multiple data paths quickly.

Hard Disk Interfaces

To connect a hard disk to a microcomputer motherboard, you must have a **hard disk interface**. This component includes circuitry that conforms to a standard recognized by both the hard disk and the motherboard manufacturer. Common standards are **Integrated Drive Electronics (IDE)** and **Small Computer System Interface (SCSI)**.

TechTalk
The SCSI (pronounced "skuzzy") standard can be used with a wide range of devices, such as a hard disk, a scanner, and a CD-ROM. As many as seven SCSI devices can be connected to one SCSI port.

Removable Storage

One of the most significant new developments in personal computers has been the advancement of removable storage. Disks and backup tapes were, until recently, the only options. Iomega's zip drive uses disks that resemble the typical 3.5-inch 1.44M (megabytes) version but with a capacity of 100M. These disks are frequently used as an alternative to tape drives for archiving, but their real advantage is in providing a way of transporting large amounts of data (such as transporting data between home and office or to a customer site or for mailing). The drives can be internal or external. Zip disks, a bit thicker than a regular floppy, have the capacity of 70 regular disks. Jaz drives are to zip drives what a hard drive is to a disk and offer storage in the range of 1G. If you like to keep a close eye on hardware trends, Web sites such as CNET have up-to-the-minute reports in computer hardware news.

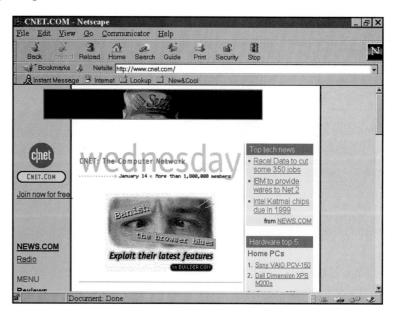

CNET provides daily updates in the computer industry especially with regard to the latest trends in hardware technology.

Zip drives are not to be confused with **zip files**. Zip files are created by compression software, such as PKZip or WinZip. Many files can be contained within a single zip file, which must also be decompressed by software.

Another major advancement in removable storage is the **nest bay**. The nest is installed in a regular 5.25-inch drive bay and accommodates several types of storage. You can insert and remove hard disk, tape, CD-ROM, zip, and Jaz drives as you need them, or transfer them between different machines.

IBM's Ramac Array Subsystem is a RAID system that contains many disks stored in special cabinets.

The Storage of the Future—Optical Disk

CD-ROM works much like the compact discs used in CD players. Just as CDs have revolutionized the music industry, **optical disks** have the potential to change secondary storage media. Based on the same laser technology as CDs, optical disks offer a medium capable of storing extremely large amounts of data. The three main types of optical disk are CD-ROM, WORM CD, and MO technology.

The most popular and least expensive type of optical disk is **Compact Disc Read-Only Memory (CD-ROM)**. As the name indicates, these disks come prerecorded and cannot be altered; CD-ROM is, in other words, a read-only storage medium. Still, CD-ROM provides an excellent way to distribute large amounts of data at low cost. CDs can store up to 650M of data, yet they can cost as little as a dollar per disk to duplicate in massive quantities.

To use a CD-ROM, you must have a computer equipped with a **CD-ROM drive**. CD-ROM towers, containing as many as 256 CD-ROM drives, are frequently attached to CD servers so that all the computers on a network can share what is stored on the CD-ROMs.

CD-ROM has been used primarily to market large applications. For example, *Infopedia* is a single CD that holds a complete encyclopedia, dictionary, thesaurus, world atlas, dictionary of quotations, world almanac, and biographical dictionary. The *Total Baseball* CD holds statistics on over 13,000 players with photographs of their trading cards and explanatory sound clips. You can tour the National Art Gallery on CD-ROM or play a variety of games.

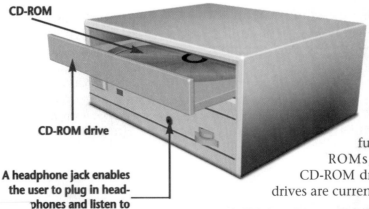

CD-ROM

CD-ROM drive

A headphone jack enables the user to plug in headphones and listen to recorded sounds.

Consumers will hear more and more about what is known as **DVD**. DVD has stood for both **digital video disk** and **digital versatile disk**, depending on which manufacturer provides the information. The most important thing to realize about a DBED is that it is the same size as a CD-ROM but offers seven times the storage capacity. DVD disks can hold full-motion video, including your favorite full-length feature film. DVD drives can read CD-ROMs, but they are much slower than the latest CD-ROM drives. Current CD-ROM drives are 24X, but DVD drives are currently only 10X.

A **Write Once, Read Many Compact Disc (WORM CD)** is purchased blank from the manufacturer and encoded using special equipment.

Courtesy of International Business Machines Corporation

The disks can't be altered after they are encoded and can't be easily duplicated because the encoding process does not actually pit the disk. Many businesses use WORM CDs to store old data files. This practice, known as **archiving**, enables old files to be deleted from the hard disk, thus freeing space for new files. WORM CDs are used most frequently for document processing with complete image processing, including replications of photos, graphics, text, and even signatures.

Until recently, recording on a CD-ROM required separate, very expensive equipment. Now drives that can write to and read a CD, called **CD-Recordable (CD-R)** drives, are available for less than $200, and prices are going down rapidly. A blank disk costs about $15. CD-R is a WORM process. The disks can be read by any standard CD-ROM unit.

If you want to create a multimedia presentation and then play it back on any available computer equipped with a CD-ROM drive, CD-R is the tool you have been looking for. With the large capacity of CD-R (roughly 600 megabytes per disk), you can create and store an entire multimedia presentation on a single disk. (Floppy disks don't have this capacity.)

CD-Rs look like standard CD-ROMs except that they are gold in color, rather than the silver of "mastered" CD-ROMs. The blank disks are made with the spiral tracks impressed on the recording surface. Because CD-ROMs are read by refraction of light, a dye layer is discolored in the recording process, which causes the area either to reflect light or to disperse it.

The technology to make **CD-Erasable (CD-E)** disks recently became available. CD-E enables users to store, access, and reuse disks in the same way that floppy disks can be used. Because of the large storage capacity of CDs, they will likely make magnetic tape, and perhaps floppy disks, a thing of the past.

Magneto-optical (MO) disks are erasable and combine the magnetic principles used on tape and disk with new optical technology. MO disks measure storage capacity in gigabytes; they are removable, portable, and durable. One of the newest MO systems—Orray produced by Pinnacle Micro—uses a storage method similar to that of RAID. Optical disks have a thirty-year shelf life and are ideal for graphics and audiovisual applications that require large storage capacity.

> **TechTalk**
> A disk drive's *access time* is usually measured in milliseconds (thousandths of a second). Access time is determined by several factors, including *seek time* (the time it takes the read/write head to locate the data) and *data transfer rate* (the rate at which the read/write head can transfer data to the computer's memory).

Courtesy of Pinnacle Micro

Pinnacle Micro's Orray is a magneto-optical (MO) system that can write simultaneously to four optical disks with a total capacity of 5.2 gigabytes. Orray's data transfer rate is 8 megabytes per second.

Storing Data in Files

No matter what storage medium or computer you are working with, everything stored on it is stored in a **file**, an area of the storage medium that is set aside to store a program or a collection of data. Files are of various types. They are always named, and they can be organized into "file cabinets" called directories. Just as a filing cabinet has different drawers to organize related information, different file directories store related types of files. This section explains what types of files are commonly used and how they are named.

Types of Files

All computers have two basic kinds of files: program files and data files. **Program files** contain programs of all kinds, ranging from system programs (such as the program used to format disks) to application programs

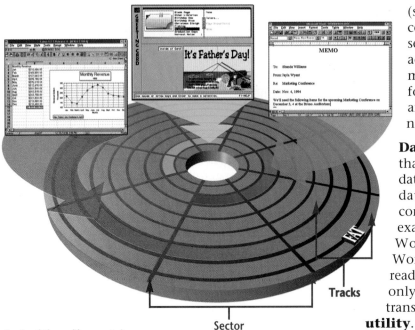

Each of these files contains a different type of data.

Sector

Tracks

(such as a spreadsheet or word processing program). Most programs use several support files. These files store additional programs and other information that may be needed in order for the program to run correctly. If any files are missing, the program may not work as expected.

Data files are created to store the data that programs use. Most programs store data in a **proprietary file format**, a data-storage format used only by the company that makes the program. For example, the word processing program WordPerfect creates data files in the WordPerfect format. These files can be read by other word processing programs only if they are equipped with a special translation program, called a **conversion utility**.

Data files can be grouped according to the kind of data they contain. Here are some common types of data files:

➤ **Configuration files** contain settings or configuration choices that a program requires in order to run correctly. You should never alter or delete a configuration file, particularly one required by a computer's operating system.

➤ **Text files** contain nothing but standard characters (letters, punctuation marks, numbers, and special symbols), such as those of the ASCII character set. Almost any application program can read a text file.

➤ **Graphics files** contain pictures in a specific graphics format used for storing digitally encoded pictures. Common graphics formats include **Joint Photographic Experts Group (JPEG)** and **Graphics Interchange Format (GIF)**. To read a graphics file, you must use a program that recognizes the file's format.

➤ **Database files** contain data that has been stored in the proprietary file format of a database program.

➤ **Sound files** contain digitized sounds, which can be played back if your computer is equipped for multimedia.

➤ **Backup files** contain copies of essential data.

TechTalk
The word *format* can describe the proprietary structure used in a file as well as the magnetic pattern used on a disk.

Naming Files

When you use an application program and save your work, you will name your file by giving it a **file name**. This is the name that the operating system uses to store and retrieve the file.

MS-DOS and Microsoft Windows 3.1 impose strict limitations on file names. You can use up to eight characters (letters and numbers) for the file name. Creating a good file name with only eight characters isn't easy. Try to choose a name that you will recognize weeks from now, when you are searching for a file you have misplaced! ESSAY1 is more descriptive than RMX9JR, for instance. A file name must be unique within the directory where the file is stored; if you save a new file with the same name as another file in that directory, the new file will replace the old file.

Optionally, you can use up to three letters as an **extension**. If you use the extension, you must separate the file name and the extension with a period, as in ESSAY1.TXT. Some applications automatically supply their own extensions, such as DOC (Microsoft Word) or WK4 (Lotus 1-2-3). A program with this capability can determine which of the files on your disk were created by that program. You still need to supply a file name, though. Table 2B.1 lists some commonly used file name extensions.

Table 2B.1	Common File Name Extensions
Extension	*File Type*
BAK	Backup file
BAT	Batch file
COM	Program file
DOC	Microsoft Word document
EXE	Program file
GIF	GIF graphics file
INI	Configuration file
JPG	JPEG graphics file
SYS	Operating system configuration file
WAV	Microsoft Windows sound file
WK4	Lotus 1-2-3 spreadsheet
XLS	Microsoft Excel spreadsheet

Microsoft Windows 95 permits users to use long file names. File names can contain up to 255 characters as well as spaces and some punctuation marks. The special characters \ / : * ? " < > | cannot be used.

Macintosh users have a 31-character limit on file names. This limitation allows a more descriptive name than is available with MS-DOS or Windows 3.1, but not as fully descriptive as Windows 95 names.

Organizing Files into Directories

As you start working with files, you will discover that they multiply rapidly. Each program on a computer is composed of a number of files. Every time you create a document with a word processing program, at least one file is created. If you don't organize the files, finding what you need will become virtually impossible.

Magnetic and optical disks keep track of files in a file **directory**. The main directory of the disk is called the **root directory**. The computer automatically updates the listing of all files in the directory whenever the contents of a magnetic disk change. However, considering the large capacity of hard drives and CD-ROMs, if all the files were in a single directory, it could be time-consuming to locate the file you want. For this reason, storage media are frequently organized into a system of directories.

Imagine that you are in charge of the video store mentioned at the beginning of this lesson. You are given the task of developing a system to keep track of all the videos. You decide to use a single card file and a three-by-five-inch index card for each copy of each video. Problems arise when you try to determine which videos are available and which have been checked out. To handle those problems, you decide to use two card files, one for the available videos and one for those that are checked out. When employees check out a video, they move the appropriate index card from the "available" tray to the "out" tray. When a video is checked in, its index card is moved from the "out" tray to the "available" tray. In essence, what you have done is to create two directories for the video index cards. When the store decides to rent games as well, you add two more card files to track the games, thus creating the equivalent of two new directories.

To further organize your computer files, you can create **subdirectories** within directories. (This structure is like a tree with a single trunk and many large branches, each containing smaller branches.) For example, suppose that you are so pleased with your organization of the video store records that you decide to organize your personal records. You could divide your database files into a subdirectory for your music CD collection, a second subdirectory for your baseball card collection, and a third subdirectory for your telephone/address book. Or you could divide your word processing documents into a subdirectory for your school work, another for personal correspondence, and another for your diary. The school work directory could be further subdivided into separate directories for each class. (Databases and word processing are covered in Chapter 5.) By creating logical subdirectories, you can locate individual files more easily.

Usually, the directory display shows the names of any subdirectories within that directory. The name, the size, and the date and time last modified will be displayed for individual files within the directory. There are several ways to find a file in a different directory. From the command line, you can tell the computer to move to the directory that contains the file, and then tell the computer the file name. Another method is to specify the name of the directory as well as the file name in your command. In a graphical interface (such as Windows 95 Explorer or Macintosh Finder), you can click the file name.

Many operating systems and graphical user interfaces include a shell or file manager utility. The shell or file manager can help you locate, move, copy, rename, and delete files easily.

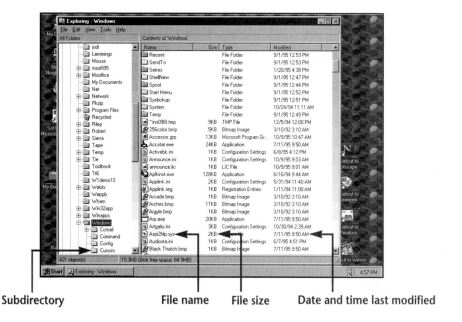

The Windows 95 Explorer.

Subdirectory   File name   File size   Date and time last modified

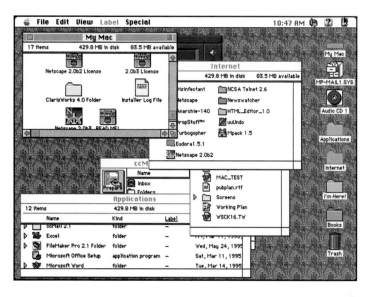

The Macintosh Finder displays this desktop opening screen.

Storage in Data Processing Applications

Most commercial computer systems have an important job to do: They keep track of transactions, such as sales, purchases, orders, and returns. In these systems, database files must keep track of transactions without error. Lost data or errors could cost a company a great deal of money; some companies have gone bankrupt because of problems with their computer systems. For this reason, data processing professionals pay close attention to the way these files are organized and used.

In data processing, computer storage is conceptualized as a **data storage hierarchy**. The smallest item of data is a single binary digit (a bit), either a 0 or a 1. Bits are combined to form a character (or byte), such as the letter *A* or the number 7. Characters are combined to form a **field**, which is a single data item such as a name or Social Security number. Related fields are combined to form a **record**, and records are combined to form a file.

Data storage hierarchy.

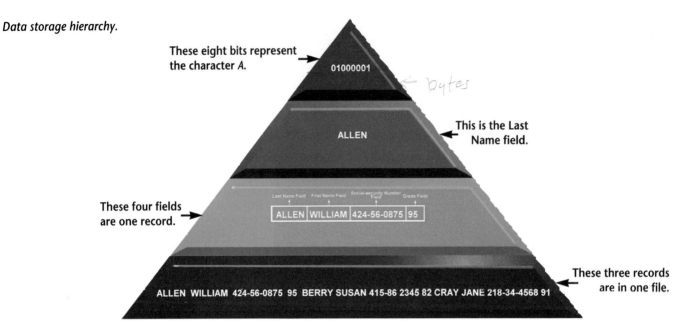

These eight bits represent the character *A*.

This is the Last Name field.

These four fields are one record.

These three records are in one file.

For example, all the data items that the school has about you are combined to form your student record. The records for each student that attends your school are combined to form the student file. In addition to maintaining the student file, the school maintains many other files, such as a class file containing a record for each class offered during the current term.

Consider another example. A library has a file of all the books it owns. This file is composed of records, one for each book. Each record contains the same four fields: title, author, publisher, and ISBN number. Each field contains a number of characters, and each character is composed of eight bits.

Types of Files in Data Processing Applications

In traditional data processing applications, data files are categorized according to the way the application uses them. The files are in five categories: transaction, master, report, output, and backup. Transaction and master files are used primarily in database and accounting applications.

A **transaction file** is used to store input data until it can be processed. The timing for the processing of the data varies. In **batch processing**, the data is keyed in and held until an entire batch can be processed at once. For example, employee time cards might be keyed into the system each week and processed twice during the month. In **real-time processing**, the data is processed as soon as it is entered. Real-time processing occurs when computers are used to control such processes as landing an airplane, running a chemical processing plant, or controlling the environment in a building. The computer recognizes the need for adjustments, makes them, and then checks to see whether more adjustments are needed.

A **master file** contains all the current data relevant to an application. For example, a customer master file contains a record for each customer of a business. The record contains such fields as name, address, current balance, and recent payments. The master file is updated when new charges and

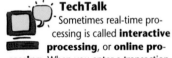

TechTalk
Sometimes real-time processing is called **interactive processing**, or **online processing**. When you enter a transaction at an automated teller machine (ATM), the machine prompts you for further data. This type of interaction is considered interactive, or online, processing.

payments are recorded. This update process can be accomplished with a transaction file or by capturing data at the time the transaction occurs. (Updating at the time of the transaction is known as **point-of-sale processing**.)

A **report file** holds a copy of a report in computer-accessible form until it is convenient to print it. Sometimes it is advantageous to keep report files instead of paper documents because the files are easier to store.

Some programs create files that will be used as input to other programs. For example, an accounts payable program accepts a transaction file of all payments made in the last week, updates the master accounts payable file, and produces an accounts payable **output file**. The accounts payable output file is then used as input to the general ledger program.

A **backup file** is a copy of a file, created as a safety precaution in case anything should happen to the original. Backing up data files regularly is extremely important. With any storage medium, the one thing you can be certain of is that it will fail—you just never know when.

Categories of Files
Transaction
Master
Report
Output
Backup

File Organization in Data Processing Applications

When a school processes grades at the end of the term, every student record in every class must be processed. When a customer calls a store and asks whether a certain item is in stock, only that item needs to be processed. And when you need to find a topic in a book, you find the correct page in the index and then scan that entire page. These three methods of searching for data illustrate three popular methods of file organization: sequential, direct (random), and indexed sequential.

Sequential File Organization

Sequential files are useful when most, if not all, of the records in the file need to be processed at the same time. The computer processes a sequential file in the order in which the data was encoded in the file. A sequential file is much like a cassette tape; you must listen to the three songs that come before your favorite song before you can hear it. In the same way, to get to the 32nd record of a sequential file, the computer must read the first 31 records in the file. Applications suitable for sequential processing include those for processing grades, payroll, and inventory.

Although the records in a sequential file do not have to be in any logical order, they often are. Usually, a unique **key field**—such as student ID, Social Security number, or inventory number—can be used to identify a record quickly. In a library's card catalog, for example, you begin by looking for a book's author, so you are using the author as the key field. Sequential files can be stored on any type of medium. In addition, they are the only type of file that can be maintained on magnetic tape.

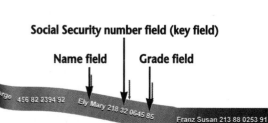

Social Security number field (key field)

Name field   Grade field

Davis George 456 82 2394 92   Ely Mary 218 32 0645 85   Franz Susan 213 88 0253 91

The Millennium Bug

Computers have been a part of our lives for the past fifty years, and their effect has been dramatic. Soon, another dramatic event will take place—the turn of the century. The change may be more dramatic in the world of computers than it is for humans, however.

In our daily lives, we often use an array of preprinted forms. Perhaps the most common of these is the personal check. As we routinely fill in the date on these checks, we don't even think about the fact that the first two digits of the year are preprinted. In another few years, those two digits will be incorrect, and we will need new checks printed, this time with the digits 20 preprinted on them.

In human terms, such a change is pretty easy. We simply buy a new batch of checks and continue with business as normal. For computers, the solution is not as easy as reprinting a few forms.

Since the early days of computers, many programs stored date information in a version of shorthand. Instead of storing the entire year, only the last two digits of the year were stored. This saved quite a bit of computer storage space when such space was expensive. The shorthand tradition was prevalent in programs written in COBOL on large computer systems in the 1950s and 1960s, but carried over into programs on smaller systems years later. To most people (programmers included), the turn of the century seemed a long way in the future.

Now programmers are faced with the problem of making sure that data generated over the past 30 or 40 years will still be usable when January 1, 2000, arrives. In addition, the programs won't be able to use their shorthand date system any more, because the two-digit year is beginning at zero again. The upshot is that programmers are now facing a huge amount of work, both in changing existing data and modifying programs so that they can generate and use new data properly.

What appears to one person as a problem can appear to another as an opportunity. A new breed of consultant is springing up to address the computing problems associated with the new century. These consultants specialize in ferreting out data that is dependent on the two-digit date shorthand. They then propose methods to modify the data, and change the programs relying on that data. It has been reported that large companies have amassed so much data that their conversion costs could easily exceed $40 million.

As the new century approaches, the need for data conversion experts and specialized data conversion software is bound to increase. For the savvy programmer and systems analyst, this presents a once-in-a-lifetime opportunity—one that others hope will never come our way again.

Direct (Random) File Organization

When records are stored in a **direct-access file**, the computer can read a specific record from that file without reading any other records first. Records in a direct-access file are stored according to a position in the file. That position is determined by the use of a mathematical computation to produce an **address** where the unique key field is stored. This process is known as **hashing**; the formula used is frequently called a hashing algorithm. Every location in primary and secondary storage is assigned a unique address; data and programs are stored and retrieved by address. Because magnetic tape is suitable only for sequential access, direct-access files must be stored on magnetic or optical disks. Direct-access files are sometimes called **random-access files** or just random files.

A special type of direct-access file, called a **relative file**, does not use a mathematical formula to determine the address of the records. Instead, the key field is a numeric integer, and it serves as the record number within the file. For example, the record for the 14th day of the year would be the 14th record in a relative calendar file.

Finding a record in a direct-access file is much faster than accessing a sequential file. Direct-access organization is excellent for such applications as an airline reservation system or an encyclopedia. The main drawback of direct-access files is that they have no sequential access capabilities. Another drawback is that there is only one way to the record—you must know the value of the key field.

Indexed Sequential File Organization

Sometimes a user wants to find a starting point in a file and then work with the rest of the file (or part of the rest) sequentially. With **indexed sequential files**, also called **indexed files**, records can be accessed either directly (randomly) or sequentially. Another characteristic of indexed sequential files is the use of multiple keys.

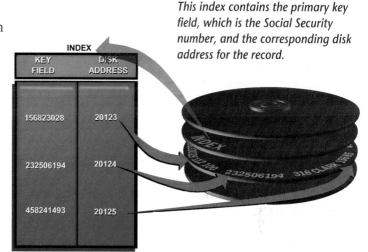

This index contains the primary key field, which is the Social Security number, and the corresponding disk address for the record.

Suppose that you want to go shopping with some friends but don't have any money with you. Therefore, you go to the bank to withdraw money from your savings account. When the teller asks your account number, you don't remember it, nor do you have your bank book with you. If the teller says that you must know the number, the bank uses a file that has only one key field. If, instead, the teller asks for your name and Social Security number, the bank uses an indexed file. The account number is the primary key, and the Social Security number is a secondary key. The system maintains two indexes for the file. Indexed sequential files require more storage space than other types of files because the indexes, which are also files, can become quite large.

Many applications are suitable for **Indexed Sequen-tial Access Method (ISAM)** files because of the flexibility of data retrieval. For example, online information services use ISAM files to maintain huge bibliographic databases. These services keep databases containing millions of items that reference publications in science, medicine, and countless other topics.

Lesson Summary

➤ Secondary storage devices provide permanent storage of programs and data.

➤ Magnetic tape can access data only sequentially.

➤ Magnetic disks provide fast, random access to data.

➤ Magnetic disks and CD-ROMs can access data sequentially or directly.

➤ Optical disks provide large storage capacity with quick data access.

➤ A computer stores data and programs as files.

➤ File names must follow rules that are specific to the operating system of the computer.

➤ Files are organized into directories and subdirectories to make data easier to locate and manage.

➤ The types of data files are transaction files, master files, report files, intermediate files, and back-up files.

➤ There is a hierarchy of data. A file is composed of records about similar items. Each record is composed of fields that contain data about an item, and each field is composed of one or more characters. Eight bits form a character.

➤ The major types of file organization are sequential, direct (random and relative), and indexed sequential (ISAM).

Lesson Review

Key Terms

access time
address
archiving
backup file
batch processing
Bernoulli disk
Compact Disc Read-Only
    Memory (CD-ROM)
CD-Recordable (CD-R)
CD-Erasable (CD-E)
CD-ROM drive
cluster
configuration file
conversion utility
cylinder
data file
data storage hierarchy
database file
direct-access file
directory
disk drive
double-density disk

double-speed drive
extension
field
file
file allocation table (FAT)
file name
floppy disk
formatting
graphics file
Graphics Interchange
    Format (GIF)
hard disk
hard disk interface
hashing
high-density disk
indexed file
indexed sequential file
Indexed Sequential
    Access Method (ISAM)
Integrated Drive
    Electronics (IDE)
interactive processing

Joint Photographic Experts
    Group (JPEG)
key field
magnetic disk
magnetic tape
magneto-optical (MO) disk
master file
online processing
optical disk
output file
platter
point-of-sale processing
program file
proprietary file format
RAID (Redundant Array of
    Inexpensive Disks)
random-access file
random-access storage
    medium
read/write head
real-time processing
record

relative file
report file
root directory
secondary storage
sector
sequential access
sequential file
Small Computer System
    Interface (SCSI)
sound file
spreadsheet file
subdirectory
text file
track
transaction file
Write Once, Read Many
    Compact Disc (WORM
    CD)
zip disk

Matching

In the blank next to each of the following terms or phrases, write the letter of the corresponding term or phrase.

_____ **1.** A file used to store program output that has the appearance of hard copy

_____ **2.** Used to locate a record in a random file

_____ **3.** A file whose contents can be accessed only in the order in which they were stored

_____ **4.** A file used to store data until it can be processed into the master file

_____ **5.** Used by the computer to determine where to store a record in a random file

_____ **6.** A file that can access a record by more than one field

_____ **7.** A single piece of data about an item

_____ **8.** A combination of one or more fields

_____ **9.** Stores records that can be accessed quickly using a specific field

_____ **10.** Formed from the combination of many records that work with the same type of data

a. sequential

b. ISAM

c. hashing algorithm

d. field

e. transaction

f. random file

g. key field

h. record

i. file

j. report

Multiple Choice

Circle the letter of the correct choice for each of the following.

1. A library stores a great deal of data about its books. Where in the storage hierarchy does information about the author or title fall?

  a. file

  b. field

  c. record

  d. program

2. Which of the following is *not* a type of file organization?

  a. random

  b. indexed sequential

  c. master file

  d. sequential

3. A transaction file is a type of _____.

  a. data file

  b. master file

  c. access method

  d. data record

4. An index-card file containing recipes in alphabetical order and separated by letter tabs is similar to what type of computer file?

  a. random

  b. sequential

  c. indexed sequential

  d. none of the above

5. Which of the following applications is suitable for sequential processing?

   a. payroll processing

   b. processing of grades

   c. inventory

   d. all of the above

6. A customer data file used to answer customer questions should *not* be stored on which of the following media?

   a. CD-ROM

   b. floppy disk

   c. magnetic tape

   d. hard disk

7. Which of the following holds the most data?

   a. byte

   b. field

   c. record

   d. file

8. Which of the following is *not* true about an ISAM file?

   a. It uses a hashing algorithm to store records.

   b. It uses multiple keys.

   c. It maintains index files.

   d. It allows sequential access of records.

9. Which of the following can store the most data?

   a. RAM

   b. magnetic tape

   c. ROM

   d. RAID

10. Which of the following is *not* an advantage of secondary storage media over primary memory?

    a. It is nonvolatile.

    b. It is faster.

    c. It has a larger storage capacity.

    d. All of the above are advantages.

Completion

In the blank provided, write the correct answer for each of the following.

1. A(n) _____ file is created as a safety precaution, in case the original file is damaged.

2. A(n) _____ file contains all the current data relevant to an application.

3. A(n) _____ is used to locate records in a random file.

4. A record is located in an ISAM file by using a(n) _____.

5. Magnetic tape can store only _____ files.

6. Secondary storage can be organized into _____ that contain _____.

7. With _____ file organization, you can access records only in the order in which they were stored.

8. A record contains one or more _____ about the same item.

9. An optical disk drive with both read and write capabilities is called a(n) _____.

10. A file name for MS-DOS can contain no more than _____ characters.

Review

On a separate sheet of paper, answer the following questions.

1. List the items in a data storage hierarchy from smallest to largest. Give an example of each item, using student information gathered when you register for courses.

2. List the five types of data files grouped according to how they are used in an application.

3. What are three popular methods of file organization?

4. Briefly explain two characteristics of indexed sequential file organization.

5. What is the advantage of organizing directories into subdirectories?

6. Why might CD storage replace magnetic tape for maintaining backups?

7. Describe how and why files are stored in directories.

8. What kind of information does the user see when a directory is displayed?

9. What is the major disadvantage of magnetic tape in comparison with magnetic disk? In what way has this disadvantage affected the use of tape?

10. How are relative files different from other direct-access files?

Critical Thinking

On a separate sheet of paper, answer the following questions.

1. If you had a telephone number but not the party's name or address, or an address but not the name or telephone number, could you look up the number or address in an ordinary telephone book? Why or why not? If so, how? If not, what would have to be changed in order to make this convenient?

2. If the telephone book were stored in a sequential data file with three fields—name, address, and phone number—in what order would the file contents have to be sorted for use by a 911 answering office? Would any other order be appropriate? Why or why not?

3. Refer to the example in the text of the video store with two card files, one for videos in stock and the other for videos checked out. Could this function be accomplished with a computer without putting two data files in separate directories? Could this function be accomplished with only one file? Briefly explain your answers.

4. When your school collects the grades at the end of the semester from all the teachers and then processes them to produce grade cards, what type of processing is being used? When you use an automated teller machine (ATM) to enter a transaction, what type of processing is occurring? Explain your answers.

5. Discuss how the evolution of storage media technology, from precomputer times until today, influenced the design of methods of storing data.

Further Discovery

How Computers Work. Ron White (Emeryville, CA: Ziff-Davis, 1995).

Encyclopedia of Graphics File Formats, Second Edition. James D. Murray and William vanRyper (Sebastopol, CA: O'Reilly, 1996).

On-line Discovery

You can access the Internet resources for the following questions by going to the Que Education and Training Web site at URL http://www.ciyf98.com/discovery. From this page, click the link for Lesson 2B and then click the link to the resource you want to access.

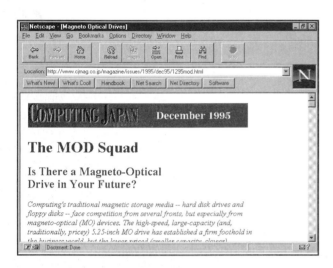

1. CD-R (or CD-Recordable) drives are more commonly used because their prices have dropped. In addition, a host of other types of storage drives, including removable hard drives and so-called magneto-optical drives, has become available. A couple of resources might help you gain an understanding of the differences in these types of storage media. The first is the **CD-Recordable Frequently Asked Questions list** (**FAQ**) at URL http://mail.ncku.edu.tw/~thlx/faq.htm. The second is an article in *Computing Japan Magazine* entitled **"The MOD Squad: Is there a Magneto-Optical Drive in Your Future"** (http://www.cjmag.co.jp/magazine/issues/1995/dec95/1295mod.html). Don't let the fact that the article is in Japanese scare you—although the prices are given in Yen, the article is in English and is quite understandable! What types of storage devices did you read about? What are the advantages and disadvantages of each? If you were to purchase a storage device for your computer, what would it be?

2. Many different formats in which files can be stored on a computer are available. Such formats enable your computer and its applications to interpret stored data as words, images, sounds, database files, and so on. Some of these file formats used for storing and representing multimedia information have become particularly popular on the Internet. Alison Zhang's **Multimedia File Formats on the Internet** (http://rodent.lib.rochester.edu/multimed/contents.htm) is a good introduction to the different types of file formats you might encounter on the Internet. Read through some of this work. What types of file formats are used on the Internet? What are some of the key differences among them?

Data In, Information Out

Outline

Learning Objectives

When you have finished reading this lesson, you will be able to

➤ Identify the most common input devices

➤ Explain why alternatives to keyed data are being developed

➤ Discuss trends in pointing devices

➤ Identify the most common output devices

➤ Distinguish between hard copy and soft copy

QUE Lab

➤ **Input/Output Devices**

When personal computers were first developed, a magazine received a letter from a reader. The reader asked the magazine to publish an article about using "those typewriter-television things." In those days, computer literacy was rare.

Even if you are just beginning to learn about computers, you know that a computer is more than an input/output device—more than a "typewriter-television thing." Still, much of what you do when you interact with a computer involves the use of input and output peripheral devices. You enter data (input) by means of input devices (such as keyboards), and you look at output on output devices (such as monitors or printers). So this chapter's examination of computer hardware includes the input and output devices of today—and tomorrow.

Input Devices

You can enter data into the computer in many ways. The most commonly used input devices are keyboards; pointing devices, such as mice and trackballs; and scanners. Many other special-purpose input devices are available, and computers often have more than one input device. For example, most personal computers have both a keyboard and a mouse.

Keyed Input

You enter most input data into the computer by using a keyboard. This input method is similar to typing on a typewriter.

Most typewriter and computer keyboards are **QWERTY keyboards**. The alphabetic keys are arranged so that the upper-left row of letters begins with the six letters *Q W E R T Y*. Designers of other keyboards claim that their boards are easier to learn than the QWERTY keyboard. The Dvorak keyboard is one example. It is not widely accepted, however, because most people have already learned the QWERTY keyboard.

The Dvorak keyboard was designed to be more efficient than the QWERTY keyboard.

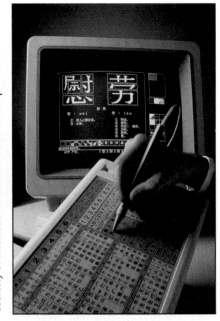

This Chinese keyboard has many more characters than the QWERTY or Dvorak keyboard.

In other parts of the world, you will find different keyboards. The coding used on the QWERTY and Dvorak keyboards works with an 8-bit code, which accommodates 256 different characters. Asian languages have many more characters. The Kanji alphabet, for example, has 50,000 characters. Japanese keyboards have to work with a 16-bit code to accommodate all the characters.

Computer keyboards include keys that are designed to perform specific tasks. These special keys include function keys, directional keys, and special-purpose keys such as Alt, Ctrl, Del, Enter, Ins, and Esc. These keys enable the user to perform complex tasks easily when using the application. For example, many applications use a function key to access online help for the user.

This computer keyboard has typewriter keys, function keys, numeric keys, directional keys, and special-purpose keys.

Courtesy of International Business Machines Corporation

Some new keyboards have 107 keys, with the three new keys designed to simplify working with Windows 95. Two of these keys, next to the Alt keys, bring up the Start menu. The third key, next to the right Ctrl key, brings up a menu of functions that are frequently accessed in whichever application is currently being used.

Prolonged keyboard use can cause wrist problems, sometimes so serious as to require surgery. To help prevent these problems, ergonomic keyboards are beginning to appear on the market. (See Lesson 8B for a more detailed discussion.)

One special type of keyboard construction is the **membrane-switch keyboard**, on which the keyboard is covered by a protective film. Membrane-switch keyboards are reliable, durable, and resistant to such hazards as liquids or grease. However, membrane keys require more pressure than keys on a standard computer keyboard. You have probably seen membrane-switch keyboards in fast-food restaurants. Membrane-switch keyboards are ideal in manufacturing situations that require little actual keying.

Courtesy of Microsoft Corporation

A Windows 95 ergonomic keyboard.

BITS
You may have heard of "computer errors" causing strange mistakes. For example, a Michigan woman received a gas bill for more than one million dollars! Almost all these errors are due to errors in keyboard data input.

Many computer systems are designed for **source-data automation**. These systems place keyboards and display units at the most convenient spot for data entry. An example is the use of point-of-sale (POS) cash registers in retail stores. POS registers send data directly to a computer file for later processing. This technique gives an advantage because most so-called computer errors are actually keying errors. Capturing data at the source minimizes errors because the people who key the data are doing a variety of tasks and are therefore less likely to make errors due to boredom.

Pointing Devices

Many people use pointing devices instead of keyboards whenever possible. Pointing devices minimize the amount of typing (and the number of errors). The many pointing devices available include the mouse, trackball, light pen, digitizing tablet, touch screen, and pen-based system.

Courtesy of International Business Machines Corporation

The Mouse and the Trackball

The **mouse** is a palm-size device with a ball built into the bottom. The mouse is usually connected to the computer by a cable (computer wires are frequently called cables) and may have from one to four buttons (but usually two). The mouse may be mechanical or optical. Mice come in many shapes and sizes. When you move the mouse over a smooth surface, the ball rolls, and the pointer on the display screen moves in the same direction. The Apple Macintosh, with its graphical user interface, made the mouse popular. Now most microcomputer systems, regardless of the manufacturer, use a mouse. With the mouse, you can draw, select options from a menu, and modify or move text. You issue commands by pointing with the pointer and clicking a mouse button. In addition to minimizing typing errors, a mouse makes operating a microcomputer easier for beginning users.

Courtesy of LogiTech, Inc.

A mouse usually has two or three buttons. Most mouse operations use the left button only.

A **trackball** is like an upside-down mouse. Used similarly to the mouse, the trackball is frequently attached to or built into the keyboard. The main advantage of a trackball is that it requires less desk space than a mouse. (Some individuals in the computer industry believe that the mouse will soon be replaced by devices that do not require as much space to use.)

The mouse is not practical for people using a laptop computer in a small space. Early alternatives, such as trackballs clipped to the side of the keyboard, have not proved satisfactory. The Apple PowerBook uses a central trackball. The IBM ThinkPad replaces the trackball with a red plastic button, called a trackpoint, located in the middle of the keyboard. You move the button with your thumbs. The newest Apple PowerBooks have a small square of plastic on the front of the keyboard that moves easily to control the pointer.

Courtesy of LogiTech, Inc.

Photographs courtesy of International Business Machines Corporation

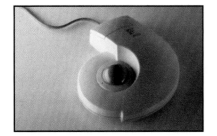  

A device that was released in 1995 enables the user to move the cursor using an infrared pen. The pen is cordless and works when it is as far as fifteen feet from the screen. Although the mouse is still the most popular pointing device, these innovations may change that.

Pointing devices include the LogiTech Trackman, the IBM ThinkPad Trackpoint, and the RISC System/6000 Spaceball.

Joysticks

A **joystick** is a pointing device often used for playing games. The joystick has a gearshift-like lever that is used to move the pointer on the screen. On most joysticks, a button on the top is used to select options. In industry and manufacturing, joysticks are used to control robots. Flight simulators and other training simulators also use joysticks.

Touch-Sensitive Screens

Perhaps the easiest way to enter data is with the touch of a finger. Touch screens enable the user to select an option by pressing a specific part of the screen. Touch screens are commonly used in grocery stores, fast-food restaurants, and information kiosks.

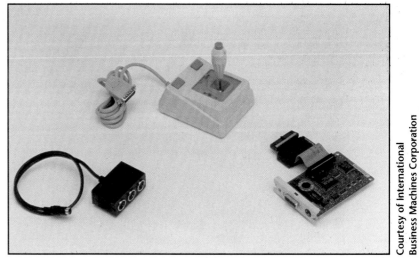

You can move the joystick in any direction to mark a location on the display screen.

Courtesy of International Business Machines Corporation

ALPS' GlidePoint Keyboard and TouchPad.

Courtesy of ALPS

Courtesy of ALPS

Pen-Based Systems

Have you received a package from United Parcel Service recently? If so, you probably signed for it on a special pad, using an electronic pen.

Pen-based systems are especially useful for people who do not like to type or who are frequently on the move. **Personal digital assistants** (**PDA**), such as the Apple Newton, are designed for people on the go. The Newton can link entries with stored files. For example, if you write "Call Margaret and wish Happy Birthday," the Newton adds a line to your "To do" list and links Margaret's phone number from your telephone directory. If your friend Ken moves, you can simply change his address and phone number. The Newton serves equally well as a calendar, calculator, and notepad.

The Apple Newton.

Pen-based systems are not perfect—they do not always register handwriting correctly. Pen-based computing is just beginning to gain widespread acceptance. For example, many stores no longer have you sign a carbon form to charge a purchase; instead you sign on a tablet that automatically records your signature.

A different type of pen called a light pen is used by many engineers and architects. The **light pen** uses a photoelectric (light-sensitive) cell to indicate screen position to the computer. You operate the pen by touching it to the screen. Light pens are frequently used for computer-aided design (CAD) applications.

This ThinkPad subnotebook computer features a monitor that interprets pen input.

Another tool used in CAD applications and other graphics applications is a digitizing tablet. A **digitizing tablet** consists of a grid on which designs and drawings can be entered. Most tablets are pressure-sensitive, and the user draws directly on the tablet using a special pen called a **stylus**, or a puck. Digitizing tablets are used to design cars, buildings, medical devices, and robots.

Digitizing tablets are used at Ford Motor Company to design new automobiles.

Courtesy of Apple Computer, Inc.

Courtesy of International Business Machines Corporation

Courtesy of Ford Motor Company

Data Scanning Devices

Optical recognition systems provide another means of minimizing keyed input by capturing data at the source. These systems enable the computer to "read" data by scanning printed text for recognizable patterns.

The banking industry developed one of the earliest scanning systems in the 1950s for processing checks. The Magnetic Ink Character Recognition (MICR) system is still used throughout the banking industry. The bank, branch, account number, and check number are encoded on the check before it is sent to the customer. After the customer has used the check and it comes back to the bank, all that needs to be entered manually is the amount. MICR has not been adopted by other industries because the character set has only fourteen symbols.

Of all the scanning devices, you are probably most familiar with **bar code readers**. Many retail and grocery stores use some form of bar code reader to determine the item being sold and to retrieve the item price from a computer system. The code reader may be a handheld unit, or it may be embedded in a countertop. The bar code reader reads the Universal Product Code (UPC), a pattern of bars printed on merchandise. The UPC has gained wide acceptance since its introduction in the 1970s. Initially, workers resisted the use of the code because the system was used to check their accuracy and speed. Today, bar codes are used to update inventory and ensure correct pricing. Federal Express uses a unique bar code to identify and track each package. Federal Express employees can usually tell a customer within a matter of minutes the location of any package.

MICR numbers

The MICR numbers appear on the bottom left of this check.

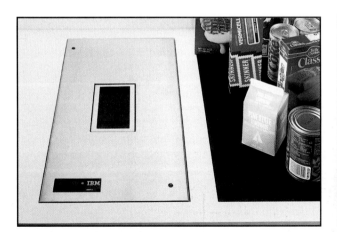

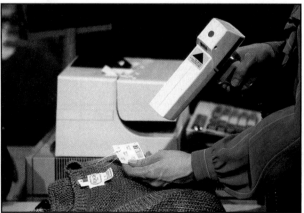

As the bar codes are scanned, the computer updates the inventory quantities.

From taking exams, you are already familiar with Mark Sense Character Recognition systems. Every time you take a test with a "fill in the bubble" Scantron form and use a #2 lead pencil, you are creating input suitable for an **optical mark reader** (**OMR**). A #2 lead pencil works best because of the number of magnetic particles in that weight lead. The OMR senses the magnetized marks, enabling the reader to determine which responses are marked. OMR is very helpful to researchers who need to tabulate responses to large surveys. Almost any type of survey or questionnaire can be designed to be suitable for OMR devices. An OMR unit can be attached to a microcomputer, and the data transferred to a file directly.

Optical scanners can scan typed documents, pictures, graphics, or even handwriting into a computer. Photographs scanned into a microcomputer appear clearly on the screen and can be displayed whenever desired. The copy that the computer has stored will never yellow with age. Early scanners could recognize only text printed in a special **optical character recognition** (**OCR**) typeface. A scanner converts the image that it sees into numeric digits before storing the image in the computer. This conversion process is known as **digitizing**.

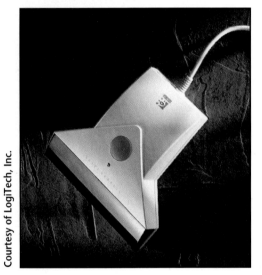

Courtesy of LogiTech, Inc.

Depending on the volume and type of material to be scanned, you can use drum scanners, flatbed scanners, sheet-fed scanners, and even small handheld scanners. The small, handheld scanners (priced at about $150) have been used most frequently with microcomputers; however, only 5 percent of all microcomputer systems are equipped with scanners. Manufacturers responded to user reluctance to use scanners by releasing in 1995 a number of new, small, paper scanners priced between $200 and $500. (In 1994, full-page scanners cost between $500 and $700.) Most of these new devices sit between the keyboard and the monitor and can interface with a fax machine, send e-mail, and store documents on disk for archive purposes.

This LogiTech handheld scanner can scan small, odd-sized items or full pages of text.

Voice Recognition Devices

Voice input and control systems have the potential of revolutionizing the way we communicate with computers. Steady progress has been made in this area, although there are still some problems. The day may soon come when we can talk to our computers the way the actors do on *Star Trek*.

Computer scientists and linguists have been working on **voice recognition systems** for two decades. The major difficulty has been that people speak with different accents and intonations. For this reason, most successful voice recognition systems require a period of "training" while the system becomes accustomed to an individual's accent and intonation.

The first systems could recognize only a few dozen words. A system recently released by IBM, known as VoiceType, is capable of recognizing as many as 32,000 words and is speaker independent.

Voice recognition devices can recognize input from individuals and be used to enter commands. These devices can also provide a picture of the sound, which helps hearing-impaired people learn to speak.

Photographs courtesy of International Business Machines Corporation

Voice recognition has unlimited possibilities and will make computers much easier to use. Speech recognition systems are already being used in many types of settings. In factories, workers use speech recognition systems to control robotic arms when the worker's own hands are busy. Speech recognition systems enable physically disabled people to use computers. A microcomputer **Voice User Interface** (**VUI**), capable of recognizing input from a variety of individuals, will be considered standard soon.

Photographs courtesy of International Business Machines Corporation

The Future of the Human-Computer Interface

One of the greatest technology think tanks in the world is Xerox Corporation's Palo Alto Research Center (PARC), which celebrated its 25th anniversary in 1995. PARC pioneered many computer innovations that we take for granted today, including the human-computer interface. Steven Jobs, Apple Computer's cofounder, visited PARC in the early 1980s and saw the Xerox Star workstation, with its mouse, graphic screen, and icons. He vowed to develop a similar computer that anyone could learn to use; the result was the Macintosh.

Stuart Card is a cognitive psychologist and computer scientist who has been developing user interfaces at PARC since its beginning. He knows how much research has gone into inventing and refining user interfaces, which at PARC date back to the early 1970s. The Macintosh, he writes, was "widely cited as the first commercially successful use of a graphical user interface. The first Apple introduction of this technology on the LISA failed, as did the second, the LISA 2, as did the third, the Macintosh 128. Only on the fourth try, the Macintosh 512, was there commercial success. But this machine had no user interface invention, it just used the design settled earlier in the series. Most of the real invention in this design, in turn, actually occurred in the designs of the Xerox SmallTalk and the Xerox Star systems and related design at PARC. . . . Some ideas in these systems can be traced back even further."[1]

A more recent innovation from PARC is the Information Visualizer, or IV. An IV is a three-dimensional, animated tool that turns the computer screen into a passageway which leads to various types of information. Card says that the old ways of retrieving information are based on content, such as words or dates. The new way is to present information in the same manner in which the brain thinks about it: in structure and context as well as content.

The PARC workstation screen presents an overview room with twelve information visualizers, or screens. Eleven are 3-D rooms; the user moves from one to another through connecting "doors." One IV room displays the Xerox organizational chart. Previously, it was an 80-page document, like one created in word processing. In the IV, it is a rotating drum with revolving names. When a person is chosen, the name is moved to the front of the screen, like a label, but the relationship to others in the organization is graphically presented.

Courtesy of Xerox Corporation

By clicking the mouse, the user can navigate closer to the individual. All screen objects, such as name labels, are interactive, which means that they can be changed or moved into various relationships, as in a work group. The view can be narrowed to the person, displaying a color photograph, biography, papers the person has written, and other public information. The view can also be widened to show the person's office, the floor plan for the work group, and biographies and other information about fellow workers. In fact, the interactive nature of the screen objects even permits showing parallels or differences between the various individuals' work.

Stuart Card believes that the ultimate goal of interface design is to make the interface vanish. Today, too much manipulation of the computer system is required. An ideal interface takes the focus off the machinery and puts it on the work.

Scientists and engineers at PARC will be the first workers who get to take advantage of IVs. But Card and his team are working to develop IVs that help visualize information for business applications.

---

1 Stuart K. Card. "Pioneers and Settlers: Methods Used in Successful User Interface Designs," a Xerox PARC monograph, Dec. 12, 1994, 6–7.

Video digitizers can capture input from virtually any type of video device, such as VCRs, televisions, and camcorders. Audio digitizers can digitize music or voice from a microphone. It is fairly easy to capture a portion of a television show, add some music that complements the picture, and play back the result on a microcomputer to create a multimedia presentation.

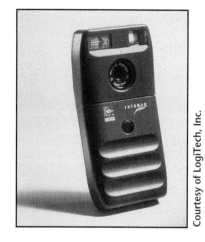

The LogiTech Fotoman is a camera that converts the "photograph" to a digital image the computer can read.

Output Devices

Output devices are as varied and as innovative as input devices. From traditional printed output to audio output and robots, there are a multitude of forms of computer output.

Most output can be divided into two categories: soft copy and hard copy. **Soft copy** is ideal when you are writing a document, playing a game, watching a video clip, or reading the latest news. Soft copy is what you see on the monitor. Soft copy is temporary; after you have finished with it, there is nothing solid to hold. You can, however, transfer soft copy to a disk to transport it. **Hard copy** can be touched and carried. Hard copy is usually some form of paper output. It is especially helpful if you need to have a colleague look at your work or you need to give your work to a supervisor or teacher.

Monitors

When you think about viewing computer output, you probably visualize a **monitor**. Monitor output is soft copy; when you have finished viewing it, you cannot pick up the output and move it. Monitor displays are the most common form of soft copy.

Sometimes, when watching television, you may notice that the picture looks a little snowy. This condition occurs because the images are not solid but rather created by configurations of dots. These dots, or **picture elements**, combine to form the image you see. The more picture elements, also known as **pixels**, the better the **resolution** of the image. The better the resolution, the clearer the picture. Computer monitors are similar to television screens.

The large monitors that you see connected to desktop computers are **cathode-ray tube (CRT) monitors**. The smaller monitors that are used on laptops and notebook computers are known as **flat-panel displays**. Flat-panel displays weigh less and consume less electricity than CRTs. Common types of flat-panel displays include **liquid crystal display (LCD)**, **electroluminescent (EL) display**, and gas plasma display. Flat-panel display monitors are still more expensive than CRTs but will eventually decrease in price. (PixelVision recently released a 16-inch flat-panel display that includes a two-million color palette and sells for $10,000.) Can you imagine hanging your monitor on the wall like a painting? It may be common in a few years.

A PixelVision flat-panel monitor.

Photographs courtesy of Radius, Inc.

Monitors are available in many sizes and shapes. Some monitors, such as the Radius dual-orientation monitor, can be rotated to provide a different view.

Most new monitors are **SVGA (Super Video Graphics Adapter)** with a pixel configuration of 800 by 600 at low-resolution mode and 1024 by 768 at high-resolution mode. (The first number designates the horizontal pixel count, and the second is the vertical pixel count.) The higher resolution with more pixels provides a clearer, more detailed image. Each pixel displays a single color at a time. Each color is represented by a numeric code (for example, bright red could be 12). If the monitor displays only 16 colors, the numeric code can be represented with only four bits. To display 256 colors (each with its own code) requires eight bits.

One monitor may look "sharper" than another even though they have the same pixel configuration. This is due to the **dot pitch**, which is the distance between pixels. (A .28 dot pitch gives a crisper image than a .30 dot pitch. The .28 dot pitch is fairly standard.) You should consider dot pitch when purchasing a monitor. The dot pitch is built in by the manufacturer and cannot be changed.

With users increasingly viewing video clips, animated objects, and complex graphics, monitors have taken on a new importance. Users now must decide how large a monitor they need. Fourteen-inch to seventeen-inch monitors are commonly used with desktop microcomputer systems. (Larger monitors are available but are expensive.)

Monitors are also categorized by whether they display in black and white (**monochrome**) or color. Monochrome monitors are rapidly becoming a thing of the past, as most applications today require color. In fact, a display of 256 colors is usually necessary for working with informational CD-ROMs and clip-art collections.

In order to connect a monitor to a microcomputer, you must have a **graphics adapter board** (also known as a video card). Each type of monitor requires a different type of board. The graphics board plugs into an expansion slot inside the computer, and the monitor plugs into the board.

In order to run today's graphics-intensive programs properly and quickly, most graphics boards come with some memory capability, known as **video memory**. It is important to realize that **video RAM** (**VRAM**) must meet higher performance specifications than regular RAM. It is recommended that instead of using RAM on a video card, the user should place VRAM or **dynamic RAM** (**DRAM**), which is slightly slower than VRAM, on a video card.

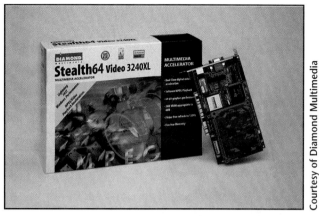

Courtesy of Diamond Multimedia

The **refresh rate** on a monitor is also important and is affected by the video card. Even a steady image is constantly regenerated, or refreshed, from top to bottom. A slow refresh rate of 60 times per second (60Hz), can cause headaches; 70Hz is a reasonable minimum. Some monitors, known as **interlaced monitors**, refresh every other line; **non-interlaced monitors** are easier on the eyes. The **Motion Picture Experts Group** (**MPEG**), has developed standards for video compression that improve the quality of the video on the monitor. MPEG drivers are available as software or as hardware built in a video card.

Audio Output

Have you ever listened to a concert or watched a television show on a computer? Audio output is a second type of soft copy. New computer systems have such good audio systems that it is possible to listen to music while you work, have the computer tell you when the printer needs paper, play games that include sound, or compose music on the computer. In order to have high-quality audio output, a good quality sound card and speakers are needed.

New sound cards even include the capability to have the computer read a text file to you while you continue working on a different application. Voice input and output have proved helpful to individuals with speech and vision impairments. Someone with a speech impairment can key a message into a computer and have the computer say it. Of course, computer-generated voices are not human; they are synthesized. **Speech synthesis**, having the computer speak, is a much simpler process than speech recognition.

Printers

The second most common form of computer output is printed documents. Although a computer can operate perfectly without a printer, it is certainly helpful to the user to have one. Because you can hold printed output, it is considered a form of hard copy.

Printers can be categorized by whether anything mechanical actually touches the paper; whether they do or do not produce a solid character; and whether they produce a page, a line, or a character at a time.

When a part of the printer presses the paper to form the character, the printer is considered an **impact printer**. Impact printers can produce carbon copies and are fairly loud, although covers are available to muffle the noise. In contrast, **nonimpact printers** are quiet. However, because nothing presses on the page, a nonimpact printer cannot produce carbon copies. This fact is usually not a problem because it is easy to produce multiple originals, but sometimes carbons are required for legal purposes.

Impact Printers

Impact printers can produce a page, a line, or a character at a time. Large computers use line printers. The main drawback to **line printers** is that they can produce only text––no graphics.

Many small computers use **character printers**. Although only one character can be produced at a time, many types of character printers can produce graphics as well as text. The most common character printers create images by using a dot pattern. These printers are known as **dot-matrix printers**. If you use a magnifying glass to look at a report created with a dot-matrix printer, you can see the small dots forming each character.

Nonimpact Printers

Nonimpact printers are increasing in popularity largely because of improvements in print quality coupled with decreasing cost. Nonimpact printers can produce both text and graphics. Because nothing actually strikes the paper, nonimpact printers are fairly quiet. Some of the most popular nonimpact printers are laser printers and inkjet printers.

Laser printers work in the same manner as copy machines; a laser beam creates electrical charges that attract toner to form an image and transfer it to paper. Laser printers come in a variety of sizes; generally the larger and faster the printer, the more expensive it is. Large laser printers are used on mainframes and minicomputers where high-quality graphic output is required. Small, "personal" laser printers are suitable for home use. Hewlett-Packard recently began production of a wireless printer. The HP5P (IBM) and HP5PM (Mac) enable the user to beam a document from a laptop to an infrared receiver in the front of the printer. The laptop needs to have a built-in infrared transmitter installed, but no cables or wires are required.

Photographs courtesy of Hewlett-Packard Company

The faster speed of the Hewlett-Packard LaserJet 5Si MX accommodates more users and higher print volumes.

The Hewlett-Packard LaserJet 5L produces high-quality reports very quickly, and its design requires little space.

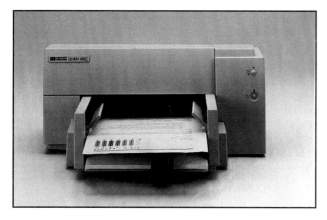

The side-by-side black and color cartridges of the Hewlett-Packard DeskJet 660C printer enable you to print in true black and color on the same page without having to swap cartridges.

Photographs courtesy of Hewlett-Packard Company

The Hewlett-Packard Color LaserJet 5 printer is useful for workgroups.

Inkjet printers are also popular for microcomputers. Although the resolution is lower on inkjet printers than on laser printers, the resolution is higher than that of dot-matrix printers. Inkjet printers are significantly less expensive than laser printers. Electronically charged ink is sprayed through a jet nozzle and passed through an electronic field, which deflects the ink to form a dot-matrix character. Color inkjet printers, which use multiple nozzles, are available at very reasonable prices. Canon recently released a color inkjet printer that weighs three pounds and stands two inches high—perfect for traveling!

A well-equipped office, at home or at work, includes an inkjet printer, a fax machine (with its own telephone), a copier, and a full-sheet scanner. A recent addition to the market is one device that does all four functions. The technology to print a document that has been faxed to you and the technology to copy a document are similar to the technology to print a document from a PC. All three technologies use similar digital patterns, and the mechanical aspects are nearly identical.

Plotters

A **plotter**, like a printer, produces hard-copy output. Plotters, which produce high-quality color graphics, are usually categorized by whether they use pens or electrostatic charges to create images. A continuous-curve plotter is used to draw maps from stored data. Computer-generated maps can be retrieved and plotted or used to show changes over time. Plotters are generally more expensive than printers, ranging from about $1,000 to $75,000 (or even more).

Microfilm, Microfiche, and CD-ROM

Storing printed reports requires a great deal of space. What can be done to save paper and storage space? **Computer Output Microfilm/Microfiche (COM)** provides one answer. **Microfilm** stores images of reports on a roll of film; **microfiche** uses four-by-six-inch sheets of film to

Courtesy of Hewlett-Packard Company

Plotters are ideal for engineering, drafting, and many other applications that require intricate graphics.

store images. Besides saving storage space, COM is less expensive than regular printed output. Producing output on microfilm or microfiche is also faster than producing printed output. COM devices can output in excess of 30,000 lines per minute. The major disadvantage of COM is that because of the small size, special readers are required to read the film or fiche.

For companies that store volumes of computer information, an alternative to COM is CD-ROM. Data Optics International offers a CD-ROM microfiche replacement service in which the computer information is recorded, indexed, and transferred to CD-ROM technology. The information can then be made available in report format through a PC or LAN network. Each CD-ROM can store one million pages, or 680M, of computer data. The advantages of this storage method are faster, simpler data retrieval and lower overall costs. Just as CDs have replaced LP records in the music industry, CD-ROM technology may eventually replace the traditional tape and microfiche methods of data storage.

Robots

Probably the most intriguing output device is the robot. Most robots are not the way you may imagine; they have little resemblance to R2D2 of *Star Wars* or Data of *Star Trek: The Next Generation*. Most robotic devices consist of a single arm that can perform a preprogrammed task. Robotic devices are frequently used in manufacturing for such tasks as spray painting or assembling parts.

Advanced robotic devices are used in scientific research. For example, Jason, a talking robot that can be seen at Epcot Center, was created for undersea exploration.

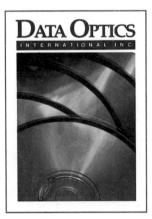

Courtesy of Data Optics International, Inc.

Courtesy of Ford Motor Company

Robots can be used for many tasks, including the assembly of other computers.

Lesson Summary

➤ Input and output devices are sometimes called peripheral devices.

➤ The most common source of computer input is the keyboard. Keying mistakes cause most computer errors.

➤ Source-data automation is the capture of data at the point where the transaction occurs and is accomplished with a minimum of keying.

➤ POS (point-of-sale) terminals are a type of source-data automation device that can be found in most department stores.

➤ A trackball or a mouse is used to point and select options that are shown on the screen.

➤ Pen-based systems are used for computer-aided design and for encoding customer signatures.

➤ Optical recognition systems enable the computer to read patterns. MICR, used by the banking industry, and Mark Sense Character Recognition Systems are types of optical recognition systems.

➤ Computers can digitize the human voice and recognize verbal instructions. Speech and voice recognition systems are especially useful in factories and in assisting the physically disabled.

➤ Hard copy is output that can be touched and carried. In contrast, soft copy output is displayed on a monitor.

➤ The display on a monitor is composed of thousands of dots, or picture elements, known as pixels.

➤ Printers are usually categorized as impact or nonimpact. With impact printers, something physically touches the paper. With nonimpact printers, nothing touches the paper but the ink.

➤ A plotter is used to produce high-quality color graphics.

➤ Robots are a type of output device.

Lesson Review

Key Terms

bar code reader
cathode-ray tube (CRT) monitor
character printer
Computer Output Microfilm/Microfiche (COM)
digitizing
digitizing tablet
dot-matrix printer
dot pitch
Dynamic RAM (DRAM)
electroluminescent (EL) display
flat-panel display
graphics adapter board

hard copy
impact printer
inkjet printer
interlaced monitor
joystick
laser printer
light pen
line printer
liquid crystal display (LCD)
membrane-switch keyboard
microfiche
microfilm
monitor
monochrome

Motion Picture Experts Group (MPEG)
mouse
nonimpact printer
noninterlaced monitor
optical character recognition (OCR)
optical mark reader (OMR)
optical recognition system
optical scanner
personal digital assistant (PDA)
picture element
pixel
plotter

QWERTY keyboard
refresh rate
resolution
soft copy
source-data automation
speech synthesis
stylus
Super Video Graphics Adapter (SVGA)
trackball
video digitizer
video memory
Video RAM (VRAM)
voice recognition system
Voice User Interface (VUI)

Matching

In the blank next to each of the following terms or phrases, write the letter of the corresponding term or phrase.

_____ 1. Output that can be viewed but not held in your hand

_____ 2. Cannot produce multiple copies

_____ 3. Capability of a computer to accept verbal instructions

_____ 4. Advanced output device

_____ 5. Paper output

_____ 6. Frequently used with microcomputers to produce hard copy

_____ 7. A picture element

_____ 8. Produces high-quality color graphics

_____ 9. Produces fast, high-quality text

_____ 10. Frequently used to produce soft copy

a. pixel

b. voice recognition

c. robot

d. soft copy

e. hard copy

f. monitor

g. plotter

h. dot-matrix printer

i. nonimpact printer

j. laser printer

Multiple Choice

Circle the letter of the correct choice for each of the following.

1. Which pointing device is likely to be most suitable for a quadriplegic (a person who does not have the use of his or her body from the lower neck down but can hold a stick in his or her mouth)?

    a. joystick

    b. mouse

    c. pen-based system

    d. trackball

2. Which of the following devices would likely be used by an instructor to grade exams?

    a. handheld scanner

    b. pointing device

    c. MICR system

    d. optical mark reader

3. Which of the following items is *not* an example of an output device?

    a. CRT monitor

    b. dot-matrix printer

    c. voice recognition device

    d. LCD

4. Which of the following statements is false?

    a. The smaller the number of pixels, the better the resolution.

    b. Images on monitors are created by configurations of dots.

    c. An SVGA screen has more than 700,000 pixels available at high-resolution mode.

    d. RGB monitors create colors by mixing red, green, and blue.

5. Which of the following is an impact printer?

    a. laser

    b. inkjet

    c. dot-matrix

    d. plotter

6. Which of the following inventions is a recent breakthrough in printing technology?

    a. fax machine

    b. wireless printing

    c. laser printer

    d. trackball

7. Which of the following is *not* used for source-data automation?

    a. POS terminal

    b. keyboard

    c. OCR

    d. UPC system

8. A plotter is used to produce which of the following?

    a. maps

    b. text

    c. microfiche

    d. soft copy

9. Which of the following is *not* a type of monitor?

    a. cathode-ray tube

    b. flatbed

    c. electroluminescent display

    d. gas plasma

10. A nonimpact printer is *not* capable of which of the following tasks?

    a. printing graphics

    b. printing text

    c. making carbon copies

    d. being used with microcomputers

Completion

In the blank provided, write the correct answer for each of the following.

1. A single dot on a monitor is known as a(n) _____.

2. A(n) _____ keyboard is the most commonly used.

3. _____ are a common source of computer errors.

4. _____ keyboards are resistant to liquids and grease.

5. In most microcomputer systems, you use a(n) _____ to point to and select options.

6. Wireless printers use _____ to receive a document.

7. MICR is used by the _____ industry.

8. Many surveys and tests are answered on a form that can be read by a(n) _____ device.

9. A(n) _____ can be used to enter a photograph into a computer.

10. A(n) _____ produces soft copy.

Review

On a separate sheet of paper, answer the following questions.

1. Describe two examples of source-data automation.

2. List four types of pointing devices. What is their major advantage over a keyboard?

3. Cite several advantages to using the membrane-switch keyboard.

4. List three types of scanners. Describe how a computer scans a document.

5. List and briefly define four output devices.

6. Why are many businesses changing to a form of source-data automation?

7. What types of operations can a PDA perform?

8. Why are trackballs becoming more popular?

9. For what is MICR used?

10. List some advantages of COM over traditional computer output.

Critical Thinking

On a separate sheet of paper, answer the following questions.

1. Imagine a visually impaired student who needs to use the computer for a word processing assignment. What types of input and output devices do you think could be helpful?

2. Cite several real-world environments where pointing devices are presently being used or could be used.

3. What types of computer input and output devices do you think could be helpful over the next fifty years in areas such as

consumer purchasing, medicine, and education?

4. Imagine a personal computer fifteen years from now. What do you think will be the input and output devices attached to that system?

5. What recent input and output devices do you think might lead to the "paperless office"? Explain how each would contribute toward this environment.

Further Discovery

PC Secrets. Caroline M. Halliday (Foster City, CA: IDG, 1996).

Peter Norton's Inside the PC, Sixth Edition. Peter Norton, Lewis C. Eggebrecht, and Scott N. A. Clark (Indianapolis, IN: Sams, 1995).

Winn L. Rosch Printer Bible. Winn Rosch (New York: Henry Holt, 1996).

Magazines such as *Byte, PC World*, and *PC Magazine* feature articles on new input/output developments.

On-line Discovery

You can access the Internet resources for the following questions by going to the Que Education and Training Web site at URL http://www.ciyf98.com/discovery. From this page, click the link for Lesson 2C and then click the link to the resource you want to access.

The Yahoo! directory page for **Input Devices** (http://www.yahoo.com/Business_and_Economy /Companies/Computers/Hardware/Peripherals/Input_Devices) points to the Web pages of many different companies that manufacture input devices. Browse several of these Web pages. What types of input devices do you see? How are they different from each other? What are the most prevalent types of input devices? Do you see any that are intended for people with disabilities?

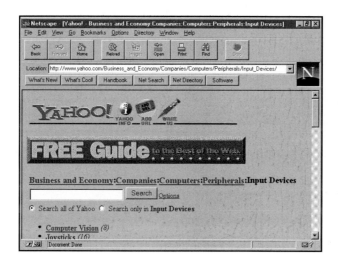

LESSON 2D

Different Needs, Different Sizes

Outline

Supercomputers
Mainframes
Minicomputers
Workstations and Microcomputers
    Workstations
    Microcomputers
Computers on the Move
Embedded Computers
Connectivity

Learning Objectives

When you have finished reading this lesson, you will be able to

➤ Distinguish among the different types of computers

➤ Define parallel processing

➤ Distinguish among a front-end processor, a host, and a back-end processor

➤ Understand the difference between a workstation and a desktop computer

➤ List the uses of embedded computers

The computer sitting on the desk in your classroom is a microcomputer. It is a small, powerful piece of equipment. Even so, the power of the microcomputer is not enough for most large organizations. The computer industry consists of more than just microcomputers.

Any classification of computers is somewhat arbitrary. Traditionally, computers have been classified by their size, processing speed, and cost. This lesson explores four commonly used classifications: supercomputers, mainframes, minicomputers, and microcomputers. Supercomputers are the largest and most powerful; microcomputers are the smallest. Because all computers are becoming more powerful and faster, any absolute measure would be ludicrous. Supercomputers are the most powerful relative to anything else currently available. Today's microcomputers can do work that required a mainframe computer 20 years ago. The microcomputer of 2010 may be equal in power to the supercomputer of today.

Supercomputers

Supercomputers are the largest, fastest, most powerful, and most expensive computers made. Like other large systems, supercomputers can be accessed by many individuals at the same time. Supercomputers are used primarily for scientific applications that are mathematically intensive. The aerospace, automotive, chemical, electronics, and petroleum industries use supercomputers extensively. Supercomputers are used in weather forecasting and seismic analysis. They are found in many public and private research centers, such as universities and government laboratories. A supercomputer was used to alert scientists to the impending collision of a comet with Jupiter in 1994, giving them time to prepare to observe and record the event. The United States Department of Energy recently contracted with IBM for an "ultrasupercomputer," three hundred times faster than any existing machine. The ultrasupercomputer will simulate nuclear explosions (eliminating the need to detonate any bombs), model global weather trends, and design power plants.

The first supercomputer was built in the 1960s for the United States Department of Defense. This computer was designed to be the world's fastest and most powerful computer of that time. The commitment to create the fastest, most powerful computer in the world is still the driving force behind the development of supercomputers. Manufacturers produce relatively few of any one model of supercomputer, and they spend millions of dollars on research and development of new machines.

Supercomputers derive much of their speed from the use of multiple processors. **Multiprocessing** enables the computers to perform tasks simultaneously—either assigning different tasks to each processing unit or dividing a complex task among several processing units. The first supercomputer had four central processing units; the **massively parallel processors** of today contain hundreds of processors.

The speed of modern supercomputers is measured in nanoseconds and gigaflops. A **nanosecond** is one billionth of a second. A **gigaflop** is one billion floating-point arithmetic operations per second. Supercomputers can perform at up to 128 gigaflops, and use bus widths of 32 or 64 bits. This capability makes supercomputers suitable for processor-intensive applications, such as graphics. Supercomputers are rarely used for input/output-intensive processing, such as accounting or record-keeping operations.

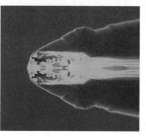

Photographs courtesy of Pittsburgh Supercomputing Center

Mordecai-Mark Mac Low, a scientist at the University of Chicago, used the Internet to access a Cray C90 supercomputer at the Pittsburgh Supercomputing Center in order to create these images. The images simulate the Shoemaker-Levy 9 comet crashing into Jupiter in July 1994.

Courtesy of Cray Research, Inc.

This Cray T3D supercomputer by Cray Research is a massively parallel processing system. The Los Alamos National Laboratory is using the T3D to run its Parallel Ocean Program global climate model.

Courtesy of Thinking Machines Corporation

The Thinking Machines' Connection Machine.

Leaders in the development of supercomputers include Cray Research Company, Silicon Graphics, Thinking Machines Corporation, Fujitsu, IBM, and Intel. Cray Research Company, founded by Seymour Cray in 1972, has been the undisputed leader in this segment of the computer industry ever since. Silicon Graphics challenged that lead in 1995. Then, in 1996, it merged with Cray, which became a subsidiary of Silicon Graphics. Cray Research recently delivered a 256-processor system to the Swiss Federal Institute of Technology. And Silicon Graphics opened a technology center, directly connected to Silicon Graphics' headquarters in California, to develop supercomputer applications in China.

Thinking Machines has produced a supercomputer called the Connection Machine, which has over 64,000 processors. The Connection Machine is reasonably priced at $5 million. Silicon Graphics is mass-marketing the Cray T90 and Cray J90 (several hundred have been sold to date) with price tags of $500,000 to $2,500,000. Supercomputers have traditionally ranged in price from $2 million to $20 million.

Supercomputer for Super Projects

Super, as in superlative, implies *awesome*. And when *super* precedes *computer*, the results are truly awesome.

A Supercomputers and Fractal Graphics class at California State University San Francisco was given an elementary algorithm to generate fractals (mathematics-oriented, computer-generated graphic designs). The students were asked to write programs for computers of their choice and then record the times required to run the programs on different systems.

The computation took 28 hours on the IBM PC or Mac Plus, 30 minutes on a Mac II with a floating-point chip, and 15 minutes on a VAX 11/750 minicomputer. The question was then asked, "How long would it take on a supercomputer?"

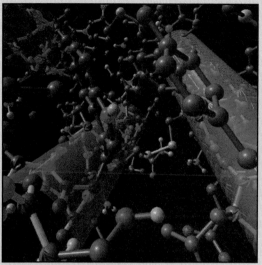

Courtesy of San Diego Supercomputer Center

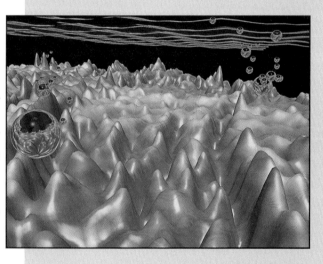

Courtesy of San Diego Supercomputer Center

With a grant from the National Science Foundation (NSF), the California State University system provided supercomputing time for the class. Enter the San Diego Supercomputer Center (SDSC) with its Cray Y-MP. The Cray generated a full-sized graphic in just one second!

Providing computer time to a class at CSU San Francisco is only one example of SDSC's activities. Established in 1985 at the University of California, San Diego, SDSC is one of five high-performance computer centers that form the National MetaCenter, an integrated national information infrastructure supported by the NSF.

According to Ann Redelfs of SDSC, more than 22,000 researchers and students at more than 500 institutions have used MetaCenter resources; more than 20,000 people have been trained at center-sponsored workshops.

A short list of the projects currently using SDSC resources includes protein structure determination, brain mapping, neurocomputation, and computational science for high school science and math teachers. Ecology researchers have simulated the ocean floor in minute detail.

SDSC MetaCenter is one of many supercomputer centers that are active worldwide. Super, indeed!

Mainframes

Since the first UNIVAC I was sold in 1951, the **mainframe computer** has been the cornerstone of the computer industry. IBM, the giant of the computer industry, captured the mainframe market in the late 1950s and made its name and fortune manufacturing mainframe computer systems. Mainframes are the most widely used type of computer in large businesses. IBM still holds an estimated two-thirds of the mainframe market.

The typical mainframe computer occupies much of a large room. Like supercomputers, mainframes require an environment with closely monitored humidity and temperature. Mainframe computers are priced between $100,000 and $2,000,000.

Courtesy of International Business Machines Corporation

An IBM ES/9000 mainframe.

For input/output-intensive operations, mainframe computers are much more suitable than supercomputers. Many modern mainframes have multi-processing capabilities; however, they are generally limited to eight or fewer processors. The processors in mainframes are slower than those in supercomputers, with speed measured in **megaflops** (millions of floating-point arithmetic operations per second) rather than gigaflops.

Front-end processor   **Back-end processor**   **Host**

Photographs courtesy of International Business Machines Corporation

Computers used at the 1996 Centennial Olympic games in Atlanta.

A mainframe computer system is usually composed of several computers in addition to the mainframe, or host processor. The **host processor** is responsible for controlling the other processors, all the peripheral devices, and the mathematics operations. A **front-end processor** is responsible for handling communications to and from all the remote **terminals** connected to the computer system. Sometimes a **back-end processor** is used to handle data retrieval operations. Although the host computer could perform all these operations, it can be used more efficiently if relieved of time-consuming chores that do not require processing speed.

Mainframe computer systems are powerful enough to support several hundred users simultaneously at remote terminals. Terminals can be located near the computer or miles away. Computers can support hundreds of users by keeping numerous programs in primary memory and rapidly switching back and forth between programs. Because computers are so much faster than people, the users never notice that the computer is handling other tasks. This capability to process many programs concurrently for multiple users is known as **multiprogramming**.

The introduction of the microcomputer and the increased capabilities of minicomputers have resulted in a decline of sales of mainframe computers. Recently, to bolster sales of mainframes, IBM started producing mainframes based on arrays of microprocessor chips and designed to be servers for giant databases used on networks of microcomputers.

TechTalk
A network server stores files that can be accessed by the other computers (clients) connected to the network.

Minicomputers

The "age of the mini" started in the late 1960s. The creation of integrated circuits suitable for computers enabled designers to shrink the size of the computer. Before Digital Equipment Corporation (DEC) released the first

DEC PDP-8 **minicomputer** in 1968, most medium-sized organizations were priced out of the computer market because they couldn't afford mainframe computers. The DEC minicomputer cost around $50,000—a considerable savings compared with the $200,000 mainframe of that time.

Courtesy of Digital Equipment Corporation

An Alpha station 600 5/266.

Like mainframes, most minicomputers are multiuser systems. Many of today's minicomputers can accommodate as many as 200 users working from individual terminals. Petrochemia Plock recently installed a Microvax 3100 minicomputer system by DEC at its fuel terminal on the northern coast of Poland. The minicomputer system will oversee the flow of fuel to distributors and dealers across the country, ensuring that deliveries of fuel are dispensed to the correct drivers. The system is similar to systems used by Esso and Shell in refinery and delivery plants throughout Europe.

The major difference between mainframes and minicomputers is in scale. Minicomputers can perform the same types of tasks as mainframes, but minicomputers are a little slower. Like mainframes, minicomputers can accommodate remote users, but not as many. Minicomputers' input, output, and storage devices look like those on mainframes; but minicomputers have slightly less storage, and the printers are slightly slower. The distinctions between these categories of computers are blurring as time passes. Minicomputers are frequently referred to as mid-range computers.

Workstations and Microcomputers

When you are working on a multiuser computer, such as a mainframe or minicomputer, you can control the input and see the output on the display, but you control nothing else. A single-user computer gives you control over all the phases of computer processing: input, processing, output, and storage. You can select the programs you want to use, and you don't have to compete with other users to gain access to the system. A single-user system is designed to meet the computing needs of an individual. Single-user computers fall into two categories: workstations and microcomputers.

Workstations

A **workstation** is a powerful desktop computer designed to meet the computing needs of engineers, architects, and other professionals who need detailed graphics displays. For example, workstations are commonly used for **computer-aided design** (**CAD**), in which industrial designers create pictures of technical parts or assemblies. To process these complex and detailed diagrams, the computer needs great processing power and much storage. Workstations are also frequently used as servers for local area networks. (For detailed coverage of local area networks, see Chapter 6.)

Image courtesy of Silicon Graphics, Inc./Sony Corp./Alias

These graphics were produced on workstation computers made by Silicon Graphics, Inc. Similar Silicon Graphics workstations produced the special effects for Jurassic Park and other movies.

Image courtesy of Silicon Graphics, Inc./CAD Center's Review

Image courtesy of Silicon Graphics, Inc.

Image courtesy of Silicon Graphics, Inc./Sideffects Software and Catapult Productions' "Land Without Books"

Workstations are small, powerful systems designed to drive networks of less powerful microcomputers and to create high-quality graphics. Workstations typically cost $5,000 to $20,000. Major competitors in this market include DEC, Hewlett-Packard, Sun, and Silicon Graphics, Inc.

The workstation has sometimes been called a "supermicro." The workstation looks very much like a desktop microcomputer, but the chips inside make the difference. Most workstations use **reduced instruction set computer** (**RISC**) microprocessors. Computer designers have discovered that by eliminating infrequently used preprogrammed instructions, they can increase the speed of the processor. Many new processor chips, including the DEC Alpha and the PowerPC, are RISC chips. RISC processors are particularly useful in special-purpose applications, such as graphics, in which speed is critical. The DEC Alpha chip was the first microprocessor designed to work with a 64-bit bus.

BITS
Powerful microcomputers with RISC chips have been referred to as "killer micros." The cry "No one will survive the attack of the killer micros!" shows the support for the RISC microprocessor chips being used in massively parallel processing computers.

A Panda workstation.

A Panda server.

People use personal computers for many household applications, such as budgeting, personal finance, and taxes.

The PowerPC 604 microprocessor wafer.

Microcomputers

It is difficult to overstate the impact of the microcomputer on the computer industry. In 1975, the microcomputer did not exist. In 1995, sales exceeded $116 billion. Microcomputers are the fastest growing segment of the computer industry.

The microcomputer segment of the industry is complex; there are different types of microcomputer platforms with varying capabilities. The most common type of microcomputer is a **desktop computer**, which is a nonportable **personal computer** that fits on top of a desk. The desktop microcomputer market has been divided into two types of computers: Apple and IBM/IBM compatible. In 1994, Power Computing Corporation began marketing Macintosh-compatible computers, raising the possibility of a new microcomputer market segment. Presently, Apple has about 8 percent of the market, IBM has about 28 percent, and IBM compatibles have most of the rest.

A few years ago, Apple Computer, IBM, and Motorola joined to develop the PowerPC chip, which enables Apple computers to run IBM applications and vice versa. Most Apple Macintosh computers and compatibles are based on this chip. IBM recently released its PowerPC chip machines. It is difficult to assess the implications of this chip on the desktop market.

Courtesy of John Greenleigh/Apple Computer, Inc.

This Power Macintosh 8100/80 uses the PowerPC microprocessor.

Recently, Intel countered with the Pentium Pro chip. (Intel's 586 chip is known as Pentium, which is Greek for 5; Intel's 686 chip is the Pentium Pro.) All the new microprocessors—Pentium Pro, PowerPC, and Alpha—are designed for 64-bit systems.

The boundary between workstations and personal computers is becoming less distinct. Today's best personal computers are more powerful and offer more precise displays than the workstations of the recent past. The new Pentium Pro microcomputers have multiprocessing capabilities. In addition, the distinction between workstations and minicomputers is becoming blurred because of the most powerful workstations. These workstations can be equipped so that more than one person can use the workstation at once, in effect making the workstation a minicomputer.

Most microcomputers enable the user to switch between tasks. This capability is known as **multitasking**—a single-user variation on multiprogramming. Multitasking can be a great timesaver. Suppose that you are using a word processor to write a term paper, and you need to do some computations on the computer and use the results in the paper. Without multitasking, you would have to close the term paper file and the word processing application, open the calculator application, make your computations, write down the results, close the calculator application, and reopen the word processing application and the term paper file. With multitasking, you simply open the calculator application, make your calculations, and switch back to the term paper file. This capability to task-swap between the paper and the calculator saves time.

People frequently refer to a personal computer as a **microcomputer**, a computer that uses a microprocessor for its processing circuitry. The term *microcomputer* originated in the late 1970s, when the only computers that used microprocessors were PCs. But today all kinds of computers use microprocessors. By this definition, most of today's computers, including some supercomputers, are microcomputers. But people usually mean PC when they use the term microcomputer.

TechTalk
A *microprocessor* is computer processing circuitry fabricated on a tiny wafer of silicon.

For many people, the abbreviation *PC* refers only to an IBM or IBM-compatible personal computer. When IBM introduced its first personal computer in 1981, the firm chose the name IBM Personal Computer—IBM PC, for short—for the product. You may still hear people say something like "Oh, she's not using a PC, she's using a Macintosh." As the people at Apple Computer are fond of pointing out, though, both the IBM PC and the Macintosh are personal computers.

Computers on the Move

The first portable computers were dubbed "luggables," and for good reason. They weighed as much as 28 pounds. Soon, reductions in size created the **laptop computer**, a more compact unit weighing roughly 10 to 12 pounds. As many people discovered to their dismay, however, 10 pounds can seem like 20 if you must carry a laptop through a large airport or for any long distance.

Photographs courtesy of International Business Machines Corporation

Portable computers provide convenience for people who work at home or travel a great deal.

Portable computing came of age with the creation of **notebook computers**, portable computers that are small enough to fit into an average-sized briefcase. At first, these computers were underpowered and didn't offer adequate storage. Today, new models offer as much processing power and storage as microcomputers and even some workstations. Weighing as little as six pounds, notebooks have become very popular. Some people use notebooks instead of desktop computers.

This IBM ThinkPad notebook computer is plugged into a docking station to access a monitor.

Photographs courtesy of International Business Machines Corporation

Some notebook computers contain slots for Personal Computer Memory Card International Association (PCMCIA) cards, such as modems and memory cards.

A **docking station** gives you the best of both worlds; you can use the notebook as a portable and then plug it into the docking station to access peripherals, such as printers, as well as full-sized keyboards and monitors. **Subnotebooks** sacrifice some storage and processing capability to bring the total weight down to three or four pounds.

Palmtop computers, sometimes called picocomputers, offer reduced size with reduced capabilities. Although some palmtops are general-purpose, many are special-purpose personal information managers, or PIMs. Special-purpose palmtops that keep phone directories and calendars and provide calculator capabilities are known as **personal digital assistants** (**PDAs**). You can use a PDA to schedule appointments, retrieve frequently used phone numbers, and jot down notes. Most PDAs are designed to accept written input by a pen; the PDA decodes what you write.

Smart cards look like ordinary credit cards but incorporate a microprocessor and memory chips. Smart cards were developed and pioneered in France about twenty years ago and are being used extensively throughout Europe. Smart cards are used to pay highway tolls, pay bills, and purchase merchandise. In France, the telecarte has virtually replaced pay telephone booths. The telecarte, which costs $7.50, is inserted into the phone, and the charge for the call is automatically deducted from the value stored on the card. Similar cards recently appeared in the United States, selling at $25 for 100 minutes and $10 for 40 minutes. Smart cards that hold personal medical history for use in an emergency are currently being tested.

Courtesy of Ameritech

A smart card has a microprocessor and a memory chip. In the future, you may use a smart card to record transactions such as purchases and work hours.

Embedded Computers

Did you know that you may have as many as a dozen computers in your home? These computers are **embedded computers**. They are built into special-purpose devices, such as video game players, microwave ovens, "smart" toasters, video cassette recorders, wristwatches, programmable furnace thermostats, and "smart" alarm clocks. In these devices, the computer is given just one task, such as getting you out of bed at the right time on Thursday morning.

If you are looking for more computers in your home, check the garage. Many people don't realize that today's cars use tiny computers to control the engine. The use of these computers has helped designers create engines that use less fuel and produce less pollution than yesterday's gas guzzlers.

Connectivity

The computers described in this lesson would be of limited use if we could not transfer data between them. Using networks or telephones to link supercomputers, mainframes, and minicomputers is commonplace. New ways to transfer data with portable computers are being developed regularly. Many people think that it is easier to send data around the world using computers than using the mail. See Chapter 6 for in-depth coverage of connectivity.

Computers are embedded in automobiles, CD players, microwave ovens, and many other pieces of equipment.

Lesson Summary

➤ Supercomputers provide the computing horsepower needed to solve complex scientific problems.

➤ The newest supercomputers use massively parallel processing designs that build many microprocessors into a single computer to tackle separate parts of a problem simultaneously.

➤ Supercomputers, mainframes, and minicomputers are multiuser computer systems.

➤ Multiprogramming segments memory and enables each user on a multiuser computer system to perform a different task.

➤ Single-user computer systems include workstations and microcomputers.

➤ Portable computers include notebooks, subnotebooks, and personal digital assistants.

➤ Embedded, special-purpose computers are found in many home electronics and in newer automobiles.

Lesson **R**eview

Key Terms

back-end processor	laptop computer	multitasking	smart card
computer-aided design (CAD)	mainframe computer	nanosecond	subnotebook
	massively parallel proces-	notebook computer	supercomputer
desktop computer	sors	palmtop computer	terminal
docking station	megaflop	personal computer	workstation
embedded computer	microcomputer	personal digital assistant (PDA)	
front-end processor	minicomputer		
gigaflop	multiprocessing	reduced instruction set computer (RISC)	
host processor	multiprogramming		

Matching

In the blank next to each of the following terms or phrases, write the letter of the corresponding term or phrase.

_____ **1.** Enables a notebook computer to use a full-sized monitor and keyboard

_____ **2.** Used by a mainframe computer for data retrieval

_____ **3.** Capability of a computer to process more than one task concurrently

_____ **4.** A million arithmetic-logic operations per second

_____ **5.** A small, handheld computer

_____ **6.** Accomplished by a computer that contains more than one processor

_____ **7.** Used by a mainframe computer to control communications to and from remote terminals

_____ **8.** A new type of microprocessor that contains fewer instructions than the traditional microprocessor

_____ **9.** One-billionth of a second

_____ **10.** The main computer in a system of linked computers

a. front-end processor

b. host

c. parallel processing

d. back-end processor

e. megaflop

f. nanosecond

g. RISC

h. docking station

i. PDA

j. multiprogramming

Multiple Choice

Circle the letter of the correct choice for each of the following.

1. Which of the following is a leader in the development of supercomputers?

   a. Cray Research Company

   b. Thinking Machines Corporation

   c. Fujitsu

   d. all of the above

2. Which of the following is *not* considered a portable computer?

   a. laptop computer

   b. notebook computer

   c. palmtop computer

   d. minicomputer

3. What is the primary use for supercomputers?

   a. input/output-intensive processing

   b. record-keeping operations

   c. mathematically intensive scientific applications

   d. data retrieval operations

4. Which of the following statements regarding a computer with a reduced instruction set microprocessor (RISC) is true?

   a. It has an increased microprocessor speed.

   b. It may require more complex programs.

   c. It is useful in special applications.

   d. all of the above

5. In your home, you probably have dozens of what?

   a. supercomputers

   b. minicomputers

   c. microcomputers

   d. embedded computers

6. What were the first computers?

   a. supercomputers

   b. mainframe computers

   c. minicomputers

   d. microcomputers

7. Which of the following is the most powerful?

   a. embedded computer

   b. workstation

   c. microcomputer

   d. PDA

8. Microcomputers are usually distinguished from other systems because they are _____.

   a. parallel processors

   b. multiuser systems

   c. single-user systems

   d. based on microprocessors

9. Space missions would most likely be controlled and monitored by what type of system?

   a. supercomputer

   b. mainframe

   c. minicomputer

   d. microcomputer

10. What is the most common type of computer?

   a. notebook

   b. minicomputer

   c. desktop

   d. workstation

Completion

In the blank provided, write the correct answer for each of the following.

1. A(n) _____ is a supercomputer that contains hundreds of processors.

2. _____ enables computers to execute tasks simultaneously.

3. A(n) _____ is one billion floating-point arithmetic operations per second.

4. The capability to transfer data between computers is known as _____.

5. A(n) _____ computer can plug into a docking station.

6. A(n) _____ looks like a credit card but has a microprocessor and memory chips.

7. A(n) _____ can be found inside many household electronic devices.

8. The first computers were _____ computers.

9. A(n) _____ can be used to drive a network of less powerful microcomputers.

10. A microcomputer is also known as a(n) _____ or a(n) _____.

Review

On a separate sheet of paper, answer the following questions.

1. Compare supercomputers and mainframes with respect to their suitability for different purposes.

2. A mainframe computer system is usually composed of several computers in addition to the mainframe, or host processor, itself. Describe the peripheral processors and their functions.

3. What are several of the operational differences between mainframes and minicomputers?

4. Describe a computer workstation.

5. Give some examples of items that contain embedded computers.

6. Can you think of some uses for smart cards that were not discussed in this lesson?

7. What is the difference between multiprogramming and multitasking?

8. How is a smart card different from a credit card?

9. Sizes of computers are sometimes known as platforms. List the platforms, from largest to smallest, that were discussed in this lesson.

10. Describe how a workstation would differ from a microcomputer found in the home.

Critical Thinking

On a separate sheet of paper, answer the following questions.

1. Draw a diagram of all the hardware components of a mainframe computer system.

2. Imagine what it might be like if all computers stopped functioning. What could be the effect on your way of living?

3. The general trend in computer technology has been toward faster and more powerful computers, while hardware has become progressively miniaturized. Do you envision some limitations in this trend?

4. Create a table contrasting the capabilities of each of the different sizes of computers discussed in this lesson.

5. What would it be like if you were required to have a portable computer that you used for all your classes? Cite some advantages and disadvantages.

Further Discovery

Computers: A Visual Encyclopedia. Sherry Kinkoph, Jennifer Fulton, and Kelly Oliver (Indianapolis, IN: Que, 1994).

The Wall Street Journal Book of Personal Technology. Walter S. Mossberg (New York: Times Books, 1995).

On-line Discovery

You can access the Internet resources for the following questions by going to the Que Education and Training Web site at URL http://www.ciyf98.com/discovery. From this page, click the link for Lesson 2D and then click the link to the resource you want to access.

1. The National Center for Supercomputing Applications (**NCSA**), located at the University of Illinois, is a research center that provides supercomputing resources for scientific research. Its home page (http://www.ncsa.uiuc.edu) provides information about the Center. What kinds of supercomputers are available at the Center? What kinds of projects have used these supercomputers? Which scientific disciplines seem to make the most use of these facilities?

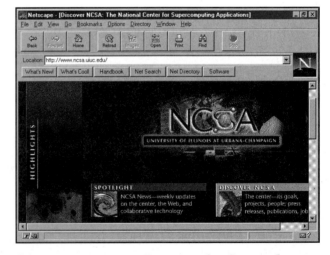

2. General Magic is a company that makes Magic Cap, state-of-the-art software that enables certain PDAs (which the company calls Personal Intelligent Communicators, or PICs) to communicate. Examine the **General Magic** home page (http://www.genmagic.com). What types of communications does Magic Cap support? Which of these features might be useful to you? How might daily life be changed if everyone carried a PDA or PIC?

PART II

Making Computers Work for You

When you fill out a job application, you will be asked what computer skills you have. Without basic skills in productivity software and a familiarity with the basics of using computers, you may have a hard time finding the job you want. Today, every career that requires a high school education or higher requires also some computer skills. Even if the company is going to train you on its computer, you need to understand how the computer works, so that you can learn quickly and efficiently.

Chapter 3   **Software and Software Development**
Chapter 4   **Systems Analysis and MIS**
Chapter 5   **Personal Productivity Software**
Chapter 6   **Advanced Applications**

CHAPTER 3

Software and Software Development

The United States faces a critical need for computer programmers, systems analysts, computer scientists, and engineers. According to the U.S. Labor Department, the demand for qualified information technology specialists is expected to double over the next ten years. The need is so critical to the continued economic well-being of our country that the president and vice-president of the United States have initiated a number of educational programs to prepare people for these occupations.

If you have any interest in a well-paying career as an information technology specialist, this chapter should be of considerable interest to you.

Lesson 3A discusses the two kinds of software: system software and application software. System software is what determines how a computer works as well as how the user works with the computer. System software is the interface between the hardware, the user, and the programs the user works with. Application software includes the programs the user works with to accomplish a particular task.

In Lesson 3B, you learn about the process of developing your own software—programming. You learn a little about the history of programming, learn about various types of programming languages, and are introduced to object-oriented programming and Web development.

Software

Outline

Learning Objectives

When you have finished reading this lesson, you will be able to

➤ Distinguish between system software and application software

➤ Identify the functions of an operating system

➤ Distinguish between operating systems and operating environments

➤ List some common popular operating systems

➤ Identify major characteristics of DOS, Windows 3.1, and Windows 95

➤ Recognize some trends in software

QUE Lab

➤ **File Management Systems**

You can use a computer to pay your bills, do your banking, communicate with people all over the world, and play games. How can a computer be so flexible? The instructions that the computer hardware follows—the software—change.

The Role of Software

Hardware needs software, or programs, to work. The type of software you use depends on the job. Software is generally one of two types: system software or application software. **System software** controls and coordinates the computer hardware. **Application software** is designed to solve a specific problem or do a specific task.

Application software includes **special-purpose programs** and **general-purpose programs**. A special-purpose program solves a specific problem, usually for a specific profession or industry. A registration program to sign up for a class is an example of a special-purpose program. General-purpose software is the backbone of the microcomputer industry. These software programs can do a variety of related tasks. Word processing, spreadsheet, and database programs are popular examples of general-purpose software and are described in detail in Chapter 4.

System Software

Programs designed to act as intermediaries between the hardware and application programs are called system software. These programs help the hardware components work together and provide support for application programs. System software includes operating systems, operating environments, language translators, utility programs, and performance monitors. The computer's operating system and the operating environment are the most important kinds of system software.

Operating Systems

An **operating system** is a group of programs that help the computer's components function together smoothly. Some parts of an operating system operate automatically, without requiring human intervention. Other parts provide utilities to the user for carrying out system maintenance tasks.

How does an operating system do its job? The operating system must first be loaded into primary storage. This process of loading is called **booting** the system. After the operating system is loaded, one part of it, called the **supervisor program**, remains in primary storage all the time. Such a program is called a **resident program**. Other parts of the operating system are kept on disk and loaded into primary storage only when needed. These programs are called **transient programs**.

When the user is working with an application program, the system software continues to manage many of the hardware components.

System software is an intermediary between the hardware and the application program.

Although operating systems are different, they have three common features. All operating systems do the following:

➤ Manage resources

➤ Control input and output processes

➤ Enable the user to communicate with the operating system

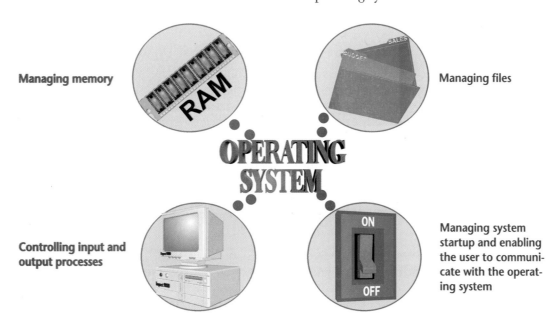

Managing memory

Managing files

Controlling input and output processes

Managing system startup and enabling the user to communicate with the operating system

Managing Resources

The resources managed by the operating system are the various hardware components, including the CPU. One important task performed by the operating system is to control the execution (running) of programs. **Multitasking** is the capability of an operating system to work on more than one task (program execution) at the same time. Whenever a task is waiting for input or output (I/O) operations to be completed, the CPU can be executing another task. Multitasking capabilities were once found only on minicomputers and mainframes. Now some personal computer operating systems, such as Microsoft Windows and Macintosh System 7.5, offer multitasking. **Multithreading** is the capability to run multiple executions of one program. Microsoft's Windows 95 has that capability. You could have the program spell-checking a large document while you continue to write in the same document.

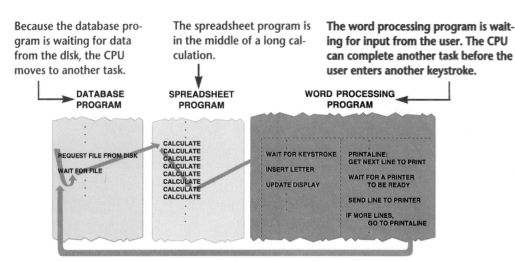

Because the database program is waiting for data from the disk, the CPU moves to another task.

The spreadsheet program is in the middle of a long calculation.

The word processing program is waiting for input from the user. The CPU can complete another task before the user enters another keystroke.

DATABASE PROGRAM

REQUEST FILE FROM DISK

WAIT FOR FILE

SPREADSHEET PROGRAM

CALCULATE
CALCULATE
CALCULATE
CALCULATE
CALCULATE
CALCULATE
CALCULATE
CALCULATE

WORD PROCESSING PROGRAM

WAIT FOR KEYSTROKE

INSERT LETTER

UPDATE DISPLAY

PRINTALINE:
GET NEXT LINE TO PRINT

WAIT FOR A PRINTER
TO BE READY

SEND LINE TO PRINTER

IF MORE LINES,
GO TO PRINTALINE

With multitasking, the CPU moves through the open programs to determine the work to be performed. If a program is waiting for input from another part of the computer system, the CPU moves immediately to another task.

Controlling Input and Output Processes

Input and output devices and storage devices require much attention. The operating system knows what a device needs and responds when the device needs it. Because input and output devices are much slower than the CPU, this immediate attention keeps the I/O devices from delaying the processing any longer than necessary.

Part of the control of the input and output devices comes from the BIOS or ROM-BIOS. The **BIOS**, or **Basic Input/Output System**, is a ROM chip that is built into the computer's memory and that checks the input and output devices when the system is started.

Communicating Between the User and the Operating System

Every operating system provides some way for the user to set the priorities of jobs and resources, respond to a problem, or tell the system what needs to be done next. On large computers, the **user interface**—the part of the system software that communicates with the user—is often called the **command interpreter**. The command interpreter is sometimes called the **job control language (JCL)**.

Operating Environments

A large part of the user interface is the operating environment. When Apple Computer introduced the Macintosh computer, it provided a different operating environment. The operating environment is the "look and feel" of using the computer and its operating system. The Macintosh offered the first popular use of a **graphical user interface** or **GUI** (pronounced gooey). Before GUIs, operating systems required the user to know many commands and what their options were. With this more user-friendly operating environment, the user was shown menus with options listed. Many times, the options were shown as icons, or pictures; the user could just point to an icon with the mouse and then click to indicate the choice. This process is called "point and click."

Microsoft recognized that GUIs were easier to use and that people learned to use them more quickly than nongraphical interfaces. The company developed Windows—and most recently Windows NT—to use this friendlier environment on IBM and IBM-compatible computers. Today's operating systems may use a command-line environment, like MS-DOS; a menu-driven environment, like a shell; or a graphical user interface environment, like Macintosh or Windows.

Commonly Used Operating Systems

Different computers use different operating systems. Many IBM and IBM-compatible microcomputers use MS-DOS alone, a combination of MS-DOS and a version of Microsoft Windows, or a version of Windows alone. Macintosh computers currently use the Macintosh System 7.5. Most computer systems—from PCs to supercomputers—can use the UNIX operating system. Table 3A.1 lists some common operating systems for microcomputers.

Table 3A.1 Common Microcomputer Operating Systems	
Operating System	*Used Primarily on These Computers*
DOS (Disk Operating System)	IBM and IBM-compatible, single-user computers
Microsoft Windows 3.1	IBM and IBM-compatible computers that are also running DOS and using an 80286 microprocessor or later (preferably a later version for better performance)
Microsoft Windows 95	IBM and IBM-compatible 486DX 33MHz or faster (preferably) with 100M of hard disk space and 16M of RAM preferred
Microsoft Windows NT (a network/multiuser operating system)	IBM and IBM-compatible, multiuser computers with 75M of hard disk space and 12M of free RAM; also works on computers with RISC chips, 90M of hard disk space, and 16M of RAM
Macintosh System 7.7	Macintosh computers
UNIX	Multiuser minicomputers and mainframes in corporate and university environments; also some personal computers

How the BIOS Works with Software

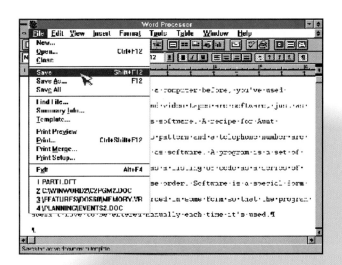

❶ When you choose the commands for saving a file in your word processor, the word processor sends the command and the data to be saved to the operating system. (In a Windows environment, Windows acts as an extension of the operating system to help handle command operations.)

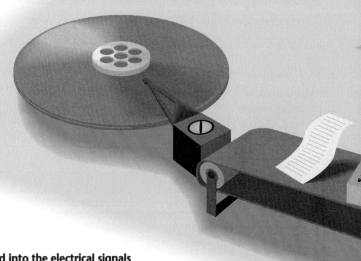

❹ The BIOS instructions are translated into the electrical signals needed to move the drive's read/write heads to the proper locations on the disk and to create the magnetic signals that record the data on the disk's surface.

2 The operating environment checks to make sure that the command to save data has no problems. For example, the operating environment makes sure that the file name is a legal one and that you're not trying to save over a file that's marked read-only. If everything is OK, the operating environment turns the job of writing the data to disk over to the BIOS.

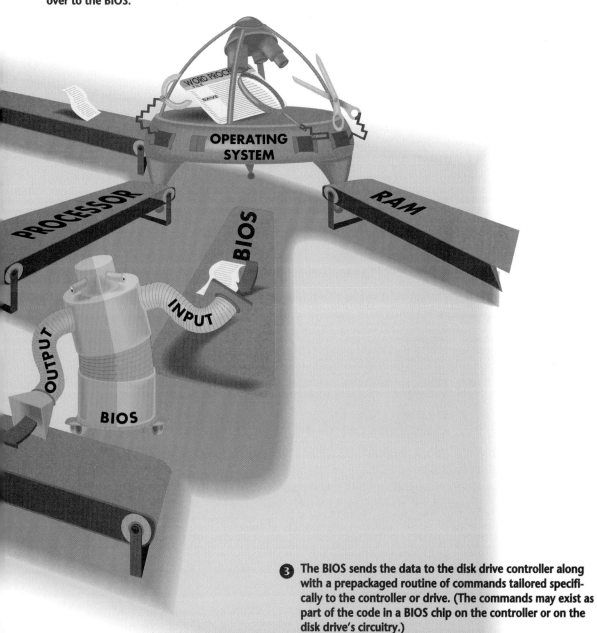

3 The BIOS sends the data to the disk drive controller along with a prepackaged routine of commands tailored specifically to the controller or drive. (The commands may exist as part of the code in a BIOS chip on the controller or on the disk drive's circuitry.)

Courtesy of Ziff-Davis Press

MS-DOS

MS-DOS (Microsoft Disk Operating System), introduced in 1981, was the standard, single-user operating system of IBM and IBM-compatible computers. MS-DOS is marketed by IBM as PC DOS, but the two systems are almost indistinguishable. Both MS-DOS and PC DOS are often referred to simply as DOS.

BITS
Early computers were designed to work with teletype machines, which printed one line of text at a time. To tell the computer what to do, the user entered a line of text at the keyboard. The computer responded by printing a line of text on the printer.

MS-DOS has a **command-line interface** that some people find difficult to use and hard to learn. Commands must be memorized and typed correctly. After you master the DOS commands, however, you can achieve a high degree of control over the operating system's capabilities.

MS-DOS restricts the user to eight-character file names with three-character extensions. You type commands at the DOS prompt; when you are finished typing, you press Enter. The prompt includes a disk drive designation and a directory designation. The format, or syntax, of the command line must be correct; otherwise, MS-DOS will not recognize it and not execute properly.

The DOS command line.

The greater-than sign (>) is called the DOS prompt.

```
MS-DOS Prompt                                          _ □ ×
T 11 x 18 ▾ [::] ⊞ ⊠ ⊠ 🗗 A

Microsoft(R) Windows 95
    (C)Copyright Microsoft Corp 1981-1995.

C:\WINDOWS>dir
```

Start | Exploring - Tech Edits | MS-DOS Prompt   12:26 AM

The first attempt to make DOS easier to use was to offer "shells" to go with the program. A **shell** is a menu-driven program that makes a command-line interface more user friendly. Instead of your having to remember what commands you want, the shell offers a menu of possible options. You choose the option you need.

Microsoft Windows 95

Microsoft Windows 95 incorporates the operating system and the operating environment into one program. With previous versions of Windows, MS-DOS was also necessary. Windows 95 is complete on its own. Windows 95 calls its basic screen a desktop. It can be as clean or as cluttered as you like. The choice of actions you can take, or "places" you can go to, are represented by icons.

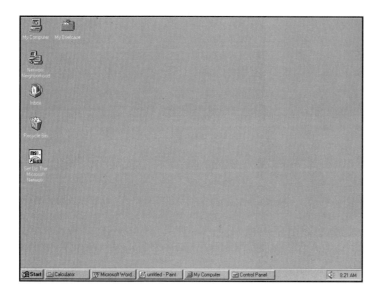

The Windows 95 desktop.

The basic computer needed to run Windows 95 is a 66MHz 486DX PC with at least 8M of RAM, but 16M is preferable. At least 60M of free hard drive space is needed for the full installation of Windows 95, and most users are not satisfied with the system's performance with less than 100M of free disk space when they start installation.

File names can contain up to 255 characters as well as some punctuation marks, such as periods, commas, and semicolons. Moving programs on and off the desktop is as simple as closing a program by clicking the X at the upper-right of the window; programs may be "put aside" on the **taskbar** at the bottom of the screen. To bring a program back onto the desktop from the taskbar, simply click the program name on the taskbar. You can also create a **shortcut** on the desktop to speed up opening an application.

The task of adding a new hardware device to your system may intimidate some users, especially novices. With the Windows 95 **Plug and Play** feature, the fear is removed. Windows 95 is designed to figure out the technical data needed to add or replace a device, make the decisions, set the switches, and configure the device to work without involving the user. Windows 95 also has an **AutoPlay** feature to start playing a CD immediately when it is inserted into the CD drive.

When you are retrieving files, an icon for "favorites" is available. Windows 95 has identified which subdirectories or files you open the most, and then maintains the list for you.

Windows 98 and Internet Explorer 4.0

Most reviews of Windows 98 rate it as little more than a small refinement of Windows 95. A collection of patches, a series of add-ons, and relatively minor improvements to hardware support are all part of the Windows 98 fine-tuning. The operating system, software compatibility, and system requirements do not reflect any major changes.

Windows 98 does promise to take full advantage of the latest advances in hardware, especially MMX technology. The implications are that audio and video files will be viewed much faster. Games requiring audio and video capabilities are to run better under the new system. Also, multiple video displays are available on a single PC.

Microsoft is promising that Windows 98 will be a more reliable system. New and updated utilities will keep hardware and software in optimal performance. Windows 3.1 used a utility known as Dr. Watson, which is reintroduced in Windows 98. It will help the user troubleshoot software problems that can freeze a machine.

The biggest addition to Windows 98 is the Web integration, which is complete and is connected directly to the operating system. Internet Explorer 4.0 is used not only to browse the Internet but to access data and run programs. The files on your hard disk can be viewed as if you are looking at a Web page.

Internet Explorer 4.0 (IE 4.0) operates exactly the same in Windows 95 and Windows 98. It is not necessary to purchase Windows 98 to get IE 4.0. It can be downloaded free from the Internet. Of course, free is a relative term, because this 22M file takes hours to download (nearly 10 hours using a 56Kbps modem).

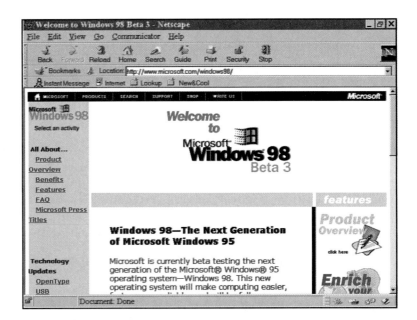

Microsoft provides up-to-date information on the latest features of Windows 98.

Microsoft Internet Explorer 4.0 is the latest in Web browsers from Microsoft.

Speedy Timing

"Gentlemen, start your engines!"

That time-honored command has signaled the start of "the greatest spectacle in racing" since the first Indianapolis 500 Race. The command hasn't changed in all these years—except to accommodate female drivers. But the sport itself has changed a great deal, largely because of computers.

The Indianapolis Motor Speedway (IMS) took IBM as a partner in its timing and scoring functions as early as 1927, when it began leasing keypunch and tabulating machines on a special one-day basis for the Indy 500. This partnership has continued without interruption and was expanded in 1956 to include the United States Auto Club (USAC).

In the late 1970s, USAC began the development of trackside computing, which has led to the current automatic timing system that, according to Arthur Graham, Vice-President of Development for USAC, "has evolved over time." The original program was written in Pascal, with later enhancements in C++ and QuickBASIC. All reporting is accomplished with Realia COBOL. The entire system runs on a PS/2 Model 95 under the control of OS/2.

The timing system process begins when data is collected from a radio-frequency transmitter mounted on the floor of each race car. As a car passes over an antenna buried in the race track, the antenna electronically identifies the transmitter and passes the signal to a trackside recording computer (TRC).

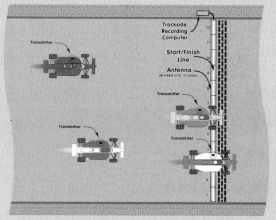

Courtesy of LogiTech, Inc.

The TRC converts the signal to a car number and records the time. This information is then passed to an IBM microcomputer that organizes the signals for all the scoring events and sends them to the IMS/USAC timing and scoring computer.

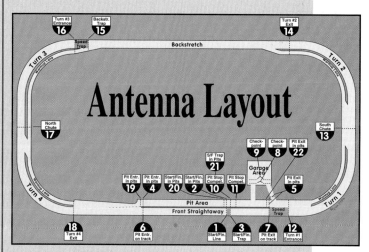

Courtesy of United States Auto Club

Each antenna is divided into twelve segments across the track, which means that the system could theoretically pick up the signals of as many as twelve cars crossing simultaneously. Because the track is less than twelve cars wide, however, this division prevents a car from being missed.

Twenty-one of these time-line antennae are in place at strategic locations around the race track, providing data that the scoring computer uses to calculate the running order of the cars, elapsed lap times and speeds, segment times and speeds, and other information. All this information can be instantly forwarded to racing officials, the race teams' pit crews, broadcast media, and fans in the stands.

USAC is revising the system to make it portable. They anticipate that a smaller version, with just 11 time-line antennae, will be ready soon for installation at tracks in Disney World, Phoenix, Las Vegas, and Laudon, PA.

How will computers be used to improve performance and times in future races? Stay tuned.

If the Deluxe Edition of Internet Explorer 4.0 is purchased on CD, the cost is minimal (about $50 and sometimes a mail-in rebate is included). The Deluxe Edition includes many of the new additions to Windows 98:

➤ Internet Assistants for Office 95

➤ Microsoft Office File Viewers

➤ Windows Desktop Update

➤ Microsoft Virtual Machine for Java

➤ Internet Connection Wizard

➤ Microsoft NetMeeting

➤ Microsoft Outlook Express

➤ Microsoft Chat 2.0

➤ Microsoft NetShow

➤ Microsoft VRML 2.0 Viewer

➤ DirectShow

➤ VDOLive Player

➤ Microsoft Agent

➤ Macromedia Shockwave Director

➤ Macromedia Shockwave Flash

➤ RealPlayer by Progressive Networks

➤ Microsoft Interactive Music Control (with MS Synthesizer Upgrade Available)

➤ Microsoft Wallet

➤ Supplemental Web Fonts

➤ Internet Explorer Sound Pack

➤ Task Scheduler

Also included on the Deluxe CD-ROM are the following:

➤ McAfee WebScanX (virus scan)

➤ Cyber Patrol (access control for children)

➤ Net.Medic (Internet monitor)

➤ Connected Online Backup (encrypted backups)

➤ Plus several other extras

Macintosh System 7.5

Apple Computer's Macintosh System 7.5 is a multitasking operating system with a graphical user interface. Its program and file-management system is called the Finder. Although the Macintosh operating system can run DOS and Windows programs, these programs perform more slowly on the Macintosh than on IBM or IBM-compatible computers. The Power Macintosh computers, which have the PowerPC microprocessor, use the System 7.5 operating system.

Macintosh Operating System Version 8

MAC OS 8 is Apple Computer's greatest success since 1984. The latest version of the Macintosh operating system is a significant improvement over its predecessors. OS 8 is part of a larger strategy related to Apple's acquisition of NeXt. Another new operating system, code-named Rhapsody, is due for release in 1998 for high-end systems.

The new operating system sports a completely redesigned desktop, although operation is essentially the same. The OS 8 package comes equipped with America Online software, Netscape Navigator, Microsoft Internet Explorer, Claris Emailer Lite, Color Sync (for color management), and even optional speech-recognition software, known as PlainTalk. Internet integration is a high priority.

OS 8 also includes push applications PointCast Network (for news broadcasts), Marimba Castanet Tuner (used to distribute and maintain software), and a channel from Excite (a search engine integrated into the Mac). PC File and Media exchange features allow the Mac to open and edit DOS and Windows files without the software used to create them.

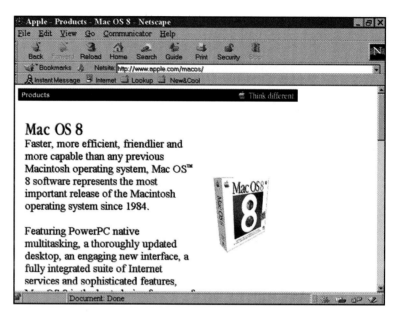

To learn more about MAC OS 8, visit the Web site for product demonstrations.

The interactive installer makes loading OS 8 a simple task. Assistant Interfaces asks questions about such things as previous Macintosh and Internet experience and uses the answers to tailor the systems. Overall, OS 8 is easily the most comprehensive Macintosh update in years.

UNIX

UNIX is a multitasking operating system used on a wide variety of computers, from mainframes to personal computers. UNIX was designed at AT&T's Bell Laboratories as a multiuser system. Its interface is somewhat unfriendly to occasional users, but shell programs are available to help these users. Because UNIX is ideally suited to multiuser applications, it is popular in systems that have linked workstations to minicomputers and mainframes. UNIX has established a successful foothold in the university and business communities.

Other System Software

As you have learned, the operating system is a very important kind of system software. System software also includes language translators, utility programs, and performance monitors. Because programmers use language translators, this type of system software is discussed in Lesson 3B.

Utility programs assist the user with system maintenance tasks. These tasks include checking the amount of available memory, formatting disks, and scanning the system for computer viruses.

When multiple users share a computer system, they depend on the quality of the system's performance—both its speed and its availability. **Performance monitors** help maximize the system's performance by keeping track of what is happening with the various hardware devices. These programs monitor how often and how quickly an application program is being executed compared to all the other programs in the system at the same time.

Application Software and Packages

Although system software is essential to running your computer, you need application software in order to do word processing, create a paycheck, or run an ATM. System software runs the hardware; application software makes the computer useful. Most of the time you spend in using the computer involves the use of application software. A **software package** is a group of programs that solve a specific problem.

Chapters 3 and 5 discuss many popular generic application software packages. These word processing, spreadsheet, and database packages account for most of the application uses on microcomputers. Application packages are designed for ease of use, often use the same interface as the operating environment, and address most of the uses people have for microcomputers.

For minicomputers, mainframes, and supercomputers, the wide variety of inexpensive, easy-to-use application software is not available. Companies that use these larger computers have a staff of programmers to create and maintain the application software they use.

The Future of Software

Over the years, software has become more useful as well as easier to use. It is also more customizable to meet an individual's needs. What will software be like in the future? The two biggest trends are to create software that supports the new work environment of workgroups and to create software that makes communications and networking easier and more natural.

The biggest challenge in making a workgroup effective is to ensure that its members can communicate more easily among themselves. Software being developed to support this need is called **groupware**. An example of groupware is Lotus Notes, which helps people present ideas, organize information, create brainstorming sessions, obtain feedback, and solve problems within workgroups. The newest way to coordinate workgroups inside a company is through intranets—networks that have the structure or look of the Internet (see Lesson 7A for more details on the Internet).

The Internet has created a category of software—Web browsers—that is changing how software is created and used. The use of World Wide Web software techniques like hyperlinks has made sharing data simpler than ever before. These tools are being used to create new applications faster than traditional tools can.

Software is making the use of a computer increasingly faster, easier, and more powerful. As more people are using the computer, it is becoming a friendlier tool, and *that* is encouraging even more people to start using the computer.

Lesson Summary

➤ Programs, or software, are the instructions to the hardware.

➤ The two types of software are system software and application software.

➤ Application software can be either special purpose, such as a payroll program or a game; or general purpose, such as a word processing program or a database program.

➤ System software acts as the intermediary between application software and the hardware.

➤ An operating system is loaded into memory—booted—when the computer is first turned on, and portions of it stay resident in memory as long as the computer remains on.

➤ Operating systems manage the hardware resources, control input and output processes, and interface with the user.

➤ The most commonly used operating systems are MS-DOS, Microsoft Windows or Windows 95, Macintosh System 7.5, and UNIX.

➤ Application software makes the computer useful to the user.

➤ The future of software is that it will continue to make the computer easier to use.

➤ The newest types of software are being developed to support workgroups, communications, and networks.

Lesson Review

Key Terms

application software	general-purpose program	operating system	special-purpose program
AutoPlay	graphical user interface	performance monitor	supervisor program
Basic Input/Output System	(GUI)	Plug and Play	system software
(BIOS)	groupware	resident program	taskbar
booting	job control language (JCL)	shell	transient program
command interpreter	multitasking	shortcut	user interface
command-line interface	multithreading	software package	utility program

Matching

In the blank next to each of the following terms or phrases, write the letter of the corresponding term or phrase.

_e_ **1.** WordPerfect and Excel

_i_ **2.** Uses icons and pull-down menus

_c_ **3.** Loading the operating system

_f_ **4.** Multiple executions of one program

_b_ **5.** A set of instructions for the hardware to follow

_g_ **6.** Checks input and output devices at startup

_d_ **7.** Running more than one program at the same time

_a_ **8.** Intermediary between hardware and application software

_j_ **9.** Program that does such tasks as formatting disks and scanning for viruses

_h_ **10.** A resident program

a. system software

b. program

c. booting the system

d. multitasking

e. general-purpose software

f. multithreading

g. BIOS

h. supervisor program

i. graphical user interface

j. utility program

Multiple Choice

Circle the letter of the correct choice for each of the following.

1. What are the two types of application software?

   a. user and professional

   b. special purpose and general purpose

   c. system and general purpose

   d. hardware and software

2. Which of the following is *not* an example of system software?

   a. language translator

   b. utility program

   c. word processor

   d. operating system

3. When is a transient program loaded into memory?

   a. when needed

   b. when the system is booted

   c. never—that's what makes it transient

   d. when the supervisor program is loaded

4. Which of the following is *not* a feature of an operating system?

   a. controlling input and output

   b. managing resources

   c. communicating with the user

   d. generating a database

5. Which of the following is *not* a commonly used operating system for microcomputers?

   a. Windows

   b. VMS

   c. MS-DOS

   d. Macintosh System 7.5

6. GUIs (graphical user interfaces) are used with which of the following?

   a. Windows

   b. UNIX

   c. Macintosh System 7.5

   d. both a and c

7. Which of the following has the job of maximizing the system's performance?

   a. GUIs

   b. performance monitors

   c. word processing programs

   d. Windows

8. The interface that most people find the most difficult to use is a _____.

   a. graphical user interface

   b. menu interface

   c. command-line interface

   d. shell interface

9. Features *new* with Windows 95 include all the following except _____.

   a. shortcuts

   b. the use of icons

   c. Plug and Play

   d. taskbar

10. Which of the following is *not* a type of application program?

    a. word processing

    b. payroll processing

    c. a language translator

    d. ATM processing

Completion

In the blank provided, write the correct answer for each of the following.

1. The most widely used system software is the _Windows 95_.

2. The process of loading the operating system when the computer is first turned on is called _booting_.

3. _Multitasking_ is the capability of an operating system to work on more than one task at the same time.

4. The part of the operating system that communicates with the user is called the _user interface_.

5. An operating system that is commonly used on computers from mainframes to personal computers is _UNIX_.

6. System software that helps maximize the computer system's performance is called a(n) _performance monitor_.

7. A list of stored instructions that tells the computer hardware what to do is called a(n) _PROGRAMS_.

8. A(n) _SHELL_ is a menu-driven program that makes a command-line interface more user friendly.

9. The greater-than prompt (>) is called the _DOS_ prompt.

10. The Macintosh operating system program and file-management system are called the _FINDER_.

Review

On a separate sheet of paper, answer the following questions.

1. What are the differences between system software and application software?

2. What is an operating system? How is it important to the computer and to the user?

3. What are the advantages of a command-line interface? What are the disadvantages?

4. What are the advantages of a menu-driven interface compared with a command-line interface? What are the disadvantages?

5. What are the advantages of a graphical user interface (GUI)? What are the disadvantages?

6. Name three types of system software other than the operating system and the operating environment system.

7. Describe some of the events that occur while a computer is booting.

8. What are the two types of application programs? What are their differences?

9. What are the three common features of operation systems? What are their functions?

10. What are the differences between MS-DOS and Windows?

Critical Thinking

On a separate sheet of paper, answer the following questions.

1. What criteria would you use to decide which operating system you would recommend for a small business?

2. How would an operating system affect the way a workgroup functions?

3. What criteria would you use to select application programs for a small business?

4. Compare the advantages of a GUI versus an operating system such as MS-DOS.

5. Experiment with both a Macintosh computer and a Windows 95 computer. How are the two operating environments similar? How are they different? Which do you prefer? Why?

Further Discovery

Inside UNIX, 2nd Edition. Chris Hare (Indianapolis, IN: NRP, 1996).

Inside Windows, 3.11 Edition. Platinum Edition. Jim Boyce, Bruce Hallberg, and Forrest Houlette (Indianapolis, IN: NRP, 1994).

Introducing Microsoft Windows 95. Microsoft Corporation (Redmond, WA: Microsoft Press, 1995).

Introduction to UNIX. George Meghabghab (Indianapolis, IN: Que Education and Training, 1996).

Macintosh Bible, 6th Edition. Jeremy Judson, ed. (Berkeley, CA: PeachPit Press, 1996).

Microsoft Windows 95 Resource Kit. Microsoft Corporation (Redmond, WA: Microsoft Press, 1995).

Running Windows NT Workstation, Version 4. Craig Stinson (Redmond, WA: Microsoft Press, 1996).

Show-Stopper! The Breakneck Race to Create Windows NT and the Next Generation at Microsoft. G. Pascal Zachary (New York: Free Press, 1994).

On-line Discovery

You can access the Internet resources for the following questions by going to the Que Education and Training Web site at URL http://www.ciyf98.com/discovery. From this page, click the link for Lesson 3A and then click the link to the resource you want to access.

1. Visit the **Microsoft Windows 95** page (http://www.microsoft.com/windows), which provides information about the Microsoft Windows 95 operating system (from a Microsoft perspective, of course). What kinds of applications are available for Windows 95? What kinds of elements characterize the Windows 95 interface? What are the hardware requirements for running Windows 95?

2. The UNIX operating system generally provides a command-line interface, often thought to be difficult for beginning users to learn, and is also known to have some obscure names for commands. However, there are many good tutorials and guides to learning UNIX aimed at beginners. One of these is **UNIXhelp for Users** (http://www.emerson.emory.edu/services/unixhelp1.3/Pages), from the University of Edinburgh. Take a look at this tutorial. If possible, obtain a UNIX account, from either your college or your local Internet service provider, and go through some of the material. Can you figure out how to look up commands in the online UNIX manual? Can you tell how to create a directory? What are "environment variables"?

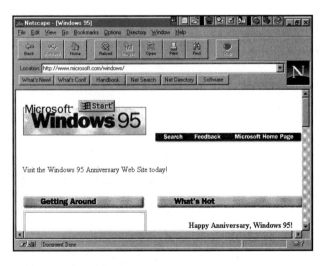
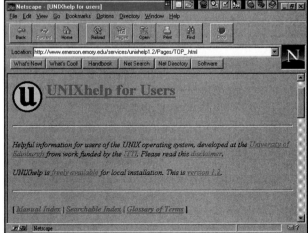

Programming

Outline

What Is Programming?
A Short History of Programming
When You Need to Develop a Program
Who Should Write a Program?
Beginning the Project
Designing the Program
     Program Logic Constructs
     Developing an Algorithm
     Program Design Tools
Completing the Project
     Coding the Program
     Testing and Debugging
     Completing the Documentation
     Implementation
     Maintenance
Types of Programming Languages
     Machine Language
     Assembly Language
     High-Level Languages
     Language Translators
     Very High-Level Languages
     Web Development Languages
Object-Oriented Languages
     What Is OOP?
     The Nature of Objects
     Basic Principles of Object-Oriented Programming
     OOP Languages

Learning Objectives

After reading this lesson, you will be able to

➤ Explain the process of programming

➤ Discuss the evolution of programming languages

➤ Identify and describe the four types of program logic constructs for a program

➤ Design a program algorithm

➤ Understand the hierarchy chart, program flowchart, and pseudocode design tools

➤ Identify languages that are suited to specific and general uses

QUE Lab

➤ **Programming**

3-21

➤ Understand the basic components of high-level languages

➤ Understand Web development languages and how they are suited for Web pages

➤ Describe the difference between object-oriented languages and other programming languages

What Is Programming?

Programming is the process of creating a list of stored instructions that tell the computer what to do. These instructions are written in a **programming language**, which is a formally designed set of symbols (often referred to as *notation*) used to create sequential instructions that can be processed and executed by the computer. The instructions programmers create with a programming language are often referred to as **code**.

Programming has been called both an art and a science. Interestingly, programming attracts people from almost every kind of educational background, from anthropology to music to physics and everything in between. Computer programming has been with us since the early 1940s, but computers were not the first machines to be programmed.

Jacquard's weaving loom was the first mechanical device programmed using wooden punched cards.

A Short History of Programming

Programming did not begin with computers; it traces its roots to the textile industry in the year 1801. This business required the talents of skillful weavers, with keen minds and nimble fingers. Creating fabrics with complex patterns was time-consuming and expensive. A Frenchman named Joseph-Marie Charles Jacquard was probably the first to program a machine. He was a weaver who dreamed of a machine that would help do his weaving more quickly, inexpensively, and with fewer mistakes.

Jacquard studied the weaving process and the machine that did it, the loom. In doing so, he displayed the analytic qualities of a good programmer. The result was a loom that could be programmed to create patterns and designs by using a punched card. Jacquard's punched card was a wooden slat with holes punched in it, shown in the following figure. In the 1940s, IBM adapted Jaquard's punched card to mechanical-electrical computers. The cards—in many cases now programmed into a magnetic stripe instead of punched—continue to be used in a number of applications, such as the tollbooths on the Massachusetts Turnpike.

Jacquard's loom demonstrated two important ideas. One, we can translate complex designs into codes, or programs, that machines readily understand. Two, in so doing, machines can be instructed to perform repetitive tasks.

Courtesy of International Business Machines Corporation

JACQUARD LOOM CARDS

When You Need to Develop a Program

Thirty years ago, the answer to "When do you develop a program?" was simple: whenever you needed the computer to do a job for you.

Commercial software was not readily available. If a company had a computer, the company also had one or more programmers available to program the computer.

Today, the software market is different. Thousands of programs and software packages are available. If you can find a program or package that meets your needs, purchasing it is probably the least expensive option. If you can't find a suitable program, you will need to write a program or a series of programs. An alternative to writing a program may be to customize an existing program.

Who Should Write a Program?

A **program** is a logical pattern of instructions to solve a problem. The figure on the next page shows the process of creating a program. Many computer hobbyists become amateur programmers. But today's businesses need efficient programmers who have been professionally trained. Many professional programmers begin with a certificate from a vocational-technical school and work their way up through experience and more training. Other professional programmers start with a two-year college degree. Some positions, however, require at least a bachelor's degree in computer science, computer information systems, management information systems, or a related major.

People frequently think of a programmer as an individual who spends all of his or her time sitting at a computer writing code. They are surprised when they read that the job specifications for a programmer includes the ability to communicate well both orally and in writing. Programming is much more than writing code.

Most of the programs written by professional programmers are complex. Relatively few are written by only one person. A lot of time is spent designing the program and working with the rest of the programming team. Studies have shown that careful design results in fewer bugs and a better finished product. So, how are programs designed?

Beginning the Project

The first step is to define the problem. Programming specifications are usually sent to a programming team. The specifications have been written by a systems analyst, who has worked closely with the person or group of people for whom the program is being written.

The specifications should include a description of the input available and the final output that the program should produce. The programming team will need to construct any intermediate screen displays and check with the analyst or the user to be certain that the displays are correct and easy to understand.

After the output has been designed and it has been determined that the required input data is available, the programming team can begin to design the program solution. The design phase of the project, if performed properly, requires 25 to 50 percent of the total time spent on the project.

The process of creating a program.

Developing a program requires six essential steps, as follows:

❶ The first step in developing a program is to define the problem. This definition must include the needed output, the available input, and a brief definition of how you can transform the available input into the needed output.

❷ The second step is to design the problem solution. This detailed definition is an **algorithm**, a step-by-step procedure for solving a problem. If a person has difficulty learning to write programs, the difficulty usually lies in developing a good algorithm.

❸ The third step in developing a program is to code the program; that is, you state the program's steps in the language you are using. The instructions must follow the language's **syntax**, or rules, just as good English must follow the rules of grammar.

SOURCE TEXT FILE

SOURCE TEXT FILE

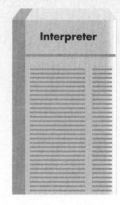

Interpreter

❹ The fourth step is to test the program to be sure that it will run correctly no matter what happens. If the algorithm is wrong or the program doesn't match the algorithm, the errors are considered **logic errors**. Any errors in a program are called **bugs**; the process of finding the bugs and correcting them is called **debugging** the program. To test or debug a program, you must create sample input data that represents every possible way to enter input.

- define problem
- design problem solution
- code the program
- test the program
- complete the documentation of the program
- implement the program

5 The fifth step in developing a program is to complete the documentation of the program. **Documentation** includes user instructions, an explanation of the logic of the program, and information about the input and output. Documentation is developed throughout the program development process. Documentation is extremely important, yet it is the area in program development that is most often overlooked.

TEXT MODULE   **TEXT MODULE**

TEXT MODULE   **TEXT MODULE**

COMPILER

OBJECT FILE   **OBJECT FILE**

OBJECT FILE   **OBJECT FILE**

LINKER

EXECUTABLE FILE

EXECUTABLE FILE

6 The last step in developing a program is implementation. Once the program is complete, it needs to be **implemented**—installed on a computer and made to work properly. If the program is developed for a specific company, the programming team may be involved in implementation. If the program is designed to be sold commercially, the documentation will have to include directions for the user to install the program and begin working with it.

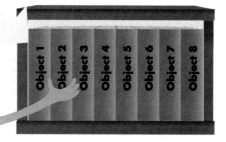

Object 1 Object 2 Object 3 Object 4 Object 5 Object 6 Object 7 Object 8

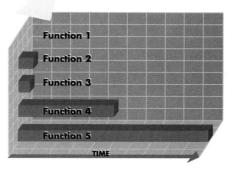

Function 1
Function 2
Function 3
Function 4
Function 5
TIME

Courtesy of Ziff-Davis Press

Even after completion, a program requires attention. It needs to be maintained and evaluated regularly for possible changes.

Designing the Program

Now that the problem has been defined, the second step in the project is to design a solution. Before you begin, it is important to know about the logic that is used in programs.

Program Logic Constructs

All programs are based on four types of **logic constructs**. It doesn't matter what language the programmer is using, or what type of application the program was designed to solve.

The first construct is known as a **simple sequence**. In a simple sequence, the instructions to the computer are designed to be executed (performed by the computer) in the order i n which they appear. Every program uses this construct.

The second construct is a **condition** (also called a **decision**). Most conditions are based on IF. . .THEN. . .ELSE logic. If a condition is true, one set of instructions is executed; if the condition is not true, a different set of instructions is executed.

The third construct is a **loop**, or **iteration**. Computer programs are valuable primarily because they can deal with large amounts of data. If you were to write a program to generate payroll checks for a company with 150 employees, you would not want to write the code 150 times! A loop enables the programmer to tell the computer to execute the same set of instructions as many times as necessary to process all the data properly.

The fourth construct is the **case**. A case is just a complex set of decisions based on a single item. For example, the IRS processes tax returns differently depending on marital status. A coded field indicates whether the taxpayer is married filing a joint return, married filing separately, single, head of household, or widowed. A case selection can be used so that the computer can determine which of those five categories a taxpayer belongs to, and then use the correct set of instructions to process the return.

Developing an Algorithm

Programmers begin solving a problem by developing an algorithm. An **algorithm** is a step-by-step description of how to arrive at a solution. You can think of an algorithm as a recipe or a how-to sheet.

Developing an algorithm can be a challenge. It is usually best for beginners to start by trying to decide how to solve the problem without a computer, and then factor in the computer later. Suppose that you want to determine your car's gas mileage. You need to know the mileage on the odometer when you last filled the car, the current mileage, and the amount of gas used. Your algorithm might be something like this:

1. Subtract the beginning odometer reading from the current odometer reading to determine miles traveled.

2. Divide miles traveled by amount of gas used to determine gasoline mileage.

We all know that a car's mileage varies depending on a number of factors, such as how fast the car was driven and whether most of the travel was in town or on a highway. How would the algorithm change if you kept track of the gas consumption and the mileage for a month? The algorithm might look like this:

1. Set miles traveled to zero.

2. Get the beginning odometer reading, the ending odometer reading, and the amount of gas used for the first tank of gas.

3. When there are more fill-ups, do the following:

   Add amount of gas used to total gas used.

   Subtract the beginning odometer reading from the current odometer reading to find the miles traveled on the last tank.

   Add the miles traveled to the total miles traveled.

   Record the current odometer reading. (The current odometer reading is the beginning reading for the next tank.)

   Repeat until there are no more fill-ups.

4. Divide total miles traveled by total amount of gas used to determine gasoline mileage.

Notice that step 3 defines a loop. The loop makes it possible to use the algorithm no matter how many times the tank is filled.

Look at one more example. A company has a number of salespeople. Each salesperson is paid a base salary plus a commission. The amount of the commission is determined by whether the salesperson has met his or her quota. An algorithm for this problem might be as follows:

1. Print report headings.

2. If sales > quota then commission = sales * .06

   else commission = sales * .03

3. Print the salesperson's name and the commission.

4. Repeat steps 2 and 3 until there are no more salespeople.

Programmers design algorithms like these to solve complex programming problems. So that other programmers can understand the design, specialized design tools for writing algorithms have been developed.

Program Design Tools

Most programs are designed in a **top-down, modular** style. This means that the programmer starts thinking generally and then works down to specifics.

Structure Charts

The design tool that shows the top-down design of a program is a **structure chart** (also called a **hierarchy chart**). Each box, or **module**, in the chart indicates a task that the program must accomplish. The top module, called the **control module**, oversees the transfer of control to the other modules.

Remember the program described earlier that calculates commissions? First, the program prints the report headings. Then each salesperson's commission is processed. After the program calculates the commission for a salesperson, it prints the salesperson's name and the commission earned. Then the loop is repeated, and the program calculates the next salesperson's commission.

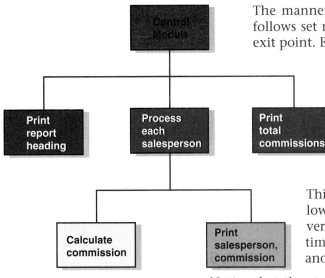

The manner in which control is transferred between the modules follows set rules. Each module has exactly one entry point and one exit point. Entry is from the module one level above in the structure chart (known as the **superordinate module**); after all the instructions in the module have been executed by the computer, exit is back to the superordinate module. Control may be temporarily transferred to a module one level down (a **subordinate module**), but must return. Control may never be passed from one module to another module on the same level of the structure chart.

This orderly transfer makes it easy for a programmer to follow the logic of programs written by someone else. That is very important because most programs are used for a long time and the original programmer may have moved on to another position.

Notice that the structure chart does not provide any detail about the program logic. Two design tools are used to show program logic: program flowcharts and pseudocode. Programmers generally select one of these tools, instead of using both.

Flowcharts

A **flowchart** is a diagram that shows the logic of a program. Programmers create flowcharts either by hand using a flowcharting template or on the computer. Each flowcharting symbol has a meaning; a diamond, for example, is used to indicate a condition, and a parallelogram indicates an input or output procedure.

A flowchart for the commission program is shown in this lesson. Notice that the symbols are evenly spaced and that the logic can be followed down the page.

A flowchart for the salesperson's commission problem.

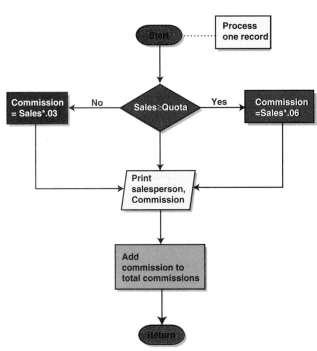

Pseudocode

Some programmers don't like flowcharting. **Pseudocode,** created in the 1970s as an alternative to flowcharts, is a stylized form of writing used to describe the logic of a program.

Pseudo means false, so pseudocode is a form of false code—in this case, code that cannot be understood by the computer. Pseudocode for the commission problem is provided in this lesson. Notice that each module that needs explanation is shown as separate pseudocode. Notice also that the words which refer to the program logic constructs are in uppercase.

Showing Logic Constructs by Using Design Tools

Recall that all programs are written with four logic constructs. Programmers incorporate those constructs into their program design, whether as a flowchart or as pseudocode. Programmers can combine the constructs; for example, a decision can be inside a loop. The four constructs are shown in this lesson in both flowchart and pseudocode form.

```
/Control Module/
BEGIN PROGRAM
     Initialize for the program
     DO WHILE there are salespeople
          Process a salesperson
     END DO
     Print total commissions
END PROGRAM

/Initialize for the program
START
     Print report headings
     Set total commissions to zero
     Read the first record: salesperson, sales, quota
STOP


/Process a salesperson/
START
     IF sales >= quota
          THEN commission = sales * .06
          ELSE commission = sales * .03
     END IF
     Print salesperson, commission
     Add commission to total commissions
     Read the next record: salesperson, sales, quota
STOP
```

The pseudocode for the sales commission problem.

Notice that there are two types of loops. In the DO WHILE loop, the decision occurs before any of the steps in the loop are executed. If the condition is not met when the loop is first encountered, the steps in the loop will never be executed. The DO UNTIL loop, however, executes the steps inside the loop before checking to see whether the condition is met. Therefore, a DO UNTIL loop is always executed at least once.

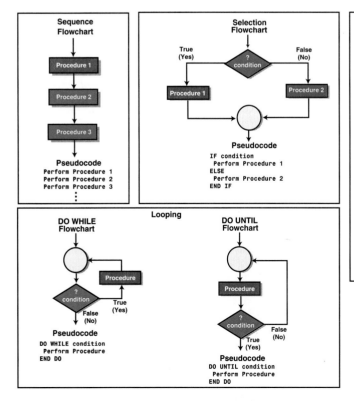

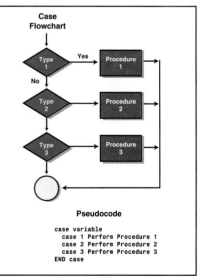

Program logic constructs shown by using flowcharting and pseudocode design tools.

Completing the Project

It is important that all members of the programming team understand and agree with the program design before proceeding. Programmers will develop and code different modules of the program, which must be combined and must work together properly. The third step in program design is to code the solution in an appropriate programming language.

Coding the Program

Many programming languages are in use today. Most computer programs are written in high-level languages. The most popular high-level languages are discussed later in this lesson. Coding is usually performed directly on the computer. (Until the 1970s, all coding was done by hand and then punched onto cards that could be read into the computer.) A program is keyed in and saved on disk as a file, and then the programmer instructs the computer to translate the program to machine language. (The language translation process is also discussed later in this lesson.) Recall that the only language a computer can understand is machine language.

During the translation process, the translator will probably detect mistakes in the code. (Only a very small percentage of programs work perfectly the first time.) These mistakes may be typographical errors, or they may be the result of the programmer failing to follow the rules of the programming language. Recall that the errors detected by the language translator are called **syntax errors**. Syntax errors must be eliminated before the program will run properly.

Testing and Debugging

The fourth step in a programming project is to eliminate all the errors. After the syntax errors are eliminated, the program will execute. The output may still not be correct, however, because the language translator cannot detect logic errors. As noted earlier in the lesson, a logic error is a mistake that the programmer made in designing the solution to the problem. For example, if a programmer tells the computer to calculate net pay by adding deductions to gross pay (instead of subtracting), that is a logic error. The programmer must find and correct the logic errors by carefully examining the program output.

Syntax errors and logic errors are collectively known as **bugs**. The process of eliminating these errors is known as **debugging**.

After the visible logic errors have been eliminated, the programming team must **test** the program to find hidden errors. Test data will check all possible outcomes for each condition. Test data should also be designed to ensure that each loop ends properly and that all computations yield the correct results. A program is ready to be used only after it has been thoroughly tested and debugged.

If the program is going to be sold commercially, it is released to a selected set of users in "beta" form for them to try out. Beta testers locate errors that were overlooked during the regular testing phase and report them to the company that is developing the program. After beta testing, the program may need additional debugging before it is released to stores.

Completing the Documentation

Now the project is almost complete. The structure chart and pseudocode or flowchart that were developed during the design phase become documentation for others who will modify the program in the future. Other documentation should have been created as the program was being coded: lists of variable names and definitions, descriptions of files that the program needs to work with, and layouts of output that it will produce. All of this documentation should have been saved and placed together for future reference.

Manuals still need to be developed to thoroughly explain how the program works. These manuals will be given to the users when the program is installed or purchased. The manuals, along with the program design work, are known as documentation.

Implementation

All that is left now is the sixth and last step: implementation. If the program has been developed for use by the company for whom the programmers work, it will still need to be tested by the users. The best-written program is useless if the user does not understand how to work with it.

If the program will be sold by a vendor, help lines should be established for buyers. If the program was written for a specific company, the program should be installed on the company equipment and the employees of the company trained so that they understand the new program.

Programming projects can be very complex, involving hundreds of programmers who produce thousands of lines of code. Programs can also be very costly to develop. A large programming project can take years to complete.

Programs should be designed carefully and users should be involved in the process so that the final product is useful.

Maintenance

Even after a program is complete, it needs to be evaluated regularly. The evaluation may lead to modifications in order to update the program or to add features for the user.

Types of Programming Languages

Programming languages have evolved greatly over the years. Each evolutionary stage is commonly referred to as a generation. To date, there are six generations of programming languages, as shown in Table 3B.1. With each passing generation, programming languages become easier to use; thus more and more knowledge workers are able to use programming languages.

Table 3B.1	The Six Generations of Programming Languages					
Generation:	1st	2nd	3rd	4th	5th	6th
Period:	1951-58	1958-64	1964-77	1977-88	1988-	1993-
Type:	Low-level	low-level, high-level	high-level	very high-level	Object-oriented	Web tools
Example:	Machine, Assembly	Assembly, COBOL, FORTRAN	BASIC, Pascal	C++, Turbo Pascal, 4GLs	Visual Basic, OOP, CASE	HTML, Front Page, Java

Different languages exist because each was designed for specific purposes. For example, some languages solve typical business problems; others perform large, complex calculations; and still others create graphics. Table 3B.2 lists some common programming languages. The following sections discuss the various types of programming languages with which you should be familiar.

Table 3B.2 Common Programming Languages

Language	Primary Users
BASIC (Beginner's All-Purpose Symbolic Instruction Code)	Nonprofessional and beginning programmers
COBOL (COmmon Business Oriented Language)	Corporate mainframe users
Pascal (named after Blaise Pascal)	Colleges and universities for teaching
FORTRAN (FORmula TRANslator)	Engineers, mathematicians, and scientists
C and universities	Professional programmers and many colleges
C++	Major software vendors
Visual Basic	Many professional programming firms

Machine Language

Electronic digital computers understand only binary arithmetic—the language of 0s and 1s that make up bits and bytes. **Machine language** is used to write programs in 1s and 0s, so it requires no translation. From ENIAC to today's most sophisticated digital computers, machine language is the same. Machine language is directly understood, or executed, by hardware. Electronic circuitry turns these 0s and 1s into the operations the computer performs. The problem was that it was extremely tedious for a programmer to sit at a keyboard and type the instructions in endless sequences of 0s and 1s.

Assembly Language

The first way this programming problem was addressed was by the assembly language. An **assembly language** uses letters, numbers and symbols to represent individual 0s and 1s. For example, where in machine language *multiply* is set as 001011, in an assembly language you just write **M**, which is translated by an assembler into the 001011 of machine language. This greatly simplified programming.

Assembly languages are powerful programming tools because they allow programmers a large amount of direct control over the hardware. They provide greater ease in writing instructions, but preserve the programmer's ability to declare exactly what operations the hardware performs.

Assembly languages are **machine-specific**, or **machine-dependent**. Machine-dependent means the instructions are specific to one type of computer hardware, so they come packaged with the computer system. Assembly code for a Hewlett-Packard computer won't work on a Compaq. Assembly code often can't even be transferred between different models built by the same manufacturer.

For the most part, assembly languages are used by systems programmers to develop operating systems and their components. Thus, one early programming problem was solved, but another remained: how to make programming languages transferable—termed **portable**—from one computer to another. The answer, in theory at least, was high-level programming languages.

What Is a "Killer Application"?

The search for the next big "killer application" has been going on ever since Dan Bricklin and Bob Frankston created the first spreadsheet program, VisiCalc, for the Apple II in 1979. A *killer app* is a program that's an instant hit, one whose usefulness is immediately apparent. Lotus Notes, a multipurpose application designed to be used by many people working together, is generally considered a killer app because it was largely the reason that IBM bought Lotus. Paul Keegan, writing in *The New York Times Magazine*, puts it this way: "Just as the Lotus spreadsheet gave companies a reason to buy IBM personal computers in the 80s, the company (IBM) is now gambling that Notes will be the leader in the next big wave of business computers. . . ."[1]

Software developers are always on the lookout for the next great killer app—perhaps because they hope to make a killing on it. Some of the software technologies that have the capability to create the future killer app include artificial intelligence, neural networks, speech recognition, international language translation, pen-based computing, and videoconferencing. As yet, none of them has reached killer status.

Perhaps the next contender is a type of software that is used to create something called the compound document. This software can almost be considered another layer of software between the operating environment and the applications. Simply defined, a compound document is a single file that has been created by two or more applications. For example, a document that has text from word processing and a worksheet from a spreadsheet *and can be opened and used by either application* is a compound document.

Both Apple and Microsoft are hotly competing in the compound document arena, creating software that works with their operating environments and applications to make the new software easy to use and versatile. Apple's software, jointly developed with IBM, is called OpenDoc. Microsoft's version is called OLE, for Object Linking and Embedding. If the compound document works, and works well, it could change the way we work with computers.

OpenDoc is a compound document component architecture. Designed initially by Apple Computer to provide an object-oriented end-user environment, the concept of a compound document has evolved far beyond the original word processing focus. A compound document in this new environment has become analogous to a structured container that allows a variety of functions or data (that is, objects) developed for different purposes to appear as a united application.

The objects referred to are portions of the document: text, graphics, a portion of a spreadsheet, and a list of names. When you click text in OpenDoc, the menu for, say, word processing tasks appears so that you can perform its specialized tasks. Likewise, if you click the graphic image, the graphics application's menu appears. The idea is that no matter what application created the objects, they can be harmoniously integrated into the compound document.

The compound document's future is promising, for it represents a step away from working with data and one toward working with information. Instead of starting a specific application to work with a document, we open documents that are served by the applications. What might be next? Is it possible that we could reach a point where applications don't actually make an appearance on-screen—don't require us to use menus or click icons—but instead work in the background? Beyond that point, is it possible that we could begin working with an idea and then let the software find the best application, or applications, with which to express that idea? Now that just might be a killer application.

1 Paul Keegan. "The Office That Ozzie Built," The New York Times Magazine, October 22, 1995, 50.

High-Level Languages

A **high-level programming language** is a way of writing programs using English-like words as instructions. High-level programming languages combine several machine language instructions into one high-level instruction. When a programmer had to correctly write a string of 0s and 1s in machine language, assembly language required only a single letter or a short **mnemonic**, a term or word that is easy to identify, such as *ADD* for addition. And where several instructions are required to program an operation in assembly code, a high-level language requires just a single statement.

Thus, as programming languages evolved, fewer written instructions and less work for the programmer accomplished more work. In other words, high-level languages are more efficient and make programmers more productive. High-level languages accomplish this through statements and syntax.

Basic Components

A **statement** is an expression of instruction in a programming language. A statement usually translates into one or more instructions at the machine language level. For example:

PRINT "Welcome to MetaSoftware version 6.0"

is a statement that tells the program to display the words in quotation marks on the screen. Each programming language includes a set of statements and a syntax.

Syntax is the set of rules governing the language's structure and statements. To write a program in any programming language, the programmer must use its statements and strictly abide by its syntax rules. These syntax rules may include how statements are written, the order in which statements occur, and how sections of programs are organized.

Human and computer languages have two major similarities:

➤ A set of words

➤ A set of language usage rules

In human language, sentences are constructed in a specific way—subject, verb, and so on. Programmers, when using a computer language, write instructions by using statements and syntax. For example, in the following statement written in a popular programming language, you must include the quotation marks around the letter Y:

answer = "Y"

This language also requires that each control structure have a beginning and a termination. So when you use an IF statement, at some point you must have an End IF statement. If you don't, it will appear that the program has a **syntax error**.

Some high-level languages also require that you organize programs in sections. A typical first section identifies the program and the programmer. This may be followed by a declaration section and then by a program section. Whatever the language requires, you must abide by its rules of syntax. The following sections touch on some of the most common high-level languages in use today.

BASIC

BASIC is an easy-to-use, high-level programming language available on many personal computers. Written to teach programming basics to beginners, BASIC has become a language that many hobbyists use to create simple programs.

BASIC began as an interpreted language so that beginners could create a program in an interactive mode, run the program, test it, and debug it. Interpreted languages are conducive to learning programming, but they run much more slowly than compiled programs. As a result, professional programmers avoided using BASIC. Newer versions of BASIC have added compilers. Microsoft's QuickBASIC and Visual Basic produce compiled programs.

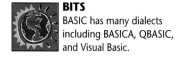

BITS
BASIC has many dialects including BASICA, QBASIC, and Visual Basic.

COBOL

COBOL is a high-level programming language specially designed for business applications. Released in 1960, COBOL is designed to store, retrieve, and process corporate accounting information and to automate such functions as inventory control, billing, and payroll. This language is the most widely used programming language in corporate mainframe environments. COBOL programs are verbose but easy to read because most commands resemble English. Versions of COBOL are available for personal computers; the newest, Visual COBOL, is an object-oriented version of the language.

FORTRAN

As a high-level programming language, FORTRAN is well suited to scientific, mathematical, and engineering applications. IBM developed FORTRAN and released it in 1957 as the first compiled high-level language. FORTRAN enables programmers to describe and solve mathematical calculations readily.

Pascal

Pascal is a high-level programming language that encourages programmers to write well-structured, modular programs. Pascal has gained wide acceptance as a teaching and application-development language. It is available in interpreted and compiled versions.

C and C++

As a high-level programming language, C is widely used for professional programming. C combines the virtues of high-level programming languages with the efficiency of an assembly language. Using C, programmers can directly manipulate bits of data inside the processing unit. As a result, C programs run significantly faster than programs written in other high-level programming languages.

C was developed by Dennis Ritchie in 1972 at AT&T's Bell Laboratories and was used to write the UNIX operating system. Because of antitrust regulations in effect before the breakup of the Bell system, Bell Laboratories was prohibited from copyrighting C or UNIX. C compilers and UNIX are therefore in the public domain and have been adopted by virtually all colleges and universities.

The original C is used so infrequently that most programmers simply refer to C++ as C. C++ contains all the elements of the basic C language but was expanded to include numerous object-oriented programming features.

```
#include <iostream.h>

void main()
{
  cout <<"Hello World!";
}
```

Language Translators

A language translator is a type of system software. Language translators include assemblers, interpreters, and compilers. The difference in these types of translators is found in the process the translator uses to produce computer-readable machine language.

In both high- and low-level programming languages, programmers write lines of programming language statements that tell the computer what to do. In high-level languages, the result is called **source code**, which can be read by people. However, the computer cannot read these instructions yet. To be readable for the computer, these instructions must be translated into **object code**, a version of the program that can be understood by the computer.

The three types of language translators are discussed in more detail here:

➤ *Assemblers*. The simplest translator is an assembler. It translates assembly language into machine language, the 0s and 1s the CPU understands.

A simple C++ program that prints Hello World! to the screen.

An interpreted program is converted into machine language object code each time it is run. It is not saved in a file.

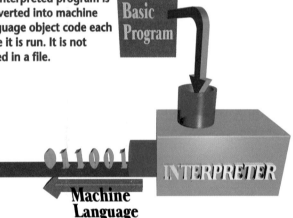

A compiled program is converted into machine language only once. It is saved in a program file and can be run whenever needed.

➤ *Compilers*. A compiler is a special type of program that translates entire files of source code into object code, which in turn becomes an executable file. An executable file is one that can be read by and run by the CPU, such as the ones that start a word processing or graphics application program.

With programs for personal computers, source code is translated directly into executable code. These files are easily recognizable in a personal computer's disk directory because their filenames end in **.EXE**. On minis and mainframes, source code is usually translated into object files, which must be linked together to create executable files.

Some advanced compilers also produce other kinds of files, such as analysis and program error files. These can be very useful to programmers, because they contain important information about how clearly the computer understands the source code as written.

➤ *Interpreters*. An interpreter translates source code one line at a time for immediate execution by the CPU. Like the compiler, an interpreter translates from the language the programmer used to write the program. However, an executable file is not created in the process, resulting in a program that runs slower. And unlike the compiler, there is no analysis and program error correction; serious errors cause the program to simply stop running. Interpreters were widely used on early personal computers, which lacked the memory capacity to run larger compiler programs.

```
C COMPUTE THE SUM AND AVERAGE OF 10 NUMBERS
C
        REAL NUM, SUM, AVG
C
        SUM =0.0
CINITIALIZE LOOP CONTROL VARIABLE
        COUNTER=0
        TOTNUM=0
C
C LOOP TO READ DATA AND ACCUMULATE SUM
  20 IF (COUNTR .GE. TOTNUM) GO TO 30
        READ, NUM
        SUM = SUM + NUM
C       UPDATE LOOP CONTROL VARIABLE
        COUNTR = COUNTR + 1
        GO TO 20
C END OF LOOP - COMPUTE AVERAGE
  30 AVG = SUM / TOTNUM
C PRINT RESULTS
     PRINT, SUM
     PRINT, AVG
     STOP
     END
```

A FORTRAN program that produces the average of ten numbers.

Popular and widely used high-level languages, such as BASIC, FORTRAN, and COBOL led to the creation of very high-level programming languages. Programming languages are very different in statements and syntax. As you read about these high-level languages, compare the four examples shown in the following four figures.

```
#include <stdio.h>

main ()
    {
        int i, num;
        float sum;

        printf("Enter numbers \n");
        sum = 0;
        for (i = 0; i <10 i++)
        {
            scanf("%d",&num);
            sum = sum + num;
        }
        printf("Sum = %3.1f\n",sum);
        printf("Average = %3.1f\n",sum
/10.0);
    }
```

A C program that produces the average of ten numbers.

```
Rem Computer sum and average of 10 numbers
Dim N(10)

Sum = 0
FOR I = 1 to 10
      INPUT N(I)
      Sum = Sum = N(I)
NEXT I

Avg = Sum / 10
PRINT "Sum ="; Sum
PRINT "Average ="; Avg
END
```

A BASIC program that produces the average of ten numbers.

Very High-Level Languages

Some very high-level languages were designed for specific purposes, whereas others were intended to set broad standards or encompass a number of computer platforms. For example, the first high-level language was FORTRAN, a science and engineering language. FORTRAN led to the development of such very high-level languages as Pascal, C and C++, each of which is a general-purpose language. Pascal led to the development of several other very high-level languages, including ADA, a special-purpose language used exclusively for U.S. Department of Defense projects.

COBOL, a business language still widely used today, led to the development of APL (A Programming Language), a very high-level language suitable for writing mathematical programs, and LOGO, used widely in education. BASIC, first developed for students at Dartmouth College, and then improved upon by Microsoft, led to several very high-level versions known variously as QuickBASIC and TrueBASIC.

A COBOL program that produces the average of ten numbers.

```
IDENTIFICATION DIVISION
PROGRAM-ID. AVERAGES.
AUTHOR. DEB KNUDSEN.
DATE-COMPILED
ENVIRONMENT DIVISION.
CONFIGURATION SECTION.
        SOURCE-COMPUTER.      HP-3000.
        OBJECT-COMPUTER.      HP-3000.
INPUT-OUTPUT SECTION.
FILE-CONTROL.
        SELECT NUMBER-FILE ASSIGN TO "NUMFILE".
        SELECT REPORT-FILE ASSIGN TO "PRINT, UR,A,LP(CCTL)".
DATA DIVISION.
FILE SECTION.
FD      NUMBER-FILE
        LABEL RECORDS ARE STANDARD
        DATA RECORD IS NUMBER-REC.
01      NUMBER-REC                     PIC S9(7)V99.
FD      REPORT-FILE
        LABEL RECORDS ARE STANDARD
        DATA RECORD IS REPORT-REC.
01      REPORT-REC                     PIC X(100).

WORKING-STORAGE SECTION.
01      END-OF-NUMBER-FILE-FLAG        PIC X(3) VALUE SPACES.
        88 END-OF-NUMBER-FILE               VALUE "YES"
01      SUM-OF-NUMBERS          PIC S9(7)V99.
01      AVERAGE-OF-NUMBERS      PIC S9(7)V99.
01      NUMBER-OF-NUMBERS              PIC 9(5).

01      WS-REPORT-REC
        05 FILLER                      PIC X(2)      VALUE SPACES
        05 FILLER                      PIC X(17)     VALUE
                                       "SUM OF NUMBERS = ".
        05 WS-SUM-OF=NUMBERS     PIC Z,ZZZ,ZZZ.99-.
        05 FILLER                      PIC X(3)      VALUE SPACES.
        05 FILLER                      PIC X(15)     VALUE
                                       "# OF NUMBERS = ".
        05 WS-NUMBER-OF-NUMBERS        PIC ZZZZ9.
        05 FILLER                      PIC X(3)      VALUE SPACES.
        05 FILLER                      PIC X(21)     VALUE
                                       "Average of numbers = ".
        05 WS-AVERAGE-OF-NUMBERS   PIC Z, ZZZ, ZZZ.99-.
05 FILLER                              PIC X(8)      VALUE SPACES.
PROCEDURE DIVISION.

100-MAIN-PROGRAM.
        OPEN INPUT NUMBER-FILE
        OUTPUT REPORT-FILE.
        MOVE SPACES TO REPORT-REC.
        MOVE ZEROS TO SUM-OF-NUMBERS.
        MOVE ZEROS TO AVERAGE-OF-NUMBERS.
        MOVE ZEROS TO NUMBER-OF-NUMBERRS.

READ NUMBER-FILE
        AT END MOVE "YES" TO END-OF-NUMBER-FILE-FLAG.

IF END-OF-NUMBER-FILE
        NEXT SENTENCE
ELSE
        PERFORM 200-PROCESS-NUMBER-FILE.
                UNTIL END-OF-NUMBER-FILE.

PERFORM 300-COMPUTE-AVERAGE
        AT END MOVE "YES" TO END-OF-NUMBER-FILE-FLAG.

300-COMPUTE-AVERAGE.
        DIVIDE SUM-OF-NUMBERS BY NUMBER-OF-NUMBERS

400-PRINT-RESULTS.
        MOVE SUM-OF-NUMBERS TO WS-SUM-OF-NUMBERS.
        MOVE NUMBER-OF-NUMBERS TO WS-NUMBER-OF-NUMBERS.
        MOVE AVERAGE-OF-NUMBERS TO WS-AVERAGE-OF-NUMBERS.

WRITE REPORT-REC FROM WS-REPORT-REC
```

Java

Java is also a very high-level language. It was initially designed to allow programmers to create *applets*, or small applications, for Web pages. Applets can be written to do just about anything, but commonly they are animated or contain sound. Some examples of applets include:

➤ Ad banners, often seen running across a Web page.

➤ Visitor counter that keeps track of Web site "hits."

➤ Image rotator or spinner, which makes a graphic or logo revolve or turn.

➤ Moving characters or animations.

➤ Text, scenes, images, or portions of screen that converge, dissolve, smear, sparkle, zoom in or out, or change colors and shapes.

Because Java is derived from C++, the code has similarities to C++. Although Java incorporates object-oriented principles, the procedural roots of Java are easily visible. Java programming is a much more traditional, procedural endeavor than programming in Visual Basic.

As Java has matured, it has become more of an object-oriented programming language (see the section, "Object-Oriented Languages") and its use has broadened. Although mostly used in Web-based application development, today programmers are using it to create a wide variety of applications, mostly on the Web, that are capable of running on many different types of computers or platforms.

```
class HelloWorld {
    public static void main (String args{}) {
        System.out.println("Hello World!");
    }
}
```

Sample Java code.

Web Development Languages

The sixth generation in programming dawned with the advent of the World Wide Web. It brought the graphical user interface you learned about in Chapter 1 to the Internet, which had previously been text-only. Everyone, from developers to entrepreneurs, were quick to see the potential for designing colorful, information-rich Web sites. As you learn in Chapter 8, the Web is based on hypertext technology. The application software you use to access Web pages is called a web browser.

The first programming language used to create, or *author*, Web pages was called Hypertext Markup Language, or HTML. Today, there are many other Web page development tools and programs. HTML programs and tools allow you to design the entire page, including background, frames, icons, buttons, text and fonts, graphics, applets, and hypertext links to other Web sites.

HTML Tools

If you're creating a simple site, such as one that is text-only or does not contain original art, graphics, or animation, you may not need a full-blown program. Some programs, such as Microsoft Word, have HTML tools built in, so you can create a Web page within Word. You can usually insert simple clip art for graphic enhancement. In addition, Netscape Navigator, a Web browser, has built-in HTML Web page by design capabilities. You can create an impressive Web page by using Netscape Navigator.

The Cathedral and the Bazaar

Eric S. Raymond is a programmer who believes in "free" software—that which can be obtained without charge. Today, most of this kind of software can be found on the World Wide Web. The title refers to the two approaches to developing software. The entire project is documented at:

```
http://www.ccil.org/~esr/writings/
cathedral-paper-1.html
```

Raymond writes, "I believed that the most important software (operating systems and really large tools like Emacs) needed to be built like cathedrals, carefully crafted by individual wizards or small bands of mages working in splendid isolation, with no beta to be released before its time." The other "seemed to resemble a great babbling bazaar of differing agendas and approaches...out of which a coherent and stable system could seemingly emerge only by a succession of miracles." Here are some important lessons Eric Raymond learned while developing an application.

1. *Every good work of software starts by scratching a developer's personal itch.* Perhaps this should have been obvious (it's long been proverbial that "Necessity is the mother of invention") but too often software developers spend their days grinding away for pay at programs they neither need nor love.

2. *Good programmers know what to write. Great ones know what to rewrite (and reuse).* While I don't claim to be a great programmer, I try to imitate one. An important trait of the great ones is constructive laziness. They know that you get an A not for effort but for results, and that it's almost always easier to start from a good partial solution than from nothing at all.

3. *"Plan to throw one away; you will, anyhow."* (Fred Brooks, *The Mythical Man-Month*, Chapter 11). Or, to put it another way, you often don't really understand the problem until after the first time you implement a solution. The second time, maybe you know enough to do it right. So if you want to get it right, be ready to start over at least once.

4. *If you have the right attitude, interesting problems will find you.* But attitude was even more important.

5. *When you lose interest in a program, your last duty to it is to hand it off to a competent successor.* Without ever having to discuss it, Carl (the other programmer Raymond worked with on the project) and I knew we had a common goal of having the best solution out there. The only question for either of us was whether I could establish that I was a safe pair of hands. Once I did that, he acted with grace and dispatch. I hope I will act as well when it comes my turn.

HTML Programs

There are hundreds of programs available for authoring Web pages, such as HoTMetaL (a play on words—hot metal refers to the way in which type was set from molten lead for linotype machines, with the letters HTML capitalized) and HTML Assistant. These programs are often made available free for use for a short period of time on the Web.

Microsoft's FrontPage 98 is another Web page authoring program. It includes a wide variety of tools to help both novice and professional Web designers easily create and manage Web sites. The Front Page Editor allows you to write text and choose fonts without having to know HTML. Like other Microsoft products, FrontPage has wizards for automating the process of completing difficult tasks, and an abundance of tools such as templates, themes, and clip art.

Object-Oriented Languages

Programming is hard work and takes time—too much time, some computer experts think. They have been working on ways to make programming simpler, easier, and faster. Object-oriented programming (OOP) languages are a recent development to improve the programming process.

What Is OOP?

Object-oriented programming differs from ordinary programming. In ordinary programming, programmers focus on the procedure the computer follows to perform an action. In OOP, programmers focus on an object, such as a dialog box on-screen. This object can be programmed to perform certain actions, such as to begin printing. The object can then be copied and used in other programs whenever needed.

OOP has actually been around for a long time, since Simula-67 was developed in 1967. The programming professional didn't pay too much attention to OOP, though, until PARC (Palo Alto Research Center, owned by Xerox Corporation) released a language known as Smalltalk in the 1970s. Smalltalk was actually the basis for both the Apple Macintosh graphical user interface and Windows. The OOP philosophy was extended to C++ and Turbo Pascal in the 1980s, and recently to both Visual Basic and Java.

Traditionally, programming languages have been procedural in nature. If you wanted a computer to accomplish a task, you figured out the logical sequence of the steps required to accomplish that task, and then programmed them into the computer. Major tasks are subdivided into smaller tasks and defined in modules. This approach is commonly referred to as **top-down design**.

OOP is entirely different because it combines top-down design with bottom-up design. OOP gained popularity and importance with the use of graphical interfaces. When you look at a Windows application, what you see is a screen with a number of objects inside a window. These objects take the form of command buttons, scroll bars, text boxes, option boxes (menus), and so on. The program awaits an event in order to take some action. The event may be a keystroke or the click of a mouse button. OOP programming is frequently referred to as **event-driven programming**. The **event** is a message that causes a **procedure** (subprogram) attached to the object to respond. These procedures are developed using traditional, top-down, procedural programming.

Programming that uses an OOP language requires adding objects to a blank form and then defining the procedures needed so that the computer will respond when an object is selected. This approach is much easier than using a procedural language that requires the programmer to develop the images on the screen, the links between them, and the procedures.

The Nature of Objects

Objects have both *attributes* and *behaviors*. For example, if the icons are buttons, when you press one with the mouse button it launches an action; that is its attribute. Its behavior might be the way it does so; for example, it might zoom the action onto the screen, or the colors might change. To make them function better, objects are organized into a hierarchy of *classes*. The class defines the kind of instructions and data found in an object; for example, some perform a specific action (such as calculating a column of spreadsheet numbers), whereas others make sure instructions, or messages, are properly carried out (such as closing a file).

For example, a COBOL programmer may write portions of the program in no particular order; that may be followed by some outlining and then going back later to "flesh it out." The programmer may find the need to write little bridge programs to link larger portions, after the fact. The result is often termed **spaghetti code**, because the code is convoluted and tangled. It may be easy for that particular programmer to make corrections or modifications later, but unfortunately, no one else may ever be able to understand the program. This has been a very common occurrence for the past 40 years and makes maintenance often very difficult.

Basic Principles of Object-Oriented Programming

OOP avoids this kind of problem by using very practical engineering techniques, much the same way an architect or engineer designs a building or an aircraft. OOP utilizes three basic principles in doing so: encapsulation, inheritance, and polymorphism.

Encapsulation

Encapsulation means that a high degree of functionality is integrated, or bundled, into each object. Encapsulation makes an object *reusable* because it is totally self-sufficient. Thus, when creating new programs or modifying old ones, it is much easier to link different objects together.

Inheritance

Inheritance means that objects within a specific class have the capability to share attributes with each other. Because the important traits have already been built in using encapsulation, it is much easier for the programmer to create a new program that is similar to an existing one. For example, if two programmers had a highly sophisticated word processing program, they could view objects, examine their encapsulation and inheritance characteristics, select specific objects, and build a desktop publishing program with them. Encapsulation assures the functionality; inheritance permits defining, or redefining, objects to suit them to the new application. A retrofit task such as this would be nearly unimaginable using a high-level language.

Polymorphism

Polymorphism lets the programmer describe a set of actions, or routines, that will perform exactly as they are described *regardless of the class of objects they are applied to*. For example, in a conventionally written application program, the exact type of printer must be defined in order to print a file— even though a dozen or more printer driver files exist. If you connect another printer and do not tell the program to change printer drivers, when you issue the "print file" command, it will not execute.

Polymorphism corrects this problem by directing the print command to address any object in the class—in other words, any printer driver—and to always print the file.

OOP Languages

Some very high-level languages have metamorphosed into object-oriented languages, such as QuickBasic into Visual Basic. Others, such as the previously mentioned Smalltalk, were conceived and implemented exclusively for OOP. Newer OOP languages, such as Borland's Delphi, have been designed as a complete, multi-purpose development environment.

Visual Basic

The BASIC programming language was developed by Professors Kemeny and Kurtz at Dartmouth in the 1960s for use in an introductory computer class. When the first microcomputers were released, they did not have enough memory to run any of the accepted languages such as FORTRAN and COBOL because of the size of their compilers. BASIC, with its small compiler that did not have to reside entirely in memory, would run on the new, small computers. BASIC quickly became the language of the micro-computer. As microcomputers grew in power, so has the BASIC language.

Visual Basic looks very different from the original BASIC from which it was derived. Visual Basic was designed by Microsoft specifically to be used in the development of applications for graphical interfaces. There are current-ly an estimated 30 million Visual Basic users. The current goal of Microsoft is to use Visual Basic to make inroads on the Internet and to gain the sup-port of the vast number of Internet users.

Like earlier versions of the BASIC language, Visual Basic is interpreted. The method used by the interpreter is not, however, the same as for previous interpreters. Interpreters for GW-BASIC, Turbo Basic, QBASIC, and QuickBasic all translated each instruction individually while the comput-er executed the program. The new Visual Basic interpreter translates each line individually, but does so as the pro-gram is being entered into the editor. An intermediate code, known as **p-code**, is produced that stays in memory until a command to execute the program is given. At that time, the p-code is translated the rest of the way into object code that the CPU can execute. This process speeds up the execution of Visual Basic programs because half of the interpretation is already completed before the program begins to execute.

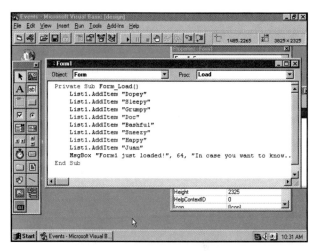

The form window is the primary win-dow used in a Visual Basic project.

Visual Basic was designed to run in a Windows environment. Visual Basic 3 runs under Windows 3.11, and Visual Basic 4 (VB4) runs under Windows 95. VB5 is designed to create OLE custom controls (OCXs) that run in browsers on operating systems other than Windows, which expands the appeal of the language.

For VB5, Microsoft has designed a smaller, faster subset of Visual Basic for Applications (VBA) that is a scripting language known as VBScript. The VBScript engine is less than 100K in size, and its source code is available free. VBScript is embedded in Hypertext Markup Language (HTML) pages as a tag. A browser downloads the script into a World Wide Web page; then the engine compiles the script and runs it.

Some concern has been expressed about the security of Visual Basic and VBScript applications. To ensure security, Microsoft is spearheading a movement among developers to develop a digital signature to verify that a component or application has not been tampered with.

One leader in the area of security is Geoffrey Rhoads, who has developed what he calls a "digital watermark" to embed a unique identifier within an image or document. Rhoads recently formed Digimarc Corporation to com-mercialize his new technology, which may be the key to securing portions of the World Wide Web and the Internet.

TechTalk
Object Linking and Embedding (OLE) permits users to easily transfer graph-ics and other objects between applica-tions.

Smalltalk

Smalltalk, as previously mentioned, is probably the best-known example of an object-oriented programming language. It was developed by Alan Kay at the Xerox Palo Alto Research Center in 1972, and it has undergone many changes and improvements on its long path to acceptance. Smalltalk pioneered the concept of programming with icons, rather than statements and syntax. Instead of the programmer typing character strings, programs are constructed by linking icons that take over the task of creating character strings—in other words, writing the code.

Most programmers feel they can develop programs using Smalltalk much faster than they can using C++. The development process permits using "what if" scenarios so that definitions may be easily refined. But because it is purely object-oriented, Smalltalk generally takes longer for programmers to master than C++. This is not due to learning the language so much as it is learning object-oriented methodology and techniques.

Delphi

Borland International has offered several powerful and innovative programming languages and tools over the years. Delphi, version 3.0, is a complete development environment, which means it is a complete set of programming tools to create an application, whether for an individual-use program to a corporatewide program, right down to compiling its own code. Delphi uses the Pascal programming language, but it is completely object-oriented. It is a powerful tool for developing Windows-based applications, in part because it includes a Visual Component Library (VCL) of commonly used icons, buttons, and menu items. In a review in *Datamation* magazine, a programmer developed an application in 20 minutes!

Java Beans

This OOP is based on the Java programming language and is a very powerful and flexible development language. Java Beans uses links to associate program elements, rather than attempting to encapsulate them. Like Java, Java Beans is a multi-platform development tool, so components written once in Java Beans can run everywhere. Java Beans has been used to build everything from small GUI applets—for example, a stock ticker—as well as network-based corporate information management systems.

Lesson Review

Key Terms

assembler	encapsulation	logic error	program
assembly language	event-driven programming	machine language	programming language
bug	executable file	mnemonic	pseudocode
case	generation	object	source code
code	high-level programming	object code	spaghetti code
compiler	language	object-oriented	statement
computer-aided software	inheritance	programming (OOP)	subordinate module
engineering (CASE)	interpreter	polymorphism	superordinate module
condition	iteration	procedure	syntax

Matching

Write the letter of the correct answer in the space provided.

_____ 1. A structured programming language

_____ 2. Can be read by the CPU

_____ 3. The manuals included with the program design

_____ 4. Most widely used object-oriented programming language

_____ 5. Combines various object code files, resolves the differences between them, and creates a finished executable file

_____ 6. Programming technique that puts together code and data to form an entity or object

_____ 7. Formally designed set of commands used to create sequential instructions that can be processed and executed by the computer

_____ 8. Translates entire files of source code in machine-readable object code

_____ 9. Programming evolved from the use of these

_____ 10. Translates source code one line at a time for immediate execution by the CPU

_____ 11. Executes a number of instructions repeatedly

_____ 12. A step-by-step solution to a problem

_____ 13. A mistake in following the rules of a programming language

_____ 14. Composed of a single task that the program must accomplish

_____ 15. Graphically shows the top-down design of a program

_____ 16. A mistake in the design of a problem solution

_____ 17. A diagram that shows the design of a program

_____ 18. Construct used for a complex set of decisions based on a single item

a. programming language

b. punched cards

c. compiler

d. linker

e. executable file

f. interpreter

g. COBOL

h. C++

i. case

j. OOP

k. algorithm

l. structure chart

m. flowchart

n. module

o. syntax error

p. logic error

q. documentation

r. loop

Multiple Choice

Circle the letter of the correct choice for each of the following.

1. As programming languages evolve, each new stage is called a

   a. mnemonic

   b. code

   c. generation

   d. compiler

2. A demonstration version of a proposed program is called

   a. an interpreter

   b. an unstructured language

   c. a pseudocode

   d. a beta

3. One of the first high-level programming languages was

   a. COBOL

   b. BASIC

   c. FORTRAN

   d. C

4. A very high-level programming language is

   a. Java

   b. Pascal

   c. APL

   d. all the above

5. The set of rules governing the way you put the statements together to make valid commands in a programming language is called

   a. syntax

   b. compiling

   c. assembly

   d. BASIC

6. High-level languages use which of the following as program instructions.

   a. 0s and 1s

   b. mnemonics

   c. binary arithmetic

   d. English-like words

7. All of the following are characteristics of objects except

   a. attributes

   b. behaviors

   c. spaghetti code

   d. derived from a hierarchy of classes

8. Web development tools and languages are characterized by

   a. HTML

   b. a graphical interface

   c. Java applets

   d. all the above

9. Object-oriented programming uses all the following principles except

   a. encapsulation

   b. spaghetti code

   c. inheritance

   d. polymorphism

10. The sixth generation of programming is primarily characterized by

   a. high-level languages

   b. polymorphism

   c. Web tools

   d. syntax errors

11. Which of the following is not one of the four program logic constructs?

   a. loop

   b. go to

   c. condition

   d. simple sequence

12. What do you call the step-by-step solution to a programming problem?

   a. recipe

   b. structure chart

   c. syntax

   d. algorithm

13. Which of the following type of error is detected by a language translator?

   a. program design

   b. logic

   c. syntax

   d. both b and c

14. Which of the following is *not* one of the steps in a programming project?

   a. design the solution

   b. select the hardware

   c. test and debug the program

   d. implement the program

Completion

In the blank line provided, write the correct answer for each of the following.

1. The language of 0s and 1s that make up bits and bytes is called _____.

2. _____ uses letters, numbers, and symbols to represent instructions the computer can understand.

3. A convoluted and tangled program is said to contain _____ code.

4. _____ enables a programmer to describe a set of actions that will perform exactly as they are described regardless of the class of objects they are applied to.

5. An easy-to-identify term or word in a programming language is called a _____.

6. An _____ is required in order to run a program.

7. The evolution of programming languages is measured in _____.

8. An example of a very high-level language is _____.

9. The basic programming language used for developing Web sites is _____.

10. A _____ translates text files into machine code and places it in an object file.

11. A(n) _____ error occurs when you do not follow the rules of the programming language.

12. Traditional programming languages such as COBOL and PASCAL are known as _____ languages.

13. Each major task in a program is called a(n) _____.

Review

On a separate sheet of paper, answer the following questions.

1. What is the difference between machine language and assembly language?

2. What is the difference between a high-level language and a very high-level language?

3. What are the three characteristics of an object in OOP?

4. Why do programmers use an editor program?

5. What is the difference between a compiler and an interpreter?

6. What is syntax, and why is it important?

7. Explain the purpose of a statement.

8. Explain the purpose of an object.

9. What does HTML stand for?

10. When would you use an HTML tool as opposed to a program?

11. Distinguish between syntax errors and logic errors.

12. Give an example to illustrate each of the four program logic constructs.

Critical Thinking

On a separate sheet of paper or in a group discussion, answer the following questions.

1. Discuss the evolution of programming languages, from early symbolic language to today's more graphic orientation. What does this tell you about who programs and what types of programs are needed today?

2. How do very high-level languages and OOP improve productivity?

3. In group discussion, describe and define a problem and a program to solve it. What type of programming language would be best?

4. Discuss how Web-based information will change the way we use programming and the programs it creates—operating systems, applications, utilities, etc.

5. Choose a language and research it on the Web (see Online Discovery). Describe five important things you learned about it that weren't in this chapter.

Further Discovery

Abort! Retry! Fail! The Top One Hundred Error Messages. Alpha Development Group (Indianapolis, IN: Alpha Books, 1992).

Decline and Fall of the American Programmer. Edward Yourdon (Englewood Cliffs, NJ: Prentice Hall, 1993).

Object-Oriented Methods. James Martin and James J. Odell (Englewood Cliffs, NJ: Prentice Hall, 1995).

Presenting Java. John December (Indianapolis, IN: Sams.net Publishing, 1995).

Programming Illustrated: The Full-Color Guide to How It All Works. D. F. Scott (Indianapolis, IN: Que, 1994).

Rise and Resurrection of the American Programmer. Edward Yourdon (Englewood Cliffs, NJ: Prentice Hall, 1996).

Show-Stopper! The Breakneck Race to Create Windows NT and the Next Generation at Microsoft. G. Pascal Zachary (New York: Free Press, 1994).

Structured Design: Fundamentals of a Discipline of Computer Program and System Design. Edward Yourdon and Larry Constantine (Englewood Cliffs, NJ: Prentice-Hall, 1979).

Sams' Teach Yourself ANSI C++ in 21 Days, Premium Edition. Jesse Liberty and J. Mark Hord (Indianapolis, IN: Sams, 1996).

Sams' Teach Yourself Java in 21 Days. Laura Lemay and Charles L. Perkins (Indianapolis, IN: Sams.net, 1996).

Sams' Teach Yourself Visual Basic 4 in 21 Days. Nathan Gurewich and Ori Gurewich (Indianapolis, IN: Sams Publishing, 1995).

 # On-line Discovery

Investigate the many aspects of programming using the Web, such as Yahoo! at www.yahoo.com/Computers_and_Internet/Software/Programming_Tools/

Explore how programs are created and how they work; for example, to see Java applet demos, go to www.sun.com/javastation/demos/

Visit some other vendor Web sites, such as Microsoft and Borland, to learn more about their products.

You can access the Internet resources for these questions by going to the Que Education and Training Web site, at URL http://ezinfo.ucs.indiana.edu/~mckimg/QUEET/onlinelinks.html. From this page, click the link for Lesson 3B and then click the link to the resource that you want to access.

---

1 *"Borland's Delphi: The Object Is Control,"* by David Vins, Datamation, May 15, 1995 (http://www.datamation.com/PlugIn/issues/1995/may15/05bbr100.html).

CHAPTER 4
Systems Analysis and MIS

Software engineering is the design, development, and implementation of production software systems—the operating systems and applications used by large organizations and enterprises. Software engineering is done on PCs, workstations, and large-scale computers. Software engineering embraces all the human aspects, from programming to management, as well as all the project details, from concept to execution to documentation. According to the Software Engineering Institute, the goal of software engineering is to decrease cycle time, increase productivity, and improve the quality of the software created.

Programmers, systems analysts, application programmers, and other software and information systems professionals take part in software engineering. So do managers and the users who work with the system. The degree of complexity and the number of steps in software engineering varies and can depend on:

➤ The size of the company

➤ The number of information systems professionals on the development staff

➤ The size and complexity of the problem that must be solved, and

➤ The number of users who use the system

Regardless of these factors, the most important point is to use the best software engineering methods and tools available to create high-quality, error-free systems in as short a time possible.

Lesson 4A explains the system development life cycle, including the coding, debugging, maintenance, and documentation stages as well as software engineering tools and techniques.

Lesson 4B explains what information technology is—who manages the information, who uses it, and how this information is best implemented.

Systems Analysis

Outline

Learning Objectives

After reading this chapter, you will be able to

➤ Discuss the steps in the system development life cycle

➤ Explain how programming tools and techniques are used for software engineering

➤ Understand various software engineering approaches to developing enterprise-wide information systems

➤ Describe some software engineering approaches and what they are used for

The System Development Life Cycle

As you learned in Chapter 3, the **system development life cycle** (SDLC) is the basis for creating computer systems. Once you understand the steps involved, you can see that it's a human process that involves both computer professionals and the users who run the systems. What usually occurs is that a department or user organization makes a formal request for an application or a system. A feasibility and cost study is performed. Once approved, the project proceeds according to the SDLC. To expand on what you've already studied, the SDLC is comprised of these steps:

➤ *Analysis*. Identifying and defining the problem.

➤ *Design*. Planning the solution to the problem.

➤ *Coding*. Writing the program.

➤ *Debugging*. Correcting program errors.

➤ *Testing and Acceptance*. Making sure the system works properly and turning it over to the users with accompanying training, as necessary.

➤ *Maintenance*. Keeping systems working properly and improving them when necessary.

➤ *Documentation*. Writing software, user, and reference documentation.

Analysis and Design

Systems analysis is the study of an activity, a procedure, even an entire business, to determine what kind of computer system would make it more efficient. **Systems design** is the activity of planning the technical aspects for the new system. This activity is usually triggered when there is a request for a new system; for example, your company's telemarketing department might ask for an application that keeps track of customer ordering information. Large companies have found that effective early planning can cut the overall program development time and costs by as much as 60 percent.

The **systems analyst** gathers and analyzes the data necessary to develop the new application. Depending on the organization and its size, he or she might also be called a systems consultant, a systems engineer, an information analyst, or a business analyst. Whatever the title, the systems analyst's tasks are to

➤ Analyze the problem to be solved, the data to be input, the expected output, and other system considerations.

➤ Interview the people who will be using the system to determine their needs, problems, and expectations.

➤ Determine which people and what kind of software, hardware, and monetary resources are necessary or available to solve the problem.

➤ Write the specifications and design the computer system and the methods for the information system to solve the problem.

➤ Guide or manage the project to a successful conclusion.

Coding

Analyzing and defining programs first involves manual tasks—easily performed without computers. Coding and debugging, which follow, are the opposite—now the pencil is put away and replaced by the keyboard. **Coding** means programming in a specific programming language, or languages—writing the *source code* for the program. The code is compiled into the language that the CPU understands.

Source code is the program, written in a specific programming language, that is sent to the computer for processing. Coding is the same as programming, but specifically refers to writing source code. By the time coding begins, the program planning stage should be finished. If the problem has been well-defined and a good design has been created, coding can often take less time than the other steps in the system development process.

Text editors. A **text editor** is an essential tool for the coding step in the system development process. It is a program used to write, erase, and manipulate words on the monitor screen. A text editor is very much like a word processor, but without many of the formatting features; in fact, word processing is the progeny of text editors.

Programming languages require certain formalities, and advanced text editors help programmers stick to the proper forms. For example, if a programming language asks that each line of source code be indented a certain number of spaces and end with a period, the text editor is set to automatically begin each line with a tab and end each with a period. Other functions, such as search, cut and paste, automatic word wrap, and automatic line spacing, also make coding a little easier.

Structured coding. **Structured coding** was the first structured writing technique, born of the need for a more organized way to write programs. Structured coding assumes that all programs can be written using three basic constructs: sequence, selection, and looping, as shown in the following figure. Programs written using structured coding techniques are easier to read, understand, and maintain. Structured coding is distinct from other structured techniques. You can use structured *coding* whether or not you use structured *design* techniques.

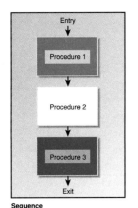

Sequence

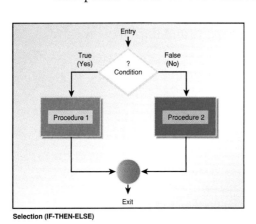

Selection (IF-THEN-ELSE)

Looping (iteration)

The three primary control structures used in structured coding.

Debugging

In the early 1940s, a programming team found a moth in a computer tube. The moth had caused a program to fail. Ever since that incident, the term *bug* has been used to describe a program or hardware problem.

Detail and precision is required, almost to the point of perfection, to make a program run successfully; therefore, bugs must be eliminated. A **debugger** is a system software that helps programmers identify errors. For example, the debugger may be used when a program runs but fails to produce the correct output. A debugger reports problems as *error messages.* The compiler also identifies program errors so that the programmer can debug, or correct, the program.

Programmers use error message listings to track down bugs. Debugging can be a costly process, consuming as much as 50 percent of program development time. Modern debugging tools, such as those found in the information engineering development environments discussed later in this chapter, help programmers spot troubles more quickly.

Testing and Acceptance

No system is truly worthwhile unless it meets the needs of the people for which it was designed. Therefore, once a system is debugged, it goes into testing so that people can see how it works. There are two types of testing:

➤ **Alpha testing** involves entering various kinds of data to see how the program reacts under different conditions. These tests are normally conducted "in-house," by the people who created the system, whether they are working in a company developing its own application or for a software publisher developing a commercial application.

➤ **Beta testing**, which presumably follows the initial alpha testing, involves users testing the system under actual working conditions— but prior to its going into production. They not only look for system malfunctions, but also for such things as ease of use, how quickly the system performs its tasks, and a number of design characteristics.

In beta testing, users are often asked to try to cause the system to fail by performing unanticipated functions—for example, opening the same file repeatedly without closing the previous one. Remember, a system should not only work as designed, it should not fail even when used improperly. When this occurs, the system should give the user an error or help message suggesting a course of corrective action.

When testing is finished and the software is ready for use, or released to production, it is given a **version** number. The first release version is numbered 1.0. Interim improvements are numbered in hundredths or tenths, such as 1.03 or 2.4.

Maintenance

Once accepted by the users, the system goes into **production**, which means it is in daily use. That does not, however, mean it is perfect. Most systems are constantly corrected, updated, and improved; this ongoing phase of the system life cycle is called **maintenance**. The users might ask that the system run faster or perform more tasks. Changing business procedures or conditions might necessitate updating or modifying the system.

Since the system is not perfect, subtle bugs may reveal themselves after the system is in use, such as during period of high-volume usage or during unanticipated types of use. Regardless of the reasons, far more is put into systems maintenance than systems design. Whether the software is a corporate-wide inventory control system or a commercial product such as a new spreadsheet, maintenance and support are essential.

Documentation

Documentation is the set of instructions that accompanies a system or an application. There are three kinds of documentation: software, user, and reference. They are differentiated by the people who use them.

Software documentation is chiefly for programmers who will maintain the program. **User documentation** and **reference documentation** are for the users who work with the program. Software documentation explains *how* a program works. User and reference documentation explains *what* a program does and *how* to use it.

Writing the documentation is the final step in the system development life cycle, but ideally it is a *process* that continues throughout development. Even though the final details cannot be written until the programming is finished, waiting until the end of the project to begin writing often results in poor documentation. Good documentation is no accident; it is the result of careful planning and development, just like the software itself. Documentation can take many forms, including conventional paper manuals or memos, on-line electronic versions, or context-sensitive help screens or messages that appear when summoned by pressing the Help key. In fact, the user often contributes to producing the system's documentation, both during and after development.

Software Engineering Tools and Techniques

Software engineering can be accomplished by using a variety of programming languages and tools. Today, software engineering is almost always accomplished using object-oriented techniques. This is because many applications in large enterprises and organizations have certain similarities; for example, the form used to take new account information may be used by sales, accounting, manufacturing, and the Web site. That form can be shared, or *re-used*, as a software *module*. Often, the place these modules are stored is called a *repository*, which is similar to a database. This saves time and money and also contributes to standard operating procedures throughout the enterprise. Here is a brief review of software engineering tools and techniques.

Structured Techniques

By the mid-1960s, government institutions and corporations were floundering in a sea of programming problems. Programs written in many individualistic styles led to chaos in software development and maintenance. The response was a variety of **structured techniques**. **Structured** programming involves a **technique** for creating more reliable and easily maintained programs that are also orderly, readable, and easily understood by others.

Y2K: The Millennium Bug

January 1, 1998, January 1, 1999, January 1, **1900**

The problem is simply date and time. Thirty years ago, it was essential for programmers to try to save space in mainframe computer storage. There was no virtual storage or extended architecture, so every byte saved was important. Since processing memory and disk space was limited, a little programming technique—dropping the first two numbers of the four-digit date (such as 1998 = 98)—was widely used. This shortcut is no longer considered clever, merely catastrophic. A survey of experienced programmers, using a scale ranging from 1 (no problem) to 5 (total economic collapse) rated the millennium problem at 3.96.

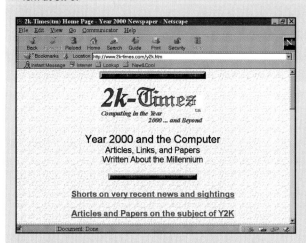

Many Web pages address the needs of those interested in the year 2000 problem.

In the 1960s, programmers never believed that their programs would still be running in full production at the turn of the century. They were still using punch cards (a limited 80-column format) and writing in a new business-oriented language, called **COBOL** (Common Business Oriented Language). It is expected that the Y2K problem will occur about once in every 50 lines of code. Each program originally cost thousands of dollars to design, write, test, and implement. Most of them are unstructured, undocumented, or poorly maintained. In order to rewrite and test these programs, approximately one million programmer-years are required, so new programmers, armies of consultants, and specialized companies must be utilized. Testing is a critical phase and is the least automated. The work is very time-consuming and expensive. It is estimated by the Gartner Group, a marketing research firm, that it will cost the United States between $50–$75 billion to correct the problem or 80 cents to

one dollar to convert each line of affected code. Worldwide, it will cost from $300–$600 billion.

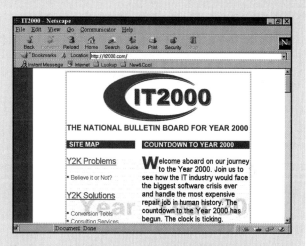

The National Bulletin Board for Year 2000 features resources for those in the IT industry.

The year 2000 problem is so widespread that it is difficult to separate critical or essential work from non-critical applications. If this is not successfully accomplished, businesses will not make the January 1, 2000, deadline. Some companies have not even started working on the problem, whereas others have already been working for several years. Pacific Gas & Electric has been working on it since 1995 and expects to be finished by the end of 1998. Bank of America, which is estimated to need $65 million in re-programming, is just beginning. Regulators have already cracked down on several small banks for inadequate preparation. Smaller banks are among the most vulnerable because of an equally small staff that's out of proportion to the problem. Insurance companies are also at risk. They have relied on computers longer than most businesses. Many are burdened with vast amounts of archaic code, legal requirements for long-term record keeping, and very old active records (such as an active life insurance policy purchased several decades ago). Many other businesses are looking to the insurance companies to cover their year 2000 losses. The insurers, on the other hand, feel a responsibility to cover the unexpected, not the obvious and inevitable. The Gartner Group estimates that 50 percent of all businesses are going to fall short of the deadline and at least five percent of these will go out of business as a consequence, resulting in a tremendous group of unemployed workers. Some have suggested that this problem could even trigger a recession.

Besides failed businesses and unemployment, there will be widespread litigation (estimated at over $1 billion). These lawsuits have already started. A grocery store owner in Michigan sued a cash register designer because of the "millennium bug." He has 10 cash registers that are not programmed to handle transactions referencing the year 2000. Credit cards that expire in the year 2000 are rejected and treated as having expired in 1900. This has resulted in a loss of 10 percent of his business. The suit has been filed against both the company that designed the cash register software and the company that sold him the system.

Although, in reality, the world may be run by mainframes, the problem is not limited to legacy systems (systems still in regular use, but developed under older technologies). All categories of computers are affected by the problem. Micro-code, operating systems, applications, queries, procedures, screens, pre-printed forms, databases, and data will all feel the impact. Most people have access to microcomputers, using them as stand-alone CPUs, nodes on networks, and terminals on larger systems. Microcomputers using older versions of DOS (3.0 or below) will not roll over to 2000. Machines such as 386 and 486 may need an upgrade to the **BIOS** (Basic Input/Output System—software that starts the computer before the operating system takes control). Even more powerful models, like Pentiums running older software, may need to be updated. Microsoft's most recent version of Access will handle the conversion, whereas Access 95 will have problems with two-digit dates. Most Macintosh computers, on the other hand, are safe from the problem.

Age and date calculations are among the most vulnerable. Ages, for example, are generally calculated by comparing the birth year to the current year. Someone born in 75 (1975) will be 25 years old in 2000, but if the computer assumes a prefix of 19__, the year 00 (2000) will be regarded as 1900 and the date of birth as 75 years in the future. In other words, you haven't been born yet. One 104-year-old woman was assumed to be 4 years old, kindergarten age, and certainly too young for social security or retirement payments. In another case, large amounts of stored food were destroyed because expiration dates such as 2001 were regarded as past their expiration (since 1901).

There is potential for havoc everywhere. The following are a few examples of areas of impact that will disrupt our lives, our jobs, and our industries:

➤ Government (federal, state, county, and municipal). Any number of old dated records and current data such as drivers license renewal dates.

➤ Telephones. Calls lasting 100 years (such as 11:59 on 12/31/99 to 12:01 on 01/01/00, if absolute values are used, neither positive nor negative, the difference between 00 and 99 is 99 years.)

➤ Medicine. Prescription renewals and blood-bank dating.

➤ Hospitals. Billing systems, insurance claims, patient records.

➤ Banks. Accounts shut down, records erased.

➤ Credit cards. Expiration dates of 00, considered expired in 1900.

➤ Air traffic control. Computer lock-ups.

➤ Prisons. Misread release dates, prisoners freed prematurely.

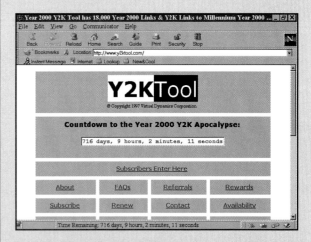

The Web offers many sites to keep surfers up-to-date on how much time is left until the year 2000.

On the other hand, this problem has become a career opportunity for many programmers, a business opportunity for numerous consulting firms, and, for the first time in years, companies are actively recruiting COBOL programmers. Even BAL (Basic Assembly Language) and PL/I (Programming Language 1) programmers are in demand. More than 50 percent of all U.S. companies are expected to require outside services to meet the year 2000 challenge. This has been an economic boon to

these segments of the computer industry, while the affected companies will not show any return for their investment. The monies expended by each company will serve merely to keep them in business.	The United States is more computerized, from government to individual, than most other nations and is far ahead of the rest of the world in dealing with the year 2000 problem. Much of the world has not yet awakened to the potential crisis.

There are a number of structured techniques, including structured programming or coding, structured analysis, structured design, and so on. Structured techniques often result in reduced program development time, increased programmer productivity, less testing and debugging, and programs that are simpler and easier to maintain. We'll look more closely at structured coding techniques in the next section. Here we'll explore a few of the more commonly used structured analysis and design techniques.

Structured analysis. **Structured analysis** uses *data flow diagrams* to chart a system's progress. By showing how data moves from one point to another, the resulting concept is that of a *logical system*. Structured analysis requires the analyst to logically think through what the system should do, before determining how it should be done. The emphasis is on the end result—what the users need from the system to perform their work. Interestingly, the logical base of structured analysis often allows the analyst to come up with more creative solutions to problems.

Structured design. **Structured design** commonly utilizes a method called the *top-down approach,* which breaks the problem into parts and arranges these parts in a hierarchy, according to their size and level of detail. The result is a *hierarchy*, or series of steps, beginning with the overall problem to be solved, and continuing in a series of increasingly more detailed parts of the problem.

Computers work by performing tasks in step-by-step fashion. For this reason, they are good at working with algorithms. An **algorithm** is a limited set of step-by-step instructions that solve a problem. Once the steps are well-defined, programmers can easily go on to write code in **modules**—distinct, logical parts of a program.

Structured techniques help us understand what we're doing before we begin writing code. They provide several kinds of road maps in various levels of detail. Structured techniques also serve as guides in coding, which is the next step in the system development process. Now that the systems analyst has defined the problem and designed the most appropriate algorithm for solving it, the next step is coding the program.

Client-Server Tools

Client-server computing is a popular platform for large scale, or enterprise, computing. A simple example of a client-server application is when you use the World Wide Web—you are using a PC, which is the client, and accessing information from any one of a number of servers that host Web sites. Some of the leading client-server tools are Oracle's Developer/2000 and Powersoft's PowerBuilder 5.0. In addition, many Java-based client-server tools are widely used, especially to develop Web-based applications.

CASE Tools

Computer-aided software engineering, or **CASE**, is a methodology especially designed for programmers in large information systems organizations. They need to quickly create new applications—or re-engineer older applications—created with spaghetti code. CASE automates the design and implementation of applications as well as the procedures linking various applications, so that they may be created more rapidly and efficiently. In this respect, CASE is similar to object-oriented programming; it differs primarily in that it is designed for applications of the high-level programming environment. CASE tools are used in three ways: for program design, re-engineering, and as an integrated set of application development tools.

Information Engineering

Information engineering is a software development methodology developed by Clive Finkelstein, an Australian information systems professional. In 1982, Finkelstein wrote, "Software engineering is intended primarily for use by analysts and programmers. It was not designed to be applied directly by users. Communication with users comes primarily through the data flow diagram. Information engineering, on the other hand, brings user department personnel, management and data processing (the Information Technology (IT) organization) together in a partnership. Its techniques draw on the experience of all three groups."[1]

Finkelstein now works with John Zachman, who was with IBM for many years. Together, they advocate a framework for enterprise architecture and information systems architecture. This framework enables managers and IT departments of organizations to work together to facilitate rapid organizational change, both for the enterprise and the computer systems that support it.

Users play an integral role in information engineering; indeed, systems cannot be designed or created without their participation. And information engineering uses the latest software tools and techniques to design and create systems; the idea is to do quality work, but to do it quickly so that the system can be put to work. Table 4A.1 compares traditional development to information engineering.

Table 4A.1 Traditional Development vs. Information Engineering	
Traditional Development	*Information Engineering*
Emphasis on coding and testing	Emphasis on analysis and design
Paper-based specifications	Computer-based specifications
Manual coding	Automatic code generation
Manual documentation	Automatic documentation generation
Often fails to meet user specs	Joint application development
Requires debugging	Automated design verification generates bug-free code
Constant code maintenance	Code regenerated according to updated design specifications

Software Engineering Approaches

There is no single method of software engineering; rather, as mentioned, it is a way of thinking about information systems development in support of business objectives. Some of the techniques or methodologies and the development tools used may be "homegrown," or developed within a business, as its own approach or for a single project; others are developed by a consultant, a software company, or a software developer.

In most cases, systems development occurs in team environments, where systems people, consultants, managers, and users collaborate to design the system. Often they use a special teamroom, such as the one shown in the following figure. Some approaches, such as those in the following examples, are common practice.

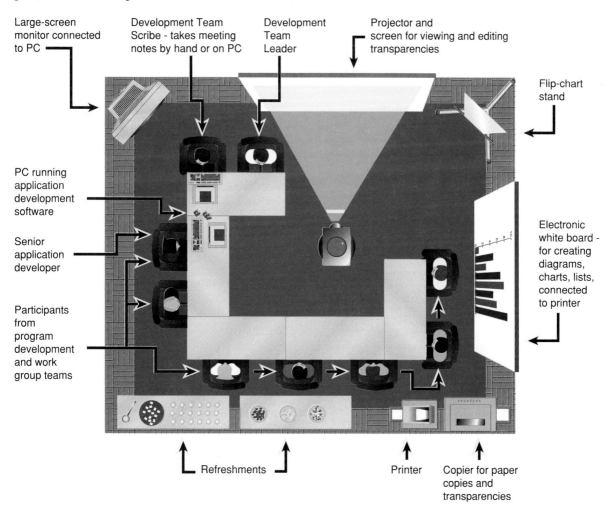

Modern development teams work in specially designed rooms, using the latest development tools to discuss, design, prototype, and test system designs.

Application Development Without Programmers

Application development without programmers refers to users creating their own applications, using languages or development tools that do not require extensive training. These tools have taken a great workload off programmers and have made it possible for users to design many everyday applications, freeing up time for the professionals to work on enterprise systems. It is common to do this kind of application development using a relational or object-oriented database with its built-in tools or languages.

One such tool is called **SQL**, for **structured query language**. SQL permits the creation of a set of queries. These enable the user obtain specific information from the database in a simple, efficient manner. SQL is easy to learn and use; it has only 30 commands, such as select, update, insert, and delete.

Microsoft Access has various tools for users and developers. Users can implement a variety of **wizards** that help automate tasks and obtain select information. Developers use Visual Basic for Applications (VBA) to design forms, reports, queries, and custom applications within Access.

One of the most common applications that users develop without programmers is the Web site. This can be created by using a Web page designer, HTML tools, Java applets, Shockwave, RealAudio, and other user-level development tools or languages.

Prototyping

Prototyping is the process of creating a working model of the new application or system. It warrants more attention, since it can be used in just about any application development environment, regardless of the methodology used. This is due to the fact that prototyping is done early in the process. Prototyping involves both users who work with the system as well as application programmers or developers. Its main purposes are to determine if the proposed system or application

➤ simulates the important interfaces between the system and user

➤ performs all the major functions

➤ can be built quickly

However, a prototype has limitations. It may not perform on par with the actual system or be able to access all the databases. It may not respond correctly to all the situations encountered when the actual application is in use. It is like a designer's model of an automobile; it has form and some function, but it can't be driven. Early prototyping tools created a prototype and nothing more. Once the users liked it, the developers had to begin again from scratch using development tools. However, that is no longer the case. The prototype is the model upon which the real system is built, and almost always evolves into the final system. In doing so, prototyping speeds the development process.

Prototyping is usually accomplished with a prototyping software development tool. This program may be a stand-alone software product or part of an integrated CASE product.

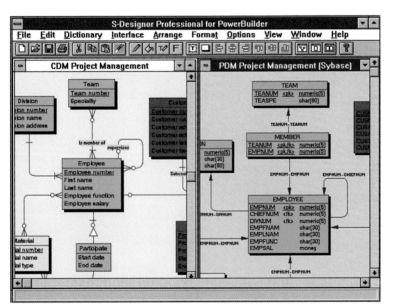

A prototyping tool at work.

Rapid Application Development

Rapid Application Development, or RAD, is an information engineering technique promoted by James Martin. Martin defines RAD as a development life cycle designed to take maximum advantage of the integrated CASE (I-CASE) tools. The goal is to produce systems of high quality at high speed and low cost. Although better/faster/cheaper is certainly the ultimate goal of computing, Martin appends this goal by saying, "A top criteria for IS must be that it never interferes with business's capability to seize a competitive opportunity. Speed is essential." Table 4A.2 shows how some companies have improved development times by using RAD approach to systems development.[2]

Table 4A.2 Steps Some Businesses Have Taken to Stay Competitive		
Company	Systems Improvement	Results
IBM Credit Corporation	Reduced financing approval time from seven days to four hours	Staff size remained the same, but productivity rose 100 fold
Wal-Mart	Reduced shelf restocking time form six weeks to 36 hours	Customers rarely find stores out of product they desire
Harley-Davidson	Reduced time to manufacture a cycle frame from 72 days to two days, at the same time raising product quality from 50% to 99%	Renewed company image for a quality product and demand soared
Motorola	Cut customer request time for a pager from three weeks to two hours	Massive increase in the volume of pager business

In the traditional development approach, the user is commonly involved in the process at the outset, *prior to design*, and then not again until the application reaches testing. In the RAD life cycle, the user is involved during the entire process; only during actual construction does user involvement diminish.

The RAD life cycle is based on four foundations—the Information Engineering methodology; high-quality software engineering tools; the utilization of the most highly skilled people; and strong management support and involvement. RAD also presumes a departure from what James Martin calls the "classical development life cycle," in which applications are built "by hand" using line-by-line coding and plastic templates.

Lesson Summary

➤ The system development life cycle includes analysis and design, coding, debugging, testing and acceptance, maintenance, and documentation stages.

➤ Software engineering can be accomplished using a variety of programming languages and tools. Today, software engineering is almost always accomplished using object-oriented techniques.

➤ Structured programming involves a technique for creating more reliable and easily maintained programs that are also orderly, readable, and easily understood by others. **Structured analysis** uses *data flow diagrams* to chart a system's progress. **Structured design** commonly utilizes a method called the *top-down approach,* which breaks the problem into parts and arranges these parts in a hierarchy according to their size and level of detail.

➤ Client-server computing is a popular platform for large scale, or enterprise, computing.

➤ Information engineering brings user department personnel, management and data processing (the information technology (IT) organization) together in a partnership.

➤ Prototyping is the process of creating a working model of the new application or system. It warrants more attention since it can be used in nearly any application development environment, regardless of the methodology used.

➤ Computer-aided software engineering, or CASE, is a methodology especially designed for programmers in large information systems organizations who need to create new applications quickly. Rapid application development, or RAD, is another information engineering technique.

Lesson Review

Key Terms

algorithm	module	source code	systems analysis
alpha testing	production	structured analysis	systems analyst
beta testing	prototyping	structured coding	systems design
coding	Rapid Application	structured design	text editor
debugger	Development (RAD)	structured techniques	user documentation
documentation	reference documentation	system development	version
information engineering	software documentation	life cycle	
maintenance	software engineering		

Matching

Write the letter of the correct answer in the space provided.

_____ **1.** Process of creating a working model of the new application or system

_____ **2.** Ongoing phase of the system development life cycle

_____ **3.** Act of planning the technical aspects of a new computer system

_____ **4.** Program written in a specific high-level programming language that is sent to the computer

_____ **5.** Set of instructions or procedures that solves a problem

_____ **6.** Study of an activity or procedure to determine the kind of computer system that can make it more efficient

_____ **7.** Information engineering technique designed to take maximum advantage of the integrated CASE tools

_____ **8.** Uses top-down approach to break a problem into parts

_____ **9.** Application development tool that permits the creation of a set of queries

_____ **10.** Software development methodology for use primarily by analysts and programmers

a. source code

b. information engineering

c. systems analysis

d. structured design

e. systems design

f. maintenance

g. algorithm

h. prototyping

i. RAD

j. SQL

Multiple Choice

Circle the letter of the correct choice for each of the following.

1. Software engineering is primarily intended for use by

  a. consulting firms

  b. analysts and programmers

  c. production software applications

  d. all the above

2. The system development life cycle is

  a. a way to be sure all seven steps are addressed

  b. no longer used in software engineering

  c. a tried-and-true means of solving a programming problem

  d. too long for today's fast-changing enterprise

3. Coding means

  a. writing the source code

  b. turning machine language into mnemonics

  c. giving users an alpha version

  d. making sure no one else understands your programming

4. Alpha testing is

  a. the highest priority

  b. done by the programming staff

  c. done by the users

  d. Version 1.0

5. One of the key uses for CASE is

   a. writing spaghetti code

   b. re-engineering older systems

   c. writing operating systems

   d. designing Web pages

6. Information engineering

   a. involves just the programming team

   b. involves just the users

   c. takes a team approach to information system design

   d. is mostly used in college courses

7. Software engineering tools for users include

   a. SQL

   b. Web tools

   c. wizards

   d. b and c only

   e. all the above

8. One of the main benefits of a prototyping tool is that

   a. users can build an application by themselves

   b. programmers don't have to write specifications

   c. the application can be built very quickly

   d. all the above

9. Client-server tools are especially useful for

   a. novices

   b. small offices and home workers

   c. Web applications

   d. military applications

10. Rapid Application Development presumes

   a. a departure from the traditional SDLC

   b. use of the Web

   c. advanced degrees in programming

   d. no need to discuss application with users

Completion

In the blank provided, write the correct answer for each of the following.

1. A release of a computer system or application for use by its intended users is called a _____.

2. A system software program that helps programmers identify program errors is called a _____.

3. A _____ is a working model of a new application or system.

4. _____ is a software engineering methodology that brings knowledge workers, management, and information systems personnel together in a working partnership.

5. Written materials that explain how a system works are termed _____.

6. The program that is written in a specific language that is sent to the computer for processing is referred to as _____.

7. When users do their own programming, it is called _____.

8. CASE stands for _____.

9. A concept that brought rigor, order, and the ability to understand a program written by someone else is called _____.

10. A powerful programming tool called _____, permits the creation of a set of queries.

Review

On a separate sheet of paper, answer the following questions.

1. What is software engineering?

2. List the steps in the system development life cycle (SDLC).

3. Define coding.

4. What is a debugger?

5. What is the difference between alpha testing and beta testing?

6. Name the three types of documentation for a system or application.

7. What are the main benefits of information engineering?

8. Define prototyping.

9. Why is application development without programmers a good idea?

10. What are the benefits of Rapid Application Development?

Critical Thinking

On a separate sheet of paper or in a group discussion, consider the following.

1. Make a list of the applications you use and write down their version numbers. (*Hint*: While the program is open, the version number can often be found by clicking on Help.) What do you think a higher version number means?

2. What are the limitations of the traditional SDLC? How do newer software engineering methods overcome these limitations? Be specific.

3. Learn more about system maintenance, possibly from a Web search, and why it's so important.

4. Learn more about one software engineering technique, possibly from a Web search, and report on how it's being used.

5. Choose a position in a hypothetical company and select an application that you use every day. Determine a need you have for an application you can develop yourself and explain what tools you would use to create it.

On-line Discovery

In order to answer some of the Critical Thinking questions from Web searches, you'll need to examine the resources available. One is www.yahoo.com, where you'll find many ways to search for suitable Web sites or information. Or you might use www.altavista.digital.com to search for keywords, such as "software engineering," "clive finkelstein," "james martin," or "client-server."

1 *Clive Finkelstein, Information Engineering, Computerworld, June 15, 1981.*

2 *Adapted from Enterprise Engineering by James Martin (Lancashire, England: Savant Institute, 1994, Volume I, 98-99.*

Managing Information Technology

Outline

Learning Objectives

After reading this chapter, you will be able to

➤ Describe the Information Technology department and its computer functions in the enterprise

➤ Describe the management and staff of the IT department

➤ Explain the way systems and applications are developed by IT

➤ Understand the concept or purpose of IT

➤ Describe some of the major trends in IT

Understanding Information Technology

Businesses first began using computer systems and setting up computer departments in the 1950s. The first computer departments were referred to by their location—the Computer Room. As the '50s progressed, International Business Machines grew to dominate business computing, so the room became known as the "IBM Room." There followed a succession of names—data processing, business data processing, information systems, management information systems (MIS), and information technology (IT). Information technology is the name most commonly used today, although one increasingly hears the term "knowledge management."

Why the computer department's name changes so frequently? It's simple—the mission, tasks, process, and implementation of computers in organizations—business or otherwise—are constantly changing. The IT department, its people, and the work they do are constantly responding to the changing needs of the organization. For many years, the computer department simply automated tasks, forms, and procedures. Then it began shaping and tailoring those tasks and procedures, making them more effective and responsive to the changing business environment. Today, it is not uncommon to see the business planners working closely with the information technology people to create cutting-edge systems that shape business strategy and create competitive advantages.

What Is Information Technology?

The term **information technology** (IT) refers to:

➤ The complex computer systems used in a modern enterprise

➤ The functional department or organization that creates and maintains those same computer systems

IT is integral to the modern enterprise. Without its systems and services, it would be difficult, if not impossible, for modern business enterprises to function. IT works with enterprise to achieve business goals. The following figure demonstrates a business process supported by an information technology system. Like the various hardware components in a computer system—such as the CPU, main memory, and peripherals—various business processes—such as order processing, accounting, manufacturing, and shipping—form a system for business.

The process shown in the figure is triggered by a sales order, which stimulates the **product definition** cycle. Each phase is supported by computer systems and software applications in the **departmental systems** linked to the cycle. The master schedule triggers the **product delivery** cycle, which is supported by additional departmental systems of the enterprise-wide management information systems until the product is shipped to the customer.

This is a custom manufacturing business process in which specialty products are created on demand for customers.

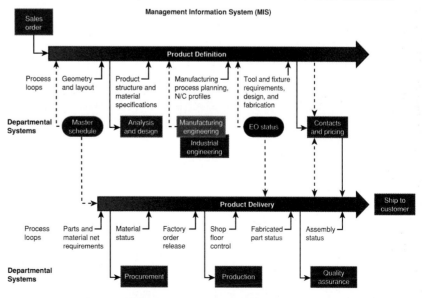

The IT system monitors, directs, and controls various processes to assure that the work gets accomplished properly and that the business achieves its goals and objectives. For most enterprises, these goals and objectives are to:

➤ Assure that knowledge workers have all the information they need to do their work in a timely manner

➤ Produce a viable service

➤ Manufacture a high-quality product

➤ Satisfy customer needs

➤ Help the company remain viable and competitive in its market

➤ Support each business process to achieve the highest levels of performance

➤ Create a profit

➤ Distribute dividends to shareholders

IT's computer systems provide data that is used by various knowledge workers in business—in the form of information—to solve problems, plan strategies, and make decisions that affect the health and livelihood of the business or enterprise. In recent years, IT's computer systems have also come to deliver products or services over the Web.

IT at L.L. Bean

L.L. Bean of Freeport, Maine, is one of the best-known mail-order outdoor clothing and equipment companies in the U.S., perhaps best known for inventing the Maine hunting boot and the chamois cloth shirt. The company ships over 13 million packages to customers each year. L.L. Bean's focus is entirely on customer service, including its IT operations, which are designed for individualized service. In 1980, L.L. Bean installed its first on-line order entry system. Its database has the answers to 92 percent of all questions asked of customer service representatives.

L.L. Bean now offers Web shopping. Customers can either order products displayed on the On-Line Product Guide (www.llbean.com) or order from a catalog directly on the Web. The Web site allows customers to create their own on-line shopper profile, providing access to the same information the customer service representatives use to allow for speedy and efficient ordering. L.L. Bean has effectively built upon its efficient IT infrastructure, using it to further facilitate its mission of providing the customer with excellent service.

In the past, customers might have to wait as long as a month for a mail-order delivery. Customer satisfaction requires speedy delivery. The on-line order system reduced product turnaround to two days, and then to 24 hours. Customers now can select their method of delivery, including Federal Express. The on-line order system captures all pertinent customer information so that address, phone number, sizes, and so on are stored and ready for the next order.

Who Manages Information Technology?

The IT department is probably the most dynamic group of people in the modern enterprise. Their influence extends throughout the organization, from the users working at PCs to the departments that obtain computer services from IT to the customers or business partners for whom the enterprise provides goods or services. As in any department, the IT department has several layers of management and staff.

The Chief Information Officer

At the head of the IT department is the Chief Information Officer, or CIO. This is usually a vice president in the enterprise, reporting to the executive vice president, chief operating officer, chief financial officer, and in some cases directly to the chief executive officer.

The CIO is responsible for all IT operations and staff. He or she must be equally familiar with the business operations and objectives of the enterprise and information technology. Similarly, the CIO must be able to communicate well with others in management—finance, marketing, manufacturing—as well as with the highly trained IT people. He or she is responsible for conceptualizing, planning, organizing, and delivering large-scale systems or applications on time, within budget, and in good working order.

Some of the other CIO's day-to-day responsibilities include:

➤ Overseeing the IT departmental infrastructure and enterprise-wide computer systems architecture

➤ Making decisions regarding use of in-house staff or to outsource IT work

➤ Creating partnerships with key IT suppliers and consultants

➤ Ensuring customer satisfaction with internal and external clients

➤ Providing professional development training for IT staff as well user training and education to ensure productive use of existing and new systems.

The *information* aspect of the CIO's job is increasingly important. Using their knowledge of both business and information technology, many CIOs have taken a leadership role in reengineering their organizations' business processes to be more productive and to make better use of information in the process. For example, CIOs are helping business people understand how they can use the Web for both internal and external purposes. CIOs are also taking a leadership role in knowledge management and the valuation of intellectual capital.

Information Technology Management

Reporting to the head of IT are the operational managers. They oversee such things as software maintenance, new application development, user training, and a number of other IT functions. These managers are often appointed to head a team of programmers working on a specific application or project. They are given specific instructions and schedules for completing portions of the projects, some of which may take years to complete.

The Chief Knowledge Officer

Thomas Davenport, a technology consultant with Ernst & Young's Center for Business Innovation, believes a new position is emerging; that of the Chief Knowledge Officer. The CKO's main job is to manage and oversee unstructured information in the form of knowledge. He or she works with or alongside the CIO, who is already busy with the IT infrastructure and systems development. The CKO must be able to create, organize, disseminate, and determine appropriate uses or applications for knowledge management. "Many companies think they don't need yet another staff position like the CKO," says Davenport, "but if no one assumes responsibility for knowledge and unstructured information, those assets won't be managed. Without someone like a CKO, organizational learning and knowledge management will continue to be rhetorical concepts, not realities."

Information Technology Staff

The IT staff has a variety of different technical skills, corresponding in many ways to similar organizational tasks in the business itself. Most staff members have completed college programs in computer science. There are systems analysts who are responsible for analyzing and designing new applications as well as complete systems. For example, the head of manufacturing might ask a systems analyst to create a system, including hardware and software, to control the entire manufacturing process of a new product.

Programmers write systems and applications with programming languages. They can be found working at mainframe or minicomputer terminals or personal computers in conventional office environments, just like any other knowledge worker.

In a Fortune 500 firm, there might be several hundred programmers working on various projects:

➤ Some are systems programmers, meaning their work involves expanding, improving or maintaining the systems software or the existing software applications, such as the accounting system or the manufacturing resource planning (MRP) system.

➤ Others are application programmers who are assigned to work with various departments in the company, such as customer service, or helping users develop new applications. For example, a company might be planning to implement an electronic commerce (e-commerce) application (discussed in more detail later in this chapter) that allows customers to buy products over the Web. Such a project involves several systems programmers working in the IT department, while assigning application programmers to order processing, inventory and shipping to set up and install the e-commerce applications.

➤ Still others are operations technicians, responsible for maintaining the hardware. Some are responsible for installing terminals and setting up personal computers, others troubleshoot malfunctioning equipment. Some are in charge of backup systems, such as changing disk packs, tapes and tape cartridges.

➤ And last, but far from least, some IT staff are Help Desk personnel, answering phones and making in-house visits to users who are having problems with their computers.

Who Uses Information Technology?

Every progressive enterprise has an IT function. It is essential for business success. IT is used in enterprises of all kinds: business, government, non-profit organizations, as well as the computer and information industry itself. IT is important in organizations large and small, but the larger the organization, the more important IT is within the organization. *InformationWeek*, a magazine for information systems professionals, ranks the top 100 IT organizations in business each year. The smallest of these IT organizations has an annual budget of $100 million; the largest is in excess of a quarter of a billion dollars.

The IT Professional Is in Short Supply

The Information Technology Association of America says there is a shortfall of 10 percent between the number of vacant positions for computer programmers, systems analysts, computer scientists, and engineers and the number of qualified workers available for those positions. In January, 1998, there were 346,000 jobs unfilled. "The problem has been getting much, much worse over the last year," says the CIO at CompUSA in Dallas. "It's harder to find people, and when you get them, they stay for much shorter periods."

Harris N. Miller, ITAA's president, says "Technical talent is the rocket fuel of the Information Age. As an information-intensive society, we cannot afford to stand by as the next wave in our economic future departs for foreign shores. Empty classroom seats, a poor professional image, finger-pointing among stockholders and other key factors are inadvertently conspiring to rewrite an American success story. We must solve this problem."

Miller believes that companies must consider hiring graduates with other academic qualifications or certified skills in specific technologies. "Whether we are talking about the programmers and systems analysts who develop IT products and services or the business and technical personnel who must use IT effectively, our findings speak for themselves. IT worker shortages continue to be a national crisis today and into the foreseeable future. To solve this dilemma requires the collective wisdom and innovative actions of employers, educators, and the government," says Miller.

The U.S. government is taking aggressive steps to help solve the problem—straight from the top. In January, 1998, Vice President Al Gore announced that he and the president were launching initiatives that "will help ensure that America has the best information technology workforce in the world," the vice president said. "Information technology is the engine of the new economy, and it is critical that American workers are prepared to take advantage of these new high-skill, high-wage jobs." The initiatives include:

Expanding industry involvement in school-to-work. The Department of Education and the Department of Labor will provide up to $6 million in grants for industry groups that expand private-sector involvement in school-to-work. This will give more young Americans the academic and vocational training they need to pursue high-skill, high-wage jobs in industries, such as IT.

Upgrading the skills of the existing workforce. The Department of Labor will invest $3 million in demonstration projects—in partnership with employers and training providers—to train dislocated workers for high-tech jobs.

Continuing the national dialogue. The Department of Commerce will convene four town-hall meetings this year in which representatives of business, academia, state and local governments, and employee organizations can discuss IT workforce needs, identify best practices, and showcase successful models others can replicate.

Vice President Gore also challenged educators and industry leaders to redouble their efforts to strengthen America's IT workforce. "Encouraging women and minorities to pursue careers in information technology, upgrading the skills of the existing workforce, and ensuring that our children excel in math and science will require new commitments from all of us," the vice president said. "America's success in the new economy depends on it."

IT systems are used by managers and knowledge workers at all levels of the enterprise. The most important objective is for IT to provide information to the right people, at the right time, to make the best decisions. Because organizations are changing, the way IT delivers information has changed, too. IT consultant and guru Peter G.W. Keen says, "Today's (IT) systems focus on alerting managers to problems and trends, answering their ad hoc questions, and providing information in the form they want, when they want it."[1]

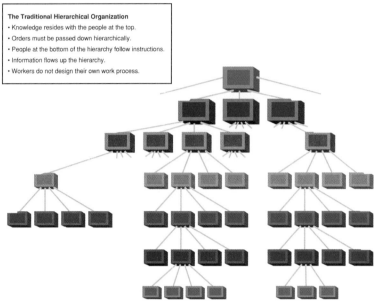

The Traditional Hierarchical Organization
• Knowledge resides with the people at the top.
• Orders must be passed down hierarchically.
• People at the bottom of the hierarchy follow instructions.
• Information flows up the hierarchy.
• Workers do not design their own work process.

The traditional hierarchical organization regards information as power to be held and dispersed by upper management (adapted from James Martin, "The Great Transitions").

Organizational Structures

The structural design of an organization affects the way that organization distributes and uses information. The following figure shows a typical organizational structure, often referred to as hierarchical. In this organization, information can only flow vertically—up and down channels. For example, for sales information to reach another department, it must flow upward to management for approval, then downward to the appropriate person for action. Information, and access to it, is much more controlled in this organizational environment.

The hierarchical organization is top-heavy with managers, and is giving way to the flattened, or clustered, organizational style, shown in the next figure. Here knowledge workers work in peer groups in which information can be readily exchanged between each other, between their group and others, and with management. In the flat organization, information is regarded as an essential asset for every employee and is shared, not controlled.

THE CLUSTER ORGANIZATION

• Value-Stream Reinvention has been done across the enterprise.

• Value-stream teams are tightly focused on the goals of their value-stream.

• Type B clusters service and facilitate the Type A value-stream teams. (Type B clusters may also be value-stream teams.)

• Planning, direction-setting, architecting, and enabling is done by the CEO team.

The modern organization regards information as a resource, to be used by those who determine a need for it (adapted from James Martin, "The Great Transitions").

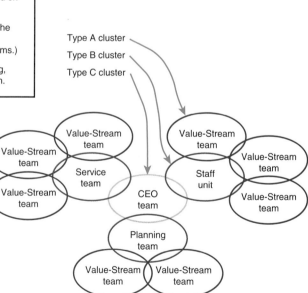

How Information Technology Is Used

As mentioned earlier, IT systems are most widely used in business, where they are often considered a strategic tool for business success. They are also used extensively in nonprofits and the public sector. Management collects business data and, with the help of IT, a system or an application is created to work with that data. A system usually involves both hardware and software. An application is software to support an enterprise activity.

Either one may be referred to by the IT organization as a **project**, or a work order to create a system. The project might be a new manufacturing system, a way for a fast-food chain to gather the daily receipts from its many restaurants, or a creating a new direct sales division with order processing on the Web site. Because many projects may be mission-critical, or needed quickly to help the enterprise become or remain competitive, it's often essential that the project be completed quickly. This is why software engineering tools and techniques are so important.

Data Collection

Once it is up and running, the new system or application collects the necessary data. Then it is stored, processed, and retrieved as strategic information. The data collected in an information system comes from three sources:

➤ *Outside sources* such as feedback from customers, sales rep surveys, magazines or trade publications, on-line database information, and the informal human networks or informal "grapevines."

➤ *Inside sources* about the company, provided by operational management concerning its productivity, resources and such, or by middle management regarding opinions or analysis of short-term goals, opportunities, and accomplishments.

➤ The *information system itself*, by feeding specific data into the computer in order to produce analyses or scenarios for senior management to set future goals, plan strategic directions, or create new competitive advantages. These are often customized information systems called *decision support systems* or *executive information systems*, designed especially for top-level managers who lack extensive computer skills.

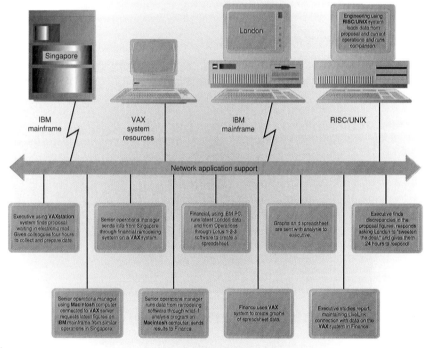

This system draws information from a variety of sources and delivers it to a variety of users.

Organizing the IT Systems

A typical large company has hundreds of different information systems in use. Although some are designed to assist customers, such as a network of ATMs at a bank, most are for internal use. In most organizations, each department or function usually has its own information system. Some of the computers used are unique to that organization while some are centralized and shared by other departments. For example, central IT systems usually provide sales figures that are used by:

> *Manufacturing* to set production goals and monitor inventory

> *Finance* to determine the firm's profitability

> *Marketing* to set quotas

> *Human resources* for employee salary evaluations

> *Accounting* or payroll, to pay salaries and sales commissions

From a management perspective, the sales information helps the operational manager know how much product to manufacture and how many workers to hire. It also helps the middle manager set goals for new products or increase market share, and it helps senior management decide on plans for expansion or growth in the future. So, in a sense, anyone who is involved in decision-making commonly uses one or more information systems.

The Information Technology Concept

The underlying concept of IT is that it is a system that works in conjunction with the business system—like an overlay that helps conceptually chart, support, and verify the business plans, directions, and strategies. It does this by asking these questions during the development process:

> What is the strategic purpose of the system or application?

> How is it going to fit in with and advance the business mission?

> In what ways does the new system complement the existing IT infrastructure?

> How compatible is the new system with the existing database and data architecture?

> Does the existing systems architecture (hardware, systems software) support the new system?

The better these questions are answered up front, the smoother the implementation of the new system. See the sidebar, "IT at Continental Airlines," for an example of such an IT plan well-executed.

IT at Continental Airlines

Continental Airlines introduced the E-Ticket, or electronic ticket, in 1995. Most airlines used, and continue to use, a paper ticket—a highly valuable document that requires an agent to prepare and print it, and then physically hand it to the customer.

The E-Ticket is an electronic document, identified by a confirmation number and customer information that is stored in the Continental database. Customers can make their reservation by phone or over the Web (www.continental.com), and then receive the confirmation number via fax or e-mail along with their itinerary.

Upon arrival at the airport, the actual ticket is obtained at the gate or retrieved from an E-Ticket machine (ETM). Additional benefits provided by this information system include pre-flight check-in, seat selection, logging the flight in the frequent flier program, and upgrades. The result of E-Ticket has been improved business processes, efficiency, and lower labor costs for Continental, more convenience for customers, and a reduction in paper.

Trends in Information Technology

All IT systems must be organized and designed to process information efficiently and economically. This is often called a computer architecture. A **computer architecture** is the design and implementation of computer systems in an organization. With the wide variety of peripherals and separate systems that must connect to the centralized computer, new computer architectures have emerged. A computer architecture is similar to a building architecture in that it determines how best to use physical facilities to help people get their work done efficiently. Many businesses have devised their own, whereas others are promoted by computer vendors. Some are enterprise-wide, whereas others have to do with specific aspects of the IT architecture. The following sections discuss a few of the current trends.

Client/Server Computing

Client/server computing is a hardware architecture that takes advantage of the processing power of two computers working together to perform a task. One is called the **client**, usually a PC, which is the "front end" of the system. The other is called the **server**, and it is the "back end" computer that holds data the client needs to process.

The server might be a mainframe, a mini, a workstation or even another, perhaps more powerful, PC. Although this architecture resembles the traditional distributed model with its mainframe and terminals, it differs significantly in that *both computers are involved in the data processing*. Each processes its data in the best way it knows how to; for example, if the user is working with a large DBMS (database management system) stored on the server, the PC downloads and uses only the data it needs; the rest stays at the server. If the server database is updated, that processing is done at the server. In addition, servers often serve more than one client PC, thus the need for more processing power.

Lawrence Shafe, author of *A Manager's Guide to Client/Server*, writes: "High-end client/server means rethinking the way in which information is distributed, accessed and presented, and also the way in which applications are developed and the tools used to develop them.

"...High-end client/server applications are critical to your business, that is, if the application stops, your business stops. These are sometimes called 'mission-critical' applications and they demand the highest standards of reliability and performance from the operating system and from development tools.

"...The justification for high-end client server is based on making the business more profitable by making the user more effective. The application of the technology is up to each organization to determine."[2]

Organizational Database Systems

DBMSs of all types are used everyday in business organizations. No modern enterprise can function without DBMS applications. In legacy systems, there was one enormous, centralized DBMS; today there still are, but there are many other specialized or departmental DBMSs as well. Here are some of the most common database systems in use:

➤ A *mainframe database* system is most useful when a homogeneous group works with the same data on a regular basis.

> ➤ A *distributed database system* is appropriate for organizations with multiple locations: offices, factories, distribution warehouses, retail outlets, and so on.

> ➤ A *client/server database* system is the most recent application for this computing architecture. DBMSs may be running on both clients and servers—wherever the knowledge workers need them.

It is often best if databases are centrally managed, even if they are primarily used by individual departments. Each department has access to the files they need, while common data can be shared between various departments. In a corporate system, there is often a centralized database that might contain accounting, employee records and other corporate data. Then there are a number of decentralized databases, specific to a department or function; for example, marketing may have its own customer database. All these databases may be running under a single DBMS application program, on a single mainframe or minicomputer.

Any data that is centralized can be shared with the decentralized databases, so everyone in the company sees a single, current file. With a DBMS, data-sharing is easier for everyone, and the data is more accurate and current. A well-managed database environment can make a major contribution to the company's success and productivity.

Data Warehousing

Data warehousing is becoming more prevalent in enterprises with vast amounts of data from which many people need to obtain information. A database has the same characteristics as a **data warehouse**, but is usually smaller and often designed and used by a single function or workgroup within the enterprise. A data warehouse collects information from the various legacy systems, a term that refers to the older databases. Often, smaller entities (termed datamarts) are built for groups. Then, as they grow, they are turned into a data warehouse.

Underlying the data warehousing process is the drive to create data-based knowledge and bring that knowledge to people who need it. The users employ a technique called **data mining** to obtain the information they need by analyzing data to discern significant patterns. While human analysts can see patterns in small data sets, specialized data mining tools are able to find patterns in large quantities of data. These tools also help analyze significant relationships that exist only when data from several sources is analyzed at the same time.

E-Commerce

Electronic commerce, or e-commerce, combines several computer and communications technologies—such as Electronic Data Interchange (EDI), electronic mail (e-mail), and the World Wide Web—to facilitate the exchange of information and to conduct business. EDI existed before the Web and provided a way for companies to exchange important business information—orders, inventory, financial information—but it was awkward and demanded that both computer systems be configured to exchange the data properly.

The Web provided a computing platform that anyone could use. It didn't take long for businesses to begin offering goods and services over the Web.

But there are many individuals and organizations that use the Web to freely dispense information and services, as well.

Thus e-commerce, whether for-profit or nonprofit, has changed the way we think about information-based transactions. It has replace many manual and paper-based operations with electronic alternatives. It has taught companies to simplify the way they present and use information. In many cases, that has led to cost savings; for example, if a company can get a customer to order information, such as a catalog, or even a product, using the Web site, that company has cut costs. They did not have to provide a toll-free phone number or a customer service representative to place the order.

IT at Amazon.com

International Data Corporation, a leading market research and consulting firm, predicts that a worldwide population explosion on the Web is underway with the number of Web users growing from 50.2 million in 1997 to 174.5 million in 2001. One e-commerce success story is Amazon.com, a virtual bookstore in Seattle, Washington. With no inventory, no books, no shelves, this company has sold nearly a million books to customers in a hundred countries over the past few years—all from its Web site (www.amazon.com). Although still striving to make a profit, Amazon.com earns substantial revenues and has taught the book publishing and bookstore industries new lessons in marketing. The next step in e-commerce is expected to be more of the big bookstore chains direct-marketing to customers—and possibly the publishers themselves.

Developing such applications puts the IT people on the forefront of marketing for the enterprise. It is their system that the customer is using, and the customer's satisfaction with that system—is it easy to use, fast, efficient, interesting—is going to make or break the sale. The Web is truly bringing the value of IT to business.

Lesson Summary

➤ Information technology (IT) refers to the complex computer systems used in a modern enterprise as well as the functional department or organization that creates and maintains those very computer systems.

➤ The IT system monitors, directs, and controls various processes to assure that the work gets accomplished properly, and that the business achieves its goals and objectives.

➤ IT systems are used by managers and knowledge workers at all levels of the enterprise. The most important objective is for IT to provide information to the right people at the right time, to help them make the best decisions.

➤ Once an IT system is up and running, the new system or application serves to collect data. Data is then stored, processed, and retrieved as strategic information.

➤ IT is a system that works in conjunction with the business system, like an overlay that helps conceptually chart, support, and verify the business plans, directions, and strategies.

➤ Trends in information technology include client/server computing, organization database systems, data warehousing, and e-commerce.

Lesson Review

Key Terms

client
client/server computing
computer architecture
data mining
data warehouse
electronic commerce
  (e-commerce)

Information Technology
  (IT)
project
server

Matching

Write the letter of the correct answer in the space provided.

_____ 1. The department or organization that provides computer systems and information services to the entire organization.

_____ 2. The head of the IT organization.

_____ 3. The act of obtaining specific information from a data warehouse.

_____ 4. A methodology and place for storing highly organized data, or information.

_____ 5. The computer that provides information to any number of users.

_____ 6. The term used to describe the design of enterprise-wide computer systems.

_____ 7. A computer that obtains information from another, but does its own processing.

_____ 8. An assignment to create a system or application.

_____ 9. The ability to do business from a Web site.

_____ 10. An emerging senior management position in the IT department.

a. project

b. CIO

c. CKO

d. information technology

e. server

f. client

g. e-commerce

h. architecture

i. data warehouse

j. data mining

Multiple Choice

Circle the letter of the correct choice for each of the following.

1. The modern computer systems that IT designs, installs, and maintains are primarily used to work with

    a. data

    b. knowledge

    c. information

    d. wisdom

2. A prevalent trend in modern enterprises is to align the IT department with business objectives to assure

    a. achieving business objectives

    b. achieving competitive advantage

    c. creating customer satisfaction

    d. all the above

3. The chief information officer

   a. programs mission-critical systems

   b. must be a male

   c. is charged with reengineering business processes to better utilize information

   d. all the above

4. The following are IT staff:

   a. programmers, business analysts, CKO

   b. programmers, system analysts, CKO

   c. programmers, system analysts, operations technicians

   d. application programmers, CKO, operations technicians

5. One of the key goals for IT is to deliver systems

   a. to senior management for approval

   b. to the right people at the right time

   c. for annual contests held by *InformationWeek*

   d. that fit into a hierarchical organizational structure

6. Typically, an IT project involves

   a. capturing data that is transformed into information

   b. processing the information to produce new, different information

   c. working quickly and efficiently to create mission-critical systems

   d. all the above

7. When applying the IT concept to business objectives, it is important to focus on

   a. strategic purposes

   b. expanding the influence of IT

   c. creating customer satisfaction

   d. working with existing systems

   e. all the above

   f. a, c, and d

8. The E-Ticket is an example of

   a. client/server computing

   b. e-commerce

   c. good use of database information

   d. how IT can streamline and improve business processes

9. The client/server architecture

   a. allows two computers to process work together

   b. requires an IT professional to work at the server

   c. always utilizes PCs

   d. is a way to avoid using legacy systems

10. E-commerce

   a. is a way to sell IT over the Web

   b. is a new marketing channel that heavily involves IT

   c. requires e-mail

   d. requires the use of more computers in the enterprise

Completion

In the blank provided, write the correct answer for each of the following.

1. The IT department was formerly known as _____.

2. The main service IT provides is the dissemination of _____.

3. The CIO must be familiar with both _____ and _____.

4. The IT staff that work in other departments to develop new applications are known as _____.

5. An important function of the IT staff in serving users is the _____.

6. There is a growing _____ of skilled and trained IT professionals.

7. A _____ project usually involves specifying both hardware and software.

8. The most important application in the enterprise is _____, or _____.

9. The CIO must determine the best _____ to supply the necessary computer systems and applications for the organization.

Review

On a separate sheet of paper, answer the following questions.

1. Explain how IT is both a concept and a functional department.

2. What is the IT organization expected to deliver to users?

3. Who is the head of the IT organization?

4. What is an emerging new occupation in the IT organization?

5. Why does it make sense to retain the best and brightest MIS knowledge workers?

6. What type of organizational structure lends itself to the best use of Information Technology?

7. What term is used to describe building a new system or application?

8. What is the most important architecture trend in IT?

9. What is the latest database trend in IT?

10. What is the latest Web-based trend in IT?

Critical Thinking

On a separate sheet of paper or in a group discussion, consider the following.

1. What makes the IT department's responsibilities so important?

2. What skills and abilities, both technical and business, contribute to the CIO's success?

3. Discuss IT's progression of managing the enterprise resource, from data to information to knowledge, and why this is significant.

4. What are the benefits to a flatter organization using a client/server architecture?

5. Discuss how the IT department, as it develops Web-based applications, is becoming more responsible for business success.

Further Discovery

Management Information Systems: Managing Information Technology in the Networked Enterprise, Third Edition. James A. O'Brien (Burr Ridge, IL: Irwin, 1996).

Information Systems: A Management Perspective. Steven Alter (Reading, MA: Benjamin/Cummings, 1996).

Management Information Systems: Organization and Technology. Kenneth C. Laudon and Jane P. Laudon (Englewood Cliffs, NJ: Prentice Hall, 1995).

On-line Discovery

Learn more about the job of a CIO and IT department at these Web sites:

➤ **www.cio.com** is the Web site for CIO magazine, a publication devoted to the senior managers of IT

➤ This Yahoo! site lists many resources for studying IT and MIS: www.yahoo.com/Business_and_Economy/Management_Information_Systems/

➤ Babson College's Center for Management Information Studies is a learning organization for IT management, educators, and students alike: www.babson.edu/cims/.

---

1 Peter G.W. Keen, *Every Manager's Guide to Information Technology*, Boston: Harvard Business School Press, 1995, p. 185.
2 Lawrence Shafe, *A Manager's Guide to Client/Server*, Wokingham, England: Addison-Wesley, 1994, pp. 1.6.

CHAPTER 5
Personal Productivity Software

Program packages that help you use personal computers to improve your work are called productivity software. You use these packages to become more productive. The number and variety of productivity software packages are growing. Word processing and electronic spreadsheets have been available for microcomputers for more than fifteen years.

Lesson 5A looks into word processing and desktop publishing. These are some of the most commonly used applications today.

Lesson 5B explores electronic spreadsheets and briefly considers the graphics they can produce.

Lesson 5C covers database management systems and file management systems. Never, until the introduction of these data-organizing tools, has collecting and manipulating data been so easy.

LESSON 5A

Word Processing and Desktop Publishing

Outline

Historical Overview: Printing Becomes a Mass Medium
Basic Features of Word Processing Software
    Writing
    Editing
    Formatting
    Saving
    Printing
Additional Features of Word Processing Software
Word Processing and Writing Quality
Desktop Publishing
    Determining Page Layout
    Entering Text and Graphics
    Formatting
    Saving
    Printing
Desktop Publishing Versus Word Processing

Learning Objectives

When you have finished reading this lesson, you will be able to

➤ Discuss the evolution and impact of printed media

➤ Describe how word processing software can help users

➤ List the tasks in producing a word processing document

➤ Explain the key features of word processing software

➤ Discuss the purpose of desktop publishing software

➤ Describe how desktop publishing and word processing software are related

QUE Lab
➤ **Word Processing**

More than 85 percent of the personal computers in existence today are equipped with word processing programs. With word processing software, you can write, edit, store, and print your work. Very few people who have tried word processing would consider going back to a paper-and-pencil method!

Learning to use a word processing program is an excellent step toward computer literacy. While you learn basic computer concepts, you learn a valuable skill also. This lesson introduces the basic features of word processing.

Historical Overview: Printing Becomes a Mass Medium

Historically, word processing can be seen as the latest step in a long process. This step has placed in the hands of the individual user the capability to print one's work.

printing press – invented by Johannes Gutenberg

The invention of the printing press and the use of movable type revolutionized communication. Johannes Gutenberg is credited with inventing the printing press in Germany in the 1450s, but movable type was used in Korea a half century earlier.

Before the invention of movable type, a person had to hand-carve the letters on blocks or stamps in order to make more than one copy of a document. The blocks were then dipped in ink and pressed onto textile or paper. Only the most important documents were duplicated. With the use of movable type, printing became a means of mass communication. Education (teaching, reading, and writing) became available to more people, and printing became the major weapon against mankind's greatest enemy—ignorance.

The printing press, however, did not make it easier for an individual to produce a document. Producing a document still required a pen or pencil. Then, in 1874, the company of E. Remington and Sons introduced the typewriter. A typewriter produced a document with characters of uniform size. Now a neater, more readable document could be produced more quickly.

Import – bring information from one program to another

The computer brought about tremendous changes. The first **word processors** were special-purpose machines designed solely to perform word processing. The special-purpose word processor included a typewriter or printer that produced top-quality printed material.

Later, **word processing software** was developed for use on general-purpose computers. This software offers several advantages over a special-purpose word processor. One advantage is that the general-purpose computer can perform other tasks besides word processing. A second advantage is that word processing software can be frequently updated with new features and capabilities. Documents produced can also be imported into other programs. As you learn in this lesson, desktop publishing programs can import documents from many word processing programs. Using a personal computer and word processing software to produce documents can dramatically improve your productivity.

 **TechTalk**
Bringing information from one program to another is called importing.

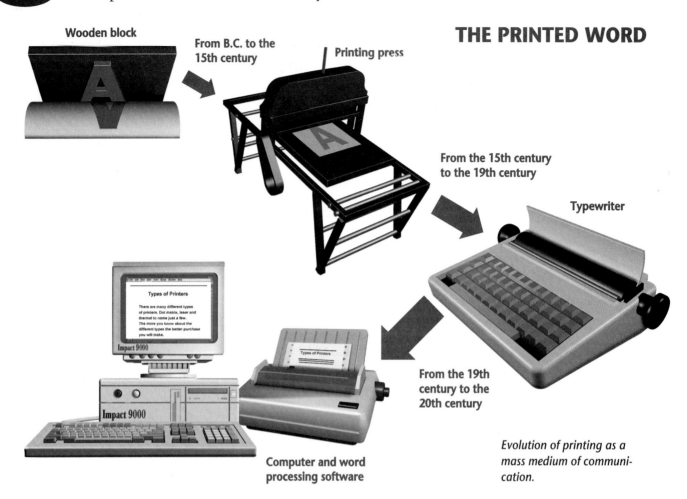

Wooden block

From B.C. to the 15th century

Printing press

THE PRINTED WORD

From the 15th century to the 19th century

Typewriter

Types of Printers

There are many different types of printers. Dot matrix, laser and thermal to name just a few.
The more you know about the different types the better purchase you will make.

Impact 9000

Impact 9000

From the 19th century to the 20th century

Computer and word processing software

Evolution of printing as a mass medium of communication.

Today, word processing programs are the most popular category of software packages. Many word processing programs are available. A few of the most popular packages are WordPerfect, Microsoft Word, and Word Pro for IBM and IBM-compatible personal computers; and Microsoft Word and MacWrite for Macintosh computers.

The Help features of today's word processing programs, such as WordPerfect, contain a great deal of information.

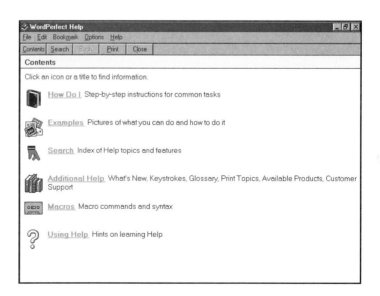

Basic Features of Word Processing Software

Word processing programs enable you to write, edit, format, save, and print a document with ease. Using word processing software, you can produce a high-quality document in much less time than if you used a typewriter. The reason is that word processing software separates document creation from document printing. With a typewriter, as soon as you type a word, that word appears on paper. If you need to correct a word in a typewritten document, you must erase the word somehow and then type the correction in the exact same spot. A word processing program, however, enables you to create a document, check it for spelling, edit it for style, format it for presentation, and save it for later retrieval. And you can do all these tasks before you print your document. The result is a more polished document that you have carefully planned, edited, and designed before you print it.

With word processing software, you can spend most of your time writing and editing your document. You can experiment with several ways of formatting the document and choose the way that looks best. Then you just press a few keys to tell the program to save and print the document.

Producing a Document
Writing
Editing
Formatting
Saving
Printing

Writing

With a word processing program, you can enter your work without being concerned about how the document will look. Instead of listening for a typewriter's warning bell to tell you when to begin a new line, you can continue to type. The software program recognizes when to begin a new line and automatically moves words to the next line. This capability is called **word wrap**. The only time you need to press the Enter key is at the end of a paragraph. In most word processing programs, whenever you press Enter, you create a new paragraph. The term **paragraph** simply means a unit of text that begins and ends with an Enter keystroke.

TechTalk In a word processing document, a paragraph can be a character, a line, or a group of sentences.

In addition, a word processing program automatically determines when to begin a new page. When you include footnotes, footers, or headers, the software adjusts the size of the page and begins each new page correctly.

Editing

Editing your document is much easier and more efficient with a word processing program than with a typewriter. While editing, you can use either insert mode or typeover mode. In **insert mode**, the software moves the rest of the text to the right as you type the new material. In **typeover mode**, the new material replaces (types over) the existing text.

Editing includes deleting text. Three ways of deleting text are possible. You can use the Delete key to delete the character to the right of the cursor. You can use the Backspace key to delete the character to the left of the cursor. Or you can mark (highlight) one or more consecutive characters and delete them all at once. With each method, the remaining characters are moved over to fill the space where the deletion occurred.

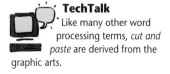

TechTalk Like many other word processing terms, *cut and paste* are derived from the graphic arts.

Editing may include moving characters, words, phrases, sentences, paragraphs, or large blocks of text from one place to another within a document or even between documents. Moving text is often called **cutting and pasting** because the process involves cutting the text from one area and pasting it in another area.

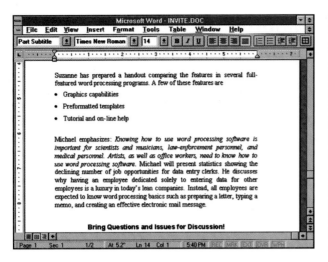

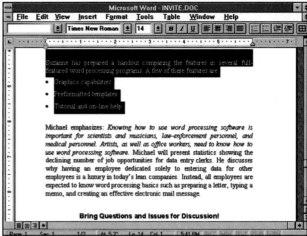

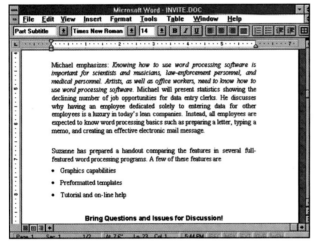

You can easily mark and move entire paragraphs with the cut-and-paste feature of word processing software.

font - complete set of character w/ same type face, style and size

default value - a common formatting value

This column uses justification for both left and right margins. This is a narrow column, and the spacing between words is distorted.

The find-and-replace feature is a handy editing tool. If you were writing a paper about "transcendental meditation," you could avoid typing that phrase by typing instead "tsm." When you are through with the paper, use find and replace to find "tsm" and replace it with "transcendental meditation." Of course, there are many other uses of find and replace.

Formatting

Formatting is the process of adjusting the appearance of the document. You can format an entire document, several paragraphs, one paragraph, or a single word or letter. Formatting includes moving and justifying margins, setting and moving tabs, adjusting line spacing, and changing fonts. Included also is the use of special effects, such as centering text, adding boldface, and underlining words. Even if you format a document while you enter it, you can change its appearance with new formatting at a later time.

Formatting options are set to commonly used values, known as **default values**, when you first load the program. Most word processing software includes default settings for margins (top, bottom, left, and right), tabs, and line spacing. You can change the settings, or you can leave the default values if they are satisfactory. For example, if your document includes numbers, your word processing software may let you use tabs to align the numbers on the decimal point. You can also change the line spacing from single to double to make your document easier to read.

Justification is the alignment of text at the left or right margin or at both margins. Left-justification aligns the beginnings of lines at the left margin; right-justification aligns the ends of lines at the right margin. Full justification aligns the text at both margins. With full justification, to align text at the right margin, a word processing program inserts extra amounts of space between words or characters.

Centering a heading or title usually takes the press of one or two keys. You can use **underlining** or **boldface** on part of a document either before or after you type the text.

A **font** is a complete set of characters with the same typeface, style, and size. Typefaces vary according to the programs you have installed. Common typefaces include Courier and Helvetica. Type styles include bold, italic, and underline.

Font size is measured in **points**. A point is 1/72 of an inch, and the size refers to the distance from the top of the tallest character to the bottom of the character that extends the lowest (such as *y*, *p*, or *q*). Generally, font sizes of 9 to 12 points are the easiest to read.

For you to use a specific font, your word processing program must be capable of generating that font, and your printer must know how to print it. With both these capabilities, you can print using the font.

> Times Roman is easy to read. Courier is a monospaced font. Helvetica and other sans serif fonts are sometimes used for headings and in tables. *Sometimes you lean toward italics;* **sometimes you feel bold;** <u>sometimes you need to underline your point!</u>

Saving

As you edit your document, you should save it regularly so that you don't lose it in case of a power failure. You usually instruct the word processing program to save your document on a secondary storage device, such as a disk. Later, you can recall the document and continue working on it.

All word processing programs restrict the size of file names. For example, DOS file names can have a maximum of 8 characters, and spaces are not allowed. Windows 95 and Macintosh file names can have up to 255 characters and can include spaces. Within these restrictions, you should use a file name that describes the contents of the document so that you can easily retrieve it again.

Printing

With word processing software, you can print your document whenever you want. It is usually more efficient to print the document after you have finished writing, editing, formatting, and saving. If you want to make changes after printing, simply make the modifications and print again.

Word processing programs include program extensions called **printer drivers**, which enable the word processing software to communicate with a printer. The printer driver translates the word processing program's formatting codes into commands that your printer can understand. Printer drivers are installed during software installation. Therefore, you don't need to worry about installing them unless you want to use a different printer. If you have a problem printing a document, make certain that your word processing software has been set up to communicate with the specific printer you are using.

TechTalk
A device driver is a software program that enables the computer system to communicate with a device such as a printer.

Additional Features of Word Processing Software

The complete list of features in a full-featured word processing program is too long to discuss in this lesson. You will learn about many of these features when you learn the specific procedures for using your program. This section describes a few special features included with most word processing programs: spell checker, thesaurus, style and grammar checker, mail merge, and macros.

A **spell checker** looks up your words in an electronic dictionary. If a word is not in the electronic dictionary, the spell checker highlights the word and asks you to make a decision. Usually, the spell checker suggests one or more replacement words with similar spelling. If the word you intended to use is listed, simply select it, and the spell checker makes the substitution. If the word is spelled correctly but is not in the dictionary, you can tell the spell checker to ignore the word, or you can add it to the dictionary.

You can ask an **electronic thesaurus** for a list of synonyms for a word if you feel that you are using a word too often. When you indicate the preferred word, the program will substitute it.

A **style and grammar checker** may be included with your word processing program. (You can also buy this kind of checker and install it to work with your program.) Style and grammar checkers are powerful programs, but you should use them wisely. Word processing programs on larger computers often have more sophisticated grammar checkers than those for microcomputers.

With **mail merge**, you can merge a list of names and addresses with a form letter, producing a "personalized" letter for each individual on the list. People who loathe junk mail may regret the development of mail merge, but using this capability can be a substantial time-saver.

Many personal productivity program packages give you the ability to create macros. A **macro** is a keystroke or series of keystrokes that you define to automate a series of actions. Using macros to automate repetitive tasks often can boost your efficiency.

Word Processing and Writing Quality

Word processing programs make writing easier. Never in history has it been so easy to present an attractive, visually appealing document. But a word processing program cannot guarantee good writing. To be effective, a document must contain a purposeful message and forceful ideas. Most of all, a document must be organized in a clear and logical manner. These tasks require human creativity and skill.

Some people think that word processing works against writing quality, encouraging poor revision habits. Instead of correcting a poorly organized paragraph, you can just add some explanatory sentences. The result is a poorly organized paragraph that's too long! Another drawback of word processing is that you can see only part of a page of text at a time; this limitation makes it hard to remember your document's overall organization.

You can offset these disadvantages by following three simple rules. First, delete poorly worded passages and start over with an improved plan. Second, use a carefully defined outline. Third, print your document and check its organization; then go back to the word processing program and reorganize the text, if necessary.

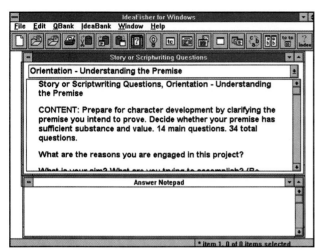 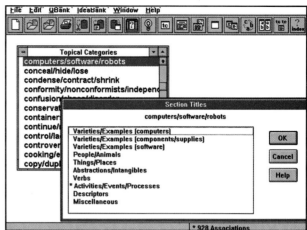

Desktop Publishing

Desktop publishing (**DTP**) combines text, graphics, and advanced formatting to create a visually appealing document. Early word processing programs were designed to work mainly with text; desktop publishing programs import text and graphics from other programs and combine them into an attractive layout. Recent releases of word processing software have incorporated many features of desktop publishing, blurring the distinction between the two applications. Therefore, many of the features described in this section are now included in both desktop publishing programs and full-featured word processing programs.

When you desktop-publish a document, you do five basic tasks. First, you determine the layout of the page. Next, you enter the text and graphics, or you import them from other sources. Then you format the document, save it, and print it.

Determining Page Layout

Before you begin working with the actual text, you should determine how you want the final document to look. It may help to sketch the layout in pencil. Some programs include a **toolbox** with icons and buttons for designing a **master page** on-screen.

Page elements include margins, columns, headers or footers, and page size. When determining margins, you must consider any folding or binding that the final document will have. You must decide whether to use one or two columns, or more than two. Layout decisions also include whether to use a header or footer and what information it should contain. The page size affects whether you should use **portrait mode** (the lines of type are parallel to the short edge of the paper) or **landscape mode** (the lines of type are parallel to the long edge of the paper).

Entering Text and Graphics

You can enter both text and graphics directly into many word processing and desktop publishing programs. However, it is usually easier to use a word processing program to enter text, and a graphics program to prepare graphics. Then you can **import** the graphics and text into the page.

IdeaFisher is a program that helps writers and speakers generate, organize, and edit ideas.

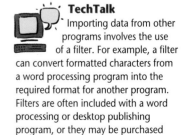

TechTalk
Importing data from other programs involves the use of a filter. For example, a filter can convert formatted characters from a word processing program into the required format for another program. Filters are often included with a word processing or desktop publishing program, or they may be purchased separately.

The New Novel

Twenty years ago, people were predicting that the computer would mean the death of the printed word. Like many other things in the Information Age, the computer has not eliminated anything, but rather has added dimensions. Take books: The printed novel—a fictional, imaginary story—continues to thrive but has also found new form in software and online versions. These new, computer-based forms involve writing, and you can be sure that the authors used word processing. Some forms include text and graphics, and others are more graphics than text.

All contribute to an emerging new art form that has many names. It has been called *hypertext* or *hypertext fiction*. Hypertext is a method of preparing and publishing text, ideally suited to the computer, in which readers can choose their own paths through the material. Hypertext applications are useful for working with massive amounts of text, such as encyclopedias. An example of nonfiction hypertext that users encounter regularly is the Help feature built into most applications. Clicking key words that appear in color or with underlining takes you to other related topics. The reader can pursue trails that fork off in alternate directions, which is why this text is often referred to as *tree-based text*. This feature becomes more interesting when you are reading a hypertext novel. Here are a few descriptions:

From "Hyperfiction: Beyond the Garden of the Forking Paths":

"Computer-based fiction ranges from straightforward electronic books with search features to highly interactive texts that invite the user to choose alternative plots, experience a scene from a different character's point of view, or call up information on topics of interest. . . . The principal publisher of the new electronic fiction is Santa Monica, California's The Voyager Co., whose Expanded Book Series repackages classics such as John Steinbeck's *Of Mice and Men* and bestsellers like Michael Crichton's *Jurassic Park*."[1]

From "Tree Fiction on the World Wide Web":

"Hypertext fiction [is] called 'tree literature,' or 'plot branching,' or 'choose your own fiction.' It consists of short sections of conventional narrative, each ending with a choice for the reader that determines what happens next and thus which section of the narrative should be read next. When presented on paper, such a fiction usually consists of numbered paragraphs connected by directions.

"Tree literature reached the masses with the publication of the 'choose your own adventure' series (beginning in 1981 with *The Circus* by Edward Packard and now numbering more than eighty titles) and the 'fighting fantasy' series (beginning in 1982 with *The Warlock of Firetop Mountain* by Steve Jackson and Ian Livingstone). Both series are adventure stories for children, almost entirely in the science fiction and fantasy genres, and presented as games rather than stories, the aim usually being to complete some task specified at the start of the book by finding the (often unique) sequence of choices that takes you from the start section to the winning section."[2]

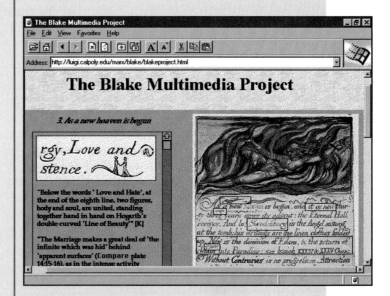

This hypertext version of the poet William Blake's illuminated manuscripts is available on the Internet at http://luigi.calpoly.edu/Marx/Blake/blakeproject.html.

---

1 Domenic Stansberry. "Hyperfiction: Beyond the Garden of the Forking Paths," NewMedia, May 1993, 52–55.

2 Gareth Rees. "Tree Fiction on the World Wide Web," posted September, 1994.

Graphics include drawings, graphs, photographs (scanned into an appropriate file format), and clip art. **Clip art** images are basic pictures of everyday objects. Several word processing programs provide clip art images that can be installed.

Graphics images are usually placed within **frames** or graphics boxes so that you can easily position the images. You can **anchor** a frame to a paragraph so that the image remains next to the appropriate paragraph even if the paragraph is moved. You can also trim, or **crop**, an image to show only part of the original image. You can determine the amount of white space to include around the image, and you can wrap text around it.

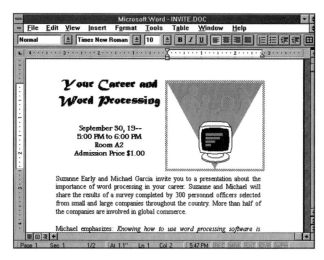

Some word processing packages include clip art images for use in documents.

Formatting

Deciding what font to use is an important formatting consideration. As in word processing software, a font is a complete set of characters with the same typeface, style, and size.

Because fonts convey different messages, it is important to select an appropriate font for your message. Some fonts are **display fonts**; others are **body text fonts**. Display fonts are eye-catching and help focus attention, but they are difficult for sustained reading. Body text fonts are not decorative; they are designed to be read easily. Frequent font changes are distracting.

DECORATING WITH STYLE

Acapella	Cache Heavy	Freshet	Jasper
Bangle	Chickadee	Fulton	Klaven
Ballet	Dayton	Gangplank	Legacy
Aeroplis	Egbert	Hamlet	Mesmer

Desktop publishing programs often include many decorative fonts.

You can use a **monospaced font** or a **proportional font**. Old typewriters have monospaced fonts. Every character takes exactly the same amount of space even though some characters are smaller and don't need as much space. Proportional fonts take different amounts of space, based on the shape and needs of each character. For example, the letter *I* requires less space than the letter *m*.

Proportional fonts place more characters on a line and closely resemble printed text. For these reasons, your proportional-text documents will look best if you follow these formatting guidelines:

➤ Use shorter lines or wider margins. For example, use 1.5 inches rather than 1 inch.

➤ Shorten the indentation for the first line of a paragraph from 0.5 inch to 0.2 inch.

➤ Use only one blank space instead of two at the end of a sentence.

Spacing generally refers to the spaces not used by the characters. For readability, you need to consider both the line length and the **leading**—the space between the lines. The longer the line, the more leading you need. **Kerning**, also called tracking or character spacing, is the

adjustment of the spaces between characters and words. The kerning that is performed automatically in the body of the text is usually adequate. In headlines or titles, however, you may want to do manual kerning to improve readability.

> Appropriate spacing between lines makes your message easier to read. The space between the lines is called leading. Leading is a printing term that originated when lead strips were inserted between lines of type to add space.

Creating a style sheet often simplifies the process of setting up a document. A **style sheet** contains such information as the font, indentation, column widths, and margin spacing. You should keep the style sheet in a separate file so that you can apply the style sheet to more than one document. One style sheet can include many different formats, which can then be applied to appropriate paragraphs in a document. A document heading, for example, would have a different format from the text within the document.

Saving

With any program, you should save the document on disk as you work. Saving the finished document before you print it is important. If you want to experiment with different effects, you can save the document under different names.

Printing

Most word processing and desktop publishing programs enable you to preview your finished document before you print it. Using the print-preview feature can save you time, paper, and frustration. When the document appears the way you want it to look, you can print only one page or the entire document. Be prepared—you will be impressed with yourself the first time your document comes out of the printer.

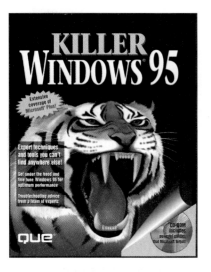

These covers were generated with QuarkXPress. The graphic elements are beyond the capabilities of most word processing programs.

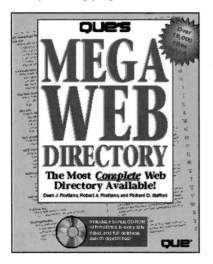

Desktop Publishing Versus Word Processing

Many word processing programs include desktop publishing features. However, a desktop publishing program can more easily handle documents that have a complicated layout, use various typefaces, and require many graphics. With a desktop publishing program, small variations in the size and spacing of type are possible. A desktop publishing program can produce more variety in type sizes and styles and more precision in spacing. Placement of text and graphics is often easier with a desktop publishing program than with a word processing program. QuarkXPress and PageMaker are examples of two popular desktop publishing programs.

Lesson Summary

➤ Word processing technology has placed printing capabilities in the hands of computer users.

➤ With a word processing program, you can write, edit, format, save, and print a document.

➤ Editing with a word processing program enables you to add text in insert mode or typeover mode. You can also move text by cutting and pasting.

➤ Formatting involves changing the appearance—for example, with justification, underlining or boldface, and different fonts.

➤ Most word processing programs enable you to check your spelling. Advanced programs add such features as an online thesaurus, grammar checking, mail merge, and macros. *repeated actions*

➤ With desktop publishing software, you can combine text and graphics to create visually appealing pages.

➤ Style sheets help the writer create a uniform appearance by controlling the spacing, the use of fonts, and the amount of indentation.

➤ Some word processing programs include desktop publishing features, but desktop publishing programs are better for complicated layouts, such as those of newsletters, newspapers, and magazines.

Lesson Review

Key Terms

anchor	font	mail merge *personalized*	style and grammar checker
body text font	formatting	master page *shows final look of document*	style sheet
boldface	frame	monospaced font *Courier*	toolbox *program w/ icon or buttons*
clip art	import	paragraph	typeover mode
crop *—to trim an image*	insert mode	point *1/72*	underlining
cutting and pasting	justification	portrait mode *short edge*	word processing software
default values *common or forced*	kerning *character spacing*	printer driver	word processor
desktop publishing (DTP)	landscape mode *long edge*	proportional font *diff amount of space*	word wrap *—automatically moves words to next line*
display font	leading *space bet line of text*	spacing *—not use by characters*	
electronic thesaurus	macro *automate one or more actions*	spell checker	

Matching

In the blank next to each of the following terms or phrases, write the letter of the corresponding term or phrase.

_____ *c* 1. Kind of typeface

_____ *b* 2. Equals 1/72 of an inch

_____ *f* 3. To bring in from another program

_____ *e* 4. Used for character spacing

_____ *g* 5. Common abbreviation for desktop publishing

_____ *a* 6. Begins and ends with Enter

_____ *j* 7. A keystroke defined to evoke *automate to bring to invoke* actions

_____ *h* 8. To align on the right margin

a. paragraph

b. point

c. Helvetica

d. crop

e. kerning

f. import

g. DTP

h. right-justification

i. Gutenberg *(printing press inventor)*

j. macro

_____ **9.** To trim a graphic image   crop

_____ **10.** Inventor of printing press   Gutenberg

Multiple Choice

Circle the letter of the correct choice for each of the following.

1. Writing, editing, storing, and printing a document using computer software are known as _____.

   a. word processing

   b. data processing

   c. productivity processing

   d. spreadsheet processing

2. Recognizing the end of a line and automatically moving the next word to the next line are known as _____.

   a. word return

   b. insert mode

   c. word wrap

   d. formatting

3. In _____, the software automatically moves the rest of the document to the right as you type new material.

   a. typeover mode

   b. editing mode

   c. insert mode

   d. justification mode

4. What do you call the program extensions that are included with word processing software to communicate with the printer?

   a. printer cards

   b. printer drivers

   c. printer helpers

   d. printer modems

5. What do you call commonly used settings that the software uses until you change them?

   a. preset values

   b. format values

   c. default values

   d. all of the above

6. What do you call the process of marking text and moving it to another area?

   a. mark and move

   b. justification

   c. formatting

   d. cut and paste

7. What feature do you use when you want to use word processing to automatically produce a "personalized" letter for a group of individuals?

   a. electronic thesaurus

   b. style checker

   c. mail merge

   d. desktop publishing

8. Which of the following combines text, graphics, and advanced formatting to create an appealing document?

   a. grammar checker

   b. desktop publishing

   c. kerning

   d. formatting

9. What do you call a complete set of characters with the same typeface, style, and size?

    a. style sheet

    b. anchor

    c. master page

    d. font

10. The words on the page are called _____; the drawings, graphs, photographs, and clip art are called _____.

    a. text, graphics

    b. graphics, text

    c. typing, displaying

    d. landscape, portrait

Completion

In the blank provided, write the correct answer for each of the following.

1. In _typeover_ mode, new material replaces existing text.

2. Adjusting the appearance of the document is called _formatting_.

3. _justification_ is the alignment of text at the left or right margin, or at both margins.

4. The feature that looks up words you type in an electronic dictionary is _spell checker_.

5. The page layout with the lines of type parallel to the long edge of the paper is _landscape_ mode.

6. When you bring already prepared text or graphics into a page, you are said to be _importing_ the text or graphics.

7. When some characters take less space to display than other characters, you are using a(n) _proportional_ font.

8. The space between the lines of text is called _leading_.

9. You can boost your efficiency by using _macro_ to automate keystrokes required to perform repetitive tasks.

10. Using word processing makes the process of typing a document separate from the final step of _printing_ the document.

Review

On a separate sheet of paper, answer the following questions.

1. What is the difference between word processing and desktop publishing?

2. What is the difference between word processing and data processing?

3. List the five tasks in producing a document.

4. What are the three ways to delete a set of characters from your document? When would you use each?

5. What does a printer driver do and why do you need one?

6. When would you use an electronic thesaurus?

7. What are the advantages of using desktop publishing software over using the advanced features of a word processing program?

8. What is a style sheet and why would you use one?

9. In what ways does word processing separate document creation from document printing?

10. What is the difference between a display font and a body text font?

Critical Thinking

On a separate sheet of paper, answer the following questions.

1. What analysis would you use to decide whether to buy a word processor or a general-purpose computer with word processing software?

2. Word processing and desktop publishing make the documents created look better than ever before, but there is still the question of the quality of the writing. How do word processing and desktop publishing improve the quality of writing? How do they lower the quality of writing?

3. It has been said that "freedom of the press is a right only if you own one." How can word processing and desktop publishing change that situation? What do you see as good and bad about that fact?

4. Find a magazine page that catches your eye. How did the editors of the magazine use graphics in the text, formatting, and layout? Support your answer with examples.

5. How do you think you could use formatting and page layout features to affect the reader's reaction to a document?

Hands-On Discovery

1. Most word processors, including ClarisWorks, WordPerfect, Microsoft Word, and Word Pro, have a "tables" feature, with which you can present information in tabular form. This is often one of the most useful, but more difficult to learn, features of a word processor. If you have access to a word processor that provides features for working with tables, use those features to try to create a table. Use the following sample data and try to make your table look similar to this example:

Team	Wins	Losses	Games Back
St. Louis	46	40	-
Houston	47	41	-
Cincinnati	39	42	4.5
Chicago	40	46	6
Pittsburgh	38	48	8

2. If you have access to a desktop publishing program such as PageMaker, Microsoft Publisher, or QuarkXPress, try to create a sample flyer for an event of some sort, such as a party, a concert, or a film. Try to make your flyer as visually appealing as you can, using graphics if you have access to some. See what your flyer looks like when it is printed.

Further Discovery

Electronic Publishing Unleashed. William R. Stanek et al. (Indianapolis, IN: Sams, 1995).

Special Edition Using Corel WordPerfect 7. Gordon McComb et al. (Indianapolis, IN: Que, 1996).

Special Edition Using WordPerfect 6.1 for Windows. Gordon McComb et al. (Indianapolis, IN: Que, 1994).

Using Word for Windows 95. Ron Person (Indianapolis, IN: Que, 1995).

On-line Discovery

You can access the Internet resources for the following questions by going to the Que Education and Training Web site at URL http://www.ciyf98.com/discovery. From this page, click the link for Lesson 5A and then click the link to the resource you want to access.

1. **Adobe PageMaker** (http://www.adobe.com/prodindex/pagemaker/details.html), **Microsoft Publisher** (http://www.microsoft.com/publisher), and **QuarkXPress** (http://www.quark.com /pi001.htm) are three very different but popular desktop publishing programs. Take a look at the Web sites for these three products. How do the sites differ? For what markets and what purposes are these sites intended? What kinds of tips and training do these Web sites provide regarding desktop publishing?

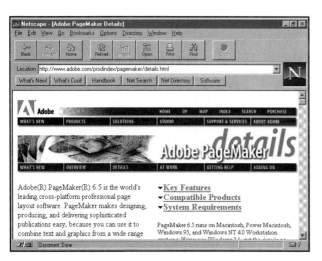
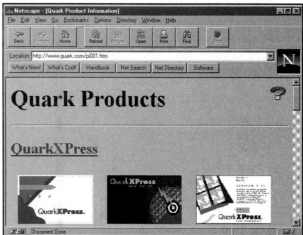

2. One of the more complex issues related to both word processing and desktop publishing is the issue of typography, or fonts. Countless fonts are available for use, and each has its own set of quirks. Not all fonts are supported by all printers or computers. Some fonts look different at different sizes, and different types of fonts are generally used for different purposes. Read some of the FAQ (frequently asked questions) about fonts from the **comp.font** Usenet newsgroup (http://www.ora.com/homepages/comp.fonts/FAQ). What are the different types of fonts, and how do they differ? What are some examples of popular fonts? What issues do font designers and users face?

LESSON 5B

Spreadsheets

Outline

Learning Objectives

When you have finished reading this lesson, you will be able to

➤ Describe the advantages of electronic spreadsheet software

➤ Discuss the features common to all spreadsheet programs

➤ List the parts of an electronic spreadsheet

➤ Explain how to create, save, and print a simple spreadsheet

➤ Describe the types of graphs that can be produced with a spreadsheet program

QUE Lab

➤ **Spreadsheets**

Pat and Tom stared intently at the computer screen. "What if we each work 15 hours a week instead of the 12 we're working now?" Pat asked. Tom typed the change into the electronic spreadsheet and looked at the monitor as the spreadsheet program automatically recalculated the totals. "It still isn't enough for that apartment near the campus," Tom observed.

Pat was getting desperate. He and Tom really wanted to move out of their parents' homes and be on their own this semester. Pat proposed, "The apartment is close enough that we can walk to classes. We could save as much as $15 to $20 a month on gasoline and parking." Again, Tom typed changes into the spreadsheet and watched as the program revised their budget. "No," Tom said, "we still won't be able to make it. Maybe if we each work 20 hours." Once more, Tom typed a new value into the computer. "That'll do it! Let's see if we can get our supervisors to agree!"

Scenarios like this one explain why electronic spreadsheet programs are used by millions of people. With a spreadsheet program, Pat and Tom just typed the column of numbers and a simple formula. The formula added the numbers in the column and displayed the sum. When they needed to change one or more of the numbers, they typed their changes, and the spreadsheet automatically recalculated the column and showed the correct numbers. Spreadsheet programs, in short, do for numerical work what word processing programs do for writing: They make it easy to revise your work until you get it just right. Many people use their spreadsheet capability to ask **what-if questions**, like the one posed in the preceding scenario.

Spreadsheets is for numerical work

Spreadsheets are used in a variety of careers and professions. For example, accountants use electronic spreadsheets to maintain and analyze inventory, payroll, and other accounting records. Businesses use electronic spreadsheets to prepare budgets and bid comparisons. Educators record grades on electronic spreadsheets. Scientists analyze the results of experiments on electronic spreadsheets. Stockbrokers use electronic spreadsheets to track stocks and keep records of investor accounts. Individuals use spreadsheets to create and track personal budgets and to calculate loan payment tables. This list is far from exhaustive, but it gives you an idea of the flexibility of electronic spreadsheet software.

Essentially, the function of a spreadsheet is to free you from tedious, repetitive computations and allow you to concentrate on analyzing and evaluating the results of those computations. Knowing how to use a spreadsheet program will not only enhance your career potential but also save you time and reduce frustration when you are working with numbers.

Advantages of Spreadsheet Software

People have long used accountant's ledger sheets to make calculations. These large sheets of paper have rows and columns for figures, along with headings that explain what these figures mean. An **electronic spreadsheet** has many advantages over a ledger pad. For example, an electronic spreadsheet, or simply **spreadsheet**, can calculate mathematical formulas automatically. You can change the numbers, and the software automatically updates the totals. You can add descriptive column headings and row labels at any time to make an electronic spreadsheet easier to understand. You can also include graphs in the electronic spreadsheet to help show trends and proportions.

productivity software
– word processing
– spreadsheets
– database management

Electronic spreadsheets can perform a variety of tasks to help people become more productive. Because of this advantage, spreadsheet programs, along with word processing packages and database management programs, are considered productivity software. Electronic spreadsheets are one of the most commonly used kinds of productivity software in the world. In fact, the success of the microcomputer is partly due to the creation of the electronic spreadsheet.

When the Apple II microcomputer was introduced in 1977, most companies viewed it as a toy. Dan Bricklin, an MBA student at Harvard School of Business, thought that the new microcomputer could help him complete his accounting assignments. He and a friend, Robert Frankston, who was studying computer engineering at MIT, decided to write a program to help with Bricklin's homework. They created the first electronic spreadsheet, known as VisiCalc (short for Visible Calculator), and formed a company called VisiCorp. Many people considered VisiCalc a major factor in making the Apple computer a success. Bricklin and Frankston later sold VisiCalc to Lotus Development Corporation. Lotus 1-2-3 has been one of the most successful spreadsheet programs on the market ever since.

Basic Spreadsheet Features

Although many different electronic spreadsheets are available, all spreadsheets work basically the same way. The features described in this section are common to all spreadsheet programs.

The Spreadsheet Screen

Different spreadsheet programs use different screen displays but have similar screen elements. The placement of the screen elements and the terminology vary, of course, from one program to another.

TechTalk
An electronic spreadsheet is sometimes referred to as a worksheet. Windows spreadsheet programs can open more than one worksheet at a time.

The Lotus 1-2-3 screen display is composed of the control panel, the work area, and the status line. The **control panel**, a special area usually at the top of the screen, contains the main menu and the edit line. The menu enables you to access the commands that are necessary for manipulating the spreadsheet, and the edit line provides information about the spreadsheet. Spreadsheets such as new versions of Lotus 1-2-3, Quattro Pro, and Microsoft Excel, which run under a GUI, provide **icons** below the control panel. You can use these icons to access frequently used commands without going through the menu system. The **work area**, where you build your spreadsheet, occupies most of the screen.

The **status line**, or status bar, is the bottom line of the screen. This line provides additional information about the status of the spreadsheet.

Operating Modes

Ready – idle and waiting for the user to enter data

Value or label mode – when user is entering data

Wait mode – when computer is doing internal computation

Spreadsheets function differently, depending on the type of operation currently being performed. These different manners of operation are known as operating modes. In Lotus 1-2-3, the **operating mode** is displayed in the status line at the bottom of the screen. A spreadsheet that is idle, waiting for the user to enter data or a command, is in *Ready* mode. When the user is entering data, the mode indicator displays *Value* or *Label*, depending on what is being entered. The mode indicator displays *Wait* when the computer is performing internal computations. Operating modes vary slightly depending on the program you are using.

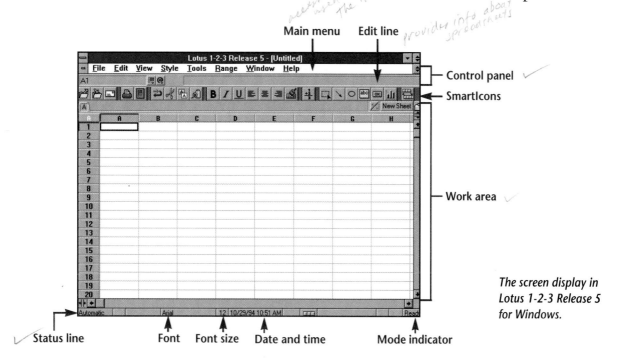

The screen display in Lotus 1-2-3 Release 5 for Windows.

Cells and Cell Contents

Electronic spreadsheets are composed of **rows** and **columns**. In spreadsheet programs, columns are designated by letters, and rows are designated by numbers.

An electronic spreadsheet contains many more rows and columns than are visible on-screen at any one time. Most electronic spreadsheets contain more than two hundred columns and several hundred rows. (After column Z, the columns are designated with two letters—AA, AB, AC, and so on.) Even though the entire spreadsheet is not visible at one time, you can work with any part of it. You use the arrow keys to move left, right, up, or down in the spreadsheet. If you need to see all of a large spreadsheet at one time, you must print it.

The intersection of a row and a column is called a **cell**. Each cell is identified by a unique **cell address** composed of the column and row designators. For example, the cell in the third row of the fourth column is cell D3. The **current cell**, also known as the **active cell**, usually has a highlighted border. When a cell is active, you can enter new data or change the data in that cell.

Different types of data can be entered into the active cell. You can enter a value, a label, a formula, or a function. A **value** is a number. Numbers are entered without symbols, such as dollar signs and commas, and then formatted so that the symbols are inserted automatically. A **label** is a heading or description that helps someone viewing the spreadsheet to understand it.

To enter values, labels, or other information into the spreadsheet, you don't type in the cell itself. Instead, you type in the **edit line**, or **cell entry line**, an area or a box usually located just above the worksheet. After you press Enter, what you typed appears in the cell.

Column C

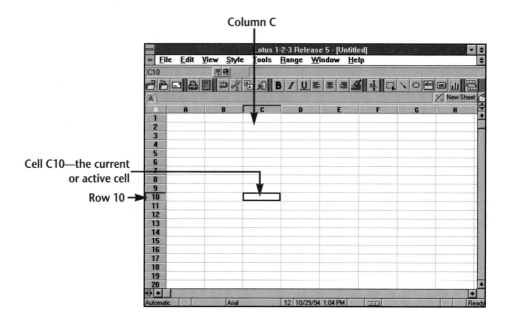

Cell C10—the current or active cell

Row 10 →

When you begin to type something in the cell entry line, the program tries to determine whether you are typing a value or a label. If you type a number, the program interprets it as a value. If you type a letter, the program interprets it as a label. To make a label consisting of numbers—for example, 1996—you must either format the cell for text, or begin typing with a special character (such as an apostrophe) that tells the program, "This is a label."

A **formula** includes one or more mathematical operators that indicate the computations to be performed. It may include operators for addition (+), subtraction (–), multiplication (*), division (/), and exponentiation (^), as well as other symbols. A formula may include cell addresses also. The advantage of including a cell address in a formula is that you can change the value in the cell referenced and immediately see the results of the change.

Formula in a cell entry line

In this Microsoft Excel spreadsheet, the student's average grade is calculated by a formula.

Label

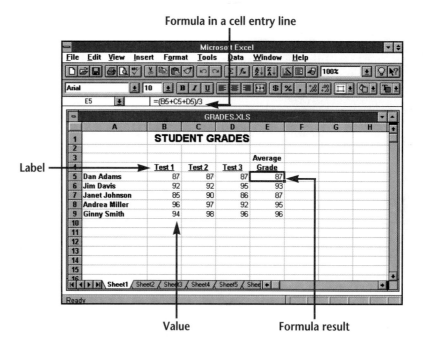

Value

Formula result

Because cell addresses begin with alphabetic characters, you must indicate when an item is a cell address instead of a label. (Recall that the program interprets as a label any entry beginning with a letter.) If the first item in a cell is a cell address, you must precede this cell address with a symbol such as a plus sign (+) or a minus sign (–). For example, the formula to add the values in cells B6 and C6 is +B6+C6. Some spreadsheet programs begin formulas with an equal sign (=).

When you enter a formula into a cell, the formula appears in the cell entry line. Only the result of the formula is shown in the cell after you press Enter.

Functions are built-in calculations that can save you time when you are entering complex formulas. Functions usually begin with a symbol such as an at sign (@) or an equal sign (=). The user then enters the range of cells on which the calculations are to be performed. Predefined functions that are commonly used include @SUM, @AVG, @MIN, @MAX, and @PMT. With Lotus 1-2-3, for example, you can enter the function @SUM(D10..D15) instead of +D10+D11+D12+D13+D14+D15.

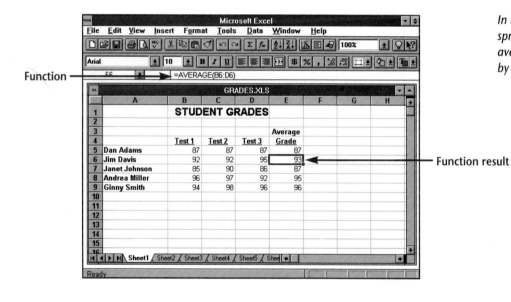

Function

Function result

In this Microsoft Excel spreadsheet, the student's average grade is calculated by a function.

Spreadsheet Navigation

To enter data into a cell, you must first move the cell pointer to that cell. In a small spreadsheet, you can use the arrow keys or the mouse to move around. In a large spreadsheet, you need a more efficient method. For this reason, many spreadsheet programs include both a vertical scroll bar and a horizontal scroll bar, which you can use with the mouse to scroll through the spreadsheet.

Spreadsheet programs also include special keys that enable you to move quickly from one location to another within the spreadsheet. Most spreadsheet programs provide a special key or a combination of keys so that you can move immediately from any cell in the spreadsheet to cell A1. With Lotus 1-2-3, you press the Home key to move to cell A1; with Microsoft Excel and Microsoft Works, you press Ctrl+Home to move to that cell. In addition, most spreadsheet programs have a function key or a pull-down menu item that you can use to go to a specific cell.

Ranges (Blocks)

Sometimes users need to perform a spreadsheet operation on a group of cells. A rectangular group of cells that is treated as a unit for a given operation is called a **range**, or **block**. A block can be formatted to look a certain way. For example, formatting a block to display percentages or dollar signs can improve the readability of a spreadsheet. You can also move or copy a block to a different location in the spreadsheet. Working with a range of cells can save time because you won't have to repeat operations for individual cells.

Commands

TechTalk
Menus in spreadsheet programs, like restaurant menus, provide lists of options from which you can make selections.

Like word processing programs, electronic spreadsheets enable you to perform many different operations on your data. You can use different spreadsheet commands to move, copy, insert, delete, format, and print the data in the spreadsheet. You use commands, for example, to change the width of columns on-screen. Commands are usually accessed through a menu system or icons.

Microsoft Excel provides examples, demos, and other help for performing basic procedures in the spreadsheet.

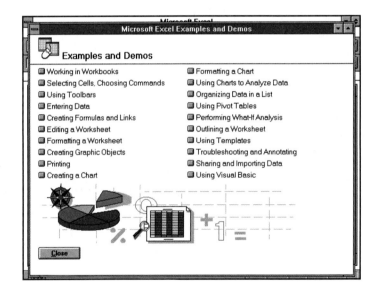

How to Create, Store, and Print a Spreadsheet

TechTalk
Microsoft Excel includes Wizards to guide you through some procedures. Wizards, also called "intelligent agents," prompt you to make choices and then provide information based on your choices.

All electronic spreadsheet programs work similarly even though each program has some unique characteristics. If you can create, store, and print a spreadsheet with one program, you can easily transfer your knowledge to another program. This section guides you through the main steps of creating, storing, and printing a spreadsheet. If you decide to create this spreadsheet, you may need more specific instructions for the spreadsheet program available to you. Most spreadsheet programs provide a Help feature for answering any questions you may have.

Remember Pat and Tom, the two friends who are trying to decide whether they can afford to move out of their parents' houses and rent an apartment together? They developed a spreadsheet to see whether they can afford the rent. What Pat and Tom learn is that they both will have to increase the number of hours they work per month (from 48 to 80) before they can make the move. How do they create the spreadsheet in the first place?

Financial Management for the Individual

One of the early justifications for getting a home computer was that you could balance your checkbook. The personal financial uses of a computer have come a long way since those days—now the computer can handle all your financial management needs.

Many stock brokerages are offering trading software that you can use to conduct all your stock transactions. One of the earliest companies to offer this type of software was Charles Schwab & Co., Inc. This company offers its StreetSmart software to anyone who keeps a required balance in his or her brokerage account or trades a certain amount of stock regularly. (For other people, the software is available at a nominal fee.) The idea behind the software is to enable you to transact stock trades and update your portfolio quickly and easily.

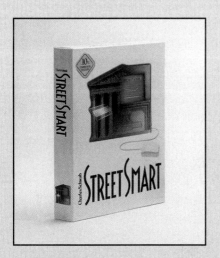

StreetSmart transactions are handled through the Charles Schwab computers. You connect to the computers using StreetSmart and your modem. This connection enables you to get the latest information and to transact your business quickly without the need for a salesperson to act as an intermediary. With StreetSmart, you can also use the Schwab financial network to get real-time quotes on various transactions. This capability enables you to determine quickly whether a transaction is in your best interests.

StreetSmart also enables you to get news and conduct research on different companies. For instance, you can download company reports on over 6,500 different companies. You can also use the software to connect to the Dow Jones News/Retrieval service or to Standard & Poor's MarketScope.

After you have conducted your transactions, your portfolio is updated automatically. Because your portfolio data is maintained by StreetSmart, you can review your portfolio any time—not just during business hours. The software can also organize information for IRS forms or print color graphs and reports.

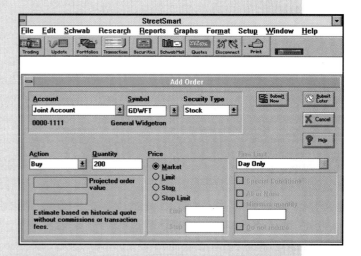

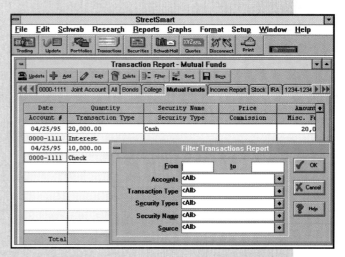

Building on the success of StreetSmart, Charles Schwab is starting to expand its software offerings. The company now also offers FundMap, which is a planning tool focusing on mutual funds. FundMap is designed to help guide your investment decisions today so that they lead to a sound retirement plan in the future.

Personal financial management has come a long way. And if the past is any indicator of the future, the ability to control your financial destiny will move more and more onto your desktop.

First, Tom types the row labels in column A and the column labels in row 3. (He uses both the mouse and the arrow keys to move between cells.) Next, he enters the values. In cell B4, he enters the number of hours that Pat works, and in cell C4, the number of hours that he works. Tom enters Pat's pay rate in cell B5, and his own pay rate in C5. He enters estimates for their expenses in cells D10 through D15. The remaining cells in the budget spreadsheet will hold the results of the calculations.

Tom begins each formula with a plus sign (+) so that the spreadsheet program will know that he's not entering a label. To calculate Pat's gross pay, for example, Tom enters +B4*B5 (Hours times Pay Rate). Deductions are calculated as 30 percent of Gross Pay (+D6*0.3). Tom then enters the remaining formulas.

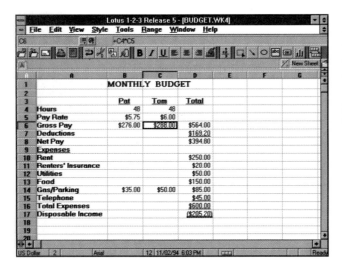

Pat and Tom's beginning budget, with each working 12 hours per week.

Pat and Tom's budget after increasing the hours each works to 20 hours per week.

From the screens, you can see that Tom has changed the data in the spreadsheet—from 48 hours to 80 hours. Notice that the results of the calculations, rather than the formulas themselves, are shown in the spreadsheet. Notice also that a negative number (Disposable Income) appears in parentheses. Do you see why working 12 hours each week is not enough for Tom and Pat to get their own apartment?

To save the spreadsheet, Tom uses the File command and then the Save As option. (The first time a file is saved, you must tell the computer the name of the spreadsheet file.) Tom names this spreadsheet BUDGET. Because he saved the file, he will be able to use it again later. Next, he uses the Print command so that he and Pat can show the spreadsheet to their parents. When the printed spreadsheet is complete, Tom exits the program.

Spreadsheet Graphics

Most people find it difficult to interpret a table of numbers. Graphics programs automatically fit the data on a single page so that it looks nice and is easy to read. With graphics capability, you can present your data as a graph and add titles and labels. Understanding a trend or a proportion is much easier when it is presented visually as a graph.

Most spreadsheet packages can produce line, bar, and pie graphs. You must identify the data block that you want the program to use; it does the rest automatically. Some spreadsheet packages can produce these images in a three-dimensional format and even rotate them. Several packages provide additional types of graphs, and some programs print the spreadsheet and the graph on the same page. Even more impressive, if you are using compatible programs, you can create a graph with a spreadsheet and copy the graph into the middle of a word processing document.

Bar graphs and **pie graphs** assist people in visualizing proportions. Bar graphs compare values. A pie graph displays each value in a range as a percentage of the total. You can "explode" a slice of a pie graph to highlight a particular value. Pie graphs are limited, however, to showing one series of data per graph. **Line graphs** provide a picture of trends over time.

The graphs included in spreadsheet packages are sufficient for many applications, but other applications require presentations that are more visually striking. Lesson 5A in the next chapter discusses more advanced graphics.

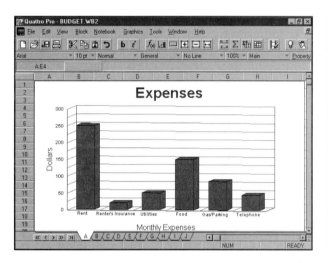

This three-dimensional bar graph shows Pat and Tom's budgeted expenses.

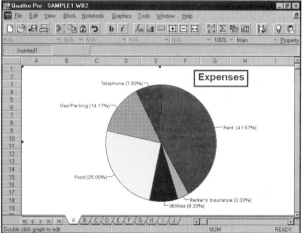

This pie graph shows Pat and Tom's budgeted expenses but expresses each expense as a percentage of the total expenses.

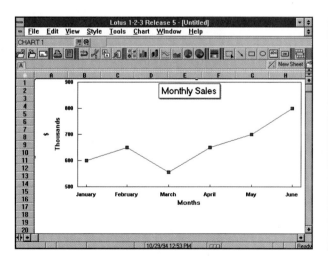

This line graph shows that monthly sales for the company declined in March and then increased in April, May, and June.

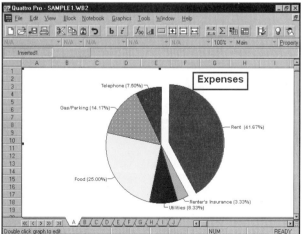

This pie graph shows the Rent expense slice exploded for additional emphasis.

BITS
Frequently, the design for a spreadsheet can be reused. A **template** is a worksheet with labels, formulas, and functions already entered. The template can serve as a form—all the user needs to do is type new data. Most spreadsheet programs come with templates for common applications.

Special Spreadsheet Features

Most spreadsheet programs enable users to develop macros. A **macro** is a set of operations that accomplishes a specific task. When you make a macro, you save the macro's keystrokes under a name that you provide. Later, when you issue the macro name, the entire set of operations is executed. Macros themselves are stored in a remote part of the spreadsheet that is not needed for data, and are saved along with the spreadsheet. Examples of tasks that can be saved as macros include printing a block of the spreadsheet, or inserting a row into the spreadsheet and copying appropriate formulas and functions into the new row.

Many new spreadsheet versions offer statistical analysis capabilities. These programs can quickly perform analysis of variance, regression analysis, and other complex statistical operations with a minimum of work by the user. The results of these operations can then be viewed and graphed.

Another special feature of many spreadsheet packages is data management. The data management capabilities of spreadsheets include creating a simple database, sorting records, and searching the database for a particular item. Each row of the spreadsheet becomes a record in the database, and each cell in the row is a field of the record. Database management is covered in detail in the next lesson.

Spreadsheet Tips

TechTalk
Lotus 1-2-3 Release 5 for Windows provides color-coded maps of several countries and cities so that users can display sales by geographical region.

Developing and working with a spreadsheet can be a frustrating experience. Use the following tips to make the experience more enjoyable and to improve the final product:

1. Plan your worksheet on paper before you begin working with the program on the computer. Think through the problem you want to solve; draw a rough sketch of the data on a sheet of blank paper or a ledger sheet. Jot down the mathematical equations you'll need to get answers. This planning saves you time, and you'll make fewer mistakes.

2. Learn to use the spreadsheet's powerful paste feature. You'll find it useful in creating a number of data entry shortcuts, and your data and formulas will be more accurate.

3. If your completed worksheet doesn't work, you'll have to edit and retest it. Copy the worksheet to another sheet, or save it with a different file name; then make corrections to the copy and test it. If the copy works, fine; if not, repeat the process.

4. When you build a spreadsheet model, even a simple one, you have created a template. Save it with the formulas but without any data; then you can use it over and over again.

5. Take advantage of the auditing function, if your spreadsheet has one. This feature is used to error-check your spreadsheet formulas.

6. Use the spreadsheet's built-in function features instead of typing complicated formulas. Functions are quicker and more accurate.

7. Enter a label in the cell above or to the left of the values you enter, to identify what the value represents.

8. If you see a cell filled with ######## characters, the column probably isn't wide enough to accommodate the data.

9. Learn to use macros, which are a way to record, save, and reuse frequently used commands, equations, and labels. With a macro, you can fill a cell with data by pressing a key or two rather than performing dozens or hundreds of keystrokes. In addition, macros are a convenient way to customize your keyboard.

10. Save your work often. If you're building a complex spreadsheet, saving each iteration as a separate sheet makes corrections much easier.

11. Check the results of formulas and functions to see whether they look reasonable. The spreadsheet will calculate results—even if you accidentally tell it to use the wrong cells!

Lesson Summary

➤ Electronic spreadsheet programs provide an easy way to work with rows and columns of numbers.

➤ The intersection of a row and a column is a cell. Every cell has an address made up of the column letter followed by the row number.

➤ Formulas produce sums and other results. If the formulas reference cells containing numbers, you can change the numbers and see the results right away.

➤ Spreadsheets can produce many types of graphs, including line, bar, and pie graphs.

➤ A range is a group of cells on which an operation is to be performed.

➤ A macro is a set of instructions that can be saved and used at a later time.

➤ Most spreadsheets include data management capabilities that enable a user to sort or search the rows of data.

Lesson Review

Key Terms

active cell	control panel	label	spreadsheet
bar graph	current cell	line graph	status line
block	edit line	macro	template
cell	electronic spreadsheet	operating mode	value
cell address	formula	pie graph	what-if question
cell entry line	function	range	work area
column	icon	row	

Matching

In the blank next to each of the following terms or phrases, write the letter of the corresponding term or phrase.

_e_ **1.** Provides information about the settings that are currently being used, as well as the date and time

_c_ **2.** A group of cells on which an operation is to be performed

_j_ **3.** A commonly used calculation that is built into the spreadsheet

_a_ **4.** Designates the intersection of a row and a column

_d_ **5.** Contains the main menu and the edit line

_b_ **6.** A group of instructions that accomplishes a specific task

_h_ **7.** A number that can be used in mathematical operations

_g_ **8.** Indicates the operation currently being performed

_i_ **9.** An equation entered into the spreadsheet by the user

_f_ **10.** The area where data can be entered or changed

a. cell address
b. macro
c. range
d. control panel
e. status line
f. active cell
g. operating mode
h. value
i. formula
j. function

Multiple Choice

Circle the letter of the correct choice for each of the following.

1. Which of the following is *not* descriptive of electronic spreadsheets?

  a. They can answer what-if questions quickly.

  b. They can include graphs to show trends and proportions.

  c. Column headings, row labels, and formulas are helpful features.

  d. They have complete desktop publishing capabilities.

2. Which one of the following types of graphs best represents trends?

  a. stacked bar

  b. bar

  c. line

  d. pie

Hands-On Discovery

If you have access to Lotus 1-2-3, Microsoft Excel, Quattro Pro, or another spreadsheet program, use it to create a simple worksheet that lists your entertainment expenses for a six-month period. Include your entertainment costs in at least four categories (such as hobbies, movies, concerts, videos, restaurants, and CDs). Experiment with various spreadsheet commands, such as those for copying and moving the contents of one cell to another, and for removing and inserting columns and rows. Try using formulas to find the total for each month's expenses and for each type of entertainment.

Further Discovery

Business Analysis with Excel. Conrad Carlberg (Indianapolis, IN: Que, 1995).

Easy 1-2-3 R5 for Windows. Trudi Reisner, revised by Janice A. Snyder (Indianapolis, IN: Que, 1994).

Excel for Windows 95 Essentials. Suzanne Weixel and Adrienne Seymour (Indianapolis, IN: Que Education and Training, 1996).

Excel for Windows 95 Essentials Level II. Jane Mack, Joyce Nielson, and Bill Brandon (Indianapolis, IN: Que Education and Training, 1996).

Managing Data with Excel. Conrad Carlberg (Indianapolis, IN: Que, 1996).

On-line Discovery

You can access the Internet resources for the following questions by going to the Que Education and Training Web site at URL http://www.ciyf98.com/discovery. From this page, click the link for Lesson 5B and then click the link to the resource you want to access.

1. **Lotus 1-2-3**, **Microsoft Excel**, and **Quattro Pro** are probably the three best-known spreadsheet applications. Examine their **product data sheets** at the following addresses:

Lotus 1-2-3	http://www.lotus.com/223.nsf
Microsoft Excel	http://www.microsoft.com/msexcel/default.htm
Quattro Pro	http://www.corel.com/products/wordperfect/cqp7/index.htm

   How do these programs differ? Can you tell what tools they offer for graphing and visualizing your data? What features do each of these three spreadsheets offer for working with the Internet?

   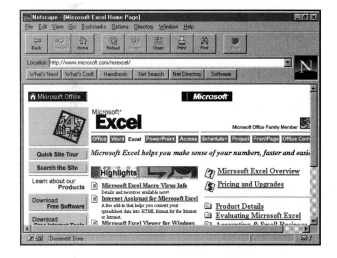

2. Take a look at the Yahoo! directory page on **Spreadsheets** at http://www.yahoo.com/ Business_and_Economy/Companies/ Computers/Software/Business/Spreadsheets. See how many completely different uses for spreadsheets you found. Are there any that surprise you? Are there any that you would find useful?

LESSON 5C

Databases

Outline

➤ **Database**

Learning Objectives

When you have finished reading this lesson, you will be able to

➤ Recognize potential uses of a database program

➤ Differentiate between a file management program and a database management system

➤ Describe four popular database structures

➤ Identify the parts of DBMS software

➤ Understand how a database is created and used

The true power of the computer lies in its capability to store, organize, and retrieve large quantities of data. Programs designed to accomplish these tasks are known as database programs. Some people associate the need to maintain large amounts of data with corporations and government offices. However, small businesses and even individuals can improve their efficiency by using database software. Both large and small companies use databases to maintain personnel files, inventory files, customer information, employee information, and accounting records.

For example, the Bulletin Boardroom maintains databases that enable stockholders to exchange views, communicate with company directors, and communicate with company representatives about issues concerning approximately 1,000 companies. (The Bulletin Boardroom was founded by Ross Kaplin in 1993, after the Securities and Exchange Commission changed the rules governing the way stockholders communicate with each other. Before this ruling, restrictions made it difficult for more than ten stockholders to confer about proxy votes.) The service, which can be accessed by modem, costs $2,000 per year. Officials anticipate 18,000 subscribers by 1997.

Imagine cataloging by hand the contents of the Library of Congress, the Smithsonian Museum, or the National Art Museum; then imagine trying to find in your catalog all references to Leonardo da Vinci. Now imagine doing the same tasks with a computer—storing all the information in a database program and then having the computer perform the search for you.

In the movie *Mission: Impossible*, the safety of all American undercover agents on assignment in Europe is endangered when a copy of a database file containing true names, as well as code names, falls into the wrong hands.

Although large organizations are major users of database management software, small businesses and individuals find them useful as well. You could use a database program to keep track of the addresses and phone numbers of friends. When they move, it's a simple matter to update the information in the database. Compare this method to using an address book, where you must cross out old addresses and telephone numbers and try to squeeze in new ones.

You can also use a database program to catalog collections, such as a baseball card or stamp collection, or a large assortment of tapes or compact discs. Another common personal use of database software is to maintain a household inventory. Think how helpful it would be to have a listing of all your valuable possessions if you became the victim of a burglary or a fire.

Even if you never develop a personal database, learning about database software is an essential component of your computer literacy. Many of the most troubling issues concerning computer use involve huge databases containing information about private citizens. Understanding how databases work can help you grasp why some people are concerned about privacy issues.

The Advantages of Databases

A **database** is a collection of data files that can be combined and treated as a unit for information retrieval purposes. As you recall from the discussion in Lesson 2B, computers use a hierarchy to store and retrieve data. Characters are combined to form a **field**, such as an item description. Related fields are combined to form a **record**.

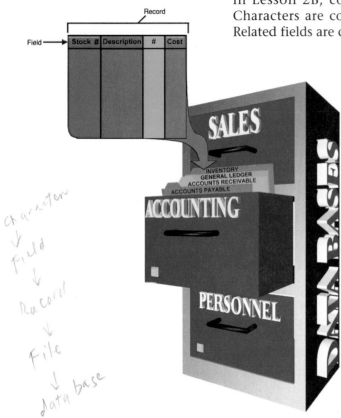

An inventory record, for instance, might include fields for the stock number, the description, the number on hand, and the cost. Records that relate to the same application are then combined to form a file, such as a company's inventory file. Files can then be combined to form a database. For example, the inventory, accounts payable, accounts receivable, and general ledger files can be combined to form a company's accounting database. An organization may have more than one database, each consisting of related files.

Traditionally, data or information was organized into separate files that were not related or combined in any way. However, this approach has three drawbacks: It produces data dependence, creates data redundancy, and does not guarantee data integrity.

Data dependence occurs when data files from different applications are incompatible and cannot be linked; the data is dependent on the application. A bank may have credit information about a customer in one application's file and have current account data in another application's file. For this reason, the credit and account data cannot be directly linked in a report.

When data is kept in a series of unrelated files, the inevitable result is **data redundancy**, or repetition of the same data items in more than one file. Repetition of data items wastes valuable storage space.

The traditional approach also endangers data integrity. **Data integrity** is the consistency of the data in all applications. When a field is repeated a number of times, all the occurrences may not be identical. Suppose that Ken moves to a new address in the same city. Soon after moving, he has new checks printed. If the bank maintains separate files for checking, savings, and loans, his address might be changed only in his checking file and not in his loan and savings files. As a result, Ken doesn't receive his car loan payment forms and doesn't pay on time.

Computerized databases reduce data redundancy and help ensure data integrity because they can link related files using a common field. In the preceding example, the bank could include a customer identification field in all checking, savings, and loan files. Then each customer would be given a unique customer identification number. Changing a particular customer's address in one file in the database would automatically change it for all the transactions involving that customer. (Ken would receive the car loan payment form at his new address.) To put this point another way, computer databases can **integrate** data from separate files. This capability to integrate files increases the flexibility of the data, reduces data dependence, and makes the tasks of modifying reports and adding new data items easier.

Database packages may also include **data security** features to protect the data from individuals not authorized to use it. Specified records or fields, as well as the entire database, can be restricted to prevent modification or access.

Types of Database Software

Two types of applications software have been developed to work with database files. File management programs can work with only one file at a time. Database management systems can work with several separate files at a time. This section describes both types of software.

File Management Programs

A **file management program** enables users to create customized databases and to store and retrieve data from these databases. File management programs come in handy when an individual or small business needs to set up a computerized information storage and retrieval system. A baseball card store, for example, could create a database of available baseball cards for customer reference.

Because file management programs are less complex than database management systems, they are inexpensive and usually easy to use. The ease of use comes at a price, though. File management programs create flat files. **Flat files** can be accessed sequentially when most of the records need to be processed, accessed randomly to retrieve a specific record, or sorted (so that the records can be accessed sequentially in a different order). The information stored in a flat file, however, cannot be linked to data in other files.

> **TechTalk**
> Similar to flat file systems that don't have subdirectories, flat database systems are not capable of accessing related tables of data or of relating information stored in two or more files.

Database Management Systems

A **database management system** (**DBMS**) can link the data from several files. A DBMS is usually more expensive and more difficult to learn than a file management program.

DBMS programs commonly use one of four database structures to link files: hierarchical databases, network databases, relational databases, and object-oriented databases.

Hierarchical Databases

Hierarchical databases, the first of the four database structures, were developed by IBM in 1968. A **hierarchical database** links data using a hierarchical relationship. In a hierarchical DBMS, a group of fields is called a **segment** rather than a record. The data element at the top of the hierarchy is known as the **parent element**. There may be several **child elements** beneath the parent element. Each of these children may, in turn, become a parent to several lower-level child elements. However, note that in a hierarchical structure, each segment can have only one parent. The structure that is created resembles a pyramid or an organizational chart.

The problem with a hierarchical database is that the data can be accessed only by following a path down the structure—access is not flexible. All the relationships among the data elements must be determined when the database is first designed. For example, suppose that a hospital maintains a hierarchical database file of all employees. Employees are categorized by the department in which they work (emergency room, intensive care unit, and so on). Within the department, employees are categorized by job function, such as nurses, doctors, and technicians. If the emergency room has a shortage of nurses one evening, producing a list of all nurses on staff would not be possible. Instead, the nurses assigned to each department would have to be determined department by department.

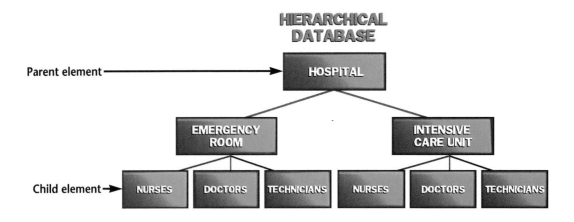

Parent element ——→ **HOSPITAL**

Child element ——→ NURSES DOCTORS TECHNICIANS NURSES DOCTORS TECHNICIANS

Many companies continue to use hierarchical databases even though the other database structures are superior. In addition, IBM still supports a hierarchical database on many of its mainframe computers.

Network Databases

The **network database** structure was developed by a **Conference on Data Systems Languages** (**CODASYL**). As in a hierarchical database, a network database organizes data in a parent-child relationship, and all the relationships among the data items must be determined during the design phase. In a network structure, however, a child can have more than one parent or no parent at all.

The relationship of students to college classes can be shown with a network structure. Each student may be enrolled in several courses, and each course includes a number of students. With a network database structure, you can produce both a student schedule (showing all classes that the student is enrolled in) and a class roster (showing all students enrolled in a class).

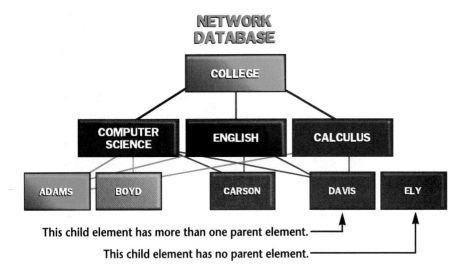

This child element has more than one parent element. ——

This child element has no parent element. ——

Relational Databases

Until recently, relational databases were considered the most flexible, and therefore most desirable, database structure. In a **relational database**, data in several files is related through the use of a common key field. The contents of a **key field** are unique to one record in the file, enabling the field to be used to identify a record. The computer uses this key field as an index to locate the records directly without having to read all the records in the files.

A relational DBMS is best envisioned as a two-dimensional table. Each row in the table corresponds to a record, and each column corresponds to a field. A relational database structure can link a customer file and an accounts payable file, for example, through the use of a common field, such as a customer account number field. The user can then request a report consisting of fields from both the customer record and the accounts payable record.

CUSTOMER FILE

Column = field

row = record

CUSTACCT	NAME	ADDRESS
101	Allen Adams	123 Row St. Cincinnati, OH 45208
102	Elizabeth Beets	Box 642 Mason, OH 45040
103	David Livesy	Hawkins St. Milford, OH 45042
104	Mollie Moore	Rogan Rd. Cincinnati, OH 45242
105	Oscar Price	Phipps Ave. Cincinnati, OH 45243

The CUSTACCT field is common to both files.

From the customer file

From both the customer file and the accounts payable file

From the accounts payable file

INVOICE	CUSTACCT	AMOUNT	PAID
1001	102	$2,500.00	NO
1002	104	$1,252.30	YES
1003	101	$250.00	YES
1004	102	$5,252.25	NO
1005	103	$1,300.50	YES
1006	105	$475.00	NO
1007	104	$325.75	NO
1008	108	$290.00	YES
1009	102	$3,468.00	NO

ACCOUNTS PAYABLE FILE

UNPAID INVOICES REPORT

CUSTACCT	NAME	INVOICE	AMOUNT
102	Elizabeth Beets	1001 1004 1009	$2,500.00 5,252.25 3,468.00
	Customer Total		$11,220.25
104	Mollie Moore	1007	$325.75
105	Oscar Price	1006	$475.00
Total			$12,021.00

Object-Oriented Databases

Object-oriented databases are the newest type of database structure and are likely to gain in popularity. In an **object-oriented database**, the result of a retrieval operation is an object of some kind, such as a document. Within this object are miniprograms that enable the object to perform tasks, such as displaying a graphic. Object-oriented databases can incorporate sound, video, text, and graphics into a single database record. This type of database is well suited for multimedia applications. A search of a health-related database, for example, could display a document that included pictures of healthful foods, videos of exercise techniques, and recorded lectures from health professionals. Object-oriented databases can have their data linked to different programs while using a hierarchical, network, or relational database structure.

Aldus Fetch 1.2 is a popular multimedia database program that supports several file formats for graphics, animation and video, sound, and text.

The Parts of DBMS Software

When properly prepared, database management systems enable people to access complex file systems with a minimum of difficulty. Most people are able to use a database management system without knowing about its

[handwritten margin notes: Components of DBMS - definition language - manipulation language - query language - report generator]

underlying structure (its fields, records, and files). This ease of access is made possible by the four components of DBMS software: data definition language, data manipulation language, query language, and report generator.

The Data Definition Language

The **data definition language** (DDL) is used to define the structure of the database. The structure, or **schema**, outlines the data to be included in the database. In the schema, each field in a record must be defined with a name, a field length, and a type. Common field types are numeric, alphanumeric, date, logical, and memo. Numeric fields can contain only the digits 0 through 9, a decimal point, and a sign. Alphanumeric fields can contain a combination of alphabetic characters, special symbols, and digits. A date field holds a single date. A logical field contains one of two possible values: Yes/No or T (true)/F (false). The value is placed there by the program as the result of a comparison or decision requested by the user. A memo field can be used to hold any type of reminder that the user might like to type.

> ### TechTalk
> A logical field assumes one of two values. For example, in a certain schema, a logical field might assume the value of Yes or the value of No.

[handwritten margin note: Schema - structure that outlines the data to be included in database]

A DDL can also define subschemas. A **subschema** outlines the fields that a user will be allowed to access. Different users can access different subschemas. The use of subschemas is an excellent way to protect the privacy of sensitive data items. For example, a payroll clerk should have access to salary data, but a salesperson should not have access to that data.

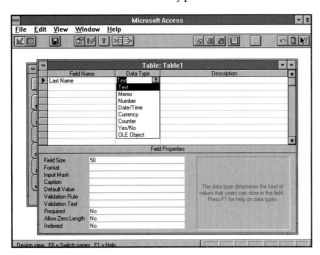

A drop-down list displays the data field types available in Microsoft Access.

The Data Manipulation Language

The **data manipulation language** (DML) includes all the commands that enable the user to manipulate and use the database. With these commands, the user can view the data, add new records, delete records, sort the records, and modify selected fields in a record. The data definition language and the data manipulation language are combined in some microcomputer database programs designed for use on only one computer because these programs have less need for security than mainframe database programs.

[handwritten margin note: DML - includes all command that users is able to manipulate and use database]

The Query Language

The **query language** enables users to ask specific questions of the database. A marketing vice president trying to decide which items to sell at a discount, for example, might ask a database program to list all inventory items with a profit margin greater than 30 percent. The most popular query language is **Structured Query Language** (SQL). SQL has been an industry-wide standard since it was first used on IBM mainframes in the 1980s. Today, SQL is used in database management systems on many platforms.

[handwritten margin note: Query - enables user to ask specific questions of the database]

The Report Generator

The **report generator** helps the user to design and generate reports and graphs in printed form. Report headings, column headings, page numbers, and totals are just some of the features that are easy to include with the report generator.

[handwritten margin note: Report Generator helps user to design and generate reports and graphs in printed form.]

Beyond the STATus Quo

Everything you ever wanted to know about a National Basketball Association (NBA) basketball game—and more—is right at your fingertips, thanks to StatMaster, a simple-to-use, online basketball statistics package.

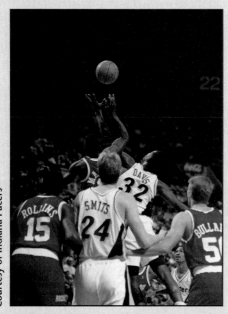

Courtesy of Indiana Pacers

StatMaster, available from an Indianapolis-based software vendor named MicroServices, automatically compiles box score statistics, percentage reports, and play-by-play running accounts of the game. The software has been used by Larry Bird in his All Star Classic and by the NBA; the software was used also at the 1987 Pan-American Games.

According to a brochure provided by MicroServices, you must enter the full rosters of both teams before the game begins; StatMaster is then ready for the opening tip-off. During the game, the actions of the players are entered into the computer, which reconfigures individual and team statistics and percentages for each period.

The running game account includes field goal/free throw percentages, rebounds, assists, steals, and turnovers for the game and the current period, as well as high scorers and the leading rebounder/scorer in the current period.

After the game, StatMaster enables you to retrieve game or summary statistics, including shooting percentages, individual/team statistics, statistics by day of the week or month, statistics versus selected opponents, statistics within the division, and opponents' winning percentages.

StatMaster even has query capability, in case you want additional information.

StatMaster accommodates unlimited remote monitors that provide media personnel with up-to-the-minute game information, including specialty statistics such as lead changes, big leads, bench points, second chance baskets, and points off turnovers.

Public relations and sports information directors like the automatic compilation of all the cumulative statistics that are kept, as well as the meaningful report formats that make next-day processing and game-day notes much easier. Media personnel like the instant video updates and immediate after-game summaries. With StatMaster, a 3- or 4-person crew can calculate statistical compilations that would ordinarily require 8 to 12 people.

Although the software is designed to serve the professional sports world, MicroServices is currently surveying amateur sporting programs in an effort to expand its market.

Now, thanks to StatMaster, you can know more about your athletic heroes than they know about themselves!

```
                    GAME MENU
                    ==== ====

        1.    PLAY BY PLAY (tm).

        2.    DEFAULT PLAYERS.

        3.    SUMMARY INFORMATION.

        4.    END OF QUARTER.

        5.    END OF GAME.

        6.    GAME REPORTS MENU.

        7.    RETURN TO MAIN MENU.

           PICK ONE: _
```

Courtesy of Ty Cheatham

```
          SEASON INFORMATION -
Team        Number      First Name        Last Name              Min
P             31         REGGIE            MILLER                2459

  g  gs fgm / fga tpm/tpa ftm / fta  off/ def  ast   st   er   pf blk  dq
 72  68 380/ 803  94/238 278/ 330    73/ 213  218   93  140  161  29   2

Double Figure Stats ..........                Category Leader (# of times)
Scoring                    Rebounding
10+  20+  30+  Hi          10+  15+  Hi            Min  Pts  Reb  Ast  St  Blk
47   16   1    36          1    0    10             15   14    1    9  24    1
              FEB 18                    Dec 23
              @ CHA                     @ ATL

High Games (Opponent & Date)
Min       Fgm        Ftm        Off        Def        Ast        St         To
48        11         11         4          7          9          4          5
Jan 15    FEB 18     Dec 23     Dec 23     FEB 23     JAN 28     JAN 28     FEB 23
@ MIA     @ CHA      @ ATL      @ ATL      @ ATL      GOL        GOL        @ ATL

OPTIONS:   A=Add    C=Change    D=Delete    S=Search   N=Next Record
              P=Prior Record    X = eXit
```

Courtesy of Ty Cheatham

Creating and Using a Database

Most databases for large computer systems are created (and maintained) by professional programmers. The users of these large-system databases are typically nonprogrammers who can access the data and produce reports but cannot modify the database program. Many database programs designed for microcomputers, however, enable nonprogrammers to create their own databases.

Creating a database involves two steps: defining the structure and entering the data. A good way to begin is to sketch the record on paper before using the database software. Include all the fields that you will need; then determine the name, type, and size for each field.

As you refine your design, consider possible future needs and the needs of other users. For example, if you are designing a library database, you would include a logical field to indicate whether a book has been checked out. Although you can modify the database structure at any time, making modifications is a time-consuming process. It is better to design carefully and minimize the need to modify the database structure.

A database for library books might include field names such as those shown in this Microsoft Access table. Because each book has a unique Library of Congress number, this field is the primary key.

After you enter the database structure into the computer, the DBMS displays a form for each record. The **form** includes the appropriate amount of space available for each field. Now the user enters into the database the data values for each field in the record. Records can be added to the database as needed.

Records can also be deleted. Deletion is usually a two-step process: You must mark the record for deletion, and you must reorganize the file to eliminate all the marked records.

Once the database is established, users can view the database records on-screen. Users can also print a report or use a query to print only selected records. In addition, they can use a query to select certain records for viewing or printing. For example, if an individual is a fan of John Grisham, the person can request a report listing all the books by that author.

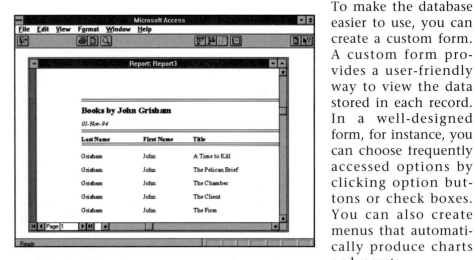

This report shows books written by John Grisham.

To make the database easier to use, you can create a custom form. A custom form provides a user-friendly way to view the data stored in each record. In a well-designed form, for instance, you can choose frequently accessed options by clicking option buttons or check boxes. You can also create menus that automatically produce charts and reports.

DBMS Tips

Designing a database can be a series of frustrating and time-consuming mistakes unless care is taken in selecting the database program and designing the files. The following tips should help to minimize problems and make good use of your time:

1. DBMS programs range from easy to learn and intuitive to extremely difficult. The simplest is the flat-file address book; the most difficult require the use of a programming language, creating the database nearly from scratch. Choose your DBMS carefully; study comparison reviews before you buy.

2. Design your database carefully and thoroughly on paper before you begin using the application. Study the design frequently to determine whether you've left out anything and to ensure that the structure is logical.

3. Define data that you'll want to search for. If you want to be able to search for an area code or ZIP code, be sure that you distinguish them as such. Otherwise, the DBMS will stop at every sequence of numbers. And if you want to sort alphabetically by last name, type the last name first.

4. If you have large quantities of existing information in another data format, you can often convert it into a format the DBMS can read. You can find the specifics for performing this task in the DBMS user manual.

5. Use forms, or templates, to enter repetitive data and automate its collection.

6. Learn the DBMS programming language to create the command files that automate your work and simplify ways to retrieve data.

7. Use the DBMS query language instead of the programming language to learn easier, quicker ways to retrieve data.

8. Explore the features of the report generator—there are many types of reports and ways to use reports. Master the various methods of formatting reports, from the use of type fonts to formats.

9. Learn to use the DBMS's relational characteristics; there are many more ways to define relationships between files than are immediately apparent.

10. Find out whether there are add-on utility programs that will assist in automating tasks you commonly perform with the DBMS.

Database Security

The data that a business stores in a database is usually essential to the operation of the organization. At least some of the data is also confidential and should not be accessed by unauthorized individuals. The most common forms of database security are elaborate passwords and user call-back systems, in which the user calls the computer, hangs up, and the computer calls the user back at a predefined phone number.

Database security can be protected also by making backups routinely. If suspected discrepancies are detected in the data, the database administrator can restore the database from the most recent backup.

Lesson Summary

➤ Database programs can store, organize, and retrieve large quantities of data.

➤ Two types of database programs are in widespread use: file management programs, which work with only one file at a time; and database management systems, which can work with more than one file.

➤ Database programs help users deal with the problems of data dependence, data redundancy, and lack of data integrity.

➤ A hierarchical database must access data following a path down through the levels of the hierarchy.

➤ A network database has a more flexible structure that allows the path to flow up or down.

➤ A relational database uses a key field as an index to locate records.

➤ An object-oriented database can incorporate sound, video, text, and graphics into a record.

➤ The data definition language (DDL) is used to define the structure of the database.

➤ The data manipulation language includes all the user commands.

➤ A query language enables users to ask specific questions.

➤ A report generator facilitates the printing of reports.

➤ Creating the database involves defining the structure and then entering the data.

Lesson Review

Key Terms

child element	data redundancy	integrate	segment
Conference on Data Systems Languages (CODASYL)	data security	key field	Structured Query Language (SQL)
	database	network database	
	database management system (DBMS)	object-oriented database	subschema
data definition language (DDL)		parent element	
	field	query language	
data dependence	file management program	record	
data integrity	flat file	relational database	
data manipulation language (DML)	form	report generator	
	hierarchical database	schema	

Matching

In the blank next to each of the following terms or phrases, write the letter of the corresponding term or phrase.

___f___ **1.** A type of database whose files are best envisioned as a two-dimensional table

___b___ **2.** Includes all the commands that the user needs to work with the database

___j___ **3.** Occurs when a data item can be used in only one application

___c___ **4.** Used to access specific data items in a database

___h___ **5.** Occurs when a data item is repeated in several files

___d___ **6.** Does not permit flexible data access

___e___ **7.** Used by file management programs

___a___ **8.** Describes the structure of a database

___i___ **9.** The consistency of data in all files

___g___ **10.** A type of database that may include text and video

a. DDL   *Definition*

b. DML   *manipulation*

c. SQL   *Query*

d. hierarchical database

e. flat file

f. relational database

g. object-oriented database

h. data redundancy

i. data integrity

j. data dependence

Multiple Choice

Circle the letter of the correct choice for each of the following.

1. Databases can be helpful in maintaining what type of information?

   a. personnel and inventory files

   b. systems programs

   c. employee/customer information

   d. a and c

2. What term is used to describe the consistency of data in all applications?

   a. data security

   b. data dependence

   c. data integrity

   d. data redundancy

3. Which of the following is *not* true about database management programs?

   a. They efficiently use linked files to share data items.

   b. They can sort files to be accessed in a particular sequential order.

   c. They can be used for independent applications.

   d. They are less expensive and easier to use than file management programs.

4. Which of the following terms does *not* describe a database structure used by a DBMS to link data from several files?

   a. hierarchical   *database*

   b. structural

   c. relational

   d. object oriented

   network

5. Which of the following is *not* one of the four components of a DBMS designed to enable the user ease of access?

    a. parent element

    b. data definition language

    c. query language

    d. report generator

6. Which of the following is true of a relational database?

    a. There is one path through the data.

    b. Sound, video, and text can all be incorporated in a record.

    c. Multiple keys can be used to index the records.

    d. Each child element has exactly one parent element.

7. When compared to a database management program, what is the main disadvantage of a file management program?

    a. Data cannot be linked between files.

    b. The structure cannot be modified after data has been entered.

    c. There is a problem with data redundancy.

    d. It uses object-oriented files.

8. What is a database?

    a. a means of producing nicely formatted documents

    b. a way to have the computer perform complex mathematical operations

    c. a collection of files that can be used for information retrieval

    d. a means of sending data over telephone lines

9. Why is security a concern when using a database?

    a. The database contains important data.

    b. The database can be accessed over telephone lines.

    c. Some data is confidential.

    d. all of the above

10. What term is used to describe the repetition of a data item in several files?

    a. data integrity

    b. data redundancy

    c. data dependence

    d. data security

Completion

In the blank provided, write the correct answer for each of the following.

1. File management programs work with ___one___ files.

2. The ___schema___ is the structure of a database.

3. A(n) ___Query___ is used to ask the database for specific information.

4. A(n) ___relational___ is used as an index to identify a record.

5. The first databases were ___DOL___.

6. A(n) ___Integrity___ is a collection of related files.

7. A(n) ___Hierachical___ database resembles an organizational chart.

8. In a(n) ___network___ database, a child element can have more than one parent element.

9. Unauthorized database access is a concern of ___security___.

10. Each ___child element___ in a hierarchical network has one parent element.

Review

On a separate sheet of paper, answer the following questions.

1. Describe three drawbacks that can occur in traditional information processing when separate, unrelated files are used.

2. How are data redundancy and data integrity linked with the failure to combine files into an integrated database?

3. What happens when database files integrate data? What are some benefits of integrating files?

4. What is a major difference between a file management program and a DBMS?

5. What is the difference between the data manipulation language and the query language with respect to what each enables the user to do?

6. What capabilities distinguish object-oriented databases from other types of databases?

7. Explain the steps required to construct a database.

8. Why is data security a concern to organizations that maintain large databases?

9. Explain how a relational database accesses records.

10. Why are object-oriented databases increasing in popularity?

Critical Thinking

On a separate sheet of paper, answer the following questions.

1. Suppose that you are the head of marketing for a company that produces cars. What type of data about your customers might be helpful? How could you use that data to increase sales?

2. List as many commands as you can that a data manipulation language would have to recognize.

3. Suppose that a business or school is storing records in separate files and has not logically related these records into an integrated database. What would be some of the consequences?

4. Suppose that you are using an object-oriented database in the registrar's office of your college. What new features might this database make available to students?

5. Consider using a database for one of your hobbies (such as a compact disc or coin collection). What would you include in your schema, or structure? How would the database be useful to you?

Hands-On Discovery

If you have access to a database management program—such as dBASE, FileMaker Pro, Microsoft Access, FoxPro, or Paradox—use the program to create a simple bibliographic database to keep track of your favorite books. Create your database with fields for author, title, publisher, year of publication, place of publication, and library catalog number. When you are finished, enter a few sample records. Create and print a simple report listing all your books. Sort your book database by author before printing.

Further Discovery

Modern Database Management, Fourth Edition. Fred R. McFadden and Jeffrey A. Hoffer (Redwood City, CA: Benjamin/Cummings, 1994).

Sams' Teach Yourself Access 95 in 14 Days. Paul Cassel (Indianapolis, IN: Sams, 1995).

Special Edition Using dBASE 5.x for Windows, Second Edition. Que Development Group (Indianapolis, IN: Que, 1995).

On-line Discovery

You can access the Internet resources for the following questions by going to the Que Education and Training Web site at URL http://www.ciyf98.com/discovery. From this page, click the link for Lesson 5C and then click the link to the resource you want to access.

1. **Switchboard** (http://www.switchboard.com) is a database of residential and business telephone book entries from around the country. Do several queries of the residential database, perhaps looking up your own phone number or the numbers of your friends. What fields are available in this database? It is likely that Switchboard uses a flat-file data model. However, if Switchboard used a relational model, data in Switchboard could easily be linked to data in other databases. In this case, what might make an appropriate key field so that the data could be linked to other databases? What other types of data might potentially be linked to the telephone directory information, and who might be potential users of this information? Do you feel uncomfortable having your telephone directory or other personal information available over the Web? Why or why not?

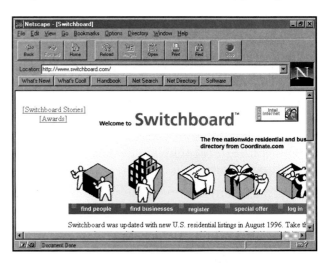

2. **DBMS Magazine** (http://www.dbmsmag.com) is an industry publication dedicated to database management systems. The magazine has a Web site, in which many of the articles are made available. Take a look at this Web site and browse some of the articles. Although many of them may be more technical than you are interested in, you will still be able to get a feel for the issues confronting those who are implementing databases in the workplace. What kinds of issues are being faced? What are some of the topics of the magazine articles? Finally, what product names do you encounter?

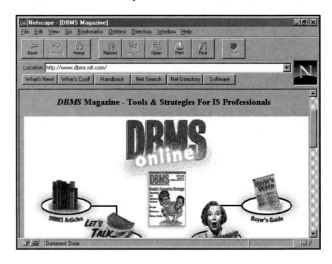

CHAPTER 6
Advanced Applications

So much can be done with computers today, beyond the use of productivity software. The use of multimedia presentation software enables individuals to create presentations that involve the audience. An ever-increasing variety of applications simplifies many otherwise tedious tasks.

Lesson 6A discusses the newest rage among personal computer users—multimedia. CD-ROM brings a new dimension to data for PCs; and if your computer has sound capability, you can integrate sound, pictures, and data.

Lesson 6B covers some of the labor-saving applications that are available. Integrated packages and software suites simplify the movement of data and graphics between programs. Personal information managers help us keep track of our busy lives. And financial packages simplify money management.

LESSON
6A

Multimedia and Presentation Packages

Outline

Multimedia
    Multimedia Hardware
    Multimedia Software
    Hypermedia
    Multimedia Applications
Presentation Packages
    Templates and Slides
    Analytical Graphs
    Clip Art
    Handouts
    Speaker's Notes
    Slide Shows

Learning Objectives

When you have finished reading this lesson, you will be able to

➤ Describe a multimedia presentation

➤ List the hardware needed for a multimedia system

➤ Explain the types of software found on CD-ROM

➤ Define hypermedia

➤ Explain how presentation packages are used

QUE Labs

➤ **Multimedia**
➤ **Presentation Packages**

Imagine sitting at your home computer working on a project for your biology class tomorrow. You have been working on this project for several days now. The topic is DNA. The entire project is presented on a microcomputer. The project begins with a five-minute video clip of a television special that you saw and recorded a couple of weeks ago. You have recorded a voice-over explanation of how the video clip ties into the project and what the reader should expect from the project. The main portion of the project is an animated guided tour through the parts of a DNA molecule. As the reader uses a mouse to point and click different parts of the display, more in-depth explanations of that portion of the molecule appear on the screen. Major points appear on the screen as bulleted items. Some of the data is supported visually with graphs. This is not a dream of how things might be in the future; this scenario is happening now, using multimedia and presentation graphics.

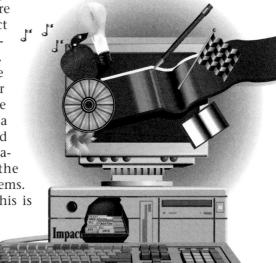

Multimedia

animation too

Multimedia systems can unite sound, text, video, and pictures to create a single multisensory experience. Although multimedia systems were originally very expensive, they are now quite reasonably priced. Most new microcomputers come with multimedia capabilities, and older systems can be upgraded with multimedia kits. (Be careful—a system with a processor any slower than 66 megahertz really is not suitable for multimedia.) Standards for multimedia systems have been set by the Multimedia PC Marketing Council (MPC). The council represents the cooperation of a number of hardware and software companies, including Fujitsu, IBM, Intel, and Microsoft.

A multimedia presentation can include files with sounds, graphics, videos, and animation to enhance the text.

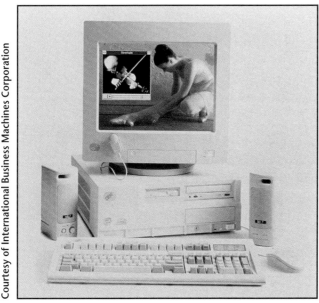

Courtesy of International Business Machines Corporation

This multimedia system includes speakers and a sound card, enabling the listener to hear the music from the violin. The system has a CD-ROM drive so that it can read discs containing huge files storing videos, sounds, animation, photographs, and graphic images.

Multimedia Hardware

A multimedia system is a computer that includes specialized audio devices, such as speakers, microphones, CD-ROM drives, and music keyboards. The system may also use television, a camcorder, videodiscs, or a VCR for video input. A multimedia system requires a sound card (also called a sound board), such as the Sound Blaster or the Pro 16 Multimedia System, and speakers to produce quality audio output. Specialized video cards are capable of capturing a full motion picture to be replayed on the monitor when needed.

A CD-ROM drive is a necessary component of almost any multimedia system. (The only way around it is to use laser discs, and they are more expensive and less popular.) Standard CD-ROM drives are currently quad-speed or eight-speed. Ten-speed drives are available but are not popular because of the added cost. The speed refers to the rate at which data can be transferred from the CD to the computer or monitor. A single-speed **CD-ROM** can transfer 150 kilobytes of data per second. Most CD drives can only play the discs, but prices are coming down on drives that can write as well as play.

A discussion about a compact disc is found in the Concise Columbia Encyclopedia in Microsoft Bookshelf, a multimedia encyclopedia available on CD-ROM.

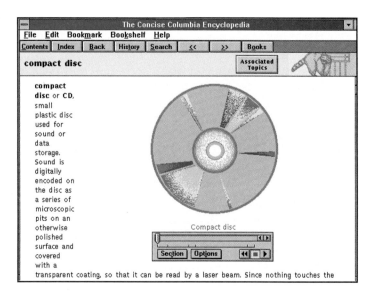

BITS

Before you can incorporate portions of copyrighted works—such as print, audio, or visual materials—into your own multimedia presentations, you must obtain written consent from the copyright holder. Failure to obtain permission is a violation of copyright laws.

A single CD-ROM can hold the entire text of an encyclopedia and video clips, enhanced with sound, to illustrate many of the items in the encyclopedia. The newest and most popular titles are interactive in nature. These products enable the user to react to the presentation and determine how it will proceed. This type of product stimulates the senses, and some studies indicate that interactive electronic books can maintain the user's attention better than traditional books.

A **sound board** is needed for the computer to produce high-quality sound. Sound boards contain sockets for microphones and external speakers. The microphone allows the user to record his or her own dialog or music. For high-quality music, MIDI is used. **MIDI**, **Musical Instrument Digital Interface**, is a standard for both cabling and communications between computers and digital musical instruments.

MIDI files can be easily shared between computer platforms, presentation packages, and electronic instruments. Some of the more sophisticated sound-editing programs allow you to mix a virtually unlimited number of sounds into your final product.

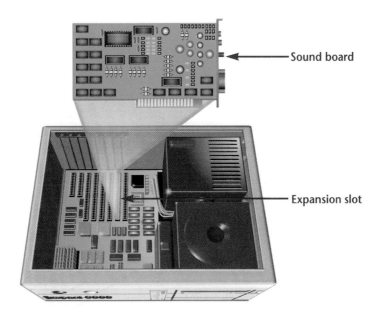

A sound board is inserted into an expansion slot on the computer's mother-board.

Sound board

Expansion slot

For those who are not musicians, a number of good sound libraries are available. The clips can be modified to fit the needs of the presentation you are designing. Amazingly, some MIDI software doesn't even require that the author know how to read music!

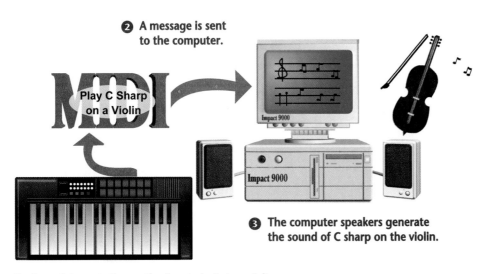

❷ A message is sent to the computer.

Play C Sharp on a Violin

❸ The computer speakers generate the sound of C sharp on the violin.

❶ A musician sets the synthesizer to imitate a violin and then plays a C sharp on the synthesizer.

Musicians use the MIDI standard to create music for movies and television and to add sound for multimedia presentations.

With Asymetrix Multimedia ToolBook, you can make a presentation that includes videos, photographs, animation, and sounds. You can program your presentation to include buttons that enable the user to move somewhere else in the presentation at any time.

Courtesy of Asymetrix Corporation

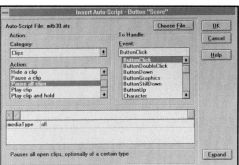

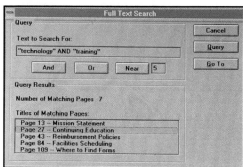

Multimedia Software

Components of multimedia presentations are combined using **authoring software**. There are many authoring programs; some good ones include HyperCard for the Macintosh, HyperScreen and Linkway for MS-DOS computers, ToolBook for Windows, and HyperStudio for the Apple IIGS. Authoring software allows individuals to blend audio files, video, and animation with text and traditional graphics.

Truly professional interactive multimedia presentations can be fairly expensive, running about $500 per minute of presentation time.

Even if you aren't a great artist, collections of clip media can make your presentation look professional. Clip media includes photos, drawings, movies, sound, and ready-to-use backgrounds. Be certain to read the licensing agreements for any clip media that you use. Some can be used freely; others cannot be used for any project that will generate income.

At the time of this book's publication, most popular software in CD format can be purchased in a variety of stores. The best-selling CDs with the longest life span are encyclopedias. Most CD products tend to have very limited life spans. Other CDs that may have some durability include the Street Atlas U.S.A. and Corel Gallery. Games tend to be big sellers, but they have limited durability. A hit will sell around 50,000 copies the first year, but many will enjoy only one year of strong sales.

The newest and most popular titles are interactive in nature. These products allow the user to react to the presentation and determine how it will proceed. This type of product tends to stimulate the senses and better maintain user attention.

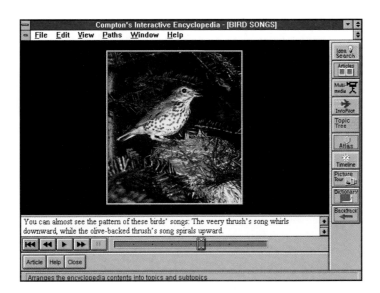

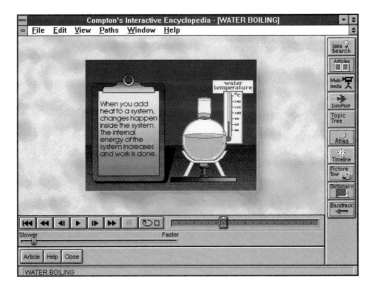

Compton's Interactive Encyclopedia includes animation, sounds, videos, and beautiful graphics to engage the viewer. The encyclopedia covers a wide range of topics from bird songs to chemical processes.

Hypermedia

Hypertext software allows a user to follow links through related topics. The concept is similar to using an encyclopedia; articles frequently end with a bibliography that references other related topics. With **hypertext**, you can click on a highlighted word in a document and go immediately to other documents that contain related text. **Hypermedia** allows the user to navigate through graphics, sound, animation, and video to find data related to a topic. One of the advantages to the user is that he or she does not need to locate the data; the user can just choose the topic, and the computer will find any related material. Some hypermedia products allow the user to interact; others simply present information to the user. Hypertext is frequently used on the World Wide Web.

Multimedia Applications

The availability of multimedia applications, along with powerful but inexpensive computers to run them, is bringing millions of computers into homes.

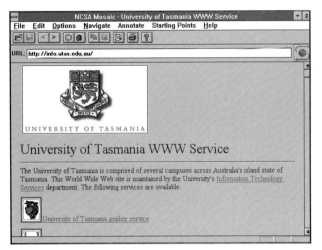

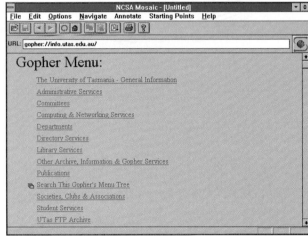

With NCSA Mosaic, users click a hypermedia link to move to an associated topic. They can browse through massive databases all over the world by using the Internet hypermedia software.

The driving force in the multimedia market is still the private consumer. A recent study by Dataquest, cited by Peter Jerram in *NewMedia* magazine (October, 1994), showed that of the $18 billion multimedia market, only $2 billion is accounted for by business. The consumer market accounts for $16 billion in mul-

Information kiosks help people make decisions on many issues. This kiosk provides information that will help a customer determine what to buy.

timedia sales annually. What are people buying? Everything from children's games to *Better Homes and Gardens* recipes (complete with audio directions) to a tour of the National Art Museum is available in multimedia form.

Multimedia is also playing a growing role in business and government, particularly in training programs. Multimedia was limited initially because it restricted interaction with the audience, but new systems have restored that capability. Infrared and radio-based controls allow a presenter to move around the room and interact with the audience instead of being tied to a mouse or a keyboard.

Information kiosks are also incorporating music, videos, and other multimedia elements. When South Africa held its first democratic elections in 1994, information kiosks were used to educate the population about the election. Thirty kiosks were moved throughout the country, dispensing information, in the individual's choice of eleven different languages, about how, when, and why to vote and about the ballot.

Business is beginning to recognize the value of visual presentations in marketing products and conveying ideas. A breakdown of business multimedia users reveals that although programmers are certainly using multimedia, they are not the largest group of users. Multimedia is most prevalent in the engineering profession, with the second largest category of users being department managers. Manufacturing accounts for 25 percent of all business use, with transportation and utilities showing only half as much use of the technology.

Some businesses are developing interactive recruiting tools on CD-ROM to be distributed to prospective employees. Advertisers and corporations are developing interactive advertisements that enable customers to explore only the products they are interested in purchasing. Multimedia products, like the Virtual Notebook System from The ForeFront Group, Inc., of Houston, facilitate videoconferencing with microcomputers in remote locations.

Experts forecast that, in the future, business use of multimedia will be primarily for communications and collaboration on projects between organizations. LAN-based e-mail systems can easily be used to distribute multimedia products.

Presentation Packages

As any student will tell you, listening to a speaker who is not using any visual aids can be boring. Trying to understand numbers presented verbally or in a spreadsheet format is not easy. Computer graphics, in the form of presentation packages, can make a speech visually compelling and display numbers in an easily understood graph or chart. The use of graphics increases the audience's attention span, comprehension, and retention of information. Studies have shown that audiences consider presenters who use visual aids to be more knowledgeable and better prepared than those who do not use any visual reinforcement.

Presentation packages enable users to create their own drawings; produce analytical graphs, such as those available with most spreadsheets; access libraries of clip art; and use a variety of colors, patterns, and text options.

Templates and Slides

The user creates a presentation as a series of **slides**. Think of a slide as an individual page in a book. Slides can be bulleted outlines of the material, text, tables of numbers, analytical graphs, or images and can include titles, page numbers, and borders. Users can prepare slides for virtually any output medium, including 35-millimeter slides, overhead transparencies, and hard copy.

Each slide follows a standard format, called a **template**, and the slides are combined to create a logical presentation. Presentation packages come with libraries of templates that vary in color and in location of titles, text, and objects. Some templates include images superimposed over a background. The user can select a template and apply it to an entire presentation.

Usually, a user creates slides by starting with an outline. Each major section in the outline becomes a new slide. The slides can be viewed individually or in a series, and individual slides can be edited as needed. When the slides are viewed in a series, the user can rearrange the slides to change the order of the presentation.

The Multifaceted Issues of a Multimedia Patent

"On again, off again" is the phrase that best describes Compton's multimedia software patent. The patent claims that Compton's New Media invented a system called multimedia that combines text, graphics, sound, and animation.

Compton applied to the U.S. Patent and Trademark Office for the multimedia patent in 1988 and received the patent in 1993. In November, Compton made an announcement about the patent at COMDEX, the world's largest computer trade meeting, that left the media world stunned.

Compton bragged to the industry that it had invented multimedia and expected to receive royalties on its invention from other multimedia publishers. The immediate reaction by other computer publishers was intensely negative.

The International Multimedia Association (IMA) and others in the industry asserted that the patent should never have been grant-

ed because multimedia technology is nonproprietary, or not exclusive. In addition, according to many in the computer industry, similar art existed at the time the patent was filed. Publishers had been creating multimedia for years, according to other industry authorities. This issue of "similar, prior art" has frequently been cited in cases where a patent's validity has been questioned.

The controversy is rooted in a philosophical question about whether software should even be protected by a patent. Computer programs, like other intellectual property, have traditionally been protected by copyright laws. Software programs contain many algorithms with complex lines of programming code. It would not be unusual for a programmer to use a previously coded algorithm, thus unknowingly breaking the law. Teachers and educators might also inadvertently break the law by using the interactive technology covered by the patent without Compton's permission.

From a practical standpoint, most software programmers have not applied for patents on their programs because they did not recognize that a patent was necessary. In addition, filing a search with the U.S. Patent and Trademark Office is a tedious process that can be expensive. Government officials who grant patents don't have access to previously created software code, which means that software patents can easily be found to be invalid. The bottom line for many people in the computer industry is that patenting software code has not been the accepted way for programmers to protect their creations.

In December 1993, after listening to the objections from the industry and reviewing the philosophical issues, the Patent Office Commissioner requested that Compton's patent be reexamined. Three months later, the U.S. Patent and Trademark Office revoked Compton's patent. Compton, however, intends to defend the patent.

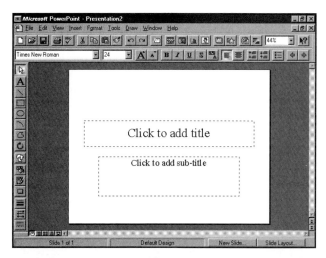

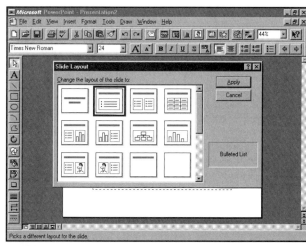

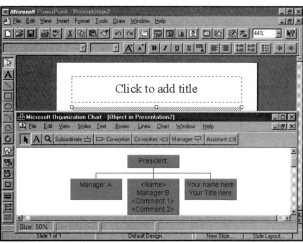

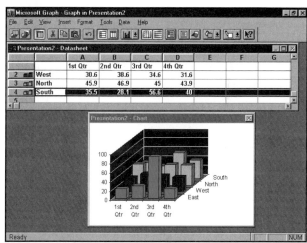

Analytical Graphs

Graphs can help viewers see trends and proportions. You can create the graphs in the presentation package or import them from another source. Commonly used types of graphs include line graphs, bar graphs, stacked bar graphs, and pie graphs. These may be displayed in either two or three dimensions. The user can rotate the image to enhance the visual impact of the data. Users can combine multiple graphs, or a graph with a supporting table, on the same slide.

Microsoft PowerPoint provides users with options to prepare slides showing bulleted lists, organization charts, and many other types of charts.

Users of WordPerfect Presentations can include several types of graphs and charts in their presentations.

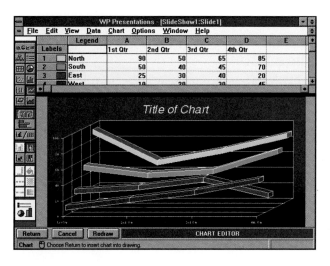

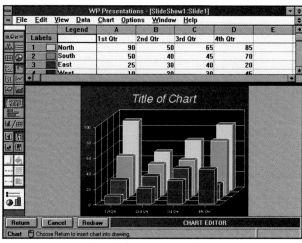

Clip Art

Images that can be incorporated into a larger presentation or slide are known as **clip art**. Clip art packages include hundreds of images that you can use, frequently with no need to acknowledge the source. Such software is known as **public domain software**. Some clip art is usually included

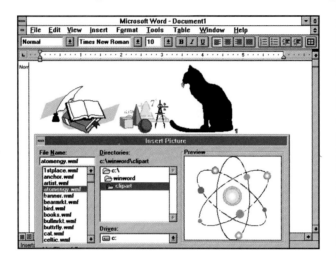

with the presentation package, and much can be downloaded from bulletin boards. Be careful, though, because not all clip art is public domain; some clip art is protected by patents and must be purchased and registered. Large collections of clip art are called **clip art libraries**.

Microsoft Word includes several clip art files that users can insert into their documents. These clip art files can be easily inserted into Microsoft PowerPoint presentations.

Clip art images can be complex and may require considerable storage space. New clip art libraries frequently come on a CD-ROM instead of a floppy disk. Incorporating clip art into a presentation is relatively simple and does not require the user to do any programming. Some presentation packages are capable of working with animated clip art and video clips.

Handouts

Most presentation packages give the user the option of producing handouts for the audience. Handouts are smaller, printed versions of the slides, usually with two, three, or six slides per page. Additional information—such as the name of the presenter, the date of the presentation, and a page number—can be included on each sheet of the handout.

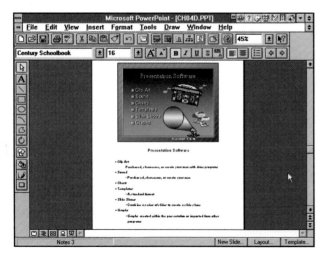

Speaker's Notes

Speaker's notes are also available through most presentation packages. The notes have a small image of a slide at the top of the page, and the speaker may incorporate typed notes on the lower portion of the page.

Slide Shows

Creating a presentation with a computer enables you to take advantage of a presentation method called a **slide show**. Using a transparent screen designed to fit on an overhead projector, or a special projection unit that attaches directly to the computer, the presenter can display the slides created with the presentation package. Pauses between slides can be timed, or the speaker can manually control the timing. Different "fade in" techniques can be used to catch the attention of the audience. For example, the current slide can fade out to a blank screen, or one screen can drop down over the preceding screen. Most presentation packages include a small **run-time program** so that a presentation can be displayed on a computer that does not have the entire presentation package loaded. This feature enables presenters to carry a presentation on a single floppy disk.

Lesson Summary

➤ Multimedia combines audio, video, text, and graphics.

➤ Multimedia requires a fast microprocessor and a large amount of storage capacity.

➤ Because of the storage requirements, multimedia software is available on CD-ROM.

➤ The consumer market for multimedia is larger than the business market.

➤ Presentation packages can add visual information to a business presentation.

➤ Clip art can be used to incorporate still images, animated images, and video into presentations.

➤ Most presentation packages enable users to easily produce outlines, slides, handouts, and speaker's notes.

Lesson Review

Key Terms

authoring software	hypertext	public domain software	template
CD-ROM	multimedia system	run-time program	
clip art	Musical Instrument Digital	slide	
clip art libraries	Interface (MIDI)	slide show	
hypermedia	presentation package	sound board	

Matching

In the blank next to each of the following terms or phrases, write the letter of the corresponding term or phrase.

_____ **1.** Used to assist in making business presentations

_____ **2.** Allows a slide show from a presentation package to be viewed on a computer that does not have the presentation package loaded

_____ **3.** Enables the user to navigate through sound, graphics, animation, and video to find data related to a topic

a. clip art

b. MIDI

c. hypermedia

d. run-time program

e. CD-ROM

f. public domain software

g. slide show

h. multimedia system

i. presentation package

j. template

_e___ **4.** Storage medium most frequently used for multimedia applications

_i___ **5.** A standard format used to create a slide show

_h___ **6.** A computer that includes special devices such as speakers, a CD-ROM drive, and a sound board

_b___ **7.** A standard for cabling and communications between computers and digital musical instruments

_a___ **8.** Pictures that can be added to a document or presentation

_f___ **9.** Usually can be used without charge and with no need to acknowledge the source

_g___ **10.** Created using a presentation package and shown to an audience

Multiple Choice

Circle the letter of the correct choice for each of the following.

1. Multimedia hardware usually includes _____.

   a. speakers, a sound board, and a CD-ROM drive

   b. television and camcorders

   c. microphones and cassette tape recorders

   d. television and VCRs

2. Hypermedia permits the user to _____.

   a. navigate through graphics and animation

   b. choose a topic and have the computer find any related material

   c. interact with the software

   d. all of the above

3. Multimedia applications that are frequently used in the home include _____.

   a. games

   b. computer marketing

   c. reference works

   d. both a and c

4. A form that can be used as the basis for a slide show is known as _____.

   a. a template

   b. clip art

   c. speaker's notes

   d. MIDI

5. _____ make(s) it easier for users to see trends and proportions.

   a. Hypertext

   b. MIDI

   c. Run-time programs

   d. Analytical graphs

6. What can you do with a presentation software package?

   a. create your own drawings

   b. create analytical graphs

   c. use a variety of text options and colors

   d. all of the above

7. A presentation package cannot produce which of the following?

   a. slides

   b. speaker's notes

   c. faxes

   d. graphs

8. Many of the pictures used with a presentation package are taken from which of the following?

   a. CAD software

   b. a clip art library

   c. a run-time program

   d. word processing documents

9. Slide shows can be viewed _____.

   a. by using an LCD panel and an overhead projector

   b. as transparencies

   c. as hard copy

   d. all of the above

10. _____ is (are) used to combine components of multimedia presentations.

   a. Run-time programs

   b. MIDI

   c. Authoring software

   d. Hypertext

Completion

In the blank provided, write the correct answer for each of the following.

1. A(n) *run-time program* enables a presentation to run even when the entire presentation package is not available.

2. Software that usually can be copied and used without any need to acknowledge the source is *public domain software*.

3. Advanced presentation packages allow the user to include *video* in the presentation.

4. Most multimedia systems are purchased by *consumer*.

5. *Hypertext* software enables a user to create links through related topics.

6. The newest multimedia applications involve the user by being *interactive*.

7. A(n) *info. kiosk* uses multimedia to make individuals aware of options or opportunities.

8. *MIDI* is used to produce high-quality music with a computer.

9. A presentation is designed as a series of *slides*.

10. A(n) *sound card* enables the computer to produce high-quality sound.

Review

On a separate sheet of paper, answer the following questions.

1. Why are most multimedia applications available only on CD-ROM?

2. What are some of the companies that have cooperated to set standards for multimedia systems?

3. What is required for a computer to produce high-quality sound?

4. Which categories of multimedia software are most popular for the home?

5. What is the concept behind hypertext software?

6. What areas within business most frequently use multimedia?

7. Why is it important to be able to run a slide show on a computer using a run-time program?

8. For what is a clip art library used?

9. Why are graphs a good presentation tool?

10. What is contained on the speaker's notes produced by a presentation package?

Critical Thinking

On a separate sheet of paper, answer the following questions.

1. Think of a presentation that you have done for a class. How could you have used a presentation package to improve that presentation?

2. If you were making a presentation, would you give the audience handouts at the beginning or the end? Why?

3. Why is it appropriate to use the term *multisensory* when discussing multimedia applications?

4. What types of software use run-time programs? What are some advantages of a run-time program?

5. See whether you can find clip art libraries that would be useful for papers and presentations in any of your classes.

Further Discovery

The Complete Idiot's Guide to Multimedia. David Haskin (Indianapolis, IN: Que, 1994).

The Winn L. Rosch Multimedia Bible, Premier Edition. Winn L. Rosch (Indianapolis, IN: Sams, 1995).

Multimedia in Practice. Judith Jeffcoate (New York: Prentice Hall, 1995).

Special Edition Using PowerPoint for Windows 95. Que Development Group (Indianapolis, IN: Que, 1995).

On-line Discovery

You can access the Internet resources for the following questions by going to the Que Education and Training Web site at URL http://www.ciyf98.com/discovery. From this page, click the link for Lesson 6A and then click the link to the resource you want to access.

1. Microsoft produces one of the most successful lines of multimedia reference CD-ROMs. Browse many of the **Microsoft** reference offerings on the World Wide Web (http://www.microsoft.com/mshome). What topics do the multimedia CD-ROMs deal with? How does Microsoft use the Web to provide periodic updates to some of the CD-ROMs? In what ways do these multimedia products use different media (such as sound, pictures, and video clips)? Finally, what other subjects do you think would make good multimedia reference CD-ROMs?

2. Macromedia Director is a popular program used to develop many multimedia CD-ROM products and even some multimedia available over the World Wide Web. Look at the **Macromedia Director** home page (http://www.macromedia.com/software/dms/index.html). What kinds of tools does the program provide for multimedia developers? What kinds of products can be created with it? If you were to create a multimedia CD-ROM, what would be its subject or theme?

Other Useful Applications

Outline

Integrated Packages and Software Suites
    Microsoft Office 97
Personal Information Managers
    Contact Management
    Calendar and Schedule Management
    Task and Project Management
    Mail Merge and Print
    Popular PIMs
Accounting and Personal Finance Programs
Network Browsers
Desktop Videoconferencing
Painting, Drawing, and Photo-Editing Programs
Additional Graphics Programs
    Computer-Aided Design and Computer-Aided Manufacturing
    Animation Graphics
Software for the Home

Learning Objectives

When you have finished reading this lesson, you will be able to

➤ Explain the advantages and disadvantages of integrated packages and software suites

➤ Discuss how personal information managers are used

➤ Explain how organizations and individuals use accounting software

➤ Discuss network browsers

➤ Explain how desktop videoconferencing works

➤ Explain the difference between images generated by painting programs and by drawing programs

➤ Explain the purpose of CAD and CAM software

➤ Discuss computer-generated animation

➤ Explain how computers are used for home entertainment

Take some time to browse through any large software store. You will notice many word processing, spreadsheet, and database programs—the subjects of the preceding lessons. But many other computer programs are also available. This chapter surveys additional popular categories of software. People are constantly finding new ways to apply computers!

Integrated Packages and Software Suites

Suppose that you need to prepare a report for one of your classes. You have a great deal of text to enter in a word processing program. You also have a table of numbers and a graph that you want to incorporate into the report. Yes, you can accomplish this task with a spreadsheet. You can export the table and graph from the spreadsheet and import them into the word processor. However, the task is relatively complex. Because combining spreadsheets, documents, and database files is required so often, programs to simplify the task have been developed. These programs, which easily combine several productivity tools, are known as integrated packages and software suites.

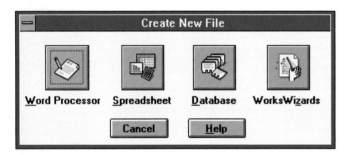

This menu from the multimedia version of Microsoft Works displays the options for word processing, spreadsheet, and database programs. WorksWizards are guides that teach users how to accomplish specific tasks.

An **integrated package** combines the features of a word processing program, an electronic spreadsheet, a database management system (DBMS), and graphics. Some of the currently popular integrated packages are Microsoft Works, ClarisWorks, and LotusWorks.

Purchasing an integrated package has several advantages over buying separate programs. An integrated package costs less than the combined cost of the separate programs. Sometimes vendors even **bundle** this software—that is, they include the integrated package with a microcomputer system as part of the system's total price. An integrated package usually requires less storage space than three or four individual programs. Because the package uses one set of commands, you can learn an integrated package more easily than you can learn individual productivity programs. And, of course, passing data from one module to another is very easy.

An integrated package does have one significant disadvantage. The modules may not be as powerful or versatile as the individual programs.

BITS
Lotus SmartSuite includes the word processing program Word Pro, the spreadsheet program 1-2-3, Freelance Graphics, Lotus Organizer, and the database management program Approach.

A **software suite** is a collection of full-featured, stand-alone programs. The programs usually share a common command structure and have similar interfaces to make them easy to learn. Programs in the suite pass data back and forth easily. Some popular software suites are Microsoft Office, Lotus SmartSuite, and Corel Office.

As a collection of programs, a suite requires more disk space and is more expensive than an integrated package. The main advantage of a software suite over an integrated package is that the individual components have the full power and versatility of stand-alone programs.

Software suites and integrated packages have been steadily increasing in popularity. Users appreciate the comparatively low cost and flexibility.

Microsoft Office Professional for Windows 95 includes Microsoft Word word processing software, Excel spreadsheet software, Access database management software, PowerPoint presentation software, Schedule + appointment book software, and Binder to help organize documents. An electronic mail program, Microsoft Exchange, can also be installed.

Microsoft Office 97

Office 97 is a faster and even more user-friendly integrated suite of programs than Office 95. (A suite is a set of programs that are designed to interface with each other.) There are three basic editions of Office 97: Standard, Professional, and Small Business. There are also other editions available, but they are primarily variations of these three.

In order to load Office 97 onto a hard drive, there needs to be at least 120M (megabytes) of space available. There has to be not only enough hard disk space for the suite, but also for **scratch space** (an area on the hard drive in which an application temporarily stores information currently being entered or modified).

The most commonly used packages within each Office 97 edition are Word, Excel, and Outlook. The other applications offered in Office 97 include PowerPoint for presentations and Access for databases.

Outlook is an information manager, which replaces the Microsoft Exchange Index and Schedule+. It is only available in the Standard and Professional Editions. It handles e-mail, phone calls, business and personal meetings, appointments, to-do lists, contacts, documents, worksheets, and contracts.

Office Art is a sophisticated drawing tool applet and is one of the outstanding new features in Office 97. It is an art tool accessible from Word, Excel, and PowerPoint. Office Art eliminates necessity for any added illustration software. Office Art can be used to draw flowchart symbols, to create 3-D shapes and shadows, and to make Bèzier curves. It is so integrated into Office applications that it does not appear to be a separate module.

IntelliMouse is Microsoft's new Office 97 mouse. It has a greater range of functions than a regular mouse. Physically, it looks the same except for the rotating rubber wheel called the wheel button. Utilizing this button, there is a choice of methods for moving through a document. Scroll bars or other controls can be used, but there is now an intelligent alternative. The wheel button can

Microsoft Outlook provides the user with a complete information manager.

Microsoft Visual Basic helps the advanced user automate repetitive tasks.

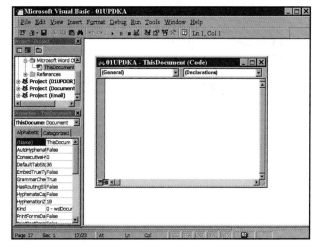

be used to scroll up or down (scroll), to drag for continuous scrolling (pan), to enlarge the screen display (zoom), and to move in and out of items in documents, worksheets, or Internet pages (DataZoom). The IntelliMouse cannot be used unless the applications software in its system has been programmed to accept these new types of commands. Obviously, all Office 97 programs support these commands.

Visual Basic for Applications (VBA) is built into Word, Excel, PowerPoint, and Access. VBA makes it easier to quickly automate any Office 97 application.

There are three versions of Office 97 available, as follows:

➤ The **Office 97 Standard Edition** includes Word 97, Excel 97, PowerPoint 97, Internet Explorer 3.0, plus Outlook 97. Besides voice narration, PowerPoint has two other notable features. One is a built-in HTML translation tool, which allows exporting to the Web; and the other is custom show, used to design mini-presentations for a variety of audiences within one PowerPoint file.

➤ The **Professional Edition** is the same as the Standard Edition but it includes Access 97, which has a new feature enabling it to import and export databases to and from the Web. Within these databases, hyperlinks can be stored.

➤ The **Small Business Edition** includes Word 97, Excel 97, Outlook 97, Internet Explorer 3.0, Publisher 97 (desktop-publishing program), Small Business Financial Manager 97 (SBFM) (accounts reporting and analysis), and Automap's Streets Plus (street-mapping software). Automap is an entirely new mapping system, using "pushpins," which allow information notes about directions, customers, meetings, and so on to be added.

Personal Information Managers

Most individuals have hectic schedules, a fact that has resulted in a large market for **personal information managers** (**PIMs**). These programs typically focus on four essential functions: contact management, calendar and schedule management, task and project management, and mail merge and print. Some PIMs also offer financial tracking and time-and-billing capabilities.

Contact Management

Contact management software is designed to help you keep track of your contacts. Information maintained by the software includes addresses, telephone and fax numbers, a notepad, automatic telephone dialing using a modem, and search and sort capabilities.

Calendar and Schedule Management

Most PIMs offer a variety of calendar formats: yearly, monthly, weekly, and daily. The amount of detail provided should increase as the time span covered decreases. A PIM usually has an alarm that can be set to serve as an appointment reminder, and the program warns the user of possible schedule conflicts. Recurring tasks are scheduled automatically, and a flexible array of calendar printing options is usually available.

Task and Project Management

Busy people tend to have several projects going at once. Sometimes keeping deadlines straight and prioritizing tasks can be overwhelming. The job of **task management software** is to organize and present tasks both graphically and in the form of "to do" lists. A PIM should enable the user to view tasks by project, deadline date, and priority. The PIM should also have the capability of automatically rescheduling overdue projects.

Mail Merge and Print

PIMs interface with different word processing and fax programs. The capability to merge documents and produce mailing labels is essential. Expanded telecommunications capabilities are appearing in the newest PIMs on the market. Users need to be aware of which programs are compatible with a particular PIM.

Popular PIMs

Some PIMs are designed for home use, some for business use, and others for a workgroup. Popular PIMs include Sidekick by Starfish Software, Lotus Organizer, Schedule+ by Microsoft, and ACT by Symantec Corporation. PIMs used for business and workgroups include ECCO Professional by Arabesque Software, Full Contact by FIT Software, and InfoCentral by WordPerfect.

Courtesy of Starfish Software

Appearing on the market are some new and exciting PIMs with unusual features. VoxMail by VoxLink enables the user to make calls with a telephone and to have all e-mail messages read aloud by the computer; this PIM even accepts verbal replies that are entered automatically into the e-mail system. The Personal Daily PlanIt series by Media Vision comes with voice-recognition capabilities and a variety of video clips, depending on the module you select. For example, PlanIt Earth begins each day with a nature video; PlanIt Adrenaline offers surfing, skiing, and other adventure videos. NetManage recently incorporated an Internet address book into its ECCO PIM.

Accounting and Personal Finance Programs

One of the first applications that businesses computerized was accounting. Although large businesses profited from having the computer do all the tedious math, smaller businesses did not enjoy that luxury until microcomputers were invented. Today, small- and medium-sized organizations use such products as QuickBooks, DacEasy, and Solomon to keep track of transactions. These transactions include accounts receivable (amounts owed by customers), accounts payable (amounts owed by the organization), general ledger (a record of all financial transactions), inventory, and payroll.

When selecting accounting software, businesses need to make certain that the software includes a full range of functions. Organizations should also consider the security features of any program that is going to maintain all their financial data.

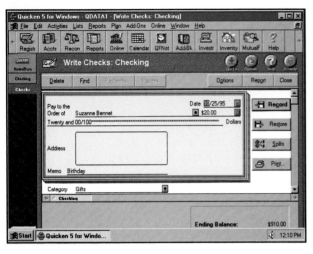

Many individuals use Quicken to write checks, track expenses, prepare budgets, and manage personal financial information.

Individuals can benefit from using the computer to keep track of such finances as checking accounts, savings accounts, and loan balances. **Personal finance programs** have built-in calculators, categorize expenditures, and print checks. These programs can automatically deduct regular monthly payments and alert the user when a payment needs to be made. Add-on packages track stocks and estimate taxes. These simplified programs have graphical interfaces and built-in help facilities. Such add-ons can make the tasks of account reconciliation and bill paying much less time-consuming. Some of the more popular home finance programs are Quicken by Intuit, Managing Your Money (MYM) by MECA Software, and Microsoft Money.

Network Browsers

A **network browser** is an application that enables the user to search locations on the Internet. In order for a browser to work, your computer must have a modem, and you must have an account with an Internet service provider. With a browser, it is equally easy to access information on a computer located in the same town, across the country, or on the other side of the world.

Some provider services, like America Online and CompuServe, contain built-in browsers. To use some other providers, like Netcom and EarthLink, you must select browser software and load it on your system. The newest versions of software suites such as the Corel WordPerfect Suite and Microsoft Office include browsers. Network browsers make finding your way through the World Wide Web easier than nongraphic access paths. The browsers that are currently most widely used are Microsoft's Internet Explorer, Netscape Navigator, and NCSA Mosaic.

Browsers format data to make it more legible and attractive. Most browsers support tables and colored backgrounds. Browsers enable you to access text, pictures, sounds, animation, and even video clips. Using a browser, the user can read or download Web pages, online magazine articles, and files. New browser features enable users to share documents; these features include both accessing and editing capabilities.

Netscape Navigator provides easy browsing for the Internet.

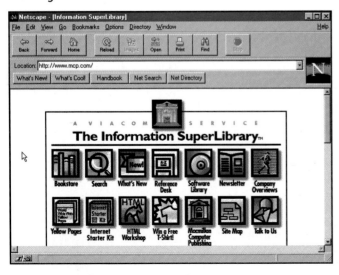

Desktop Videoconferencing

Just a few years ago, we thought that it was wonderful to be able to send e-mail from one location to another; now that capability isn't enough. People want to be able to see each other and discuss a document that they all can see on their computer screens; they want to have **desktop videoconferencing.**

For a little while, only businesses could afford to have videoconferencing capabilities. With software now costing under $100, that limitation no longer applies. Organizations have discovered the benefits of allowing employees to see each other while they work on the same document from different locations. However, individuals have also decided that it is more comfortable to chat with someone you can see.

Desktop videoconferencing software can be run alone, permitting users to hear each other, or with a camera mounted on top of the monitor to transmit a picture. Software enables individuals to work on a one-to-one basis or in groups.

Courtesy of Dan Bosler, Tony Stone Images, Inc.

Painting, Drawing, and Photo-Editing Programs

Painting, drawing, and photo-editing programs enable the user to create illustrations with the computer. **Painting programs** create an image by turning individual screen pixels (picture elements) on or off. This technique is called **bit mapping**. Painting programs give the user a greater range of creativity than drawing programs provide. The user can vary the background to simulate different types of canvas. Painting is possible by copying different styles and techniques such as paint, airbrush, chalk, crayon, and colored pencil. Lines can be blended or smeared. The user can erase portions of the picture but cannot manipulate individual objects. Some paintings are difficult to distinguish from those produced with traditional techniques.

Drawing programs plot the points required to create an object and then automatically draw lines between these points. The graphics created are called **vector graphics**. You enter images into the computer with a mouse or with a stylus and **digitizing tablet**—a peripheral device that converts graphics into data that the computer can process. Objects can be easily moved around the screen or erased. Complex illustrations can be created by combining or overlaying objects. Most drawing packages have the capability of incorporating text.

A rose is created with a painting program.

The enlarged image reveals the pixels that make up the picture.

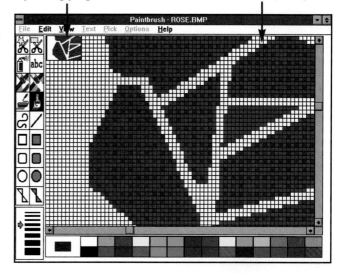

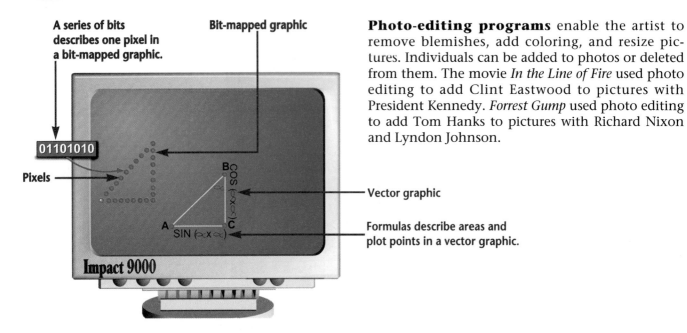

A series of bits describes one pixel in a bit-mapped graphic.

01101010

Pixels

Bit-mapped graphic

Vector graphic

Formulas describe areas and plot points in a vector graphic.

Impact 9000

Photo-editing programs enable the artist to remove blemishes, add coloring, and resize pictures. Individuals can be added to photos or deleted from them. The movie *In the Line of Fire* used photo editing to add Clint Eastwood to pictures with President Kennedy. *Forrest Gump* used photo editing to add Tom Hanks to pictures with Richard Nixon and Lyndon Johnson.

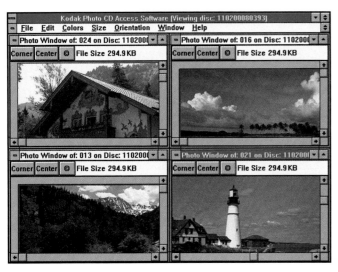

Kodak Photo CD.

WordStar PhotoFinish.

Additional Graphics Programs

This book has already discussed spreadsheet graphics, graphics available with presentation packages, and illustration programs. Other types of graphics can be created with computers as well.

Computer-Aided Design and Computer-Aided Manufacturing

Computer-aided design (**CAD**) and **computer-aided manufacturing** (**CAM**) software is used to create architectural drawings, product designs, landscaping plans, and engineering drawings. CAD programs are frequently used for manufacturing applications, commonly referred to as CAD/CAM.

Engineers can design products as varied as automobiles, bridges, and sky-scrapers with CAD/CAM software. CAD/CAM programs can zoom in on one portion of a drawing, rotate the image, and display it in two or three dimensions. CAD/CAM enables designers to work much faster than they once worked, creating in a day designs that used to take weeks. The entire manufacturing process is quicker when a computer is used because designs can be tested with a computer-assisted engineering (CAE) program before manufacturing. Many CAM programs can estimate manufacturing costs before production and can control assembly-line robots.

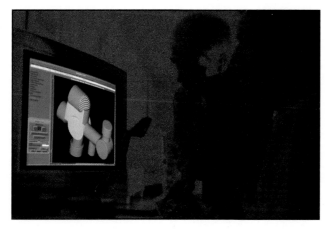

Courtesy of EDS

Animation Graphics

Every second of an animated cartoon requires approximately thirty individual images. Simple math reveals that creating a thirty-minute cartoon show will require that illustrators draw 54,000 images (thirty images per second × sixty seconds per minute × thirty minutes). Traditionally, each image was first outlined and then painted by hand. Needless to say, this was a time-consuming undertaking. Using a computer, it is not necessary to create an entirely new image just to make a small change. Using computer animation, an illustrator can even merge photographs with cartoons. (Remember Roger Rabbit?)

Animated computer graphics are also used extensively in movies and advertising. The feather shown at the beginning and end of the movie *Forrest Gump* is a computer-generated graphic image. The movie *Virtuosity*, which deals with virtual reality, used computer-generated animation liberally; and *Toy Story* was created entirely by computer animation.

Morphing is a special animated graphics technique in which one image appears to change and become something entirely different. Morphing originated from the technique of *warping*, which was used to correct satellite images from space. The Michael Jackson video *Black and White* uses morphing to show him change into a panther and to change the images of people. Television commercials use morphing as well; one commercial shows a man shaving, and as he shaves, his face changes.

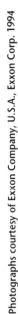

Photographs courtesy of Exxon Company, U.S.A., Exxon Corp. 1994

A morphing program was used to blend the image of the automobile into the image of the tiger. The first step in the process is to digitize both images. Starting and ending points are then identified. Mathematical formulas are used to change values and calculate positions of key points in the changing image. The original image is warped along a mathematically calculated path until it is blended into the final image.

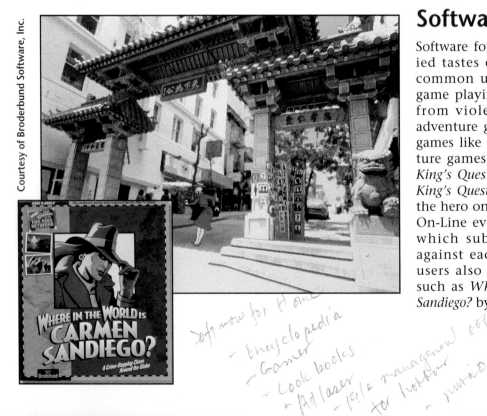

Courtesy of Broderbund Software, Inc.

Software for the Home

Software for home use reflects the varied tastes of users. One of the most common uses of home computers is game playing. Computer games range from violent, graphically complex adventure games to simple, traditional games like solitaire. Action and adventure games are quite popular, such as *King's Quest* by Sierra On-Line, Inc. In *King's Quest*, the user plays the part of the hero on a dangerous mission. Sierra On-Line even developed a network on which subscribers can play games against each other. Home computer users also enjoy educational games, such as *Where in the World Is Carmen Sandiego?* by Broderbund.

The GPS Phenomenon

GPS is an acronym for Global Positioning System, a navigational system developed by the U.S. Department of Defense beginning in the late 1970s. GPS is implemented through a series of 24 satellites. These satellites transmit toward the earth radio signals that can be received by special GPS equipment. At any point on the earth, receivers can detect 5 to 8 GPS satellites. The signals from these satellites, when received, indicate the receiver's position and can be used to calculate direction and velocity of the receiver.

The GPS system started as a military project to aid in positioning ships, planes, vehicles, and personnel around the world. The system is also used for targeting devices on weaponry. Since its inception, however, GPS has proved to be a beneficial technology in many fields, including civilian navigation, hunting, hiking, mapping, and surveying.

Courtesy of Magellan Systems Corp.

The GPS satellites transmit two signals. The most accurate signal is referred to as the Precise Positioning System (PPS). This signal is encrypted and is for military use only. It provides accuracy to within 18 meters horizontally and 28 meters vertically. The other signal, the Standard Positioning System (SPS), is made less accurate on purpose by the Department of Defense to deter enemy forces from using the technology against the United States and its allies. The SPS signal provides accuracy to within 100 meters horizontally and 156 meters vertically. The only difference between the signals is their accuracy. They both transmit three-dimensional coordinates from which the latitude, longitude, elevation, and time of day can be determined.

Courtesy of Magellan Systems Corp.

Commercially, a wide array of products that use the SPS to display information has been released. These range from handheld navigational devices used by campers, hikers, and hunters to more expensive units used in automobiles, boats, and airplanes. There are even devices you can hook into your portable computer to display where you are and where you are going. You can use these devices and the associated software to indicate where you want to go, and the software will tell you how to get there from your current location.

Understanding that the SPS signal is inaccurate has allowed many companies to develop GPS devices that correlate satellite data with ground-based transmitters at a known location, such as an airport. This technique gives much better accuracy—to within one millimeter! In tests, these devices have been linked to on-board airline computers and used to land airplanes accurately and safely without human intervention. After the testing phase is through, it is possible that we may see such applications used widely on transportation vehicles of the future.

Home education is becoming increasingly popular. Young children can learn the alphabet and acquire reading skills with computer games. Teenagers can prepare for college entrance exams. CD-ROM programs with video clips teach foreign languages, and encyclopedias and atlases are available on CD-ROM. The *Auto Almanac*, published annually by CE3, provides prospective buyers with information on more than 1,500 automobiles.

Specialized file management software is used at home by hobbyists to keep track of their collections, such as coins, stamps, baseball cards, CDs, and videos. Many cookbooks are available on disk, and most of them enable users to add their favorite recipes to the collection.

Home users can subscribe to information services that provide electronic mail, news, stock quotes, movie reviews, and access to shopping malls. Private bulletin boards enable users to exchange views on topics of interest, send e-mail, and share public domain software. (Chapter 6 discusses in more detail the use of home computers for communications.)

Lesson Summary

➤ Integrated packages combine features of common productivity software, including word processing, electronic spreadsheet, and database management system programs.

➤ A software suite is a collection of full-featured, stand-alone programs.

➤ Integrated packages and software suites enable the easy transfer of data between applications.

➤ Personal information managers (PIMs) are designed to maintain telephone and address information, keep track of appointments and projects, keep notes, perform mail-merge operations, and print.

➤ Accounting and personal finance software keeps track of financial transactions and prints checks.

➤ A network browser makes it easy for individuals to locate information on the Internet.

➤ Desktop videoconferencing allows users in different locations to see each other while working on a project together.

➤ Painting, drawing, and photo-editing programs are specialized graphics programs that permit artistic expression with the computer.

➤ Computer-assisted design and computer-assisted manufacturing software is used to design new products, estimate costs, and control assembly-line manufacturing with robots.

➤ Home computers are used for games and education. Hobbyists keep track of collections, and cooks maintain their recipes on home computers. Information services and bulletin boards deliver news and facilitate communication.

Lesson Review

Key Terms

bit mapping	contact management	morphing	photo-editing program
bundle	software	network browser	software suite
computer-aided design	desktop videoconferencing	painting program	task management software
(CAD)	digitizing tablet	personal finance program	vector graphics
computer-aided manufac-	drawing program	personal information	
turing (CAM)	integrated package	manager (PIM)	

Matching

In the blank next to each of the following terms or phrases, write the letter of the corresponding term or phrase.

_i_ 1. Permits people to see each other and work on a project from computers at different locations

_d_ 2. Software to assist in keeping track of appointments and scheduling

_b_ 3. Individual applications that can exchange data easily

_e_ 4. Creating a picture by turning individual pixels on and off

_j_ 5. Enables an artist to remove blemishes and add coloring

_h_ 6. A graphics technique that causes an image to appear to change into something different

_c_ 7. A collection of program modules that use a standard set of commands

_a_ 8. Makes it easy to find your way around the Internet

_f_ 9. Graphics created by plotting the points required to create an object and then connecting lines between the points

_g_ 10. Can be used to estimate manufacturing costs before production begins

a. network browser

b. integrated package

c. software suite

d. PIM

e. bit mapping

f. vector graphics

g. CAM

h. morphing

i. desktop videoconferencing

j. photo-editing program

Multiple Choice

Circle the letter of the correct choice for each of the following.

1. Which of the following is a capability of a personal information manager?

   a. calendar and schedule management

   b. financial tracking

   c. CAD/CAM software

   d. all of the above

2. Calendar and schedule management includes which of the following?

   a. an alarm to serve as an appointment reminder

   b. automatic telephone dialing

   c. automatic scheduling of recurring tasks

   d. a and c

3. Which of the following is *not* true about PIMs?

    a. Most PIMs have Internet access.

    b. PIMs should be able to reschedule overdue projects automatically.

    c. PIMs are designed to interface with different fax programs.

    d. none of the above

4. Painting programs offer many capabilities, including which of the following?

    a. simulating the appearance of paint, airbrush, chalk, crayon, and colored pencil

    b. altering backgrounds to simulate different types of canvas

    c. blending and smearing of lines

    d. all of the above

5. Computers are being used increasingly at home for which of the following?

    a. access to stock quotes, movie reviews, and recipes

    b. management of hobbyists' collections

    c. games and education

    d. all of the above

6. Which of the following is *not* an example of a network browser?

    a. Navigator

    b. PIM

    c. Explorer

    d. Mosaic

7. Desktop videoconferencing allows users to _____.

    a. see each other

    b. work on the same project

    c. hear each other

    d. all of the above

8. Without a graphical network browser, the commands for the World Wide Web would look like _____.

    a. a GUI screen

    b. UNIX commands

    c. a spreadsheet

    d. bit mapping

9. What do you call the process of creating an image by turning individual pixels on and off?

    a. CAM

    b. bit mapping

    c. vector graphics

    d. digitizing   *graphics to data*

10. What would an engineer use to assist in testing a new automobile before production?

    a. CAE

    b. CAD

    c. morphing

    d. bit mapping

Completion

In the blank provided, write the correct answer for each of the following.

1. Most network browsers provide a(n) __*graphic*__ interface for the Internet.

2. Software that can be copied and used without any need to acknowledge the source is __*public domain*__

3. Vendors frequently __*bundle*__ software and include it with the purchase of a computer.

4. A(n) __*accounting and personal finance*__ program is useful for home budgeting and keeping a checkbook.

5. __*task management*__ software is used for scheduling and prioritizing projects.

6. __*Painting*__ programs create an image using bit mapping.

7. A cartoon and a photograph can be merged using ___animation graphics___.

8. Project teams can work together from different locations using ___video conferencing___.

9. A(n) ___digitizing tablet___ is used to convert graphics into data that can be processed by a computer.

10. ___CAD/CAM___ programs are used to design products and analyze those products before production.

Review

On a separate sheet of paper, answer the following questions.

1. Cite some advantages of buying an integrated software package rather than separate programs.

2. What is the main advantage of a software suite over an integrated package?

3. What capabilities may be found in personal information management software?

4. Businesses need accounting software for what types of functions?

5. In what ways can CAD/CAM programs be helpful to engineers?

6. What results can be achieved with animated computer graphics programs?

7. What uses can you think of for desktop videoconferencing?

8. How could PIM software be useful to you?

9. What can be accomplished using a photo-editing program?

10. What is the major difference between a painting program and a drawing program?

Critical Thinking

On a separate sheet of paper, answer the following questions.

1. What effect might computerized photo editing have on photos and videos that are used as evidence in criminal cases?

2. Can you think of any advantages or disadvantages to using only integrated software in college labs?

3. How might you efficiently use the contact management feature of a personal information manager?

4. What have you heard about the different network browsers? Which do you think would be best for you?

5. Can you think of any disadvantages to having desktop videoconferencing capabilities on every computer in a business?

Further Discovery

CorelDRAW! 6 Expert's Edition. Gary Bouton (Indianapolis, IN: NRP, 1995).

The Little Quicken Book. Lawrence J. Magid and Louis G. Fortis (Berkeley, CA: PeachPit, 1996).

Special Edition Using Lotus Notes 4. C. Richards (Indianapolis, IN: Que, 1996).

Special Edition Using Novell PerfectOffice 3. Bill Bruck (Indianapolis, IN: Que, 1995).

Special Edition Using Microsoft Office Professional for Windows 95. Rick Winter and Patty Winter (Indianapolis, IN: Que, 1996).

Using ACT! Lori Jaworski (Indianapolis, IN: Que, 1995).

Using Lotus SmartSuite 3, Special Edition. Daniel Gasteiger et al. (Indianapolis, IN: Que, 1994).

On-line Discovery

You can access the Internet resources for the following questions by going to the Que Education and Training Web site at URL http://www.ciyf98.com/discovery. From this page, click the link for Lesson 6B and then click the link to the resource you want to access.

1. Emerging software is clearly driven by the companies and types of companies that make up the software industry. *The Economist*, an influential British business magazine, published **"A World Gone Soft: A Survey of the Software Industry,"** in May 1996. After taking a look at this survey (http://www.economist.com/surveys/software/index.html), what do you think will be some of the important new software genres in the near future? Will the companies that do well be small or large? Will the companies that own media content (such as publishers, film studios, and television producers) dominate the software market?

2. Browse the Yahoo! directory page on **Software** (http://www.yahoo.com/ Computers_and_Internet/Software), which provides links to information about many different types of applications. See whether you can find three applications of computer software that are new to you. Are there any that you think would be useful in your home or office?

3. Personal finance applications have become very popular recently. Many of these applications even work with online banking services offered by banks, savings and loans, and credit unions. Using these services, you can manage your accounts, check balances, download statements, and pay bills, all from the same program. Two of the most popular personal finance programs are **Intuit's Quicken** and **Microsoft Money**. Look at the Web sites for these products: http://www.intuit.com for Quicken and http://www.microsoft.com/moneyzone for Microsoft Money. What electronic banking features do these programs provide? Do they work with only certain financial institutions? Think about using such software in your own household and explore the potential problems and difficulties that might emerge with doing all banking and finance on the computer. Contact your own bank or credit union and find out whether it offers any on-line banking services.

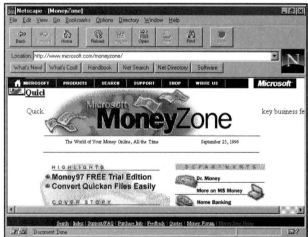

PART III

Getting Connected

Have you "surfed the Net" or "browsed the Web" yet? No? Then what are you waiting for? The world is shrinking as people from around the world are communicating with each other, regardless of national borders or historical differences. All it takes to join in is a computer with basic hardware and software, a telephone line, and an Internet service provider. You can be part of the communications revolution.

CHAPTER 7

Data Communications

The world is shrinking. Computers and their capability to communicate with each other have removed distance from our consideration. People anywhere in the world can use their computers to "talk" to someone nearby or halfway around the world.

In Lesson 7A, you learn about the hardware and software used when computers "talk" to other computers.

Lesson 7B tells you about the networks that are being created to connect computer systems: local area networks (LANs), wide area networks (WANs), and intranets.

Telecommunications

Outline

Hardware
    Modems
    Modulation Protocols
    Channels
        Transmission Media
        Transmission Modes
    Digital Telephony
Software
Uses of Telecommunications
    Telecommuting
    Electronic Mail
    Bulletin Boards
    Online Information Services
    Teleconferencing
    Facsimile Transmissions
The Impact of Telecommunications

Learning Objectives

When you have finished reading this lesson, you will be able to

➤ Describe the hardware necessary for communications between computers

➤ Define modulation protocols

➤ Describe the various types of transmission media

➤ Explain the difference between synchronous and asynchronous transmission modes

➤ Define Integrated Services Digital Network

➤ Discuss communications software

➤ Describe the various uses for telecommunications

QUE Labs

➤ **Networks**

➤ **Internet**

➤ **World Wide Web**

➤ **Building a Web Server**

Suppose that you are interested in knowing the price your auto dealer pays for those neat new Ford Probe GTs. If you had that information, you would be able to negotiate a better price. Can your computer help? There's nothing on your computer pertaining to that subject. But the computer can do something else besides store and retrieve data. Equipped with communications hardware and software, your computer can communicate with other computers—making data on other computers available directly to you. And new possibilities exist! By contacting an online information service, such as CompuServe, you can join a car-buying forum (a discussion group) that provides dealer invoice prices for all currently available cars.

Computers can communicate in two ways: telecommunications and networks. With **telecommunications**, two computers establish a link through the telephone system. In a **computer network**, discussed in Lesson 6B, the computers are linked directly by high-speed cables.

Linking computers through the telephone system isn't an ideal solution, as you will see. The telephone system is designed for the human voice, not for data. The system transmits data at a very slow rate, but the connection is cheap and flexible. Millions of people use telecommunications every day to expand their reach—so can you.

Hardware

To link two computers through the telephone system, a hardware accessory called a **modem** is necessary. The hardware is needed because the telephone system conveys information by using analog techniques rather than digital techniques.

Modems

Computers are **digital** machines. Any information that goes into a computer must be expressed in digits, or numbers. As discussed in Lesson 1A, computers work only with binary numbers. Telephone wires, however, are designed to carry analog signals. **Analog signals** are electrical representations of sound waves.

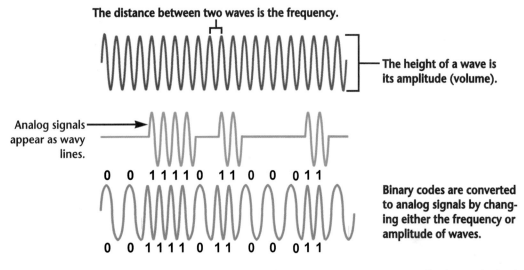

The distance between two waves is the frequency.

The height of a wave is its amplitude (volume).

Analog signals appear as wavy lines.

0 0 1 1 1 1 0 1 1 0 0 0 1 1

Binary codes are converted to analog signals by changing either the frequency or amplitude of waves.

0 0 1 1 1 1 0 1 1 0 0 0 1 1

Efforts are under way to convert the telephone system from analog to digital. The job will not be complete until well into the next century. As long as your communications company is still using analog equipment, your message must be sent in analog signals. Linking two computers through the analog telephone system requires that both computers be equipped with modems. Using a process called **modulation**, a modem transforms the computer's digital signals into analog tones that can be conveyed through the telephone system. On the receiving end, the process used is **demodulation**, in which the other modem transforms this signal from analog back to digital. Modems can play both roles, modulation and demodulation. In fact, that's where the name *modem* comes from. It's short for modulator/demodulator.

Modems are of two kinds, internal and external. An **internal modem** is designed to fit within one of your computer's expansion slots. It gets its power from the computer's expansion bus. An **external modem** has its own case and power supply. For this reason, external modems are slightly more expensive.

Most of the modems sold today can send and receive faxes as well as computer data. These modems are called **fax modems**. For more information on faxing and fax modems, see the section "Facsimile Transmissions" later in this lesson.

Courtesy of Hayes Microcomputer Products

This Hayes OPTIMA FAX modem is fast enough to transfer large data files, graphic images, and multimedia.

Modulation Protocols

To establish communications, modems must conform to standards called **modulation protocols**. These protocols, set by international standards organizations, ensure that your Brand A modem can communicate with another modem, even if it is made by a different manufacturer.

Several modulation protocols are in common use. Each protocol specifies all the necessary details of communication, including the **data transfer rate**. This is the rate by which the two modems can exchange data. The rate is measured in **bits per second** (**bps**). You may encounter the term *baud rate* when a modem's data transfer rate is discussed, but the technical definitions of baud rate and bps rate differ. The correct measurement of a modem's data transfer rate is the bps rate. The baud rate is the maximum number of changes that can occur per second in the electrical state of a communications circuit.

The standard modulation protocol, called **V.34**, established in 1994, permits two similarly equipped modems to exchange data at a rate of 28800 bits per second. An earlier standard, **V.32 bis**, established a rate of 14400 bps. Standards before V.32 regulated communication at 9600, 2400, 1200, and 300 bps.

Two modems can communicate only if both follow the same modulation protocol. If your modem follows the V.34 protocol, your modem cannot communicate at 28800 bps unless the modem on the other end observes the same protocol. However, most modems can **fall back** to a lower rate. When a modem attempts to establish a connection, it automatically negotiates with the modem on the other end. The two modems try to establish which protocols they share, and then they use the fastest rate that both modems have. If a computer with a 9600 bps modem is connected to a computer with a 14400 bps modem, the data would be transferred between the two computers at 9600 bps.

TechTalk

V.34 and V.32 bis are versions of the codes established by an international body of standards governing modems. The term *bis* means "in addition to." Therefore, V.32 bis provided additional functionality to V.32 modems. International standards enable a modem in the U.S. to communicate with modems in other parts of the world.

Channels

The **communication channel** is the physical link between the two computers. Two important characteristics of communication channels are the transmission medium and the transmission mode.

Transmission Media

Transmission media in widespread use are wired media and wireless media. Wired transmission media include twisted-pair cable, coaxial cable, and fiber optic cable. **Twisted-pair cable** is a simple and inexpensive medium, but it is slow and susceptible to errors. **Coaxial cable** (coax) is faster and stronger than twisted-pair cable but is more expensive. Coax is used by cable television. **Fiber optic cable** is the newest and fastest transmission medium. Instead of wires, thin glass fibers with a width less than that of a human hair are used. Light pulses, rather than electrical signals, are sent on the fibers.

Dish antennas transmit and receive data with communications satellites that are orbiting more than 20,000 miles above the earth.

Courtesy of Thomson Consumer Electronics

Wireless transmission media include cellular telephone systems, microwave relay transmission, and satellite transmission. **Cellular telephone systems** enable portable computer users to keep in touch with central offices while they are working in the field. **Microwave transmission** is used by telephone companies and computer networking utilities to provide long-distance data and telephone communication. Microwaves are limited to straight-line transmission; they cannot travel through buildings or mountains. **Satellite transmission** can blanket the earth with computer connectivity; any person using a suitably equipped portable computer can originate and receive messages through satellite transmission.

An important characteristic of any transmission medium is its bandwidth. **Bandwidth** relates to the data transfer capacity of the medium (how many messages it can carry at one time). Bandwidth is usually measured in kilobits per second (Kbps), megabits per second (Mbps), and gigabits per second (Gbps). A **gigabit** is one billion bits.

The rate at which twisted-pair cable can transfer data is much slower than the rate at which a floppy disk transfers data into your computer's memory. Coaxial cable is faster than twisted-pair cable. Fiber optic cable has a very high bandwidth. Some experimental systems are capable of transferring more than 5 Gbps. That is enough to transmit the text of a 32-volume encyclopedia in the blink of an eye.

Courtesy of Sony Electronics Inc.

Mounted four stories above Times Square in New York City, this Sony video screen is programmed to run a seven-day loop of video segments. The files are transferred by modem to a separate system that cues the screen to run specific video spots at a scheduled time.

Transmission Modes

The **transmission mode** enables the receiving computer to know where one byte ends and the next byte begins on the transmission medium. The two transmission modes are asynchronous and synchronous.

With **synchronous transmission**, the two computers synchronize themselves so that a given unit of data is relayed during a set time period. Synchronous transmission is more commonly used with minicomputers and mainframes. With **asynchronous transmission**, each byte is marked with a start bit and a stop bit. Asynchronous transmission is slower than synchronous transmission because 20 percent more data must be sent (ten bits are required to convey an eight-bit character). Asynchronous transmission, however, is simpler to implement. Modems use the asynchronous transmission mode.

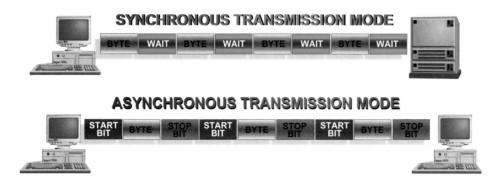

SYNCHRONOUS TRANSMISSION MODE

BYTE | WAIT | BYTE | WAIT | BYTE | WAIT | BYTE | WAIT

ASYNCHRONOUS TRANSMISSION MODE

START BIT | BYTE | STOP BIT | START BIT | BYTE | STOP BIT | START BIT | BYTE | STOP BIT

In synchronous transmission mode, data is transmitted between computers at timed intervals. Synchronous transmission mode is faster and more accurate than asynchronous transmission but requires more expensive equipment.

In asynchronous transmission mode, data is transmitted at irregular intervals. Start and stop bits are used to identify individual bytes.

Digital Telephony

The telephone company is going digital—eventually. Most people do not realize that major portions of the long-distance telephone system have already been converted from analog to digital. The problem, which is called the **last-mile problem**, lies in local service delivery, where analog services prevail. The standard telephone wires that deliver services to most homes and businesses are twisted-pair. A huge capital investment, estimated to top $325 billion, would be required to convert all the twisted-pair wiring to high-bandwidth media, such as fiber-optic cable. Don't count on it happening soon.

An interim solution to the last-mile problem is already available. It is called **Integrated Services Digital Network** (**ISDN**). ISDN provides digital telephone and data services to homes and offices but uses today's twisted-pair wiring. ISDN telephone users enjoy noise-free, CD-quality sound. They can view a TV-like picture of the person on the other end of the line. Using twisted-pair wiring, ISDN cannot convey data very quickly, but no modulation or demodulation is necessary. In place of today's modems, ISDN computer users have **digital modems**. These devices are not really modems because they do not modulate and demodulate. They help the linked computers to synchronize data transmission and provide error correction. ISDN services are becoming available throughout the U.S. for as little as $32 per month after the payment of an installation fee. ISDN is becoming popular enough that a term to describe the standard analog service has been coined: **Plain Old Telephone Service** (**POTS**).

A more controversial topic surrounding ISDN concerns the capability to wiretap, or intercept telephone calls. Digital services make wiretapping virtually impossible without some built-in help. The FBI asked the communications companies to build in that wiretapping capability for the sake of national security. Because using a wiretap requires a court order, the FBI argued that individual rights are protected, yet an important tool in finding and prosecuting criminals and international terrorists is still available to the authorities. Critics argued that not having the capability to wiretap absolutely protects individual rights of privacy. These critics said that illegal use of wiretapping would be too easy. A bill called the Digital Telephony Act of 1994 was approved by Congress, giving the FBI the wiretapping capability it sought.

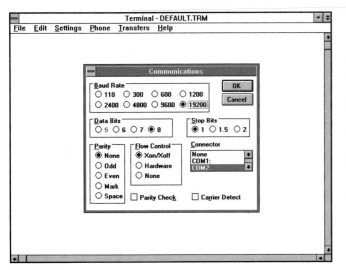

The Terminal communications program is available with Microsoft Windows.

Software

A **communications program** enables a computer to communicate with other computers through the telephone system. In effect, the program transforms a computer into a remote terminal of the distant computer. A **remote terminal** enables the user to operate the distant computer, just as if that person were sitting in front of the distant computer and using its keyboard.

A good communications program provides utilities that make telecommunications easy. The program directs the modem to dial the telephone number needed. The program also enables the user to choose communications settings, such as the data transfer rate. When a PC is being used as a terminal with a minicomputer or mainframe computer, software makes the PC emulate (act like) a terminal. This emulation is necessary because the operating systems of the minicomputer and mainframe expect to work with terminals, not microcomputers. A good program includes the capability to emulate many widely used computer terminals. The program also has features that enable the user to store and print the received data.

Uses of Telecommunications

Telecommunications is changing the way many things are accomplished and even inventing new things to do. The following is a brief look at some areas affected by telecommunications.

Telecommuting

Telecommuting is the combination of telecommunications with commuting. When you telecommute, you use your personal computer and telephone lines to connect to the computer at work and do work-related tasks at home. Then you can send your results to the computer at work through the telephone lines.

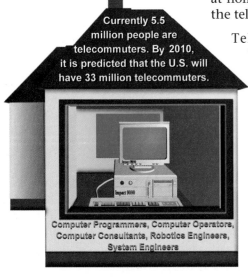

Many computer professionals are joining the growing number of telecommuters.

Telecommuting has pros and cons. The pros are impressive. Telecommuting can facilitate work for people who have disabilities that limit mobility or require special adaptive equipment. If one-fourth of all workers were to telecommute rather than drive to work, cities and states could save billions of dollars on road construction. Reducing the number of cars on the roads by 20 percent would improve air quality, and the United States could reduce its dependence on foreign oil.

As you might expect, however, some bosses don't like telecommuting. How does an employer know whether an employee is really working or just sitting around watching television talk shows? Some workers do not like telecommuting. In many firms, advancement requires putting in "face time" and creating a positive impression. That's hard to do through a computer. Another drawback is that some telecommuters report problems in drawing a line between work at home and family responsibilities. For them, it's easier to work at the office, where such conflicts do not occur.

Electronic Mail

Electronic mail (**e-mail**) enables you to send messages from your computer for access at someone else's computer. Both the sender and the recipient must be part of the e-mail system. One such system is MCIMail, a subscription-based electronic mail service that uses telecommunications access.

In use daily by millions of people, electronic mail has led to a renaissance of letter writing. Compared to the postal service, electronic mail has many advantages:

➤ *It's fast.* Most systems can relay your message to the recipient in a matter of minutes or seconds. Many systems let you check to see whether the recipient has accessed your message.

➤ *It's easy.* When you contact the service, you see a list of the messages you have received. You read the first message and then decide how to respond. You can reply to the message if you like, or just delete it if it requires no reply. You can save it or print it. You can even forward the message to others.

➤ *It's fun.* International electronic mail systems enable you to find "pen pals" all over the world.

➤ *It's cheap.* Worldwide electronic mail access is available through services such as CompuServe; these services charge less than you would expect to pay for monthly telephone service. At a college or university, worldwide e-mail service may be available for registered students at a nominal price.

➤ *It's flexible.* You can send a message to more than one person if you like.

E-mail does have disadvantages. Some e-mail systems require you to be part of the same system to receive your message. However, if you have Internet access, that e-mail system will allow communications with any other Internet user, around the world. The **Internet**, a global network of computer networks, is fast emerging as the Grand Central Station for world e-mail. Networks are discussed in Lesson 7B, and the Internet is discussed in Chapter 8.

Another, more serious disadvantage is that electronic mail lacks the privacy protection given to first-class mail. Although a federal statute protects electronic mail privacy, it does so only during transmission, not during storage. Anyone with legal access can access and read your messages once they have been stored on disk. Activist groups such as the Electronic Frontier Foundation (EFF) are working to extend to e-mail the same protections that are extended to first-class mail. Recent court decisions have said that company management may read the e-mail of any of its employees on the company's e-mail system. If you don't want other people to read your message, don't send it by e-mail.

E-mail is becoming so common that it is changing the way we communicate. An e-mail message is easily forwarded to others and can be incorporated into other messages or word processing documents. When a

Using America Online, you can read the mission statement of the Electronic Frontier Foundation.

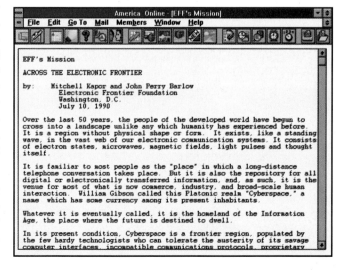

message is sent, the recipient often responds quickly, perhaps without giving the answer all the thought it deserves. Communications and writing classes in high schools and colleges are adding discussions on tips and tricks on using e-mail.

Bulletin Boards

Electronic **bulletin board systems** (**BBSs**) are a new means of casual communications for computer users. A BBS is a computer system—often just a PC equipped with a modem and special software—that enables computer users to access the system, send and receive e-mail messages, and obtain computer files. If you have a personal computer, communications software, a modem, a telephone line, and the telephone number of a BBS, you can explore the BBS world. According to one estimate, there are more than 45,000 BBSs in the U.S. alone. Some are free, but most charge a modest fee.

To use a bulletin board, you use your communications program to call the bulletin board telephone number. When the BBS answers, you see a menu listing the available options, such as electronic mail, games, and file libraries. Many BBS systems offer extensive libraries of **public domain software** (noncopyrighted software that anyone may copy), **freeware** (copyrighted software that can be freely copied but not sold), and **shareware** (copyrighted software that requires the payment of a registration fee if you decide to use it). You can download this software for your use. (In **downloading**, you transfer a file from the remote computer to your own.) Users contribute to a BBS's richness when they upload software. (In **uploading**, you transfer a file from your computer to the remote computer.)

BBSs raise interesting legal questions. Is the BBS operator legally responsible for messages and files that have been left by the system's users? If the BBS is like a newspaper, the operator is responsible. A newspaper is responsible if it prints something illegal, such as a defamatory statement. If the BBS is like a telephone system, the operator is not responsible. The courts have ruled that a telephone company cannot be held responsible for illegal messages. At present, it is not clear whether courts will consider BBSs more like newspapers or telephone companies.

On-line Information Services

An **on-line information service** is like a BBS that can accept calls from thousands of subscribers at a time. With more than two million subscribers, CompuServe is the oldest on-line information service. Subscribers to on-line information services can exchange electronic mail with other users, download files from extensive file libraries, engage in real-time "chatting" with other computer users, get the latest stock quotes, and find information on thousands of topics. Other leading services include America Online, Prodigy, and Delphi.

Thousands of people can be connected to an online information service at the same time. A bank of modems collects information from all the users and forwards it to the central computer.

Interactive Television: TV You Can Get Your Hands On

Until recently, any attempts to talk to your television went unheard—at least by your TV. Current developments, however, are changing that situation.

GTE, the first telephone company to offer video services in the U.S., began testing interactive television and traditional video services in Cerritos, California, in 1988. More than twenty interactive programs were developed for broadcast during the trials. Catalog ordering services have been among the most popular programs with viewers.

The trials, scheduled for a wide range of markets across the U.S., are primarily aimed at testing consumer response to the services, not the technologies themselves, according to an article in the June 1994 issue of *Computer Graphics World.*

As a result of this testing, GTE now has a cable station—GTE Main Street, Center Screen—which is an expanded pay-per-view channel. The company is also planning to build a video network projected to include at least 77 million homes in 66 key markets in the next 10 years. By the year 2003, the company projects 2 million residential subscribers.

In 1995, GTE/AT&T initiated a trial in Manassas, Virginia, to include such applications as video on demand, home shopping, multiplayer and multihousehold games, information services, and educational programming. AT&T planned another trial with Viacom International on its cable system in Castro Valley, California. Both trials used AT&T transport equipment, fiber optics, and coaxial cable. Some trial sites will also test StarSight, an electronic on-screen programming guide.

Services provided by Interactive Networks (IN) enable subscribers to predict the plays in sporting events and to compete with the contestants in some popular game shows. IN has also developed interactive programming for soap operas, news, documentaries, and dramas. Ultimately, IN plans to extend its interactive capabilities to permit give-and-take discussion among home viewers and TV talk shows, such as *Oprah* and *Larry King Live.*

Microsoft, a strong advocate of interactive television, has joined with Tele-Communications Inc. (TCI) to establish their own cable system. This system will enable viewers to select programs at their convenience, regardless of the preset time slot. Viewers will also be able to request lists of offerings by category and by actor and actress. Hughes-Avicom has also made plans to offer Microsoft Interactive TV (MITV) for in-flight entertainment.

Not all interactive television is entertainment-oriented. A growing number of colleges throughout the world are offering courses to remote sites via interactive television. Malaysia has started a nationwide interactive education network designed to provide an electronic library system to schools throughout the country.

The architecture and infrastructure for all these systems haven't been finally determined, but most predictions about hardware requirements for interactive television include cable and wiring, a computer server, a communication switcher, and a set-top box. Whether that box will rest on a television set, a computer, or some hybrid of the two remains to be seen.

Teleconferencing

A **teleconference** is a meeting in which the participants do not meet physically but use telephones and computers to meet. Conference call capability has been available from telephone companies for many years. The computer conference is similar to a bulletin board system. When one computer sends a message, all the other participants can receive it at the same time.

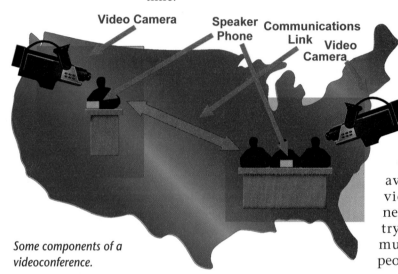

Some components of a videoconference.

The next step in teleconferencing is **videoconferencing**. Videoconferencing involves sending video signals as well as telephone and computer data signals. Videoconferencing did require special hardware and special digital telephone lines, but recently, POTS videoconferencing has become available. The widespread use of videoconferencing could have a negative impact on the travel industry because videoconferences are much cheaper than transporting people to a meeting place.

Facsimile Transmissions

Facsimile transmission—or **fax**, as it is popularly known—enables you to send an image of a document over the telephone lines to anyone who has a fax machine. The sending fax machine makes a digital image of the document, converts it to analog for the telephone system, and sends the analog signals. The receiving fax machine converts the analog signals to digital signals, converts the digital signals to an image of the document, and prints that image.

A HyperTerminal screen.

Most of the modems sold today include fax capabilities. If you install fax software on your computer, you can send and receive faxes from it. One drawback is that you can send only those documents that you have created with your computer, unless your computer is equipped with a scanner.

The Impact of Telecommunications

In the telecommunications age, messages can be sent to India as easily as to Indiana. Two citizens of the world can "chat" with each other using telecommunications regardless of where in the world they live. The result isn't welcomed by totalitarian governments, which can survive only if they limit communication between individuals.

In the former Soviet Union, for example, "underground" bulletin boards provided a crucial forum for free speech and accurate information. The bulletin boards may have even played a role in the Soviet Union's downfall. In China, computer networks and fax machines told the world the truth about the brutal suppression of the student democracy movement. With global telecommunications available, governments are finding it harder to hide the facts and interrupt the exchange of ideas.

Lesson Summary

➤ Telecommunications refers to the linking of two computers through the telephone system. A modem and communications software are required.

➤ Modems translate the computer's digital signals into the analog signals that the phone system was designed to carry. Today's modems can transfer data at up to 32,600 bits per second. New digital telephone services will facilitate higher transmission speeds.

➤ The communication channel is the physical link between two computers and includes the transmission medium and transmission mode.

➤ The transmission medium is either wired or wireless. Wired media include twisted pair, coaxial, and fiber optic cable. Wireless media include cellular telephone, microwave, and satellite transmissions.

➤ The bandwidth of a medium refers to how many messages it can carry at one time. Some experimental fiber optic systems can transmit at more than five gigabits per second.

➤ The transmission mode is either synchronous or asynchronous. Synchronous transmission uses time control, and asynchronous transmission uses start and stop bits to mark each byte. Modems use asynchronous mode.

➤ Integrated Services Digital Network (ISDN) uses existing transmission media but transmits digital signals. ISDN uses digital modems and synchronous transmission.

➤ Electronic mail, or e-mail, allows messages sent from your computer to be accessed by the recipient at his or her computer, as long as you both have access to the same e-mail system. The Internet is providing a base for interconnecting many e-mail systems.

➤ Telecommuting involves using your computer at home attached by telecommunications to the computer at work.

➤ Bulletin board systems (BBSs) enable independent computer users, using telecommunications, to interact with each other through a central contact.

➤ On-line information services are national or international services that provide BBS services, e-mail, and often access to the Internet.

➤ Teleconferencing and videoconferencing provide meetings with the participants' not physically coming together, but sharing voice, video, and computer information.

➤ Telecommunications technology has raised many legal questions that the courts will have to settle.

Lesson Review

Key Terms

analog signal	download	Internet	telecommunications
asynchronous transmission	e-mail	last-mile problem	telecommuting
bandwidth	electronic mail	microwave transmission	teleconference
bits per second (bps)	external modem	modem	transmission mode
bulletin board system (BBS)	facsimile transmission	modulation	twisted-pair cable
cellular telephone system	fall back	modulation protocol	upload
coaxial cable	fax	on-line information service	V.32 bis
communication channel	fax modem	Plain Old Telephone	V.34
communications program	fiber optic cable	Service (POTS)	videoconferencing
computer network	freeware	public domain software	
data transfer rate	gigabit	remote terminal	
demodulation	Integrated Services Digital	satellite transmission	
digital	Network (ISDN)	shareware	
digital modem	internal modem	synchronous transmission	

Matching

In the blank next to each of the following terms or phrases, write the letter of the corresponding term or phrase.

_____ 1. Another name for e-mail

_f_ 2. Computers linked by high-speed cables

_c_ 3. Uses light pulses

_g_ 4. Facsimile transmission

_h_ 5. Requires a digital modem

_b_ 6. Bits per second

_d_ 7. One billion bits

_a_ 8. Needs start and stop bits

_i_ 9. Videoconference

_e_ 10. Called modulation

a. asynchronous transmission

b. data transfer rate

c. fiber optics

d. gigabit

e. digital to analog

f. computer network

g. fax

h. ISDN

i. teleconference

j. electronic mail

Multiple Choice

Circle the letter of the correct choice for each of the following.

1. What is telecommunications?

   a. any linking of two computers

   b. linking two computers through the telephone system

   c. linking two computers with direct high-speed lines

   d. all of the above

2. A modem is necessary because _____.

   a. computers are digital

   b. telephone systems transmit analog waves

   c. telephones aren't fast enough without them

   d. both a and b

3. If a computer with a 9600 bps modem is communicating with a computer with a 14400 bps modem, the communications is occurring at what rate?

   a. 9600 bps

   b. 14400 bps

   c. both a and b

   d. Communications cannot occur.

4. Which of the following wired transmission media is the fastest?

   a. twisted-pair

   b. coaxial

   c. fiber optics

   d. cellular telephone

5. To know where one byte ends and the next one begins, the communications must establish _____.

   a. transmission channel

   b. transmission media

   c. transmission mode

   d. transmission mean

6. When data is sent during set time periods, what do you call the transmission mode?

   a. synchronous

   b. asynchronous

   c. protocol

   d. none of the above

7. Digital transmission using today's technology can be accomplished with which of the following?

   a. analog equipment

   b. remote terminals

   c. Integrated Services Digital Network

   d. asynchronous transmission

8. What do you call the combination of video signals, voice signals, and data signals?

   a. teleconferencing

   b. bulletin board systems

   c. the Internet

   d. videoconferencing

9. Which of the following is true when you download data using a bulletin board system?

   a. You must be using a fax modem.

   b. You are transferring a file from a remote computer to your computer.

   c. You are transferring a file from your computer to a remote computer.

   d. You are breaking copyright laws.

10. When must you use a modem?

    a. when the communications link includes analog signals

    b. when you are using fiber optics

    c. when the bandwidth is wide

    d. all of the above

Completion

In the blank provided, write the correct answer for each of the following.

1. _analog signal_ are electrical representations of sound waves.

2. The rate by which two modems can exchange data is called the _data transfer rate_ bps.

3. The physical link between two computers is called the _communication channel_.

4. The number of messages that a transmission medium can carry at one time is known as its _bandwidth_.

5. Using your computer at home to communicate with the computer at work instead of going to work is called _telecommuting_

6. The fast-growing global network of computer networks is the _Internet_.

7. Noncopyrighted software that anyone may copy is called _public domain_ software.

8. You can send an image of a document over telephone lines using _fax_.

9. CompuServe and America Online are examples of _online information service_

10. Modem is a combination of modulation and _demodulation_

Review

On a separate sheet of paper, answer the following questions.

1. Explain why modems are necessary for telecommunications.

2. How do modulation protocols work? Why are they necessary for modems to communicate?

3. What is the difference between wireless transmission and wired transmission? Give examples of each.

4. What is the relationship between transmission media and bandwidth?

5. How does the last-mile problem affect telecommunications?

6. Why does a computer need communications software for telecommunications to occur?

7. What is telecommuting? What are some advantages and disadvantages of telecommuting?

8. What are some advantages and disadvantages of e-mail over the postal service?

9. Cite some examples of the impact of telecommunications.

10. How do teleconferencing and videoconferencing differ?

Critical Thinking

On a separate sheet of paper, answer the following questions.

1. Do you think e-mail should have the same privacy protection that the U.S. mail has? Why? Or why not?

2. Should the federal government have the power to demand that companies build wiretapping capability into digital networks, which are nearly impossible to wiretap without help?

3. Should governments ban some messages, such as pornography, from on-line information services? How could such a ban be administered?

4. What are the advantages of using a fax modem to fax documents? What are the disadvantages?

5. When the majority of the people in the world have access to computers and telecommunications, how might the roles of governments and the relationships among governments change?

Further Discovery

LAN Times Guide to Telephony. David D. Bezar (New York: Osborne/McGraw-Hill, 1995).

Special Edition Using ISDN. James Y. Bryce (Indianapolis, IN: Que, 1995).

Understanding Data Communications. Gilbert Held (Indianapolis, IN: Sams, 1996).

On-line Discovery

You can access the Internet resources for the following questions by going to the Que Education and Training Web site at URL http://www.ciyf98.com/discovery. From this page, click the link for Lesson 7A and then click the link to the resource you want to access.

1. The **Center for Democracy and Technology** (**CDT**) at URL http://www.cdt.org is an advocacy group for free speech rights and civil liberties with respect to telecommunications technologies and policies. The group maintains an extensive archive on government censorship of telecommunications, particularly in connection with the Communications Decency Act. While being aware that this advocacy group has a certain point of view, read some of the texts in this archive (http://www.cdt.org/cda.html). What does the Communications Decency Act censor? What are the principal arguments for and against the Act? Under what conditions should the government censor the content of telecommunications transmissions?

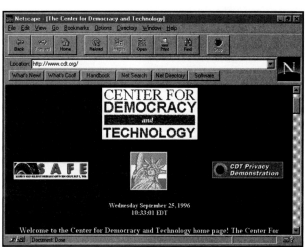

2. Videoconferencing is one of the most exciting areas of development in telecommunications, with applications ranging from business to government to education to home and family. **PictureTel** (http://www.picturetel.com) and **VTel** (http://www.vtel.com) are two of the largest companies that sell videoconferencing equipment. Look through these two companies' home pages, both of which contain good introductions to important videoconferencing concepts and terminology. What kinds of equipment are required for video-conferencing? What kinds of telecommuni-

cations lines are required? What applications do the companies emphasize? In what ways would videoconferencing affect your life? Would you be willing to communicate this way regularly? When you talk on the telephone, do you wish you could see the people with whom you are communicating? Will increased use of videoconferencing really result in a reduction in travel and travel expenses? Why or why not?

LESSON
7B

Computer Networking

Outline

QUE Lab

➤ **Networks**

Learning Objectives

When you have finished reading this lesson, you will be able to

➤ Describe the components that make up a computer network

➤ Explain how networks transmit data and information

➤ Discuss the standards that make it possible for computers to communicate across networks

➤ Discuss the components of a local area network

➤ Define three types of network topologies

➤ Discuss the physical media for wide area networks

➤ Explain the hardware and applications for wide area networks

➤ Explain the differences between intranets and LANs and WANs and discuss the benefits of an intranet

➤ Describe the different types of computer networking software

The first time two computers communicated with one another was May 1, 1964, at Dartmouth College in Hanover, New Hampshire. It was 4 o'clock in the morning when Professor Tom Kurtz successfully transmitted a portion of a BASIC program from one teletype terminal to another.

From this simple beginning, computer communications has become not only essential and ubiquitous, but has blurred every distinction between communications media. Today, we not only send data over telephone lines, but we can conduct voice conversations over the Internet and send and receive interactive data via satellites through the medium of television.

Computer communications have become easier, as well. The technical difficulties of configuring two computers to "talk" to one another have been surmounted, primarily through software design. Moreover, it has become possible for many different types of electronic devices to communicate with other electronic devices—computers to fax machines, telephones to televisions, VCRs and laser disc players to computers.

Communication channels have also become interconnected—telephone lines connect to fiber optic cable to microwave dishes to satellites to cellular phones and modems. Telecommunications use **switched lines** through the telephone companies' PBXs (Public Branch Exchanges). Even though the computerized PBXs can carry more than simple voice communications, you need a **computer network** for fast computer connections.

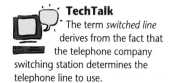

TechTalk
The term *switched line* derives from the fact that the telephone company switching station determines the telephone line to use.

Courtesy of The Bettmann Archive

Courtesy of AT&T

Telephone companies use switched lines at stations known as PBXs. These photographs contrast an early 1900s PBX with today's computerized PBX.

Local area networks can be connected to form a wide area network.

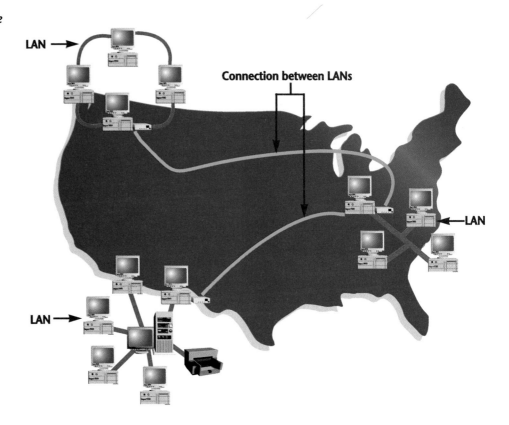

The Purpose of Networks

Because computers process data so quickly, you can justifiably say that they "conquer time." With a computer, you can perform calculations in seconds that would have taken days, weeks, or even years by hand. Computer networks also enable us to conquer another dimension—space. Here are some examples:

➤ Researchers at a small state university need a supercomputer to calculate the results of a sophisticated problem. But they don't have the money to travel to a major supercomputer facility. In the past, these researchers would have to give up. Today, they can send their data to a supercomputer center through the Internet. The next day, they receive the results.

➤ A Massachusetts-based insurance company has discovered a place where many young, educated workers live. Even better, these workers do not mind taking clerical jobs, such as processing insurance claim forms. The place? Ireland. The company sends forms from Massachusetts to Ireland through a satellite network. Workers process the forms there and send them back to Massachusetts through the same network.

➤ You need some information from the Smithsonian, but you don't have the time to visit it. With the aid of the Web, you can tour several Smithsonian collections while sitting in front of your computer. You will see beautiful, full-color graphic images of sculptures, photographs, and paintings.

The United States is becoming abundantly networked for business, government, personal communications, and entertainment purposes. And as it does so, computer networking is changing the very fabric of society. Richard Civille, Director of the Center for Civic Networking in Washington, DC, writes:

> A National Information Infrastructure, designed for Democracy, will help our country work smarter with a better informed citizenry more fully engaged in life, liberty and the pursuit of happiness. Americans will enjoy more efficient, less costly government; (there will be more) high-quality jobs and educated citizens to fill them. We will pave a road away from poverty and promote life-long learning. Such a promise fulfilled will improve the public health, the cultural life of our communities and revitalize our civic institutions. This is the civic promise of information infrastructure—not simply "video dial-tone," 500 channels of movies, home shopping, or interactive video games.

Such an "information infrastructure" is based on computers networked together, as they are in the Internet. According to a 1998 Harris Poll, over 26 percent of all U.S. adults now have an e-mail address, up from 12 percent in the poll taken in 1996. The availability of Internet access is, in large part, responsible for the increase. Internet use rose from 28 percent to 36 percent, and the use of PCs at home rose from 54 percent to 64 percent since the 1996 poll.

In this lesson, you learn more about computer networking as it applies to large enterprises and organizations, governments, and the world. Computer networking is changing the world in every way, turning local communities into a global village. Another prime example is the local or regional Internet service providers (ISP), usually small entrepreneurships that provide e-mail and World Wide Web services for their community.

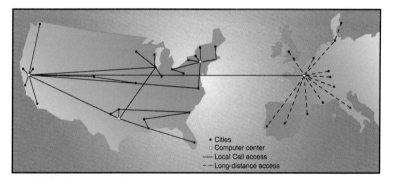

A nationwide network can provide voice and data communications via many different types of computers and network devices.

According to an International Data Corporation (IDC) research study of worldwide Internet use, "We are at the beginning of a high-stakes game of 'Internet leapfrog' in which regions that have a high percentage of aggressive Internet users will be positioned to leap ahead of others in production and profitability growth."

What Is a Computer Network?

A **computer network** is an electronic system that uses hardware, software, and communications devices to connects various terminals together in one or more communications channels in order to share data, information, or both. Computer networks normally speed connections between computers. A computer network links two or more computers with a direct, high-speed connection. Networks are physically composed of terminals and communications channels, both discussed in the following sections.

Terminals

In order for computers or any other communication device to communicate, there must be two or more terminals, connected by a communications channel. A **terminal** is an input and output device connected to a separate processing device. Typically, a *dumb terminal* is a keyboard and monitor. A PC is an *intelligent terminal* because it can perform its own processing. A terminal can be simple or complex; for example, two tin cans, connected by a communications channel made of a length of string, are simple terminals. Today, it is common to see terminals that include telephones, PBXs, PCs, and larger computers.

Communications Channels

A **communications channel** is the means of transmitting data or information between the terminals. The simplest communication channel in use today is two copper wires, called *twisted-pair*, used in basic telephone service. A better channel is *coaxial cable*, used in various television applications. Better yet is *fiber optic cable*, used by phone companies, the telecommunications industry, large business, government, colleges and universities, and other commercial concerns.

These three communications channels are hard-wired; that is, a physical connection between terminals. A fourth channel is *microwave*, which transmits signals through the air between earth stations or satellites. For example, DSS satellite television uses the microwave communications channel.

Twisted-pair wiring is the oldest and slowest. Fiber optic and microwave can provide all the bandwidth necessary for the most sophisticated information delivery.

Methods of Computer Communications

Most communications channels use **asynchronous communications** to transmit data, meaning the data is transmitted one at a time, from start to stop until everything is completely transmitted. This method is contrasted with *synchronous communications*, which transmits data by coordinating it to start and stop with an internal clock signal from the computer. Most modern computers and PCs use asynchronous, and older mainframes use synchronous communications.

The better the communications channel, the more data and information it can transmit. The terms used to describe better channels are bandwidth and transmission speed.

Bandwidth Issues

Bandwidth refers to the capacity of a communications channel to carry data or information. Bandwidth is measured in cycles per second, or *Hertz* (abbreviated Hz). Voice bandwidth is not much of an issue; the frequency range of the human voice is quite narrow, about 300–3,000 Hz. But what happens when a friend tries to play music for you, with a frequency range of 20–20,000 Hz, over the phone? Chances are it doesn't sound quite as good as your stereo. Obviously, twisted-pair has a limited bandwidth.

Bandwidth is measured in two ways. The first is the *number of messages* the channel can carry, whether voice or data. The more messages carried, the better. This is distinct from transmission speed (discussed next) because the type of message determines the number of messages a channel can carry and how quickly the message can be delivered. For example, a credit card authorization request is typically 1K, or 1,000 bits, and takes only an instant. However, if you are downloading a still photograph or even a full-motion video clip from the Web, it could range upward of several megabits and take minutes or even hours. In such cases, files are often compacted using *data compression* techniques to save space and speed up transmission. A commonly used program for data compression is WinZip.

The second way bandwidth is measured is by the *nature and quality of the signal*. Data must have a very clear channel; what you hear as noise on the phone line can completely corrupt a data transmission. Coaxial cable can be affected by inclement weather, and falling autumn leaves can downgrade microwave transmissions. Imagine the significance of this to a bank that is electronically transferring several billion dollars. In addition, full-motion video used in multimedia applications requires very high bandwidth channel capabilities. Thus, the communications channel must be as wide—and as clean—as possible to accommodate a large number of complex signals.

Courtesy Nico Mak Computing, Inc.

WinZip is a popular program for data compression and extraction that can reduce file size for quick and efficient transfer.

Transmission Speeds

Communications bandwidth is measured in kilobits per second (kbps) or gigabits per second (gbps), tending toward the higher speeds all the time. When considering bandwidth and speed, the channels are classified into three categories:

➤ *Narrow band transmission*, the slowest at 45–150 baud; used by telegraph and teletype machines; commonly twisted-pair wires.

➤ *Voice-grade transmission*, the middle speed at 300–9,600 baud; the human voice is in this range, thus so are telephones as well as inexpensive or home-use modems; commonly twisted-pair wires.

➤ *Wideband transmission*, for highest speed at 19,200 baud to 500 Kbps or more; this is for commercial grade channels used in business, finance, the government, and, in particular, the World Wide Web. As the Web grows more graphical and delivers more video and sound, bandwidth will continue to be an issue. Coaxial cable is being used for satellite and cable wideband transmissions, and fiber optic or microwave transmission, or T1 or T3 links from common carriers, is mostly used for computer networks.

Networking Protocols

Protocol refers to a prescribed manner of doing something. Networking **protocols** refer to a set of *standards* that ensure data and information are properly exchanged between communicating computers. The most common *protocol standard* is referred to as X.25, which is used worldwide. Although most adhere to the X.25 standard, there is no single protocol used by all. Protocols refer to means of transmission, which have improved over the years. The following protocols are listed in chronological order:

➤ **Simplex**, or one direction only, for example from host to recipient

➤ **Half-duplex**, meaning one direction *at a time* although both directions are possible

➤ **Full-duplex**, meaning both directions at the same time

Today, most voice and data communications channels are full-duplex; the need for information and instantaneous feedback requires it. However, the computer-to-printer channel is simplex, and most large host-to-terminal computer systems still use half-duplex.

There are several specific techniques for data exchange within the full-duplex protocol. The first is *circuit switching*, which routes data along a prescribed path from source to destination. The more common method is **packet switching**, which sends data in small blocks, or packets, each separate, along the most expedient route to the destination, where they are reassembled in proper order. Although seeming more complex, packet switching is far more efficient.

Nodes, Switches, and Devices

There is often a need for various devices in a computer network to help facilitate getting data or information through the communications channel, from one computer to another. It all begins with a **node**, which is any point of connection in a computer network. A node may be the originating computer, the destination computer, any computer in the communications channel through which data or information passes, or any one of a number of switches of devices in the channel that help facilitate the data transfer. Most of these switches and devices are designed for different applications—for example, the data center in the Information Technology department, for a workgroup, or for an individual PC. Here are a few examples:

➤ *Switches*. A **switch** receives incoming transmissions arriving at a node and redirects them through the network to their proper destinations. Switches typically have a prescribed bandwidth that allows them to handle different volumes of transmissions. There are different switches for different types of networks, such as LANs and WANs.

➤ *Routers*. A **router** is used in packet-switching networks to examine the packet and its addressing, and determine how to send it on its way to the proper destination.

➤ *Smart Hubs*. A **hub** is any node on a network, but a smart hub replaces separate switches and other network hardware devices that make it simpler to create and maintain networks, such as LANs, or to interconnect incompatible networks, such as a high-speed WAN and a lower-speed LAN.

➤ *Remote Access Devices*. Remote access devices are used to connect remote users to central or enterprise computers and data centers—for example, the traveling businessperson using a notebook computer. Remote access devices are special dial-up modems, switches, bridges, routers, hubs, and servers that are designed to ensure security, proper access (to one's workgroup LAN, the corporate database, and so on), with the most speed and efficiency and the lowest cost.

➤ *Internet Devices*. Internets and intranets (within the enterprise) require special communications devices, such as the **firewall** to ensure security and prevent unauthorized access, special servers for different types of information—a CD-ROM jukebox or a video server, for example—and routers and switches specially configured for Internet and intranet uses.

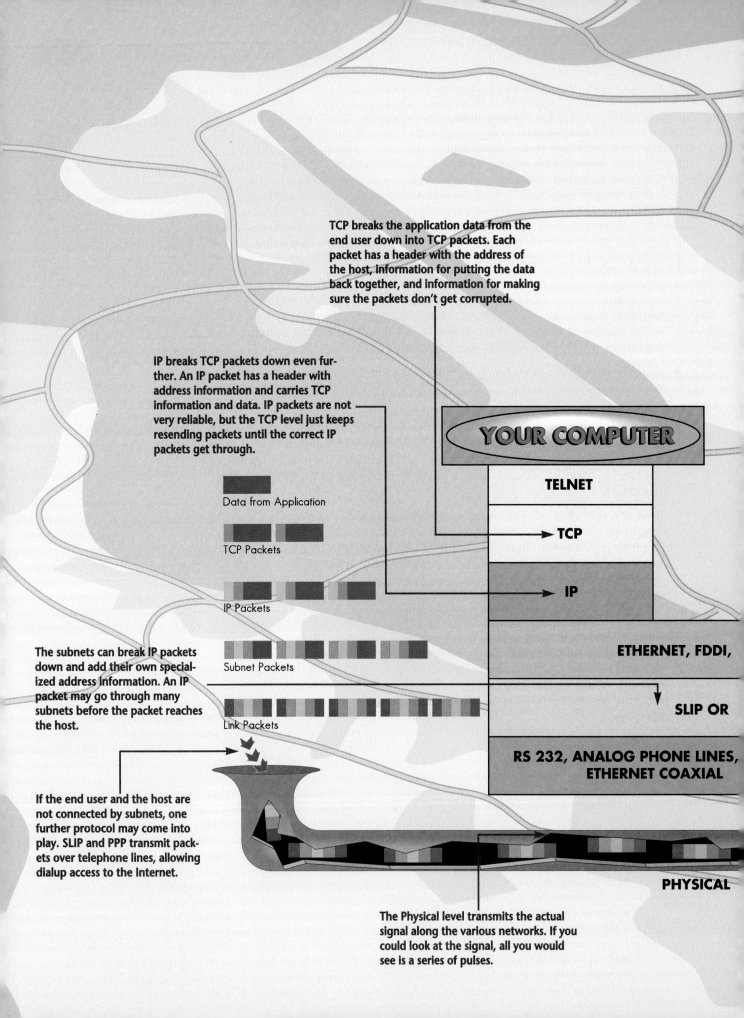

TCP breaks the application data from the end user down into TCP packets. Each packet has a header with the address of the host, information for putting the data back together, and information for making sure the packets don't get corrupted.

IP breaks TCP packets down even further. An IP packet has a header with address information and carries TCP information and data. IP packets are not very reliable, but the TCP level just keeps resending packets until the correct IP packets get through.

Data from Application

TCP Packets

IP Packets

The subnets can break IP packets down and add their own specialized address information. An IP packet may go through many subnets before the packet reaches the host.

Subnet Packets

Link Packets

If the end user and the host are not connected by subnets, one further protocol may come into play. SLIP and PPP transmit packets over telephone lines, allowing dialup access to the Internet.

YOUR COMPUTER

TELNET

TCP

IP

ETHERNET, FDDI,

SLIP OR

RS 232, ANALOG PHONE LINES, ETHERNET COAXIAL

PHYSICAL

The Physical level transmits the actual signal along the various networks. If you could look at the signal, all you would see is a series of pulses.

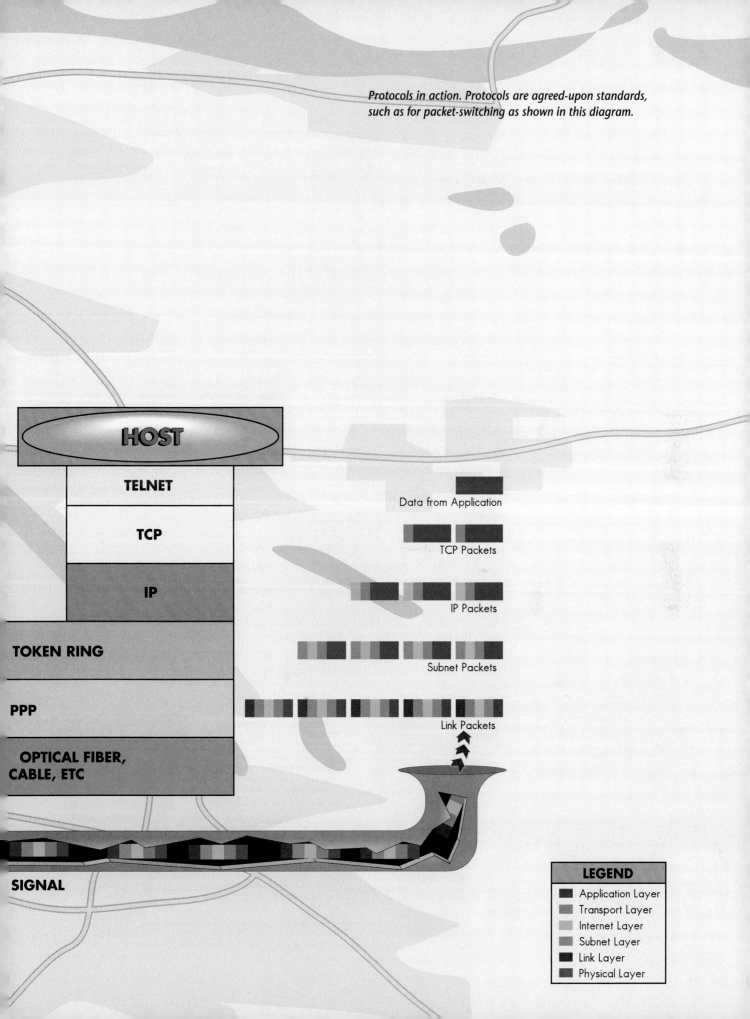

Protocols in action. Protocols are agreed-upon standards, such as for packet-switching as shown in this diagram.

HOST

TELNET

TCP

IP

TOKEN RING

PPP

OPTICAL FIBER, CABLE, ETC

SIGNAL

Data from Application

TCP Packets

IP Packets

Subnet Packets

Link Packets

LEGEND

Application Layer
Transport Layer
Internet Layer
Subnet Layer
Link Layer
Physical Layer

Network Standards

Communications network standards are the rules and guidelines for achieving satisfactory performance and communication between different networks and computer systems. Each new communications technology or application seems to require its own standards. Here is a sampling of network standards:

➤ ASCII, for data file transfer

➤ FDDI, for high-speed fiber optic transmissions

➤ T1 (and T3) for wideband circuits

➤ SMTP (Simple Mail Transfer Protocol) for electronic mail message handling

➤ SNA, for IBM mainframe communications

➤ DECNET, for Digital minicomputer communications

These are just a few, and there is no practical reason for you to know them all. However, for the purpose of understanding the importance and usefulness of standards, we will study one that attempts to bring uniformity to data communications: OSI.

The basic premise underlying all computer networks is that they are "open," or available to any type of computer system. **Open Systems Interconnect**, or **OSI**, is a standard that separates computer-to-computer communications into seven layers or levels, each building one atop the next. The OSI model was created by the European International Systems Organization in the 1970s, and in the 1980s came to be regarded as a solution, not just for communications, but for the enterprise-wide open systems issue. As its name implies, its stated goal is to make differing systems "open" from the hardware through the application, as shown in the following figure.

Dr. Peter G.W. Keen, author, professor and consultant on communications, says of OSI, "The OSI model has generated several of the most important and useful standards in the telecommunications field. The architecture, not OSI, is the strategy, although OSI may be a key element of the architecture."

The seven layers of OSI. When properly implemented, the only layer the user interacts with is the Application layer.

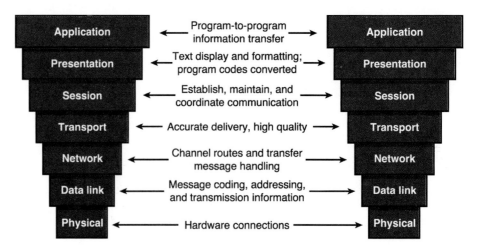

The ATM Standard

With the advent of the 1990s, the number of people using computers in networks exploded. Workgroup computing became popular, and users wanted to share information across the network with co-workers. Moreover, the applications they used were changing, as well. Windows and the graphical user interface made it possible to create value-added files—spreadsheets with charts, word processing files that used different fonts and sophisticated formatting. Multimedia became the buzzword, followed in short order by the World Wide Web.

Suddenly, the face of networking changed dramatically: Users were consuming ever more bandwidth. "Applications aren't getting any smaller," says Brian Young, director of marketing at ZeitNet, based in Santa Clara, California. "As people push the usefulness of various applications, those applications will continue to push the bandwidth of the networks."

Enter ATM, or **Asynchronous Transfer Mode**. Rather than being based on packet-switching, ATM was designed from the ground up with an entirely different approach—cell switching. An ATM cell is a small, fixed-size packet in a uniform format that allows it to be transferred rapidly over any ATM network. The ATM network uses a cell switching technology to create and maintain the cell flow through media. If the information needs to be re-routed through a packet-switched network, a bridge or router is used to convert cells to packets and packets back to cells.

ATM is a sophisticated broadband networking technology that supports data, voice, and video traffic at extremely high transfer rates. As such, it's ideally positioned to support the multimedia computing work that is becoming more and more prevalent. ATM's greatest potential may yet be realized in those networks requiring the convergence of multimedia services through central points of distribution, such as commercial and campus backbone nets.

An example is London-based Cinesite, providing digital film production services for the motion picture industry. Some of Cinesite's movies include *Mission: Impossible*, *Space Jam*, and *First Knight*. A typical rendering is a composite of live action and computer-generated scenes or characters—for example, when Bugs Bunny meets Michael Jackson in *Space Jam*. A single frame might have four or five layers of compositing, averaging 12M; a 10-second rendering can run quickly into two-digit gigabytes.

Key to the Cinesite operation is the Ampex DST high-speed tape device. Tapes hold 30 to 100G, and are the easiest media to use for file transfer and backup in the rendering process. The Ampex can store data at up to 17M per second. Typically, a film segment is scanned from the original 35mm negatives and archived on the Ampex, then downloaded as needed to a Silicon Graphics workstation for rendering the special effects—FX, as they are known in the business.

Time is of the essence: Both access and processing must be accomplished quickly over the network in order to render and finish a shot. In 1994, Cinesite found that its network backbone was "maxed out," according to Martin Weaver, computing services manager. "We can't do our work without a high-speed network. We had to expand," he says. "This is a shared network, so we only had so much bandwidth. We needed switching capabilities."

Cinesite selected Cabletron Systems to install its Asynchronous Transfer Mode (ATM) network, "because they offered us a single solution," says Weaver. The switches and cabling were ordered, installed, "and it worked straight off, which was a pleasant surprise," he says. In just three months, Cinesite doubled its workload capacity, which made it possible to undertake an additional new film project.

Types of Computer Networks

This section explores LANs and WANs in detail. It then discusses the large-scale networks that commonly support WANs and LANs, including public networks, private networks, value-added networks, the Internet, and intranets.

Local Area Networks

With a local area network, several computers can share a printer and access files on another computer.

A **local area network** (**LAN**) uses direct, high-speed cables to share hardware, software, and data resources. With a LAN, the connection spans a short distance and doesn't use wires owned by a telephone company. Typically, a LAN connects the computers in a department, a building, or several buildings situated near each other. Each hardware device on a LAN, such as a computer or printer, is called a **node**. A LAN integrates anywhere from two or three computers up to several hundred computers.

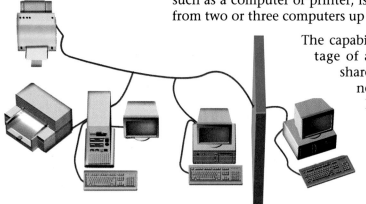

The capability of sharing resources is a major advantage of a LAN. Because the computers in a LAN share hardware, several people can use the same network printer. Because the computers in a LAN share software, only one copy of a software package is needed, as long as that package is designed and licensed to be used on a network. Sharing data means that all the LAN users can access one database and get the most up-to-date data.

LAN Hardware

In addition to computers, the hardware components needed to create a LAN include the network cable, a cable interface unit, and network interface cards for each computer. The **network cable** can be twisted-pair cable, coaxial cable, or fiber optic cable. The **cable interface unit**, sometimes called a hub, sends and receives signals on the network cable. This unit is a box outside the computer.

BITS
Some LANs are wireless. Wireless LANs use infrared or radio wave transmission. Although wireless LANs are more prone to errors and interception, they do not require laying cable and moving it when a node is relocated.

The **network interface card** is inserted into an expansion slot inside the computer. The interface card sends and receives messages to and from the LAN. The card is connected to the cable interface unit by wire.

LANs can be connected by a bridge, a router, or a gateway. If two LANs are similar, you use a **bridge** to connect them. With two or more similar LANs, you use a **router** to connect them. With two dissimilar LANs, you use a **gateway**. The gateway translates the LANs' different data formats.

In a star topology, all the computers in the network are attached to the host computer. The host can be a mainframe or a smaller computer.

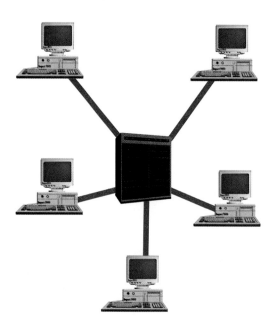

LAN Topology

The physical layout of a local area network is called its **topology**. The three most common topologies for LANs are star, ring, and bus.

A **star topology** has a **host computer**, which is responsible for managing the network. Usually, the database and printer are part of this host computer. The other nodes are attached to the host and all messages are routed through the host. If the central computer fails, so does the network.

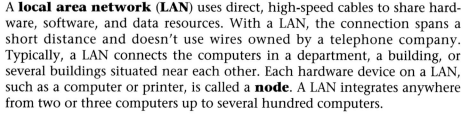

A **ring topology** has all nodes attached in a circle, without a central host computer. Messages travel around the ring until they reach the computer to which they are addressed. If the ring is broken, the network fails.

A **bus topology** does not use a central or host computer. Instead, each node manages part of the network. Information can be transmitted from one computer directly to another without traveling through every other node. Bus topology is the most popular LAN topology because the failure of one network computer does not affect the other network computers.

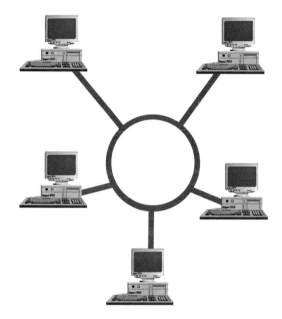

In a bus topology, the failure of one network computer does not affect the other network computers.

In a ring topology, the computer nodes are attached in a circle without a host computer.

LAN Models

Regardless of the topology, LANs usually follow one of two models: client/server or peer-to-peer.

A **client/server model** uses one or more computers as servers, and the other computers on the network are clients. The **server** is a high-capacity, high-speed computer with a large hard disk capacity. It contains the **network operating system**, the software required to run the network. The server also contains network versions of programs and large data files. **Clients**—all the computers that can access the server—send requests to the server. Here are some common services that clients request:

TechTalk
A client computer is sometimes called a workstation.

➤ Storing and retrieving files on the server's hard disk

➤ Running programs that are stored on the server's hard disk

➤ Printing to a network printer

The client/server model works with any size or topology of LAN and does not tend to slow down with heavy use.

With the **peer-to-peer model**, all computers on the network can access public files and printers connected to other computers in the network. (A **public file** is one that a user has made available for others to access.) No one computer is in charge of the network; all computers share the network management tasks. A peer-to-peer network tends to slow down with heavy use, and keeping track of the information on each computer can be difficult. Therefore, this model is used with small networks.

Peer-to-peer networking is ideally suited to workgroups.

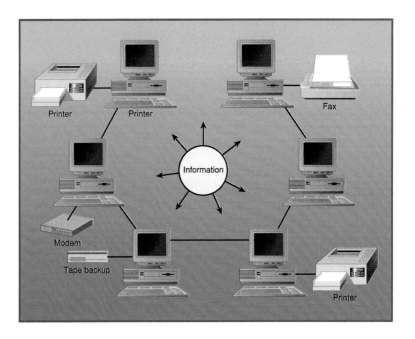

A network can also be a hybrid combining elements of both client/server and peer-to-peer models.

The Impact of LANs

As the use of computers increased during the 1960s and 1970s, the value of information became more obvious to businesses and other computer users. Mainframes and minicomputers became more powerful, and new databases that were created grew to be very large. The department that was responsible for maintaining the data in a database wanted to be able to access the data quickly at any time. Users began to demand more control over the database. The mainframe computer, however, still required experts to maintain it, and most of these experts worked in the data processing department.

BITS
Smart terminals have processing capabilities; some have disk drives for users to download information. **Dumb terminals** interact with the remote computer but cannot process any information.

The solution was to add terminals, input/output devices consisting of a keyboard and a monitor. Users could access the data through their terminals, but the maintenance of the computer was the responsibility of the data processing department. Because the data processing department continued to control the data, hardware, and software, other departments using the data found that changing hardware or software could be cumbersome and slow. This difficulty created real problems for these departments.

Today, many companies are changing the storage of and the responsibilities for their data. A LAN, with data distributed among the responsible departments, is less expensive than a mainframe computer. The necessary software is often easier to use than the software for the mainframe and can be readily upgraded or changed. As a company grows, adding new computers to the LAN is easier than adding new terminals to an overworked mainframe or minicomputer.

In some ways, maintaining a LAN is similar to maintaining a mainframe. For example, like mainframes, LANs require a knowledgeable person to keep them working. Some companies have purchased a LAN and then found that they did not have an employee who could address the day-to-day problems and questions of the LAN users. In addition, both mainframes and LANs require periodic backups of the data and the software in case of a disk failure. Procedures to back up and recover data must be provided for both LANs and mainframes.

Some people in the computer industry have predicted that personal computers, especially with LANs, will completely replace the minicomputers and mainframe computers. Networks have already replaced many mainframe and minicomputer installations, but powerful mainframes are still needed for huge tasks, such as keeping track of airline reservations. There is, however, no doubt that LANs have dramatically changed the nature of data processing.

Wide Area Networks

A **wide area network** (**WAN**) is a computer network that directly connects computers separated by long distances—more than a mile and as much as half the globe. WANs require special media, which are provided by telephone companies and other firms that specialize in this service. WANs also require special hardware.

Physical Media for WANs

Wide area networks use special-purpose telephone wires, fiber-optic cables, microwaves, or satellites for communications.

The simplest WANs use dedicated lines. A **dedicated line** is a specially conditioned telephone line that directly and permanently connects two computers. Dedicated lines provided by telephone companies are called **private lines**, or **leased lines**. For example, a computer in a Vancouver store may send transactions to the main office computer in Toronto over a leased line. A leased line can handle as much as 64,000 bits per second. Some special-purpose dedicated lines can handle as much as 64 million bits per second.

Microwaves, as mentioned earlier, are radio waves that have a very high frequency. Besides warming your pizza, they can transmit data. The chief disadvantage of microwaves is they depend on line-of-sight transmission. No obstruction can get in the way. Furthermore, microwaves can travel only about 50 miles. For both of these reasons, some networks build microwave relay towers. You have probably seen these towers, bristling with antennae, atop the highest hill in the area.

Communications satellites are placed in a **geosynchronous orbit** thousands of miles above the earth. In this orbit, the satellite rotates with the earth so that it is always above a given spot. The latest WANs use long-distance fiber optic cables. For example, a fiber optic cable linking two U.S. universities transmits 5 billion bits per second.

WAN Service Providers

Dedicated lines, microwave communications, and satellite services are available from a variety of companies, including the **common carriers** (telephone companies such as AT&T, Sprint, and MCI). Increasingly, telephone companies are offering dedicated Integrated Services Digital Network (ISDN) connections to businesses and large organizations. (For more information on ISDN, see the section later in this chapter, "Integrated Services Digital Networks.")

When an organization wants to offer communications services to others, it submits a tariff to the government. (A **tariff** is a list of services and charges for the services to be offered.) When the government has accepted the tariff and approved the organization to offer communications to others, that organization is known as a common carrier.

Some firms specialize in providing dedicated lines. These companies lease dedicated lines, add services to enhance the communications, and then sell that enhanced service. This service is called a **value-added network**; see the later section, "Value Added Networks."

A **public data network (PDN)** builds its own high-speed data highways using microwaves, satellites, and optical fiber. A PDN can send data at rates of one million bits per second or more. See the later section, "Public Networks."

WAN Hardware

WANs require some special hardware items. A **multiplexor** is a hardware device that enhances the usefulness of a WAN connection. A multiplexor combines input signals from as many as several dozen computers and sends the combined signal along the communications channel. On the other end, an identical multiplexor decodes the signal and sends the messages to their correct destinations.

Routers work with packet switching networks. They receive packets and examine their addresses. Based on routing data kept in an automatically updated table, the router decides where to send each packet.

Front-end processors handle all the communications tasks for large computers, which would otherwise get bogged down by sending and receiving messages. These processors also provide security to prevent unauthorized access.

Uses of WANs

Like LANs, WANs enable file exchange, remote database access, electronic mail, teleconferencing, and discussion groups. Businesses have found other uses for WANs.

Electronic Data Interchange (EDI) is a procedure by which companies can exchange standard documents such as invoices or purchase orders. If two companies have compatible systems, they can establish a connection through which company A sends a purchase order to company B by means of EDI—computer to computer. When company B ships the product, company B sends an invoice by EDI to company A. Company A can then pay by electronic funds transfer through its bank. The entire operation occurs without any paper changing hands.

If two companies do not have compatible systems, they can use an intermediary EDI company to change the code so that the two companies can communicate. Very large manufacturing companies often require as a condition of purchase that their suppliers have EDI systems compatible with the company's system. The buyer can order parts to be delivered just in time to be used. This capability enables the buyer to shorten the length of time between buying the parts and selling the finished product and receiving payment. Thus, using EDI can reduce a company's costs.

International Networks

WANs can be worldwide. Connecting with a computer outside your own country's borders, though, has potential for difficulties. Although standards for protocols have been established, there are no international standards for tariffs. When you communicate across national borders, the tariffs are determined by all the countries that provide services to you.

Virtually all countries have recognized that to be part of the world economy, they must be part of the world communications system. Therefore, companies, either native to the country or invited foreigners, are establishing systems for data communications. In many situations, the communications systems are being built before the roads and other infrastructures in the country.

Public Networks

A **public network** is an *open* communications network available for use by anyone, usually on a fee basis. The U.S. Sprint, MCI, and AT&T telephone networks are examples of public networks. They span the United States and the world. Overseas, many countries have a state-owned and operated public network for telephone, telegraph, e-mail and Internet communications (and the mails, too), often referred to as PTT, which is French for Poste Telegraphique et Telephonique. Even though originally designed for voice messages, these public networks carry a large volume of data communications traffic today.

In France, the telephone network was intentionally turned into a computer network by a project called Teletel. It was launched in 1981, when the French telephone and post office department put a terminal called "Le Minitel" in every home in France. Over 4 million have been installed.

Initially, Teletel was to replace printed phone books by giving people on-line directory assistance. However, enterprising companies soon realized they could provide other on-line services to the public. The program was a success: The number of on-line services in France has jumped from 200 to over 9,000. One popular service is called Dialog, which allows people to form groups and have typed on-line conversations.

Data Communications Networks

In the United States, some networks are used exclusively for computer communications. An example mentioned earlier is the packet-switching network. In the U.S., the most prominent packet-switching networks are Tymnet and Telenet. In Canada, it's Datapac. The first packet-switching network was ARPANET, created in the 1960s by the U.S. Department of Defense Advanced Research Projects Agency. It links various government agencies, research labs and universities. Today, it is called the Internet, and it links hundreds of locations and millions of computers in North America.

Integrated Services Digital Networks

ISDN, or the Integrated Services Digital Network, is a completely digital communications network. It was first introduced by AT&T in the 1980s, but is gradually gaining more favor. ISDN supports multiple voice and data carriers in what are termed bearer channels (B channels). There is also a separate data channel (D channel) available.

There are two basic types of ISDN service. Basic Rate Interface (BRI), with two B channels and one D channel, for most home and small business uses. This means you could conduct a telephone conversation and have your computer connected to the Internet simultaneously, on the B Channel, with a single ISDN line. Primary Rate Interface (PRI), with up to 23 B channels plus one D channel, is for larger enterprises. The following figure shows how ISDN channels work.

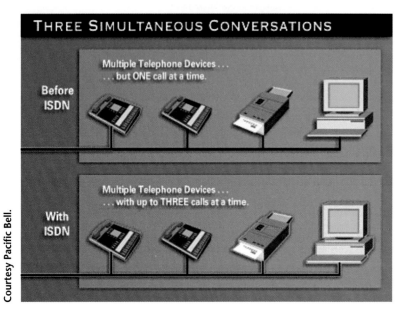

Courtesy Pacific Bell.

The advantages of ISDN.

To access BRI service, users must obtain an ISDN phone line, which usually means being within about 3.4 miles or 5.5 km of the telephone company central office. Longer distances require repeater devices. Customers will also need special equipment, such as ISDN terminal adapters or routers, or a PC adapter card, to communicate with the phone company switch as well as with other ISDN devices. ISDN calls are usually (in the U.S.) charged by the minute, even for local calls. Rates can vary from state to state. Whatever the cost, ISDN is truly digital, which means no modems are needed and connection speeds are five times faster than conventional analog-to-digital connections.

Private Networks

In addition to public networks, many private networks exist in the United States. A **private network** is a *closed* communication system, usually confined to a particular company, governmental entity, or other group.

An example of a private network is American Airlines' SABRE reservation service. SABRE stands for Semi-Automated Business Research Environment. Developed by IBM in the mid-1960s, SABRE now has more than 68,000 terminals that connect 8,000 reservation operators and 14,000 travel agents around the world. Over 470,000 reservations are made daily on SABRE. Many are made over the Internet using services such as America Online. During a 1997 fare war, SABRE was processing 4,100 transactions per second.

Several types of private networks exist in business today, serving a variety of needs for knowledge workers. These networks, large or small, are categorized in two ways. One way is by topology, or the physical layout of network devices and nodes. The other is by the proximity of the devices and nodes to each other.

Value-Added Networks

Value-added networks, or VANs, are semi-private networks designed to act as more than simply a communications channel; hence, they add additional value to the networking process. An example is electronic data interchange, or EDI, which is used to transmit business data from remote sites to corporate headquarters. However, VANs are, in large part, being replaced by the Web and intranets.

The Internet

What we use today is called the Internet, or Internet I. What we'll use tomorrow is being called *Internet 2*, and the University Corporation for Advanced Internet Development is creating it. Some of its objectives include

➤ Demonstrate new applications that can dramatically enhance researchers' ability to collaborate and conduct experiments

➤ Demonstrate enhanced delivery of education and other services (such as health care, environmental monitoring) by taking advantage of "virtual proximity" created by an advanced communications infrastructure

➤ Support development and adoption of advanced applications by providing middleware and development tools

➤ Facilitate development, deployment, and operation of an affordable communications infrastructure

➤ Promote experimentation with the next generation of communications technologies

➤ Encourage transfer of technology from Internet 2 to the rest of the Internet

Internet 2 is expected to be deployed around the year 2002. See Chapter 8, "Connecting the World," for a full description of the Internet.

Intranets

An **intranet** is simply an Internet within the secure confines of an enterprise. It provides services to users from a corporate or organizational server, and is often connected to the Internet through a secure firewall. As with the Internet, the networking infrastructure is built in. Remote employees can use the intranet in the same way they would use the Internet, except that it is proprietary and secure. More and more enterprises are establishing intranets as a way of providing a wide range of computing applications and services to users and corporate partners or customers without the cost of building proprietary networks. Table 7B-1 shows some typical transmission speeds for various applications.

Table 7B.1 Typical Transmission Speeds for Computer Communications		
Application	*Bandwidth*	*Type of Channel*
Corporate LAN	Multi-gigabits/sec	fiber optic, microwave
Campus LAN	20–100 megabits/sec	fiber, coax
Metropolitan	40–50 mpbs	local carrier lines
Regional (gov't, corp)	5–50 mbps	leased lines, T1, T3
National	56kbps–2mbps	leased lines
International	9.6kbps–64kbps	PTT, VAN services

The Expanding Intranet Market

Because most organizations have a need for more dynamic ways to link people and information, the intranet market is expanding. Estimates of the combined corporate Internet and intranet markets show a jump of $12 billion in 1995 to $208 billion by the year 2000, with more than 70 percent of that jump from intranet use.

Organizations of all sizes are facing major communication challenges, requiring easy and quick access to department, corporate, and customer information. With intranets, employees and business partners can share information and software, communicate effectively, and do so inexpensively.

Benefits and Uses of Intranets

With an intranet, all of an organization's computers—whether they are stand-alone systems, connected to a mainframe, or part of a LAN or WAN—can communicate with each other. There is no need to adjust the network when a new user joins. This capability allows for growth without pain, and flexibility without sacrifice. The internal web works with the same software as the World Wide Web and therefore requires no additional training for users.

Web software, used with intranets, will interface with most applications and databases, so an organization's existing software can still be used. Web technology is available for almost all operating systems and hardware platforms and is modestly priced. Security with several encryption packets is available. Generally, the cost of intranet software and hardware is often less than $50 per user.

Users can put the information on their Web pages onto the intranet, and all interested parties can access the information, read it, and download it without wasting the paper to copy it, or the time to make and circulate the copies. Members of a workgroup located across the world can brainstorm or exchange ideas collectively or individually. Employees can enroll in a new benefits package without leaving their desks or demanding attention from the benefits clerk unless they have a problem. Customers can request information and receive an immediate response automatically. As you can see, intranets are changing the face of communications within organizations.

Computer Networking Software

As with all computer systems, computer networking requires an operating system and separate and distinct applications. Most operating systems are proprietary or designed to run on specific computer hardware. In this chapter, you learn about the most widely used network operating systems. Applications are more ubiquitous, and in keeping with the open systems philosophy, have been designed to operate on just about any computer platform.

Network Operating Systems

Microsoft Windows NT has become the most widely used network operating system, or NOS. Windows NT is designed for multiple users and platforms. It is contrasted to Windows 95 and 98, which are both designed for the individual PC user. Windows NT is a client-server NOS; that is, there is an NT Server version and an NT Workstation version. The latest release, Workstation 5.0, significantly extends its reliability, security, networking, and performance advantages.

Windows NT Workstation 5.0 includes all the familiar tools, utilities, and application support of Windows 95/98, including Windows Explorer, plug and play hardware management, power management, and broad application support. It also features IntelliMirror, a set of management technologies that combine the power and flexibility of distributed computing with a tightly managed environment. IntelliMirror works by "intelligently mirroring" a user's data, applications, system files, and administrative settings on Windows NT 5.0-based servers.

A case in point is the University of Washington's Department of Computer Science & Engineering, a strong teaching and research organization that uses Windows NT. For years, the department used the UNIX operating system, but in 1993, it implemented changes. Beginning with the instructional program and moving into the research facilities, the CS&E Department began integrating desktops and servers to Windows.

Today, Department Chair Ed Lazowska says most of the department's computers and many of its file servers are Windows-based. They have migrated the core infrastructure of e-mail and Web servers to the Windows NT Server NOS.

The department's computing environment is a number of LANs that use switched Ethernet with 100Mbps service. In the primary instructional computing lab, seven Windows NT Server-based machines provide file services, print spooling, and application support to 60 PCs running Windows NT. They coexist on a single subnet along with numerous UNIX hosts and X Windows terminals.

A separate CS&E research lab, used largely by faculty and graduate students, includes 14 Windows NT Server-based machines along with numerous Windows NT Workstation-based desktops. The servers provide **Microsoft SQL Server**, **Microsoft Internet Information Server** (IIS) and **Microsoft Systems Management Services** support, digital video support, and other services. A separate introductory programming lab, used for the introductory CS&E course, runs Windows 95.

Most administrative desktops in the department also run Windows NT-based and the full suite of Microsoft Office applications. In all, more than 500 Windows-based systems have been installed in the department over the past three years.

Networking Applications

Most users want to use applications with which they are already familiar, and there is no reason not to do so in a networked computing environment. Many applications are delivered from the network server, or may run on a client PC and be mirrored to other PCs or servers. These applications include word processing, spreadsheet, Web browser, and so forth.

Perhaps the most important application in a networked environment is the **DBMS**, or **database management system**. Large enterprises may have hundreds of databases in use, the products of a number of different vendors such as Oracle, Sybase, or Informix. Users need data manipulation tools, such as **SQL**, fourth-generation languages, or a spreadsheet to work with the data. All this is accomplished in the same way as a user working at a stand-alone PC or a terminal.

A new category of software, called **middleware**, performs interactive tasks between users at their client machines and the Internet or a Web site. For example, a user might have a middleware virtual office with a Web address that allows him or her to check messages, post reports, pick up files, and interact in virtual meetings with other users, regardless of their location. An example is the Netopia Virtual Office, shown in the following figure.

A virtual office is accessible over the Web, wherever you are in the world.

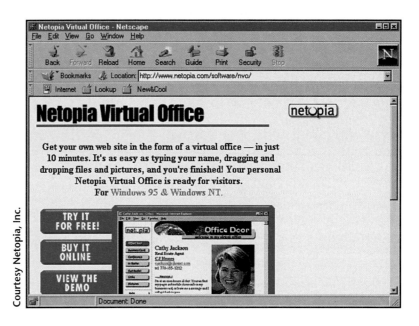

Courtesy Netopia, Inc.

Middleware is becoming increasingly important as more companies expand existing client-server, mainframe, and simple Web-based information systems into new electronic commerce and order-entry applications. For example, Talarian offers a **Java** version of its SmartSockets publish-subscribe middleware, which allows developers to build Java programs that can communicate with programs written in almost any programming language on any platform.

Another type of user middleware is BusinessVue (and its cousin, StockVue) from Alpha Micro. It automatically pulls together data from multiple Internet sites so users can gather a wide range of strategic information about competitors and their business plans. Middleware is undoubtedly the first of many new, innovative applications that allow users and developers to use the information provided on the World Wide Web in more useful, productive ways.

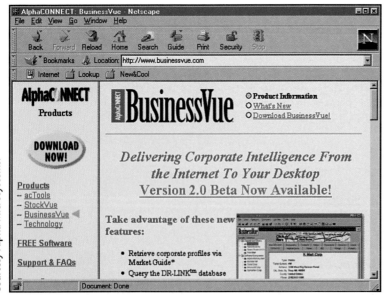

Courtesy Alpha Microsystems.

BusinessVue is a middleware application that uses intelligent agents to locate and organize information you need from Web sites.

Computer Networks and Closed Societies

Personal computers have long been a tool for disseminating information. In the early days of the PC revolution, the computer placed the means to gather, organize, and publish information into the hands of more people than any other previous publishing medium. In 1989, the student uprising at Tiananmen Square was due, in part, to the distribution of information the government sought to suppress. This distribution was facilitated through the use of the PC, and PC users were the ones who made the Western world aware of what had happened.

With the growth of computer networks, such as the Internet, the effects of the PC are being felt in more countries. Traditionally closed societies are finding it hard to remain closed. For instance, Saudi Arabia and many other Arab countries have very strict rules concerning politics, religion, and sex. These topics have been controlled through state-run television, radio, and newspapers, or through strict laws with heavy punishments attached.

The Internet is a different story, however. It can best be described as "orderly anarchy," where anyone can discuss or distribute anything at any time. All three of the taboo subjects are discussed openly and candidly on the Internet, and this has led to problems for these countries. Many officials want to ban the Internet entirely, but others insist that doing so would leave the countries technologically hobbled. Governments are left with the predicament of keeping a tight reign on the moral fiber of their society and allowing the free exchange of information using the latest technology available.

Different countries have taken different approaches to the problem. In Kuwait, people can sign up for local Internet access, with no restrictions, for around $200 (U.S. currency) per month. Likewise, the United Arab Emirates and Bahrain have opened their doors to the Internet. In Saudi Arabia, the government has chosen to regulate Internet access as though it were a controlled substance. Those who want access to the Internet must apply to the government and sometimes wait years for approval (if they get it at all). In addition, access lines to the Internet run at slow speeds to discourage the proliferation of contraband images and information in the country.

The roadblocks to free access placed in the Arab world have not slowed some computer-literate people. Many have learned that they can dial into the Internet by placing long-distance calls to neighboring countries or by dialing directly to the United States. Such connections are obviously feasible only for those with quite a bit of money, but the connections are happening nonetheless. Many observers indicate that even though the doors to the Internet are opening slowly in traditionally closed societies, they are still opening. The results can only be guessed, but it appears that these countries won't remain closed too far into the future.

Lesson Summary

➤ Computer networks provide high-speed, direct links between computers.

➤ Bandwidth refers to the capacity of a communications channel to carry data or information. Bandwidth is measured in cycles per second, or *Hertz* (abbreviated Hz).

➤ Communications network standards are the rules and guidelines for achieving satisfactory performance and communication between different networks and computer systems. Each new communications technology or application seems to require its own standards.

➤ Local area networks (LANs) use direct, high-speed cables to share hardware, software, and data within a short distance. Each hardware unit in a LAN is called a node.

➤ The hardware components needed to create a network include the computers, the network cable, the cable interface unit, and network interface cards.

➤ Topology is the physical layout of the network. A star topology has a central, host computer. A ring topology has nodes connected in a circle. A bus topology, which is the most popular, has a direct connection from any node to any other node.

➤ The two most common models of LANs are client/server, which has the central computer as server; and peer-to-peer, which is used most often with small LANs, with no central computer.

➤ Wide area networks (WANs) directly connect computers separated by long distances.

➤ The physical media of a WAN can include dedicated lines from the telephone company, microwave connections, fiber optics, and communications satellites in geosynchronous orbit.

➤ Common carriers, such as AT&T, MCI, and Sprint, may offer services such as ISDN, value-added networks, public data networks, and packet switching networks.

➤ Intranets connect computers and networks within an organization by using hardware and software used on the Internet.

➤ Intranets use hyperlinks and communication techniques like those on the World Wide Web to connect users in an organization.

➤ Computer networking requires an operating system, and separate, distinct applications. Most operating systems are proprietary.

➤ Microsoft Windows NT has become the most widely used network operating system, or NOS. It is designed for multiple users and platforms.

Lesson Review

Key Terms

asynchronous communications	dedicated line	microwave	ring network
asynchronous transfer mode (ATM)	dumb terminal	middleware	ring topology
bandwidth	Electronic Data Interchange (EDI)	multiplexor	router
baseband coaxial cable	fiber optic cable	network cable	server
bridge	firewall	network interface card	simplex
broadband coaxial cable	front-end processor	network operating system	smart terminal
bus topology	full duplex	node	star network
cable interface unit	gateway	open systems interconnect (OSI)	star topology
client	geosynchronous orbit	packet	switched lines
client/server model	half duplex	packet switching network	tariff
coaxial cable	host computer	peer-to-peer model	terminal
common carrier	hub	private line	topology
communications satellite	Integrated Services Digital Network (ISDN)	private network	twisted-pair cable
computer network	intranet	protocol	value-added network (VAN)
connectivity	leased line	public data network (PDN)	wide area network (WAN)
cyberspace	local area network (LAN)	public file	
		public network	

Matching

In the blank next to each of the following terms or phrases, write the letter of the corresponding term or phrase.

___f___ 1. Leased line

___d___ 2. Host computer

___g___ 3. Geosynchronous orbit

___a___ 4. Internet within the secure confines of an enterprise

___b___ 5. The capacity of a communications channel to carry data or information

___j___ 6. Standard document exchange

___h___ 7. AT&T, MCI, and Sprint

___e___ 8. Server

___i___ 9. Packet switching

___c___ 10. Gateway

___l___ 11. A device for data communication; may be dumb or smart

___n___ 12. The most common protocol standard

___o___ 13. Completely digital communications network

___m___ 14. A type of communication channel

___p___ 15. The most common method of transmission in communications channels

___k___ 16. A device that redirects messages at a node

a. intranet

b. baseband

c. similar function of a bridge

d. star topology

e. client

f. private line

g. communications satellites

h. common carriers

i. public data network

j. EDI

k. switch

l. terminal

m. coaxial

n. X.25

o. ISDN

p. asynchronous

Multiple Choice

Circle the letter of the correct choice for each of the following.

1. When computers are linked with a direct, high-speed connection, what is the result called?

   a. telecommunications

   b. a network

   c. a connection

   d. an information system

2. What are the two types of networks?

   a. LANs and WANs

   b. highway and systems

   c. local area networks and wide area networks

   d. both a and c

3. Computers process data so quickly that they are said to conquer time. With connectivity, what else do computers conquer?

    a. people

    b. business

    c. space

    d. data

4. Which of the following is a major advantage of a local area network?

    a. It is the easiest way to use a computer.

    b. It is cheaper than a single computer.

    c. It can share resources such as printers and databases.

    d. All of the above.

5. What do you call the physical layout of a LAN?

    a. connectivity

    b. interface

    c. bridge

    d. topology

6. An intranet is easy to use because it _____.

    a. uses the same software as the World Wide Web

    b. is just another name for a LAN

    c. uses the Internet

    d. all of the above

7. Since the advent of local area networks, mainframe computers have _____.

    a. become less popular

    b. become more popular

    c. been unaffected

    d. disappeared

8. If two computers need to be connected but are too far away for a LAN connection, which of the following statements is true?

    a. They cannot be connected unless they are moved closer together.

    b. They can be connected by a wide area network.

    c. They can be connected only by public telephone switched lines.

    d. This situation has never occurred.

9. What do you call a telephone line set by the telephone company to permanently connect to computers?

    a. a packet

    b. the Internet

    c. a dedicated line

    d. a switched line

10. If companies have compatible systems, they can use _____ to electronically communicate documents such as purchase orders, invoices, and payments.

    a. packets

    b. processors

    c. Electronic Data Interchange (EDI)

    d. Integrated Services Digital Network (ISDN)

11. Bandwidth is measured

    a. in Hz

    b. the wider it is, the poorer the quality

    c. according to the number of messages

    d. by the quality of the signal

    e. all of the above

    f. all except b

12. The most common networking protocol is

    a. X.25, full duplex, packet switching

    b. X.400, full duplex, packet switching

    c. X.25, half duplex, packet switching

    d. X.25, half duplex, circuit switching

13. A node may have the following

    a. switch, router, hub

    b. switch, computer, router, hub

    c. only a switch

    d. only a router

14. In order for computer networks to be open, they must employ

    a. ASCII

    b. SMTP

    c. OSI   *Operating system interface*

    d. all of the above

Asynchronous Transfer Mode

15. ATM is ideally suited for

    a. replacing existing packet-switched networks

    b. using the Internet

    c. networks without much bandwidth

    d. multimedia

Completion

In the blank provided, write the correct answer for each of the following.

1. A group of two or more computers connected together and in close proximity is probably a(n) *Local area* network.

2. Each hardware device on a LAN is called a(n) *Node*.

3. For a computer to be connected to a LAN, the computer must have a card known as the *network interface card*

4. To connect two similar LANs, you use a device called a(n) *bridge*.

5. In a star topology, the central computer that has everything routed through it is called a(n) *host* computer.

6. A file that has been made available for other users to access through the LAN is called a(n) *public* file.

7. A computer network that directly connects computers separated by long distances is called a(n) *Wide area network WAN*

8. A special telephone line that directly and permanently connects two computers in a WAN is a(n) *dedicated* line.

9. A(n) *tariff* is a list of services, plus the charges for those services, that is filed with the government.

10. A set of standards for communication is called a(n) *protocols*.

11. The most popular use for wideband transmission today is *www*.

12. The point of connection for any type of computer, switch or device is a *node*.

13. An example of a network topology is *star, bus, ring*

Review

On a separate piece of paper, answer the following questions.

1. What is a computer network and what purpose does it serve?

2. What is the difference between a LAN and a WAN? Why do we need both types?

3. What is the Internet and how is it controlled?

4. List the major hardware components of a local area network and briefly describe what each component does.

5. Name and describe three typical topologies of a local area network.

6. What is the difference between the client/server model and the peer-to-peer model?

7. Why have companies started using intranets?

8. Describe the services that communications companies provide for WANs.

9. What is EDI and how can it reduce a company's costs?

10. Define and describe *multiplexor*, *router*, and *front-end processor*.

11. What is the purpose of a firewall?

12. What is a primary advantage in having ISDN?

13. Explain the differences between network operating systems (NOS) and individual operating systems, and between networking applications and stand-alone applications.

Critical Thinking

On a separate sheet of paper, answer the following questions.

1. What security problems do you think a LAN or a WAN could create? How could an organization protect itself from these problems?

2. Two nearby college campuses want to connect to share resources. What hardware would be ideal for each campus to have? What hardware would they need to make the connection?

3. What is the difference between telecommunications and networking?

4. What effect do you think networks, especially international networks, will have on political boundaries around the world?

5. Describe an example of how bandwidth affects you when you're using the Web.

6. Visit your campus's information technology department and learn what kind of networks are in use across your campus.

7. Do some occupational research to learn what needs the country has for skilled networking specialists and programmers, and what opportunities might be there.

Further Discovery

Absolute Beginner's Guide to Networking, Second Edition. Mark Gibbs (Indianapolis, IN: Sams, 1994).

Client/Server Computing for Dummies. Doug Lowe (Foster City, CA: IDG, 1995).

Communications and Networking for the PC, Fifth Edition. Larry Jordan and Bruce Churchill (Indianapolis, IN: NRP, 1994).

Complete Idiot's Guide to Networking. Dan Bobola (Indianapolis, IN: Que, 1995).

Inside Netware 4.1, Second Edition. Doug Bierer (Indianapolis, IN: NRP, 1995).

PC Learning Labs Teaches Netware. Ziff-Davis Development Group (Emeryville, CA: Ziff-Davis, 1994).

PC Magazine Guide to Connectivity, Third Edition. Frank J. Derfler (Emeryville, CA: Ziff-Davis, 1995).

On-line Discovery

You can access the Internet resources for these questions by going to the Que Education and Training Web site, at URL http://www.ciyf98.com/discovery. From this page, click the link for Lesson 7B and then click the link to the resource you want to access.

1. Web66, a project aimed at integrating the World Wide Web into K–12 classrooms, has produced a simple **Network Construction Primer** (http://web66.coled.umn.edu/Construction/ Construction.html) that introduces elementary LAN concepts and terminology. In addition, Novell, the largest vendor of LAN software, makes available a **Networking Primer** (http://corp.novell.com/bg/apr96/bg10000.htm) and a **Glossary of Networking Terms** (http://corp.novell.com/market/glossary.htm). Using these resources, or any others you can find on the Internet, see if you can come up with a basic list of equipment that a small business (of about two dozen people) would need for setting up a LAN in the office to share files and printers. What terms or concepts are hard to understand?

2. Many people hope that Integrated Services Digital Network (ISDN) will eliminate many of the problems with slow access to the Internet and other networks from the home and office. However, ISDN has also been long in coming to many areas. Dan Kegel, from CalTech, maintains an **ISDN Web page** (http://www.alumni.caltech.edu/~dank/isdn) with many links to information about ISDN and to issues surrounding ISDN. Although this page is full of the author's opinions, it is one of the best collections of ISDN resources available. Take a look at some of these resources. How fast is ISDN, compared to a typical 14.4 or 28.8 modem? Where is ISDN available? You may want to call your own telephone company and find out whether ISDN is available in your area. If you connect to an information service (such as America Online or Prodigy) or if you connect directly to the Internet through an Internet service provider (ISP), the service that you connect to must also support ISDN in order for you to make the best use of its speed and features. Does the service that you subscribe to support ISDN? Finally, what technologies on the horizon may replace ISDN?

CHAPTER 8
Connecting the World

The Internet is growing and evolving rapidly. More and more people use the Internet for business and personal use every day. To many it is not only a tool to increase productivity, but a necessity.

Lesson 8A explores the Internet and the services it can provide users. This section recalls the Internet's brief history, from its origins as an academic research tool to its current role as a communications and leisure medium for the masses.

Lesson 8B introduces the fastest growing part of the Internet—the World Wide Web. Find out about the different functions that the Web enables you to perform, and learn how to do thorough and efficient research online.

LESSON
8A

The Information Superhighway and the Internet

Outline

Learning Objectives

When you have finished reading this lesson, you will be able to

➤ Define the term *infrastructure* and explain its economic benefits

➤ Explain what the Information Superhighway is and what benefits it will bring

➤ Enumerate the most popular uses of the Internet

QUE Lab

➤ **Internet**

Do you have enough entertainment and information resources available in your home now? Are television, radio, telephone, books, and a computer enough? In 1940, most Americans thought that radio, telephone, and books were enough, but today, according to the 1990 census, more Americans have television in their homes than have indoor plumbing. As time passes, what people want and expect changes. The computer industry, the communications industry, and the entertainment industry (and several others) are betting that you will want even more entertainment and information resources—once you see how convenient it is to get them.

The question now is how to meet the need. The proposed answer has been called the Information Superhighway. An **Information Superhighway** is a high-speed digital transmission system capable of providing connectivity to homes, schools, and offices. In the United States, plans call for the construction of a **National Information Infrastructure** (**NII**). The NII will be capable of delivering text, graphics, video, and sound almost instantaneously.

Infrastructures in Society

An **infrastructure** provides the means for transporting goods and information. Today, in most countries, infrastructure includes roads, railways, airlines and airports, shipping lanes and ports, telephones, telegraphs, television, radio, and newspapers.

Who owns the infrastructure? In America, government agencies own some pieces of the infrastructure—the roads, primarily. Many other pieces are privately owned but regulated by the government. Some pieces, such as newspapers, are privately owned and unregulated. All countries have some mix of privately and publicly owned infrastructure.

An Information Infrastructure

Infrastructures promote economic gain and increase a country's competitive edge with other countries. The rationale for constructing a National Information Infrastructure is also economic. An NII may fuel economic growth, as previous infrastructures have. With an NII, businesses can compete more effectively. They can lower transaction costs by conducting transactions electronically. They can reduce shipping costs by delivering documents and software electronically. Finally, they can obtain the latest information to enable them to compete effectively with foreign firms.

Unfortunately, the NII will be very expensive to build. The problem isn't so much with continent-spanning **backbone networks**—the "trunk lines" of the Information Superhighway. In fact, these networks already exist. The problem, called the **last-mile problem**, lies in the local delivery system. Most homes, schools, and offices are served by analog telephone lines and cable TV connections. Neither is suited to high-bandwidth multimedia communications. An investment of up to $325 billion may be required to replace these connections with fiber optics.

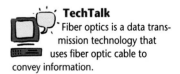

TechTalk
Fiber optics is a data transmission technology that uses fiber optic cable to convey information.

Funding for the NII

The U.S. Congress has already approved legislation to construct a **National Research and Educational Network** (**NREN**), which will enable linked universities to exchange billions of bits of data per second. From this project are expected to emerge the experience and knowledge that will stimulate NII development.

The construction of the NII will probably be left to the private sector. To repay their investment, the companies that construct the NII will charge fees for access. For this reason, some people fear that the NII will create an "information elite," consisting of those who have the means to pay. One study has found that early NII plans leave out poor and minority neighborhoods, expecting that few households in these neighborhoods could afford to subscribe.

The Internet: What Is It?

The **Internet** does not exist—at least, not in the way many people think it does. There is no home office or central computer. It is not a service owned and operated by a business or government agency. The Internet is basically a set of rules for connecting networks. You can also think of it as the set of networks connected according to those rules. The World Wide Web is simply a way of using the Internet.

When the government established the **ARPANET** (for Advanced Research Projects Agency NETwork) in 1969, it connected scientists at a few major universities. In the 1970s, **e-mail** (electronic mail) quickly became popular and the **File Transfer Protocol** (FTP) was established to facilitate the download of files from one computer to another. Gradually, more and more sites and networks were connected to the network (200 sites by 1981). By 1984, academic and research users were already outnumbered 2 to 1 by commercial users. When ARPANET was dissolved in 1989, it was only part of a fast-growing *internet*work. The only physical aspect of the Internet was the "backbone" of major lines that carried communications between the networks. It was still an exotic tool used by technicians. As it became more sophisticated and accessible, simple text menus became common.

The **World Wide Web** was developed in Europe for nuclear scientists in the early 1990s. The Web is a **GUI**-based (graphical user interface) system using **hyperlinks** (highlighted words and icons that connect to another document, sometimes at another location). The pre-Web Internet was like a computer operating under DOS with simple text-based menus and commands. The relationship between the World Wide Web and the Internet is like using Windows on a computer. It's still the same computer, but the way the user interacts with it is different. The World Wide Web is simply that part of the Internet that operates using this interface. Just as DOS software was redesigned to work under Windows, older Internet sites have been adjusted to be compatible with the Web.

Ease of access and faster communications made the Internet and World Wide Web take off in the late 1980s and early 1990s. When America Online began offering Internet access in 1989, the established

Hyperlinks used to connect the user to another page on the Que Education & Training Web site.

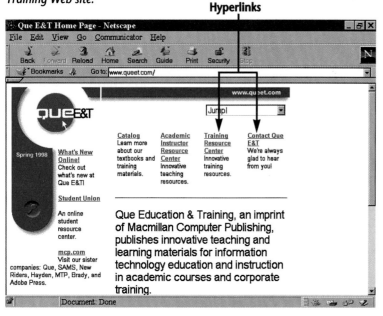

base of more technical users resented the newcomers; but the populariza-tion of the Internet proceeded rapidly. Today, **Internet service providers (ISPs)** are everywhere and most peoples' view of the Internet consists entirely of World Wide Web sites. Schools, libraries, and even some stores and restaurants provide terminals with Internet access, and every business wants to establish its presence. New computers are routinely equipped with modems. The 1980s made computers commonplace. History will most likely record the 1990s as the decade in which we began living in an online world.

Using the Internet

Most people access the Web from their home computers through the com-mercial online services such as America Online, CompuServe, Prodigy, and the Microsoft Network. These services include Internet access as part of their service. In addition, many users connect through Internet service providers, evenly split between national and regional/local providers. Some ISPs are in business solely to provide Web access, but many other types of businesses, including a number of telephone companies and newspapers, also offer an Internet access service. You pay a fee for the right to dial in to the provider. Service providers usually provide customers with a piece of software, known as a **Web browser**, which facilitates access and naviga-tion. The two most popular browsers are Netscape Navigator and Microsoft Internet Explorer.

You can begin your Internet journey by clicking on a word or icon or by entering an Internet address. This address is a **URL (Uniform Resource Locator)** such as "http://cnn.com" (which reaches the home page of the Cable News Network) or "http://www.microsoft.com" (which takes you to Microsoft's home page). The letters, **http**, stand for **hypertext transfer protocol**. This is a signal that you are accessing a World Wide Web docu-ment or Web page. FTP addresses begin with "ftp://." Addresses for e-mail (see Lesson 7A) begin with your ID and @ (the "at" sign), for example, user@microsoft.com. In the examples, "cnn" and "microsoft" are the actual addresses that you are trying to reach (many, but not all, begin with "www"). The type of site is identified by a **domain name** ("com" in the examples). The most common domain names are the following:

.com	Commercial sites
.org	Nonprofit or private organizations
.net	Networks
.edu	Educational institutions
.gov	Government agencies
.mil	Military

Outside of the United States, the domain name is followed by a country abbreviation (for example, "jp" for Japan).

Today, about 90 percent of all registered sites are commercial (.com). In order to accommodate the proliferation of Internet addresses, several new domain names are expected to be added shortly. These include

.info	Information services
.firm	Firms and businesses

.store	Retail businesses
.arts	Cultural
.rec	Recreational
.nom	Individual or personal nomenclature
.web	WWW-related

The domain name may be followed by other designations, separated by slashes to identify specific pages.

The primary address for a site leads to its **home page**. **Hyperlinks** can take you to other pages or other sites. Normally, when you pass your cursor over a link, the address it leads to appears in a bar at the bottom of your screen. Your browser keeps a list of those that you have accessed, which allows you to reestablish yourself at an earlier site simply by clicking on the address. Addresses of sites that you expect to visit in the future can be saved in a **bookmark** list. When you want to go back to it, simply open the list and select the site. When you connect with a site, you may be handed a **cookie**. A cookie is a small piece of data sent to your hard disk by the Web site. In most cases, the cookie is used to help your system to use the site. It may record registration information or save you the trouble of reentering passwords. Cookies can also be used to track your usage of the site for marketing purposes. You may never be aware of them unless you set your browser to alert you whenever one is sent.

The Web can be an endless source of information and might even help you find a job (see Online Discovery, Lesson 10A). Addresses for Web sites are widely available in magazines and books. Even many television shows, commercials, and ads in newspapers and magazines now include Web addresses.

Another way of finding information on the Web is through a **search engine** (see Lesson 8B and Online Discovery). The search engines help you find almost anything on the Web. Many people are using **People Finders** to locate e-mail addresses, phone numbers, and street addresses of friends and relatives. Excellent examples of People Finders are Four 11 (www.four11.com) and Switch-board (www.switchboard.com). These types of services can be used to locate businesses.

The addresses of hyperlinks appear at the bottom of the Web browser.

Home page   Primary address of site

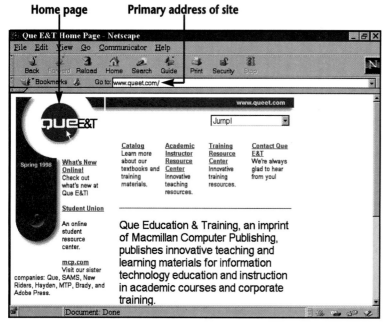

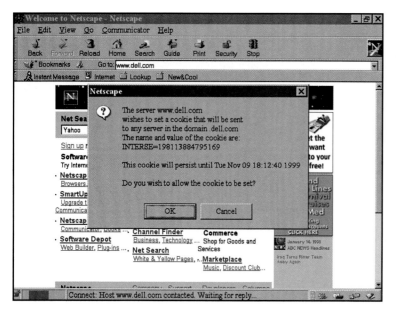

A "cookie" warning is received when a site places data on your hard disk.

In addition to the World Wide Web, many Internet users still employ some of the Internet's older, more specialized tools, including Usenet, Telnet, and File Transfer Protocol (FTP).

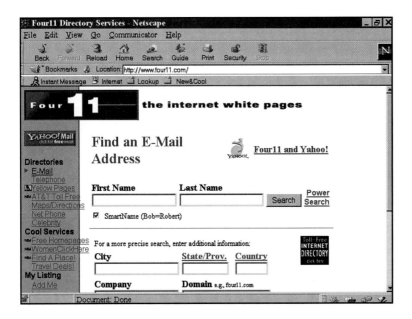

Four 11 established by Yahoo! is used to find people all over the United States.

Usenet

Usenet is a collection of more than 20,000 **newsgroups**, or discussion groups, on every conceivable subject. For example, some newsgroups are self-help groups for victims of cancer or sexual abuse, and others give the latest in gossip about show business personalities. Anyone can contribute a message, called an **article**, to a Usenet newsgroup or post a reply, known as a **follow-up post**, to an existing article. With the aid of a **newsreader** (a program designed to access Usenet newsgroups), you can read an entire **thread**—all the replies to an interesting article. Most Web browsers, including Netscape Navigator and Microsoft Internet Explorer, include built-in newsreader capabilities.

Over the years, Usenet old-timers have developed a largely unwritten set of rules they call **netiquette**. These rules are intended to enhance the quality of discussion. If you break them, you may receive critical electronic mail. Netiquette rules are really simple courtesy. Be sure to consider the other users when you are trying out Usenet.

BITS
Rules of netiquette provide courtesy guidelines for network users. One rule, for example, discourages flaming, the writing of angry messages to other network users.

Telnet

Telnet is the service of the Internet that allows you to access remote computers outside your area. Many computers on the Internet are set up to allow Telnet access. Some require login names and passwords, but many do not have any restrictions. Through Telnet, you may access libraries, databases, and other public services all over the world. **Hytelnet** is a tool that helps you access the various sites through Telnet. The World Wide Web lets you access sites through Telnet and use FTP to retrieve documents you find.

The Internet's Protocols

Your computer sends data to, or receives data from, a host computer over the Internet. A program such as Telnet breaks up the data into packets. Protocols, which are standards on which the computing community has agreed, specify how packets should be layered, or packaged, into even smaller packets. Different layers of packets address a variety of software and hardware needs in order to send information over different networks and communication links.

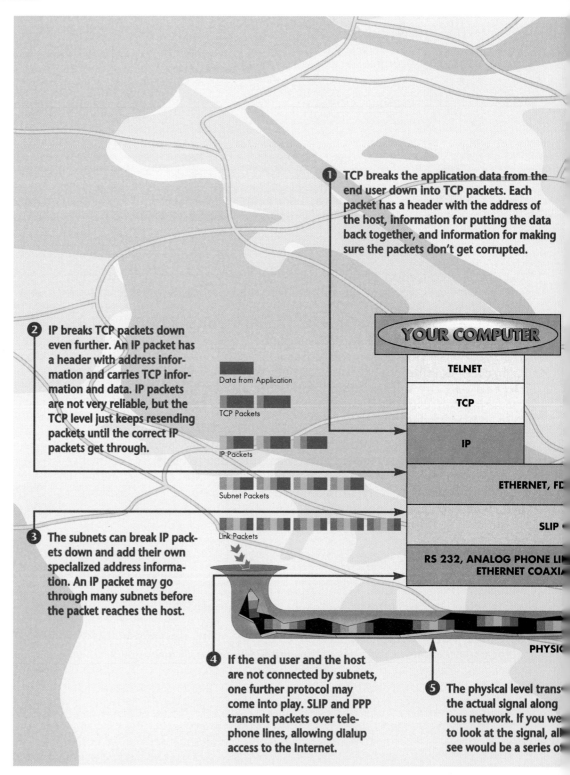

❶ TCP breaks the application data from the end user down into TCP packets. Each packet has a header with the address of the host, information for putting the data back together, and information for making sure the packets don't get corrupted.

❷ IP breaks TCP packets down even further. An IP packet has a header with address information and carries TCP information and data. IP packets are not very reliable, but the TCP level just keeps resending packets until the correct IP packets get through.

❸ The subnets can break IP packets down and add their own specialized address information. An IP packet may go through many subnets before the packet reaches the host.

❹ If the end user and the host are not connected by subnets, one further protocol may come into play. SLIP and PPP transmit packets over telephone lines, allowing dialup access to the Internet.

❺ The physical level trans the actual signal along ious network. If you we to look at the signal, al see would be a series of

Data from Application

TCP Packets

IP Packets

Subnet Packets

Link Packets

YOUR COMPUTER

TELNET

TCP

IP

ETHERNET, FD

SLIP

RS 232, ANALOG PHONE LI
ETHERNET COAXI

PHYSIC

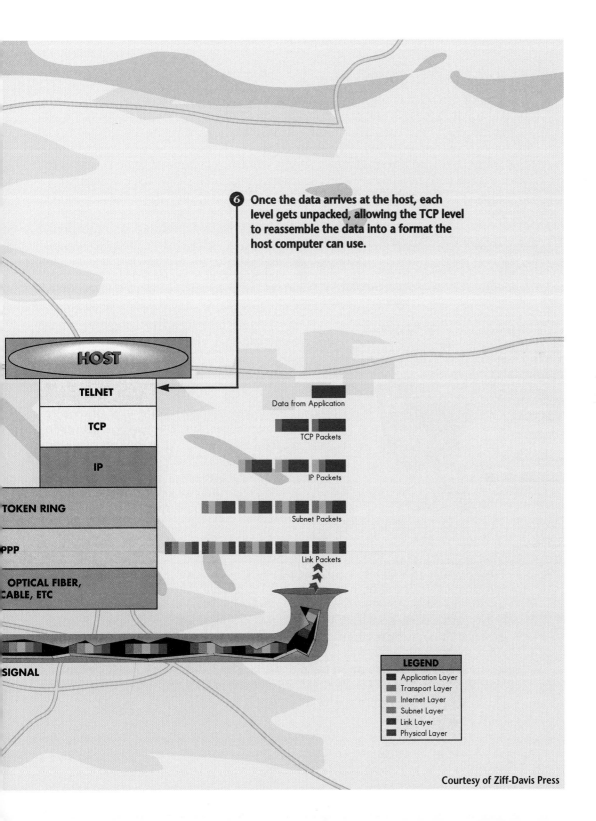

6 Once the data arrives at the host, each level gets unpacked, allowing the TCP level to reassemble the data into a format the host computer can use.

HOST

TELNET

TCP

IP

TOKEN RING

PPP

OPTICAL FIBER, CABLE, ETC

SIGNAL

Data from Application

TCP Packets

IP Packets

Subnet Packets

Link Packets

LEGEND
- Application Layer
- Transport Layer
- Internet Layer
- Subnet Layer
- Link Layer
- Physical Layer

Courtesy of Ziff-Davis Press

File Transfer Protocol (FTP)

Another common use of the Internet is to obtain computer programs and files by means of **File Transfer Protocol** (**FTP**), one of the Internet's many standards. With the aid of an FTP **client program** or Web browser, you can access **public file archives** located on computers throughout the world. These archives are directories of computers that have been set aside to provide free public access to programs and files. If you aren't sure where to find a given file, a program called **Archie** can tell you the addresses of all the archives that have a copy of that file.

Push Technology

One of the most significant recent developments in Internet access is **push technology**. Push refers to content automatically sent to you (as opposed to searching the Web and pulling in information). One of the most prominent push offerings is The PointCast Network (www.pointcast.com). PointCast is an Internet news service that replaces your screensaver with news, weather, sports, stock information, and, of course, advertising. Updates are automatic for businesses and institutions with direct Internet connections. For most people who use dial-up Internet through an ISP, updates are scheduled or requested. Graphical advertising increases download time, and the downloaded material may take up more disk space than you might like. The benefit is that PointCast, like broadcast television, is supported by its advertising and is free to users.

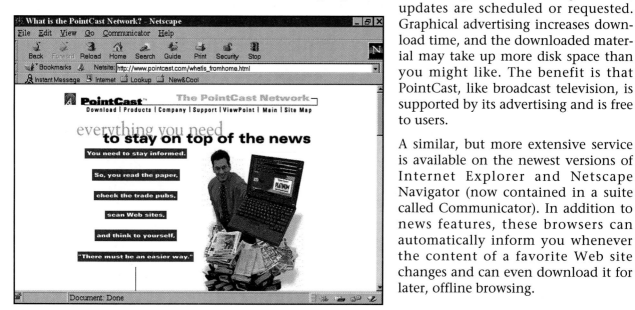

A similar, but more extensive service is available on the newest versions of Internet Explorer and Netscape Navigator (now contained in a suite called Communicator). In addition to news features, these browsers can automatically inform you whenever the content of a favorite Web site changes and can even download it for later, offline browsing.

The PointCast Network—one of the oldest and best Internet news servers.

Net Safety

The Internet has opened up a world of information, but not all of that information is useful or accurate or even desirable. Information on the Web has no more guarantee of accuracy than print or word of mouth. Con artists and sexual predators can function anonymously. Several companies produce software that can block selected material in order to shield children from undesirable material on the Web. Companies that allow employees freedom of access have often been disturbed by reduced productivity caused by idle browsing. The Internet is a revolutionary tool, but users should keep in mind that not everyone uses it responsibly.

Netiquette

Netiquette refers to online manners and behavior. We should treat other people in cyberspace as respectfully as we do in everyday situations, and in some cases our manners need to be better. After all, other cyberspace citizens cannot see you or hear your voice inflections—all they know is what you type. So follow these simple rules to avoid offending, angering, or hurting others:[1]

1. Before you write, think about your reader, yourself, and your image. Remember, the person on the other side is human, too. Make sure that your messages use a tone and language your readers will understand and appreciate; the way you write to your teacher is probably not the same way you write to a fellow student. Be sure that your communications present you in the way you want—and be willing to stand behind what you say.

2. Treat e-mail that you receive as confidential unless the sender specifically gives you permission to share it with others.

3. Respect the copyright and license agreements of material written by others. If you quote someone from a book or magazine, mention your source.

4. Do not participate in chain letters. Doing so could result in a loss of online privileges.

5. Typing messages in ALL CAPS is equal to shouting. Don't shout! A single word in uppercase for emphasis is fine, but not much more.

6. Use abbreviations sparingly; overuse can make your message difficult to understand.

7. Be careful with humor. Use emoticons, or smileys, such as :) or the <g> symbol for "grin," if you think your tone is unclear or if you want to emphasize that you're being friendly or kidding around.

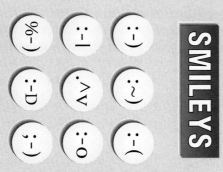

Smileys: when you care enough to let them know your mood.

8. Reply promptly to e-mail received from others. Let them know that their messages got through and that you value their correspondence.

9. When replying to specific topics in another person's message, include only the pertinent phrases or sentences. Don't return the entire message in your reply—it is a waste of resources and usually unnecessary. Preface reply portions with a greater-than arrow (>).

10. If you receive a message that was intended for another person, either return it to its sender or forward it to the recipient—but let both parties know that you received it in error.

11. Don't "flame" or reply to a provocative message when you're upset. Wait a while to cool down before answering. Always assume that every word you send is part of a permanent document. Don't say something you'll be sorry for later.

Flaming is the most serious breach of online netiquette.

12. Before participating in chats, forums, or e-mail on services like America Online or Prodigy, make sure that you are familiar with their rules of netiquette.

---

1 Donald Rose. Adapted from Minding Your Cybermanners on the Internet *(Indianapolis, IN: Que), 20–40.*

Net Access

You can access your Internet service provider through your modem, which converts digital computer signals into telephone analog signals and back again at the other end (Lesson 7A). The current standard is the 33.6Kbps modem. It transmits data at 33.6 kilobits per second (or 33,600 bits per second). Several other modem speeds, however are becoming available or are in development.

56Kbps modems function like 33.6Kbps modems when sending information. Their speed advantage is only for incoming data. This advantage is useful because the volume of incoming data is much greater when receiving elaborate page images from Web sites. The speed that you actually get depends upon many factors, including the quality of telephone lines and connections, distance from the phone company's switching station, and the equipment at the other end. Performance at your house may be substantially different than that only a block away. Most 56Kbps modems reach about 50Kbps 10 percent to 20 percent of the time. In fact, they only make it to 40Kbps about half of the time. Worst of all, there are two incompatible, competing standards for 56Kbps modems (from U.S. Robotics and Rockwell). A world standard for 56Kbps will not be established until late 1998.

ISDN (Integrated Services Digital Network, see Lesson 6A) offers 64–128Kbps performance. ISDN, because it transmits digitally, does not use a modem. It does, however, require special equipment at a relatively high price. Installation can cost $200 with a $45 per month fee, plus a one-cent per minute usage charge—all of which is over and above your Internet access fees. Additionally, unlike regular phone connections, ISDN does not supply its own power.

Digital Subscriber Lines (DSL, also ADSL and several other versions) is a much newer technology that promises even higher performance, but at an even higher price. It is currently available only in limited areas.

33.6Kbps and 56Kbps modems, ISDN, and DSL use regular telephone company copper wires. A potential alternative is the **cable modem**. This works on your cable connection, instead of phone lines. Speed estimates vary widely with uploads rated at 300Kbps to 10Mbps and downloads rated from 1.5Mbps up to 30Mbps. One reason for this variation is that cable speeds are reduced according to the number of systems using the line. A recent test found that a cable modem at least matched the performance of a dedicated 1.5Mbps line while downloading an image. If you give this performance a score of 100, a DSL line earned a 75, an ISDN line a 13, a 56Kbps modem a 5, and a 33.6Kbps modem a 4. Clearly, cable modems are a technology to watch.

The options discussed certainly do not exhaust all the possibilities. Satellite service can function at 400Kbps, but can only download. One company in England is even experimenting with Internet access through electric power lines. **WEB-TV**, recently purchased by Microsoft, provides 33.6Kbps Web access and e-mail without a computer by using your television set.

The Internet in Industry

The development of the Internet was a tremendous leap in bringing people and information together. Internet technology is also helping to connect businesses with their employees and customers.

Intranets (Lesson 7B) are networks internal to a company, college, hospital, or other institution. They look like the Internet and use the same rules and technology. They provide quick, easy communication between departments and co-workers. An online expense form, for example, can be filled out by an employee, approved by a manager, and processed by the Accounting department with no use of paper or physical mail. Intranets are currently in use in over 60 percent of Fortune 500 companies.

Internal networking has also made possible the use of **network computers (NCs)**. These range from what are essentially stripped down PCs (for example, IBM's Network Station, which has only a 33MHz CPU), to very powerful models. They lack CD-ROM and floppy drives and are sealed. Their only function is to access the network server where all files and software are stored and where the work is actually done. One of the major complaints of network managers is user-added hardware and software. Network computers cost less initially, are easy to maintain and replace, and allow greater control of the computing environment.

Intranets provide a standard that permits Web-based information to be used internally and to connect with other intranets. **Extranets** are a bridge between the Internet and the intranets. They provide limited, outside access to corporate networks. Extranets can function as a collaborative link between intranets for conferencing and joint projects, a window to the intranet for employees on the road or working as telecommuters (Lesson 7A), or as a gateway for customers and suppliers.

Extranets can reduce the need for mail, telephone tag, and unnecessary travel. Physicians can file insurance claims online. Airlines can allow travelers to select prices and schedules themselves. Federal Express advertises the fact that customers can track the progress of their own packages. Access to extranets can be customized to give users access to just the relevant areas they need without requiring them to extract it themselves from a glut of information. The data can be presented in a way that is most useful to each user without compromising security.

The online world is a product not only of technology but also of the innovative ways in which people apply that technology. This is only the beginning.

Lesson Summary

➤ Infrastructures are the means of transporting goods and information from one place to another.

➤ The Information Superhighway is the name that has been given to a proposed infrastructure for using computers and telecommunications technology to transport information anywhere in the world.

➤ Using high-capacity, high-quality communication lines, computers can be connected to exchange data, opinions, or news.

➤ A prototype of the Information Superhighway is the Internet, an existing international network of networks, which operates with little or no control.

➤ The Internet enables users to share e-mail, chat on various topics, exchange programs or data files, and access the world's research facilities.

➤ Other networks in America, such as Prodigy and America Online, offer some services similar to those of the Internet and provide their subscribers some degree of access to the Internet.

➤ Protocols used by the Internet are Transmission Control Protocol (TCP) and Internet Protocol (IP), called TCP/IP.

➤ The Internet is a packet-switching network.

➤ Connections to the Internet are by direct access (an IP connection) or dialup access.

➤ Dialup access is inexpensive but requires downloading files from a direct access computer.

➤ Direct access, an IP connection, allows access to files and e-mail to come to your computer. Direct access can be through telephone lines using SLIP (Serial Line Internet Protocol) or PPP (Point-to-Point Protocol) or through a LAN with Internet connectivity.

➤ UNIX is the most commonly used operating system for Internet host computers.

➤ Basic services of the Internet are e-mail, Telnet, and File Transfer Protocol (FTP).

➤ Programs added to the Internet that use the basic services include Archie, Gopher, WAIS, and the World Wide Web (WWW).

➤ E-mail is personal communication, anywhere in the world, to another Internet user. The two parts of an e-mail address are the user name and the domain name.

➤ Usenet is e-mail at a group level, consisting of more than 5,000 newsgroups on a multitude of topics.

➤ Telnet enables you to access remote computers outside your area, such as libraries' computers or databases.

➤ Using FTP, you can get programs and files from other computers copied to your computer.

➤ The World Wide Web (WWW) uses Usenet, Telnet, and FTP access to create a hypermedia system.

Lesson Review

Key Terms

Archie
article
asynchronous transfer
  mode
backbone network
client program
dialup access
dialup IP
direct Internet access
domain name

File Transfer Protocol (FTP)
follow-up post
hypermedia system
Hytelnet
Information Superhighway
infrastructure
Internet
Internet protocols
last-mile problem
National Information
  Infrastructure (NII)

National Research and
  Educational Network
  (NREN)
netiquette
newsgroup
newsreader
packet-switching network
Point-to-Point Protocol
  (PPP)
public file archive

Serial Line Internet Protocol
  (SLIP)
TCP/IP support
Telnet
thread
Usenet
user name
World Wide Web (WWW)

Matching

In the blank next to each of the following terms or phrases, write the letter of the corresponding term or phrase.

_____ i 1. Means for transporting goods and information

_____ d 2. Rules for communication

_____ g 3. Internet protocols

_____ e 4. Inexpensive access to the Internet

_____ a 5. A collection of discussion groups

_____ j 6. Allows access to remote computers

_____ b 7. Worldwide hypermedia system

_____ f 8. First part of an e-mail address

_____ h 9. Last part of an e-mail address

_____ c 10. Piece of information on the Internet

a. Usenet
b. WWW
c. packet
d. protocols
e. dialup
f. user name
g. TCP/IP
h. domain name
i. infrastructure
j. Telnet

Multiple Choice

Circle the letter of the correct choice for each of the following.

1. A high-speed digital transmission system capable of providing connectivity to homes and offices may be called a(n) _____.
   a. interstructure
   b. Information Superhighway
   c. telephone system
   d. none of the above

2. The biggest problem in developing a National Information Infrastructure is in _____.
   a. getting people to agree there is a need
   b. building the continent-spanning backbone
   c. wiring for local delivery
   d. developing the technology that could do the job

3. Computers on the Internet must _____.
   a. be of the same type
   b. be able to connect to one Internet server for the country
   c. connect to a coaxial cable connector
   d. use the same protocols

4. When the Internet began as ARPANET in 1969, it was _____.
   a. government sponsored
   b. used by the Department of Defense
   c. linked to university research centers
   d. all of the above

5. You can connect to the Internet through _____.
   a. direct access
   b. dialup IP
   c. a connected LAN
   d. all of the above

6. The three basic services available from the Internet include all of the following except _____.
   a. on-demand video
   b. e-mail
   c. Telnet
   d. File Transfer Protocol

7. If someone had an e-mail address of sue_cit@hud.gov.us, you probably would assume that she worked _____.

    a. for the U.S. government

    b. underseas

    c. in a remote village in the tundra

    d. You couldn't tell from the address.

8. If you want a shareware program that is available on a computer on the Internet, you could transfer the program to your computer by using _____.

    a. Usenet

    b. FTP

    c. Telnet

    d. the U.S. Mail

9. Archie is a program available on the Internet that _____.

    a. helps you find files

    b. hooks you up to newgroups

    c. identifies comic book references

    d. helps route e-mail

10. The World Wide Web is a hypermedia system because it _____.

    a. is hyperfast

    b. links to other computer resources

    c. can be used only to bring in video material

    d. none of the above

Completion

In the blank provided, write the correct answer for each of the following.

1. A prototype of the Information Superhighway is the __Internet__.

2. Roads, railways, airlines, telephones, radio, and television are some of what makes up a country's __Infrastructure__.

3. The network of networks that connects computers all around the world is called the __Internet__.

4. The pieces of information that are sent over the Internet are called __packets__.

5. The operating system most commonly associated with the Internet is __Unix__.

6. The symbol that separates the user name from the domain name in an e-mail address is __@__.

7. If the last part of the domain name of an e-mail address is edu, you can assume that the address is at a(n) __educational institution__.

8. Behavior on Usenet is expected to conform to a set of rules, not necessarily written anywhere, called __netiquette__.

9. The World Wide Web document that a business can use to communicate with its customers is also called a(n) __Web site__.

10. Using the Internet to send a written message to another Internet user is called __e-mail__.

Review

On a separate sheet of paper, answer the following questions.

1. Why is the United States considering building a National Information Infrastructure? How will this NII affect the Internet?

2. Describe the Internet.

3. Why was the Internet designed with no central office or computer?

4. Describe the difference between dialup access and direct Internet access.

5. Contrast the two ways of obtaining direct access to the Internet.

6. List the three basic services available through the Internet.

7. Describe the parts of an e-mail address.

8. Compare Usenet and Telnet.

9. Why is the World Wide Web called a hypermedia system?

10. What technologies are being suggested to speed up the Internet and the Information Superhighway?

Critical Thinking

On a separate sheet of paper, answer the following questions.

1. What is the difference between the Internet and the Information Superhighway? Why are they being discussed as two separate entities?

2. How do you think widespread use of the Internet or Information Superhighway will affect the various government agencies in your country?

3. What would you propose to deal with the social stratification that widespread use of the Information Superhighway could cause?

4. What effect do you think popular use of the Information Superhighway could have on the socialization of people in close physical proximity as well as those separated by long distances?

5. How do you see yourself using the Internet over the next five years?

Further Discovery

The Complete Idiot's Guide to USENET. Paul McFredies (Indianapolis, IN: Alpha Books, 1995).

How the Internet Works, All New Edition. Preston Gralla (Emeryville, CA: Ziff-Davis, 1996).

Internet Report. Mary Meeker and Chris DePuy (New York: HarperBusiness, 1996).

Internet Research Companion. Geoffrey W. McKim (Indianapolis, IN: Que Education and Training, 1996).

The Internet Unleashed 1996. Sams Development Group (Indianapolis, IN: Sams.net, 1996).

Que's Mega Web Directory. Dean J. Rositano, Robert A. Rositano, and Richard D. Stafford (Indianapolis, IN: Que, 1996).

Special Edition Using the World Wide Web, Second Edition. Bill Eager (Indianapolis, IN: Que, 1996).

Students' Guide to the Internet. David Clark (Indianapolis, IN: Alpha Books, 1995).

On-line Discovery

You can access the Internet resources for the following questions by going to the Que Education and Training Web site at URL http://www.ciyf98.com/discovery. From this page, click the link for Lesson 8A and then click the link to the resource you want to access.

1. The Internet Society (ISOC) is an open-membership organization charged with promoting the use and globalization of the Internet. Many ISOC subcommittees are charged with governing certain aspects of the Internet, including technical standards. Browse the **ISOC** home page (http://www.isoc.org). What are some of these subcommittees, and what aspects of the Internet are they responsible for coordinating? The ISOC Forum is the electronic newsletter of the ISOC. Look at several of the back issues available on the Web site. What issues does the ISOC deal with? What are some of the controversies reported on in the ISOC Forum?

2. The World Wide Web Consortium (W3C) is an industry group that promotes the use of the Web, disseminates information about the Web, and develops standards for it. Examine the **World Wide Web Consortium** home page (http://www.w3.org/pub/WWW). In which areas does the consortium develop standards? Who participates in the standards-making processes? The World Wide Web Consortium home page also contains much information on the history of the Web. Where did the Web see its beginnings? What are some resources available to people wanting to put information on the Web?

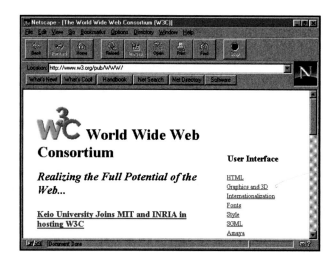

The World Wide Web

Outline

Learning Objectives

When you have finished reading this lesson, you will be able to

➤ Describe the World Wide Web and explain how it is related to the Internet

➤ Define some common terms used on the World Wide Web

➤ Explain what hypertext is and how it is related to the World Wide Web

➤ Define a Web browser and explain how it is used

➤ Describe some of the most popular search engines used on the World Wide Web

➤ Describe what a Web page is and explain how it differs from a Web site

└QUE Labs

➤ **World Wide Web**

➤ **Building a Web Server**

You hear it on television and radio: "Visit us at our Web site." Many advertisements on television and in the print media include the company's Web address. McCormick/Shilling invites you to try recipes at http://www.mccormick.com, and the city of Santa Fe offers its free visitor's guide at http://www.santefe.org. California is trying an experiment in offering sample ballots over the Web. When Aunt Jane has to have her gall bladder removed, the whole family can get the latest on her condition by checking Uncle Joe's Web site. The World Wide Web (WWW) has captured the attention and imagination of millions of people. More than half of the people getting on the Internet are accessing the Web.

The Relationship Between the World Wide Web and the Internet

As you learned in the preceding lesson, the Internet is a network of networks that anyone can access. In its beginnings, the Internet was used by researchers at colleges and universities to communicate with the United States government. The faculty and students at the colleges and universities soon branched out and began communicating with each other. The World Wide Web began in 1989 as a project by high-energy physics researchers in Switzerland to distribute research results over the Internet to fellow physicists. Since then, the Web has rapidly moved into the forefront of Internet technologies. More people use the Web on the Internet than all other technologies on the Net combined. To most of the general public, the Web is synonymous with the Internet itself and is, in fact, thought by many to have played the dominant role in moving the Internet from an academic research tool to a household word.

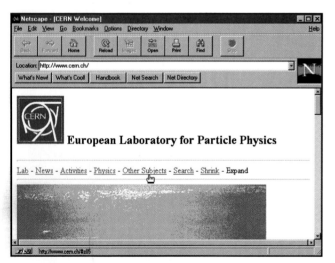

CERN, the birthplace of the World Wide Web.

The overall structure of Web technology is **client-server architecture**. This means that the technology of the Web consists of two parts: a client and a server. The server is where the information that the user accesses is actually stored. If you want to make information available to others over the Web, you put the information on a server. If you want to access the information, you get the information from a server. The client is the piece of software that allows you to access the information. Generally, you run the client on your own computer, and the server exists somewhere out on the Internet.

The client gets information from the server by means of a **transaction**. The client makes a connection to the appropriate server over the Internet and sends a request for a resource from the server. The server then sends the requested resource back to the client, and the client breaks the connection with the server. Usually, all of this happens in a few seconds.

The World Wide Web clients—the software that enables you to access resources on the Web—are called browsers. Popular browsers include Netscape Navigator, Mosaic, Lynx, and Internet Explorer. The resource requests sent by the client to the server are in the form of Uniform Resource Locators (URLs). URLs are strings of characters that determine which of the thousands of servers to connect to and which resource on that server to find. After the server locates the resource specified by the URL, the server sends the resource (the document) to the client, which displays it for you to work with, print, or save.

The documents sent by the server to the client are written in a language called **HTML**, or **Hypertext Markup Language**. HTML is a language designed to transmit documents that can contain different media formats in the same document: text, graphics, movies, sounds, and hypertext links to other documents and other resources. Your Web browser receives the HTML, allowing you to move around in the document and follow the hypertext links to the linked-to documents.

Basic Terminology

As with most new technology, the Web has generated and popularized many terms that most people don't fully understand. Using the Web is easier if you know the meaning of some of the language of the WWW.

Hypertext: Click here to go there.

The Web uses a writing technology called **hypertext.** Traditional text, such as a paper document, is linear. You begin at the beginning and finish at the end, and there is only one order in which to read the document—the order determined by the author. Hypertext frees the reader from the linear nature of text.

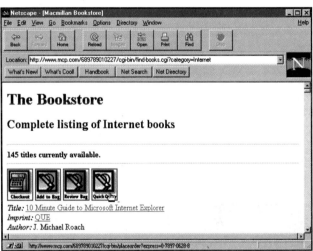

Hypertext uses links, also called **hyperlinks**. You can be reading a hypertext document and come across a link. It is then your choice to continue in the document or follow the link. This link could go to another part of the document or to another document entirely. If you have many documents, all linked to many other documents, you have a network (or web) of text, with no fixed beginning, no fixed ending, and no fixed way to browse the text.

The software that enables you to go from one resource to another by following hyperlinks is known as a **Web browser**. The most popular browsers—such as Netscape Navigator, Internet Explorer, and Mosaic—are graphical browsers and are being adopted for use within organizations to access intranets. The basic capabilities of a browser are to retrieve documents from the Web, jump to links specified in the retrieved document, and save and print the retrieved documents.

Mosaic was the first popular GUI browser.

If the computer you are using cannot handle graphics, you will need to use a nongraphical browser. This type of browser will be able to retrieve documents that contain graphics, but will just ignore the graphics and display the rest of the document. The Web is capable of offering full multimedia, but if your computer can't deal with all the media, you can still access the text material. Lynx is a popular nongraphical browser.

A code developed to identify resources on the Internet is called the **Uniform Resource Locator**, or **URL**. A URL is similar to the library catalog call number of a book. If you know the call number of a book, you can find the book at the library. If you know the URL of a resource on the Internet, you can find that resource.

The URL has three parts:

> ➤ *The tool used to access the resource.* Tools include telnet (for Telnet-based resources), ftp (for FTP-based resources), news (for Usenet newsgroups), gopher, and http (for Web-based resources). For example, if a URL begins with gopher, you know that the resource is a Gopher resource and you need to use a Gopher browser to access the resource. The tool identifier is usually followed by two slashes (//).

> ➤ *The address of the computer on which the resource is located.* This address uniquely identifies the computer on which the resource is located, anywhere on the Internet.

> ➤ *The optional path name of the resource itself.* The path name tells you the names of the directories and subdirectories on the computer where the resource can be found. This piece of information may not be present if it is not needed.

URLs are given to help you find specific resources on the Internet. The addresses provided at the start of this lesson were the URLs found in advertisements in a popular magazine. If you are doing research for a paper in a class and you find information on the Internet, you should cite the source of that information. Include the author's name or the organization's name (if no author is given), the date of the item or the date you referenced it, the name of the article, and the URL for the resource. URLs are provided in the Online Discovery sections at the ends of the lessons in this book.

Data is moved within a network or between networks according to established rules, called protocols. The protocol of the World Wide Web is **HTTP or Hypertext Transfer Protocol**.

A document (or file) you create that can be accessed by a Web browser is called a **Web page** or **Web site**. The tool you use to build your Web page is HTML. When you "surf the Net" with a Web browser, you are locating and looking at Web pages built by other people. If you don't want a Web page of your own, you don't have to create one in order to use and enjoy the Web. You learn more about creating your own Web page later in this lesson.

Java is a programming language that can be used to add dynamics to a Web page. The Java program is included in the Web page in a binary form that makes the program execute regardless of what computer it is on. Java programs can add animation, sounds, or interactive programming to a Web page.

What You Can Do on the Web

The World Wide Web is a part of the Internet, and through the Web, you can use any of the Internet's options. You can use the Web to find information, make commercial transactions, send and receive e-mail, tour museums, make reservations, and contribute information. Keep in mind, though, that the Internet and the Web are growing rapidly and their contents can be easily changed. What was there yesterday could be gone today, and what isn't there today could be there tomorrow. Two of the most intriguing activities on the Web are doing research and creating Web pages.

Research on the Web

There are two ways to find information on the Web: searching and browsing. When you know exactly what you want, you can search for it. If you have only an idea of what you want and you need to look around to see what is available, you need to browse.

Consider an analogy. When you start a research paper, you may know that you are going to write about diabetes. Then you can go to the library and look up *diabetes* in the subject card catalog or in the *Readers' Guide to Periodical Literature*. In this case, you are *searching*. If you know only that you want to do your paper on a genetically influenced disease, you might start reading some journals or looking at some books—just to see what looks interesting. This approach is known as *browsing*.

To find information on the Web, you may need to use a search engine. A **search engine** is a piece of software that gives you the ability to search for Internet resources. Search engines are usually accessed through Web browser software. Each search engine provides different searching options and has its own look. Search engines also differ greatly in the number of resources they allow you to search. Some search engines have both searching and browsing capabilities.

Search tools can be categorized as **subject directories** or **Web databases**. Subject directories are manually compiled by staff of the directory and by users who submit entries. Web databases are compiled by software "robots," or intelligent agents, that roam the Web and collect information for the databases. Both approaches to search engines have created effective products. The search engines highlighted here are currently popular or have historical interest. However, new search engines may be worth using, so be watching for them.

Subject Directories

Search engines that are subject directories of resources classify subjects according to broad categories and multiple levels of subcategories. Two such engines are Yahoo! and the World Wide Web Virtual Library.

Yahoo!

Yahoo! started as a personal project for two Stanford graduate students and has grown into a popular destination on the Net and a commercial endeavor for its founders, David Filo and Jerry Yang. The beginning screen has fourteen major categories to choose from. Each category is divided into subcategories, several levels deep. Many of the resources include a short description and the links to the site. You can use Yahoo! to search directly if you don't want to browse through subject categories.

Yahoo! can take you to many Web sites.

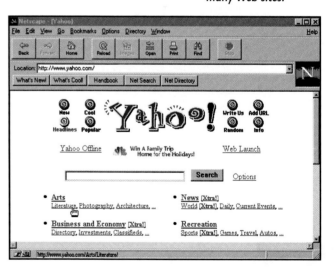

The World Wide Web Virtual Library

The WWW Virtual Library is the oldest Internet subject directory. The maintenance of its subdirectories has been delegated to people who are knowledgeable in the subject area and committed to maintaining the directory. You know that you are accessing The WWW Virtual Library because each location with a subdirectory carries the visual symbol of the Virtual Library, an open book in front of the globe. The subdirectories may be located on computers anywhere in the world.

Networking on the Internet

Would you like to send your resume to more than 20 million potential readers? Do you hesitate because you can't afford the postage? Don't despair. A new online service is available for just this purpose.

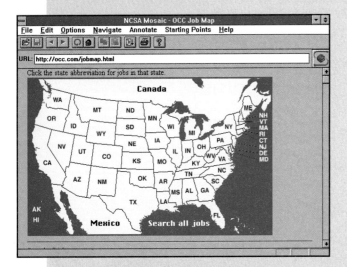

Online Career Center, Inc., known as OCC, provides such a service. Based in Indianapolis, Indiana, it is a unique, nonprofit employer association that provides services not available through the Internet alone.

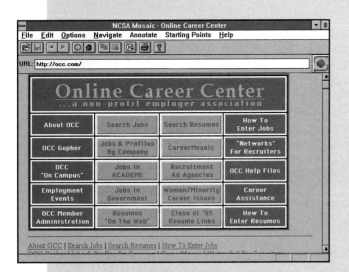

OCC offers desktop access to the Internet with an e-mail address for each account. The association has a database on the Internet that enables an applicant or employer to make information available to more than 20 million Internet users. Job listing and resume databases are provided with online keyword searching to assist both employers and applicants in using the Internet effectively. Also offered is a database of company information and profiles, as well as unlimited employment advertising and e-mail. In addition, OCC provides an electronic connection to the Internet and other networks such as Prodigy, CompuServe, and America Online.

Corporate recruiters formed OCC to reduce recruitment costs, thus allowing them to play an active role in the design, development, and direction of online services for recruitment and human resource management. Member companies can run unlimited recruitment advertising and place company profiles on the database. The companies can also gain access to the resume database.

Employers can submit ads directly on the Internet by e-mail to OCC or by phone, fax, or mail. Like most newspaper classified services, OCC also handles blind ads.

The service is free for a job seeker with a computer. All that's necessary is to be able to access the Internet, send an e-mail message to occ-info@msen.com, and type *info* on the subject line. The system then responds with instructions.

Job seekers who do not have access to a computer can mail a typed resume to Online Resume Service, 1713 Hemlock Lane, Plainfield, IN 46168. For a small fee, a resume of up to three pages (including a cover letter) will be posted on the Internet for ninety days.

Company recruiters access the center's database to post job openings or sort through resumes by region, profession, or other criteria. Not limited to computer industry jobs, the career service is backed by more than forty major corporations plus a number of small businesses.

"There are probably over 3,000 companies using the Internet for employment," said OCC executive director William O. Warren, according to the Associated Press. "What we're doing is organizing all that."

For many people, the flexibility of the clearinghouse idea is a major advantage. In the *Washington Post* (1993),

continues

Warren was quoted as saying, "The idea for a centralized job database grew out of the interest that various companies had in tapping the labor force laid off by large companies. This gives small companies the chance to look at this pool of talent."

OCC has published a 20-page booklet, "Recruiter's Guide to the Internet." The brochure explains the Internet and OCC and assures potential OCC users that they don't need to be computer experts. The system is menu-driven, with help files for every menu screen.

Because the Internet is worldwide, OCC's services are available worldwide with a strong presence in Canada, Europe, Asia, Australia, and Pacific Rim countries. OCC is available also on almost every college campus in America, as well as colleges and universities in many foreign countries.

Ads can be posted as "text only" and as "display" ads with graphics, logos, and color. The World Wide Web technology of the Internet is hypermedia with graphics, sound, and text. With so much technology at hand, the old rules for preparing an eye-catching resume no longer apply. How to make an electronic resume stand out is yet to be defined.

Popular job search wisdom claims that networking is everything. With OCC, this advice takes on a whole new meaning.

The advantage of this search tool is the expertise of the individuals who maintain a specific subject directory. The disadvantage is that the organization of the subjects does not let you search the entire WWW Virtual Library; moving from one subject to another can be awkward.

Web Databases

As noted, Web databases are built by software "robots," or intelligent agents, that travel over the Web to look for subjects and information that can be downloaded into a database automatically. The quality of a search tool that uses database technology is determined by how comprehensive the database is and how well the search engine—the software that does the searching for you—finds what you need and presents it to you. Alta Vista and Infoseek Guide are two popular database search tools.

AltaVista

AltaVista, one of the newest Web databases, is highly ranked by most surveys of search engines. The Web robot (called Scooter) for this database searches the Web and Usenet newsgroups on the Internet, indexing over 16 million Web pages. AltaVista offers both simple and advanced search options, including Boolean operators.

Infoseek Guide

Infoseek is available, by button, from the Netscape Navigator Web browser. Infoseek is a Web database, but the "Guide" is the beginning of a subject directory. Infoseek Guide is developing into a search tool that uses both database and subject directories.

Using a Search Engine Effectively

With any of the search engines, you can do a simple search for one or more words or even a phrase, and the engine will return the best results it can. But you may find that many of the sources returned are not what you want. If you get a hundred sources to look at and fifty of those are irrelevant, you are going to waste a lot of time narrowing the list to just those sources of potential value.

BITS
Boolean logic was named for George Boole, the mathematician who developed it.

To help you focus your search and avoid most of those unwanted sources, search engines offer a system known as **Boolean logic**, which enables you to combine search terms in different ways. By using the **Boolean operators** AND, OR, or NOT, you can describe the logical relationship of two or more terms. AND means that both terms must be present; OR means that either term must be present but that both are not necessary; and NOT means that the term should not be present (if it is, the source should be excluded).

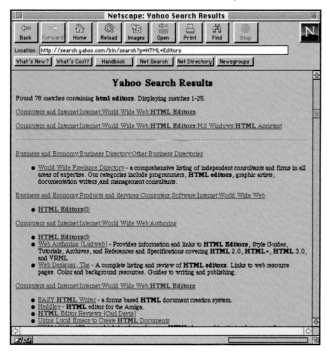

The results of a search with Yahoo!

If you wanted to see sources on the Easter Bunny, you could request *Easter* AND *Bunny*. If you did not include the AND operator, you would get every reference for *bunny* and every reference for *Easter*. The AND reduces the number of sources found, so you don't have to read a lot of material you don't want. If you use the OR operator, you will get every reference with either term. If, for example, you requested *movie* OR *film*, you would get all *movie* and *film* references. If you wanted to find references to stars but only those in astronomy, you might use *stars* NOT *movie*. This search would not remove references to rock stars, but it would reduce the number of irrelevant matches.

When you use the search engines, be aware of a few terms that are related to searching. Words that describe your search topic are known as **search items**. **False drops** are items that are found in a search but are not what you want; words with two meanings often result in false drops. **Hits** are returned items that match your search terms. **Results ranking** is an attempt to put the resources returned by the search in an order based on each resource's relevance to your query.

Web Pages and Web Sites

Until now, the discussion has been about how to get information from the World Wide Web. Suppose that you want to publish information on the Web for others to see. To do this, you need to create a Web site or Web page. Think of a Web site as the umbrella organization of your home page and Web pages.

Originally, your **home page** was the place (the document or file) where you stored addresses of Web pages or sites you had visited and thought you might want to visit again. The home page was like a personal address list for you. With the development of Web browsers, the home page has evolved into the page that tells someone accessing your site about *you*. When you use a browser to go to a Web site, the home page is the first page or document you see.

The Web page is the document—including text, graphics, sound, animation, and video—that you create to share with anyone who finds your page. Anything you can store on a computer can be included in a Web page. The terms *location* and *document* may be used interchangeably with the term *Web page*. They all refer to the information you get from a World Wide Web address. The browser is the tool you use to go from one page to another on the Web.

Creating a Web page can be as easy or challenging as you want to make it. Online services like America Online, Prodigy, and CompuServe have tools that provide a template you can fill in and save as your Web page. Each service offers subscribers 1M or more of space on which to create your Web page. If you connect through an Internet service provider (ISP), most providers give each customer at least 1M of space for a Web page, as long as the customer maintains a Web account. With an ISP, you can create your Web page in one of three ways: You can use HTML to create the page, you can use word processing software, or you can use Web-authoring software.

The more appealing the information (and its presentation) on your Web page, the more visitors you are likely to get. But having a great Web page will not guarantee you a popular Web site. To be popular, you have to tell everyone that you are out there, and what you have that people will want to come and see. Many search services will let you provide keywords in their Web databases so that anyone searching for a particular keyword or phrase will have the option of accessing your page.

A Web site is a group of related Web pages. The Web site is the master address, and the individual Web pages are like subdirectories to that root directory. Many businesses are creating Web sites for their customers to use. These sites may include price lists, information about products, and comparisons of product features with those of competing products. Many sites even allow customers to order products over the Web. Because your site is representing *you* on the Web, you will want the site to look impressive. For a professional-looking site, you may want to hire a firm that creates Web sites. Such firms employ HTML experts as well as graphic designers and marketing specialists.

TechTalk
Large companies may have a *Webmaster* on staff to create and maintain the Web site.

A word of caution: Web pages contain information you can access, but you have no assurances that what is printed there is accurate or true. There are no rules or laws—except the general libel and slander laws—that govern what is on the Web.

Get On and Go

Are you ready to join the millions of other people surfing the Web? What do you need to get on and go? You need a computer, a modem, a telephone line, and an Internet service provider or online service. You can get on the Internet with any computer, but the older, slower computers require a lot of compromises for use on the Net. The ideal computer is one with an operating system that provides a graphical environment—such as the Macintosh, a PC running Windows 95, or a UNIX machine running the X Window environment.

The faster your modem, the more you will enjoy the Web. A 14.4Kbps is the minimum speed you will be willing to tolerate for very long, and a 28.8 or 33.6Kbps modem is much better. The slower the modem, the longer it takes to download files. If you have only one telephone line for both your voice phone and your modem, you will probably miss a lot of calls. A second line will cost you a one-time installation fee (usually up to $100) and then a minimum monthly service charge. The line into the modem will not need any of the costly extras you might have on your voice line.

Choosing an Internet service provider or an online service (such as America Online or CompuServe) is a matter of shopping around to get the one that best meets your needs, at the lowest price available. Online services are usually more costly than an ISP, but they are simpler to use for the novice and provide additional services beyond Internet access. Online services are generally more expensive than an ISP if you are online more than twenty hours a month. An ISP provides a local number to call to access the Internet, as well as some space for a home page. The charge for time online varies from unlimited free use with your monthly fee, to a limit of twenty or more hours free and a per-hour charge after that.

Once you are online and ready to use the World Wide Web, you can find a Web browser that is available to download from the Internet at no charge. With your Web browser loaded, you are ready to "catch a wave" and surf the Web. Enjoy!

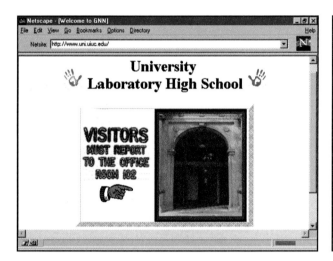
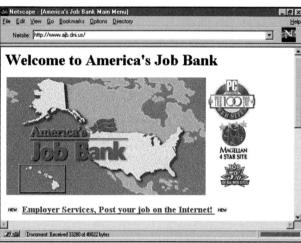
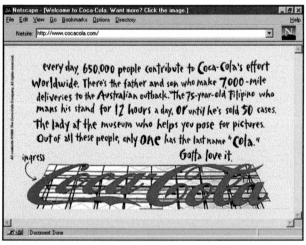

Some sample Web sites.

Lesson Summary

➤ The World Wide Web is the dominant technology on the Internet.

➤ The overall structure of Web technology is client-server architecture. The client is the software that allows you to access information, and the server is the place where the information is stored. The documents on the server that are accessed by the client are written in HTML, or HyperText Markup Language.

➤ World Wide Web clients are called browsers. The most popular browsers are Netscape Navigator, Internet Explorer, and Mosaic. The basic capabilities of a browser are to retrieve documents from the Web, jump to links specified in the documents, and save and print the documents.

➤ Hyperlinks connect documents created by HTML, enabling you to move to another part of the document or to a different document.

➤ The Uniform Resource Locator (URL) is the address of a resource on the Web. Included in the URL are the tool to access the resource, the address of the computer where the resource is located, and the optional path name of the resource on the computer where the resource resides.

➤ HTTP (Hypertext Transfer Protocol) is the protocol of the World Wide Web.

➤ Java is the programming language used on the Web to add animation, sound, and interactive programming to a resource.

➤ Research on the Web can be done by searching or browsing. Searching involves looking for key terms and identifying Web locations that use those terms. Browsing involves looking around for interesting items.

➤ Search engines are categorized as subject directories or Web databases. Subject directories, such as Yahoo! and The World Wide Web Virtual Library, are built by staff and include Web addresses in subject directories and subdirectories. Web databases, such as Alta Vista and Infoseek Guide, are built by software "robots" that roam the Web looking for key terms and placing them in databases.

➤ Web pages are documents, with hyperlinks, that are stored on the Web and retrieved by browsers. A home page is the page first encountered when a Web browser finds a Web site.

➤ The best computer to use for getting on the Internet and the World Wide Web is capable of using a graphics interface, a fast modem, a telephone line, and either an Internet service provider (ISP) or an online service.

Lesson Review

Key Terms

Boolean logic	Hypertext Markup	Java	Uniform Resource Locator
Boolean operators	Language (HTML)	results ranking	(URL)
client-server architecture	Hypertext Transfer Protocol	search engine	Web browser
false drop	(HTTP)	search item	Web databases
hit	hyperlink	subject directories	Web page
home page	hypertext	transaction	Web site

Matching

In the blank next to each of the following terms or phrases, write the letter of the corresponding term or phrase.

_____ f   1. Network of networks

_____ c   2. Technology of the World Wide Web

_____ j   3. Address of a server

_____ a   4. Client software that accesses the Web

_____ i   5. Protocol of the Web

_____ b   6. Language to create animation

_____ g   7. Software to search for Web resources

a. browser

b. Java

c. client-server architecture

d. Yahoo!

e. hyperlinks

f. Internet

g. search engine

h. AltaVista

_____d_____ **8.** Subject directories   **i.** HTTP

_____h_____ **9.** New Web database   **j.** URL

_____e_____ **10.** Connects Web pages

Multiple Choice
Circle the letter of the correct choice for each of the following.

1. In reference to the World Wide Web, the server is _____.

   a. where the information is actually stored

   b. a piece of software that allows you access to information

   c. the document you retrieve

   d. the network that runs the Internet

2. The software that you use to access information on the Web may be called a _____.

   a. server

   b. client

   c. browser

   d. both b and c

3. A "create your own adventure" book, which could have several endings depending on your answers to questions in the book, could be an example of _____.

   a. linear text

   b. hypertext

   c. marked-up text

   d. both a and b

4. If a URL starts with http//, you know _____.

   a. that it is an FTP-based resource

   b. that it is a Web-based resource

   c. that it is not available anywhere on the Internet

   d. nothing—that isn't enough information

5. If, on the Web, a document has text, graphics, and sound, you can assume that the document was created using _____.

   a. a client

   b. HTML

   c. URL

   d. HTTP

6. If a Web page includes animation, probably _____ was used in creating it.

   a. Java

   b. Hypertext

   c. URL

   d. HTTP

7. Two ways of finding information on the Web are _____.

   a. transferring and searching

   b. browsing and networking

   c. searching and browsing

   d. networking and transferring

8. You can use the Web to _____.

   a. send and receive e-mail

   b. make reservations

   c. search for information

   d. all of the above

9. Subject directories are built by _____; Web databases are built by _____.

    a. people, software robots

    b. software robots, people

    c. HTML, HTTP

    d. Infoseek, Yahoo!

10. When a Web browser finds information on the Web, the first place it finds the information is on the _____.

    a. Web site

    b. Web page

    c. Web home page

    d. hypertext

Completion

In the blank provided, write the correct answer for each of the following.

1. A search _____ is a piece of software that gives you the ability to search for Internet resources.

2. In a search, the returned items that match your search terms are called _____. *HITS*

3. The terms AND, OR, and NOT are called _____. *Boolean operators*

4. Yahoo is an example of a(n) _____. *search engine (subject directories)*

5. The professional who creates and maintains Web pages and Web sites for companies is called a(n) _____. *graphic designers / marketing specialist HTML experts*

6. Another name for the software robots that roam the Web to collect data for Web databases is _____.

7. The protocol of the World Wide Web is called _____. *HTTP*

8. The software that allows you to go from one resource to another by following hyperlinks is called a(n) _____. *Browser*

9. A code developed to identify resources on the Internet is called the _____. *URL*

10. When you give an address of a resource on the Internet, the tool code (such as http or gopher) is followed by _____. *(2) slasher*

Review

On a separate sheet of paper, answer the following questions.

1. What is the difference between a client and a server?

2. Explain how hypertext is used to link documents together on the Web.

3. What is a Web browser?

4. How are Uniform Resource Locators (URLs) used on the Web?

5. Define *search engine*.

6. Explain how subject directories and Web databases differ.

7. How can Boolean operators help you search for information on the Web?

8. What is the purpose of a Web page?

9. Compare Web pages and Web sites.

10. What hardware do you need to get on the Web?

Critical Thinking

On a separate sheet of paper, answer the following questions.

1. How could you use the World Wide Web to help you prepare a paper on the political climate in the Near East?

2. What do you think are the dangers of the popularity of the World Wide Web?

3. What would you put on your home page?

4. When would it be better to use a subject directory search engine rather than a Web database search engine?

5. If you get information from the Web, how would you ensure that it is correct?

Further Discovery

Most Popular Web Sites: The Best of the Net from A2Z. Lycos Press (Indianapolis, IN: Que, 1996).

Que's Mega Web Directory. Dean J. Rositano, Robert A Rositano, and Richard D. Stafford (Indianapolis, IN: Que, 1996).

Special Edition Using the World Wide Web, Second Edition. Bill Eager (Indianapolis, IN: Que, 1996).

Sams' Teach Yourself Web Publishing with HTML 3.2 in 14 Days. Laura Lemay (Indianapolis, IN: Sams.net, 1996).

 # On-line Discovery

You can access the Internet resources for the following questions by going to the Que Education and Training Web site at URL http://www.ciyf98.com/discovery. From this page, click the link for Lesson 8B and then click the link to the resource you want to access.

1. **Yahoo!** (http://www.yahoo.com) and **The World Wide Web Virtual Library** (http://www.w3.org/pub/DataSources/bySubject/Overview.html) are two Internet search engines that use subject directories and were described in the chapter. Look at both of these search tools and browse the subject directories provided. Does either of these tools provide categories representing the subjects you are interested in? Do you notice any gaps in their subject coverage? Yahoo! enables you to search its catalog of Web sites. Do a sample search for a subject that you would like to learn more about. Did you find anything?

2. **AltaVista** (http://altavista.digital.com) and **Infoseek Guide** (http://guide.infoseek.com) are two popular Web database search tools that were discussed in the chapter. **Lycos** (http://www.lycos.com) and **HotBot** (http://www.hotbot.com) are similar search tools. Think of a topic you would like to retrieve information on (for example, your favorite television show, movie, or hobby), and perform a search for that topic, using all four search engines. How did the results from each search differ? Every search engine has a help screen of some sort that describes the different search options available to help you improve the accuracy of your search. Take a look at the help screen for each of these tools. What kinds of options are available? Are there any options that look particularly useful to you? Any that you don't understand?

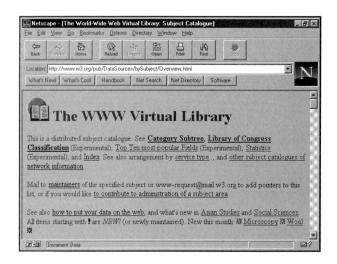

PART IV

Computers Shaping Society and Your Future

Computers are changing our society. Along with all the exciting, positive things that computers can do, they can also have a negative effect. Governments are trying to pass laws to keep under control the problems that computers cause. Laws have been passed to try to stop children from being exposed to pornography, protect citizens' rights to privacy, and protect the environment. To be able to decide whether the proposed laws are what you want, you need to understand the problems the computer can cause and how computers are used.

CHAPTER 9
The Social Challenge—Now and Tomorrow

Computers help us do many wonderful things. However, like any invention, computers also have the potential to cause harm. You wouldn't dream of sitting in front of a television set eight hours a day, yet many people work with a computer monitor for that length of time. This prolonged exposure can be harmful. In the same way, we need to be careful in how we use the data stored on computers—to protect our right to privacy. Furthermore, the dangerous materials that are used in computer hardware must be disposed of properly—to protect our environment. Despite the potential for harm, the potential for good is much larger.

Chapter 9 looks at the dangers of computers—dangers posed to our health, our environment, and our privacy—as well as the promise that these amazing machines hold for the future.

Lesson 9A considers the ethical problems surrounding access to and use of computers containing privileged information. Lesson 9B considers the possible harmful effects of computers to our health. The text also gives suggestions of what we can do to minimize potential problems. Lesson 9C examines ways in which computer access and data security can be protected. Lesson 9D looks at some of the new areas in which the computer is being used to create a brighter future.

Ethics—Doing the Right Thing

Outline

What Is Ethics?
ACM Ethical Standards
Ethics for Computer Users
    Software Piracy
    Unauthorized Access
    Public and Private Networks
Ethics for the Computer Professional
    Professional Standards
    Programmer Liability
Ethics for Businesses
The Ten Commandments of Computing

Learning Objectives

When you have finished reading this lesson, you will be able to

➤ List the values computer professionals use to define ethical computing behavior

➤ Explain when copying software is ethical and when it is not

➤ Discuss the potential harm that can come from unauthorized computer access

➤ State the computer professional's code of ethics

➤ Apply ethical reasoning to ethical dilemmas in your own computer use

Can you imagine an electronic "love triangle" making headlines? That's just what happened after an incident on the WELL, a computer network based in northern California. A male user had been involved in electronic "romances" with at least two female users. Neither woman was aware of the other, and none of these people had ever met. The "romances" consisted solely of ardent electronic mail exchanges. But when the two women discovered that they had the same "lover," they posted his name—and urged other female subscribers to delete his mail. The resulting tumultuous debate made the cover of *Newsweek*!

This incident may seem amusing—unless you happen to be one of the people involved. They didn't think it was so funny! But it does point out one of the challenges of new technologies. They push existing ethical and moral ideas into unpredicted areas, where it's far from certain just what rules apply. The "two-timing" man didn't feel that he was doing anything wrong because the "romances" existed only in cyberspace. But the women (not to mention many male and female observers) disagreed; they pointed out that electronic mail friendships and romances can reach surprising emotional depth. Who's right?

Many people have been trying to answer questions like these, and a new field of ethics—computer ethics—is emerging. This lesson surveys the basics of ethical thought and outlines ethical guidelines for computer users and computer professionals.

What Is Ethics?

Ethics is the branch of philosophy that deals with the determination of what is right or wrong, good or bad. To behave ethically is to live one's life in accordance with a set of ethical principles, which are based, ultimately, on moral values.

Over the centuries, philosophers have proposed many competing theories of ethical conduct. Some philosophers believe that ethical behavior must be grounded in absolute moral principles, such as "Behave toward others as you want them to behave toward you." Others believe that ethical behaviors are required because they lead to the greatest good for the greatest number of people. Still others believe that ethics must be founded in religious values.

ACM Ethical Standards

Because computers raise special ethical problems, people who work with computers tend to avoid the theoretical issues. Computer professionals prefer to set practical guidelines for ethical behavior. In an attempt to formulate a set of ethical principles for computer professionals, the ACM (Association for Computing Machinery) developed a statement of the ethical values of its members. The *ACM Code of Ethics and Professional Conduct* contains twenty-four rules, or imperatives, with eight general moral imperatives.

According to these values, an ethical person does the following:

1. Contributes to the improvement of society and to the well-being of human lives

2. Takes care not to harm others

3. Speaks the truth and merits trust

4. Treats others with fairness

5. Honors the intellectual property rights of others

6. Gives proper credit when using the intellectual property of others

7. Respects the right of other individuals to privacy

8. Honors confidentiality

Many computer professionals believe that these basic values can provide clear guidance for ethical computer use.

Based on these principles, do you think that the electronic "two-timer" behaved unethically? His behavior was dishonest and inconsiderate. He wanted to carry on as many "electronic affairs" as possible without considering that his behavior could hurt somebody.

Ethics for Computer Users

You may not think that sitting down at a personal computer raises ethical issues, but it does. Almost every computer user will sooner or later be faced with an ethical dilemma concerning software piracy, for example. Other ethical issues are pornography and the Internet and unauthorized access to computer systems.

Software Piracy

For computer users, one of the most pressing ethical issues concerns the duplication of computer programs.

Some programs are offered free to anyone. This software is said to be in the **public domain**, and you can legally copy public domain software. The software is free because the person who created it chose to make it available free to everyone.

Another type of software is called shareware. **Shareware** has been copyrighted, and the creator offers it to anyone to copy and try out. In return, the creator asks the user to register and pay for the software if he or she continues using it. Some shareware providers then send software upgrades and corrections to registered users.

Most software, however, is **copyrighted software**, legally protected against copying or being used without paying for it. **Software piracy** involves making illegal copies of copyrighted software. Software piracy is a felony offense.

Courtesy of Software Publishers Association

Most software companies do not object to your making a backup copy of their software, in case a disk or file is later damaged. Most software is designed to be copied or installed on your hard disk for you to use. Many software publishers allow you to copy software to your desktop computer and your laptop. You may *not* make copies to give to other people or to sell, however. If software is on the computers in the college's computer lab, you may *not* copy it onto disks for your use elsewhere.

CTE LICENSE

The Issue Was Plagiarism

Plagiarism is the unauthorized use of another person's original words or ideas. You may have heard discussions at your college about plagiarism, for it has been around a long time. People sometimes plagiarize by copying another's writing from a book or a term paper. Plagiarism is not only unethical behavior; it is also a violation of copyright law—a form of intellectual theft. Unfortunately, the Information Age and word processing have made plagiarism much easier.

For example, a college student loaned a fellow student the disk containing her bibliography for the class term paper. He used it for his term paper and then passed it along to ten other students. The professor saw identical bibliographies in their papers, and all received a reprimand for their actions. This accessibility means that each student must take more stringent measures to avoid plagiarizing, even unintentionally.

All kinds of information are distributed on floppy disks and optical disks these days. This information includes magazine articles, the works of William Shakespeare, book excerpts, works from the Internet—the list goes on and on. In addition, it is not uncommon to obtain information from electronic sources over the telephone lines. When using this information responsibly and ethically, you must cite the source—whether your work is a paraphrase or a direct quotation—in a reference or citation, providing the author's name, the article title, where it was published, the date, and so on.

Most information can easily be plagiarized simply by copying portions of text into a word processor and creating a file. The plagiarist may simply put his or her name on the document. Some try to obscure the plagiarism by changing a few words, modifying some sentences, adding or deleting a paragraph here and there, and calling the result an original work. But the plagiarist knows that he or she has committed an unethical act. And although a short-term goal may have been met—that of getting a term paper in on time—the long-term goal of acquiring knowledge through the learning process and disseminating it through the effective use of language has not. Plagiarism, like other unethical acts, really hurts the plagiarist most of all.

A recent college graduate was hired as a staff writer of a well-known investment advice newsletter. Key to the newsletter's success were its original insights into the market and its unique perspective on investments. This young woman worked hard but often ran late on her deadlines. Fearful that she would not have an article done in time, she plagiarized an article from a magazine published by an investment services company, typing it into her word processor and submitting it as her own work. The editor immediately sensed the lack of insight in the work and challenged its originality. The woman confessed that she had plagiarized the work, and although her editor understood the reason, the plagiarism was the grounds for dismissal. The writer couldn't be trusted to report and write ethically and responsibly again, and thus her career as a writer and journalist came to an abrupt and unfortunate conclusion.

Organizations with many computers can buy software for all the computers at a reduced price per unit. This agreement, called a **site license**, is a contract with the software publisher; the contract allows multiple copies of software to be made for use in the organization. Taking copies outside the organization violates the contract.

Does copying software really do any harm? Yes! Writing a software package takes a long time and a great deal of effort. Most packages are created by a team of programmers, analysts, and other experts. These experts need to be paid a salary while writing the programs. Often the time between the start of the project and the time money starts to come in from sales is two to four years or longer. If people copy the software from someone else instead of buying their own copies, the software publisher will not earn enough money to make the effort worthwhile. This fact can discourage companies from developing new, exciting software. Software piracy adds to the cost of software packages and inhibits the development of new software. Everyone loses with software piracy.

Unauthorized Access

A **computer hobbyist** is someone who enjoys pushing his or her computer skills to the limit. And sometimes that means trying to get past the security precautions that prevent unauthorized access to computer systems. In all the states of the U.S., unauthorized computer access is a crime.

The term **hacker** was originally coined to refer to computer users who experimented with computer programs to test their limits. When some of these users began to experiment with illegally accessing systems, the news media used the term *hacker* to mean people who attempt to gain unauthorized access to computer systems. The term **cracker** has been proposed to refer to this computer criminal, with *hacker* applied to the ethical computer user.

Some crackers have argued that breaking into a company's database to prove that it is vulnerable is a legitimate behavior. When the behavior is evaluated with the ethical principle of not doing what you would not want everyone else to do, unauthorized access is difficult to justify. True, a company may want to test its security against crackers. A computer security company, such as the one depicted in the movie *Sneakers*, can provide the test.

Crackers may persist in their behavior out of the belief that no one is being hurt. That thought is small consolation to the people who are trying to store confidential or sensitive information on a computer system. A cracker who alters or vandalizes key data in a hospital records system may endanger lives. Whether or not harm is done, cracking is wrong because it violates the ethical principle of respecting the privacy of others.

Public and Private Networks

With the growth of online information services such as CompuServe and America Online, public networks such as the Internet, and bulletin board systems, the question of appropriate material for posting online has become an issue. The most volatile issue is pornography, now often called **cyberporn**. The question is whether adults have the right to publish pornography on these online systems where minors can get to it. The biggest problem area is the Internet. Services like CompuServe, Prodigy, and America Online have established guidelines for their users and have the means to enforce those limits. The Internet, however, was designed to have no single authority and has no capability for enforcing rules or standards.

The fact that the Internet is an international network adds to the complexity. People from countries with stricter codes will be at the mercy of people from countries with more lax codes, as long as no method exists to restrict material from the network. To many people, the strength of the Internet is its open forum—the fact that it cannot be censored.

Currently, the best way for parents to protect their children from cyberporn and for individuals to avoid material they do not choose to see is to control access in the home. Simply avoid the places on the Internet where cyberporn is located. One tool to aid in this effort is **PICS**, or **Platform for Internet Content Selection**, a voluntary ratings system that is widely endorsed by companies contributing to the Internet. A second tool is **filtering software** available at many software outlets. Some packages are Cyber Patrol, CYBERsitter, The Internet Filter, SurfWatch, Net Nanny, and WebTrack. Purchasing, installing, and registering these packages entitle you to frequently updated lists of sites to be avoided.

Ethics for the Computer Professional

"The hardest person to protect against is a knowledgeable employee." This statement is an axiom of computer security. The person who built your security system knows its weaknesses. Computer professionals include programmers, systems analysts, computer designers, and database administrators. Computer professionals have so many opportunities to misuse a computer system that ultimately the only protection is for the computer professional to act ethically. Computer professionals have been aware of this problem for as long as they have been working on computers; therefore, computer professional organizations have developed codes of ethics for the profession.

Professional Standards

The codes establish several standards. The most important are competency and professional responsibility. **Competency** requires a professional to keep up with the latest developments in the industry. Because the computer industry encompasses so many areas and advancements are occurring constantly, no individual can be competent in all areas. Therefore, the code requires professionals to keep up with their areas of specialization to the best of their abilities and to seek help from other experts when encountering something unfamiliar.

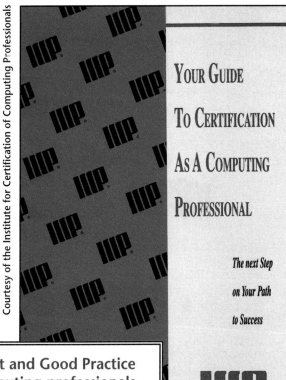

Courtesy of the Institute for Certification of Computing Professionals

YOUR GUIDE

TO CERTIFICATION

AS A COMPUTING

PROFESSIONAL

The next Step

on Your Path

to Success

Institute for Certification
of Computing Professionals

Codes of Conduct and Good Practice for certified computing professionals

The essential elements relating to conduct that identify a professional activity are:

A high standard of skill and knowledge.

A confidential relationship with people served.

Public reliance upon the standards of conduct established practice.

The observance of an ethical code.

Therefore, these Codes have been formulated to strengthen the professional status of certified computing professionals.

Excerpt from the Code of Ethics of the Institute for Certification of Computing Professionals.

Professional responsibility involves doing the best possible job even though the user may not immediately recognize the difference between the best job and a poor job. This standard means making sure that a program is as correct as possible, even if no one else is likely to find bugs for months—or even years. Professional responsibility also means informing the purchasing company if a program could have an adverse effect on the public. A third aspect of professional responsibility is honoring the privacy of the company when leaving a job. When leaving a company, a professional does not take programs he or she developed for the first company; nor does the professional tell the new company about projects being developed by the other company.

A computer professional has access to the company's greatest asset: its data and the equipment to manipulate the data. Professionals also have the knowledge to use these assets properly or to misuse them. Most companies do not have the resources to check on the actions of their computer experts. To keep the data safe and correct, the company is dependent, to some degree, on the ethics of the computer professionals.

Programmer Liability

Even the most ethical programmer can produce a program with errors. Most complex programs have so many possible combinations of conditions that to test the program for every combination is not feasible. In some cases, the tests would take years; in other cases, no one can think of a test for all the possibilities. All experienced programmers know that all programs of any size have bugs. Programmer liability arises out of the need to determine whether the bugs were inevitable or the result of negligence on the part of the programmer. Usually, the question of programmer liability comes up in a court of law.

Consider this situation. An airplane flying in poor visibility uses a computer to guide the plane—a common occurrence. The air traffic control system controlling the plane is also a computer system—a technique now used by larger airports. The plane crashes. A minor bug is discovered in each software package. If the plane had been dealing with a person in the tower rather than a computer, the bug would not have come up. If the air traffic control program had been interacting with a human pilot, the bug would not have occurred. Both bugs were determined to be inevitable. Where does the liability for the loss of life and property lie?

Conscientious programmers who have written programs to control systems on which people's lives depend often have nightmares about making a fatal mistake. They usually demand several levels of peer review of their work to be sure that every effort has been made to eliminate the bugs in the program.

Ethics for Businesses

A business or organization must protect its data from loss or damage, from misuse or error, and from unauthorized access. Otherwise, the organization is not serving its clients effectively.

To protect data from loss, an organization must have proper backup procedures. Backup procedures to make copies of data files and databases for protection are discussed in Lesson 9C.

Protecting data from misuse or error is difficult for any organization; misuse can come from different sources. One type of misuse is not using the appropriate software or not using software properly. A company or organization has a responsibility to maintain the data that is as complete and correct as is reasonably possible. For all data to be absolutely correct is impossible, but whenever an error is discovered, it must be corrected as quickly as possible.

Data that has not been properly maintained can have serious effects on the individual or organization it relates to. Errors in data can and do occur. It is the responsibility of the organization dealing with the data to ensure that its data is as correct as possible.

The second type of misuse of data occurs when an employee or company fails to keep data confidential. Do you get junk mail? Junk mail is mail sent to you without your requesting it. It includes advertisements, contests, offers of services, and occasionally free samples. How do the advertisers get your name and address? They buy lists from businesses.

A breach of confidentiality occurs when an employee looks up data about a person in the database and uses that information outside the specific job. Many companies have developed specific rules of conduct for their employees and actively enforce them. For example, any employee of the IRS found using data outside of his or her specific job is subject to immediate dismissal.

The Ten Commandments of Computing

The Computer Ethics Institute in Washington, D.C., has attempted to codify these principles into a set of "commandments" for computer users and computer professionals alike. The Institute has formulated the following guidelines:

1. Thou shalt not use a computer to harm other people.

2. Thou shalt not interfere with other people's computer work.

3. Thou shalt not snoop around in other people's computer files.

4. Thou shalt not use a computer to steal.

5. Thou shalt not use a computer to bear false witness.

6. Thou shalt not copy or use proprietary software for which you have not paid.

7. Thou shalt not use other people's computer resources without authorization or proper compensation.

8. Thou shalt not appropriate other people's intellectual output.

9. Thou shalt think about the social consequences of the program you are writing or the system you are designing.

10. Thou shalt always use a computer in ways that show consideration and respect for your fellow humans.

Reprinted by permission of the Computer Ethics Institute

Lesson Summary

➤ Ethics concerns the definition of right and good actions.

➤ Computer professionals stress the values of contributing to the improvement of society, avoiding harm to others, respecting the truth and the privacy of others, behaving fairly, honoring confidentiality, and honoring the intellectual property rights of others as well as giving credit when using those intellectual properties.

➤ Copyrighted software is legally protected against copying. Software piracy is the felony offense of copying copyrighted software.

➤ Public domain software is offered free to anyone.

➤ Shareware is software that is copyrighted but available to copy and try out. If you keep it, you should pay a registration fee.

➤ Hackers are computer enthusiasts who try to test software and hardware to its limits. Those hackers who try to get unauthorized access to systems or databases are called crackers.

➤ The Internet has created new issues of freedom of speech and the transmission of pornography, sometimes called cyberporn. There are laws to control the pornography, but there are many problems in enforcing the proposed bans.

➤ Organizations for computer professionals have developed codes of ethics for the profession. The two major provisions of the codes are competency and professional responsibility. Competency requires that professionals keep up with the latest developments in their areas of expertise, and professional responsibility requires doing the best job possible every time.

➤ One reason for professional ethics is the liability of programmers. Because an error in a program could be devastating, programmers must follow all reasonable steps to ensure the correctness of their programs.

➤ Businesses have an ethical mandate to protect their data from loss or damage, from misuse or error, and from unauthorized access.

➤ The Computer Ethics Institute in Washington, D.C., has summarized the ethical standards for businesses, computer professionals, and computer users in ten guidelines, or "commandments," for computer professionals and computer users.

Lesson Review

Key Terms

competency	cyberporn	Platform for Internet	shareware
computer hobbyist	ethics	Content Selection (PICS)	site license
copyrighted software	filtering software	professional responsibility	software piracy
cracker	hacker	public domain	

Matching

In the blank next to each of the following terms or phrases, write the letter of the corresponding term or phrase.

_e_   **1.** Legally protected software

_g_   **2.** One who tests the limits of a computer system

_c_   **3.** Software that you can copy and then pay a fee

_f_   **4.** An agreement that gives you the right to make a limited number of copies

_____   **5.** Pornography on a computer network

a. ethics

b. public domain

c. shareware

d. software piracy

e. copyrighted software

f. site license

g. hacker

h. programmer liability

_____h_____ 6. The legal responsibility to write correct code

_____d_____ 7. Unauthorized copying

_____i_____ 8. The responsibility to keep up with innovations in the field

_____b_____ 9. Software that can be copied for free

_____a_____ 10. Philosophy that deals with knowing right from wrong

i. competency

j. cyberporn

Multiple Choice

Circle the letter of the correct choice for each of the following.

1. When dealing with questions of right or wrong behavior, you are working in which of the following areas?

    a. standards

    b. ethics

    c. principles

    d. none of the above

2. Which of the following does *not* constitute ethical computer use?

    a. avoiding harming others

    b. honoring confidentiality

    c. speaking the truth

    d. borrowing software so that you can make a copy

3. What does it mean to give proper credit when using the intellectual property of others?

    a. including the name of the software package a system is based on

    b. not telling secrets that were in a file you saw

    c. not copying software

    d. all of the above

4. Which of the following is software that you can copy legally?

    a. public domain software

    b. shareware

    c. a and b

    d. It is illegal to copy any software.

5. Software piracy is _____.

    a. a misdemeanor

    b. a felony

    c. a capital crime

    d. legal

6. Making a copy of software to put on your desktop computer and another copy on your laptop computer is usually _____.

    a. a misdemeanor

    b. a felony—software piracy

    c. a capital crime

    d. legal

7. What is hacking?

   a. the crime of breaking into a computer system

   b. testing the limits of computer systems

   c. copying software illegally

   d. a and b

8. When a computer professional asks an outside expert for help, the professional is exhibiting _____.

   a. competency

   b. professional responsibility

   c. liability

   d. fear of keeping up in his or her area

9. Which of the following is true regarding programmer liability?

   a. It involves programs that have failed.

   b. It questions whether the programmer should have found the bug in the program.

   c. It comes up in a court of law.

   d. all of the above

10. If a business maintains its data according to proper ethical standards, which of the following is true when an error in the data is detected?

   a. The ethical standards have been violated.

   b. The business is subject to fines.

   c. The business will take proper steps to correct the data.

   d. a and b

Completion

In the blank provided, write the correct answer for each of the following.

1. The branch of philosophy that deals with the determination of what is right or wrong, good or bad, is _ethics_____.

2. Software that is legal to copy and free to anyone is in the _public domain_

3. _Shareware_____ is copyrighted software that you can try for free, but you pay a registration fee if you are going to keep it.

4. Making illegal copies of copyrighted software is called _software piracy_

5. A contract to buy software to make several copies to use in an organization, at a reduced per-copy price, is called a(n) _site license_

6. Pornography that can be downloaded from public or private networks is sometimes called _cyberporn_____.

7. A(n) _crackers_____ attempts to gain unauthorized access to computer systems or databases.

8. A(n) _hackers_____ attempts to test the limits of computer systems.

9. Keeping up with the latest developments in an area of expertise is known as maintaining _competency_.

10. Professional _responsibility_ involves doing the best job, even if the user would not necessarily know whether the best job was performed.

Review

On a separate sheet of paper, answer the following questions.

1. List the eight general moral imperatives the ACM developed for computer professionals and users to follow.

2. Why is software piracy considered a crime? Who gets hurt by this crime and how?

3. What is the difference between a hacker and a cracker?

4. What are two important standards for computer professionals, as established by computer professional organizations?

5. Why are the standards for professional ethics important for computer professionals?

6. What is programmer liability? How could the issue of programmer liability arise?

7. From what perils do organizations and businesses need to protect their data?

8. Name at least five commandments of computing as established by the Computer Ethics Institute in Washington, D.C.

9. What are the issues regarding pornography and public networks?

10. What is a site license? How does a site license affect the copying of software?

Critical Thinking

On a separate sheet of paper, answer the following questions.

1. Give examples of what might be considered a breach of confidentiality.

2. Under what circumstances could a person copy copyrighted software and not violate the law or the standard code of ethics?

3. Suppose that you are the manager of a department in an insurance company. Your employees are responsible for looking up personal details about clients and reporting the details to other authorized departments. What ethical code of behavior would you give your employees? How would you make sure that they followed the code?

4. What action would you suggest to deal with the problem of cyberporn? How would you enforce any laws you propose?

5. Propose an additional commandment to the ten commandments of computing. Justify why your new commandment is needed.

Further Discovery

Computer Ethics, Second Edition. Tom Forester and Perry Morrison (Cambridge, MA: MIT Press, 1995).

Computer Privacy Handbook. Andre Bacard (Berkeley, CA: PeachPit Press, 1995).

Sex, Laws, and Cyberspace. Jonathan Wallace and Mark Mangan (New York: Henry Holt, 1996).

 # On-line Discovery

You can access the Internet resources for the following questions by going to the Que Education and Training Web site at URL http://www.ciyf98.com/discovery. From this page, click the link for Lesson 9A and then click the link to the resource you want to access.

1. The University of California at Fullerton provides a large collection of resources related to ethics (and not just computer ethics) on its **Ethics on the World Wide Web** page (http://www5.fullerton.edu/les /ethics_list.html). This collection includes conference proceedings, ethics guidelines, case studies, and many other types of information. Using these resources, attempt to find three case studies of ethical dilemmas or case studies related to computer ethics. One of the pages pointed to is a collection of computer usage policy statements. Look at several of these from an ethical standpoint. What common ethical principles do they assume? How do they differ from each other?

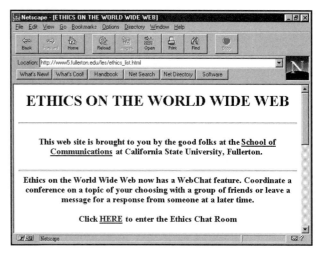

2. **Computer Professionals for Social Responsibility** (http://www.cpsr.org/dox/home.html) is a group that has tried to promote both ethical conduct and awareness of the social impact of computers in society. What kinds of issues does this group find important? How might some of these issues affect computer ethics?

3. For another perspective on computer ethics, take a look at the home page of the **Software Publishers Association** (SPA) at URL http://www.spa.org. The SPA is the primary clearinghouse for anti-software-piracy information. Contrast the ethical principles that the SPA promotes with those promoted by the Computer Professionals for Social Responsibility or the Association of Computing Machinery. The SPA home page even provides a toll-free number and an e-mail address for reporting suspected software piracy. Under what circumstances would you report someone who copied software illegally?

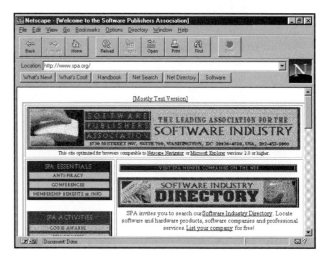

The User, the Computer, and the Environment

Outline

Learning Objectives

When you have finished reading this lesson, you will be able to

➤ Understand the health risks associated with prolonged computer use

➤ Tell why programs and data should be backed up

➤ Be responsible for a microcomputer system

➤ Discuss the environmental concerns associated with computers

If you drive a car, you expect that it will eventually need repair. You expect that your refrigerator and CD player will eventually break. And you expect that you will get sick from time to time. Likewise, you can expect that your computer will either break or develop problems at some point. And, unfortunately, you need to be aware that your computer may contribute to your chances of developing health problems—unless you take precautions.

This lesson explores the ergonomics of working with computers. The 1994 edition of Merriam-Webster's *Collegiate Dictionary* defines **ergonomics** as "an applied science concerned with designing and arranging things people use so that the people and things interact most efficiently and safely." In this lesson, you consider the safety of the computer user, the proper care of a computer, and the impact of computers on the environment.

Caring for the User

No one knows the potential health implications of sitting two feet in front of a television set, forty to fifty hours a week, year after year. It would be difficult, though, to find a doctor who would recommend it. Yet many of us who work with desktop computers do just that! The health problems are becoming apparent. A computer can negatively affect your health in two ways. First, a computer monitor emits radiation. Second, the use of a computer day after day can wear your body down, causing eyestrain and stress injuries. Fortunately, devices have been developed to help.

Radiation Dangers

Cathode ray tube (CRT) monitors emit low-level electromagnetic fields (a form of radiation) that have been associated with a variety of illnesses, including leukemia. Thanks to strict radiation regulations passed by Sweden in 1990, many manufacturers have designed new monitors that meet those standards by emitting less radiation than older models. Users are warned not to sit too close to the sides of the monitor where the electromagnetic fields are the strongest. Add-on filters are available to diminish the radiation. Zenion Industries, Inc., has even developed a unit, known as the Screen ELF, that sits on top of the monitor and uses a "pulsed plasma field" to replenish the air supply within a six-foot radius.

Courtesy of Zenion Industries, Inc.

The Screen ELF.

Eye Problems

Many people who use computers for prolonged periods complain of blurred vision and eyestrain. Most of these eye problems are a result of focusing up close for long periods of time. Other factors that contribute to eyestrain include poor lighting and glare. Monochrome monitors can cause a photochemical change in the retina that results in an after-image in a color complementary to the screen color. This can result in a mild form of color blindness. Interlaced monitors show flicker more than noninterlaced monitors and are a contributing factor to eyestrain and headaches. **Computer vision syndrome (CVS)** is characterized by symptoms typical of eyestrain such as dry eyes, irritated eyes, blurry vision, and headaches.

TechTalk An interlaced monitor first scans every other line and then comes back and scans the lines it misses. The eyes perceive a slight flicker or shimmer.

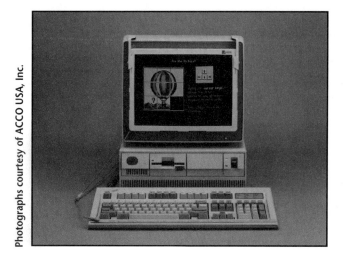

Photographs courtesy of ACCO USA, Inc.

A glare screen filter.

A copyholder.

What can you do to protect your eyes? Monitors with higher refresh rates are easier on the eyes than those with lower refresh rates. (The computer refreshes the image on the screen regularly.) Glare screens are available that will prevent reflections on the monitor, and many glare screens include radiation guards. Using a stand to hold any hard copy that you are using can also help prevent eyestrain.

Exercises may help prevent eyestrain. One simple exercise is to rub your hands together until the palms are warm. Place your warm palms over your eyes without applying any pressure. The warmth will relax your eyes, and the break will be good for them as well. A more vigorous eye exercise requires that you focus on something distant and then switch to something close; repeat this exercise ten times. Switching your focus exercises all the eye muscles and allows your eyes to refocus easily on the monitor.

Repetitive Stress Injuries

Too many hours of keying can result in **repetitive stress injury (RSI)**. During keying, wrist motion is limited, which results in wrist strain. A variety of injuries may occur. The most common is **carpal tunnel syndrome**, a painful swelling of the tendons and the sheaths around them, usually caused when the median nerve is pinched. Carpal tunnel syndrome results in tingling, numbness, and pain and frequently requires surgery.

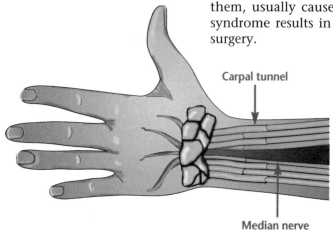

Carpal tunnel

Median nerve

Although there is no sure way to avoid RSI, some developments are worth considering. A wrist rest placed in front of the keyboard helps reduce the risk of carpal tunnel syndrome. The wrist rest helps to ensure that the wrists are held flat, rather than at an angle.

Keyboard drawers and recessed keyboards help in the same manner as the wrist rest. Bucky Products makes a rest called the Bucky Wristpillow, filled with buckwheat hulls (a traditional Japanese stuffing) that adapt to your form. Several manufacturers are developing ergonomic keyboards that can be positioned in different ways to vary the wrist position.

Courtesy of ACCO USA, Inc.

The MouseMaster combines a wrist rest, mouse pad, and desk organizer.

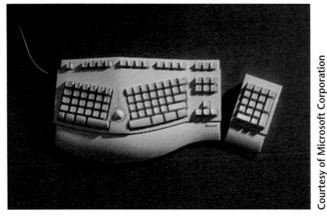

Courtesy of Microsoft Corporation

The Microsoft natural keyboard.

Musculoskeletal Pain

A myriad of musculoskeletal problems can develop because of poorly designed work areas. An ergonomic chair enables the user to adjust the seat height, the back, and the armrests. The chair should be adjusted so that the person's feet are flat on the ground or on a footrest and the backrest supports the lower back. Good posture is extremely important in avoiding back, neck, and shoulder pain. In addition, position the monitor at a comfortable level for your neck and eyes and at the proper distance.

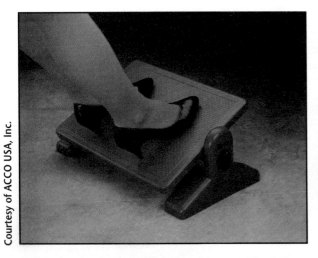

Courtesy of ACCO USA, Inc.

This adjustable ergonomic footrest can reduce muscle strain. The footrest is especially useful when the chair cannot be adjusted.

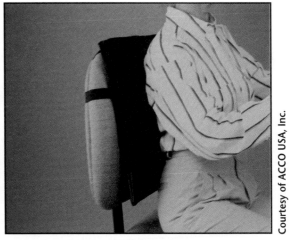

Courtesy of ACCO USA, Inc.

This back cushion is contoured to reduce muscle strain and promote better posture.

Caring for Your Computer

Caring for a computer involves both the care of the hardware and the care of the stored programs and data. Most large organizations develop security policies and procedures for their information systems. Anyone responsible for a computer system needs to do the same.

Taking Care of the Hardware

Maintaining accurate records about the computer system is important. You should keep all the technical manuals for the computer in one handy location. Keep near the manuals the warranties and records for all additional hardware that was not part of the original system.

One of the most common causes of computer failure is a battery that needs replacing. Microcomputers store internally information about the devices attached to the system. This information is maintained by battery power; there is a small battery on the system motherboard. Although new batteries are supposed to have a five-year life span, some fail before that time. When the battery starts to fail, the system first loses the date and time. As the battery power decreases, the system loses other information—for example, the type of hard drive attached to the system. You should print copies of essential files, such as AUTOEXEC.BAT and CONFIG.SYS, and the system setup to save time in case you ever need to recover from a battery failure.

A typical AUTOEXEC.BAT file.

```
C:\>type autoexec.bat
@ECHO OFF
SET SOUND = C:\SB16
SET BLASTER=A220 I10 D1 H5 P330 T6
SET MIDI=SYNTH:1 MAP:E
C:\SB16\DIAGNOSE /S
C:\SB16\SB16SET /P /Q
PROMPT $p$g
PATH=C:\;C:\DOS;C:\WINDOWS;C:\WINDOWS\COMMAND; C;\QEMM
PATH=%PATH%
SET TEMP=C:\DOS
SET MOUSE=C:\MOUSE
C:\WINDOWS\COMMAND\MODE CON:RATE=32 DELAY=1
```

```
C:\type config.sys
DEVICE=C:\WINDOWS\HIMEM.SYS
DEVICE=C:\WINDOWS\EMM386.EXE RAM I=B000-B7FF
FILES= 100
DOS=UMB
DEVICEHIGH /L:1,26928 =C:\SB16\DRV\CTSB16.SYS /UNIT=0  /BLASTER=A:220 I:7 D:1 H:5
DEVICEHIGH /L:3,10416 =C:\SB16\DRV\CTMMSYS.SYS
DEVICEHIGH /L:2,12048 =C:\WINDOWS\SETVER.EXE
DOS=HIGH
SHELL=C:\COMMAND.COM C:\ /E:2048 /P
DEVICE=NEC_IDE.SYS /D:MSCD001 /P:1FOS /I:14 /V /N:1 /M:S
```

A typical CONFIG.SYS file.

In addition to using an internal battery, the computer draws power from an electrical outlet. The amount of electricity flowing into the computer can vary; electrical systems experience both surges and brownouts. A **surge** occurs when a large amount of power flows through the outlet. A surge can occur, for example, when lightning strikes nearby or when power is restored after a blackout or brownout. A **brownout** is a period of low voltage resulting in less power. An easy and inexpensive way to protect your computer hardware is with a **surge protector**, or surge suppressor. A surge protector contains several outlets and has a voltage switch to absorb any extra current. All the plugs attached to the computer hardware should be plugged in to the surge protector. Actually, you may want to use surge protectors for all your expensive electronic equipment, such as stereos and televisions. The surge protector does not guard against loss of power, but the loss itself is not dangerous to your hardware.

If a power failure occurs, a surge protector cannot protect data that is in memory. (Remember that RAM is volatile.) If you live in an area that experiences frequent power outages, or if a business requires that a computer system continue to function even when the power fails, a UPS (uninterruptible power supply) is needed. A UPS costs considerably more than a surge protector, but it will protect what is in RAM and enable you to continue to use the computer for several hours without power.

A surge protector.

Courtesy of ACCO USA, Inc.

You should follow some common-sense precautions to protect your hardware. Largely because of the fan inside, a computer attracts dirt, dust, and smoke particles. Do not smoke near a computer. A smoke particle is large enough to cause a hard drive crash! Use a soft cloth to keep the computer and the surfaces around it clean. Do not spray household cleaners near the computer. Do not spray glass cleaner on the monitor. Instead, spray the glass cleaner onto a cloth and then wipe the monitor. The com-

Keep in dust cover when not in use.

Do not place food near disks.

Avoid dust, direct sunlight, and pet hair.

SECURITY X-RAY

Do not place heavy objects on disks.

Do not write on disks with pencils or ball-point pens.

Avoid the X-ray machine at the airport. Hand carry disks.

puter should be opened and cleaned regularly; how frequently you clean it depends on how well the immediate environment is maintained. Once a year is adequate for most systems. To clean your computer, open the case and clean the inside by using compressed air and a special vacuum.

Do not eat or drink near a computer. The crumbs can find their way into the fan and then into the system. Spilled liquids can ruin a keyboard or an entire system. If you are hungry or thirsty, take a break!

The monitor is susceptible to a phenomenon known as burn-in. **Burn-in** occurs when an image is left on-screen for a long period of time, creating an after-image. A number of screen saver programs on the market are designed to prevent burn-in. These programs display a constantly changing image; no image remains on-screen long enough to do damage. The screen saver starts automatically after a specified amount of time has elapsed without any keyboard activity, and disappears when the user begins to use the keyboard again.

Disks also need proper care. Floppy disks should be kept away from electronic devices other than the computer. Keep disks in a dust cover or a case when they are not being used. Use only a felt-tipped pen when writing on labels; if you press hard, a ball-point pen can damage a floppy disk.

If a disk contains important data, secure the write-protect tab so that the data cannot be accidentally erased. Occasionally, a floppy disk will develop a **bad sector**, a portion of the disk that is flawed and can no longer be used to store data. In this case, you need to copy any important files to a new disk and then discard the old disk. Protect your valuable data by storing your floppy disks in a disk/media storage tray.

A multimedia tray.

Hard disks are a little more difficult to care for. Like a floppy disk, a hard disk can develop bad sectors, but it is too expensive to discard and replace. Many utilities are available to help detect bad sectors and direct the computer to avoid storing data in those sectors. Spinwrite, Norton Utilities, and Microsoft Scandisk are a few programs that detect disk problems and provide solutions.

Disks can also become fragmented over time. **Fragmentation** occurs when programs are stored on the disk and erased, and then new programs are stored. If the new file is larger than the one previously occupying that space on the disk, the operating system may have to divide the new file and store it on different parts of the disk. Fragmentation slows down data retrieval and is hard on the disk drive. Running a **defragmentation program** reorganizes the files on the disk so that each file is located in adjacent clusters on the disk. The reorganization speeds data retrieval and helps prolong the life of the hard disk. Many programs are available to accomplish this task; operating systems often provide a built-in defragmentation program.

Protecting the Programs and Data

The programs and the data stored on a computer are the most valuable parts of the computer system. The computer itself is replaceable and is frequently insured, but the data can be both irreplaceable and invaluable. You can legally make a copy of a program for backup purposes. However, when a program is installed on a hard disk, the original can be stored and used as a backup. Make certain that all backups are stored in a safe place.

Large organizations spend considerable time and effort in protecting the security of their data. Aside from the possibility of malicious damage, data and programs are susceptible to accidental damage. It is fairly easy to decide to delete all the files from a floppy disk—and instead delete all the files from the current directory of the hard disk! If you are the person responsible for a computer system, the most important thing you can do is to make certain that backup copies of the programs and the data exist. Again, many backup programs are available, and most operating systems come with a backup program.

Extremely large hard disks are time-consuming to back up onto floppy disks. Suppose that you have a 1.2G hard drive on a microcomputer. You would need more than 800 floppy disks to back up that hard drive! Tape backup drives make the backup process a simple and relatively painless task. That same 1.2G hard disk can be backed up onto one or two tapes. Prices are coming down on writeable CD-ROM drives; soon they should become popular as backup media. Backups should be stored at a different location from the computer in case of fire or burglary.

Backing up the system regularly is very important. Remember that hard disks are accessed mechanically. The question is not *whether* a hard disk will fail, but *when*. An intelligent computer user prepares for a failure in advance. In addition to making backups, you should keep a disaster recovery disk. The **disaster recovery disk** should include the essential operating system files, along with the files necessary to restore the system from the backup.

GLOBE: Student Monitors of the Earth

In Dorothy's immortal words, "There's no place like home." Although our street addresses, towns, states, and even our countries may be different, all people share one common address: Planet Earth.

Because we all share ownership of this planet we call home, each of us must accept the responsibility for keeping it habitable and productive. To this end, an international science and education partnership has come together in a program called GLOBE. The vision for GLOBE was first stated by Vice President Al Gore in his book *Earth in the Balance*, in which he proposed a program that would use school teachers and their students to monitor the entire earth.

GLOBE, an acronym for Global Learning and Observations to Benefit the Environment, is a network of students throughout the world; these students make environmental observations, share the resulting environmental images with each other, and provide useful data to environmental scientists. The students around the world make environmental observations at or near their schools, as well as conduct scientific experiments from which global environmental images can be created and relayed back to the students. The data helps the students understand earth systems and aids environmental researchers throughout the world.

More than two thousand schools in the U.S. have joined with schools around the world to study the environment. More than a hundred countries around the world have already expressed an interest in GLOBE, and over twenty nations have signed bilateral agreements to participate in the program.

More than 90 percent of GLOBE's long-term funding is expected to come from foreign governments, international sources, and nongovernment sources in the U.S. Each foreign government, if able, pays for its own country's participation. For countries that cannot afford to implement GLOBE in their schools, resources are available from the private sector. A nonprofit organization is the focal point for U.S. private sector contributions.

Courtesy of Jade Albert/FPG International

Existing environmental education programs throughout the world are incorporated into GLOBE. It makes use of the Internet, direct satellite communications, television, and other technology to ensure that all schools and students can participate.

No matter where we call home, we are all connected by computers into one global village.

Computers and the Law

Computers have opened up other unlikely occupations, such as lawyers who deal with the Internet and the law. Digital signatures (personal encryption codes, indecipherable code for security purposes), third-party certifiers (verify the signer's identity), and electronic watermarks (electronic code embedded into a document) are now necessary for Internet business transactions or on-line marketing. These three items have been the subject of legal determinations. Eighteen states have already enacted digital signature laws, because the common practice of scanned signatures can easily be copied, cut, and pasted.

The Internet has no geographical boundaries. There are unprecedented legal issues because the documents are electronic rather than physical. The law has not yet caught up to the technology. Technology is outpacing the capability of regulating the flow of personal information. Huge amounts of private and supposedly secured data are easily accessible to anyone at any time by just the click of a mouse. Credit records, driver's licenses, property records, criminal histories, shopping lists, magazine subscriptions, and medical records (in some states) are but a few of these personal data items.

Other types of information are also available on the Internet. Children are at risk from the flood of adult-oriented material. E-mail has lead to defamation, discrimination, and harassment suits, as well as claims of invasion of privacy. In one Internet case, Boston University is suing eight Web-based sites that customize research papers. The college claims that these businesses are breaking a 1973 Massachusetts law that makes it illegal to sell term papers to Massachusetts' students. This lawsuit was filed in federal court in October 1997. It not only accuses the term paper sites with racketeering, but with wire and mail fraud.

Issues that never would have been considered 20 years ago are now prevalent and pressing problems. The computer, and most lately the Internet, have changed how we look at the dissemination of information.

Computers and the Environment

Computer technology was once thought to be a "clean" industry, producing comparatively little pollution. But there are so many computers today that problems are mounting.

Energy consumption is a major concern. The Environmental Protection Agency (EPA) has estimated that 80 percent of the time when monitors are turned on no one is looking at them! New monitors automatically go into a "sleep" mode when there is no keyboard activity, which helps to save some energy. Screen savers that revert to a blank screen are more energy efficient than those that display images. Turning off the monitor is even more energy efficient than using a screen saver. A good strategy is to have a screen saver installed, but turn off the monitor whenever you leave the room for a long time.

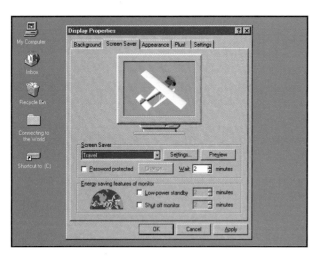

An Energy Star screen saver.

Most of the major manufacturers have joined the Energy Star Program defined by the EPA. Any computer component that consumes less than 30 watts in an idle state earns an Energy Star. Unfortunately, the increased use of computers also has indirect implications for energy consumption. Because computers generate heat and require cool temperatures for operation, extra electricity is required to cool offices.

Floppy disks should be reformatted and used over and over. Backup file disks and program disks will last for years if they are stored and cared for properly.

Although there was much discussion about a "paperless office" when computers first became popular, the use of paper has actually increased. Users need to be responsible about their use of paper. Try to do as much editing as possible before you print a document. To help eliminate errors, run the spell checker and grammar checker before printing. Also use the print preview feature of the application to see whether the output is the way that you want it. If paper is used on one side only, turn it over and use the back as scrap paper.

Recycling toner cartridges for laser printers is good for the environment and can save money too. Recycled cartridges are less than half the cost of new toner cartridges. Several laser manufacturers have developed new printers that are kinder to the environment. Okidata laser printers have a separate toner barrel that needs to be replaced only one-fourth as many times as most toner cartridges. The new Ecosys printer by Kyocera Corporation has a cartridge that should last the lifetime of the printer.

None of these suggestions requires much sacrifice from computer users. With just a little care, we can help improve our planet for future generations.

Home Computers

Approximately 60 percent of American households currently owning a computer are still using 486-or-older machines. Only 50 percent of these PC households are using Windows 95; the rest are using Windows 3.1 or other operating systems, such as MAC OS. Both the hardware and software for these older CPUs are becoming outdated. Soon these systems will be unable to run newer programs at any acceptable speeds and will eventually run out of hard disk space.

Because personal computers are replaced about every four years, should money be put aside yearly toward the purchase of a new PC? If so, how much should be saved? These are personal questions to be answered. Keep in mind that there will always be an additional cost for new peripherals, such as printers, scanners, modems, and digital cameras. Historically, PC prices have stayed about the same; but their capabilities have increased substantially. In 1981 a 4.77MHz IBM PC with 64K of RAM cost $2,665. Compare this to a modern example: two PCs from a major direct-mail vendor, each with a sound card and speakers. They both include Windows 95 and a software bundle that includes Microsoft Office 97:

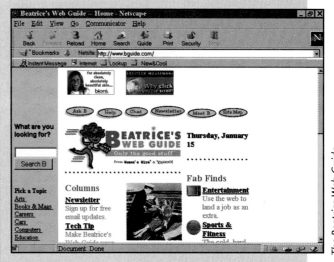

The Beatrice Web Guide.

Computer #1	Computer #2
200MHz Pentium MMX	300MHz Pentium II
32M RAM	64M RAM
4.3G hard drive	8.4G hard drive
17-inch monitor	19-inch monitor
4M Video RAM	8M Video Ram
24X CD-ROM	32X CD-ROM

Total cost:
Approx. $1,900   Approx. $3,200

Technology will continue to progress at a rapid speed increasingly affecting society. The question remains: How will society continue to adapt to this change?

Lesson Summary

➤ Computer users need to be aware of the health hazards associated with prolonged computer use.

➤ Computer hardware needs to be kept in a clean, safe environment.

➤ Backups of computer programs and data should be made regularly.

➤ Computers should be used in a socially conscious manner that is friendly to the environment.

Lesson Review

Key Terms

bad sector	computer vision syndrome	disaster recovery disk	repetitive stress injury (RSI)
brownout	(CVS)	ergonomics	surge
burn-in	defragmentation program	fragmentation	surge protector
carpal tunnel syndrome			

Matching

In the blank next to each of the following terms or phrases, write the letter of the corresponding term or phrase.

_h_ **1.** Dry eyes, irritated eyes, blurry vision, and headaches

_j_ **2.** A period of low voltage

_e_ **3.** Occurs when the same image appears on the monitor for a prolonged time

_i_ **4.** A part of a disk that can no longer be used to store data properly

_g_ **5.** Carpal tunnel syndrome

_b_ **6.** Slows down data retrieval from a disk

_a_ **7.** The science concerned with people and things interacting efficiently and safely

_c_ **8.** A swelling of the tendons in the wrist

_f_ **9.** Contains all essential system files

_d_ **10.** A type of monitor that minimizes flicker and reduces eyestrain

a. ergonomics

b. fragmentation

c. carpal tunnel syndrome

d. noninterlaced

e. burn-in

f. disaster recovery disk

g. RSI

h. CVS

i. bad sector

j. brownout

Multiple Choice

Circle the letter of the correct choice for each of the following.

1. Which of the following statements is true regarding computer care?

   a. You should keep technical manuals and records of purchases in one handy location.

   b. You should copy essential files as well as the system setup.

   c. You should use a surge protector.

   d. all of the above

2. Screen saver programs prevent _____.

   a. brownouts

   b. burn-in

   c. screen flickering

   d. bad sectors

3. Which of the following is *not* true?

   a. Fragmentation occurs when stored programs are erased from disk and replaced with new programs that are usually larger.

   b. Fragmented files can be reorganized into adjacent clusters on the disk.

   c. Only hard disks develop bad sectors.

   d. Disk life can be prolonged by using defragmentation programs.

4. Which of the following are potential health problems associated with computers?

   a. stress-related injuries

   b. problems caused by a monitor's electromagnetic fields

   c. blurry vision and headaches

   d. all of the above

5. Wrist rests and ergonomic keyboards might help prevent _____.

   a. radiation dangers

   b. carpal tunnel syndrome

   c. blurred vision

   d. none of the above

6. One of the most common causes of computer failure is _____.

   a. battery failure

   b. faulty cabling

   c. monitor failure

   d. fragmentation

7. Which of the following is associated with keying?

   a. CVS

   b. musculoskeletal pain

   c. carpal tunnel syndrome

   d. all of the above

8. Which of the following is *not* a danger to floppy disks?

   a. dust

   b. hair

   c. x-ray machines

   d. surge suppressor

9. What do you call a disk that contains all the essential system files?

   a. disaster recovery disk

   b. backup disk

   c. defragmentation program

   d. database disk

10. Many people who use computers for a long time experience which of the following?

    a. headaches

    b. blurred vision

    c. eyestrain

    d. all of the above

Completion

In the blank provided, write the correct answer for each of the following.

1. A(n) _defragmentation_ program is used to reorganize the files on a disk.

2. An after-image on a monitor is a result of _burn in_.

3. _WRIST REST_ and _KEYBOARD DRAWER_ (ergonomics) can reduce the risk of carpal tunnel syndrome.

4. Monitors emit a(n) _radiation_ that might be hazardous to the user's health.

5. The risk of _color blindness_ is increased when a monochrome monitor is used.

6. It is important to keep a(n) _back up_ of programs and data files.

7. You can protect computers and other expensive electrical devices by plugging them in to a(n) _surge protector_.

8. It is wise not to _sit_ or _close_ near a computer.

9. The energy consumption of computer _monitor_ is a concern addressed by the Energy Star Program.

10. An ergonomic chair can reduce _musculoskeletal pain_.

Review

On a separate sheet of paper, answer the following questions.

1. What concerns should you have in caring for computer hardware?

2. What can cause burn-in? What precautions can you take to prevent burn-in?

3. What is fragmentation and when can it occur?

4. Discuss some important issues related to making backups.

5. Cite some health problems associated with the use of computers.

6. What type of recycling of computer products does the text recommend?

7. What are some precautions that you can take to protect your floppy disks?

8. Which type of monitor discussed in this lesson is best for your eyes?

9. How should a person sit when using a computer to minimize musculoskeletal pain?

10. What should you do if a floppy disk develops a bad sector? What about a hard disk?

Critical Thinking

On a separate sheet of paper, answer the following questions.

1. Ergonomics is sometimes referred to as "human engineering." How does this definition relate to machine use, people, and environments?

2. Carefully analyze a computer workstation. Cite several physical characteristics of the equipment that have been shown to result in less fatigue and strain.

3. The "intelligent building" is designed to have features that reduce stress in the work environment (for example, wall colors). Cite some ways in which customizing the work environment can reduce stress and minimize health problems.

4. What steps can you take to protect your data and programs from accidental damage?

5. Visit a computer lab on your campus. What ergonomic features do you see? What other changes could be implemented?

Further Discovery

Computer Resources for People with Disabilities. Alliance for Technology Access (Alameda, CA: Hunter House, 1994).

Help! My Computer Is Killing Me. Sheik N. Imrhan (Dallas, TX: Taylor, 1996).

The Trouble with Computers. Thomas K. Landauer (Cambridge, MA: MIT Press, 1995).

On-line Discovery

You can access the Internet resources for the following questions by going to the Que Education and Training Web site at URL http://www.ciyf98.com/discovery. From this page, click the link for Lesson 9B and then click the link to the resource you want to access.

1. Dan Wallach at Princeton University maintains a **Typing Injury FAQ** (http://www. cs.princeton.edu/~dwallach/tifaq), a list of frequently asked questions, in which he provides information and pointers to other documents about computing injuries. Explore the different problems this FAQ deals with. What kinds of guidelines for comfortable computing are offered? What kinds of devices are available to make using the computer more comfortable? Compare the FAQ with another ergonomics-related page—the **Computer Related Repetitive Strain Injury** page (http://engr-www.unl.edu/ee/eeshop/rsi.html).

2. The previously mentioned Web sites deal primarily with ergonomics problems related to typing and using pointing devices on computers. For a broader perspective on ergonomics, look at **ErgoWeb** (http://www.ergoweb.com) at the University of Utah. Through this site, you can see how pervasive and important ergonomics issues are in the workplace. See whether you can find out which laws and regulations affect office ergonomics. Which government agencies regulate these issues. If you were to design an ergonomically correct computer workstation for an office, what resources and references would you have at your disposal?

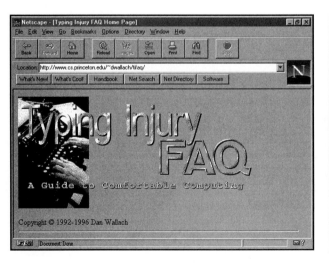

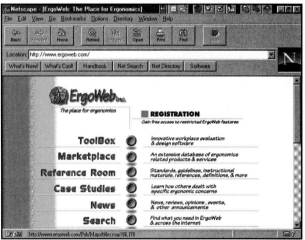

Security and Privacy

Outline

Learning Objectives

When you have finished reading this lesson, you will be able to

➤ Describe the controversy surrounding computers and possible invasion of privacy

➤ Explain the purpose of the Clipper chip

➤ Describe privacy concerns in the areas of data communications, databank access and accuracy, and electronic funds transfer

➤ Name some basic ways in which to protect computer systems from natural disasters and unauthorized physical access

➤ Define and describe the different types of computer viruses

➤ Recognize your rights concerning the use of private data

In the Sunday newspaper, you see a questionnaire that promises free items and coupons if you just fill it out and send it in. Looks like a great deal! So you fill out the questionnaire and mail it. Without your knowledge, the firm that placed the ad types your responses into a computer database—and then sells the information to anyone who wants a custom-tailored mailing list! Several weeks after responding, you receive the items; then the junk mail starts flooding your mailbox. Hundreds of companies now know that you make over $30,000 a year, you like outdoor sports such as skiing, and you buy approximately ten cases of soft drinks per year.

Consider another example. Suppose that you purchase a house. A few months later, you start receiving letters in the mail from lenders trying to convince you to refinance your mortgage or borrow against the equity in your home. Somehow, they all know the amount of your loan, the interest rate you are paying, and even the exact amount of your monthly payments!

These two examples illustrate ways of distributing information that violate our privacy. Most people accept these types of occurrences as common-place. To what extent should we allow our privacy to be compromised? Should the availability of information be limited? These are some of the issues addressed in this lesson.

The Need for Information

When all transactions were on a cash basis, a business had no need to know anything about its customers. With today's "cashless society," businesses need to be able to verify that checks and credit cards are valid. Furthermore, information must be accessed quickly and easily.

In the same manner, individuals expect to be able to call government offices and businesses to inquire about personal matters, such as how much you owe on your charge card bill. People expect companies to resolve prob-lems in a timely manner, but that would not be possible if the information were not readily available.

Large databases of information are necessary for the normal functioning of our society. The entire world depends on the ready availability of up-to-date information. That's not going to change. But what can we do to pro-tect individual privacy?

The Right to Privacy

Privacy was defined by Alan Westin in his book *Privacy and Freedom* (1967) as "...the rights of persons to control the distribution of information about themselves." According to this definition, invasion of privacy would include the collection or distribution of information in such a way that the person to whom it pertains finds it objectionable. Although we assume that individuals have the right to privacy, that right is not explicitly stated in any government document.

Individual Privacy in the Information Age

We live in an age of marketing, where everyone seems intent on selling something. It is no wonder, then, that computers are being used to help target individuals and companies as potential buyers of various sales and services.

Courtesy of TRW Information Services

Over the past twenty or thirty years, marketing and direct mail firms have improved their skills and honed their tools to the point where they can target virtually any demographic group in the world. Particularly in first-world countries, where much of business is highly computerized and many citizens use electronic means to pay for purchases, the buyer's every step is tracked and analyzed.

Courtesy of TRW Information Services

For instance, when you purchase an item over the phone with your credit card, chances are good that your purchase is added to a record of the types of things you like to buy. Marketers can amass quite a bit of information about you simply from tracking your purchasing history and combining it with other public information, such as your address, occupation, and age. A company can learn a lot about you also by matching records and combining facts from different databases, such as your banking records and payroll records. All of this detailed information can then be used to target specific marketing information to you.

In the future, such highly targeted marketing could be used in interactive video systems that show you only the products in your price range (not the "cheaper" stuff). The company can maximize its profit—and you would never have the opportunity to make a decision to purchase a less expensive alternative.

Many people view such comprehensive data gathering as an invasion of privacy. They cite the potential for the information to be used inappropriately or for purposes unrelated to that for which the information was originally disclosed. For instance, it may be possible to correlate a medical database with an insurance database to learn the names of policyholders who had a positive result on a particular medical test. The fear is that the insurance company could then cancel your policy based on the test results.

Buying and selling data and matching services are a big business. Although most countries have laws to prohibit the release and cross-matching of information in government agency databases, there are no corresponding laws to cover data kept in private-sector databases. Proponents of privacy point out a need for stricter laws, whereas marketers play down any potential misuse of information.

Wiretapping and Data Encryption

Wiretapping—breaking into a communications wire to read a message addressed to someone else—has become an important issue in current discussions about privacy and the use of computers. Digital communications are much more difficult and more expensive to intercept than the analog communication systems that telephone companies have traditionally used. Because of this difficulty, the FBI and the U.S. Department of Justice are asking the telephone companies to make the **Clipper chip** a standard. This chip will automatically encrypt all data received or sent over digital communication lines. It seems likely that government agencies, such as the Internal Revenue Service, will be the first to be required to use the chip. Access to those agencies through modem or fax lines may then require use of the chip. Eventually, the chip could become a standard in the United States.

To intercept an encoded transmission, the government would have to get a warrant, just as it does for tapping ordinary phone lines (approximately 1,000 warrants are issued each year). Civil liberties organizations point to abuses in which government agencies have engaged in unauthorized wiretapping. Politicians of one party, for example, could theoretically coerce law enforcement agencies into spying on the activities of political rivals to learn information that could prove advantageous in an election. These civil liberties experts believe that citizens have the right to protect themselves against government surveillance, which is sometimes misguided and potentially tyrannical. They believe that the Clipper chip would make it too easy for these agencies to listen in on the private communications of individuals. Controversy over the Clipper chip started over two years ago and continues today.

> **TechTalk**
> To *encrypt* data means to translate it into secret code that cannot be deciphered without a key.

The Clipper chip (also called the Key Escrow microcircuit).

Courtesy of Mykotronx, Inc.

Electronic Mail Privacy

A related area of concern is electronic mail, or **e-mail**. Millions of employees routinely use electronic mail to send messages to colleagues in their companies and to others outside the firms. Recent court decisions ruled that this mail is not private and that company personnel may review messages to be certain that they pertain to company business.

Some information services screen messages before placing them into "forums" where they can be read by other users. The information services have taken the position that they are at least partly responsible for what is printed on their networks. Some individuals believe that e-mail should have the same privacy protection as postal mail.

Many individuals are concerned about unacceptable materials, such as pornography, being distributed publicly. In July of 1994, a research computer in California was shut down when it was discovered that more than one thousand pornographic images had been stored on it and were available to the public over the Internet. Immediately following the discovery, the images were erased, and two employees were fired.

The problem of pornography has become so pervasive that a new term, **cyberporn**, has become common. The issues of pornography and restriction of access to areas of an adult nature are at the center of growing public concern. Several large computer software companies have joined to form the Information Highway Parental Empowerment Group to create standards for software filters that make it possible for parents to restrict their children's access. The controversy over privacy and freedom of speech as it relates to computer files will probably not be resolved for years.

Record Matching

Communications and data transmissions are not the only areas in which the use of computers has caused concern for personal privacy. There has been a great deal of concern about the use of computerized databanks for record matching. In **record matching**, dissimilar computer databases are searched to try to match one record with another on the basis of a common name or Social Security number. An example of record matching is the recently adopted policy of the Internal Revenue Service to match income tax returns with Social Security numbers of parents who are delinquent in child-support payments—and then send any tax refunds to the court system to be paid toward the overdue child support.

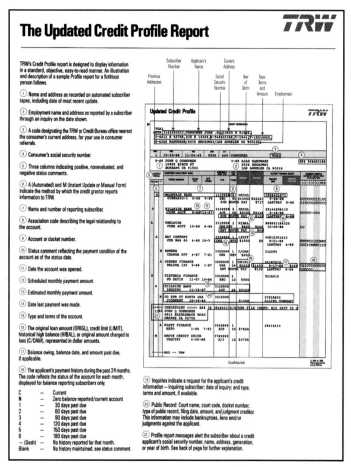

Courtesy of TRW Information Services

Credit Reporting

Private databases are also surrounded by controversy. Credit information agencies are regulated by the *Fair Credit Reporting Act of 1970*, which gives individuals the right to review and correct credit reports. The problem is that individuals are frequently not aware of errors in their credit reports until they are applying for a loan. Delinquent debts incurred by individuals with similar names sometimes cause serious problems. The time required to correct an error may result in a delay in loan approval or in other hardships for the applicant.

Electronic Funds Transfer (EFT)

Electronic funds transfer (EFT) systems maintain complete records of all transactions that affect customer accounts. For example, when your paycheck is deposited to your checking account, the transaction is recorded. When you withdraw funds from an automated teller machine, the transaction is recorded. And when you use your ATM card at the service station or grocery store, the transaction is recorded. Although the system needs to track all these transactions, the resulting record paints a very clear picture of your spending habits.

Questions about who should have access to an individual's EFT records are currently the subject of debate. The availability of this information presents a potential for invasion of privacy. Some European countries, including Sweden, France, and Germany, have passed legislation to create commissions that license computer databanks, receive citizen complaints, and enforce the right to privacy.

TRW: Giving Credit Where It's Due

Whenever you open a new line of credit—to apply for a credit card, finance a car, or mortgage a home—the chances are good that TRW will provide your credit history to the lender.

TRW, an information service with headquarters in Texas, maintains and manages records on approximately 190 million consumers. It then sells the information to its clients as they request it. If you request a loan or credit card, a credit report from TRW will probably determine whether your request is successful. (TRW will provide a personal credit report to any individual, free of charge, once each year, and the individual may challenge negative items and include an explanation of the objection in the credit report.)

A giant in the information industry, TRW has been able to grow to its great size through the use of technology and automation. An example of this up-to-date automation is the robotic hand that files and retrieves data on request. Consumer and business credit information is stored in magnetic tape cartridges in one of a dozen Storage Technology Automated Tape Cartridge Systems at TRW Information System & Services' national data center in Allen, Texas.

Courtesy of TRW Information Services

The Allen data center has a maximum storage capacity of 12 trillion 960 billion bytes, making it one of the world's largest databases. With this amount of confidential data, the company is constantly working to protect the privacy of the individual who is the subject of the data and to keep the data secure from unauthorized access.

One example of TRW's concern for privacy is its attitude toward telephone numbers. Other credit agencies include the individual's home telephone number on a credit report, but TRW does not because many consumers have unlisted numbers and the company thinks that those numbers should remain private.

TRW has adopted a set of Fair Information Values that the company and all its employees use to establish and follow policies that balance privacy and security with the consumer's need for credit. TRW is also aware of the potential of unauthorized access from outside the company. Data centers are protected by a variety of physical security measures including electronic access systems, closed-circuit television monitoring, data encryption, and logical data access controls. The database includes a number of software protection techniques such as artificial intelligence monitoring systems and services for detecting fraudulent applications and suspicious addresses and Social Security numbers.

Security

You've learned that the rights of individuals about whom data is stored on computers must be protected. Computers also need protection—from natural disasters, acts of sabotage, theft, and unlawful access. Some of these concerns are applicable to home computer systems as well as computer systems in organizations.

Natural Disasters

Computer systems should be protected with surge protectors to guard against surges in the power lines. If power outages are common, or if a system is essential to the operation of the organization, an **uninterruptible power supply** (**UPS**) is also needed. The UPS will provide power to the system for several hours if the power fails. Smoke detectors and fire extinguishing systems should be installed for maximum protection against fire. Businesses frequently join in a mutual-support disaster contingency system so that if one company loses its computer system, the company will be able to use another company's system for essential processing.

Access Control

Acts of sabotage may be directed against either hardware or software. Large organizations generally protect their hardware by restricting access to the rooms where the equipment is kept. Security systems should be installed wherever computers hold sensitive data.

Most large computer systems require that users enter a user name and **password** to log on to the system and use it. In the same way, the majority of local area networks require a user name and password. Programs can be installed on stand-alone microcomputers to require passwords to access programs and even individual files. Passwords should not be obvious (such as the user's name or birthday) and should be changed frequently. Users should also be encouraged to lock their doors and their microcomputer systems when they leave the workplace. In some environments, it may be necessary to bolt hardware to desks to prevent theft.

An active badge and a network receiver.

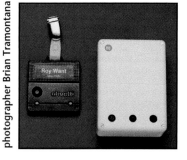

Courtesy of Xerox PARC and photographer Brian Tramontana

Another approach to restricting access to certain areas is for employees to wear "active badges" that track their locations. At Xerox Palo Alto Research Center (PARC), employees wear active badges that emit infrared or radio signals, which are picked up by a central system. These badges tell the system exactly where the employee is at any given time. Thus, active badges prevent unauthorized employees from gaining access to restricted areas.

A technology like the active badge offers many conveniences. For example, employees are instantly identified when they approach electronic information centers such as the LiveBoards installed at Xerox PARC. An individual can stop to receive a message from a LiveBoard, reply to the message, and then continue walking to another location.

Decisions about how society will incorporate this kind of technology fuel the debate about privacy versus security. Although this technology gives us faster access to information, the technology also provides other people with detailed information about our whereabouts. Employers will be able to watch over the location of each employee who is wearing an active badge at all times during the day.

Courtesy of Xerox PARC and photographer Brian Tramontana

A Xerox PARC LiveBoard.

Data Backups

As previously mentioned, software is subject to damage and destruction from natural disasters, acts of sabotage, theft, and unlawful access. To prevent the loss of data, computer personnel and users should back up programs and data regularly. Backups should be stored away from the computer system so that they are not susceptible to the same hazards as the system.

Full backups of everything stored on the computer should be made at least once each month. **Incremental backups**, which back up only those changes since the last incremental backup, should be made regularly too, usually daily in a business environment. Most companies do a good job of backing up large systems and file servers. The challenge is to maintain all the essential data stored on desktop computers scattered throughout the organization. What is needed, but not yet available, is a program that can automatically back up all the hard disk storage of an organization, wherever it is located, to a designated backup server.

Large organizations should also establish a **disaster recovery plan**. The plan should be written and have complete detailed instructions. The plan should also include an alternate computing facility that can be used for emergency processing until a destroyed computer can be replaced.

Network Control

Although networks facilitate the sharing of files, networks also present some challenging security considerations. Networks are accessible from many locations within an organization; most networks are even accessible by modems from remote locations. Computer files can be vulnerable to unauthorized individuals.

Most networks are capable of supporting private user account numbers and passwords. The use of passwords helps discourage crackers (computer criminals who break into systems to do damage) and competitors from tapping into the network, but it is still vulnerable to disgruntled employees. **Callback systems** can ensure that an employee is calling from a recognized telephone on specific days of the week and during certain hours. In a callback system, the user calls the computer and enters his or her account number and password, after which the computer terminates the connection. The computer verifies the user ID and password, the day, and the time of day. The computer then calls the user back at the telephone to which that user is assigned.

Firewalls are becoming the security method of choice for many business intranets. (An **intranet** is designed to facilitate communications within an organization, as well as with customers and partners.) A **firewall** is software designed to protect files and data from unauthorized access. Firewalls are usually used to protect a local area network from unauthorized access through the Internet. Firewall security software, available from a number of software companies, usually includes several protection features. Encryption scrambles proprietary information so that unauthorized users cannot read it. Intrusion protection and authorization features control access and maintain a log of unauthorized access attempts. Although expensive, these systems can be a significant deterrent to misuse of data and system sabotage.

Computer Viruses

A **computer virus** is a program designed to alter or destroy the data stored on a computer system. It takes its name because of its behavior, which is similar to the way in which real viruses work. Both real and computer viruses reproduce themselves, infect another system, and do damage to it. Computer viruses normally copy themselves to a hard disk and then onto other floppies used on the same computer before any symptoms are apparent. Their activation may depend upon the number of times they have spread to other disks.

A virus can be designed to strike after certain commands are issued or become active on a certain date. Friday the 13th is a favorite virus date. A virus normally reaches your system through floppy disks and downloads. For example, once a computer virus was inserted onto the Internet through a terminal; the virus infected 6,000 computers and destroyed millions of dollars of research data in less than 24 hours. The person who wrote the virus was prosecuted and convicted.

Some viruses are relatively harmless and merely display a message, whereas others may scramble or erase files and directories. The BONES virus will scramble your hard drive if an uninfected floppy is accessed on the 7th of the month. The MDMA virus will delete several Windows files (including Help files) upon closing a document after the 20th of the month. The Anticmos virus will erase your computer's startup instructions.

Types of Viruses

Viruses can be divided into several categories. These include worms, Trojan horses, time bombs, file infectors, and boot sector viruses.

> ➤ A **worm** is a virus designed to take control of a system temporarily. The harm that a worm does may not be purposeful, but it often corrupts data and causes irreparable damage. It is said that the first worm was distributed on new software near Christmas; the virus displayed the banner "Peace on Earth" along with a picture of the Earth turning, and then erased itself.

BITS
Trojan horses are named for the first Trojan horse, which concealed Greek soldiers. Disguised as a gift to the city of Troy, the huge, wooden horse was welcomed inside the walls of Troy, whereupon the Greek soldiers emerged and destroyed the city.

> ➤ A **Trojan horse** is disguised as a useful program, but it contains hidden instructions to perform a malicious task instead. Sometimes a Trojan horse is disguised as a game or a utility program that users will find appealing; then, when the users begin running the "game," they discover that they have loaded another animal entirely. A Trojan horse may erase the data on the hard disk or cause other damage.

> ➤ **Time bombs** and logic bombs are designed to sit harmlessly on a system until a certain event or date causes the program to become active. The most famous time bomb is the Michelangelo virus, named after the great artist. On the artist's birthday (March 6) each year, this virus is designed to destroy the contents of any hard drive that it is hidden on.

> ➤ Most viruses are **file infectors** that spread from program to program and do damage to code, data, and directories. A file infector virus hidden on a floppy disk will transfer itself to any hard disk that the floppy comes into contact with. When another floppy disk is inserted into the computer containing that hard drive, the virus will copy itself onto that floppy disk. You can see why viruses can spread rapidly through an organization.

➤ A **boot sector virus** will load each time the computer is booted and can make the data stored on the disk inaccessible.

TechTalk
The boot sector of a disk is reserved for use by portions of the operating system that are needed to boot the system from that disk.

Precautions Against Viruses

Viruses pose a serious threat to computer systems. Hundreds of viruses are in existence, and more are being written each day. In addition, some new viruses are self-modifying so that each new copy is slightly different from the previous one, making it very difficult to protect the computer.

Anti-virus packages, often called vaccines, refer to a database of known viruses. When they recognize a virus, they alert the user and, normally, remove the virus. If the virus cannot be removed, the file containing it must be deleted. New viruses are always appearing so it is important to keep anti-virus software up-to-date.

Other precautions can be taken as well. Scan all disks and downloaded files. Setting the write protect tab on disks that you are only reading will block the virus from infecting it. If a virus does succeed in damaging your system, you can minimize the impact if your files are backed up regularly.

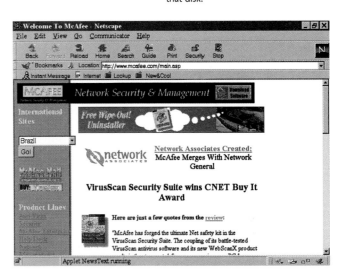

McAfee is just one of many companies that offers a complete line of anti-virus packages for business and personal use.

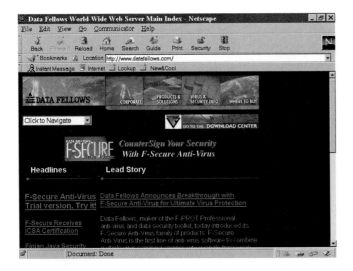

Data Fellows offers a list of the currently known viruses on its Web site.

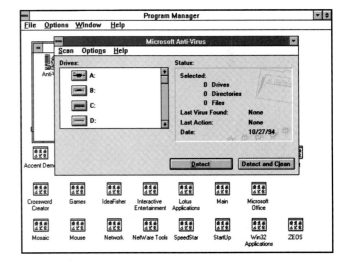

Microsoft Anti-Virus, provided with some versions of Microsoft Windows, scans for over 1,200 different viruses.

Legislation

A number of privacy laws addressing computer concerns have been passed since 1970. Other privacy legislation regarding the related areas of cable television and telephone transmissions has also been passed. These related laws are not discussed because they are beyond the scope of this text.

United States Privacy Legislation

Many laws protecting individual privacy have been passed in the last twenty-five years. Privacy is *not* specifically covered in the Bill of Rights, but that does not mean that U.S. citizens don't possess this right. The Bill of Rights, after all, specifically states that its enumeration of basic human rights is not intended to rule out the existence of other basic rights. The right to privacy has been consistently upheld as a right in various decisions of the U.S. Supreme Court. Here are brief summaries of privacy legislation regarding computer data:

➤ *Fair Credit Reporting Act of 1970.* Restricts the use and dissemination of information by credit bureaus. Credit agencies may share information with anyone that they feel has a "legitimate business need." Unfortunately, legitimate is not explicitly defined. The law also gives individuals the right to access and correct their own credit records. (Credit bureaus must, on request, release a copy to the individual once each year with no charge.)

➤ *Freedom of Information Act of 1970.* Gives a citizen the right to request copies of data files that the federal government has stored about him or her.

➤ *Privacy Act of 1974.* Prohibits federal agencies from using data collected about an individual for a purpose other than the one for which the data was originally collected. Specific exceptions permit some federal agencies to share data.

➤ *Right to Financial Privacy Act of 1979.* Sets rules that federal agencies must follow when examining bank customer records.

➤ *Computer Fraud and Abuse Act of 1986.* Permits prosecution of individuals who use computer systems they are not authorized to use.

➤ *Computer Matching and Privacy Act of 1988.* Sets procedures for the use of computer data to verify eligibility for federal benefits or to recover delinquent debts.

Many nongovernment organizations that have large databanks are not covered by any existing legislation. Privacy is still considered primarily a matter of ethics rather than law. The Code of Fair Information Practices, developed in 1977, has been adopted by many private organizations but has not been written into law. Briefly, the code states the following:

1. There will be no secret databases maintained.

2. Individuals will have the right to access records about themselves.

3. Information gathered about individuals must be used for the purpose for which it was originally obtained.

4. Individuals have the right to correct or dispute records about themselves.

5. The organization will take reasonable precautions to ensure that data is correct and is not misused.

European Privacy Legislation

The concern for privacy is high in Europe, where Nazi abuses led to a heightened awareness of the ways that governments can misuse information. For example, Nazis used telephone records to find and arrest Jewish citizens, many of whom were sent to die. For this reason, in many European countries today, you cannot obtain an itemized list of the calls for which you are being billed. Laws prevent telephone companies from collecting this information.

Since the late 1970s, several European nations have adopted privacy legislation specifically related to computers. Currently, Italy, Belgium, Spain, Portugal, and Greece have no privacy legislation in place relating to computers. The European Commission has proposed legislation that is much more rigid than any being considered in the United States. That legislation would do the following:

1. Require organizations to establish security systems to protect data from unauthorized access.

2. Prevent an organization from maintaining data about an individual without that person's consent.

3. Allow an individual to withdraw consent from an organization to maintain and use information pertaining to that individual.

4. Ban electronic profiles of individuals based on buying patterns.

5. Forbid transmission of data to countries that have not adopted similar legislation.

Neither the Code of Fair Information Practices nor the European Commission proposal has been adopted, but both are being considered. The world as we know it could not exist without the capability to transfer and maintain computer records. We need to ensure, however, that computers do not violate the sanctity of individual privacy.

Lesson Summary

➤ One of the challenges presented by computers is to balance the need for information and the right to privacy.

➤ The Clipper chip provides a data encryption and decryption standard that can be easily interpreted by U.S. government agencies.

➤ There is considerable controversy over the privacy of e-mail and the transmission of pornographic computer files.

➤ A field common to two databases can be used as a key for record matching.

➤ EFT systems maintain a log of transactions that could compromise an individual's privacy.

➤ Computers should be protected from natural disasters.

➤ Access to computers can be controlled by requiring passwords and restricting physical access to equipment.

➤ All computer data should be backed up regularly.

➤ Companies should have a well-defined disaster recovery plan.

➤ A computer virus is a program designed to damage data and files stored on computers. Common types of viruses include worms, Trojan horses, time bombs, file infectors, and boot sector viruses.

➤ A number of laws have been passed to protect privacy and address concerns regarding computer use. Additional laws are currently under consideration.

Lesson Review

Key Terms

boot sector virus	disaster recovery plan	incremental backup	Trojan horse
callback system	e-mail	intranet	uninterruptible power
Clipper chip	file infector	password	supply (UPS)
computer virus	firewall	record matching	vaccine
cyberporn	full backup	time bomb	worm

Matching

In the blank next to each of the following terms or phrases, write the letter of the corresponding term or phrase.

_h_ 1. A system in which the computer calls the user at a preset phone number

_c_ 2. A virus hidden in a program such as a game

_i_ 3. Software designed to protect files and data on a local area network from unauthorized access through the Internet

_d_ 4. A complete copy of the data and files stored on a disk

_a_ 5. A program designed to damage the data and files stored on a disk

_b_ 6. A means of preventing a user from accessing a file that the user should not see

_e_ 7. A virus that is set to execute at a certain date and time

_j_ 8. A program that will delete viruses from a disk

_g_ 9. A copy of all data and files that have been altered recently

_f_ 10. A virus designed to take control of a system temporarily

a. computer virus

b. password

c. Trojan horse

d. full backup

e. time bomb

f. worm

g. incremental backup

h. callback

i. firewall

j. vaccine

Multiple Choice

Circle the letter of the correct choice for each of the following.

1. Which of the following does *not* serve as a precaution against the consequences of natural disasters?

    a. mutual-support disaster contingency system

    b. virus scanning program

    c. fire extinguishing system

    d. uninterruptible power supply

2. Which of the following is a virus?

    a. worm

    b. Trojan horse

    c. file infector

    d. all of the above

3. Which privacy legislation permits citizens to request copies of data files that the federal government has about them?

    a. *Privacy Act of 1974*

    b. *Freedom of Information Act of 1970*

    c. *Fair Credit Reporting Act of 1970*

    d. *Computer Matching and Privacy Act of 1988*

4. Consider a scenario in which a federal environmental agency chooses to examine bank records for a manufacturing firm based in New England. The guidelines that the agency would have to follow are described under which of the following?

    a. *Right to Financial Privacy Act of 1979*

    b. *Computer Fraud and Abuse Act of 1986*

    c. *Freedom of Information Act of 1970*

    d. none of the above

5. Consider the statement "Information gathered about individuals must be used for the purpose for which it was originally obtained." This statement would be found under the _____.

    a. Code of Fair Information Practices

    b. *Freedom of Information Act of 1970*

    c. *Privacy Act of 1974*

    d. none of the above

6. Which of the following is *not* indicative of a "cashless society"?

    a. ATMs

    b. credit cards

    c. the Clipper chip

    d. EFT

7. Which privacy legislation permits prosecution of individuals who access computer systems they are not authorized to use?

    a. *Privacy Act of 1974*

    b. *Freedom of Information Act of 1970*

    c. *Computer Fraud and Abuse Act of 1986*

    d. *Computer Matching and Privacy Act of 1988*

8. Which of the following is *not* addressed by the Code of Fair Information Practices?

    a. secret databases

    b. privacy of e-mail messages

    c. the use of information about an individual

    d. a person's right to know what information is kept about that person

9. What do you call a program used to eliminate viruses from a disk?

    a. defragmentation program

    b. backup

    c. disaster recovery plan

    d. vaccine

10. Which of the following is *not* a type of access control?

    a. active badge

    b. password

    c. UPS system

    d. locking door

Completion

In the blank provided, write the correct answer for each of the following.

1. _privacy_ is the right of a person to control the distribution of information about himself or herself.

2. The _Clipper chip_ is used for encryption of computer data.

3. Companies have recently been granted the right to look at employees' _e-mail_ messages.

4. The increased use of ATMs poses a possible threat to individual privacy because of the _____ maintained.

5. _Cyberporn_ is pornographic material distributed through the use of computer files.

6. A(n) _active badge_ worn by an employee can be used to restrict access to areas containing computer hardware and storage media.

7. A(n) _virus_ is designed to damage the data and files stored on a computer.

8. _boot sector_ load each time the computer is started.

9. Legislation proposed by the _several European nation_ would prohibit transmission of data to countries that have not adopted security and privacy legislation.

10. A(n) _Backup_ is an important component of a disaster recovery plan.

Review

On a separate sheet of paper, answer the following questions.

1. Define the term *privacy*. In what ways does the Clipper chip help reduce invasion of privacy? In what ways does the Clipper chip facilitate invasion of privacy?

2. What is an EFT system? What steps have some European countries taken concerning EFT systems?

3. With regard to security issues, what are some of the ways that computers and computer data need to be protected?

4. What is a computer virus? How are computer viruses spread?

5. What is stated in the Code of Fair Information Practices?

6. What is record matching? What data items might be used for data matching?

7. Explain how passwords help to protect computer data.

8. What is meant by backing up data? Develop a backup schedule for a microcomputer used in a small business.

9. Why do you think an incremental backup would be preferred over a full backup daily?

10. What is the purpose of an uninterruptible power supply?

Critical Thinking

On a separate sheet of paper, answer the following questions.

1. How do you feel about the court decision ruling that e-mail within a company is not private and may be scrutinized by company personnel?

2. How do you feel about restrictions on freedom of speech as they relate to e-mail and networks?

3. How might our system be improved to enable individuals to check more easily their own credit reports for errors?

4. Do you believe that the records of an EFT are a complete and true indicator of your spending habits?

5. Comment on the logic behind statement 5 of the proposed European Privacy Legislation. (The statement forbids transmission of data to countries that have not adopted similar legislation.)

Further Discovery

Actually Useful Internet Security Techniques. Larry J. Hughes, Jr. (Indianapolis, IN: NRP, 1995).

Building in Big Brother: The Cryptographic Policy Debate. Edited by Lance J. Hoffman (New York: Springer, 1995).

Computer Related Risks. Peter G. Neumann (Reading, MA: Addison-Wesley, 1995).

Privacy and Freedom. Alan F. Westin (New York: Atheneum, 1967).

The Right to Privacy. Ellen Alderman and Caroline Kennedy (New York: Knopf, 1995).

On-line Discovery

You can access the Internet resources for the following questions by going to the Que Education and Training Web site at URL http://www.ciyf98.com/discovery. From this page, click the link for Lesson 9C and then click the link to the resource you want to access.

1. The Electronic Frontier Foundation (EFF) is an organization that supports civil liberties on the Internet and also lobbies the government for laws protecting the rights of Internet users. The organization's home page provides access to detailed case files on various controversies in which the organization has been involved. Examine **The Electronic Frontier Foundation** home page (http://www.eff.org) and find three different issues the EFF has confronted. For each issue, try to find on the home page a specific incident that illustrates the issue. Finally, as a challenge, try to find a Web site for another organization that deals with similar issues but has a different perspective.

2. The Computer Emergency Response Team (CERT) is an organization that works with the Internet community to respond to computer break-ins and other security problems. Browse the **CERT Information Center** Web site (http://www.cert.org). What kinds of security problems does CERT deal with? What kinds of resources does it provide to network administrators for dealing with security problems?

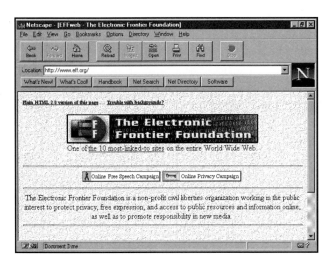

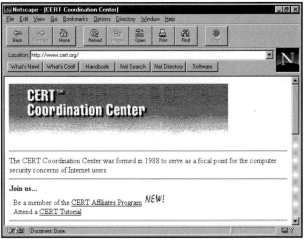

LESSON 9D

A View Toward the Future

Outline

OLE - object linking embedding

OOP -

Learning Objectives

After you have finished reading this lesson, you will be able to

➤ Discuss the historical development of artificial intelligence

➤ Explain what expert systems can and cannot do

➤ Define neural networks and indicate likely future applications

➤ Explain how fuzzy logic can improve a machine's performance

➤ Identify likely future advances in computer hardware

➤ Point out promising areas of development in computer software

➤ Identify new areas of development in computer-based communications

Let your imagination take you into the twenty-first century. You are returning home from a shopping trip. No sooner do you step in the door than the telephone rings, as usual—if "ring" is the right word. There's no such thing as a phone now; in its place, an artificially intelligent neural net computer stands ready to assist you with many tasks, including communications.

Throughout the house, flat translucent panels illuminate, and you hear a gentle chiming sound. Then you hear a pleasant voice saying, "Your friend, Timothy, is calling. Shall I display the call on-screen?" You say, "Sure, computer, but wait a second until I have put the groceries in the refrigerator."

You close the refrigerator door, making a distinctive sound that the "phone's" neural net has learned to recognize. Tim appears on-screen, in beautiful color, and you hear his voice in clear, stereo sound.

Tim asks, "Movie tonight?"

"Sure," you say, "what are you in the mood for?"

"Let's take a look at some twentieth-century flicks again, just for fun," Tim says. "How about *Star Trek XXXII*?"

"Hear that, computer? Download it, and we'll watch it at 7."

Is this scenario plausible? Perhaps, but technological futures are especially difficult to predict. Radio, for instance, was originally thought to have no use other than to broadcast Sunday sermons. It took imagination and vision to see a world in which radio waves brought news, sports, weather, and music into every home and automobile.

Generally, short-range predictions of technological progress are much easier than long-range ones. This lesson examines some probable short-range advances, those that you're likely to see in the next decade or two, and offers some guesses about long-range possibilities.

Already in existence are primitive versions of technologies that, some believe, may transform the nature of computing. These technologies include artificial intelligence, artificial life, and virtual reality.

Artificial Intelligence—Computer or Human?

How far away is an artificial intelligence, a machine or computer program that can mimic some or all of the characteristics of human intelligence? If you're talking about a robot that can converse in many languages and ponder its own fate, this type of artificial intelligence is very far away (if it is even possible). Still, efforts continue in giving computers at least some of the attributes of human intelligence. And some efforts have been partially successful.

In 1950, the British computer scientist Alan Turing proposed a test to determine whether a computer could be called intelligent. In the **Turing test**, a person sits at a computer and types questions. The computer is connected to two other hidden computers. At one, a human being reads the questions and types responses. At the other, a computer with no human assistant runs a program that also gives answers. If the person typing the question can't tell the difference between the human's answers and the computer's answers, Turing said, the computer is intelligent.

Turing's definition of intelligence assumes that if a computer acts in an intelligent way, it is intelligent. By this standard, computers have long ago passed the Turing test. In the mid-1960s, Joseph Weizenbaum, a computer scientist at MIT, wrote a simple program called ELIZA. This program mimics a human therapist. If you type "I'm worried about my girlfriend," the program responds, "Tell me more about your girlfriend." The program is actually very simple. If the user types a word on the program's built-in list, such as *girlfriend*, *father*, *guilt*, or *problem*, the program copies this word and puts it into the response.

A Session with ELIZA the Therapist

Men are all alike.

IN WHAT WAY

They're always bugging us about something or other.

CAN YOU THINK OF A SPECIFIC EXAMPLE

Well, my boyfriend made me come here.

YOUR BOYFRIEND MADE YOU COME HERE

He says I'm depressed most of the time.

I AM SORRY TO HEAR YOU ARE DEPRESSED

It's true. I am unhappy.

DO YOU THINK COMING HERE WILL HELP YOU NOT TO BE UNHAPPY

I need some help, that much seems certain.

WHAT WOULD IT MEAN TO YOU IF YOU GOT SOME HELP

Perhaps I could learn to get along with my mother.

TELL ME MORE ABOUT YOUR FAMILY

From *Computer Power and Human Reason*, by Joseph Weizenbaum.

ELIZA can't fool people for long, but today's programs are larger and more resourceful. In the First Annual Loebner Prize Competition, held at the Boston Computer Museum in 1991, ten human judges tried to determine which of eight display screens showed text produced by people and which ones displayed text produced by the computer. An advanced program called PC Therapist tricked half the judges into thinking that the program was a human being.

Many people will never be satisfied by the Turing test. Mimicking intelligence is one thing, they say—but being intelligent is another. Our intelligence, we like to think, is characterized by self-awareness—we are conscious. We know we exist, and we can reflect on that fact. A computer program might be capable of mimicking a person's words, but it is far from being self-aware. But some artificial intelligence researchers disagree. They believe that our self-awareness is just the result of our very complex programming.

Of all the technologies on the horizon, the most far-reaching in its potential impact is **artificial intelligence** (**AI**). Computer scientists working in the field of artificial intelligence believe that the one area of human intelligence which is at the core of human intelligence is what is often called "common sense." But they do not agree on what that is or, more important to them, how to achieve it in a "computer." In the United States, two groups of AI teams are currently working on diverse attempts at creating AI in a computer. One approach is to imitate human thought, and the other approach is to create the same effect as human thought, regardless of how that is done.

Rodney Brooks of M.I.T. is developing a machine, named Cog, that has cameras for eyes; a "skin" that has sensory input; and a brain of eight 32-bit, Macintosh-type processors. Cog is learning the way humans learn, by trial and error. The object is an AI machine that can do diverse tasks and think the way humans can.

Courtesy of International Business Machines Corporation

Douglas Lenat of Austin, Texas, is developing a machine, called CYC, that is being fed all the rules of "human consensus reality," or common sense. Instead of having CYC learn by experience, the knowledge of the experience is being input. Lenat believes that once CYC has about two million common sense rules, it will be able to do much of its own learning. For example, CYC can read the encyclopedia and then ask questions about anything it didn't understand—and its common sense will be strong enough to tell it what it did or didn't understand.

CYC represents the top-down approach to AI, that the basis of human thought is symbolic knowledge. Intelligence can be created by coding the logical structures we use to apprehend the world. Cog represents the bottom-up

Cog, an artificial intelligence machine.

approach to AI. This approach encourages programs to work more like biological structures than logical structures. The programs build a lot of small, simple programs and let them interact and learn which interactions are successful.

The capability that both AI approaches are trying to develop is to infer from known facts. If a software package is able to infer, it can be of great help to humans. One of the first applications of this inference power is in **intelligent agents** that are being developed, especially for the Internet. For example, an agent could peruse the Internet and put together a customized newspaper for you to read when you get up every morning. You would select topics you are interested in reading about, give them priorities, and specify the total length of the newspaper. The agent would find the articles of greatest interest to you and put together your own newspaper (on your computer screen or printed on paper).

One computer, called Deep Blue, has been programmed to play chess at the world-class level. In 1996, World Chess Champion Garry Kasparov was able to win his match with Deep Blue, barely. But the same machine could not drive itself to the match, talk to the press about the significance of the match, and then play world-class chess. Only Kasparov could do that. Computers are being developed to exhibit human intelligence, but not to replace humans.

Research that scientists are performing in several related areas is advancing our knowledge of artificial intelligence. These areas include natural language, expert systems, robots, neural networks, and fuzzy logic.

Natural Language

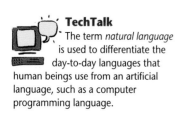

TechTalk
The term *natural language* is used to differentiate the day-to-day languages that human beings use from an artificial language, such as a computer programming language.

Even if we cannot define intelligence adequately, we can recognize some aspects of human intelligence, such as the abilities to reason; to solve problems; to learn; and to use a **natural language**, such as English or Chinese, to communicate.

In *Star Trek IV*, Scotty, the engineer, time-travels back to twentieth-century San Francisco. He picks up a Macintosh computer's mouse and, thinking it is a microphone, attempts to give the computer a verbal command. His astonished onlookers do not realize that such things are commonplace in the twenty-fourth century!

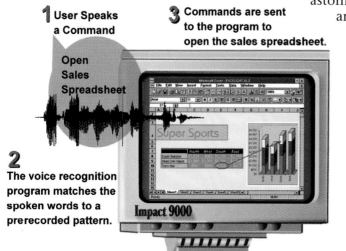

1 User Speaks a Command

Open Sales Spreadsheet

2 The voice recognition program matches the spoken words to a prerecorded pattern.

3 Commands are sent to the program to open the sales spreadsheet.

Impact 9000

Considering the slow progress in computer voice recognition, creating a computer that we can talk to is not about to happen in the near future. Today's computer voice recognition systems can "understand" a few hundred verbal commands, such as "Open window" or "Start program." But that capability is very different from a person's being able to say, "Computer, show me all my appointments for next Tuesday, OK? And by the way, who makes the best pizza in town?"

What's holding back the computer's capability to recognize a natural language? Human languages are so complex that linguists have not agreed on a single model of a natural language grammar system. Although some computer programs do accept natural language input, the sentences must be phrased to conform to fairly strict syntax rules.

Expert Systems

As you have learned in this book, computers work with data and transform it into information. An **expert system** is a computer program that uses a database of knowledge to draw conclusions. In other words, an expert system reasons.

Part of human knowledge consists of rules that have an if-then structure:

➤ *If* you are trying to start your car, *then* press and release the gas pedal before turning on the ignition.

➤ *If* the car does not start the first time, *then* do not press the gas pedal before turning on the ignition again.

An expert system is a computer program that relies on a **knowledge base**, a database of if-then knowledge. To use the expert system, you supply information to the program. Based on the information you supply, the program consults its knowledge base and draws a conclusion, if possible.

Expert systems have been very helpful in diagnosing diseases, especially rare diseases or diseases that medical experts do not routinely see. Expert systems can outperform human experts in some highly restricted areas of knowledge, but expert systems do not have common sense, the background knowledge that people have and use every day. In addition, a high proportion of human expertise is based on rules of thumb learned by experience. Computer scientists have tried to give expert systems common sense and experiential rules of thumb, but these attempts have not been successful. For now, expert systems are valuable only for very limited assignments, such as diagnosing a specific disease, processing insurance claims applications, or checking credit applications for fraud.

Robots

Robots have been in the movies and on television for years. However, those "show business" robots are not necessarily true representations of working robots. A **robot** is a computer that outputs motion instead of information. Robots do not need to look, move, or act like humans.

Today's robots include input sensors that detect light, sound, touch, and heat. These sensors enable the robot to change its motion based on outside stimuli.

Don't worry about robots taking over the world in your lifetime. In the absence of artificial intelligence, today's robots are not very smart. They can perform a few manual tasks repeatedly and rapidly, but they can do only the tasks they are programmed to do. Cog, mentioned earlier in this lesson, may be a prototype of future robots because it combines sensory input and AI-like thinking.

As you learn in Lesson 10B, robots have many applications in industry. For example, spot-welding machines are nonmobile robots that move an "arm" (a manipulating mechanism) while the base is fixed to a track or a holding base. In general, robotic systems can do precise tasks accurately and consistently. Like Dante II, discussed in Lesson 10C, robots can perform tasks that are dangerous for humans. Robots can also do repetitive tasks without getting bored and careless. Although robots are expensive, they work 24 hours per day, do not go on strike, do not show up to work with a hangover, and do not require health insurance and pensions. For these reasons, companies like robots very much. As robots grow more capable, the opportunities for unskilled and semiskilled employment are sure to decline.

BITS
Czech playwright Karel Capek coined the term *robot* in 1923 to describe intelligent, human-shaped machines that eventually rebelled against their human masters. The term *robot* derived from the Czech *robota*, which means "forced labor."

Robots are used to make many computer parts, such as circuit boards and chips.

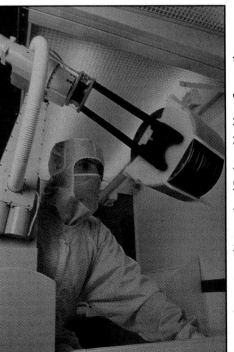

Photographs courtesy of International Business Machines Corporation

Neural Networks

Key advances in artificial intelligence will most likely come from neural nets. A **neural network** (or just **neural net**) is a computer that does not use the linear IPOS (input-processing-output-storage) design used by almost all computers of today. Instead, a neural network mimics the structure of the human brain.

Although little is known about how the human brain works, its physical structure has been explored. Anatomists know that the brain contains billions of brain cells, called neurons. These neurons are connected by current-conducting nerve fibers called ganglia. Often, a single neuron has many ganglia attached to it, forming a dense and complex network of interconnections. Scientists believe that when people learn things, some connections are reinforced and grow stronger, while others do not receive reinforcement.

In a neural net, thousands of computer processing units are connected in multiple ways, just as the neurons in a brain are connected. Neural nets aren't programmed; they're trained. The net "learns" by trial and error, just the way humans do. An incorrect guess weakens a particular pattern of connections; a correct guess reinforces the pattern. After the training is finished, the neural net "knows" how to do something, such as operate a robot. Neural nets behave much the way brains behave. In fact, neural nets exhibit electromagnetic waves that are surprisingly similar to the brain waves in humans. None of today's neural nets, however, approaches the complexity of even an animal's brain, but more complex neural nets are planned.

Ordinary computers are very good at solving problems that require linear thinking, logical rules, and step-by-step instructions. Neural nets are very good at recognizing patterns, dealing with complexity, and learning from experience.

Japan has been developing uses of neural networks since 1988. The Japanese have integrated neural networks into devices ranging from air conditioners to rice cookers to word processors. Neural networks have also been used to help decide when to buy and sell securities, to ensure the best quality of a photocopy, and to classify welding defects.

Fuzzy Logic

Along with neural networks, computer scientists have been trying to get computers to make decisions by using fuzzy logic. Traditional computers make binary decisions: yes or no, right or wrong, on or off. But humans make decisions according to a scale. You are not 100 percent happy or sad; you are more happy than sad. Not polarizing decisions but evaluating by degree is called **fuzzy logic**.

Computer scientists are trying to develop rules for fuzzy logic and use them with neural networks to apply to artificial intelligence problems. An example of an application of fuzzy logic is the circuitry that enables a handheld video camera to adjust to jiggling and show a steady picture. The circuitry figures out what probably should and should not move and adjusts the image accordingly. Another application is antilocking automobile brakes; the brakes sense when they should release or continue pressure to keep the car from sliding out of control.

Artificial Life

Computer viruses, as you learned in Lesson 9C, are programs that can "infect" a computer by propagating in unseen ways. Some viruses are malicious and can destroy data. Others are merely irritating. But according to some researchers, all viruses have at least one of the key characteristics of living organisms—the capability to reproduce.

Computer viruses have inspired a new area of research—**artificial life** (also called **a-life**). In a-life research, researchers create a "life-form" within the computer. These life-forms are currently one-celled "creatures" that can move themselves and reproduce themselves by their own "will." They have been used to test evolutionary theories and to test theories of life-form behavior.

One outgrowth of artificial life research is experimentation with **genetic algorithms**. As you know, an algorithm is a procedure for solving a problem. The biggest challenge in computer programming is to produce an effective algorithm for solving a program. In genetic algorithm research, scientists are letting the computer mimic nature.

According to evolutionary theories of biology, organisms try to survive. Occasional errors in the genetic code introduce mutations, leading to change. Sometimes these changes are advantageous and give the organism a better chance to survive. The organisms with an advantageous genetic code predominate because they have more opportunities to reproduce.

Genetic algorithm research mimics nature in the following way. A number of algorithms are placed into a computer "environment" and are given the potential to mutate in random ways. All the algorithms compete to try to solve the problem. Over time, one of the algorithms emerges as the best at tackling the problem.

Virtual Reality

Virtual reality (**VR**) is a computer technology that uses multiple sensors for input and output and interactively adjusts the output based on the input. In a typical VR system, the user wears glasses with twin television screens (one for each eye), stereo headphones, and a glove. The glasses and headphones immerse the user in the pictures and sound of an imaginary environment. The user alters the environment by moving the glove.

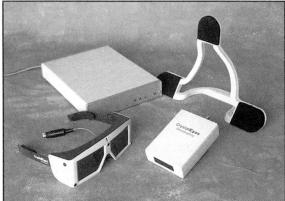

Courtesy of Stereo Graphics Corporation

Virtual reality glasses and headphones.

VR has been embraced by game makers as a great new toy; however, VR has serious uses as well. While an architect is designing a building, the buyer may not be able to visualize the structure well enough to say whether some feature will be satisfactory. With VR, the buyer can "walk through" a building while it is still being designed. The most important application of VR made to date is in training doctors; the doctors can practice a procedure as many times as needed to master it satisfactorily.

Tomorrow's virtual reality systems may transform the nature of entertainment. Instead of watching a movie on a flat screen, you will feel as if you're in the movie yourself, with the action going on all around you! The possibilities are limitless—and so are the concerns. Virtual reality could very well become the "designer drug" of the twenty-first century, producing sensory addictions that could be hard to shake. Why study or work when you can don a VR suit and experience just about anything you like?

Virtual reality users can surround themselves with an environment they can fashion at will.

Photographs courtesy of Stereo Graphics Corporation

Virtual reality technology enables people to design cities by changing the plans based on simulated structures.

Tomorrow's Technology

Additional advances in computing technologies include hardware developments, software developments, and major improvements in communications. Several of these are described in this section.

Hardware

At the same time that computers are getting more powerful, their price is declining. If the automobile industry had made the same progress since 1955, a new Rolls Royce would cost $2.50, would go 16,000 miles per hour, and could travel to the moon and back on one tank of gas.

Much of this progress has been made possible by advances in the semiconductor industry. These advances have enabled the computer hardware industry to mass-produce miniature electronic devices of fabulous complexity. There's every reason to expect this trend to continue, up to the point where designers start running into the physical limits of miniaturization.

Hardware advances include larger capacity for RAM, faster processing speeds using optical computing and parallel processors, optical storage media with huge capacity, and much smaller processors using nanotechnology. Here's a taste of what's to come.

Memory

Nathan Myhrvold, Vice President of Advanced Technology at Microsoft, predicts that in two to four years, the size of RAM in desktop computers will be 120M to 500M. The processing speeds will also increase by about 100 times.

Virtual Reality Is More Than Fun and Games

Children born with physical conditions that limit their mobility are doubly handicapped. Research in the last 25 years has demonstrated that self-locomotion experience plays an important role in a child's development, according to an article written by Dr. Dean P. Inman and his colleagues at the Virtual Reality Labs of Oregon Research Institute.

Skills such as spatial and depth perception, shape recognition, visually guided reaching, awareness of self-motion, and problem solving in multidimensional space are all developed through mobility. These skills form an important part of how we interact with and use our environment. Children with limited mobility cannot have these learning experiences. Computer-generated virtual reality (VR), however, provides a way to substitute simulated experiences for actual mobility. Thus, VR enables physically handicapped children to develop spatial perceptual abilities.

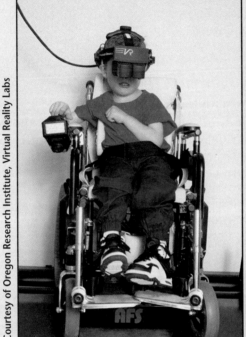

Courtesy of Oregon Research Institute, Virtual Reality Labs

In the Virtual Reality Labs, a program that provides these missing mobility experiences for orthopedically impaired children is under way. The program trains the children to operate motorized wheelchairs in virtual reality. Using this technology, the children can "move" freely and independently within different environments, according to Dr. Inman and his colleagues.

Virtual reality software generates three-dimensional images that respond to input from the student's joystick and head position. In addition to the simulated reality responses, the student's actions generate several real-world responses.

The wheelchair is placed on rollers that enable the chair's back wheels to rotate independently at normal speeds (a frame prevents the chair from actually moving). Irregularities in the surfaces of the roller cause the chair to vibrate slightly, simulating a sidewalk or carpet.

To simulate the experience of "crashing" into objects or walls, the software signals a brake to stop the wheels from turning. This braking jolts the student driver as if a real crash with an immovable object had occurred, with no danger to the driver or others.

A helmet contains two video screens, one for each eye, in its visor to present a three-dimensional view of the virtual reality world. Two earphones, one for each ear, supply stereophonic sound effects.

The software is designed to develop a child's skill in driving a motorized wheelchair safely and independently in the school and community, on the way to reaching the child's full potential.

Speed

Using light instead of electrons is the idea behind **optical processors**. Because light can travel much faster than electrons, optical processors should be several hundred times faster than the electronic circuits used today. Researchers in laboratories are experimenting with optical processing chips with thicknesses of 40 atoms.

Parallel Processing

One limitation of processor design is that processing occurs in series. **Parallel processors** now being designed and built can greatly increase the **MIPS**—millions of instructions per second—the computer can accomplish. Today, supercomputers are being designed around microprocessor chips arranged in a parallel pattern, not a serial pattern. The biggest drawback to parallel processors is that a new approach to software logic will have to be used to design programs for these processors. Programmers who want to develop software for these processors will have to be retrained.

The combination of RISC (reduced instruction set computing) chips and parallel processing can greatly increase the speed of supercomputers, as well as microcomputers. RISC chips are faster than CISC (complex instruction set computing) chips because RISC chips are limited in what they can do. When you are using chips in parallel, you can use parallel RISC chips for many processing functions and CISC chips for other functions.

Digital Video Discs (DVDs)

Digital discs, which hold 7 to 12 times the amount of data on a CD-ROM, can transfer data faster than the fastest CD-ROM today, record data at your computer, and play your old CDs—does this sound like an "off in the distant future" dream? This technology is being built today. In 1995, industry representatives from around the world met and agreed on a standard for the emerging digital video disc (DVD) format. Both the motion picture industry and the computer industry proposed detailed specifications for digital discs. All these specifications were met in the accepted DVD format. DVD standards include discs with the same diameter, thickness, and durability of current CDs.

A DVD can contain an entire movie in high-quality video on a single side of a disc (up to 2 hours and 13 minutes), with the capacity to include digital sound in three languages, plus subtitles in four additional languages, and no need to turn the disc over. When used for data storage for computers, DVD-ROM has 4.7 gigabytes of storage on a single layer and 8.5 gigabytes on a dual-layer disc—12 times the capacity of a CD. The prices of DVD-ROM products are expected to be comparable to current CD-ROM products.

Tiny "nanomachines" may someday be constructed with atoms and released into the bloodstream to cure various diseases.

Nanotechnology

The technological advance in the more distant future is **nanotechnology**, or **molecular manufacturing**. In the U.S. and Japan, research in computer technology based on devices that use atom switches is moving quickly. An **atom switch** moves a single atom and bonds it in the new location, and then later moves the atom back if needed. Nanotechnology involves building a processing chip up from the atomic level. The physics has been proved; a technique for setting atom switches has been proved. The current problem is the mechanics for actually building something at that level. A prediction for the future of nanotechnology is that a unit the size of a sugar cube will include hundreds of processors working in parallel at incredible speeds. In the United States, scientists at IBM, Xerox PARC, and other places are working on nanotechnology—how to build it, control it, and apply it to problems.

Software

Software hasn't been improving as fast as hardware, and for good reason. Creating a good application program is a huge job, requiring in some cases the equivalent of hundreds of years of human effort to complete. The sheer complexity of today's huge programs creates problems for software developers and users alike. Some major growth areas in software are the increasing use of graphical user interfaces and the use of software development tools such as object-oriented programming and natural language processors.

Graphical User Interfaces

Although the use of **graphical user interfaces** (**GUIs**), such as the Macintosh interface and Microsoft Windows, has been growing, the full power of this type of platform has not been explored. The next few years will bring a parade of software products that use GUIs to simplify the interface between the user and computer. Millions of people have not started to use the computer, but the pressure to join the technology is mounting. Software that makes computing easier will be increasingly important.

One recent product that simplifies the interface between application packages is **object linking and embedding** (**OLE**). OLE is a tool for joining applications. For example, you can embed part of a spreadsheet in a word processing document. The power of OLE is that it remembers where it places that spreadsheet part; if you update the spreadsheet, OLE also updates the portion of the spreadsheet in the word processing document. You can also update the spreadsheet in the document, and OLE updates the original spreadsheet. With OLE, you can seamlessly merge results from several applications.

New Programming Languages

Techniques that improve the development of new software are being created but with much less hype than hardware developments, because software development techniques initially affect fewer people. As mentioned in Lesson 3B, object-oriented programming (OOP) is being used to create generic building blocks of a program (the objects) and assemble different sets of objects as needed to solve specific problems. This approach can make constructing a program a task for the end user rather than the exclusive area of a programmer or software engineer. The programmers can construct the building blocks, and the end users can assemble them as needed.

The next anticipated level of software development is fifth-generation languages. In **fifth-generation languages**, the user gives the instructions to the computer in a natural language—English, Japanese, and so on.

Communications

Communications is the fastest-growing, fastest-changing area of computer use. Changes occurring now are the emergence of wireless transmission; the development of videoconferencing; and the creation, transmission, and reproduction of digitized documents.

Wireless Transmission

The old copper telephone wires are being replaced by fiber-optic wire for nonmobile users and by **wireless transmission** for mobile computer users. Like cellular phone technology, wireless transmission uses radio waves. Most wireless communication is over relatively short distances. The current use of wireless transmission is to create local area networks (LANs) with nodes (individual PCs connected to the LAN) that can be moved around without rewiring. Cellular phones can also create wireless transmission; a portable fax machine in your car can use the cellular phone in the car to send a fax.

Bill Gates (CEO of Microsoft Corporation) and Craig McCaw (a leader in the cellular telephone industry) have formed a company called Teledesic. They plan to use hundreds of satellites to create a worldwide wireless network for voice, data, and video transmission. The cost is several billion dollars, and the technical challenges include launching satellites weekly for several years. Wireless transmission may be the answer for countries that can't afford to upgrade their traditional telephone systems.

Desktop Videoconferencing and Networked Video

Videoconferencing enables people who are physically separated to hold a conference. When one person is talking, everyone sees that person. When someone else speaks, that person appears on everyone's video. Because the technology has been so expensive, videoconferencing centers have been created. New technology has enabled videoconferencing on microcomputers. Now the conference can be among people on a LAN or geographically distant. (Some hardware does require the connection to be ISDN.)

The next breakthrough will be to have an on-screen window for each conferee. This capability will increase the level of satisfaction for communications such as distance learning.

Technology suppliers and communications companies are forming alliances to provide live video to interested customers. Intel Corporation and the Cable News Network offer a service that delivers live television over microcomputer networks. The service, called CNN at Work, delivers Headline News or CNN broadcasts in addition to selected stock quotes and text messages from the local area network administrator. The service can be obtained without adding hardware or wiring.

With CNN at Work, users can capture live video and store it on their hard disks for later retrieval.

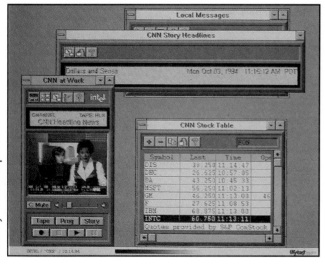

Digital Transmission of Documents

Have you heard of the "paperless office"? For years, the prediction was that computer technology would eliminate the need for paper. That prediction does not seem probable today, but bypassing paper can save time. When you save a document on paper and then need to alter or manipulate the text by computer, you must recapture the document in computer-readable form (digital form). For a document to be sent by fax, the fax machine must first digitize the document, then send the digital form, and finally reconstruct the document at the end machine. A built-in fax modem can send a form stored in the computer (of course, in digital format) or receive a digital form and keep it in its digital format.

Xerox Corporation has developed equipment that in one operation can send documents in digital form over any distance and then reproduce as many paper copies as needed. If the original is on paper only, a scanner can digitize the document first.

This technology has an added value. Sometimes codes in the document may be stored in digital form but not appear on the paper copy. This technique stores these codes on the paper copy when it is reproduced. Symbols called **glyphs** are coded in the document. These glyphs cannot be seen by the human eye, but a scanner can "see" them. Instead of sending a spreadsheet with just the numbers shown, you can send and have stored on paper the formulas that calculated the numbers, as well.

Lesson Summary

➤ Artificial Intelligence (AI) is software or hardware behaving as if guided by human intelligence. Computer scientists have been attempting AI since computers were first developed.

➤ Alan Turing created the Turing test of AI—if a human cannot determine whether material is being generated by a computer or by a human, the computer shows artificial intelligence.

➤ AI experts are using a top-down approach to build a computer with millions of logical structures coded in. Then the computer can learn on its own.

➤ Another group of AI experts is trying the bottom-up approach to build a computer with sensory input capability and parallel processors to learn from its own experiences, from the beginning.

➤ Many applications of computer technology use some aspect of artificial intelligence. These include natural language, expert systems, robots, neural networks, and fuzzy logic.

➤ Natural languages are the languages humans use to converse with each other. Natural languages are difficult for computers because of complex syntax rules; therefore, it is difficult to design an algorithm for syntax rules for the computer to follow.

➤ An expert system is software that uses a database of knowledge to draw conclusions, attempting to mimic how an expert in a field would draw on his or her experiences to make knowledgeable decisions.

➤ Robots are computers that output motion instead of information. Although robots use very little intelligence today, they do perform boring, routine, or dangerous tasks and have replaced non-skilled and low-skilled jobs.

➤ A neural network, or neural net, is designed to work like the human brain. Circuits are connected in the way neurons in the brain are connected. The neural net reinforces successful connections and thereby learns successful behavior, as brains do.

➤ Using fuzzy logic is how humans often make decisions, instead of using the binary (yes or no) logic of computers. Fuzzy logic is based on degrees on a scale rather than on absolutes.

➤ In hardware advances, the direction is toward larger capacity for RAM, faster processing speeds using optical computing and parallel processors, digital video discs, and much smaller processors using nanotechnology.

➤ Software advances include the increased use of graphical user interfaces (GUIs) and software development tools such as object-oriented programming (OOP) and natural language processors.

➤ In communications, the major improvements are in wireless transmission and the digitizing and transmitting of documents over telephone lines.

Lesson Review

Key Terms

artificial intelligence (AI)	genetic algorithm	molecular manufacturing	optical processors
artificial life (a-life)	glyph	nanotechnology	parallel processors
atom switch	graphical user interface	natural language	robot
digital video disc (DVD)	(GUI)	neural net	Turing test
expert system	intelligent agent	neural network	virtual reality (VR)
fifth-generation language	knowledge base	object linking and embed-	wireless transmission
fuzzy logic	MIPS	ding (OLE)	

Matching

In the blank next to each of the following terms or phrases, write the letter of the corresponding term or phrase.

_____g_____ **1.** Natural language

_____e_____ **2.** To evaluate by degrees rather than binary logic

_____l_____ **3.** Has greater storage capacity than a CD-ROM

_____c_____ **4.** Has motion for output

_____ 5. A tool that enables you to update changes made in an embedded document and have those changes automatically reflected in the original document

_d_ 6. Acts like neurons

_b_ 7. Needed by expert systems

_a_ 8. Measured by the Turing test

_____ 9. Uses the atom switch

_h_ 10. Used to create generic building blocks of a program

a. artificial intelligence

b. knowledge base

c. robot

d. neural net

e. fuzzy logic

f. nanotechnology

g. fifth-generation language

h. OOP

i. DVD

j. OLE

Multiple Choice

Circle the letter of the correct choice for each of the following.

1. Which of the following is a major element of intelligence?

   a. reasoning and problem solving
   b. ability to learn and remember
   c. natural language and common sense
   d. all of the above

2. Which of the following is true about the attempts by computers at natural language?

   a. They are generally successful.
   b. They lack common sense.
   c. They can handle Japanese but not English.
   d. They can understand but not speak.

3. Which of the following must be included in an accurate description of robots?

   a. They output motion instead of information.
   b. They look and act like humans, but not as smoothly.
   c. They are not used in useful applications yet.
   d. They are unable to hurt a human being.

4. What do you call computer circuits that act like the circuits in the human brain?

   a. expert systems
   b. artificial intelligence
   c. neural networks
   d. intelligent agents

5. A program uses which of the following to decide when the rice that is cooking is done?

   a. artificial life
   b. virtual reality
   c. a timer
   d. fuzzy logic

6. Which of the following is currently being developed in computer hardware?

   a. a processor using light instead of electrons
   b. circuits working in a parallel pattern instead of a serial pattern
   c. memory capacity of 500 megabytes
   d. all of the above

7. Which of the following is an innovation in software development being used today?

    a. fifth-generation languages

    b. intelligent agents

    c. object-oriented programming

    d. all of the above

8. The latest medium in high-capacity storage is the _____.

    a. 8-inch diskette

    b. glyph

    c. digital video disc

    d. CD-ROM

9. Nanotechnology involves working _____.

    a. at extremely fast speeds

    b. with extremely small computer devices

    c. on extremely large computers

    d. none of the above

10. Which of the following is an essential feature of intelligent agents?

    a. They record what you need for later reference.

    b. They warn you of security breaches.

    c. They interpret your directions, but don't need exact directions.

    d. They give you back about 10 percent of all the data you give them.

Completion

In the blank provided, write the correct answer for each of the following.

1. Languages used by humans, rather than by computers, are called _natural_ languages.

2. Software that asks questions, compares the answers to a database of knowledge, and then suggests the actions an expert in the area would probably suggest is known as a(n) _expert system_.

3. A computer that outputs motion rather than information is a(n) _robot_.

4. A computer that mimics the structure of the human brain is known as a(n) _neural_.

5. A(n) _a-life_ is a life-form that is created in a computer, can move itself and reproduce, and is not a virus.

6. _virtual reality_ is a computer system that uses multiple sensors for input and output and that interactively adjusts the output based on the input.

7. A(n) _atom_ switch moves a single atom and bonds it in the new location, and then later moves the atom back if needed.

8. The newest storage technology, DVD, has a capacity that is _7-12x_ than that of CD-ROM.

9. Small pieces coded into a document that can be transmitted with the document are called _glyphs_.

10. When a LAN is created with nodes that can be relocated without any rewiring, the network is using _wireless_ transmission.

Review

On a separate sheet of paper, answer the following questions.

1. Explain how the Turing test might be applied to ELIZA.

2. What is the relationship between artificial intelligence and natural language?

3. What are the similarities between the way neural networks and the human brain work?

4. Compare binary logic with fuzzy logic.

5. How are scientists using artificial life to study nature?

6. What are some of the advances expected in hardware in the next few years?

7. What are some of the advances occurring in software?

8. What are some of the advances occurring in communications?

9. What is nanotechnology and how does it work?

10. What are the advantages of using robots? What are the disadvantages?

Critical Thinking

On a separate sheet of paper, answer the following questions.

1. Describe the decision process that an expert system might use to determine whether a check should be accepted by a cashier.

2. What do you think is holding back the development of neural networks that work at the same level of function as the human brain?

3. How could fuzzy logic be applied to the problem of driving a car?

4. Explain the concept of an intelligent agent. How would you use an intelligent agent?

5. What would be the advantages and disadvantages of having computers with artificial intelligence? Is this concept something humans should fear? Why or why not?

Further Discovery

Contemplating Minds: A Forum for Artificial Intelligence. Edited by William J. Clancey, Stephen W. Smoliar, and Mark J. Stefik (Cambridge, MA: MIT Press, 1994).

Java Developer's Guide. Jamie Jaworski (Indianapolis, IN: Sams.net, 1996).

Java Sourcebook. Ed Anuff (New York: Wiley, 1996).

Virtual Reality Technology. Grigore Burdea and Philippe Coiffet (New York: Wiley, 1994).

On-line Discovery

You can access the Internet resources for the following questions by going to the Que Education and Training Web site at URL http://www.ciyf98.com/discovery. From this page, click the link for Lesson 9D and then click the link to the resource you want to access.

1. The Yahoo! directory page on **Artificial Intelligence** (http://www.yahoo.com/Science /Computer_Science/Artificial_Intelligence) provides a wealth of information about AI available over the Internet. Using these resources, can you tell what the current areas of artificial intelligence research are? Where is this research being conducted? What are the major problems being worked on by people who study AI? In particular, make sure that you browse the sections on expert systems, fuzzy logic, natural language processing, robotics, and neural networks.

2. Of all the areas of future development in technology, one of the most controversial is nanotechnology. It is characterized by more than its share of hype, and it has many detractors. Brad Hein of Iowa State University has put together an impressive array of nanotechnology resources on his **Nanotechnology** page (http://www.public.iastate.edu/~bhein/nanotechnology.html). Which institutions are studying nanotechnology? Are any journals or publications focusing on nanotechnology? Can you find the voices of any of the nanotechnology detractors in these documents? Finally, what are some reported advantages of nanotechnology?

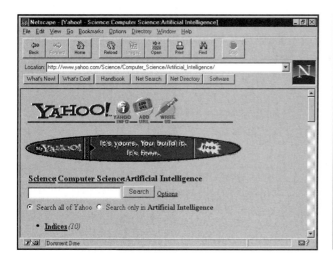

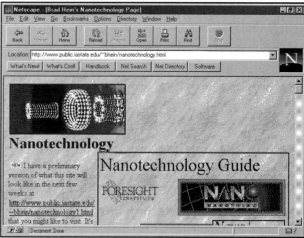

CHAPTER 10

Traditional Uses of Computers

Since elementary school, people have asked you what you wanted to be when you grew up. You may still not be certain of the answer to that question. That's all right; most people change careers at least twice. But no matter what you do, computers will be a part of your working experience.

From retail stores to manufacturing plants to the courtroom, the computer is changing the way we work. Imagine exploring space or the depths of our own planet—without computers. Computers are even helping doctors repair broken bones and cure diseases.

During the next ten years, the number of jobs related to the computer industry will increase dramatically. It is hard to imagine all the jobs that will be in demand then, but for a start, you can look at the jobs that involve computers now.

Lesson 10A explores current jobs in the computer industry and computer career paths, including typical education requirements. This lesson also looks into the future to see where job opportunities may occur.

Lesson 10B explains some new and exciting ways in which computers are used in business, industry, and the legal profession.

Lesson 10C looks at recent discoveries and changes in science and medicine that would have been impossible without computers.

10A

Careers in the Computer Industry

Outline

Learning Objectives

When you have finished reading this lesson, you will be able to

➤ Describe the three areas in which computer professionals have traditionally found jobs

➤ Describe the new computer careers that are opening up because of rapid technological advancement

➤ Explain the educational requirements for typical computer careers

➤ List ways that computer professionals keep up with constant innovations in the computer field

➤ Discuss the effects that computers have had on general employment

Just take a look at the "Help Wanted" columns. In almost every job category, you will see ads that include phrases such as "Computer knowledge a plus" or "Lotus 1-2-3 skills preferred." Or you will see statements such as "Microsoft Office skills put you at the top of the list." The knowledge that you gain from this course will help you in any profession, but you might want to consider a career in the computer industry itself.

This lesson explores careers in the computer industry, beginning with traditional computer career paths. The lesson continues with a discussion of new computer careers created by advances in technology and concludes by examining the impact of computers on overall employment.

The computer technology revolution has an essential and unavoidable part to play in the advancement of our world, yet society's acceptance of this fact has proved to be a slow and difficult process. Ninety percent of the United States workforce does not have true computer competency. These people are reluctant to deal with computers, fearing, as most people do, what they do not understand. Many people are so frightened by the world of fast-paced technological advancement that they threaten to reject it entirely. This irrational fear and aversion to computers is widely known as **cyberphobia**. There are in fact, surprisingly few people who accept computers for what they truly are, a necessity rather than a luxury.

Many jobs are very procedural and can be easily computerized. In many cases, job security will be based upon the development of logical thinking, creativeness, and conceptual skills. Otherwise, without this knowledge, the current workforce will be left behind. Many businesses and industries have not implemented potentially beneficial computer applications, because their workforce has been resistant to change and has not had the proper education.

Jobs in the Computer Industry

With annual revenues of over $100 billion, the computer industry is one of the largest and most successful industries in the world. As you might expect, computer hardware and software firms are themselves major employers. Outside the computer industry, jobs are also available in companies and organizations that use hardware and software products. Many large firms have an information systems department that employs computer professionals. Smaller firms hire computer professionals as consultants on a work-for-hire basis.

Table 10A.1 shows the mean salaries of a number of careers in the computer industry.

Table 10A.1 Mean Salaries in the Computer Industry	
Computer Career	Mean Salary
CIO	$124,670
Manager, Systems and Programming	$77,500
Network Manager LAN/WAN	$67,380
Project Leader	$60,860
Data Center Manager/Operations Manager	$67,560
Software Engineer	$52,990

continues

Table 10A.1 Continued	
Computer Career	Mean Salary
Network Administrator	$53,750
Client Server Programmer/Analyst	$52,840
Programmer Analyst	$42,270
Telecommunications Specialist	$44,780
PC Applications Specialist	$42,110
Systems Analyst	$48,240

Source: Data from DataMasters 1996 Computer industry salary survey.
Web site: http://www.webpress.net/dm/survey.html#northeast

According to the Bureau of Labor Statistics, much of the growth in employment through the year 2005 will be the result of a rising demand for computer specialists. The following list describes the basic responsibilities of various computer specialists:

> **Data entry personnel** key in data from source documents. Job opportunities in this area have declined as **optical character recognition (OCR)** technology has developed. OCR devices scan written or typed text and transform it into computer-readable form.

> **Computer operators** keep computer equipment—whether minicomputers, mainframe computers, or network servers—functioning smoothly on a day-to-day basis.

> **Computer repair technicians** deal with breakdowns in computers and related equipment.

> **Systems analysts** look at the entire scope of a firm's information processing activities—the data, the people, the way the work is organized, and the information to be produced. Systems analysts try to devise computer approaches to improve productivity and deliver better service to customers. Analysts may have programming skills, but programming is not their chief responsibility.

> **Programmers** follow a systems analyst's recommendations. They create, test, and document custom computer programs that precisely meet an organization's needs, as determined by the analyst. Programmer-analyst jobs combine the two functions. Software developers are programmers and analysts who develop software such as productivity tools or computer games.

> **Database administrators** ensure that data is entered correctly, develop procedures for the analysis of data, and ensure database security. This job is an important one; the organization's ability to function may depend on it!

People with computer skills and knowledge enjoy a wide variety of career options.

Categories of Computer Careers

Traditionally, computer careers are divided into three areas: computer information systems, computer science, and computer engineering. These careers differ in the nature of the job, education required, and typical career path.

Computer Information Systems (CIS)

Careers in the **computer information systems (CIS)** field involve jobs in the information systems department of an organization. The focus is on designing computer systems that will control the organization's information, process its data, support its procedures, and then keep the systems working smoothly.

CIS professionals typically major in business with a specialty in computers, programming, and systems analysis. Generally, a bachelor's degree is expected; however, some entry-level positions may require only an associate's degree and some experience or aptitude for programming. Higher-level programming jobs and systems analyst jobs usually require on-the-job experience and at least a bachelor's degree, and preferably a Master of Business Administration (MBA) or a Master of Management Information Systems (MIS).

The entry-level position, with a bachelor's degree in business and a specialty in CIS, is programmer. From programmer, three paths are often available: senior programmer and supervising programmer, systems analyst and project leader, and user liaison. The top management positions, such as chief information officer (CIO), are usually filled by CIS professionals within a company because they know the firm's business best.

Computer Science

Computer scientists develop systems software and personal productivity software. The focus is on the relationship of hardware and software, as well as on developing software that makes the best use of hardware while enabling users to accomplish their jobs. Traditionally, computer scientists

BITS
Demand is especially strong for programmers who know how to write programs for client/server architectures.

developed operating systems, database management systems, language translators, and artificial intelligence programs. Today, there are also opportunities in developing software packages that solve productivity problems. Opportunities are also available in developing software packages that increase productivity, such as word processing programs and communications programs. Applications outside business, such as medical applications or special computer graphics, are more likely to be developed by computer scientists than by CIS specialists.

At most colleges and universities, computer science programs grew out of mathematics programs. The training is highly technical and usually involves several semesters of higher mathematics such as calculus, as well as training in several programming languages and theoretical topics such as programming language structure and artificial intelligence. A minimum of a bachelor's degree is necessary, and a master's degree is valued.

Careers in computer science are less likely to lead to management positions, but such careers have more levels of expertise than CIS careers. The opportunities for promotion are in lead programmer, designer, or project leader in developing new systems. Senior computer scientists are highly paid, a fact that reflects the value of the special talent needed in this area.

Computer Engineering

A **computer engineer** designs new computers and peripheral hardware. CIS and computer science careers are software-oriented, whereas computer engineers are hardware-oriented. Like all engineers, computer engineers use programming, but software development is not the primary thrust of their jobs.

Engineering is divided into many areas of specialization. Computer engineering and electrical engineering are the two fields most pertinent to the computer industry. Computer engineers develop hardware systems, and electrical engineers specialize in designing electronic circuitry (including microprocessors). Any engineering discipline requires a bachelor's degree and may take five years to complete.

Project leader and design leader are typical promotion paths for computer engineers. In an engineering-oriented company, managers often rise from the engineering staff as well.

Certification Specialists

Licensing and certification is becoming more relevant for certain jobs. While Formal education is a requirement, but it is also necessary to have the proper certification. This is not an unusual demonstration of competence. For years, engineers, accountants, and lawyers have been required through formal testing to show certain levels of professional competency. If successful, they became, respectively, registered professional engineers, certified public accountants, and members of the bar. Many others must be licensed to legally perform their jobs, such as doctors, private investigators, hairdressers, plumbers, and electricians.

Now, quite a few computer organizations offer a variety of certifications. Two of the more prominent companies, Microsoft and Novell, have become leaders in certifying information technology professionals. Some of the certifications are as follows:

MOUS (Microsoft Office User Specialist)

MCT (Microsoft Certified Trainer)

MCSE (Microsoft Certified Systems Engineer)

MCSD (Microsoft Certified Solution Developer)

MCPS (Microsoft Certified Product Specialist)

CNI (Certified Novell Instructor)

CNA (Certified Novell Administrator)

CNE (Certified Novell Engineer)

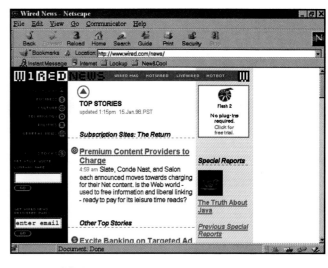

New Career Paths

Evolving technology has created new career opportunities in addition to altering traditional jobs. The microcomputer explosion has resulted in new jobs in repairing microcomputers, installing them, building communication links between them, and helping people when they have difficulties using them. The Internet has opened up new career opportunities such as Webmaster and network research specialist.

To keep up-to-date on the latest in computers in today's society, visit the Wired magazine Web site.

Microcomputer specialists often work with end users, helping them purchase, install, and use their computers. They can also implement security and backup procedures.

Many computer software and hardware makers have help lines that people can call when they have trouble. The people who work these help lines, called **customer support technicians**, are in great demand.

Telecommunications specialists have found a growing job market. Now that companies have all these microcomputers on their desks, management is looking for ways to connect the computers with each other, as well as with minicomputer and mainframe computer systems. The job of the telecommunications specialist is to establish all the capabilities of communication within a company. Many companies that make international connections need an international telecommunications specialist's help.

The Internet is becoming an important path for a company to communicate with potential and current customers. The **Webmaster** is responsible for the visual layout, the written content, the links to other locations, and often the techniques to follow up on the customer's inquiry. Companies with large Internet business may have a Webmaster staff of several employees.

Network research specialists, or information brokers, will conduct your research on the Internet and other online services and then write a report on the results. With online services growing at such a rapid pace and with so much information available, these specialists are filling an emerging need. Most of these specialists currently work as independent contractors, but large companies, especially in the medical field, may be employing network research specialists soon.

A Lifetime of Learning

When you are preparing for a computer career, keep one thing in mind: You are hitching your life to a wild horse. Change, not continuity, is the norm. New technological developments will create new kinds of jobs—and make old ones obsolete. In a computer-related field, chances are that you will work at as many as five or six different jobs before you retire.

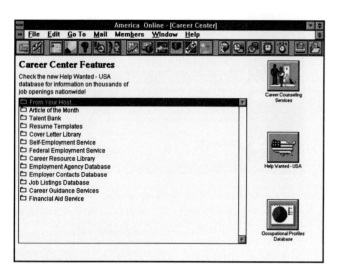

Thousands of career opportunities are listed in America Online's Career Center. The databases are not limited to computer careers; one can search for career openings in many specialties.

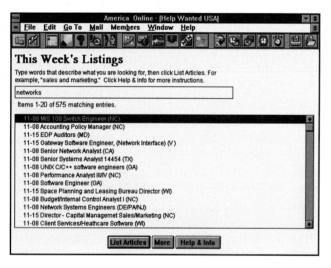

Consider CIS professionals. Twenty years ago, they worked in a central computing facility, where they wrote programs or designed systems. When the microcomputer came along, these professionals had to decentralize. They moved away from the central mainframe computer to microcomputers installed in the end users' area. Instead of writing programs, CIS professionals installed software packages, customized those packages to work best for the user, and acted as resident computer experts for the user. For many of these professionals, this adjustment wasn't easy.

The biggest challenge to anyone in a computer-oriented career is to keep up with the rapid advancement of technology. Studies of personalities in various professions have found that people in computer-related careers are noticeably different from the general population. These people are more interested in learning new things than in having more responsibilities. Having this interest is an advantage because there is always something new to learn in computers.

Using an on-line information service is one way for users to learn about new advances in technology and associated career opportunities. Many on-line information services provide databases with career information. A growing number of people are using these databases.

The most common ways to keep up with the new technology are to take seminars, access on-line services, read computer periodicals, attend conferences and shows, and join a professional association.

Seminars

Computer-related seminars, usually lasting from one day to one week, are widely available. Typically, they are presented by the developer of a new hardware or software product or by a company specializing in training in a new technology. Most companies recognize the value of sending their staff to these seminars.

More extensive training may be required. Many colleges, universities, and training institutes offer a series of courses leading to a certificate. One example is the Novell Certificate, which was designed by Novell (a network software company) and is licensed by Novell to institutions which show that their staffs have the necessary training and equipment to train students in their software. Other software manufacturers offer certificate programs through institutions.

On-line Services

The Internet and other on-line services have information concerning the latest breakthroughs in technology. When you need to be up-to-the-minute, accessing on-line services is the easiest and fastest way to get the information you have to know.

Computer Magazines, Newspapers, and Journals

Many computer magazines, newspapers, and journals are published weekly, monthly, or quarterly. Some, such as *ComputerWorld*, cover the entire spectrum of computer issues. Others, such as *PCWorld*, *Datamation*, and *InfoSystems*, are aimed at a specific part of the computer industry—for example, microcomputers, technology management, or office automation. Over a hundred of these periodicals are now in print. If you have a particular area of interest, you can probably find a periodical that covers the newest and best happenings in that area.

Conferences and Shows

One way to keep in touch with your profession is to attend conferences and trade shows. **Trade shows** are annual meetings in which computer product manufacturers, designers, and dealers showcase their products. COMDEX, for example, is an annual event held in various locations around the world. The COMDEX in the fall is held in Las Vegas, Nevada. With over 1,500 exhibitors and over 150,000 attendees at a COMDEX show, several companies "roll out" their newest products. Besides displays and brochures about various products, many workshops and product demonstrations are offered at COMDEX. Trade shows can serve as a crash course in what is happening in the area of computer technology that interests you.

New products are often presented at COMDEX.

Professional Organizations

Joining one of the many professional associations can help you keep up with your area of interest, as well as provide valuable contacts for your career. Some associations have local chapters, and most offer publications, seminars, training, and conferences for members. Here are some of the most important organizations:

➤ **Association for Computing Machinery** (**ACM**). Focusing on computer science, this organization features many special-interest groups (SIGs) in such areas as databases, artificial intelligence, microcomputers, and computer graphics.

➤ **Data Processing Management Association** (**DPMA**). This is the premier organization for CIS personnel and managers.

➤ **Institute of Electrical and Electronic Engineers** (**IEEE**). This is the premier professional society for computer engineers.

Interview with Tonya Antonucci

Tonya was born on March 30, 1968, in Biloxi, Mississippi, and now lives in Kirkland, Washington. She graduated from Stanford University in 1990 with a B.A. in political science and a minor in economics.

Interviewer: Where do you work?

Tonya: I'm a product manager in the Online Group at Starwave Corporation. I'm responsible for *Outside Online* on the Internet's World Wide Web. It's an on-line publication for outdoor enthusiasts, offering current news on adventure sports and environmental issues, forum discussions with outdoor experts, advice on traveling and buying gear, and the ability to read and search issues of *Outside* magazine.

Interviewer: What's your job like?

Tonya: Marketing on-line publications is unlike traditional marketing in a few key ways. First, the on-line publication isn't a finished product that ships to target markets. It evolves and changes daily. So I meet with the editorial staff of *Outside Online* almost every day to discuss and plan upcoming content, contests, and on-line surveys, to name a few. I write press releases and prepare informative documents explaining our publication. I'm on-line a lot, generating awareness about *Outside Online* on the Internet and with various communities of users on commercial services, such as America Online. Other activities on any given day include buying advertising, securing new content, forming partnerships for promotional activities, working on long-range marketing plans, and attending trade or consumer shows.

Interviewer: What do you like about your employer and your work?

Tonya: Starwave is a start-up technology company, founded in 1993. We're young people, we work long hours, and we're dedicated to delivering products we believe in. What's uniquely attractive is our market position. We've established ourselves as early leaders in on-line publishing, and there's a certain pride or "top dog" mentality that motivates everyone to keep improving and stay ahead of the curve.

Interviewer: Where do you think future opportunities lie?

Tonya: Given the explosive growth of publishing on the Internet and on-line services, there are opportunities in all facets of my industry. Demands will be high for programmers, writers, editors, and business majors savvy in advertising, marketing, customer support, and operations.

Interviewer: What advice would you give today's college student?

Tonya: If you hope to graduate and move directly into the field of electronic publishing, you face some competition from old-school print publishers and other media professionals who are crossing over to the new medium. Some will be your parents' age, with loads of editing, marketing, and general business experience. College students have access to cutting-edge technology and resources that bring you quickly up to speed. Take advantage of that and get some experience, too. At the same time, be sure you're sharpening your basic

continues

communication skills. Although the electronic medium is different, being able to speak and write intelligently and cogently is still an asset.

Interviewer: Tell us about your computer system.

Tonya: I use a Hewlett-Packard xm2 (486DX2-66 MHz) with 32MB of RAM, running Windows 95. I use Microsoft Excel and Word a lot, but I'm always connected to the Internet via a T-1 line and have 14.4bis external modem connection to America Online, Prodigy, and the Microsoft Network (MSN).

Interviewer: What are your favorite nonwork uses for the computer?

Tonya: Games are a hit with me. I enjoy *Myst*—of course, who doesn't? I have an instructional rock-climbing CD, and I have to admit I'm partial to the new Sting CD we've produced here at Starwave.

Interviewer: What do you do for fun?

Tonya: Soccer is my part-time obsession. I've played soccer ever since I was eight years old. I was assistant coach for the Stanford Women's Soccer team the first year they went to the NCAA final four tournament. I'm still extremely competitive, and that continues to motivate me on the soccer field. I play in a women's league with other former college players, and I'd like nothing more than for our team, the Saints, to win a national championship.

The Impact of Computers on Overall Employment

Although computers are creating new job opportunities, they're also making many old jobs obsolete. One purpose of advanced technology is to free humans from drudgery and make work more efficient, but as a result, fewer workers may be required. For instance, computer-guided robots are taking over many manufacturing jobs that people once held. Those workers fortunate enough to retain their jobs may find that they suffer **deskilling**. Their expert skills have been made obsolete by **automation** (the replacement of human workers by machines), and they now receive lower pay.

The jobs most likely to be eliminated by computers involve repetitive, semiskilled tasks. Consider an example. Some discount stores once required customers to place an order with a clerk. The clerk typed the order into a computer, which relayed the order to the stock room. Stock room workers put the product on a conveyer belt, where the customer picked it up. The stores' management realized that most customers were computer literate enough to punch in the orders themselves, so they replaced almost all the clerks (retaining a few for the computer illiterate) and put the computers where customers could use them directly.

When advancing technology makes an entire job category obsolete, **structural unemployment** has occurred. Structural unemployment differs from the normal up-and-down cycles of layoffs and rehires. People who lose jobs because of structural unemployment are not going to get them back. Their only option is to retrain themselves to work in other careers.

Who will survive—and flourish—in a computer-driven economy? The answer is simple. The survivors will be people with three characteristics:

They are highly educated, they know that education is a lifelong process, and they adapt quickly to change.

The impact of computers on employment isn't all negative. Computers have also opened up opportunities. Many people with disabilities are able to work and support themselves, leading lives they choose, because of support from computers. An extreme example is the Englishman Stephen Hawking. Dr. Hawking is a brilliant theoretical physicist who suffers from a rare neuromotor disease that has left him increasingly paralyzed. He communicates through a computer and slight hand movement. Using this tool, he wrote *A Brief History of Time*, a best-selling book explaining some of his theories of space and time. (One drawback to the technology, says Professor Hawking, is that the voice synthesizer he used was built in America and therefore speaks with an "American accent." For a British citizen, this took getting used to, but now Hawking says that he has completely identified with "his American voice.")

Lesson Summary

➤ Computers have provided an interesting and constantly changing array of job opportunities for people in the computer industry.

➤ The three traditional career areas are computer information systems (CIS), which is business-oriented; computer science, which focuses on hardware and software; and computer engineering, which is oriented to the design of hardware.

➤ Computer engineers and computer scientists are the professionals who are designing the next innovations.

➤ New computer careers that use the latest technology include microcomputer specialist, customer support technician, telecommunications specialist, Webmaster, and network research specialist.

➤ Computer professionals keep up with the latest technology by attending seminars, reading professional periodicals, attending conferences and shows, and participating in professional associations.

➤ Computers create jobs, but they also eliminate them. Technology has created more diverse jobs but has also replaced workers with machines.

➤ Deskilling has resulted in displaced workers. But computers have created more employment opportunities for disabled people by giving them the help they need.

Lesson Review

Key Terms

Association for Computing Machinery (ACM)
automation
computer engineer
computer information systems (CIS)
computer operator
computer repair technician
computer scientist
customer support technician
data entry personnel
Data Processing Management Association (DPMA)
database administrator
deskilling
Institute of Electrical and Electronic Engineers (IEEE)
microcomputer specialist
network research specialist
optical character recognition (OCR)
programmers
structural unemployment
systems analyst
telecommunications specialist
trade show
Webmaster

Matching

In the blank next to each of the following terms or phrases, write the letter of the corresponding term or phrase.

_____ 1. Field most concerned with designing hardware

_____ 2. COMDEX

_____ 3. Is concerned with widespread computer issues

_____ 4. Computer science organization

_____ 5. CIS organization

_____ 6. Results from automation of job

_____ 7. Special interest group

_____ 8. Is concerned with data security

_____ 9. Specializes in systems software

_____ 10. Has mostly microcomputer coverage

a. database administrator
b. computer scientist
c. computer engineering
d. *ComputerWorld*
e. *PCWorld*
f. trade show
g. SIG
h. ACM
i. DPMA
j. deskilling

Multiple Choice

Circle the letter of the correct choice for each of the following.

1. Which of the following personnel key in data from source documents and have a poor career outlook?
   a. computer operators
   b. microcomputer specialists
   c. data entry personnel
   d. data librarians

2. Which of the following computer career areas usually requires education in business as well as computers?
   a. computer information systems
   b. computer science
   c. computer engineering
   d. all of the above

3. Which of the following computer careers involves designing new hardware?

    a. computer information systems

    b. computer science

    c. computer engineering

    d. all of the above

4. Which of the following is a professional organization for computer engineers?

    a. Association for Computing Machinery (ACM)

    b. Data Processing Management Association (DPMA)

    c. Institute of Electrical and Electronic Engineers (IEEE)

    d. none of the above

5. The career that involves creating and maintaining a company's Web page on the Internet is called what?

    a. Webmaker

    b. World Wide Web specialist

    c. Webmaster

    d. telecommunications specialist

6. Which of the following is *not* true about systems analysts?

    a. They are concerned about all information processing in an organization.

    b. They are primarily concerned about programming systems.

    c. They devise new approaches to process data.

    d. They are concerned about data, people, and processes.

7. How do computer professionals try to keep up with changes in their field?

    a. reading magazines, newspapers, and journals

    b. attending trade shows

    c. belonging to professional organizations

    d. all of the above

8. Which of the following is *not* a new career in the computer industry?

    a. systems programmer

    b. customer support technician

    c. telecommunications specialist

    d. microcomputer specialist

9. What characteristic will people who are most likely to do well in the new job market have?

    a. computer literate

    b. adaptable to change

    c. educated

    d. all of the above

10. Which computer career area does the most systems software development?

    a. computer information systems

    b. computer science

    c. computer engineering

    d. all of the above

Completion

In the blank provided, write the correct answer for each of the following.

1. The employment outlook for computer programmers is _____.

2. The job that combines the duties of computer programmers and systems analysts is known as _____.

3. The technology that is reducing the opportunities for data entry personnel is _____.

4. Within the computer information systems area, the preferred educational level for systems analysts is _____.

5. The annual meeting in which computer product manufacturers, designers, and dealers showcase their products is called a(n) _____.

6. The professional organization for CIS personnel and managers is _____.

7. Computers have helped employment opportunities for people with _____.

8. The replacement of human workers with machines is called _____.

9. When automobiles reduced the use of horses and therefore the demand for blacksmiths, the resultant unemployment would be called _____.

10. Overall, the employment opportunities in the computer industry are projected to be _____.

Review

On a separate sheet of paper, answer the following questions.

1. What is the difference between a career in CIS and a career in computer science?

2. How does computer engineering differ from computer science?

3. How does the typical computer professional adjust to the constant change in the computer industry?

4. List some computer-related professional organizations and their areas of focus.

5. What are the negative effects that computers are having on general employment?

6. What are three new career opportunities in the computer industry? What is the major focus of each of these?

7. List the most common ways for a computer professional to keep up with new technology.

8. What is the difference between a computer operator and a computer repair technician?

9. How do the educational requirements for the three traditional computer careers differ? How are they similar?

10. What are the differences between the job of telecommunications specialist and database administrator?

Critical Thinking

On a separate sheet of paper, answer the following questions.

1. What is the difference between being a computer operator and a computer user? What is the focus of each role?

2. If careers in the computer industry have such a good outlook, why doesn't everyone go into those careers? How important is aptitude and personality when selecting a career?

3. If you were an official for a union in an industry that was just starting to automate, what would you establish as your long-term goals for your union membership?

4. What education and training would you think a company would want for a customer service technician?

5. What effect do you think computers will have on the career you are currently preparing for?

Further Discovery

The Computer Consultant's Workbook. Janet Ruhl (Leverett, MA: Technion Books, 1996).

How to be a Successful Computer Consultant. Alan R. Simon (New York: McGraw-Hill, 1994).

Occupational Outlook Handbook, 1994-1995 Edition. U.S. Department of Labor, Bureau of Labor Statistics (Lincolnwood, IL: Passport Books, 1994).

The Programmer's Job Handbook. Gene Wang (Berkeley, CA: Osborne, 1996).

 # On-line Discovery

You can access the Internet resources for the following questions by going to the Que Education and Training Web site at URL http://www.ciyf98.com/discovery. From this page, click the link for Lesson 10A and then click the link to the resource you want to access.

1. The **Association for Computing Machinery** (**ACM**) is the foremost professional association for people in the computing professions, and its members come from both industry and academia. The ACM home page (http://www.acm.org) provides much information for computing professionals, including publications, conferences and events, and career information. Browse the ACM home page and particularly the "Career Opportunities and Development" section. What kinds of careers did you find out about? What kinds of organizations hire computing professionals and in what capacities? How might you get started establishing yourself in a computing profession?

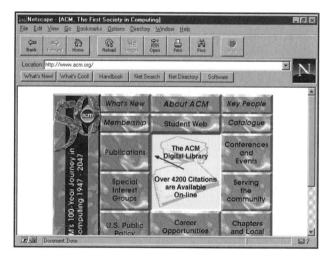

2. **CareerWEB** (http://www.cweb.com) is a job-posting service available over the Web. Companies with jobs available can post them through CareerWEB, and people wanting jobs can post their resumes and even submit them electronically to companies with positions to fill. CareerWEB positions can be searched by both location and job category. Perform a search for positions available in the computing fields. What kinds of job titles are common? What kinds of skills and degrees are generally called for? What types of companies most commonly have computing positions available?

LESSON
10B

Business and Industry

Outline

Retail
Banking and Finance
The Stock Market
Computers and the Law
Manufacturing

Learning Objectives

When you have finished reading this lesson, you will be able to

➤ Explain the UPC code and its advantages

➤ Understand the advantages of point-of-sale terminals

➤ Discuss different forms of electronic banking and potential problems associated with electronic banking

➤ List uses of the computer in the stock market

➤ Discuss different ways in which computers are used in the legal profession

➤ Understand how computers have changed manufacturing procedures

Business and industry have changed dramatically since the first computer was sold in 1951. Today, it is difficult to imagine how businesses could operate without computers. The current growth in international business and industrial development would not be possible without computer communications. Our entire economy is based on the availability of data, whether it is credit, financial, organizational, or legal data. Without the computer, we would be adrift and sinking in an ocean of paper.

Retail

In the past twenty-five years, computers have transformed retail marketing. One of the newest tools in retail marketing is the interactive kiosk. The kiosk presents the customer with a number of interactive video screens and adapts to the customer's choices. Macy's in New York recently installed a five-foot-tall interactive information kiosk in the boys' department. Young shoppers can use a touch-screen to indicate their height and weight in order to determine the perfect size pants. The kiosk also plays music and runs promotional videos on other screens. Nabisco Foods used four seven-foot-tall kiosks to promote its products at the National Restaurant Association trade show. Because information kiosks require expertise to design and program, many companies go to outside firms that specialize in this new form of marketing.

Courtesy of International Business Machines Corporation

Point-of-sale terminals can be adapted to meet the specific inventory needs of restaurants and various merchandising businesses.

Courtesy of International Business Machines Corporation

Courtesy of International Business Machines Corporation

Think about the last time you went shopping. Gone is the conventional cash register. Today's "cash registers" are really **point-of-sale (POS) terminals** connected to a central computer. The central computer locates the product in a database stored on disk, determines the current selling price, and automatically updates the store inventory.

Home on the Range

We know that computers are making an impact in every part of our lives, but we often think this impact is greatest on "city folks." However, computers and technology are also making big changes in farming and ranching.

Computer technology has been used for years to help identify animals. Zoos, horse breeders, research labs, and pet owners have long had the option of inserting a microchip under the skin of their animals. These microchips, called **transponders**, are about the size of a grain of rice. Each transponder contains unique identification information that enables someone to prove ownership of the animal. When a scanner is passed over the transponder, it picks up a radio frequency generated by the scanner. This energizes the chip, and it sends back the identification number contained within it. The scanner can either display the identification number or send it to an attached personal computer. When the identification number is retrieved from a computerized registry, it indicates any stored information about the animal, including ownership.

The same technology has been used in Thailand to help crocodile farmers. In Asia, crocodile farms are big business—there is a large demand for goods made from crocodile skin as well as for the meat of the animal. After the United Nations implemented regulations restricting the trade of wild crocodiles to protect them, the Thai government required farmers to place microchip identification tags under the tail skin of the farm-raised crocodiles shortly after birth. These tags satisfy United Nations requirements of protecting the wild animals. (The farm-raised variety enjoy no such protection.) Farmers and food processors can use the microchip identification later to prove that a crocodile was raised on a farm instead of caught in the wild or smuggled into the facility.

Photographs courtesy of InfoPet Identification Systems, Inc.

In the American West, a variation on the implanted transponder is being used by cattle ranchers to help manage their herds. Instead of being planted under the skin, the microchip is encased in a capsule about the size of a dinner mint, and then attached to the ear of the cattle shortly after birth. (Government restrictions do not allow implanting in animals destined for the dinner table.) The chip contains information about the sex, birth date, heredity, ownership, and potential health problems of the animal. As the cattle move through the ranch, sensors register the information from the microchip and send it to a PC. Thus, ranchers can track movement and

continues

collect information such as weight (if the animal passes over a scale) and dietary supplements received. It is only a short step from there for ranchers to calculate costs on an animal-by-animal basis—a feature that is much more difficult with traditional branding or tagging.

As an industry, transponder technology for animal management and tracking is still in its infancy. Costs for the chips are relatively high (around $10 to $15 per chip, implanted) but should become lower as their use becomes more widespread. The universal use of such devices will occur eventually as standards among different manufacturers are developed.

In Lesson 2C, you learned that the computer can access the cost of an item based on the **universal product code** (**UPC**) encoded on a label or tag and either keyed by the checker or read with a scanner. The UPC identifies the item with a series of bars. The code is based on the width of the bars and the space between the bars. Use of the UPC code has resulted in faster processing of items, fewer price errors, and decreased inventory costs.

Some stores allow customers to use a **debit card** to purchase groceries. The debit card entered in the store's computer directs your bank to transfer funds electronically from your bank account to the store account. Some of the more sophisticated debit card devices show your itemized bill and run a video advertisement for the store.

When you first order a prescription from a pharmacy, the pharmacist enters your personal data, including insurance information, into a computer. All prescriptions that you order from that pharmacy are tracked in your computer record. Using the computer makes it easy for the pharmacy to bill insurance companies and renew prescriptions. The charges for the medicine are determined from a UPC label. All the data is entered into the store computer, so inventory is updated automatically.

Experts predict even more changes in the retail industry as "social computing" becomes more popular. **Social computing**, a term coined by William Bluestein of Forrester Research, is the capability to order goods electronically. A consumer in Los Angeles, for example, can browse the offerings of a gourmet food store located in Hong Kong by using a microcomputer to access an information service. The order is placed electronically, and the items are automatically billed to the customer's charge card and delivered to the customer's door.

A more complex form of social computing known as **electronic data interchange** (**EDI**) is used by companies that exchange information with suppliers and manufacturers using information services. EDI enables a purchasing department to electronically enter an order with a supplier. The supplier's computer informs the production department that the order needs to be filled, and informs the shipping department where the completed items should be sent. Recent studies conducted by the Energy Department's Lawrence Livermore Laboratory in California show that more than 100,000 companies use EDI regularly.

Banking and Finance

Millions of dollars are transferred electronically within the United States every day. The "cashless society"—long predicted by computer experts—is quickly becoming a reality.

BITS
Using MICR systems, banks process over forty billion checks in the United States every year.

The banking industry was a pioneer in using computers for data input. The Magnetic Ink Character Recognition (MICR) system, which you learned about in Lesson 2C, was invented in 1956. Despite the speed and efficiency of MICR, many banking customers are moving away from using checks. **Electronic funds transfer** (**EFT**) systems and **automated teller machines** (**ATMs**) account for a growing percentage of all banking transactions. EFT enables employees to have their payroll checks automatically deposited to their accounts or have regular monthly payments deducted automatically.

Imagine that you are out shopping on a Saturday and you see the CD player you have been wanting—on sale for an unbelievable price. You don't have the money in your checking account to pay for it, but you do have some extra money in your savings account. You have to be at work at 8:00 A.M. on Monday morning, you have a meeting late Monday afternoon, and your bank is open from 10:00 A.M. to 5:00 P.M. In the past, you would hope that your check didn't clear until Tuesday, or you would not purchase the CD player. With EFT, this problem doesn't exist. You purchase the CD player, go home, call the bank, and electronically transfer the money from your savings account to your checking account to cover the check.

BITS
ATMs are available 24 hours a day, 7 days a week. ATM networks link the ATMs of many different banks so that customers have a wide range of banking locations.

If you don't like to bank over the telephone, you can stop at a convenient ATM on your way home. An ATM is a specialized computer terminal that enables customers to make deposits and withdraw funds without having to wait inside the bank. Customers can also use the ATM to transfer funds between accounts.

ATMs can be found both inside and outside banks, stores, shopping malls, hotels, and casinos. The availability of ATMs has introduced new dangers. A customer inserts a debit card and then keys in a **personal identification number** (**PIN**). ATMs are vulnerable to electronic theft, and customers are vulnerable while conducting their transactions. Bank customers are warned not to keep their secret personal identification numbers with their ATM cards. (The ATM card cannot be used without the PIN.) AT&T is pioneering an ATM (developed by NCR, which AT&T purchased in 1991) that identifies customers by voice. Sensar Inc. has developed a security system for ATMs, known as IrisIdent, that can identify customers by scanning the iris of a person's eye. The scanned image is compared with a large database to verify the match. Both of these new ATMs have been designed to help protect bank customers from thieves using stolen ATM cards. Both are a part of a new field known as **biometric identification,** which uses unique physical characteristics, instead of a driver's license, credit cards, or debit cards, to confirm an individual's identity.

The use of EFT and ATMs raises concerns about privacy. When a customer uses these computerized banking tools, a complete chronological record of all transactions is maintained. This could, conceivably, permit a bank or the government to monitor the customer's lifestyle and location.

A new form of debit card that will help to protect individual privacy and bring about the "cashless society" is currently being tested. Imagine never needing to handle coins or checking to be certain that you have received the correct amount of change from a purchase. In the English town of Swindon, this is already a reality. People pay for everything from McDonald's hamburgers to clothing by using a bank card. The system, known as Mondex, is being tested by two of Britain's leading banks. The Mondex card disburses money that has been loaded onto a microchip from an ATM. The system results in quicker transactions, fewer errors, and freedom from dealing with bills and coins. Of course, there is also a downside to the Mondex system: If lost or stolen, the money loaded onto the card can be spent by anyone, just like cash. Banks in the United States are negotiating to use the Mondex system.

The Stock Market

One of the foundations of the free enterprise system is the stock market, which enables individuals to purchase shares in the equity (worth) of a company. When millions of people purchase shares, companies can raise the money necessary to make massive investments—investments big enough to build railroads, create airlines, and manufacture automobiles.

BITS
Stock markets exist in a number of countries. Japan, England, and the United States have the largest stock markets. Computers have opened these markets to international trading.

Computers are changing the way investors trade shares. All transactions are maintained and tracked with mainframe computers. Brokers place their orders electronically, and computers determine appropriate changes in stock prices based on trading activity. Speculators can track the performance of stocks, access current prices, and place buy and sell orders by using their microcomputers.

Soon the trading floor itself will be transformed. Both the American Stock Exchange (AMEX) and the New York Stock Exchange (NYSE) are experimenting with wireless cellular technology. Traditionally, brokers have shouted their transactions across the floor. Now brokers can use personal digital assistants (PDAs) to process orders and transmit information. The result—less paper, less noise, and increased accuracy.

Computers provide investors and financial advisors with instant access to financial data and analysis.

Not everyone agrees that computers have been good for the stock market. Investment firms use **program trading** to analyze stock market trends and obtain buy and sell recommendations on a minute-by-minute basis. Many computers that use this software may say "sell" at the same time, which can lead to wild swings in stock prices. Program trading was identified as a leading cause of the 1987 stock market crash, in which investors lost millions of dollars. Today, some stock exchanges forbid the use of program trading if stock prices rise or fall more than fifty points.

Computers and the Law

Law firms deal with vast amounts of information. To best serve the needs of clients, lawyers must be able to access data quickly, and it must be accurate. In addition to managing large amounts of data pertaining to client cases, law firms must keep abreast of constantly changing laws. And keeping track of calendars and client billing is a nightmare without a good computer program. Legal offices would be drowning in paper files if it weren't for magnetic storage media.

A relatively new legal profession is paralegal services, ranked in the ten fastest-growing occupations by the U.S. Bureau of Labor Statistics.

Paralegals assist with legal research, create legal documents, and use spreadsheets for analyses related to cases. Knowledge of microcomputer applications is a necessity for paralegals.

Increasingly, legal research is accomplished on a microcomputer that uses telecommunications to link with one of several excellent legal databases. The most well-known legal databases are Westlaw and Lexis. Both provide detailed case information available through a variety of search techniques. Databases like these can be searched for cases that are similar to the current case, and those cases can often be cited as precedents.

Even the judicial system has been transformed by the use of computers. Courts calculate alimony and child support payments, keep track of case information, and maintain calendars with specialized computer programs.

The most crucial use of the computer for lawyers is in litigation support. Depositions, which are statements made under oath by parties involved in a legal action, are keyed directly into the computer. Scanning permits evidence and photos to be stored and categorized for easy retrieval. Multimedia, computer graphics, and computer simulations have been found to have significant impact on juries. Eyewitness Animations, a company located in Florida, specializes in computer videos that simulate crime scenes. Animators create a two-dimensional image through a CAD program and import those images into Autodesk's 3D Studio program. Virtual reality may be the next step in crime re-creations.

Photographs courtesy of Autodesk, Inc.

Scenes can be modified and re-created with Autodesk's 3D Studio program. For example, the program enables users to view a hillside with or without buildings.

Manufacturing

Computers are also transforming manufacturing. The use of computers on the manufacturing floor means that fewer workers are needed to create products and that companies can respond quickly to rapidly changing, competitive pressures. A modern assembly floor may contain many robotic arms performing repetitive tasks, supervised by a single human.

Manufacturers are using multimedia to improve their operations. Engineers develop multimedia presentations that show workers exactly what is occurring in the manufacturing processes. In addition to revealing areas that need improvement, graphical presentations can provide a clearer picture of a potentially hazardous condition before it erupts, thereby safeguarding workers.

In the past, a lengthy time gap separated the design of industrial parts (such as an automobile's suspension components) and the retooling of machines for their manufacture. Thanks to computers, that gap is narrowing. As you learned in Lesson 5B, computer-aided design (CAD) applications enable engineers, architects, and artists to create or modify objects quickly. In CAD, the computer monitor replaces a manual drafting table and enables the designer to create three-dimensional images that can be rotated.

Courtesy of Ford Motor Company

An automobile assembly line consists of many computer-controlled robots.

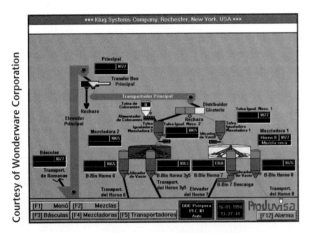

Courtesy of Wonderware Corporation

Glass bottle manufacturing plant (Venezuela)

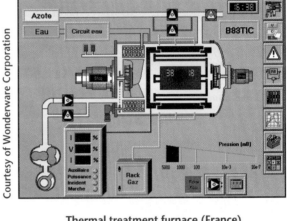

Courtesy of Wonderware Corporation

Thermal treatment furnace (France)

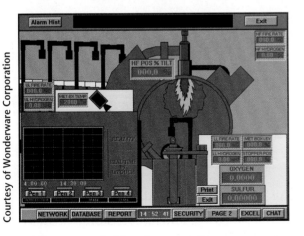

Courtesy of Wonderware Corporation

Molten copper holding furnace making copper rods

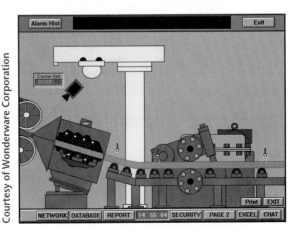

Courtesy of Wonderware Corporation

Rolling machine turning copper rods into copper wire

Wonderware Corporation provides highly graphical and animated representations of manufacturing processes for companies throughout the world. Screen labels, buttons, and menus appear in the operator's native language (shown here in Spanish, French, and English). Workers can view the manufacturing processes and know exactly what is happening without having to understand complicated formulas and math. Alarm buttons alert workers to potential problems.

The CAD output becomes input to computer-aided manufacturing (CAM) equipment that automatically makes modifications to production equipment. CAD/CAM software has been available for mainframes and minicomputers for a long time; only recently have full-featured packages become available for microcomputers and workstations.

Using CAD/CAM applications facilitates the automation of a portion of a manufacturing process. Integration of computer technology into the entire manufacturing process is known as **computer-integrated manufacturing** (**CIM**). CIM uses computers to link the entire procedure, from order entry to production and even to warehousing and distribution. CIM compresses production times into amazingly brief spans. Production cycles that once required weeks or months can be accomplished in days or hours.

Just-in-time (**JIT**) **manufacturing** monitors inventory and triggers the manufacturing process only when inventory levels are sufficiently diminished. JIT enables manufacturers to order supplies as they are needed for production and to maintain minimal inventory levels.

The user views a stereoscopic image through the head-mounted display. The sensor glove permits the user to manipulate objects in the virtual environment.

Manufacturers are also using virtual reality to test various designs. **Virtual reality** (**VR**) is a computer system that immerses the user in the illusion of a computer-generated world. The user, wearing a special **head-mounted display** (**HMD**) and a sensor glove, navigates through this world at will. The computer interactively adjusts the output according to the user's input. Using virtual reality, manufacturers can perform many different tests on various designs without destroying expensive models. Just-in-time manufacturing and the testing of designs using virtual reality systems reduce production costs.

Courtesy of Ford Motor Company

Courtesy of Ford Motor Company

Lesson Summary

➤ Retail stores use point-of-sale terminals to retrieve product prices and update inventory.

➤ Customers use debit cards to transfer funds directly from their accounts to the store's account.

➤ Social computing and EDI enable customers and suppliers to exchange order information electronically.

➤ Many bank transactions are performed electronically using EFT or ATMs.

➤ The speed of stock trading has been increased by the use of computers.

➤ Law offices use computers for research, billing, and producing legal documents.

➤ Manufacturing firms use computers in every aspect of the manufacturing process.

Lesson Review

Key Terms

automated teller machine (ATM)
biometric identification
computer-integrated man- ufacturing (CIM)
debit card

electronic data inter- change (EDI)
electronic funds transfer (EFT)
head-mounted display (HMD)

just-in-time manufac- turing (JIT)
personal identification number (PIN)
point-of-sale terminal (POS)

program trading
social computing
transponder
universal product code (UPC)
virtual reality (VR)

Matching

In the blank next to each of the following terms or phrases, write the letter of the corresponding term or phrase.

_____ 1. Equipment that automatically makes modifications to production equipment

_____ 2. What an individual using an ATM must key in to access funds and conduct a transaction

_____ 3. Electronic monitoring of inventory to trigger the manufacturing process when needed

_____ 4. Using computers to analyze and trade stocks

_____ 5. Transferring funds between accounts using telecommunications

_____ 6. A marketing tool that contains interactive video displays

_____ 7. Bar codes placed on items to facili- tate computer identification

_____ 8. Companies exchanging information with suppliers and manufacturers electronically

_____ 9. Integration of computer technology throughout the manufacturing process

_____ 10. Using the computer to create and modify three-dimensional images

a. CAD

b. JIT

c. EDI

d. program trading

e. PIN

f. CAM

g. EFT

h. information kiosk

i. UPC

j. CIM

Multiple Choice

Circle the letter of the correct choice for each of the following.

1. Which of the following groups contain items that do *not* belong together?

   a. POS terminals, UPC, debit card

   b. EFT systems, banking industry, ATMs

   c. ordering goods electronically, EDI, social computing

   d. CIM, ATM, program trading

2. Which of the following is *not* a true statement?

   a. Use of the UPC code has decreased inventory costs; however, the number of price errors remains the same.

   b. The debit card enables a store's computer to direct your bank to transfer funds from your account to the store's account.

   c. Social computing is the capability to place an order for goods electronically.

   d. a and b

3. Which of the following represent(s) concerns mentioned in this lesson?

   a. ATMs are vulnerable to electronic theft.

   b. Computerized records of all transactions might permit a bank or the government to monitor a customer's lifestyle and location.

   c. New voice IDs, which have replaced the PIN approach, are inaccurate.

   d. a and b

4. In which of the following ways do lawyers use computers?

   a. to key depositions directly into the computer

   b. to scan photos and evidence into computers

   c. to search databases for cases with similar characteristics

   d. all of the above

5. Transferring dollars electronically is *not* associated with which of following?

   a. EDI

   b. cashless society

   c. just-in-time approach

   d. social computing concept

6. What is program trading?

   a. individuals sharing and copying computer programs

   b. using the computer to analyze and trade stocks

   c. a term to describe selling used programs

   d. a part of JIT processing

7. What do you use a debit card for?

   a. to borrow money from a company for a short time

   b. to gain access to a hotel room

   c. to transfer money from your account to another account

   d. to identify an individual for insurance purposes

8. Point-of-sale terminals have replaced what?

   a. bank tellers

   b. MICR equipment that banks used

   c. cash registers

   d. credit cards

9. What do you call the new marketing tool that features interactive video screens?

   a. information kiosk

   b. presentation package

   c. CAD/CAM program

   d. ATM

10. What are Magnetic Ink Character Recognition systems used for?

   a. to read UPC codes

   b. to research legal cases

   c. to program robotic equipment for manufacturing

   d. to process checks

Completion

In the blank provided, write the correct answer for each of the following.

1. A user wears a(n) _____ and _____ when experiencing virtual reality.

2. _____ is the ability of individuals to order goods electronically.

3. ATMs and EFT are indications that the _____ society is becoming a reality.

4. A(n) _____ can be used instead of cash to pay for goods.

5. _____ are used in manufacturing plants to assemble products.

6. All stock transactions are maintained and tracked using _____.

7. A(n) _____ and a card are required to use an ATM machine.

8. _____ immerses the user in a computer-generated world.

9. _____ is the most crucial use of computers for lawyers.

10. A(n) _____ assists in legal research and document preparation.

Review

On a separate sheet of paper, answer the following questions.

1. What is a UPC code? What are some of its advantages?

2. In what ways do computers aid stock market transactions?

3. How are CAD and CAM related?

4. How does JIT manufacturing work together with CIM?

5. How are computers helping paralegals?

6. How are information kiosks used?

7. What is the difference between a debit card and a credit card?

8. How is virtual reality used in manufacturing?

9. What is a PIN and how is it used?

10. What is EDI?

Critical Thinking

On a separate sheet of paper, answer the following questions.

1. Do you think that defendants in criminal cases will be aided or harmed by having juries exposed to case-related multimedia, computer simulations, and crime reenactments?

2. What kinds of tasks do you think a robot would do well in the automobile manufacturing process?

3. What advantages and disadvantages can you see in using computerized databases to search for law cases with characteristics similar to those of the current case?

4. Do you foresee problems with returning goods, especially foods, through the social computing approach?

5. How have EFT transactions changed the way the banking industry conducts business?

Further Discovery

The Digital Economy: Promise and Peril in the Age of Networked Intelligence. Don Tapscott (New York: McGraw-Hill, 1996).

Frontiers of Electronic Commerce. Ravi Kalakota and Andrew B. Whinston (Reading, MA: Addison-Wesley, 1996).

Global Advantage on the Internet: From Corporate Connectivity to International Competitiveness. (New York: Van Nostrand Reinhold, 1996).

Information Systems: A Management Perspective. Steven Alter (Reading, MA: Benjamin/Cummings, 1996).

No Chairs Make for Short Meetings and Other Business Maxims from Dad. Richard Rybolt (New York: Plume Books, 1994).

The Reengineering Revolution. Michael Hammer and Steven Stanton (New York: HarperBusiness, 1995).

Team-Based Problem Solver. Joan P. Klubnik and Penny F. Greenwood (Homewood, IL: Irwin, 1994).

 # On-line Discovery

You can access the Internet resources for the following questions by going to the Que Education and Training Web site at URL http://www.ciyf98.com/discovery. From this page, click the link for Lesson 10B and then click the link to the resource you want to access.

1. **Hoover's Online** (http://www.hoovers.com) is a useful source of business information available via the Web. Although Hoover's is a commercial resource and requires payment for most services, it also provides much information free of charge. Use Hoover's to explore three companies of your choice. What types of information does Hoover's provide about your companies? Do they have sites on the World Wide Web? What other information about your companies does Hoover's link to? Finally, if you were an amateur investor, how might a service like Hoover's Online help you in choosing companies to invest in?

2. **CommerceNet** (http://www.commerce.net) is a not-for-profit organization that provides information to companies wanting to do business over the Internet. CommerceNet has collected on its home page many resources related to commerce over the Internet. What kinds of issues do companies wanting to do business on the Internet face? What kinds of resources does CommerceNet provide?

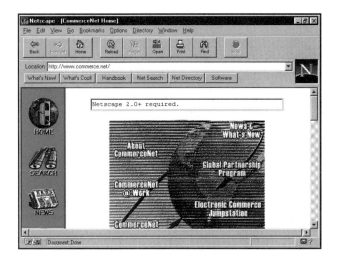

LESSON 10C

Science and Medicine

Outline

Learning Objectives

When you have finished reading this lesson, you will be able to

➤ Explain how computers are aiding scientific research

➤ Discuss how computer simulations are extending the frontiers of human knowledge

➤ Provide examples of how computers are aiding patients and diagnosing medical conditions

➤ Discuss the role of computers in medical research

➤ Provide examples of how computers are helping the disabled be more independent

➤ Explain why computers are playing a growing role in sports and improving individual performance

When Galileo aimed his crude telescope at the heavens, a new age of science began—an age in which technology extends the scientist's range of perception. Instruments such as electron microscopes enable us to perceive the shapes of atoms, and radio telescopes show us the far reaches of the universe. Today, the computer is bringing about another revolution in science. Thanks to the computer, we can tackle problems so complex that they could not have been investigated without the computer's help.

The results are sure to affect your life. Increasingly, the challenges we face have one thing in common: They are unbelievably complex. Cancer, for instance, isn't just one disease; it's a loose collection of thousands of diseases, and their different causes are bound up in the fabulous complexity of the human genetic code. Without the computer, it would have taken dozens or even hundreds of years of human labor to sift through known genetic patterns to make a match that is suspected to contribute to disease. Now a supercomputer can do the job in minutes.

Science

Computers are extending scientists' reach by enabling researchers to pool knowledge, use exploratory robots, track complex behaviors, and simulate complex systems.

Pooling Knowledge: The Human Genome Project

The **Human Genome Project** is one of the most exciting research efforts undertaken in many years, perhaps ever. This project seeks to map the complete genetic plan of a human being. Such a goal would not be possible without the computer's aid.

Deoxyribonucleic acid, or DNA, is known as the thread of life. It is a spiral-staircase-shaped molecule found in the nucleus of cells of living things. The specific makeup of DNA determines what that living thing is. Like all living things, every human has a specific DNA pattern. The objective of the Human Genome

Courtesy of The Perkin-Elmer Corporation, Applied Biosystems Division

The ABI 373 DNA Sequencer is used to sequence, size, and quantitate DNA.

Project is to determine what pieces human DNA has and what each of these pieces (genes) contributes to the human.

This research project is being carried out by scientists around the world. One tool that has given the project worldwide scope is the Internet. When a laboratory in Paris, France, has a breakthrough, the scientists immediately communicate their findings, through the Internet, to scientists in the United States, Japan, Australia, the United Kingdom, and other countries. Once the findings are independently verified, the other groups know to work on other gene pairings.

The ABI 394 DNA synthesizer uses software that can be customized for specific research requirements.

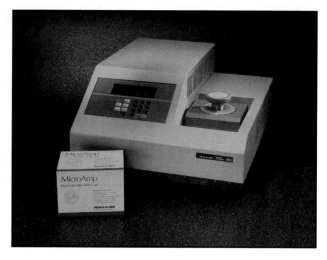

The GeneAmp PCR System 9600 is a microprocessor-controlled system for Polymerase Chain Reaction (PCR). It is used in the Human Genome Project, biomedical research, genetic analysis, and other demanding applications.

Because billions of pairs of genes are in the human genome, careful records of identifications of pairs must be kept. Maintaining these records ensures that no effort will be wasted on identification duplication and that no pair will be overlooked. The database that controls the records is also on a computer.

Exploring the Unknown: Robotics

A robot named Dante II was used by scientists to try to monitor volcanic activity in Alaska's Mount Spurr. The spiderlike robot was controlled by commands sent by satellite from Anchorage, many miles away. Dante II's mission was to creep up to the edge of this volcano, which had erupted in 1992 and 1993, and peer over the volcano's edge to transmit images to scientists. Dante II used a laser imaging system and video cameras to transmit the images to satellites. These images were then forwarded by satellite to Anchorage and to the Ames Research Center in California.

Although the robot had difficulty with the terrain, the scientists discovered information about active volcanoes by using robots as remote explorers. Dante II is being modified to explore the surface of Mars or the moons of Jupiter.

Scientists used the Internet to guide Dante II into Mt. Spurr in Alaska.

Dante II (ten feet tall and ten feet wide) was used to descend into the crater of a volcano.

Robots have also been used to study underwater environments. Oceanographers used a robot, computers, and computer communication—specifically the Internet—to explore the bottom of the Gulf of California. The robot was controlled by computers on a nearby ship. Data from the robot was communicated through the Internet from the ship to researchers around the world.

Most scientific breakthroughs are not as much of a result of the data collected as they are of the analysis of the data. When observations are shared with researchers around the world, the chances of major breakthroughs are greater.

Images were transmitted by satellite from the volcano to the scientists.

Tracking Complex Phenomena

Farmers in eastern Oregon are working with scientists to analyze data from satellites in order to understand crop growth. The computers are used to interpret data about solar ray reflections to determine areas of active photosynthesis. The results can show irrigation equipment failure, drainage problems, pest infestations, and nutrient stress. Solar ray reflections can also be interpreted to aid in analyzing land use, assessing flood damage, and predicting avalanches.

Conserving the environment requires understanding many aspects of wildlife in the wilderness areas of earth. Natural scientists are tracking various species of wildlife to determine their movements and the effects of weather patterns on their lives. The key to this research is the ability to observe large numbers of wildlife and to observe the behavior of single animals in groups—both without the observer's presence influencing the animals' behavior. One effective way to accomplish this goal is to tag individual animals in their environments and then use satellite **tracking devices** to track either a group of animals or an individual animal. The signals picked up by the satellite contain the data necessary for either method of tracking. The enormous amount of data that the satellite picks up can be processed by a computer—a task that would overwhelm an individual or even a group of individuals.

In physics labs around the world, scientists are trying to prove theories on the nature of matter. They have been able to isolate and describe *quarks* as the basis of atomic particles. Currently, they are closing in on the last quark, called the top quark. Because quarks are subatomic in size, they are not visible. Physicists "find" them by tracking billions of atomic collisions per second and tracing the results back to extrapolate about the behavior of the quark. One scientist compared it to starting with the U.S. national debt and processing it down to $12. Such tracking and processing are possible only with the processing power of computers.

Simulating Complex Systems

Models and simulations are tools that scientists have been using for years. Now computers can enhance these models and simulations by using much larger bases of data. The result is greater accuracy and precision than ever before. The computer processing does not improve the correctness or appropriateness of the model; that is up to the community of scientists. But the scope and clarity of the model or simulation are enhanced by use of the computer.

Meteorologists have been predicting the weather based on models of the earth's atmosphere for years. Today, they can collect observations from people, measuring devices, and satellites. Meteorologists can then process the data, apply it to a model, and get more accurate predictions. The model has not changed a great deal, but the amount of data that can be fed into the model is much greater and has fewer "blind" spots. The result is greater accuracy.

Communicating over the Internet, scientists and other interested people could discuss the collision of the Shoemaker-Levy 9 comet with Jupiter.

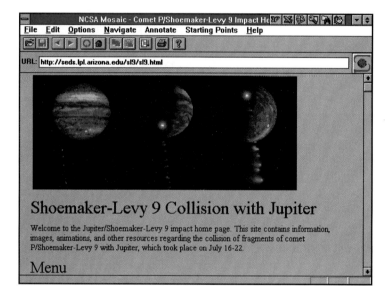

The many photographs you may have seen of Mars or Jupiter are also simulations. The data from the Hubble Space Telescope is sent back to earth as binary numbers (called digital form). Here computers interpret those numbers and create the pictures you have seen. The pictures from that digital form are not the clear, colored pictures that were published; the original images were much less distinct. The computers used mathematical models to interpret the data and fill in areas that were not clear. Astronomers were more interested in the data that was sent back, used to interpret levels of various gases emitted and radiation levels. Again, computers were used to interpret the data.

TechTalk
An AutoCAD program is a computer-aided design program developed by Autodesk and widely used for professional CAD applications.

Archeologists recently used an AutoCAD program with a surface-mapping program to capture detailed information about the Sphinx in Egypt. Combining the new information with previously known historical data, the archeologists were able to create photographs that re-create the image of the original Sphinx. The data and models can be used when the Sphinx requires maintenance and repair from deterioration.

Medicine

Computers are used in medical research, in medical education, and in aiding people with limitations because of medical conditions. Do these uses add up to a health care breakthrough? You be the judge.

Patient Care

Patient care includes the diagnosis and treatment of medical conditions. **Imaging devices** are important tools for diagnosis. Unlike X-rays that take one image of the body part, imaging devices today take a number of images.

Images are produced in digital form for the computer to analyze. The picture that the computer builds is much more complete than any picture generated before the use of computers. The level of detail helps medical experts diagnose some diseases earlier than was previously possible. Early diagnosis significantly improves a patient's chance for recovery. These imaging devices include the CAT (computerized axial tomography) scanner, MRI (magnetic resonance imaging), and ultrasound imaging.

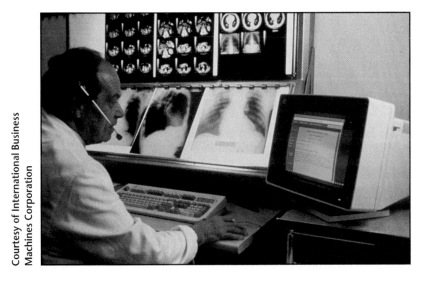

Courtesy of International Business Machines Corporation

Computerized imaging devices provide many images.

Although imaging devices, based on computer technology now several years old, are accepted tools, they are not always enough. One limitation to these devices is that they still need to be read and interpreted by a radiology expert. A recent addition to the imaging field is **teleradiology**. The imaging signals are sent, in binary form, over fiber-optic communication lines to imaging output equipment some distance away so that the radiology expert can read and interpret the images. Using this computer technology can help reduce overall radiology costs.

Computers are also used to help doctors explain problems and suggested treatments to patients. Decision support systems have been developed to answer patients' questions about upcoming surgical procedures. Patients can access these systems to help them make informed decisions.

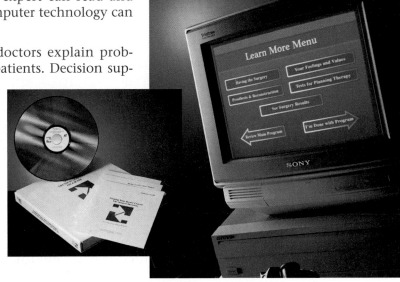

Photographs courtesy of Sony Electronics, Inc.

Decision support systems provide critical information to patients who are trying to determine which option to choose.

Computers Predict the Weather

In many places in the United States, the saying is "If you don't like the weather, wait ten minutes and it will change." That saying illustrates the challenges faced by those who predict the weather.

According to the National Climatic Data Center (NCDC), which manages and disseminates global environmental data, evidence is mounting that the global climate is changing.

Improvements in data sensor technology and communications provide the NCDC with huge volumes of data. One of its major challenges is to receive and process the digital data in real time. The new collected data is added to historical archive data to create reference databases for use in climate change research.

The NCDC is one of three National Oceanic and Atmosphere Administration (NOAA) data centers. The others are the National Oceanographic Data Center in Washington, D.C., and the National Geophysical Data Center in Boulder, Colorado. The mission of the NOAA is to describe and predict changes in the Earth's environment, manage the nation's ocean and coastal resources, and promote global stewardship of the world's oceans and atmosphere.

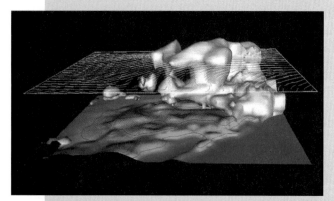

Courtesy of San Diego Supercomputer Center

NOAA's research depends on advances in high-end computing and on the collection and dissemination of environmental data. Increased computing power will enable higher resolution in the current models of the Earth's atmosphere-ocean system, making possible more accurate representation of weather fronts and ocean eddies and eliminating distortions due to clouds. More accurate NOAA models will improve understanding of climate and weather systems.

Using the Internet, NOAA researchers access massively parallel supercomputer systems at distant locations. Geographically distributed researchers collaborate to share resources and data by accessing these systems remotely from high-performance workstations.

NOAA's Forecast Systems Laboratory has developed models to provide high-resolution forecasts on both national and regional levels that support operational and aviation meteorology. These models are useful to both the Federal Aviation Administration and the National Weather Service.

The NOAA Central Computer Facility is managed and operated by the National Meteorological Center, which is part of the National Weather Service (NWS). It runs models that track hurricanes, ocean wave height, and short-term climate changes, such as those associated with hurricanes and tornadoes. Model output typically consists of predicted rainfall, winds, temperature, and humidity at various forecast intervals.

A Cray C90 supercomputer was added to the NWS hardware arsenal in May of 1994. The C90 is useful in tracking hurricanes, as well as routing airplanes around turbulent weather. Precipitation forecasts benefit agricultural and marine activities. Marine predictions using the Cray include the continued development of a wave forecast model. Sea ice prediction models are also being tested.

Courtesy of International Business Machines Corporation

Another of NOAA's projects is to operate the United States' environmental satellites. The primary user of the satellite data is the NWS, but information is also shared

continues

with various other federal agencies (Agriculture, Interior, Defense, and Transportation Departments); other countries such as Japan, India, Russia, European Space Agency members, and the United Kingdom; and the private sector.

As they say, the only thing that's certain about the weather is that it's going to change. And it probably did in the time it took you to read this.

Not only patients but also medical students can use computerized systems for learning. A computerized animated anatomy of the entire human body has even been developed. Run on a personal computer, the program enables patients and students to peel away—one layer at a time—the skin, muscles, internal organs, and skeleton, which can then be manipulated on-screen. It's an autopsy without the cadaver! Medical students can repeat the procedures as often as needed before working on real bodies.

A similar tool is available from the University of Colorado and can be accessed through the Internet with the proper authorization. The database contains 1,771 cross sections of a male cadaver; a similar database is being developed for a female cadaver.

The Johns Hopkins University School of Medicine and the University of Maryland Medical Center have created a special network to consult interactively on the diagnosis and treatment of patients with a specific problem. The first application of this network benefited children born with abnormal skulls. Network linkups like this will enable doctors anywhere who have the communications equipment but not the special expertise to tap into the knowledge base of experts elsewhere. Such networks also enable doctors to consult with other experts without extensive travel. All the data that they need for reference is portable.

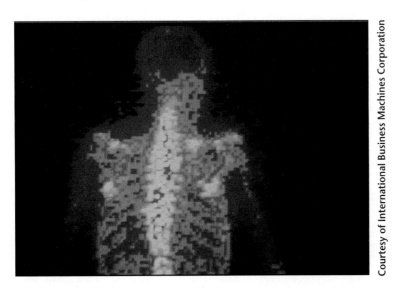

Courtesy of International Business Machines Corporation

Complex images can be transmitted to medical experts for consultation through computers using a special network.

Computers have been used as tools to collect and manipulate data for decades, but doctors are now finding ways to use that simple computer power to improve patient care and reduce costs. HMOs are using computers to track care for clients with diseases such as diabetes and cancer. In an HMO setting, profits are maximized when the health of the clients is maximized. Tracking patients with diabetes to ensure that they have their eyes and feet checked regularly and have blood sugar screening tests periodically can reduce the number of complications from the disease, thereby reducing the cost of caring for the client over the long term. HMO giant Kaiser Permanente has recently created such a database and anticipates saving money as well as lives.

 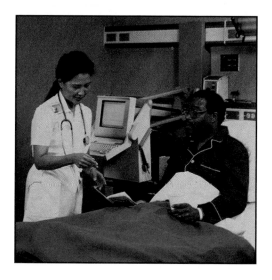

Computer-controlled devices have vastly improved the precision of many surgical procedures, thus shortening the patient's recovery time.

Orthopedic surgeons use computers to control the contouring of a joint, such as a hip joint, during surgery. The technology is similar to the way computers control lathes or milling machines in factories. Computers also control lasers when they are used to treat cataracts. The precision of a computer-controlled tool is much greater than anything the surgeon can do unaided.

Research

The computer is a common tool used during medical research. Researchers can use computers to control an experiment, to record the data and analyze it, to communicate with other doctors around the world, and to model molecules. Research in cardiology, being conducted at Techion/Israel Institute of Technology in Haifa, Israel, is finding people who are at risk for sudden heart attacks that are often fatal. The doctors are using a computer to analyze data from electrocardiograph (EKG) equipment. The output variations, which are too small for the human eye to discern, are proving to be predictors of later severe heart attacks. And the people at risk do not necessarily exhibit other indicators associated with the likelihood of a future heart attack. Identification before the attack is saving lives.

Computers can interpret data to create the structure of a molecule, especially complex molecules such as proteins. As a result, drugs can be designed that will bind to a protein molecule and thus act as an inhibitor against some viruses. Part of this drug development is performed on the computer. The process saves time in trying thousands of drug variations to find the best one with the fewest side effects.

The computer can be used to collect data from patients who are taking experimental drugs or trying other therapies. The data can be collected faster, and correlations can be found more quickly. The doctors can conclude whether a treatment is promising and should be continued or whether it needs to be abandoned.

MEDLINE is a computer database developed by the National Library of Medicine. The database has a memory bank of references to 6 million articles from 3,500 medical journals worldwide. With MEDLINE available, doctors no longer have to rely on memories of an article they read somewhere that said something about a more reliable test for a condition they think a patient has. The doctor can use MEDLINE to look up the condition and get all the latest research and case studies published on the condition.

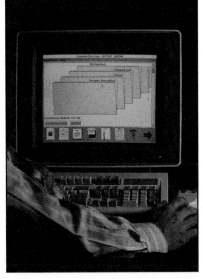

Computerized medical records systems help doctors to quickly find, review, and analyze a patient's medical condition.

Photographs Courtesy of International Business Machines Corporation

Computers and Special Needs

For people with disabilities, the computer is a valuable tool. Computers can speak as output, rather than print to a monitor, so that the visually impaired can use them. Computers have voice synthesizers to speak for those users who cannot.

Current research being performed in both Japan and Austria involves the use of brain waves to control computers. Research has verified that our brains emit a low-level electric signal when we think. Scientists, in experiments around the world, are learning how to harness this signal and use it to command a computer. Using this technique to instruct the computer to do certain tasks, a person with limited mobility can be more independent. Another possible application is to bypass an injured spinal cord and use brain waves to activate muscles.

Sports and Sports Medicine

As early as the 1984 Olympics, computers have been used to analyze the athletic performance of a person and show where the movements were

Medical personnel can access databases all over the world for the most current information about a disease or medical condition.

less than ideal. With analysis from the computer, along with constant monitoring, an athlete can improve performance and reduce the likelihood of injury. While in the dugout, Houston Astro relief pitcher Rob Murphy enters into his laptop computer every pitch he has thrown. This record helps him know what works and doesn't work against any hitter he has faced before.

Computers are banned on the sidelines of National Football League games. Perhaps one reason is David Hillman. Hillman integrated his computer science background and work with artificial intelligence for the U.S. Air Force to develop a program that analyzes the teams playing against the Washington Redskins, his favorite team. Hillman's program predicted what plays the opposing team would run against the 'Skins, with close to an 80 percent accuracy record.

Whether the computer is designing the hull of an America's Cup sailing ship, helping the crew of the same ship sail the fastest route, or helping athletes stay injury-free, there is no doubt that the computer is changing the face of sports and sports medicine.

Lesson Summary

➤ The Human Genome Project, mapping the three billion pairs of genes in human DNA, is supported by computers and computer communication.

➤ Computer-controlled robots can go places that humans dare not go. Space exploration and underwater exploration would not be as advanced as they are today without computers.

➤ Computers and communications technology have been vital in tracking complex phenomena such as environmental conditions, the movement of wildlife, and subatomic particles called quarks.

➤ The calculation capability of computers makes possible simulations to predict the weather or picture distant planets.

➤ In medicine, computer processing is an important part of many imaging tools, such as CAT scans and MRI.

➤ Teleradiology enables doctors to send images to experts located in distant places, to be read and interpreted. Computer-based communications support teleconferencing to consult with distant medical experts.

➤ Computers have been key in creating and tracking patient databases and controlling surgical tools with vital precision.

➤ When conducting medical research, the computer is used to track data and simulate molecular structure to design new drugs.

➤ Medical databases such as MEDLINE can help doctors around the world stay current with the latest medical findings.

➤ Computers are being adapted to help disabled people read and speak and activate muscles.

➤ Computers are being used to improve sports performances and the analysis of games.

Lesson Review

Key Terms

Human Genome Project MEDLINE tracking device
imaging device teleradiology

Matching

In the blank next to each of the following terms or phrases, write the letter of the corresponding term or phrase.

_____ 1. Tracked by Human Genome Project

_____ 2. Used for medical reference

_____ 3. Used AutoCAD for restoration

_____ 4. Like a computer-controlled tool for orthopedic surgery

_____ 5. Imaging device

_____ 6. Makes weather predictions

_____ 7. Activity indicated by solar ray reflections

_____ 8. Used for volcano exploration

_____ 9. The process of communicating imaging output

_____ 10. Subatomic particles

a. computerized axial tomography

b. photosynthesis

c. DNA

d. MEDLINE

e. quarks

f. teleradiology

g. milling machine

h. simulations

i. Dante II

j. Sphinx

Multiple Choice

Circle the letter of the correct choice for each of the following.

1. Which of the following is the worldwide project to map human DNA?

   a. Universal Genome Project

   b. Human Genome Project

   c. Human Gene Project

   d. World Gene Project

2. Robots, controlled and monitored from a distance, are used in which of the following locations?

   a. underwater

   b. in volcanoes

   c. in space

   d. all of the above

3. Active photosynthesis can be detected, determining plant growth activity, by interpreting which of the following?

   a. sun spots

   b. holes in the ozone layer

   c. solar ray reflections

   d. oxygen levels in the air

4. The improvement in the accuracy of meteorologists' weather predictions is a result of which of the following?

   a. better models

   b. better data

   c. new computers

   d. weather has become more stable, and therefore more predictable

5. CAT scans, MRI, and ultrasound are examples of diagnostic tools called _____.

    a. scanners

    b. imaging devices

    c. asynchronous transfer modes (ATMs)

    d. MEDLINE

6. Which of the following makes teleradiology, the long-distance reading of radiology images, possible?

    a. fiber-optic communication lines

    b. laser optics

    c. any telephone line

    d. a combination of b and c

7. Recent research of brain waves has shown that these waves can be used for which of the following?

    a. to emulate microwave ovens

    b. to control computers

    c. to predict heart attacks

    d. none of the above

8. Which of the following is *not* a way in which computers are used in sports?

    a. designing the hull of sailing ships

    b. analyzing athletic performances of Olympic athletes

    c. on the sidelines of National Football League games

    d. in the dugout, analyzing each pitch thrown

9. How do computers help physicists discover the nature of quarks?

    a. by tracking atomic collisions

    b. by showing quarks bigger than they are

    c. by showing quarks smaller than they are

    d. all of the above

10. Why are doctors using databases to track patients with specific illnesses?

    a. to monitor the care they are receiving

    b. to see whether they are still alive

    c. to see whether they have spread the illness

    d. to be able to charge them again

Completion

In the blank provided, write the correct answer for each of the following.

1. The Human Genome Project is determining the makeup of human _____.

2. Scientists share findings on various projects from anywhere in the world by using the _____.

3. Volcanoes, underwater, and outer space are being explored by _____.

4. Archeologists used _____ to map the Sphinx in Egypt to help preserve it.

5. _____ involves sending imaging signals over fiber-optic communication lines so that a radiology expert can interpret the image without traveling to the patient.

6. CAT, MRI, and ultrasound are all examples of _____.

7. The _____ is the database of millions of articles from medical journals, developed by the National Library of Medicine.

8. Physicists are using computers to track subatomic particles called _____.

9. Studying the migration patterns of wildlife can be performed using tags affixed to the animals and tracking devices located in _____.

10. Digital data sent by the Hubble Space Telescope and interpreted by computers using a simulation, or _____, created the "photographs" of Mars and Jupiter.

Review

On a separate sheet of paper, answer the following questions.

1. How are computers aiding the Human Genome Project?

2. How can robots be used to explore areas too dangerous for humans to explore? What are some of the advantages of using computer technology in this way?

3. How are satellites being used to help farmers and scientists monitor the environment?

4. How is the use of computers in predicting weather and in planet exploration similar?

5. How are computers being used to help educate patients and medical students?

6. How are computer databases helping with patient care?

7. How are computers being used to aid in developing new drugs?

8. How are computers being used to find subatomic particles?

9. In what ways can computers help people with disabilities?

10. How are computers being used in sports?

Critical Thinking

On a separate sheet of paper, answer the following questions.

1. Considering the way computers are being used to help find environmental problems, what other environmental problems do you think computers could help solve?

2. Do you think using computers in sports is taking the "sport" out of it? Why or why not?

3. What are the advantages in using the Internet for worldwide coordination of scientific research? How do you think this might affect political boundaries?

4. What problems do you see in using computers in medical care? What are the advantages?

5. In addition to helping students learn anatomy, what other ways could the computer be used to help medical students and doctors learn new medical care techniques?

Further Discovery

Levitating Trains and Kamikaze Genes: Technological Literacy for the Future. Richard P. Brennan (New York: Wiley, 1994).

The Way Science Works: An Illustrated Exploration of Technology in Action. Foreword by John Durant (New York: Macmillan, 1995).

On-line Discovery

You can access the Internet resources for the following questions by going to the Que Education and Training Web site at URL http://www.ciyf98.com/discovery. From this page, click the link for Lesson 10C and then click the link to the resource you want access.

1. The Human Genome Project is one of the largest-scale scientific research projects in history. An introduction to the project can be found at http://www.nhgri.nih.gov, the home page of the **National Center for Human Genome Research** (**NCHGR**). The actual information collected from the project, the map of the structure of human DNA, is stored in a very large object-oriented database called the **Human Genome Database** (**GDB**) at http://gdbwww.gdb.org. After looking at the database and the introductory text, see whether you can figure out what kinds of information this database contains. In what ways can researchers query the database?

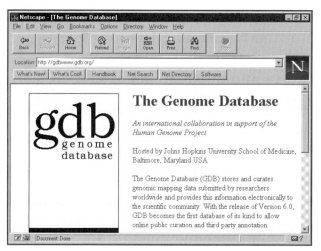

How do researchers contribute information to the database? Finally, this project has long been considered somewhat controversial. Try to find out what some of the social issues or controversies surrounding this database are.

2. The **Stanford Public Information REtrieval System** (**SPIRES**) is a collection of databases and information-sharing tools for the high-energy physics research community. SPIRES is located at http://www-spires.slac.stanford.edu/find/spires.html. Perhaps the most significant feature of SPIRES is the preprint archive—an archive of scholarly publications made available to the high-energy physics community before they are published in journals. This archive was one of the first uses of the World Wide Web, long before most people had even heard of the Web. How are scholars able to retrieve documents from this archive? What other resources are available through SPIRES to high-energy physics? How could the availability of shared archives like this one over the Internet affect scientific research? Can you think of other research communities that might benefit from such a resource?

3. The **National Library of Medicine**
(**NLM**) is a major provider of information
for medical researchers over the Internet.
NLM is located at http://www.nlm.nih.gov.
Most of the databases are available only to
those appropriately authenticated (and
often those who have paid the fee).
However, the NLM provides some introductory information, through which you can
gain an understanding of the different
resources available. Resources of interest
include the **Visible Human**
(http://www.nlm.nih.gov/research
/visible/visible_human.html) and **Internet
Grateful Med** (http://igm.nlm.nih.gov).
Internet Grateful Med is the Internet-based
version of MEDLINE, the database of research in the medical fields. Explore these two resources,
as far as you can without an account. Who are the intended audiences for these databases? What
kinds of information are available?

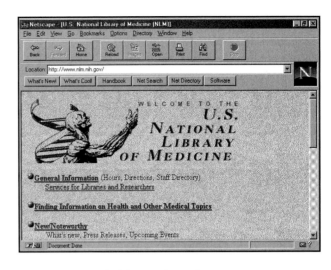

CHAPTER 11
A Hardware Buyer's Guide

Experts forecast that within this generation, microcomputers will become as commonplace as television sets. Just as you can expect to purchase a television set during your life, you can expect to purchase a microcomputer. The system may be for your work or for your home. How will you go about selecting a microcomputer? What will you look for? Chapter 11 is designed to assist you in making a well-informed purchasing decision.

Lesson 11A presents strategies for becoming an educated shopper before you purchase a microcomputer. The lesson discusses current popular microcomputer systems, including both the Macintosh and the IBM families of microcomputers.

Lesson 11A Strategies for Selecting Hardware

LESSON 11A

Strategies for Selecting Hardware

Outline

Learning Objectives

When you have finished reading this lesson, you will be able to

- List the steps to follow in determining computer needs

- Understand how software needs influence buying decisions

- Understand how IBM-compatible and Macintosh systems differ

- Determine your hardware requirements

Computers aren't just for business anymore. Although you may not be thinking about buying a computer today, the odds are that you will buy one sometime. Buying a computer can be a frightening experience. The vendors speak "computerese," and each claims that his or her product is obviously better than the competition. Every computer has a variety of features—some that you need, some that you want, and some that you don't need or can't afford. This lesson discusses factors you should consider before buying a microcomputer.

Before You Go Shopping

Most people would not think of making a major purchase without first researching what is available and analyzing what they need or want. Think of all the time that goes into preparing to purchase a car. Like buying a car, purchasing a computer requires considerable thought, along with some careful research, before a wise decision can be made. You can break the process into four steps: analyze your needs, learn about computers, determine the appropriate software, and select the hardware.

Your Needs Come First

The most important thing about a computer system is that it enables you to do all the tasks you want to accomplish. It doesn't matter whether someone else thinks that a feature isn't necessary; it may be necessary for you.

What You Need Now

What do you intend to do with a computer? You should always answer this question before you buy a computer. Begin by making a list of all the tasks that you (and anyone else who will use the computer) want the computer to accomplish. This process is known as a **needs assessment**.

Consider how a family of four might use a computer. Assume that David is a business manager who uses a computer at work to produce documents, financial reports, and presentations. Joyce is an architect who uses computers at work to design buildings. Joyce is also a talented artist who is interested in learning more about computer-generated graphics. Both adults agree that tracking the family checking account manually is too time-consuming. The two children, Aimee and Jeff, want to do research, write reports for school, and read multimedia books. Aimee and Jeff are also interested in computer games, and the parents are interested in exploring the concept of "edutainment." All of them agree that they would use an information service. Table 11A.1 shows the needs assessment or "want list" that this family has generated.

Table 11A.1 The Needs Assessment for Purchasing a Computer	
Need/Want	*Type of Software*
Documents and written reports	Word processing
Financial reports	Spreadsheet
Presentations	Presentation
Computer-generated graphics	Graphics
Checking account	Personal finance

continues

Table 11A.1 Continued	
Need/Want	Type of Software
Research	Multimedia encyclopedia
Entertainment	Games and multimedia books
Internet	On-line service

Next consider where you are going to use the computer. Can it stay in one room? Does it need to be portable? Besides the traditional desktop micro-computers, a number of portable computers are available. Many of the lap-top or notebook computers adapt to fit in a **docking station** that consists of a full-size monitor and keyboard. Using a portable computer with a dock-ing station makes it easy to carry large files between home and work.

When you buy a computer, determine which software programs you want to use and whether you would like to be able to work at home.

Many different types of laptops are available, including those with multimedia capabilities.

What You Will Need Later

Can you envision your use of the computer in two or three years? If you are the type of individual who likes to learn new things, you may need a computer capable of running all the latest programs. If you are just interested in getting a computer to do what you want, and know that you will be reluctant to go through the learning cycle again, the newest and most powerful software may not mat-ter to you.

Second, Learn about Computers

The family described in this lesson has some computer knowledge already. You are beginning to gain some knowledge by taking a class and reading this text. Before you buy a computer system, you should do some more research. Read some computer magazines, talk to friends who own comput-ers, visit computer stores where you can play with the demo systems, talk to computer vendors, and attend a local user group meeting. All this research will take some time, but it will be time well spent.

By researching computers, you will learn what is currently available and when new models are expected. Whenever a computer based on a new microprocessor is released, the older models go down in price. Weigh whether you need the newest technology that costs more, or whether older technology is sufficient for you. No matter what your decision, the computer that you buy today will not take care of all your computing needs forever. Computer technology changes rapidly, and your needs will change as computers become capable of doing more.

Some people adamantly prefer Apple Macintosh computers, whereas other people are equally adamant in their preference for IBM compatibles. On Macintosh systems, you just plug in the peripherals, and you're ready to go. The Windows 95 system has the new **Plug and Play** technology jointly developed by Intel Corporation and Microsoft that makes the process much like that of a Macintosh. As time goes by, the differences between Windows-based systems and the Macintosh are becoming less apparent.

Software Comes Third

After learning about computers, you should reevaluate your needs assessment. Revise your list if you have learned about other types of programs that you would like to have.

Apple microcomputers and IBM-compatible microcomputers run software programs with similar capabilities. But some programs will run only on one of these two "families" of micros. If you want specific software packages, make certain that they run on the family of microcomputers that you prefer.

First on the needs assessment in Table 11A.1 is a way to create documents and written reports. This type of work is usually accomplished with a word processing program. A number of good programs are available. Find out which ones are taught at the local college (where usually only the most popular, reliable programs are taught), talk to friends and colleagues about the programs they use, read magazine reviews, and try some programs in computer stores. The word processing programs that are most widely used on IBM-compatible computers are Microsoft Word and WordPerfect; most Macintosh users run Microsoft Word for the Macintosh.

Some software suites include presentation programs.

Consider whether you want specific application programs or an integrated suite of programs. As you learned in Lesson 5B, a program suite generally consists of a word processing program, a spreadsheet program, and a database management system. In addition, presentation software is often offered in a suite. The advantages of a suite are that all the programs work in a similar manner (making them easy to learn) and the files are easily moved between the different programs in the suite. A suite might be a good idea for the family described in this lesson.

Also on the family's needs assessment is the checking account. A number of specialized financial packages for home accounting are available, as well as different packages for business accounting. Determine all the budget information that you would like to track on the computer, and then see what some of the packages offer. Most home accounting packages will keep the checkbook, track income and expenses, graph expenses by category, remind you to pay monthly bills, and print checks. It might be worthwhile when selecting a home accounting package to decide whether you would like to do your own income taxes on your computer; if so,

Courtesy of International Business Machines Corporation

there are tax programs that are compatible with specific home accounting packages.

An information service is often of interest to first-time computer buyers. You can subscribe to an information service to keep up with the news, do research, discuss hobbies, and "surf" the Internet. Compare prices and see what is offered by such services as America Online, Prodigy, and CompuServe. There are also a large number of local access services. Many information services offer thirty-day free-trial packages; you can compare these services and decide which one you prefer. If you intend to subscribe to an information service, you will need to get a modem.

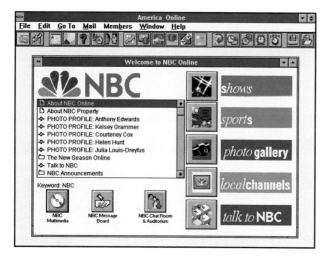

On-line information services provide current news for subscribers.

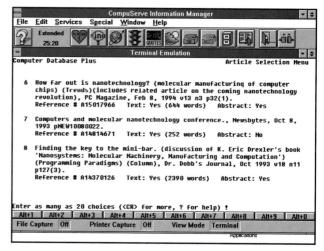

Subscribers can use an on-line information service to research interesting topics.

In the example, Aimee and Jeff want to read multimedia books and play computer games. Many games are available, and some of these are educational. Multimedia reference works and picture collections are also popular. Multimedia products require a sound card, speakers, and a CD-ROM drive.

Grandma and Me (Living Books).

Computer games such as MYST by Broderbund are specifically designed for CD-ROM and require an SVGA monitor and a sound card.

Hardware Is Fourth

After you know the types of software that you need, you can decide more easily on the hardware. All the electrical cords (known as cables) should come with the system.

Now you know why a needs assessment is important. It helps you focus on the software that you need, and the software determines the hardware that will be required.

Microprocessors

The microprocessor is the heart of a microcomputer system. A microprocessor is designed to run at a certain clock speed. The **clock speed** is the rate at which the computer's tiny internal clock ticks a beat; the purpose of this mechanism is to synchronize internal data movements. The Pentium 133 runs at 133Mhz. One megahertz is one million clock ticks per second.

Be aware that looking at clock speed isn't necessarily a good way to compare two computers. A 486DX running at 25MHz, for example, is much faster than a 386DX running at 33MHz. The reason is that the 486DX can process more data with each clock cycle. Clock speed provides a useful comparison only when you are comparing computers built around the same microprocessor. A 90MHz Pentium is faster than a 60MHz Pentium; a 486DX-66 is faster than a 486DX-50.

IBM PC and compatible microcomputers use Intel microprocessors (or microprocessors made by other companies that imitate Intel's design). The following is a quick overview of the microprocessors in common use:

➤ *486DX and 486SX.* These are the outgoing standard, entry-level Intel microprocessors. The DX model includes a numeric coprocessor, which the SX model lacks. The DX2 models run at much faster clock speeds than the SX models, and the DX4 models are the fastest of the 486 microprocessors.

➤ *Pentium (or 80586).* This is Intel's most popular microprocessor, which runs approximately twice as fast as the 486.

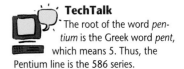

TechTalk
The root of the word *pentium* is the Greek word *pent*, which means 5. Thus, the Pentium line is the 586 series.

➤ *Pentium Pro (or 80686).* This is the newest of Intel's chips. Recently introduced, this microprocessor is the fastest and most expensive of the IBM-compatible systems currently on the market. The first of these chips ran at 133MHz; newer P6S models run at 200MHz.

➤ *P68.* This microprocessor is currently in development. To be released in 1997, the P68 chip may reach speeds approaching 300MHz.

The most important consideration to keep in mind when buying a personal computer is the first part of the "code," such as 486DX4, which refers to the microprocessor. More than anything else, the microprocessor determines the computer's overall performance. Learning about the differences in microprocessors can help you make rational buying decisions.

Macintoshes use Motorola 68000 series microprocessors, and Power Macintoshes use the new PowerPC chips jointly designed by Motorola, IBM, and Apple Computer. In Power Macintoshes, the PowerPC runs software designed for 68000 series microprocessors by using a technique called **emulation**. With emulation, a program "tricks" the software into thinking that it is running with the microprocessor for which it was designed. The more powerful Power Macintoshes, such as the 7101 and 8101 models, can run Microsoft Windows software by using a different emulation program. However, there is a performance penalty when emulation is used.

The following provides a quick overview of the Macintosh microprocessors in common use:

➤ *68040.* A faster microprocessor than the 68030, this chip's performance is similar to that of the Intel 486 chips.

➤ *PowerPC 601.* This first PowerPC microprocessor now powers several Power Macintosh models.

➤ *PowerPC 603e.* Designed for Apple's line of notebook computers, this chip runs at 100–117MHz.

➤ *PowerPC 604.* This chip offers improved performance over the PowerPC 601 and 603 chips.

➤ *PowerPC 620.* This is the most ambitious PowerPC chip, offering full 64-bit processing capabilities and performing twice as fast as earlier PowerPC models.

The PowerPC 601 chip was created for use in both IBM and Macintosh computers.

Courtesy of International Business Machines Corporation

Memory

The next item to consider when buying a computer is the amount of memory you need. Two important issues are how much random-access memory (RAM) you need and whether to use a temporary storage place for your programs.

RAM—How Much Is Enough?

If you are buying an IBM PC-compatible system, you need to consider whether you plan to run Windows 3.1 or Windows 95. Most new systems come with Windows 95, and this "choice" may soon become your only option. If you are running Windows 3.1, the system will need at least 8M of RAM. If you want to use a CD-ROM, use graphics programs, or take advantage of Windows 95 multitasking capabilities, 16M of RAM is preferable. The same is true for Macintosh computers; 4M is the practical minimum, but performance improves significantly with 8M of RAM.

Cache

Many of the better-designed IBM PC-compatible systems come with a **cache** (pronounced "cash"), a temporary storage place for frequently accessed program instructions. The use of a cache brings big payoffs in overall system performance. With some careful shopping, you should be able to find a system offering a 128K or 256K cache for just a few dollars more than a system without a cache.

Disks

A common mistake made by first-time buyers is to underestimate the amount of disk storage they will need. Today, 500M sounds like a lot, but you won't believe how quickly you will fill it up. Generally, you can estimate that you'll need approximately 50M of disk space for each major application you run. This amount allows ample room for file storage. If you plan to run five applications (such as word processing, spreadsheet, database, telecommunications, and graphics), you will need 250M. It is also important to remember that your operating system requires a considerable amount of space. Consequently, you won't have much room left for new applications or games.

Getting a larger hard disk for your system doesn't cost much more than a smaller disk. For a little money, you can upgrade your system to include a one-gigabyte hard disk. Another option is to add a second hard disk later. Hard disk prices are lower now than ever before, running less than $.50 per megabyte.

You should also consider the **hard disk interface**—the circuitry that connects your hard disk to the rest of the computer. With IBM PC and compatible computers, the most popular hard disk interface is the **IDE** (**Integrated Drive Electronics**) interface. For superior performance, but at additional cost, you can get a **SCSI** (**Small Computer System Interface**) adapter that lets you run SCSI-compatible drives. On Apple Macintosh systems, the SCSI interface is standard.

Of course, a floppy disk drive is a necessity. Almost all that you will find on the market today are 1.44M drives. New drives capable of working with higher-density disks have been developed and are becoming available in stores.

Video Cards and Monitors

The computer's **video card** determines the quality and resolution of the display you see on your monitor. The current standard display for an IBM or IBM-compatible computer is a Super Video Graphics Array (SVGA) card with a resolution of either 800 by 600 or 1024 by 768; the **resolution** is a measurement indicating the sharpness of an image or the degree of detail. With higher resolutions, you can see more detail on-screen.

Advanced systems offer a special bus design that directly connects the video circuits with the microprocessor, speeding performance considerably. Two such designs are the **VESA local bus** and the **PCI local bus**. (The term *local* indicates that the video circuits are kept close to the microprocessor.) If you plan to run Microsoft Windows, look for a system that has a **graphics accelerator**. Built into the video card, this accessory can improve Windows' performance by as much as two or three times.

This monitor has its own programmable microprocessor that enables you to set your own preferences.

Courtesy of Nanoa Corporation

On Macintosh systems, video resolution depends on how much **VRAM**, or **video RAM**, is installed in the system. The amount of RAM also affects the number of colors you can display. Today's Macintoshes have separate video memory circuits, ranging in size from 256K to 2048K (2M). Table 11A.2 shows the relationships among the amount of VRAM, the screen resolution, and the number of colors that can be displayed. For example, a Macintosh with 1M of VRAM can display more than 16 million colors with a resolution of 640 by 480. Standard Macintoshes come with only 512K of VRAM, but you get much better color (more colors and higher resolution) with a minimum of 1M.

TechTalk
VESA is an acronym for Video Electronics Standards Association. PCI stands for Peripheral Control Interface.

Table 11A.2   Macintosh Monitors

| VRAM | Number of Colors Displayed for Various Resolutions | | | | | |
	512 x 342	640 x 480	832 x 624	1024 x 768	1152 x 870	1280 x 1024
256K	256	16	16			
512K	32768	256	256	16	16	
768K	32768	32768	256	256	16	16
1024K	16777216	16777216	32768	256	256	16
2048K	16777216	16777216	16777216	32768	32768	256

The dot pitch on the monitor is also important. It can affect the ease with which you can read the display. The most widely used dot pitch today is .28.

Monitors are available in different sizes. You can purchase anything from a 14-inch to a 21-inch monitor. Usually, a 15.5-inch monitor will provide adequate clarity. Individuals who intend to do a lot of desktop publishing or use CAD applications may prefer a 17- or 21-inch monitor. Store clerks may try to convince you to purchase a large monitor to watch television, videos, or animated graphics; for most users, a television set with a VCR is preferable.

Modems

You need a modem so that your system can communicate with other computers. A faster modem will save you connect time, and therefore usually money, compared to a slower modem. Today, a fast, reasonably priced modem will work at a 28.8 baud rate.

CD-ROM Drives and Multimedia Kits

The newest CD-ROM drives are 8x speed or 10x speed (eight times or ten times faster than the original CD-ROM drives). Remember that in order to play a CD and hear the audio portion of it, you need to have a sound card and speakers in addition to the CD drive. These three components make up a "multimedia kit." This kit is a fairly expensive add-on to your basic system. However, as new applications become larger, CD drives become more essential.

Courtesy of International Business Machines Corporation

Now Go Shopping

Shop around and compare prices. Before buying, always research the vendor's reputation. Call the Better Business Bureau; try to find out how long the company has been in business in your city. Ask about warranties; compare the warranty period and service that the manufacturer provides with those of other manufacturers and vendors. Find out what procedure you must follow if you have a problem with the computer.

Ordering a computer system by mail can be a good option; several reputable companies sell only through the mail. Most mail-order companies even have an 800 telephone number that you can call if you need help. However, when you order through the mail, you must set up the system yourself.

TechTalk
A *bay* is a space in the system that can hold a hard drive, floppy drive, tape drive, or CD-ROM.

When you purchase a system, make certain that you receive original floppy disks or CDs and manuals for the operating system, as well as for all the programs on the hard drive. Possession of the original disks ensures that you have a license for the programs.

Remember that systems can be upgraded. If you want a feature but it is too expensive to purchase now, look for a system that can be easily expanded. Read the computer's specifications to determine the maximum amount of primary memory the computer can hold. Make certain that the system has enough **bays** to hold another hard drive, a tape backup, or a CD-ROM drive.

You are taking a risk when you purchase a used computer. Computers become outdated rapidly, and it is difficult to predict when one will have a problem. Many of the new applications will not run on older systems. It is usually better to save your money until you can purchase a new system.

Buying a Microcomputer

Vendor _____   Date _____

Length of time in business   _____
Duration of warranty   _____
Type of service (on-site, carry in) _____

	Speed/Size	Cost
Microprocessor	_____	_____
RAM	_____	_____
Hard drive	_____	_____
Monitor	_____	_____
Video card	_____	_____
Floppy drive(s)	_____	_____
CD-ROM drive	_____	_____
Modem	_____	_____
Printer	_____	_____

Software:	Program	Cost
	_____	_____
	_____	_____
	_____	_____
	_____	_____

Total Cost of Microcomputer   _____

System Case:
Number of bays   _____

Motherboard:
Bus size   _____
Expansion slots   _____
Maximum RAM   _____

General Remarks:
(Impression of vendor knowledge, willingness to help, service policy, quality of product brand, and so on)

_____
_____
_____
_____

A worksheet for buying a microcomputer.

Lesson Summary

➤ It is important to determine what you need a computer for before purchasing one.

➤ The software that is run on the computer will determine the hardware that is required.

➤ Be sure that you purchase a system with enough memory (RAM) to run the operating system and the programs you want to use.

➤ It is important to purchase a computer with enough bays to accommodate extra devices such as a hard drive, tape backup, or CD-ROM drive.

➤ The video card will affect the number of colors that can be displayed and the speed with which a display will appear on the screen.

Lesson Review

Key Terms

bay	graphics accelerator	PCI local bus	VESA local bus
docking station	hard disk interface	Plug and Play	video card
cache	IDE (Integrated Drive	resolution	video RAM (VRAM)
clock speed	Electronics)	SCSI (Small Computer	
emulation	needs assessment	System Interface)	

Matching

In the blank next to each of the following terms or phrases, write the letter of the corresponding term or phrase.

_____ 1. Measured in megahertz

_____ 2. Describes the clarity of the display on a monitor

_____ 3. Manufactures the microprocessor for the Macintosh

_____ 4. Used to hold secondary storage devices

_____ 5. Fast, temporary storage for frequently used instructions

_____ 6. Manufactures the microprocessor for IBM-compatible computers

_____ 7. A method used by one computer to duplicate the function of another computer

a. cache

b. emulation

c. Intel

d. Motorola

e. microprocessor

f. docking station

g. Plug and Play

h. clock speed

i. resolution

j. bay

_____ **8.** The "heart" of the microcomputer

_____ **9.** Provides a full-sized keyboard and monitor for a notebook computer

_____ **10.** Capability of a computer to recognize new devices that are added to it

Multiple Choice

Circle the letter of the correct choice for each of the following.

1. Before you buy a computer, which of the following tasks should you perform first?

    a. select the computer hardware

    b. analyze your needs

    c. determine the appropriate software

    d. learn about the kinds of computers available

2. In buying software, which of the following tasks should you _not_ perform?

    a. try some programs in a computer store

    b. find out which software programs are taught in the local college

    c. buy software that will match your needs in five to ten years

    d. talk to friends and colleagues to see which programs they use

3. Which of the following items is necessary if you want to subscribe to an online service?

    a. printer

    b. cable

    c. modem

    d. bay

4. To upgrade a system in the future, you should consider which of the following when you buy a computer?

    a. the maximum amount of primary memory the system can hold

    b. the number of bays in the current system

    c. the number of cables the current system requires

    d. a and b

5. Which of the following statements concerning your choice of a computer vendor is _not_ true?

    a. A vendor's reputation is important.

    b. You should ask about the warranties the vendor provides.

    c. Ordering a computer system by mail is never a good idea.

    d. Ask about the procedure to follow in case you have a problem with the computer after you buy it.

6. Which of the following is a hard disk interface?

    a. SCSI

    b. IDE

    c. PCI

    d. a and b

7. You must have sufficient hard disk space to store _____.

   a. programs

   b. data

   c. the operating system

   d. all of the above

8. The bays in a computer system hold all of the following except _____.

   a. a disk drive

   b. a modem

   c. a CD-ROM drive

   d. a tape backup

Completion

In the blank provided, write the correct answer for each of the following.

1. A(n) _____ is a list of what you want to use a computer to accomplish.

2. When you run out of hard disk space, you should _____.

3. A(n) _____ is required in order to use an information service.

4. One _____ is one million clock ticks per second.

5. A(n) _____ on the video card will make Windows and other graphics programs run more efficiently.

6. The _____ and _____ determine the system speed.

7. The _____ by Apple can emulate an IBM-compatible computer.

8. It is important to _____ before purchasing a computer.

Review

On a separate sheet of paper, answer the following questions.

1. What items might you include in a needs assessment?

2. What are some things you might do just before purchasing a computer system?

3. Name two advantages of a software suite over separate applications programs.

4. What is the Pentium chip?

5. What is meant by emulation?

6. What concerns should you keep in mind when shopping for a computer?

7. What considerations do you need to think about before purchasing a computer through the mail?

8. How much RAM would you need if you were purchasing a computer? Justify the amount that you stated.

Critical Thinking

On a separate sheet of paper, answer the following questions.

1. Consider the tasks you now do for school-related commitments, job duties, and personal endeavors. State your own needs assessment.

2. Talk to some friends. Do they use Macintosh or IBM microcomputers? Why did they choose one over the other?

3. In what areas do you foresee the most growth in hardware and software? How will they affect your computer purchases?

4. What features do you think Intel or Motorola might put into any new microprocessors within the next three years?

5. What types of applications or tasks in our society might require more memory, retrievable storage, and greater speeds of processing?

Further Discovery

Every Family's Guide to Computers. Winston Steward (Emeryville, CA: Ziff-Davis, 1995).

PC Magazine 1996 Computer Buyer's Guide. John Dvorak (Emeryville, CA: Ziff-Davis, 1995).

Upgrading and Repairing PCs, 4th Edition. Scott Mueller (Indianapolis, IN: Que, 1994).

Upgrading Your PC Illustrated. Allen Wyatt (Indianapolis, IN: Que, 1994).

On-line Discovery

You can access the Internet resources for the following questions by going to the Que Education and Training Web site at URL http://www.ciyf98.com/discovery. From this page, click the link for Lesson 11A and then click the link to the resource you want to access.

1. Many guides to buying computers are available through the World Wide Web. Some guides are associated with computer-related companies that sell or take advertising for computer equipment; others are created by individuals with advice to share. Two such guides are **Dave's Guide to Buying a Home Computer** (http://www.css.msu.edu /pc-guide.html) and **PC Today Online** (http://www.peed.com/pccatalog.yahoo.html). Browse these two guides. What kinds of options are available for a user who wants to purchase a computer? To what degree do the user's needs determine the type of computer and options purchased? If you were to purchase a computer for yourself, what kinds of equipment would you purchase?

2. Many personal computer manufacturers offer complete information about their products through the World Wide Web. Examples of Web sites that provide complete specification information include those of **Apple Computer** (http://product.info.apple.com/productinfo /datasheets); **Gateway 2000** (http://www.gw2k.com), which allows you to build interactively the configuration you want; **Dell Computer** (http://www.dell.com); and **IBM** (http: //www.pc.ibm.com). Take a look at several of these pages. What are some of the options that these computer companies are offering? What kinds of price differences do you see among the brands? Over the last couple of years, notebook computers have greatly increased in sophistication, and they now rival full-sized desktop computers in functionality and features. What high-end features are these computer companies offering in their notebook computers? Finally, what kinds of features are available on Apple Macintosh computers, compared with the features of PC-compatible brands?

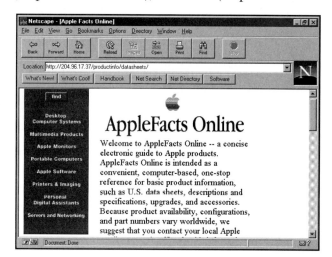

CHAPTER 12

Emerging Uses of Computers

This chapter shows you new ways in which computers are used in a variety of professions—some that you may not normally associate with computers. From elementary school through college, and beyond, computers are changing the way we learn. They also change the way we travel and the way we relax. They even change the manner in which our safety is protected.

Lesson 12A discusses how computers enhance education, both in and out of the classroom.

Lesson 12B looks at new ways in which computers are being used to improve our transportation systems.

Lesson 12C examines the exciting use of computers as an aid in law enforcement.

Lesson 12D considers how computers are used to enhance the fine arts and entertainment.

Computers in Education

Outline

Learning Objectives

When you have finished reading this lesson, you will be able to

➤ Discuss edutainment

➤ Tell how computers can help children learn

➤ Discuss the uses of computers in colleges

➤ Explain how computers are used in school administration

➤ Describe ways to use computers at home to enhance education

The year is 2005, and your child is just beginning school. What do you want his or her classroom to look like? What will the "perfect" classroom look like in ten or twenty years?

Imagine this: The front of the room is a clean white wall; it can be used to show a video clip, project a computer screen image, or even write on with special pens. The wall is touch-sensitive, and a printer is attached to it that can be used to print whatever is currently displayed. This wall is part of a network with direct access to the personal digital assistants (PDAs) of each child. At enrollment, each child receives a PDA, which is returned when the child moves to a different school. The PDAs can directly capture text sent from the instructor's computer. This capability may sound unrealistic, but it is already possible, and it is a teacher's dream. Why? What is the advantage of having computers in the classroom?

Courtesy of Smart Technology, Inc.

Computers to Teach Young Children

The first few years of a child's education are crucial. Research has shown that lecturing (talking at students) is not the most effective way to transfer knowledge, and that many people do not learn by sitting still and listening. Every student, regardless of learning style, needs to be visually stimulated and actively involved. Fortunately, visual stimulation and active involvement are two of the things that computers do best. This section of this lesson highlights a number of products that help children learn.

Colorful interactive screens engage interest while children learn new skills.

When is the best time to expose a child to computers? Computers can be beneficial from the time children begin to learn colors, numbers, and letters. A number of different multimedia products, incorporating sound and animation, help preschool and kindergarten children learn to read. *Alphabet Blocks* by Sierra On-Line helps children learn the alphabet and the sounds of letters. *Sound It Out Loud (Volumes 1 and 2)* by Conexus begins by having children work with three-letter words. The program uses cartoon characters who speak the words as they appear on-screen. The Living Books series from Broderbund includes the Dr. Seuss books, *Aesop's Fables*, the Berenstein Bears books, *Arthur's Teacher Troubles, Little Monster at School*, and *Grandma and Me*. Recognizing that learning a language is easiest for the young, the Living Books products provide an opportunity for children to learn different languages; the opening screen of each offers a choice of English, Spanish, or Japanese. Besides teaching reading, word pronunciation, and narrative structure, many of these books teach a value lesson. These programs are not merely adaptations of textbook lessons; they're exercises in **participatory learning**.

Courtesy of International Business Machines Corporation

*Little Monster at School
is one of Broderbund's
Living Books.*

Click the drawing to watch the character dance.

Click the astronaut
to see him float.

Click any word to hear
it pronounced.

Early in the morning, Mom wakes me
and says, "Get up, Little Monster, it's time
for school."

Click the number 1 to
go to the beginning.

Click the arrow to move
to the next page.

Courtesy of Davidson & Associates

Courtesy of Davidson & Associates

In Davidson's **Math Blaster: In Search of Spot,** *children develop problem-solving and math skills by helping Blasternaut rescue his robot friend, Spot.*

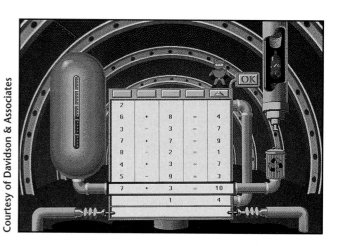

Courtesy of International
Business Machines Corporation

	Super Bubble	Big Chew	Mr. Cavity	No Sugar	Flavored Gravy	Overall Averages
9	34.30	27.25	10.20	65.40	45.34	36.50
10	35.60	45.67	11	70.50	46	41.75
11	47.54	55.40	14.54	63.45	48.10	45.81
12	50	60	16.80	87	52.65	53.29
13	60.10	57	18.97	94.20	55.40	57.13
15	45.51	49.06	14.30	76.11	49.50	46.90
16	25.80	32.75	8.77	30.75	10.06	21.63

Pyet BUBBLE.WK1
B9   :+34.300000

Spreadsheet examples using imaginary data help students understand a real-world activity.

In most elementary schools, overworked teachers teach more than thirty children at a time. Not everyone learns at the same pace or from the same type of material. The teacher simply cannot keep repeating a lesson in different ways until he or she is sure that all the children understand the concept. But a computer can.

Computers let every child learn at his or her own pace. If a child does not show mastery of a concept on a test, the computer can present the same concept differently and then administer the test again.

Computer programs can turn the abstract into the concrete. Imagine trying to lecture to fifth-grade students about how the stock market works. Now imagine putting the students into groups and giving each group a set amount of "money." Stocks and stock prices are entered into a computer spreadsheet. Each group chooses a stock and uses the spreadsheet to track the value of its holdings over a four-to-six-week period. The concept of stocks and investments becomes much easier to understand when children can learn as they enjoy participating in a game that uses the computer as a tool.

Teachers can use educational video clips on CD-ROM to show famous paintings to a class, parts of the world the class is studying, or a relevant portion of last night's news broadcast.

Photographs courtesy of International Business Machines Corporation

Educational CD-ROMs are available to help students learn about Greek mythology, music, and many other subjects.

Slightly older children can benefit from **edutainment**, which is a cross between education and entertainment. Such games as *Where in the World is Carmen Sandiego?* present children with facts within the framework of a game. (*Carmen*, featured in several video games, now stars in an educational animated television show as well.)

Isaac Asimov Science Adventure by Knowledge Adventure is edutainment that presents a fascinating merging of fact and fiction. *Science Adventure* has been described as a virtual-reality science environment.

Isaac Asimov Science Adventure II *explores a myriad of fascinating topics from embryos to fiber optics.*

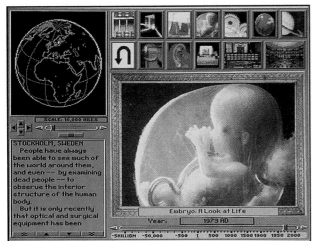

Photographs courtesy of Knowledge Adventure, Inc.

Multimedia: The New Textbooks

You are there—shivering with Washington at Valley Forge, riding with General Grant at Appomattox, performing with Mozart for the King of Prussia, walking on the moon with Neil Armstrong, fiddling with Nero as Rome burns.

Showing documentaries is a valid method of education. The use of dramatic presentations (multimedia programs) earns high praise from teachers and school administrators worldwide. Statistics show that these programs greatly improve student comprehension and retention (*T H E Journal*, March, 1994).

One of the most powerful applications is the creation of interactive tutorials. Many different tutorial programs enable students to create presentations using text, graphics, images, narration, sound, choice buttons, and even video. A photo-editing program supports collages, and animation is also an option. This capability has never before been available to educators. These programs are available for Mac, Windows, and MS-DOS hardware.

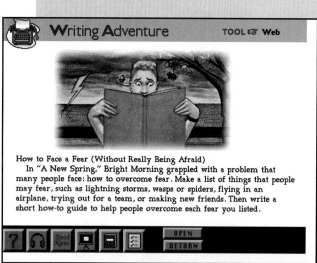

How to Face a Fear (Without Really Being Afraid)
In "A New Spring," Bright Morning grappled with a problem that many people face: how to overcome fear. Make a list of things that people may fear, such as lightning storms, wasps or spiders, flying in an airplane, trying out for a team, or making new friends. Then write a short how-to guide to help people overcome each fear you listed.

Courtesy of Computer Curriculum Corporation

In addition to creating "homemade" multimedia presentations, instructors can purchase at reasonable prices hundreds—maybe thousands—of commercially prepared titles on CD-ROM. Again, most can be bought in Mac, Windows, or MS-DOS format.

With a Microsoft disk called *Musical Instruments*, viewers can both hear and see almost every musical instrument invented. Another musical Microsoft product is *Multimedia Beethoven*. *PC Computing* (December, 1993) reviews these programs: "The interface is clean and lets you explore the instruments thoroughly, and the scholarship is sound. . . . Once you've experienced the addition of sound to a music textbook, you'll never look at a textbook the same way again."

Humans thrive on multiple input. Educators have long recognized that we remember 10 percent of what we read, 20 percent of what we hear, 30 percent of what we see and hear, 50 percent of what we see someone do while explaining it, and 90 percent of what we do ourselves, even if it's only a simulation (*PC World*, October, 1993).

The educational world—from preschools to professional schools—is adopting multimedia at various rates of speed.

Exeter-West Greenwich (EWG) Junior/Senior High School in Rhode Island has taken a "total immersion" philosophy (*Technology & Learning*, October, 1993). The nearly four-to-one student-to-computer ratio enables every student to have ready access to computers for multimedia authoring.

EWG has a multidisciplinary approach to projects. In creating multimedia projects, students not only learn research and presentation skills—they also learn how to work together as a group toward shared goals.

At Bakersfield (CA) College, President Rick Wright's class in general psychology is the first on his campus to use multimedia. He offers all materials through interactive computer presentations (*T H E Journal*, October, 1993).

Dr. Wright and a colleague team-teach a large section of 225 students. They capture digital audio from CDs or audiotape; they digitize images from photographs and

continues

slides. They also use motion videos from psychology videotapes collected over the last twenty years, and they use video discs. "We try to sort out the best of the material to use as clips in our lectures," President Wright said. "This technology lets you clip the pertinent things and insert them in your lecture where you want them. Multimedia clip making is a stroke of genius, because if you can capture just what you need from the videotapes for each topic in your lecture, it gives you incredible power—everything is integrated."

Response has been overwhelmingly positive. Students are requesting more multimedia classes. Teachers find that through images, animation, and motion video, they can cover more material in greater detail than with traditional methods. Multimedia classes are cost-efficient because a teacher can handle larger classes.

Dr. Wright explained, "I think the lesson is that young or old, human beings generally process visual images much more efficiently than text or spoken words."

Courtesy of International Business Machines Corporation

Does edutainment have value? Should education be fun? The answer to both of these questions is an emphatic "Yes!" Learning can and should be fun; students learn more and challenge themselves to go beyond what is required if they are having fun.

Computers in High Schools and Colleges

High school and college students also benefit from computer-based learning experiences. The way older students use the computer is very different from the way younger children use it, however. Programs are less entertainment-oriented but still exciting and challenging.

One valuable program is WORKLINK, designed for high school students who plan to enter the work force after high school. WORKLINK enables students to develop personal records that include transcripts; ratings of work habits, such as attendance, punctuality, and motivation; and results of job-specific skills assessment tests. These records are made available to employers who are a part of the WORKLINK project. WORKLINK is a joint project of the Education Testing Service (ETS) and the National Association of Secondary School Principals (NASSP).

Using the computer to provide intelligent tutoring is increasing in popularity in both high schools and colleges. An **intelligent tutoring program** can adapt based on student responses to review areas where the student is weak and to skip areas where the student has already mastered the material. **Computer-based tutorials** (**CBT**) are helpful to students no matter what their level of subject mastery. Advanced students are not bored by questions that seem repetitive and simplistic, and students having more difficulty with the subject will be asked more questions in order to reinforce concepts. A student will receive immediate feedback from the computer, enabling him or her to see the correct answers while the question is still fresh in the student's mind.

Computer Curriculum Corporation offers creative multimedia programs for older students.

Photographs courtesy of Computer Curriculum Corporation

Many colleges are offering introductory computer classes similar to the one in which you are using this book. More and more colleges are requiring that all students learn word processing. Additionally, colleges are changing their curriculum requirements to ensure that all graduates are computer literate. Students at a few colleges, like Carnegie-Mellon University, are required to purchase a computer on entering the institution.

Courtesy of Indiana University Purdue University Indianapolis

College computer labs offer a wide variety of software programs. Labs enable students to work independently at their own pace.

In the Classroom

Remember dissecting a frog in high school biology? Today, students can "dissect" the frog by using a computer simulation. Students can design a frog, build an animal with the behavior patterns of a frog, teach the animal, stimulate its muscles, and learn about the frog without having to dissect a dead animal. Interestingly, this idea of "constructing" a frog (and learning by building) was developed and computerized by Media Lab of MIT through funding by Interlego (the Danish manufacturer of Lego toys).

Educators can also get CD-ROM programs that show a frog being dissected; the illustrations are interspersed with theoretical explanations and line diagrams further illustrating the dissection. Many areas of science such as botany, chemistry, and anatomy can be taught effectively using multimedia presentations.

Photographs courtesy of Indiana University-Purdue University Indianapolis

Students can use computer programs to explore biology and anatomy topics.

In large classrooms, lecturers can use multimedia instructional portable systems for assistance in presenting a class project.

CD-ROM–based interactive problem-solving programs help students develop critical-thinking skills. One such program, by Video Discovery, enables a class to analyze the symptoms of employees who attended a company picnic and became ill. The class can choose different people to interview in order to arrive at a diagnosis. (As it turns out, the chef didn't clean the cutting board, and all the employees have salmonella poisoning.) A myriad of these problem-solving cases are available for various subject areas.

Computer labs permit students to learn computer skills, and to use computers to assist in classes that are not directly computer-related. Term papers, resumes, and accounting are all easier when using the computer. Computer labs that feature networked computers provide a social learning experience and opportunity for discussion that is both different and superior to the solitary experience of a single user.

Simulation Games

Simulations are games that reflect an aspect of the real world. One of the first, and most popular, simulation games enabled the user to "fly" an airplane. A number of realistic and educational flight simulation games are available. Simulation games have been developed also to teach aspects of business such as production and marketing. Most simulations involve the students in small decision-making groups that compete against each other to produce the most profit.

A fairly new simulation known as *ICONS* (International Communication and Negotiation Simulation) involves lower-division college students from around the world. Teams from more than a dozen countries participate in a simulation designed to focus on the difficulties that western Europe and post-Communist nations are experiencing in the current global political climate. Teams communicate daily using the Internet. There is no winner; when the game is ended, teams are allowed to see all the communications that have occurred, with each team submitting an analysis of one aspect of the negotiations. Such simulations encourage cross-cultural awareness and involve students in a manner that increases the number of students who complete a class.

For Research

The most tedious part of a term paper or a science project traditionally has been to find source material. Using computer communications capabilities, students can access primary sources from their school library, classroom, or home. Wireless technologies are making access from remote locations effortless. The University of California at Santa Cruz recently installed its Richochet network made by Microcom. About two dozen small radios mounted on poles provide access to the college network for all the dormitories and other on-campus areas popular with students.

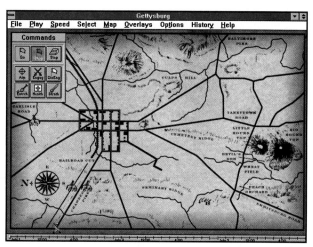

Students can research historical topics from a wealth of resources on CD-ROM.

Using a computer to access the Internet, it is possible for a student to contact an expert on a topic and engage in a dialog, using e-mail. Libraries can offer on CD-ROM a wealth of resources that the school could not otherwise afford to purchase. Research skills developed in this way prepare students for the world of work.

Online information services have encyclopedias and a wealth of current articles. The Internet offers users access to libraries around the world. In 1969, only three computers were connected to the Internet; today there are more than three million. In discussing the Information Superhighway at the Electronic Media Summit in January 1994, Vice President Gore stated that every classroom in the nation will be connected by the year 2000—at no charge. Many high school and college libraries already have access. As a result, research today is faster, more complete, and more rewarding than it was a decade ago.

Students are also using computers to create projects. Computer-based projects can incorporate text and graphics to explore any topic of interest to a student. Students can narrate the presentation as it appears on the computer monitor. Instructors can use the projects to determine subject mastery and student skills. Computer-based projects are excellent for individual or group activities.

For Distance Learning

Distance learning, taking the classroom to the student, has been tried without much success over the last twenty years. The idea has merit; students who live long distances from college campuses find it difficult to get an education, and distance learning can help. Adult students, working and supporting families find it difficult to attend classes at fixed times. The primary problem with the first distance learning experiments was the absence of interaction between the instructor and the students. The students watched a television show and sometimes went to the college campus to take a final exam. The new computer-assisted form of distance learning looks considerably different. Using videoconferencing, students gather at a center where a satellite transmission is received. The students see the instructor and the entire room where the instructor is located. On the opposite end of the transmission, the instructor can see the students and the room where they are located. Students and instructor can also talk to each other. The opportunity for interaction increases the amount of learning that occurs.

Today, college students can take video courses using their home computers. This form of distance education was first used successfully by the Open University of the United Kingdom in the early 1970s. The model established by the OUUK has been adopted by colleges in many countries, including the Information Technologies Institute of New York University's School of Continuing Education. At NYU, faculty featured in the courses are located throughout the United States. The first course of study established was a 16-unit Advanced Professional Certificate in Information Technology. Students work independently but communicate with faculty and other students by e-mail. Homework assignments are frequently posted, and turned in, using e-mail.

A consortium of community colleges has developed similar materials to enable students to complete an associate of arts degree at home, and more consortiums are being established now. The "**virtual university**" is fast becoming a reality, as colleges throughout the world begin to use this form of distance education.

Administrative Uses of Computers

With the increase in population, schools could not function without computers. Some of the ways in which educational institutions use computers are fairly obvious; others are not. Computers make it easier for instructors to maintain student grades, develop lesson plans, and create homework assignments. Schools use computers to maintain all student records, assign students to classes, assign classes to rooms, and pay employees. These tasks alone make the computer a necessity. Colleges are also required to use the computer for financial aid reporting procedures.

Additionally, the computer is used for all the research performed on campus. Research includes tracking groups of students to determine graduation rates and graduates' occupations. Schools conduct studies on the performance and attitudes of students in order to improve the educational process. Studies also provide information for accountability reporting.

Colleges need to maintain their enrollments. A new marketing strategy is to distribute to high schools and community colleges a CD-ROM that enables students to see the campus, hear students and professors talking about the school, and learn about financial aid opportunities. Some colleges are paying for virtual-reality technology that gives a prospective student the opportunity to walk through the campus. Many colleges have home pages on the World Wide Web to inform prospective students about their campuses.

College campuses are beginning to feature information kiosks that provide campus maps, listings of college activities, and personal enrollment information to students. The programs displayed by the kiosks can be updated regularly to provide students with current information.

Education Outside the School

Education does not stop in the classroom. Many programs, disguised as games, are excellent educational tools. When young people are exposed to learning in an enjoyable setting, they want to learn more. Some of the better educational programs include *Thinking Things* and *KidDesk Family Edition* by Edmark Corporation, *Kids Studio* by Cyberpuppy Software, and Knowledge Adventure's *3D Dinosaur Adventure* for small children.

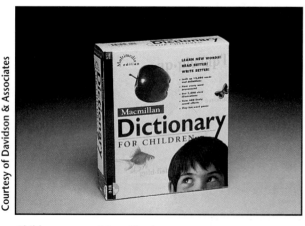

Courtesy of Davidson & Associates

Children can use Macmillan's Dictionary for Children to find the definitions of words.

And how many teenagers understand the way a city is planned? Some teens understand a great deal after using a game made by Maxis. *Sim City 2000* uses realistic graphics and sound to teach users about underground water systems, transportation systems, landscapes, and city services.

Addison-Wesley's *Real World Math: Adventures in Flight* has youngsters earning flying miles by answering math problems pertaining to airplanes and common situations encountered in a flight hanger before a flight. Those who play *Alge-Blaster 3* from Davidson use algebra to defend against invading Red Nasties on the planet Quadratics.

Older children and adults enjoy *Oceans Below* by Software Toolworks, a tour that covers the world in search of exotic fish, mammals, and plant life. A highly educational tour of the body is available with Softkey International's *Bodyworks*.

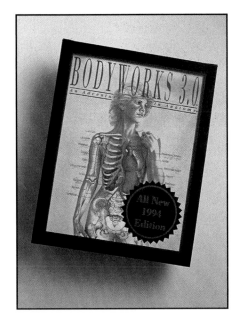
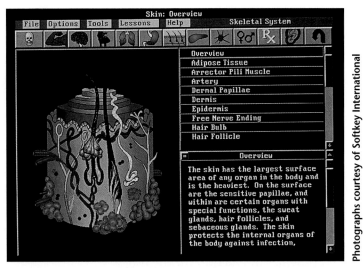

Bodyworks 3.0 provides an adventure in anatomy. Users can zoom in for more detail on a topic of interest, such as the skin.

Reference materials can also prove fascinating and educational when presented in video. Older learners will be mesmerized by the *Picture Atlas of the World* from National Geographic and *PC Globe Maps 'n' Facts* from Broderbund. Understanding current events becomes fun with *Newsweek Interactive* by Software Toolworks, an ongoing series that releases a new edition with new topics quarterly. Encyclopedias become fascinating when you can see and hear a video of a famous person or an animal. (Encyclopedias on CD-ROM are also much less expensive and contain more current information than encyclopedias in book form.) All these products prove that learning is fun and should not be confined to the classroom.

Lesson Summary

➤ People learn better when they are actively involved and visually stimulated rather than when they are passive listeners.

➤ Computer programs are available to assist preschool children in learning the alphabet and reading.

➤ Edutainment provides educational material in a setting similar to a game so that education becomes entertainment.

➤ Computer simulations enable students to learn in an interactive, group environment that mirrors a part of the world, such as a particular business enterprise.

➤ Computers facilitate research by making sources easily available.

➤ Educational administrators use computers to help run the institution.

➤ Education should not stop in the classroom. A variety of games, reference materials, and special-interest programs enhance learning at home.

Lesson Review

Key Terms

computer-based tutorial (CBT)

distance learning

edutainment

intelligent tutoring program

participatory learning

simulation

virtual university

Matching

In the blank next to each of the following terms or phrases, write the letter of the corresponding term or phrase.

_____ 1. A computerized model that reflects one aspect of the real world and provides interaction for the user

_____ 2. Can adapt based on a student's responses, with the computer selecting material for the student to review

_____ 3. Provides access to encyclopedias and libraries of material

_____ 4. Can provide information to students about college enrollment records and campus activities

_____ 5. A computer program that uses sound and graphics

_____ 6. Small electronic device that can send and receive signals to similar devices

_____ 7. A program that helps students to prepare for and locate jobs

_____ 8. Games that are educational

_____ 9. A simulation that teaches international negotiations

_____ 10. The use of computer technology to teach students who are in a remote classroom

a. edutainment

b. distance learning

c. simulation

d. information kiosk

e. PDA

f. WORKLINK

g. *ICONS*

h. Internet

i. multimedia

j. intelligent tutoring

Multiple Choice

Circle the letter of the correct choice for each of the following.

1. Which of the following is true of edutainment?

    a. Facts may be set within the framework of a game.

    b. It is a cross between education and entertainment.

    c. It enhances learning and encourages students to challenge themselves.

    d. all of the above

2. Which of the following groups contain words or concepts that are *not* associated?

    a. multimedia, speaking cartoon characters, Living Books series

    b. games, edutainment, education

    c. link to instructor's computer, PDA, computers on loan to students

    d. none of the above

3. Some new marketing strategies include programs that enable students to do which of the following?

    a. view college campuses

    b. listen to professors and students talking about their school

    c. take a "virtual reality" walk through a college campus

    d. all of the above

4. At educational institutions, computers can be used to do which of the following?

    a. maintain student records

    b. designate rooms for courses

    c. track graduates after graduation

    d. all of the above

5. Which of the following does *not* represent an educational program for very young children?

    a. *Oceans Below*

    b. *KidDesk*

    c. *Kids Studio*

    d. *3D Dinosaur Adventure*

6. Which of the following is true about simulation games?

    a. They teach one aspect of the real world.

    b. They can involve students in a group effort.

    c. They can involve students from different locations.

    d. all of the above

7. People learn best by which of the following activities?

    a. listening to a lecture

    b. active involvement

    c. repetitive drill

    d. watching others

8. Which of the following enables students in remote locations to attend classes without commuting?

    a. edutainment

    b. PDAs

    c. distance learning

    d. simulation games

9. Which of the following would *not* be a way to learn about biology?

    a. edutainment

    b. distance learning

    c. a simulation

    d. WORKLINK

10. Which of the following is not edutainment?

    a. *Alge-Blaster 3*

    b. *Where in the World is Carmen Sandiego?*

    c. *ICONS*

    d. *Sim City 2000*

Completion

In the blank provided, write the correct answer for each of the following.

1. _____ programs combine sound and graphics.

2. The cross between education and entertainment is known as _____.

3. A program that reproduces a part of the real world is a(n) _____.

4. Programs that challenge students to find solutions to problems enhance _____ skills.

5. _____ is a program that helps high school seniors prepare to enter the workforce.

6. Colleges are modifying their curricula to require that all graduates are _____.

7. *Sim City 2000* is an example of _____.

8. Some day students will be able to share files in the classroom using their _____.

9. _____ enables students in remote classrooms to interact with the instructor and with each other.

10. Colleges can keep students informed of current events and graduation requirements by using _____.

Review

On a separate sheet of paper, answer the following questions.

1. What is a PDA? How is it useful?

2. What types of currently existing computer aids are related to biology lab dissections?

3. In what ways are computers being used educationally by high school and college students?

4. What has been the major improvement in the area of distance learning?

5. What is edutainment? Why is it successful?

6. How can an information kiosk be useful on a college campus?

7. How can computers enhance critical-thinking skills?

8. How do college administrators use computers?

9. How do instructors use computers to make their jobs easier?

10. What are some of the benefits of computer simulation games?

Critical Thinking

On a separate sheet of paper, answer the following questions.

1. Give an example of a real-life situation that could be presented interactively on CD-ROM to help students build problem-solving skills.

2. Can you envision any problems or concerns in implementing distance learning and satellite-transmitted classrooms?

3. How do you feel about the clean white classroom wall, mentioned at the beginning of the lesson, that would be used for showing computer images and writing on with special pens? Would you still need or want a traditional chalkboard or whiteboard? Why or why not?

4. How do you feel about WORKLINK? Could it be beneficial to you? In what ways?

5. What are your feelings about doing actual dissections versus using computer simulations?

Further Discovery

Alone But Together: Adult Distance Study through Computer Conferencing. Daniel Eastmond (Cresskill, NJ: Hampton Press, 1995).

Instructional Media and Technologies for Learning. Robert Heinick, Michael Molenda, James D. Russell, and Sharon E. Smaldino (Englewood Cliffs, NJ: Prentice Hall, 1996).

The Monster Under the Bed. Stan Davis and Jim Botkin (New York: Simon and Schuster, 1994).

That's Edutainment: A Parent's Guide to Educational Software. Eric Brown (Berkeley, CA: 1996).

Theory and Practice of Distance Education, 2nd Edition. Börje Holmberg (New York: Routledge, 1995).

The World Wide Web for Teachers. Bard Williams (Foster City, CA: IDG, 1996).

The monthly magazine *T H E Journal: Technical Horizons in Education* is regularly an excellent source of information.

On-line Discovery

You can access the Internet resources for the following questions by going to the Que Education and Training Web site at URL http://www.ciyf98.com/discovery. From this page, click the link for Lesson 12A and then click the link to the resource you want to access.

1. **Teaching and Learning on the Web**, from the Maricopa Community Colleges, is a directory of sites in which the World Wide Web is actually being used for teaching and learning. This directory, at URL http://www.mcli.dist.maricopa.edu/tl /index.html, can be searched by keyword and browsed by academic subject. Pick two different subjects and compare the ways in which the Web is being used for teaching and learning in these two subjects. How is the use in the two subjects different? How else could the Web be used?

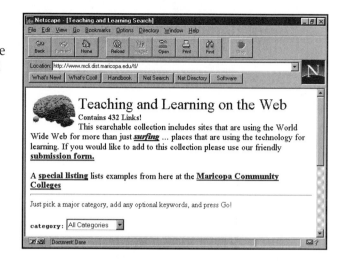

2. Many teachers have made information about computer-based resources for math and science education available on the Internet. Sites such as the **Center for Science and Mathematics Teaching** home page (http://www.tufts.edu/as/csmt) and **The Cornell Theory Center Math and Science Gateway** (http://www.tc.cornell.edu/Edu /MathSciGateway) provide some great starting points for locating resources for teachers and students of math and science. The Yahoo! directory page on **Math and Science Education** (http://www.yahoo.com/Education /Math_and_Science_Education) also provides some pointers. Take a look at several sites related to math and science education. What are the best resources you found? For what grade levels are the resources aimed?

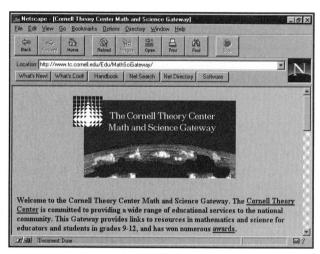

Computers in Transportation

Outline

On the Road
    Smart Cars
    Car Navigation
    Smart Streets
In the Air
    Airplanes
    Air Traffic Control
    Airline Reservation Systems
    Airports
On Land and Sea
    Logistics
    Trains
    Travel Guides
Toward the Future

Learning Objectives

When you have finished reading this lesson, you will be able to

➤ Discuss what makes a smart car "smart"

➤ Explain how cars are being equipped to navigate in areas where the driver has never been before

➤ Define a "smart" street and tell how the U.S. government is attempting to create smart streets

➤ Explain how computers are used to build and fly airplanes

➤ Discuss the air traffic control system and explain how computers are used to support the ATC system

➤ Discuss how trains, planes, and automobiles are being developed for the next decade

As you are cruising down the highway late one night, you are too drowsy to notice the slower moving car in front of you. Your car, alert to the danger, slows down, and that wakes you enough to realize that you want to pass. As you signal and start to swing to the left to pass, your car, again sensing danger, warns you of the car that is in your blind spot to the left. As you approach the off ramp that you want, your car alerts you that you need to get off here. The display map of the area you are entering shows where you are and where you want to go. The map automatically routes you around the construction project that blocks the major road you would have taken.

Does this scenario sound like something from a science fiction story? All the devices mentioned are being tested in labs or are available on cars today.

The Information Superhighway moves information around the world. But people and products still have to be moved also. The "old-fashioned" super-highways, airways, shipping lanes, and railways are still important. And they have been affected by computers. This lesson looks at how technology is affecting trains, planes, and automobiles.

On the Road

Automobile transportation allows great personal freedom of movement, but it also has costs. Automakers and governments around the world are look-ing for ways to reduce these costs. Engineers and computer scientists are making cars safer, more reliable, and easier to operate. Three major areas of research and development are making cars "smarter," connecting them into navigation systems and maps, and making the streets "smarter."

With Avis' Heads-Up Display, you can keep your eyes on the road by viewing important driving information on the windshield.

Smart Cars

Smart cars can help the driver maintain control of the vehi-cle, control the car's environment, and anticipate and warn the driver about traffic problems. Microprocessors are making cars capable of controlling themselves and interacting with their environment. Embedded computers enable cars to diagnose their own internal problems, operate safely, warn the driver of potential problems, and keep track of where in the world they are.

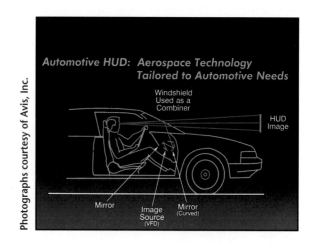

Photographs courtesy of Avis, Inc.

All these devices, of course, add to the cost of the automobile. Average spending on a new car has exceeded $20,000 for the first time ever, and the average American family now spends more than half its annual income for a new car.

Designing the car of the future uses the tools of the future. The use of CAD/CAM in automobile design led the way to automation of manufacturing; today automakers are designing cars by using laser-generated holograms and simulations to predict such details as the sound of the doors shutting and the level of engine noise inside the car when it is accelerating. Simulations even make crash tests possible before the car is built. Wind tunnel simulations performed on a design make it possible to minimize the wind drag and thereby improve the fuel economy.

Currently, cars include microprocessor-controlled **ABS (antiskid braking system)** brakes and computer-controlled fuel injection. ABS brakes are being taken to the next level with the **Automotive Stability Management System** (**ASMS**) being tested in Sweden and Michigan. ASMS uses sensors that detect and control sideways momentum, steering-wheel position, rotation of each wheel, and cornering rate of the car to overcome any driver error and make skidding virtually impossible—even on the slippery surface of light snow over ice.

Multiplex central wiring is a continuous-wire system with one wire making a complete circle throughout the machine with separate locations for every function. This technology allows for microprocessor control of the entire auto and treatment of the car as an integrated unit. Sensors placed throughout the vehicle can track and record wear on parts and systems, even sensing when tire pressure is too low. These central wiring systems allow for even better self-diagnosis than before. As problems are sensed, demands on a system can be switched to other systems, averting problems before they occur.

This kind of wiring also allows for personalizing. Just turning on the car starts adjustments of seat and steering wheel positions, interior temperature settings, choice of CDs, and even ride suspension and steering effort. The Lincoln Continental has 24 features available for personalizing.

The "central nervous system" of an automobile can also protect the vehicle from outside dangers. Blind spots from side mirrors can be eliminated by using an infrared sidelight on the driver's door. A passing vehicle causes a reflection of the light back to a receptor and triggers a warning. Over a million cars already have a self-adjusting electrochromatic rear-view mirror that protects the driver from the glare of headlights from cars behind him. The manufacturer of these mirrors is currently working on window glass that can, at the flip of a switch, protect against sun glare.

A recent agreement of automotive industry people has established a multiplexing standard. Now microprocessor chip makers can work on developing one set of chips that enables standard communications with the engine. This communication is necessary for the controlling chips to "talk" to the exhaust emission scanners, for example.

Car Navigation

In Japan, drivers are already testing car navigation gear, mounted on the dashboard, that can show you where you are and display a detailed map of how to get where you want to go. American automaker General Motors is offering a similar system as an option in some models of Oldsmobile. The two necessary pieces for this system are the following:

➤ The **global positioning satellites** that circle the earth, with the necessary transmitting and receiving equipment in the vehicle

➤ A digital map of the area with coordinates that correspond to the satellite signals

The global positioning satellites are in place and have been working for several years. The U.S. military put 24 satellites in orbit so that from anywhere in the world at least three satellites are accessible. Airplanes, cars, tanks, ships, submarines, or stationary objects can use the satellites as needed.

Detailed maps are not as easily available. Several companies are currently working on detailed maps of the United States. Maps are available for Japan. Maps of other areas of the world will become available when the mapmaking companies feel that the car buyers of the area are going to spend the money to get the navigational packages included in their cars. In mid-1995, prices were still around $2,000 (U.S. currency). The maps can be as simple as a line-drawn map or as fancy as video pictures from the driver's view. Hertz and Avis car rental companies are now making navigational packages available at an added price on many of their rental cars.

Avis' new car navigational system, now offered in many U.S. cities, includes on-screen maps, highlighted routes, and a voice prompt.

Courtesy of Avis, Inc.

The next step beyond the use of maps with automobile navigation systems is a **geographic information system** (**GIS**). Maps of the United States combined with demographic data from the 1990 U.S. census can be used with special software to help companies choose sites for new stores, manufacturing plants, and other facilities or to plan transportation routes. In the past, such systems cost around $100,000, but with the work performed for other uses helping to pay for some of the effort, the complete package for IBM-compatible PCs is under $2,000.

Smart Streets

The U.S. government is helping to pay for developing an **Intelligent Transportation System** (**ITS**) to develop smart streets as well as smart cars. These streets have sensors tied into processors to determine when there is traffic congestion; the sensors can transmit that data to the navigation system of oncoming cars or to other portable electronic devices, such as personal digital assistants (PDAs) or wristwatch pagers. The navigation system could, of course, rework a driver's route to avoid the congestion. A consortium of electronic and computer companies is working with state and federal government agencies in the Seattle area to develop a prototype system. Orlando, Dallas, and Las Vegas are trying additional models. Smart streets and systems to warn travelers of congestion and alternative routes are being built and tested in cities around the United States and around the world.

The supporters of ITS predict that the various technologies of smart cars and smart streets could reduce highway fatalities by as much as 8 percent by 2011, as well as reduce traffic congestion and pollution. Critics say that reducing congestion and simplifying driving will only encourage more drivers and therefore negate the positive effect on pollution, fossil fuel consumption, and reduced congestion.

In the Air

When the Information Superhighway won't do the job, the next choice for rapid travel is the air. Airplanes can take you quickly to any place you want to go. Many innovations are making air travel safer and more comfortable than ever.

Airplanes

Airplanes, like automobiles, are designed with the use of computers. Simulations of wind tunnel tests are completed before the aircraft is built, even as a model. Boeing's newest planes were tested for more than two years before any construction began.

Pilots are trained using computerized **flight simulators**. The program is designed to act like the aircraft on which the pilot is training. A flight simulator can create thousands of conditions and present the trainee with realistic situations. The pilot's reactions to the situations can be recorded, analyzed, and replayed until the pilot naturally reacts in the best possible manner for each situation. And all this training is accomplished without the pilot's ever leaving the flight simulator.

Air Traffic Control

The biggest lifesavers for airplanes are the navigation systems. Some of the technology was tested during Desert Storm; other systems were designed and tested for civilian flights. The heart of airplane safety is the **Air Traffic Control** (**ATC**) system. Originally, people performed all air traffic

Traffic Signal Control

Freeway Management

Emergency Management Services

Traveler Information

Transit Management

Electronic Payment

Electronic Toll Collection

Incident Management

Highway-Rail Crossing Protection

Icons provided courtesy of the U.S. Department of Transportation

Components of an Intelligent Transportation System.

control tasks, but ATC systems are changing to computers as air traffic increases and the capability of computers expands. With the enormous size differences between a single-passenger aircraft and a 300-passenger airbus, it is difficult for aircraft pilots to be aware of all the planes behind, above, and below them. Commercial aircraft are now required to have installed, to use, and to obey the **Traffic alert and Collision Avoidance System** (**TCAS**). Although the software has made mistakes and given avoidance maneuvers to aircraft in no danger, TCAS has averted many accidents.

Photograph by David Ximeno Tejada, Tony Stone Images, Inc.

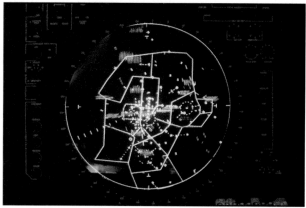

Photograph by Wayne Eastep, Tony Stone Images, Inc.

In addition to TCAS, ATC systems are also being replaced by automated systems. Airplanes are equipped with a **transponder** (transmitter/receiver) that communicates with the ATC system. The newest ATC system integrates airplane information with weather information so that airplanes can be warned of bad weather cells or possible wind shears, as well as other aircraft in the area.

Computers have invaded the passenger compartment also. Take any flight, and you will see laptop and notebook computers come out as soon as the plane is in the air. The biggest problem for the computer-user traveler is power. The battery pack just doesn't last long enough. The airlines are negotiating to retrofit planes with power plugs at each seat. The power is not the problem; the hang-up is the standards for the cable and plugs. Airlines have also been offered computer equipment capable of showing a dozen or more movies to passengers on individual screens on the back of the seat in front of them.

Airline Reservation Systems

Historically, one of the pioneer efforts in using large computer complexes with large databases and thousands of terminals worldwide was the **airline reservation system**. Today's airline reservation system does not just reserve a ticket for a seat on a flight; the system also reserves hotel rooms and rental cars for travelers. The reservation system drives much of the activity of the airline personnel. The system schedules supplies—from food to fuel—for the flight, sets staffing, determines flight plans, and requests take-off and landing reservations from the terminals.

Airports

The latest use of computers with air travel is at the airport. Denver's international airport was delayed in opening nearly a year because of glitches in the computerized luggage-handling system. The system was designed to have 4,000 computer-guided carts carrying suitcases along 22 miles of track, delivering 60,000 bags an hour to and from dozens of gates and carousels. Software apparently was at the root of the problem, which was finally resolved. In Brussels, a new terminal with a computerized baggage facility with a capacity of handling 9,600 bags per hour opened without incident.

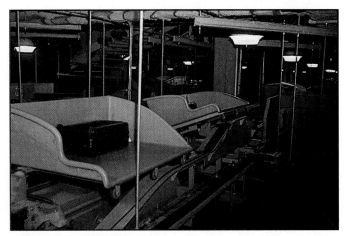

Photograph courtesy of Denver International Airport

On Land and Sea

Cars and planes are not the only way computers are used with transportation. Yacht racing is safer because of the global positioning satellites. In the event of an accident, an emergency beacon can pinpoint the boat's location and signal it to listening posts around the world, such as the Maritime Rescue Coordination Centre in Canberra, Australia, which monitors the Southern Ocean. Trains are controlled by computers, shipping companies monitor every package they are handling, and even tourists can use computerized travel guides.

Logistics

Logistics is the planning and carrying out of a complex scheme, usually involving moving material and people from one location to another. Express delivery is a growing $18 billion a year business that depends on computers. The two biggest carriers are Federal Express and United Parcel Service, which together control 70 percent of the U.S. overnight delivery market. How can these carriers guarantee overnight delivery from anywhere to anywhere? They depend on computers to route the packages and track them. Anyone with a PC and a modem can order pickups, print shipping labels, and track delivery. The software is free from the delivery service.

Once the package is in the hands of the service, it is shipped to a central sorting hub, sorted by computers using optical scanners, and then trucked or flown to its overnight destination. Whenever the sender or receiver wants to know the location of the package, he or she can access the computer, and the tracking system has all the information.

Photograph courtesy of Federal Express Corporation

Computerized Routing Systems

Computers have been used to automate many tasks previously performed by hand. Whether we are typesetting, processing checks, or making morning espresso, computers have changed the way we conduct our business and live our lives. One area where computers have had a huge impact is in automated routing systems.

Automated routing is nothing more than the use of technology (specifically computers) to speed the way physical objects are routed. The size of the objects doesn't particularly matter—they could be as small and ethereal as electronic messages, as mundane as your letter to Aunt Martha, or as large as freight trains. Routing systems are used extensively in many businesses. For example, the new Denver International Airport uses computers to manage its people-mover trains, which run between terminals of the facility. Computers control the starting, stopping, and speed of the trains so that no human drivers are necessary. The airport uses computers also to automatically route baggage from one flight to another in a matter of minutes.

Perhaps the leader in the area of automated routing is Federal Express. This forward-looking company has used technology extensively in its package-handling operations. In fact, Federal Express has computerized every step of handling a package. The key to the system is a unique bar code placed on every package. The bar code is created either by the sender (using free Federal Express software) or by the couriers when they pick up the package. The bar code indicates information such as the package ID, billing specifics, the package weight, the sender, and the recipient. The bar code is scanned six times, on average, during the shipment of the package.

The bar code on the package is first scanned by the courier using what Federal Express calls the SuperTracker. This device then relays the package information by satellite to the main computer system in Memphis. When the package is transferred to the local Federal Express office, it is scanned again, and then again when it arrives at one of their hubs. There are five major hubs in the United States, which collectively handle over 2.4 million packages per day. As a package moves through the hub, the bar code is read by overhead

scanners that aid in routing the package to the proper airplane. Once the package arrives at the destination Federal Express office, it is scanned again as it is placed on the delivery truck. Finally, it is scanned for a last time when it is delivered to the recipient.

Photograph courtesy of Federal Express Corporation

The purpose of each scan is to allow the proper routing of the package, as well as to document tracking information. This is why you can use Federal Express software or call Federal Express to determine the precise location of your package as it makes its way toward its destination.

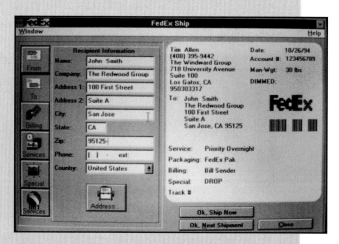

Photograph courtesy of Federal Express Corporation

continues

If a package is destined for international delivery, automation also helps in preparing customs documentation. This helps Federal Express avoid lengthy delays in clearing international borders. The heart of the customs system relies on EDI (electronic data interchange) to transact quickly and reliably the necessary documentation for the shipment.

Routing systems are getting more sophisticated, and their use is becoming more common in many different fields. They will become even more common as their prices continue to drop in relation to their capabil-ities.

Photograph courtesy of Federal Express Corporation

Trains

Whether in San Francisco, New York, London, or Paris, the scene is similar. As you approach the train depot to board the commuter train or the Chunnel train, you use your ATM or credit card at a machine to get a debit card to cover your fare. You put your debit card into the slot at the turnstile, and it returns the card to you on the other side with the fare deducted. A recorded message, played by the computer as it senses the incoming train, alerts you to its arrival and the next destinations. After you board, the computer pulls the train out of the station and on its way. When you get off the train, if you owe more fare, the exit turnstile takes your debit card, deducts the remaining fare, and returns the card to you on the other side.

Travel Guides

If your travels take you to France, the *Michelin: France* guide to restaurants and hotels is now available in a pocket-computer version (for about $200). Besides offering information in several languages—French, English, German, Spanish, and Italian—the guide can calculate exchange rates in 21 currencies and give special information, such as hotels with balcony rooms or restaurants with vegetarian fare. Updates are provided as needed.

Toward the Future

Although the innovations discussed so far are new and exciting, there are more to come. A goal of the U.S. government is to produce automobiles with fuel economies of 80 mpg by the year 2004, while maintaining performance and the cost of today's cars. Alternative fuels will be needed, along with microprocessor control of fuel systems. This project is the Supercar program, which is expected to cost about $1 billion to develop.

Another project under development but not ready for the open market is a car that can drive itself. Japanese automakers are working on a prototype. A European coalition is working on a project called Prometheus, and the U.S.

A smart car named ALVINN.

is developing a vehicle called **Autonomous Land Vehicle in the Neural Network**, or **ALVINN**. The current prototype of ALVINN uses a three-stage process. First, ALVINN is driven over the road, using laser and sonar waves and taping the view. Next, ALVINN replays the tape and data thousands of times, developing the car's neural networks. Finally, ALVINN drives the road itself, handling the acceleration, braking, and steering. The biggest problem is that ALVINN can't handle anything it hasn't seen before.

Air travel is due for major changes. The current air fleet is aging rapidly. New planes now in design stages in Europe, America, and Japan share several improvements. The new planes will be more economical to fly, getting better fuel economy than today's gas guzzlers. They will be larger than today's planes, with passenger capacities of 200 to 600, and they will be faster. A manager of Kawasaki Heavy Industries predicts that by the year 2010 regular supersonic service between London and Tokyo will take about 3 hours rather than the 13 hours the trip takes today.

A worldwide satellite-based air traffic control system will make travel safer, but one loss will come on the ground. Most airports are inadequate to handle the larger planes, and most are not planning expansions. All the time gained from the faster planes may be spent getting into, around, and out of the airport with your luggage.

Cruise ships are increasing in popularity. Cellular communications keep the ship at sea in touch with the rest of the world. Computers are adding to the amusements available; for instance, virtual reality movie houses give passengers tired of being at sea a chance to experience flying through the Grand Canyon or over Alaskan glaciers and then returning to their seagoing adventure. With better navigation than ever, computer controls to smooth out the ride, and a plan to cater to the passengers' enjoyment, cruises are expected to be twice as popular in the next five years.

Rail travel will get faster, smoother, and easier in the coming century. The French TGV (train grande vitesse) Atlantique travels in excess of 500 kph. The Japanese are experimenting with a superconductive magnetism-powered train that simply floats above the rails and runs at 550 kph. In Europe, the biggest change will be the new standardized high-speed lines that allow seamless travel between countries.

Lesson Summary

➤ Automobiles are being equipped with navigation systems that use global positioning satellites and digital maps. Smart streets include sensors in the street to recognize congestion and signal navigation systems or personal digital assistants.

➤ Computerized flight simulators are used to train pilots.

➤ Automation is moving into the air traffic control (ATC) tower with automated equipment, and airplanes are being equipped with the Traffic alert and Collision Avoidance System (TCAS). Computers are being integrated into the airport operation, including new baggage-handling systems.

➤ The express delivery companies are improving their services by using computers.

➤ New commuter trains and high-speed trains are possible because of computer controls.

➤ Supersonic airplanes will be capable of traveling from London to Tokyo in three hours. Trains also will be faster and more convenient. Cruise ships will include better contact with the outside world so that passengers will enjoy longer cruises.

Lesson Review

Key Terms

Air Traffic Control (ATC)
airline reservation system
ALVINN
antiskid braking system (ABS)
Automotive Stability Management System (ASMS)

Autonomous Land Vehicle in the Neural Network
flight simulator
geographic information system (GIS)
global positioning satellite

Intelligent Transportation System (ITS)
logistics
multiplex central wiring
smart cars

Traffic alert and Collision Avoidance System (TCAS)
transponder

Matching

In the blank next to each of the following terms or phrases, write the letter of the corresponding term or phrase.

_____   **1.** A pilot training tool

_____   **2.** Antiskid braking system

_____   **3.** A program to develop smart streets

_____   **4.** Allows personalization of a car's settings

_____ 5. Uses neural network to "learn" how to drive

_____ 6. Uses microprocessors to help drivers drive more safely

_____ 7. Used to locate cars, planes, and boats

_____ 8. Being developed in the U.S. to help navigate cars with the use of global positioning satellites

_____ 9. Keeps planes flying safely as a primary responsibility

_____ 10. Software to integrate maps and demographic data

a. smart car

b. multiplex central wiring

c. ABS

d. global positioning satellites

e. geographic information system

f. digital maps

g. Intelligent Transportation System

h. flight simulator

i. air traffic control

j. ALVINN

Multiple Choice

Circle the letter of the correct choice for each of the following.

1. A(n) _____ car can warn you of traffic in your blind spot and correct for oversteering on ice.

   a. computer
   b. intelligent
   c. smart
   d. German

2. Which of the following is used to test an automobile's design before it is built?

   a. simulation
   b. model
   c. video car
   d. crash dummy car

3. Using microprocessor chips to control braking is called what?

   a. antiskid braking system
   b. simulated braking
   c. Automobile Stability Management System
   d. a and c

4. Which of the following consists of a continuous-wire system throughout the car, with one wire making a complete loop with addresses for various functions?

   a. personalized wiring
   b. parallel wiring
   c. multiplex central wiring
   d. nervous system wiring

5. Which of the following is a type of rear-view mirror that can self-adjust for the glare of headlights from behind?

   a. flip mirror
   b. electromagnetic mirror
   c. multiplexing mirror
   d. electrochromatic mirror

6. Which of the following systems consists of maps combined with demographic data and used by special software?

   a. global positioning system
   b. map-planning system
   c. geographic information system
   d. digital mapping system

7. Automobile navigation systems already being used in some cars need two components. One is access to the global positioning satellites. What is the other component?

   a. infrared sensors

   b. personal digital assistants

   c. a smart road

   d. digital maps

8. A major tool used in training pilots is _____.

   a. the test airplane

   b. the flight simulator

   c. the air traffic control system

   d. all of the above

9. Which of the following is the famous European travel guide that has been computerized?

   a. *Michelin: France*

   b. *Passport* guide

   c. transponder

   d. *Perelli* guide

10. In the future, where will air traffic control systems be based?

   a. on satellites

   b. on the planes themselves

   c. in five countries around the world

   d. on ocean-going ships

Completion

In the blank provided, write the correct answer for each of the following.

1. A car that can monitor its own internal workings is called a(n) _____.

2. The area behind the driver and to the left is sometimes called a(n) _____.

3. Satellites that send signals which enable a properly equipped car to determine its location are called _____.

4. When sensors in the streets can determine traffic congestion and transmit that information to oncoming cars, the streets are said to be _____.

5. The transmitter/receiver that enables airplanes to be tracked by an air traffic control system is called a(n) _____.

6. Commercial aircraft flying in the U.S. are required to use a system to tell them when to take evasive action to avoid an air crash. The system is called _____.

7. Staffing and supplying an aircraft before it takes off is part of the system that sells travelers their tickets. The system is known as a(n) _____.

8. _____ is planning and carrying out a complex scheme, usually involving moving people or things.

9. A prototype of a car that can drive itself is named _____.

10. _____ communication enables passengers on cruise ships to keep in touch with the rest of the world.

Review

On a separate sheet of paper, answer the following questions.

1. What are the characteristics of a smart car?

2. How can using simulations of cars before they are built improve their safety?

3. Multiplex central wiring can make what kind of car personalization possible?

4. What equipment is needed so that a car can tell a driver his or her location?

5. How is a smart street supposed to act?

6. How do flight simulators make pilots better able to fly planes?

7. Why was the Traffic alert and Collision Avoidance System created? How can it help make air travel safer?

8. When airplanes are bigger and faster, what problems will air travelers have in getting to their final destinations?

9. How could global positioning satellites help boats in races be safer?

10. How are computers being used to help make rail travel easier?

Critical Thinking

On a separate sheet of paper, answer the following questions.

1. Will having "smarter" cars reduce the problems that we have because of cars—such as traffic, pollution, and use of fossil fuels? Or will smart cars make it easier to travel by car and just encourage the use of more cars?

2. Besides a travel guide, such as *Michelin: France*, what other electronic or computer-based devices do you think would make traveling easier?

3. What advantages and disadvantages do you see with traveling on a 500-passenger supersonic airplane?

4. Do you think that navigation systems with maps make cars more or less safe? Why?

5. What aspects of a car would you like to personalize? Why?

On-line Discovery

You can access the Internet resources for the following questions by going to the Que Education and Training Web site at URL http://www.ciyf98.com/discovery. From this page, click the link for Lesson 12B and then click the link to the resource you want to access.

1. The **Texas Transportation Institute** (**TTI**) does research and development in integrated traffic control systems. The TTI home page (http://herman.tamu.edu) illustrates the research that is occurring there and describes in detail several of the most interesting projects. What are the most significant projects being worked on at TTI? How will these developments change traffic patterns, both in the city and on the highway? Services like the "Houston Area Real-Time Traffic Report" (available from the TTI home page) would presumably be most useful if available in the car. When do you think such a service will be commonly available to motorists? How much would you be willing to pay for a vehicle that had such systems integrated? How would the service look to the driver?

2. New developments in electronic commerce, including electronic data interchange (EDI), electronic banking, and the capability to order goods over the Internet, actually create additional needs for rapid transportation of goods across the country (and the world). Look at the home pages of several shipping companies, including **Airborne Express** (http://www.airborne-express.com), **UPS** (http://www.ups.com), **Federal Express** (http://www.fedex.com), and the **United States Postal Service** (http://www.usps.gov). How do these organizations use technology to improve shipping speed and service? What services are available to customers right from their own computers? Do any of these organizations offer services directly over the Internet?

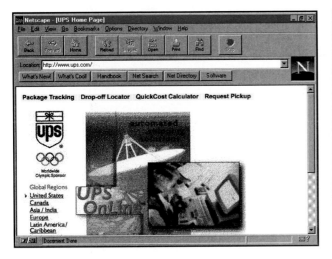

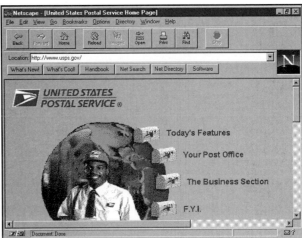

LESSON 12C

Computers in Law Enforcement

Outline

Learning Objectives

When you have finished reading this lesson, you will be able to

➤ Discuss software piracy

➤ Understand how governments are cooperating to develop standards for dealing with computers and computer crime

➤ Explain how computers are used to identify criminals

➤ Define computer matching and explain how records are matched

➤ Explain how police departments use MDTs

➤ Discuss computer fraud and credit card fraud

➤ List some of the dangers of telecommunications

➤ Discuss problems encountered by law enforcement officials in seizing computers

Like any invention, computers have the potential to be used for both good and evil. Computer systems provide security for data from modification, destruction, and misrepresentation. Unfortunately, computers have also been used for virtually every imaginable type of crime: fraud, theft, sabotage, murder, forgery, espionage, and embezzlement. Despite geographic distance, law enforcement agencies throughout the world face similar threats from those wanting to use computers for wrongdoing.

Legislation is being developed, law enforcement officials are being trained, and computers are being used to combat those who would use them irresponsibly. Computer groups have reacted in various ways to proposed legislation. The Electronic Frontier Foundation tends to react negatively to any legislation that seeks to curtail computer use. Computer Professionals for Social Responsibility looks more favorably on that kind type of legislation.

The International Picture

Governments throughout the world are faced with computer crime. In November 1993, for example, two computers in the Kashiwazaki Kariwa atomic power plant in Japan were infected by the data-destroying virus Cascade. This incident is just one of many similar occurrences at other locations.

The most common computer crime is piracy of copyrighted software. The Software Publishers Association (SPA) estimates that 95 percent of the software in Pakistan is pirated, 89 percent in Brazil, 88 percent in Malaysia, and 82 percent in Mexico.

TechTalk
Software piracy is the unauthorized and illegal copying of copyrighted software without the permission of the software publisher.

In May 1995, the Italian government conducted a nationwide crackdown on private bulletin board systems. Italian customs officials converged on dwellings where FIDONET system operators lived. Approximately sixty FIDONET BBSs were shut down, and more than one hundred computers and thousands of floppy disks, CD-ROMs, and WORMs were confiscated. The charge was **software piracy**.

Russia passed a law against software piracy in 1990 and is currently cooperating with the U.S.-based Business Software Alliance to enforce that law.

To combat computer crime, law enforcement agencies representing Canada, Europe, Japan, and the United States are cooperating to develop security guidelines. The completed document, known as the *Common Criteria for Use with Information Technology Products*, will be submitted to the International Standards Organization (ISO) for approval. *Common Criteria* will address such issues as networking, database operations, data security, and encryption.

Twenty-three countries participate in the International Conference on Computer Evidence, which holds annual meetings. However, according to Detective Frank Clark, a participant in the conference representing the United States, "electronic meetings take place daily." Participants have formed five committees to develop international standards for software, data, communications, forensics evidence, and legislation.

Unfortunately, law enforcement agencies face serious challenges in fully using computer capabilities to fight crime. An international conference on criminal justice sponsored by Great Britain and the United States in May 1995 highlighted some of those problems. Police forces do not have the funds that organized crime has at its disposal; this lack results in law enforcement organizations working with inferior computer equipment. Another problem is that police attempting to track a computer crime that crosses international boundaries run into legal obstacles, and cooperation between the police forces of the countries involved is not always the best.

Some impressive advances are being made in the use of computers by law enforcement. In the Netherlands, a unique approach to putting more police on the streets by minimizing paperwork has been developed. Small computers, resembling ATM machines, have been placed on street corners so that citizens can walk up and report a crime. Over 3,000 reports were logged on just one of the systems in the first month of operation. The **compucops** are built around a 486 microprocessor. The systems accept both voice and typed data on the same phone line. Law enforcement agencies in France, Norway, the United Kingdom, and Hungary are considering installing similar systems.

Federal Use of Computers

A 1939 presidential directive made the Federal Bureau of Investigation (FBI) the national clearinghouse for data relating to internal security. Subsequently, the Civil Identification Division began to collect fingerprints of arrested criminal suspects. Today, more than 173 million sets of fingerprints are on file in the FBI computer database. Through the International Exchange of Fingerprints, the FBI shares criminal identification information with law enforcement agencies from more than eighty foreign countries.

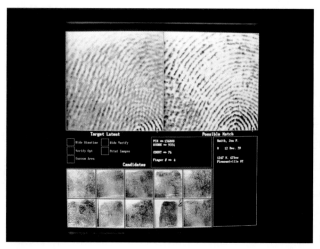

Photograph by Alan Abramowitz, Tony Stone Images, Inc.

The National Crime Information Center

The National Crime Information Center (NCIC) is located at FBI headquarters in Washington, D.C. NCIC is the computer hub of a communications network that is accessed by federal, state, and local law enforcement agencies throughout the United States. NCIC maintains a comprehensive database of information on crime and criminals; this database is available to law enforcement officials in a matter of seconds.

Taking a Byte out of Crime

Computer scientists represent some of the newest recruits of the Federal Bureau of Investigation, due to the fact that many phases of FBI activity are going online, using sophisticated new hardware and software.

For example, a geographic information system (GIS), using software that performs geographic analyses, has been linked with an arson information database. The GIS isolates spatial and time-related patterns and generates maps that are both easy to read and easy to reproduce. These maps have helped eliminate the use of pin-map tracking of arson crimes, which are often inaccurate and unmanageable. Complex serial arson cases in Washington state, Minnesota, Florida, Tennessee, and the New England area have been solved with the help of these computer programs.

The FBI is also using the computer to develop the Integrated Automated Fingerprint Identification System (IAFIS). This system, scheduled for full implementation in 1997, will enable experts to analyze electronically 65,000 fingerprints a day. The goal is to create a pool of more than 200 million fingerprints and provide law enforcement officials across the nation with online access to these records.

Another phase of the project will convert the FBI's current collection of 36 million cardboard fingerprint records to an electronic format.

Courtesy of International Business Machines Corporation

Computer technology is also helping the FBI improve its National Crime Information Center (NCIC). With this system, online crime information, including fingerprints, will be available from a police squad car within seconds. Other services provided by the enhanced system include automated records validation, new databases of probation and parole files, and an intrusion safeguard for the system itself. With the system, the FBI plans eventually to serve more than 72,000 agencies.

Computer layout and design techniques were also used on an FBI wanted poster. A magazine designer at *PC World* used a desktop publishing software program to redesign a wanted poster that he saw displayed at the post office. As part of an attempt to help catch the criminal, the new poster and the information about the felon were featured in *PC World*.

Our world is becoming an even safer place, now that computers are taking a byte out of crime.

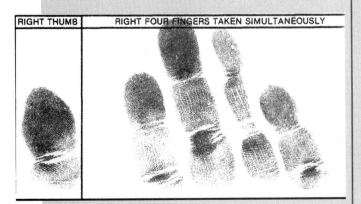

Courtesy of Caitlin Brown

Recently, the FBI was able to discover an alleged CIA mole named Rick Ames by using "electronic surveillance of Ames' personal computer." The FBI will not reveal exactly how this surveillance was accomplished. They could have planted a bug in Ames' computer to record keystrokes as they were entered, or they might have accessed the computer over modem lines from a remote location when it was turned on, and perused the contents of the hard drive. Whatever method was used, it was successful, and Ames never knew that the computer had been accessed.

The IRS—Internal Security

The Internal Revenue Service (IRS) has developed software to lock hard drives in order to protect data that might be valuable in a criminal investigation. The IRS has also written software to assist investigators in executing search warrants in cases involving computers.

Computer matching is used by the federal government to cross-link the information stored in different computers. Social security numbers, sometimes jokingly referred to in the computer industry as the **universal identifier numbers**, are used to cross-link databases. For example, the IRS and the Department of Justice use computer matching to recover overdue child support from individuals before tax refunds are issued. Computer matching has also been used by the government to find employees who have defaulted on student loans.

State and Local Use of Computers

Walk into a modern police department, and you will see a computer on every desk. Reports must be filled out on every suspected crime, and word processing software saves a considerable amount of time. Many reports are saved directly to disk and archived in a database; those that are not saved directly are usually scanned into a database from hard copy. The Indianapolis Police Department uses Kodak's QuickSolve software to aid in its criminal investigations. QuickSolve provides electronic storage and retrieval of evidence, including crime scene photographs, fingerprints, crime lab reports, and mug shots.

The Kodak QuickSolve software.

Courtesy of Eastman Kodak Company

In Iowa, a state that has invested heavily in distance education, parole hearings are held using videoconferencing technology. (Parole hearings are usually held to determine whether an individual has violated the terms of his or her parole.) Two judges are able to handle all the parole hearings for the state. Hearings are held in classrooms throughout the state that are connected to the Iowa Communications Network. Both judges like the distance hearings; they save the judges time on the road, enabling them to be more productive and saving the taxpayers money.

In an interstate effort to control gang activities, a new law enforcement database known as GREAT (Gang Research Evaluation And Testing) has been developed. GREAT allows agencies to access information quickly about known gang members from three states: California, Hawaii, and Nevada. So far, over 250,000 gang members have been entered into the system. One of the problems of apprehending gang members in the past has been their mobility—but no more, thanks to GREAT.

With the Kodak QuickSolve system, you can do selective printing.

Courtesy of Eastman Kodak Company

Mobile Data Terminals

Most law enforcement vehicles are equipped with a computer terminal or a microcomputer. The remote terminal (called a **mobile data terminal**, or **MDT**) has access to a mainframe computer at the agency's headquarters; the mainframe has a database containing vehicle and driver's license information, including outstanding warrants and criminal records. This information has helped officers apprehend suspects in cases not related to the vehicular violation for which the system was initially queried.

Local police departments maintain their own databases in addition to accessing state and federal databases. Local databases may contain gang membership information, including tattoos; track movements of individuals in ongoing cases; and track leads in ongoing cases. Local police also make use of **expert systems** to assist in identifying patterns that might lead to the arrest of serial killers and rapists.

Photograph by Jim Pickerell, Tony Stone Images, Inc.

Photograph by Keith Wood, Tony Stone Images, Inc.

Digitized Criminal Investigations

A new service, called **Image APB**, is currently being tested by a number of agencies. Image APB broadcasts images through paging channels. A sketch or photograph of an individual—for example, a missing child—can be sent to every officer who has a portable computer and a pager. An entire police force can be provided with a photograph in a matter of minutes. The system is affordable—a microcomputer can be equipped for about $300—so we are likely to see it becoming a standard for law enforcement agencies.

Challenges Posed by Computers

Many crimes are committed using computers. Law enforcement officials need to know how to expose the perpetrators and how to access any evidence stored on computer systems.

Computer Fraud

One of the most common types of white-collar computer crime is fraud. The first known large-scale **computer fraud** was committed by Equity Funding Corporation. Company management decided to boost stock prices and attract investors by overstating company sales and profits. The lies compounded, with the number of phony insurance policies growing and company officials falsifying medical records. By the time the company was shut down in 1973, more than $2 billion in phony insurance policies had been entered into the computers. The Equity Funding Corporation computer fraud was the subject of a high-quality, made-for-television movie entitled *The Billion Dollar Bubble*.

Unscrupulous employees have used computers to embezzle funds from their employers, steal from company customers, falsify data, and gather data to use for blackmail.

The Computer Fraud and Abuse Act of 1986 defines activities that fall within the definition of computer fraud, and specifies maximum penalties for perpetration of computer fraud. One of the first cases tried under the Computer Fraud and Abuse Act was that of Robert Morris. Morris was found guilty of introducing into the Internet a virus that attacked thousands of computers and destroyed millions of dollars of data. Morris' defense was that the virus was not purposely designed to do harm but had a bug that caused it to replicate and destroy data. He was sentenced to three years of probation and ordered to perform four hundred hours of community service.

Credit Card Fraud

One specialized type of fraud being perpetrated with the assistance of computers is **credit card fraud**. Credit card numbers are accessed by unauthorized individuals and used to purchase items. Sometimes the credit card information is distributed over telecommunications lines, and the numbers are used by different people. Most vulnerable to this type of fraud are telephone credit card numbers, which allow computer criminals to place hundreds of hours of long distance calls without incurring charges.

Illegal Telecommunications Activities

One of the dangers, which was discussed earlier in this chapter, is the practice of copyrighted software being pirated and distributed using telecommunications services.

Another danger was pointed out by President Clinton in his speech to the American Association of Community Colleges in April 1995. In that speech, while talking about the bombing of the Federal Building in Oklahoma City, the president stressed the dangers of "the airwaves," referring to telecommunications services as well as other public access media, being used by radical groups for illegal purposes.

Recently, a number of cases have appeared in the news involving stalking of individuals over telecommunications services, distribution of pornography, and children being lured into situations where they can be abducted. One solution under discussion is banning the use of nicknames so that individuals must disclose their real names.

Seizure of Information Stored on Computers

Software has been developed to execute search warrants and process seized property. Police routinely seize computers and software discovered at the scene of a crime. They may even seize computers from businesses suspected of illegal activities. Unfortunately, this practice can result in serious disruption of the business and cause severe problems even if the charges are dismissed. It is very difficult for a business with all its accounts receivable and payable encoded on a computer to function without that computer and the software that it contains.

Training of Law Enforcement Officials

One of the biggest challenges facing law enforcement agencies is proper training of officers. Agencies have not developed training programs, and officers must travel to attend workshops. Many departments are understaffed and underfunded; they have trouble sending personnel for the needed training.

Investigators need to know when and how to seize a computer system. They also need to learn how to make copies of the data stored on a system without physically seizing the system or damaging the data on it. A comprehensive manual entitled *Federal Guidelines for Searching and Seizing Computers* was published by the Department of Justice in December 1994. The manual covers when seizure is legal and explains how to seize a computer system or the data stored on a computer system.

One of the fastest growing fields of expertise within the law enforcement profession is the investigation of computer crime.

Lesson Summary

➤ Governments throughout the world are cooperating to develop standards for dealing with computer crime.

➤ Criminals frequently have computer equipment superior to that of law enforcement agencies.

➤ NCIC, located at FBI headquarters, maintains criminal files for the U.S.

➤ Computer matching of databases assists law enforcement agencies in tracking individuals who have broken the law.

➤ There is concern about the use of telecommunications for criminal activity, as well as a demand for investigators trained in computer crime procedures.

Lesson Review

Key Terms

compucops   credit card fraud   mobile data terminal   universal identifier number
computer fraud   expert system   (MDT)
computer matching Image APB   software piracy

Matching

In the blank next to each of the following terms or phrases, write the letter of the corresponding term or phrase.

_____ 1. Used by citizens to call police and report a crime in progress

_____ 2. Unauthorized distribution of credit information over telecommunications lines

_____ 3. A privately run computer service for e-mail and file exchange

_____ 4. Cross-linking the information in different computers

_____ 5. Used to distribute images pertinent to a crime through paging channels

_____ 6. The U.S. clearinghouse for data relating to internal security

_____ 7. Using the computer to deprive others of what is rightfully theirs

a. MDT
b. NCIC
c. compucop
d. software piracy
e. computer fraud
f. FBI
g. computer matching
h. BBS
i. credit card fraud
j. Image APB

_____ 8. Agency that maintains the U.S. database of criminal information

_____ 9. Illegal duplication of computer programs

_____ 10. A computer terminal located in a police patrol vehicle

Multiple Choice

Circle the letter of the correct choice for each of the following.

1. Software piracy refers to _____.

    a. individuals stealing computer floppy disks

    b. criminals stealing computer chips

    c. programmers copying code from other programs

    d. individuals copying copyrighted programs

2. Computers can help catch criminals by _____.

    a. keeping logs of leads in cases

    b. analyzing serial crimes

    c. keeping criminal history records

    d. all of the above

3. The most widespread computer crime is _____.

    a. software piracy

    b. credit card fraud

    c. embezzling funds

    d. theft of computer systems

4. The governments cooperating to develop the *Common Criteria* security guidelines include all of the following except _____.

    a. Canada

    b. China

    c. Japan

    d. the United States

5. _____ is using compucops to aid in crime reporting.

    a. The United States

    b. Japan

    c. The Netherlands

    d. Russia

6. The _____ is the federal agency responsible for the internal security of data.

    a. CIA

    b. NCIC

    c. Department of Justice

    d. FBI

7. Problems relating to telecommunications include all of the following *except* _____.

    a. distribution of pornography

    b. software piracy

    c. use by groups engaged in illegal activities

    d. inability to cross national boundaries

8. The IRS has written programs for law enforcement agencies to assist in _____.

    a. detecting crimes involving computers

    b. processing seized computer hardware and software

    c. writing search warrants

    d. locating criminals using their fingerprints

9. The _____ does not believe in the regulation of computer users.

    a. Electronic Frontier Foundation

    b. International Standards Organization

    c. Computer Professionals for Social Responsibility

    d. NCIC

10. Challenges facing law enforcement include all of the following *except* _____.

    a. funding

    b. training of officers

    c. international recognition that a problem exists

    d. cooperation between agencies

Completion

In the blank provided, write the correct answer for each of the following.

1. The _____ maintains a database of millions of sets of fingerprints.

2. The _____ will be responsible for approving standards for computer security.

3. _____ is the illegal duplication of copyrighted software.

4. Many police vehicles are equipped with _____ to communicate with mainframe computers at headquarters.

5. Telecommunications services run by private individuals are known as _____.

6. The _____ is sometimes referred to as the universal identifier number.

7. It is important that law enforcement officers know how to _____ hard drives on computer systems that are involved in a crime investigation.

8. Police officers use _____ software to write crime reports.

9. _____ software is used to maintain data such as criminal records and fingerprints.

10. Banning _____ has been suggested to reduce the dangers of communicating with strangers using telecommunications services.

Review

On a separate sheet of paper, answer the following questions.

1. What is software piracy?

2. Discuss some of the ways in which unscrupulous individuals are using telecommunications services for illegal purposes.

3. How are computers used to commit credit card fraud?

4. How can law enforcement officials determine whether a computer is being used to commit a crime?

5. What are the areas for which the ISO is going to adopt standards?

6. What are some of the obstacles that law enforcement agencies need to overcome to be able to fight computer crime effectively?

7. How does computer matching help to find individuals who have broken the law?

8. What is Image APB?

9. How are expert systems used in criminal investigations?

10. What is the name of the manual that presents guidelines for law enforcement in dealing with computers involved in criminal investigations?

Critical Thinking

On a separate sheet of paper, answer the following questions.

1. How would you suggest that individuals who use telecommunications services be protected from others who would take advantage of that use?

2. What are some of the uses that law enforcement agencies make of databases? What other uses of database software might be of assistance to law enforcement agencies?

3. For each of the five areas relating to computer crime, think of one standard that you would like the International Standards Organization to adopt.

4. Do you think that compucops are a good idea? In your opinion, would they work in the United States? Why or why not?

5. What types of problems do businesses face when a computer system is seized?

Further Discovery

25 Years of Criminal Justice Research. National Institute of Justice (Washington, DC: U.S. Department of Justice, 1994).

Computer Crime. David Icove, Karl Seger, and Willaim VonStorch (Sebastopol, CA: O'Reilly, 1995).

Investigating Computer Crime. Frank Clark and Ken Diliberto (Boca Raton, FL: CRC Press, 1996).

Sex, Laws, and Cyberspace. Jonathan Wallace and Mark Mangan (New York: M&T Books and Henry Holt, 1996).

On-line Discovery

You can access the Internet resources for the following questions by going to the Que Education and Training Web site at URL http://www.ciyf98.com/discovery. From this page, click the link for Lesson 12C and then click the link to the resource you want to access.

1. **CopNet** (http://police.sas.ab.ca) is a Web page of resources primarily of interest to law enforcement officers. Although CopNet is from Canada, it contains resources from all over the world, including pointers to law enforcement agency home pages from many countries. Look at some of these resources. Does the police department in your home town or city have a home page? If not, pick the police department home page from a different city. What kinds of resources does the home page provide? Does it provide a way for citizens to communicate with law enforcement officers about problems in their communities?

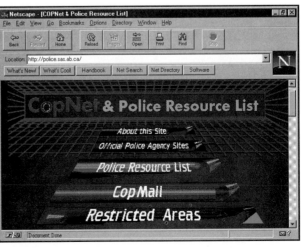

2. The **Federal Bureau of Investigation** (**FBI**) provides informational resources to local law enforcement officers; many of these resources are computer databases. Browse through the **FBI** home page (http://www.fbi.gov). What databases does the FBI make available? What information is available in these databases? Can you think of any other ways in which national databases might help law enforcement officers?

Arts and Entertainment

Outline

Performing Arts
 Music
 Dance
 Theater
Fine Arts
 Creating Art
 Restoring Art
Photography
Are Computers Improving the Arts?
Movies and Television
 Movie Magic
 Special Effects
 Animation
 On-Demand Television
Fun and Games
 Interactive Television
 Multimedia Entertainment
 Games for the Young Child

Learning Objectives

When you have finished reading this lesson, you will be able to

➤ Discuss how artists can use computers as tools

➤ Describe what MIDI does and how musicians use it

➤ Explain how computers can help a choreographer design a dance

➤ Discuss how computers are pivotal in efforts to restore works of art by the old masters

➤ Explain how computers can be used to enhance and alter photographs

➤ Discuss how computers are used to create "movie magic"

➤ Describe how computer technology can reduce costs and increase the power in television and moviemaking

➤ Discuss how computer games can help develop skills

➤ Describe how some people view the future of computers in the entertainment field

Art in its various forms is a means for humans to express emotions and elicit emotional responses in others. Because the computer is incapable of emotions, it cannot create art. The computer can, however, be a powerful tool in the hands of an artist.

Have you ever played marbles or tag? How about jacks or hopscotch? These children's games have helped many generations of children develop muscle and hand-eye coordination as they grew into adulthood. Today, computer games do the same thing. Tomorrow's adults need to be able to manipulate a computer, and computer games start teaching the physical coordination necessary to accomplish this task.

The movie industry also has profited from computer techniques. Think about the special effects of recent movies. Have you ever asked yourself how they do that?

This lesson explores the many ways that computers are used by artists, craftsmen, and artisans. The lesson also looks at some of the directions computer games are taking and at ways computers are being used in the entertainment industry.

Performing Arts

Performing arts require, as the name implies, a human performance. The computer can play a role in these art forms by being a useful tool in organization, reproduction, and record keeping. In the area of music, there has been experimentation with the computer as the performer.

Music

Where would music be today without synthesizers and other computer equipment such as MIDI and sound boards? Today's music would probably sound like the music of the '50s and '60s.

A **synthesizer** or electronic keyboard uses FM (Frequency Modulation), sampling, or waveguiding technology to produce a sound pattern. This sound pattern may be simple (sounding like one instrument) or complex (sounding like several instruments). The sound pattern is sent into the computer through **MIDI (Musical Instrument Digital Interface)**.

Courtesy of International Business Machines Corporation

MIDI is a standard for the cabling and hardware that connect computers and electronic instruments and for the method used to pass the sound pattern between these devices.

Music is regulated electronically through MIDI, and MIDI data can be generated through a MIDI-capable keyboard, wind instrument, guitar, or percussion controller. MIDI data can also be generated through a **sequencer** (a software program used to play MIDI files) that has recorded the MIDI data, or a sequencer playing back a file.

When the musician plays a song on an electronic instrument, each note is sent through the MIDI to the computer, along with the note's length, the amount of attack, the tempo, pitch, and decay time. In digital form in the computer, the MIDI file for the song can be changed easily. For example, it is easy to transpose the song from one key to another or to repeat sections.

Musicians commonly use MIDI standards for creating music for television or movies, or for adding music and sounds to video or computer games or multimedia presentations.

To process music, the computer may need a **sound card**, or **sound board**. The sound card is inserted into an expansion slot of a PC. Macintosh computers often come with a sound card built in. The card has outlets—called jacks—through which a microphone, MIDI, or speakers are connected to the sound card and therefore into the computer. The sound card converts analog sounds, such as sounds from a microphone, into digital signals to be processed by the computer; then the sound card converts the signals back into analog signals for the speakers. Sound cards are often the central connection point for multimedia hardware.

Dance

Have you ever wished that you could see *Swan Lake* danced the way it was a hundred years ago? You could hear an orchestra play the music the same way it was played then if the musicians used the score from that time. Choreographers usually don't record dance, however, so dance is often passed on by teaching it to the dancer. If a teacher forgets movements, they could be lost forever. There are ways of noting choreography, but the task can be extremely time-consuming. Even the "new" technology of video recording can miss nuances in timing and spatial relationships.

Photograph by Anthony Edgeworth, The Stock Market

The application of the computer to this problem has resulted in a dance notation called **DOM (Dance on Microcomputer) notation**. DOM produces an animated figure performing the dance routine. A program called Life Forms creates a three-dimensional figure; the choreographer can experiment with this figure and then save only the movements that "work."

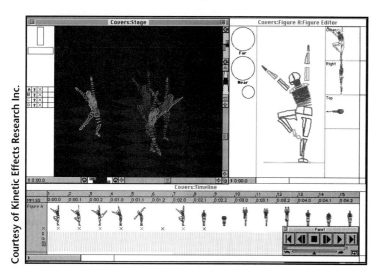

Courtesy of Kinetic Effects Research Inc.

A Life Forms screen.

Merce Cunningham, a pioneer of modern dance, has experimented with Life Forms to create a complete dance program. In 1994, he premiered a 90-minute dance called "Ocean," which he created with Life Forms. Because the dance is performed in the round (with the audience and the orchestra encircling the stage), the choreographer must be aware of all the angles of every dancer all the time. Tracking that level of detail would be extremely challenging without the use of the computer.

With Life Forms, the choreographer develops the three stages of the dance—creating the sequence, integrating with the other dancers, and doing time adjustments—by using the Sequence Editor, the Stage View, and the Time Line to record and replay a figure performing the routine in stages. Individual movements are created and recorded using the Sequence Editor. This editor also allows slow down, speed up, rotation of view, and stop action any time during the routine. After several figures' routines have been recorded, they can be integrated and viewed with Stage View; which also allows rotation and tilt for viewing at any angle. Time Line allows each dance sequence to be adjusted in relative time.

Cunningham prefers to have the individual dancers or small groups of dancers rehearse separately and have the entire performance, including the orchestra, come together for one dress rehearsal before the performance. This approach keeps the dance fresh but makes seeing the entire performance early, for adjustments, impossible. Life Forms gives the choreographer that capability.

Theater

Many of the sophisticated stage presentations in theaters today are supported by computers. Three major uses of computers in the theater are the design of the sets, the control of the lighting, and the production of special effects.

Set designers start with rough sketches from the director, playwright, and set designer. The designers use CAD programs to design the sets in detail. Set designers then use software that converts a set of CAD drawings into a three-dimensional drawing so that the director can preview all the sets before construction begins. This software shows views of the sets from all the viewing angles the audience may have. Changes are easily made until everyone is satisfied. Construction is then based on the CAD drawings.

Lighting can make or break a live theater performance. Often sets are painted screens, and incorrect lighting makes them invisible to the audience. Lighting must follow the action on the stage and the timing of the performance. To do that, the basic lighting controls are put into the computer; then the lighting technician lets the computer do all the predictable things and needs to worry only about the unpredictable events.

Special effects—such as ghosts, fog, or lightning—can do a great deal to improve a stage presentation. You are aware of the special effects in movies and on television. Theater special effects are not as complex as those, but they can set the mood or create the focus the director wants in key places.

Fine Arts

The fine arts—including painting, sculpture, and architecture—have been an area of human expression since the beginning of civilization. Today, the computer is used as a tool to help create pieces of art and to help recover, restore, and protect works of art by the old masters.

Creating Art

The computer can be used as an art medium. Artists can use software like Macintosh's MacDraw and MacPaint to create "freehand" art. The computer is a tool, just as a paintbrush or pencil is a tool. In sculpture, a CAD drawing can help the creator visualize the project from all angles before creating the sculpture itself.

Restoring Art

Art restorers had hoped that the capabilities of the computer to catalog, analyze, and simulate could be applied to the problems of saving the works of the old masters, but critics of the use of computers scoffed. The restoration of Michelangelo's frescoes in the Sistine Chapel proved the value of the computer. Techniques developed by NASA to enhance satellite photographs sent from space made possible the capability of the computer to "see" beneath centuries of grime, oxygenation, and even abuse.

A technique called **computerized infrared reflectoscopy** has been used to solve mysteries of art history. The fact that some pigment colors are "invisible" under infrared light has allowed art historians to "see" the sketches and repaintings of the original artist. Details unseen until recently are now being viewed, opening new insights to the art students who study them. For example, studying Titian's *Albertini Madonna and Child* showed a praying saint hiding under the baby's chubby legs.

With the help of experts from Olivetti, Fiat, and IBM, Italy has become the center of expertise in the area of art restoration using computers.

Photograph by Joachim Messerschmidt, FPG International

Photography

At the Adams family reunion, Uncle Fred finally gets the whole family together for a picture. But every time he tries to snap the picture, someone moves and ruins the shot. Is he ever going to let everyone go? If he has a digital camera, no problem. He can take several shots. Then, using either the floppy disk from his electronic camera or photo CDs from his photo CD camera, he can load the pictures into his PC. There he can easily manipulate the pictures any way he wants. He can exchange places for Cousin Joe and Aunt Flo and completely remove Cousin Larry from the shot. The old saying that "the camera doesn't lie" is changing. Cameras, or specifically pictures, can say anything you want—true or not.

One use of digitally altered photographs is to help track missing children. If a child is abducted at age three, a photograph may not be much help looking for the child six years later. But with digital enhancement and a few educated guesses based on photographs of siblings or parents at age nine, a "photograph" of the child as she looks today can be created. These enhanced photographs have helped locate several children years after they disappeared.

This new photography technique may one day make the old family picture album obsolete. The pictures can be put on CD-ROM and shown on television monitors or a computer monitor. Even old photographs can be preserved this way, by using a scanner. Now the family history can be safe from time, flood, and other damage.

Are Computers Improving the Arts?

Photograph by Mug Shots, The Stock Market

Artistic expression through music, dance, theater, painting, sculpture, and other media is at least as old as mankind's recorded history and sometimes is all that exists of a people's history. Is the computer a necessary tool for artistic expression? Shakespeare's plays have been entertaining audiences for several hundred years without computer-produced ghosts. Bach and Mozart created their music without the need of a synthesizer or MIDI.

The question for today's artists is this: Is the computer making the artists better able to express themselves, or is it distracting them from their art? Time will have to be the judge.

STEPS TAKEN TO PRODUCE A
COMPUTER AGE-PROGRESSION OF
A MISSING CHILD'S PHOTOGRAPH

Step 1: The initial step in considering an age progression of a missing child's facial image is the collecting of family photographs and videotapes. When available, they should portray only the biological Mom, Dad, and older siblings, at the missing child's present age. By keeping the selection within the biological family, valuable information is imparted to the computer age-progression specialist that reflects growth, family likeness, and unique features and facial patterns influenced by heredity. The quality of photo images should be good and in the same pose as the missing child. The importance of this initial step is seen in the preceding procedures that involve the use of the computer software.

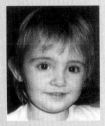

Step 2: Last known photograph of child before abduction at 3 years old

Step 3: Child's photograph scanned into computer and stretched for merging with 9-year-old father

Step 4: 9-year-old father

Step 5: 3-year-old stretched photo merged with 9-year-old father

Step 6: Result of merger

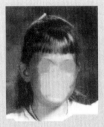

Step 7: Photograph of a 9-year-old girl from reference file chosen for hairstyle and dress

Step 8: Merged to transfer hair and dress to missing child's aged image

Step 9: Final age-progressed image as 9-year-old

Step 10: Recovery photograph

The Artful Balance: The Classic Piano and the Computer

Piano lovers aren't singing "those old piano roll blues" anymore. The player piano is back, and it's better than ever. This time it's computerized!

Courtesy of Yamaha Corporation of America, Keyboard Division

Piano lovers are singing the praises of these new devices, now dubbed "reproducing pianos" because of their uncanny capability to reproduce individual nuances of an artist's original performance. Yamaha's Disklavier is built into the piano at the factory, whereas PianoDisc offers kits that can transform any piano, grand or upright, into a high-tech player piano.

A large selection of prerecorded disks is available for each system, and both systems can be controlled with wireless remotes. PianoDisc offers a Symphony option that provides instrumental accompaniment for the piano, and Disklavier has interactive educational software to help you learn to play the piano. Both systems are often used as "invisible accompanists" for soloists and vocalists.

Both Disklavier and PianoDisc can record as well, storing the computer-coded performance data on standard 3.5-inch disks. (PianoDisc also offers a playback-only system that uses compact discs.) As music is recorded, a series of sensors scans every characteristic of the performance, including pitches, timing, touch, duration, and pedal depression. With 127 levels of expression per note, each system records and re-creates musical thought and feeling with striking fidelity—imitating the exact tone, richness, and projection of each performance. It's as if the artist were sitting there, invisibly performing a recital just for you.

This recording capability is the feature that piano teachers are raving about. Teachers can create "model" disks for their students to play back as reminders of how particular musical phrases should sound. "My students no longer have to rely on their minds' ears!" one teacher exclaimed.

Students can also record music themselves to compare their performances with their teachers' or with earlier versions of their own efforts. In addition, stored performances by some of the great pianists can be played back, allowing aspiring students to compare themselves with greats such as Horowitz and Rubenstein.

These superpianos can also communicate back and forth with other computerized musical devices (such as sequencers, drum machines, synthesizers, and even a PC), allowing composers and arrangers to literally play their arrangements directly onto sheet music or to create a whole new brand of orchestral arrangements from their piano keyboard. The possibilities are endless—no wonder PianoDisc calls it "a 21st century version of the player piano." Honky-tonk piano rolls it's not!

Courtesy of Kent Lacin Media Services

Movies and Television

The financial bonanza of 1994, *Forrest Gump*, illustrates several ways the movie industry uses computers. The most obvious effect was to insert star Tom Hanks, who played Forrest Gump, into historical film footage. Gump appears with U.S. Presidents Kennedy, Johnson, and Nixon, as well as with other important figures.

Photograph by Michael Simpson, FPG International

The computer can merge separate shots. The computer first breaks down the scenes digitally, then manipulates the elements in the scenes, and finally reconstructs the scene to include the desired elements. A similar technique enabled Hanks to appear in a scene with a napalm explosion. Again, two shots were digitally merged. Another ongoing effect in *Forrest Gump* involved digitally erasing the legs of Gary Sinise, the actor playing an amputee.

Movie Magic

The digital manipulation of elements in a scene is called **morphing**, a special effect created by computer animation that smoothly transforms characters into other shapes as you watch. Originally used in the movie *Willow*, morphing also appears in *Terminator 2: Judgment Day*. The morphing programs enable moviemakers to establish the starting image and the ending image; then the program creates the intermediate frames necessary to change the picture. The technique was developed at Industrial Light & Magic with the use of large, powerful workstation computers. You can now find at your local software retailer morphing programs that can run on 386-based PCs or higher.

Digital techniques can ensure that a movie can be finished regardless of the health of the leading actors and actresses. Before a project begins, the stars go into a studio and are filmed making a series of motions and talking. If something happens and the star cannot finish all the scenes for the project, the computer uses the test film to digitally put the star into any remaining scenes, with dialog if needed.

Another emerging use of morphing is to film actors and actresses approximately every ten years during their careers. Then if a seventy-year-old actor, for example, has a role that requires him to appear at a younger age, the computer can use the earlier test films to create the scenes with the same actor as a younger person. Today, because this technique is new, a younger actor has to be hired and aged using makeup.

Special Effects

One of the major results of using computer technology in movie and television production is the reduction in costs. In the *Young Indiana Jones* series, George Lucas used computer technology to generate backgrounds for "period pieces" and augment the crowd scenes. As a result, Lucas spent $10,000 for scenes that would normally cost $30,000 to $40,000.

Photograph by James Porto, FPC International

If a movie costs a minimum of $30 million to make, only established moviemakers can find investors to back movie projects; consequently, very few innovative movies or movies made by novice directors can be made. Reducing average production costs by using computer effects can help this situation.

Animation

When the Disney Studio made *Snow White* and *Cinderella*, each production took more than two years and hundreds of animators and illustrators. Computer-generated **animation** provides faster results and requires less manpower. Most Disney animation movies use computer-generated background, but humans still draw the characters. An exception to this is *Toy Story*. *Toy Story* was made using computer-generated animation. The computer also enables the merging of live action and animation, as demonstrated by *The Mask*, starring Jim Carrey. Although Hollywood has been making movies that combined live action and animation since Gene Kelly danced with Jerry the Mouse, movies like *The Mask* have taken the process to the point that part of Jim Carrey—his heart—was animated, and the rest was real Jim Carrey.

On-Demand Television

Merging cable television with telephone service is the next big area of expansion in the entertainment industry, according to executives of companies like Time Warner, AT&T, and Viacom. In Britain, American telephone companies have teamed up with British cable TV companies to wire the country for voice, data, and video. In the future, this capability will enable subscribers to call into a computer database and order movies or shows "on demand." Today, you must wait until the movie you want is available and then request access to it. The **on-demand television** system in Britain is serving as a prototype for a system in the United States.

Implementation of **interactive television** in the United States will be one more step in building an Information Superhighway (I-way). The cable television companies, the telephone companies, and the computer game companies are moving toward a system that can connect most American homes with a computer network using the cable television connection. The current vision, in initial testing, is a PC connection to the television, which is connected by cable to a mainframe computer that has a large database. To see a movie or show, you will send a message to the central computer, and the movie will come over your TV. Shopping, games, financial news, and stock information are other options you may have access to through the network. The cable, PC, and television hookup become your entrance onto the I-way.

Fun and Games

Using the computer for games and interactive entertainment is a major area of computer development. Game systems—from Sega Genesis and Nintendo to **multimedia games** such as Wing Commander III—and 3-D graphics provide a strong economic drive to develop new technology.

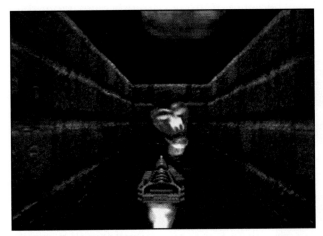

Photographs courtesy of Electronic Arts

Interactive Television

The computer games described in the preceding paragraph are just the beginning. Suppose that you want to play chess against a human opponent. Using your cable hookup, you request an opponent. The network connects you with someone of your skill level from anywhere in the world.

A very controversial application of interactive television is just beginning to be developed today—gambling through television cable. Americans gambled close to $340 billion last year. Subsequently, Gaming Entertainment Television and the Game Show Channel are both working on ways to operate within the FCC rules and enable viewers to gamble interactively.

Multimedia Entertainment

CD-ROM has given the world the latest in game playing by providing a higher level of integration of sound and graphics. *Myst* was the first big selling CD-ROM game. Movies are recorded on CD-ROM and then played on a PC so that movie segments can be included in a game. Until recently, the technology was too slow to be useful. A recent development, however, has improved the controlling of motion pictures being played from CD-ROM by personal computers.

The idea of computer games creating innovations in computer technology is not new. Computer games have been around as long as computer programmers. When work became too intense, programmers would fiddle around, trying to create something fun on the computer. Even the UNIX operating system is rumored to have been developed by programmers to support a game they had written.

Multimedia, the merging of CD-ROM and sound, was developed because of a desire to improve games. An early predecessor to a multitasking environment on PCs came from a "panic button" on a game. If the boss came by, you could click the button, and the screen would show an impressive-looking spreadsheet; the screen would then return to the game when you clicked the button again.

Game makers, interested in getting more games into households, have helped fund the development of the Information Superhighway. Computer games are providing the impetus to develop many exciting new products with a wide variety of uses. The game industry currently does more than $15 billion a year in business and is growing.

Photograph by Mark Scott, FPG International

Games for the Young Child

Games often provide the early introduction of computers to young children. Children enjoy using the computer; when games are fun and educational, parents can encourage their child's interest in the computer through games. Many computer games build some of the same skills that reading builds, such as maintaining focus, problem solving, and developing imagination. These games also build skills in using a keyboard and a mouse, understanding the limits and restrictions of breakable equipment, and developing the hand-eye coordination appropriate for using computers—all skills necessary in life. Just like books, movies, and television, however, some games are not appropriate for children. Parents need to guide their children to products that teach the lessons they feel their children should learn.

Lesson Summary

➤ In performing arts, the computer is useful in organization, record keeping, reproduction, and simulation.

➤ In music, MIDI (Musical Instrument Digital Interface) is the interface from the instrument to the computer. Once MIDI has turned the music into digital form, the computer can process it.

➤ In dance, DOM (Dance on Microcomputer) notation and Life Forms have allowed dances to be created and preserved on computer for future dancers to study and then re-create.

➤ Theater uses computers for designing sets, controlling lighting, and creating special effects.

➤ In the fine arts, painters and sculptors use computers as an artistic instrument or a visualization tool.

➤ Computers have been important in saving, restoring, and studying works of art from the past.

➤ Photography has been changed by the use of digital cameras and computers to manipulate the digital output from those cameras. Applications such as "aging" missing children and manipulating pictures to represent anything the photographer wants are changing the idea that "cameras don't lie."

➤ Art can be affected by computers, but the ultimate expression of the emotion is in the hands of the human artist.

➤ Computers can help in a variety of ways to create movie magic. They can merge several pictures to create a scene that never occurred, or add scenery and people that weren't there.

➤ Morphing is the process of transforming an object into another object before your eyes.

➤ Animation that uses computers versus animation drawn by hand can save thousands of hours of labor and months in development time.

➤ On-demand television will enable viewers to request television programming whenever they choose, not just at set times.

➤ The computer game industry, including arcade games, home game systems, and games for personal computers, is more than a $15 billion industry, and it continues to grow.

➤ Interactive television will give gamers the opportunity to play with other players around the world.

➤ Using multimedia PCs has increased the realism of computer games as well as their complexity.

➤ Computer games for very young children provide education and training in skills that children will use throughout their lives.

Lesson Review

Key Terms

animation
computerized infrared
  reflectoscopy
DOM (Dance on Micro-
  computer) notation

interactive television
morphing
multimedia games
Musical Instrument Digital
  Interface (MIDI)

on-demand television
sequencer
sound board

sound card
synthesizer

Matching

In the blank next to each of the following terms or phrases, write the letter of the corresponding term or phrase.

_____ 1. Used in making *The Mask*

_____ 2. Used in making *Forrest Gump*

_____ 3. Used in making *Toy Story*

_____ 4. Helps find missing children

_____ 5. Rotation and tilt viewing

_____ 6. Defines multimedia

_____ 7. Allows morphing to occur

_____ 8. Reveals mysteries of art history

_____ 9. "Freehand" art

_____ 10. Records individual movements

a. MacDraw

b. digital manipulation

c. merged historical shots with current ones

d. computer-generated animation

e. merged animation and live action

f. computerized infrared reflectoscopy

g. digitally altered photographs

h. CD-ROM and sound

i. Sequence Editor

j. Stage View

Multiple Choice

Circle the letter of the correct choice for each of the following.

1. Altering elements of a scene usually involves which of the following?

   a. manipulating digital elements

   b. erasing the negative

   c. changing colors

   d. You can't alter elements of a scene.

2. When making movies or television shows, what do you call the transformation from one shape to another by computer?

   a. magic

   b. melting

   c. morphing

   d. animation

3. What do you call the capability to request a movie or television show at any given time?

   a. on-demand television

   b. cable television

   c. computer games

   d. personal television

4. Digital manipulation of elements is being used in moviemaking to do which of the following?

   a. erase body parts of characters on the screen

   b. finish a picture when something happens to an actor

   c. add background to a scene

   d. all of the above

5. Which of the following is one way to reduce costs in producing movies?

    a. digitally alter the background and crowds

    b. remake movies that were popular before

    c. have George Lucas make the movie

    d. none of the above

6. What is the purpose of MIDI?

    a. to make computers capable of composing songs

    b. to electronically regulate music through the computer

    c. to connect multimedia devices to the computer

    d. to make animation move to the rhythm of the music

7. What is the biggest computer-aided art restoration to date?

    a. stripping Van Gogh's self-portrait

    b. restoring Michelangelo's frescoes in the Sistine Chapel

    c. restoring Duchamp's *Nude Descending a Staircase*

    d. restoring Mona Lisa's smile

8. A new type of camera that allows photographs to be manipulated by computers is a _____.

    a. digital camera

    b. Polaroid camera

    c. microcamera

    d. CD-ROM camera

9. Which of the following is true regarding computer control of lighting during live theater productions?

    a. It is impossible because so much is unpredictable.

    b. It is used for the basics, and a human controls the rest.

    c. It is used for everything so that nothing will be missed.

    d. none of the above

10. Which of the following is a consideration about using computers in creating painting, sculpture, and architecture?

    a. Computers are creating neater and more valuable art than humans are today.

    b. Computers are of no use because they have no emotions.

    c. Computers are being used as a tool in the hands of humans.

    d. No one has tried to use computers in this area.

Completion

In the blank provided, write the correct answer for each of the following.

1. CD-ROMs, sound cards, and speakers are often referred to as _____.

2. Special effects created by computer animation that transforms shapes into other shapes are called _____.

3. Young children are often introduced to computers by using _____.

4. For a computer to merge two or more scenes, the pictures must first be in _____ form.

5. Multimedia and 3-D graphics are examples of developments that were encouraged by the _____ industry.

6. A more commonly used name for Musical Instrument Digital Interface is _____.

7. Multimedia hardware needs a(n) _____ for a central connection point.

8. A set designer could use a computer with _____ software to design the sets in detail.

9. For an analog signal to be manipulated by computer, the signal must be changed to _____ form, a procedure often performed by a sound card.

10. Entire dances have been created using a program called _____.

Review

On a separate sheet of paper, answer the following questions.

1. How can digital manipulation help in making movies and television shows?

2. Cite examples of how morphing has been used in movies.

3. Describe on-demand television.

4. Describe interactive television.

5. How can young children benefit from computer games?

6. How are the three stages of developing a dance accomplished using Life Forms software?

7. How can set designers use computers to help create sets for theatrical productions?

8. How has computerized infrared reflectoscopy been used to solve some mysteries of art history?

9. How does computer-controlled lighting enhance a theater presentation?

10. How can a sculptor use a computer in creating a work of art?

Critical Thinking

On a separate sheet of paper, answer the following questions.

1. Has the use of computers improved theater productions? Why or why not?

2. When the computer is part of the creation process, can the result still be called art, because it is no longer strictly a human process?

3. Because computer games are just computer-generated pictures and don't involve real people, should the games be required to have rating codes like those for movies to make people aware of violence and sexually explicit content?

4. What do you see happening as a result of making gambling available on interactive television? What regulations do you think might be needed with interactive gambling?

5. Most computer games for older children and adults appeal more to boys and men than to girls and women. What effect is this difference in appeal likely to have? What would you suggest to alter this result if you were in charge of a company designing computer games?

Further Discovery

How Computer Graphics Work. Jeff Prosise (Emeryville, CA: Ziff-Davis, 1994).

The Magic of Computer Graphics. Mike Morrison (Indianapolis, IN: Sams, 1995).

The Multimedia Casebook. Mary Fallenstein Hellman and W. R. James (New York: Van Nostrand Reinhold, 1995).

Photoshop Artistry: A Master Class for Photographers and Artists (San Francisco: Sybex, 1995).

On-line Discovery

You can access the Internet resources for the following questions by going to the Que Education and Training Web site at URL http://www.ciyf98.com/discovery. From this page, click the link for Lesson 12D and then click the link to the resource you want to access.

1. Most digital-film and video-effects production companies at some point use 2-D and 3-D graphics production software from Alias|Wavefront. Such movies as *Species*, *Judge Dredd*, and *Crimson Tide* have made use of this software and the effects it can generate. Explore the **Alias|Wavefront** home page (http://www.aw.sgi.com). What kinds of effects can the software be used to produce? What other kinds of uses besides digital effects for film can this software be used for? How do you think these types of software programs will affect movies of the future? In addition, browse the home pages of some of the production companies that create these effects. A list of these companies, along with links to their home pages, can be found at the **Visual Effects Headquarters** site (http://www.vfxhq.com). Are you surprised to find that many scenes which look real were actually digital effects created on a computer?

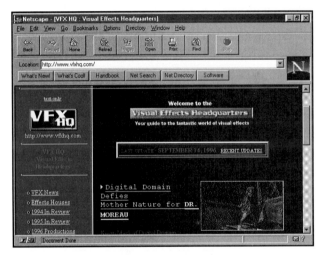

2. In the last couple of years, many films made for the mass audience have companion sites on the World Wide Web. The Web sites for movies such as **Armageddon** (http://www.armageddon.com), **Titanic** (http://titanicmovie.com), and **Lost in Space** (http://www.Lostinspace.com) provide background information, production information, fan discussion forums, and, of course, advertisements for derivative products. Browse several of these movie pages. What kinds of background information do they provide? Are these sites little more than advertisements and product order forms, as many critics have accused them of being?

GLOSSARY

access time A combination of seek time, rotational delay time, and transfer time.

active cell In a spreadsheet program, the cell in which the cell pointer is located.

adapter A circuit board that provides additional capabilities for a computer; also called an expansion card.

address A location in a computer system, identified by a name, number, or code label.

address bus A set of wires running from the central processing unit (CPU) to random-access memory (RAM).

airline reservation system A computerized reservation system that uses large computer complexes with large databases and thousands of terminals worldwide.

Air Traffic Control (ATC) A computerized system that performs air traffic control tasks; ATC was necessitated by increased air traffic and enabled by the expanding capabilities of computers.

algorithm A step-by-step mathematical or logical procedure.

a-life See *artificial life*.

American Standard Code for Information Interchange (ASCII) A standard computer character set consisting of 96 upper- and lowercase letters along with 32 nonprinting control characters.

analog signal Electrical representation of sound waves.

analytical engine A device planned by Charles Babbage in the nineteenth century. Never completed, this device would have been a full modern computer with an IPOS cycle and punched cards for data input.

anchor To fix text or a graphic in an absolute position on the page.

animation The creation of animated characters, objects, and other visual effects by computer. Computer-generated animation, which provides faster results and requires less manpower, is used in most visual media, from multimedia games to motion pictures.

antiskid braking system (ABS) A microprocessor-controlled system in cars that controls braking and prevents skidding; also called an antilock braking system.

application program/application software A program or software that performs a specific task, such as word processing or database management.

Archie A program that lets the user search an index of files that can be downloaded from other servers using anonymous FTP.

archiving The practice of storing old data files on separate disks to make room for new files on the hard disk. Businesses often use WORM CDs for archiving.

arithmetic-logic unit The portion of the central processing unit that makes all the decisions for the microprocessor, based on the mathematical computations and logic functions that it performs.

article A message contributed to a Usenet group.

artificial intelligence A computer science field that tries to give computers some characteristics of human intelligence, such as the capability of understanding natural language and reasoning.

artificial life (a-life) A new area of research in which a "life-form" is created within the computer and is used to test evolutionary theories or theories of life-form behavior.

ASCII See *American Standard Code for Information Interchange*.

assembler A program that transforms an assembly language program into machine language so that a computer can execute the program.

assembly language A program language in which each program statement corresponds to an instruction that the processing language can carry out.

Association for Computing Machinery (ACM) An organization featuring many special-interest groups in such areas as databases, artificial intelligence, microcomputers, and computer graphics.

asynchronous transfer mode (ATM) A wide area network design that uses high-speed switching devices to route messages.

asynchronous transmission One of two transmission modes in which each byte is marked with a start bit and a stop bit. Because this method results in lower communication speeds, telephone lines use asynchronous communication.

atom switch A switch that moves a single atom, bonds it in the new location, and later moves the atom back if needed.

authoring software Software that enables the user to blend audio files, video, and animation with text and traditional graphics.

automated teller machine (ATM) A specialized computer terminal that enables customers to make deposits, withdraw funds, and transfer funds between accounts without having to interact with a human teller.

automation The replacement of human workers by machines.

Automotive Stability Management System (ASMS) A system that uses sensors to detect and control sideways momentum, steering-wheel position, rotation of each wheel, and cornering rate of a car in order to overcome any driver error and make skidding virtually impossible.

Autonomous Land Vehicle in the Neural Network (ALVINN) An experimental smart car, being developed in the U.S., that can drive itself.

AutoPlay A Windows 95 feature that automatically begins playing a CD when it is inserted into the CD drive.

backbone network The "trunk lines" of the Information Superhighway.

back-end processor One of several processors in a mainframe computer system that is used to handle data retrieval operations.

backup file A copy of a file created as a safety precaution in case anything happens to the original.

bad sector A flawed portion of a disk that can no longer be used to store data.

bandwidth A measurement, expressed in cycles per second or bits per second (bps), of the amount of information that can flow through a channel.

bar code reader An input device that scans bar codes and then converts the bar code into a number on-screen.

bar graph A graph with horizontal or vertical bars, commonly used to show the values of unrelated items.

baseband coaxial cable A cable capable of carrying one signal at a time at a rapid pace.

Basic Input/Output System (BIOS) chip A ROM chip that is built into the computer's memory and that checks the input and output devices when the system is started.

batch processing The processing of one program instruction after another without user intervention.

bay A space in a computer system that can hold a hard drive, floppy drive, tape drive, or CD-ROM drive.

benchmark A standard measurement used to test the performance of different brands of equipment.

Bernoulli disk A removable hard disk, consisting of a single platter encased in a plastic cartridge.

binary digit A number that uses a base 2 number system rather than a decimal (or base 10) number system.

biometric identification A new field that uses unique physical characteristics to confirm an individual's identity instead of using a driver's license, credit cards, or debit cards.

BIOS See *Basic Input/Output System (BIOS) chip.*

bit The basic unit of information in a binary numbering system.

bit mapping The turning on or off of individual screen pixels in order to create an image.

bits per second (bps) A measurement of transmission in asynchronous communication.

block A rectangular group of cells that is treated as a unit for a given operation.

body text font A font used for the main part of a document, designed to be easily read.

boldface A character emphasis visibly darker and heavier in weight than normal type.

Boolean logic A system that uses the Boolean operators AND, OR, and NOT to refine the scope of an on-line search.

Boolean operators The logical operators AND, OR, and NOT, used to specify the logical relationship between two quantities or concepts; used in on-line searching. Boolean operators are also called logical operators.

boot To load an operating system into primary storage and prepare a computer for use.

booting See *boot.*

boot sector virus A virus that loads each time the computer is booted and can make the data stored on a disk inaccessible.

bpi Bytes per inch.

branch prediction A module that tries to predict the most effective way to route an instruction through the microprocessor.

bridge In local area networks, a device that enables two similar networks to exchange data.

broadband coaxial cable A cable capable of carrying more than one signal at a time.

brownout A period of low-voltage power flow.

bubble memory A magnetic representation of data on the surface of semiconductor chips. Each bubble represents a binary 1; the absence of a bubble represents a binary 0.

bug A programming error that causes a program or computer to perform erratically, produce incorrect results, or crash.

bulletin board system (BBS) A computer system that enables computer users to access the system, send and receive e-mail messages, and get computer files.

bundle The inclusion of software with a computer system as part of the system's total price.

burn-in A phenomenon that occurs when an image is left on-screen for a long time, creating an after-image.

bus A highway of parallel wires along which signals are sent from one part of the computer to another.

bus topology The physical layout of a local area network that does not use a central or host computer. Instead, each node manages part of the network, and information is transmitted directly from one computer to another.

bus width The number of bits, such as 16 or 32, that can travel through the bus at the same time.

byte Eight bits grouped together to represent a character (a letter, number, or symbol).

cable interface unit An interface unit that sends and receives signals on the network cable.

cache A temporary storage space for frequently accessed program instructions.

cache memory A specialized chip used with the computer's memory to provide a storage area that keeps frequently used accessed data or program instructions readily available.

callback system A method of network control that serves as a deterrent to misuses of data and system sabotage by verifying the code and telephone number of the individual trying to access the system.

carpal tunnel syndrome A painful swelling of the tendons and the sheaths around them in the wrist, usually caused when the median nerve is pinched.

case A programming construct in which a complex set of decisions is based on a single item.

cathode-ray tube (CRT) monitor The large monitor connected to a desktop computer. The monitor's vacuum tube uses an electron gun to emit a beam of electrons that illuminates phosphorus on-screen as the beam sweeps across the screen repeatedly.

CD-Erasable (CD-E) CD-ROM technology that enables users to store, access, and reuse disks in the same way that floppy disks can be used.

CD-Recordable (CD-R)   CD-ROM technology that enables users to write to as well as read a compact disk.

CD-ROM   See *Compact Disc Read-Only Memory (CD-ROM)*.

CD-ROM drive   A read-only disk drive designed to read the data encoded on compact disks and to transfer this data to a computer.

cell   A rectangle formed by the intersection of a row and column in a spreadsheet. You enter text or numbers into a cell.

cell address   A letter and number combination, such as B4 or D7, that identifies by column and row a cell's location on a spreadsheet.

cell entry line   An area or box usually located just above a spreadsheet.

cellular telephone system   A system of transmitting data by means of portable computers and telephones.

central processing unit (CPU)   The computer's processing and control circuitry.

character   Any letter, number, punctuation mark, or symbol produced on-screen by the press of a key on the keyboard.

character printer   A printer that produces only one character (a letter, number, punctuation mark, or symbol) at a time.

child element   A lower-level segment, or group of fields, in a hierarchy.

client   On a network, any computer that can access the server.

client program   A program that runs on a computer and helps the user use File Transfer Protocol (FTP).

client/server architecture   The structure of Web technology, consisting of two parts: a client and a server. The server is where information that a user accesses is stored; the client is software that enables a user to access the information.

client/server model   A model that uses one or more computers on the network as servers and uses the other computers on the network as clients.

clip art   A collection of graphic images stored on disk and available for use in a page layout or presentation graphics program.

clip art libraries   Large collections of clip art.

Clipper chip   A chip that automatically encrypts all data received or sent over digital communication lines.

clock speed   The number of times that a computer's internal clock pulses in one second.

closed bus system   A bus system that comes with established ports into which cables attached to peripheral devices can be plugged.

cluster   The basic unit of storage on a floppy or hard disk; a cluster includes two or more sectors.

coaxial cable   A high-bandwidth connecting cable in which an insulated wire runs through the middle of the cable.

column   A vertical block of cells in a spreadsheet, usually identified by a unique alphabetical letter.

command interpreter   Another term for the user interface, the part of the system software that communicates with the user; also called the job control language (JCL).

command-line interface   An interface for which commands must be memorized and correctly typed.

common carrier   Telephone companies such as AT&T, Sprint, and MCI that offer dedicated lines, microwave communications, and satellite services.

communication channel   The physical link between two computers.

communications program   A program that enables a computer to communicate with other computers through the telephone system.

communications satellite   A satellite placed in a geo-synchronous orbit and rotating with the earth so that the satellite is always in the same spot relative to the earth.

Compact Disc Read-Only Memory (CD-ROM)   A popular and inexpensive optical disk that comes prere-corded and is a read-only storage medium.

compatible   The capability of a device, program, or adapter to function with or substitute for a given make and model of computer, device, or program.

competency   A professional standard requiring a computer professional to keep up with the latest developments in the industry.

compiler   A program that reads the statements written in a human-readable programming language and translates the complete program into a machine-readable executable program.

complex instruction set computer (CISC)   A central processing unit that can recognize as many as 100 or more instructions and carry out most computations directly.

compucops   Small computers, with 486 microprocessors and resembling ATMs, that are used on street corners in the Netherlands for reporting crimes.

computer   A machine that can follow instructions to alter data and perform at least some operations without human intervention.

computer engineer   A hardware-oriented professional who designs new computers and peripheral hardware.

computer fraud   The access of a computer by an unauthorized individual. Examples of computer fraud include embezzling funds, stealing from customers, falsifying data, and gathering data to use for blackmail.

computer hobbyist   An individual who enjoys pushing his or her computer skills to the limit.

computer information system (CIS)   A computer system in which all the components are designed to work together.

computer literacy   Sufficient computer knowledge to prepare an individual for working and living in a computerized society.

computer matching   A method used by the federal government to cross-link the information stored in different computers.

computer network   A system of two or more computers linked with a direct, high-speed connection.

computer operator   A person who keeps computer equipment functioning smoothly.

Computer Output Microfilm/Microfiche (COM) A cost-efficient and fast means of producing and storing computer output by using microfilm or microfiche.

computer professional An individual who has taken intermediate and advanced courses in computer education. Computer professionals apply their training to improve the performance, ease of use, and efficiency of computer systems.

computer repair technician An individual who deals with breakdowns in computers and other related equipment.

computer scientist A computer professional who develops systems software and personal productivity software.

computer virus A program designed to alter or destroy the software or data stored on a computer system. Computer viruses can be passed from one computer to another on floppy disks, over networks, and over remote modem connections.

computer vision syndrome (CVS) Vision problems that result from focusing closely on a computer screen for long periods of time, from poor lighting, or from glare.

computer-aided design (CAD) Software used to create architectural drawings, product designs, landscaping plans, and engineering drawings.

computer-aided manufacturing (CAM) Software used in the manufacturing of products.

computer-aided software engineering and computer-aided systems engineering (CASE) Software that provides tools to help with every phase in systems development and enables developers to create data flow diagrams, data dictionary entries, and structure charts; also a methodology that uses microcomputers and software, as well as procedures to aid the systems developer.

computer-based tutorial (CBT) A type of intelligent tutoring program that is tailored to the student's level of subject mastery and can provide immediate feedback.

computer-integrated manufacturing (CIM) The integration of computer technology with manufacturing processes.

computing process Everything and everyone necessary for a computer to perform a useful task.

condition A programming construct in which one set of instructions is executed if a condition is true, and a different set of instructions is executed if the condition is false; also called a decision.

Conference on Data Systems Languages (CODASYL) A conference that led to the development of the network database.

configuration file A file, created for an application program, that stores the choices you make when you install the program so that they are available each time the program starts.

connectivity The extent to which a computer or program can function in a network.

contact management software Software designed to help keep track of contacts by maintaining a list of addresses, phone numbers, and fax numbers. Information is also maintained through the use of a notepad, automatic telephone dialing with a modem, and search and sort capabilities.

control module The top module (or box) in a structure chart used to indicate tasks a program must accomplish. The control module oversees the transfer of control to the other modules.

control panel In Lotus 1-2-3, a special area at the top of the screen that contains the main menu and the edit line.

control unit A component of the central processing unit that obtains program instructions and sends signals to carry out these instructions.

conversion utility A special translation program that enables word processing programs to read files.

copyrighted software Software legally protected against copying or being used without paying for it.

cost/benefit analysis An analysis of the cost of something and the benefits, both tangible and intangible.

CRT See *cathode-ray tube (CRT) monitor*.

cracker Someone who tries illegally to break into a secure computer system.

crash conversion The changing over of existing data files to the format of a new system by abruptly stopping the old system and starting the new system. See also *direct conversion*.

credit card fraud The use of a credit card or its number by an unauthorized individual to purchase items or acquire funds.

crop To trim an image to show only part of the original image. Cropping may involve determining the amount of white space to include around the image, as well as wrapping text around it.

current cell The cell in which the pointer is positioned.

customer support technician A person who works help lines in order to answer customer questions and solve problems.

cutting and pasting Moving text by deleting it from one location and inserting it in another.

cyberphobia An extreme and irrational fear of computers.

cyberporn On-line pornography.

cyberspace The virtual space created by computer systems.

cylinder All the tracks and sectors in the same relative location on a disk pack.

data Some kind of unorganized material that can be entered into a computer.

data access time The time needed for a computer to locate and transfer data to primary memory.

data bus A bus that connects the CPU and memory, providing a pathway to the computer's peripherals.

data definition language (DDL) One of four parts of a database management system (DBMS) used to define the structure of the database.

data dependence The dependence of data on the application in which the data is stored; data dependence occurs when data files from different applications are incompatible and cannot be linked.

data entry personnel Individuals who key in data from source documents.

data file   A file, created by a program, in which data is stored.

data integrity   The validity and consistency of the data in all applications.

data manipulation language (DML)   One of four parts of a database management system (DBMS); DML includes all commands that enable a user to manipulate and use the database.

Data Processing Management Association (DPMA)   The premier organization for CIS personnel and managers.

data redundancy   The repetition of the same data in two or more data records.

data security   Features included in database packages to protect data from individuals not authorized to use it.

data storage hierarchy   The organization of data from smallest (bit) to largest (database).

data transfer rate   The rate at which two modems can exchange data.

data transfer time   The time required to transfer data to primary memory.

database   A collection of related information electronically stored and organized in a useful manner that acts as a base for retrieving information.

database administrator   The person who oversees a database. The database administrator ensures that data is entered correctly, develops procedures for the analysis of data, and ensures database security.

database file   A file containing data that has been stored in the proprietary file format of a database program.

database management system (DBMS)   A program that organizes data in a database, providing information storage, organization, and retrieval capacities.

debit card   A credit card used to transfer funds electronically from a bank account to a business account.

debug   The process of finding and fixing bugs (errors) in a computer program.

debugging   See *debug*.

decision   A programming construct in which one set of instructions is executed if a condition is true, and a different set of instructions is executed if the condition is false; also called a condition.

decision support system (DSS)   A tool to help management analyze data to make decisions on semistructured problems.

dedicated line   A special conditioned telephone line that directly and permanently connects two computers.

default value   A common formatting value that a program uses when some other formatting value isn't specified.

defragmentation program   A utility program that reads all files on a disk and rewrites some of them so that all parts of each file are contiguous.

demodulation   In telecommunications, the process of receiving and transforming an analog signal into its digital equivalent so that a computer can use the information.

deskilling   The replacement of jobs by machines through automation and advanced technology.

desktop computer   A nonportable microcomputer that fits on top of a desk.

desktop publishing (DTP)   The combination of text, graphics, and advanced formatting to create inexpensively a visually appealing document.

desktop videoconferencing   Conferencing by computer; software enables conferees to see each other and discuss a document viewable on all their screens. Desktop videoconferencing software can be run alone, permitting users to hear each other, or with a camera mounted on top of the monitor to transmit a picture.

dialup access   The use of a personal computer and a modem to connect with a computer having direct Internet access.

dialup IP   A form of direct access in which a modem and a telephone line are used.

difference engine   A steam-driven calculating machine created by Charles Babbage in the nineteenth century and capable of solving equations and printing tables. Technology at the time had not advanced enough to produce this invention.

digital   A number representation for something in the real world, such as temperature or time, so that counting can be performed precisely.

digital modem   A device that helps linked computers synchronize data transmission and provide error correction.

digital video disc (DVD)   A disk that can hold seven to twelve times the amount of data on a CD-ROM, transfer data faster than the fastest CD-ROM today, and record data at your computer.

digitizing   The conversion process by which scanners convert images into numeric digits before storing them in the computer; the process of converting data into digital form.

digitizing tablet   In computer-aided graphics, a peripheral device used with a pointing device to convert graphics into data that a computer can process.

direct-access file   A file in which records are stored according to a position in the file, enabling the computer to read specific records from the file; also called a random-access file.

direct conversion   The changing of existing data files to the format of another application.

direct Internet access   The capability of a computer of sending and receiving Internet data packages without an intermediary.

directory   An area on a disk where you can store files. A directory listing shows the directory contents by file name. The files in a directory can be programs or data documents.

disaster recovery disk   The essential operating system files along with the files necessary to restore the system from backup files in the event of a computer failure.

disaster recovery plan   An organization's written plan, with detailed instructions, specifying an alternative computing facility to use for emergency processing until a destroyed computer can be replaced.

disk drive   A mechanism designed to store and retrieve information on a floppy disk.

display font   An eye-catching font, often used for headings and captions, that is larger than the body font of the document.

distance learning   A technique that uses computers and telecommunications to take the classroom to the student at a remote location.

docking station   A cabinet containing disk drives, video circuits, and specially designed receptacles for housing a portable computer so that it can use peripheral devices.

documentation   The instructions, tutorials, and reference information that provide the information a user needs in order to use a computer system or application.

DOM (Dance on Microcomputer) notation   A computer program that produces an animated figure for performing dance routines.

domain name   The name that identifies the computer system on which the user has an account.

dot-matrix printer   An impact printer that forms text and graphic images by hammering the ends of pins against a ribbon in a pattern (matrix) of dots.

dot pitch   The distance between pixels.

double-density disk   A disk capable of storing twice as much data as a single-density disk.

double-speed drive   A drive providing the minimum level of retrieval speed for multimedia applications.

download   To transfer a file from a remote computer to your own computer.

downwardly compatible   A capability of hardware or software that runs without modification when using earlier computer components or files created with earlier software versions.

DRAM   See *dynamic RAM*.

drawing program   A program that uses object-oriented graphics to produce line art.

dumb terminal   A terminal that interacts with the remote computer but cannot process any information.

dynamic RAM (DRAM)   A random-access memory chip that is slower than VRAM and is often used on video cards to store video information.

EBCDIC   Extended Binary Coded Decimal Inter-change Code.

edit line   An area or box, usually located just above the spreadsheet, that provides information. To enter values, labels, or other information into the spreadsheet, you type in the edit line; also called a cell entry line.

edutainment   A cross between education and entertainment that provides educational material in the form of a game so that the education becomes entertainment.

EEPROM (Electrically Erasable PROM) chip   Electrically Erasable Programmable Read-Only Memory chip.

electrochromatic   A feature of a car rear-view mirror that adjusts the mirror automatically and protects the driver from the glare of headlights.

electroluminescent display (EL)   A small, flat-screen monitor used on laptop computers.

electronic data interchange (EDI)   A procedure for the electronic exchange of standard documents through information services.

electronic funds transfer (EFT)   A process that enables employees to have their payroll checks automatically deposited to their accounts or have regular monthly payments deducted automatically.

electronic mail (e-mail)   The use of a network to send and receive messages.

electronic spreadsheet   A computerized version of an accountant's pad; a general-purpose accounting program that enables you to type headings and numbers for calculation.

electronic thesaurus   An on-line thesaurus providing lists of synonyms for words.

e-mail   See *electronic mail*.

embedded computer   A computer built into another device, such as a video game player, microwave oven, toaster, VCR, or wristwatch.

emulation   The duplication of the functional capability of one device in another device.

end user   An individual who uses a computer and its applications to perform tasks and produce results.

end-user development   A systems development technique in which the end user develops the system by using a personal computer.

enterprise-wide operation   The highest level of operation involving two or more operations within a company that are integrated to improve the operation of the enterprise.

EPROM (Erasable PROM) chip   Erasable Programmable Read-Only Memory chip that can be programmed and reprogrammed with a special electronic device.

ergonomics   The science of designing machines, tools, and computers so that people find them easy and healthful to use.

ethics   The branch of philosophy dealing with the determination of what is right or wrong, good or bad.

even parity   An error-checking technique that sets an extra bit to 1 if the number of 1 bits in a byte adds up to an odd number.

event   In object-oriented programming, a message that causes a procedure (subprogram) attached to the object to respond. The event may be a keystroke or the click of a mouse button.

event-driven programming   A term frequently used for object-oriented programming (OOP).

executive information system (EIS)   A system that supports management's strategic planning function.

expansion card   A circuit board that provides additional capabilities for the computer.

expert system   A computer that uses a database of knowledge to draw conclusions; an expert system reasons.

Extended Binary Coded Decimal Interchange (EBCDIC)   Character-set coding scheme used to represent 256 standard characters.

extension   A three-letter suffix added to a DOS file name; often supplied by the application and indicating the type of application.

external modem A modem with its own case, cables, and power supply, designed to plug into the serial port of a computer.

facsimile transmission (fax) The sending and receiving of printed pages between two locations, using a telephone line.

fall back In modems, to decrease the data transfer rate to accommodate communication with a slower modem.

false drop In an on-line search, items that are found but are not what you want; words with two meanings often result in false drops.

fax See *facsimile transmission*.

fax modem A modem that can send and receive faxes as well as computer data.

fiber optic cable A network cable made from tiny strands of glasslike material that transmit light pulses with very high efficiency and can carry massive amounts of data.

field A space reserved for a specified piece of information in a database record; a column in a database.

fifth-generation language A new level of programming language in which the user gives the instructions to the computer in a natural language, such as English or Japanese.

file A document or other collection of information stored on a disk and identified as a unit by a unique name.

file allocation table (FAT) A hidden on-disk table listing every cluster on a floppy or hard disk.

file infector A virus that is spread from program to program and that damages code, data, or directories.

file management program A program that enables you to work with, organize, and control files, directories, and disks by displaying a disk's directory structure and listing files.

file name A name that you assign to a file when the file is first written on a disk.

File Transfer Protocol (FTP) An Internet standard that ensures error-free transmission of program and data files through the telephone system.

filtering software Software that prevents access to places on the Internet where cyberporn is located.

firewall A security method that is used to protect a local area network from unauthorized access through the Internet. Firewall security software usually includes several protection features.

flat file A file that does not permit the information stored within it to be reorganized or linked to data in other files.

flat panel display A smaller monitor that is used on laptops and notebook computers.

flight simulator A program designed to act like the aircraft on which the pilot is training.

floppy disk A removable data storage medium; a magnetically coated flexible circle of mylar plastic.

flowchart A diagram that shows the logic of a program.

follow-up post A reply posted to a Usenet group.

font A complete set of characters with the same typeface, style, and size.

form A user-friendly means of viewing the data stored in a record that makes the database easier to use.

formatting One of the basic tasks handled by the computer's operating system that establishes a pattern for the display, storage, or printing of data; the process of adjusting the appearance of a document.

formula In a spreadsheet program, a cell definition that defines the relationship between two or more values.

fragmentation The storing of a file in noncontiguous sectors on a disk. After files are erased, the operating system divides files and stores them in the first available spaces; the result is slower disk operation.

frame A rectangular area absolutely positioned on the page and containing text, graphics, or both.

freeware Copyrighted software that can be freely copied but not sold.

front-end processor A processor responsible for handling communications to and from all the remote terminals connected to a computer system.

full backup Backing up of everything stored on the computer, recommended at least once a month.

function Built-in calculations that can save you time when entering complex formulas in a spreadsheet program.

fuzzy logic Not a definitive yes or no, on or off kind of logic, but a degree or evaluation kind of logic.

gateway A device that connects two dissimilar LANs or connects a LAN to a wide area network, minicomputer, or mainframe and then translates the different data formats.

general-purpose program A program used to perform a variety of tasks. Examples are word processing, desktop publishing, electronic spreadsheet, and database programs.

genetic algorithm Research in which scientists let the computer mimic nature in its quest for a solution to a problem.

geographic information system (GIS) A system in which maps of the United States combined with demographic data from the 1990 U.S. census can be used with special software to help companies choose sites for new stores, manufacturing plants, and other facilities or to plan transportation routes.

geosynchronous orbit An orbit in which a satellite rotates with the earth so that the satellite is always above a given spot.

gigabit A unit of measurement approximately equal to 1 billion bits.

gigabyte A unit of measurement approximately equal to 1 billion bytes.

gigaflop One billion floating-point arithmetic operations per second.

global positioning satellite A satellite that circles the earth and enables a properly equipped car, boat, or plane to determine its location.

glyph A symbol, coded in a document, that cannot be seen by the human eye.

graphical user interface (GUI) A design for the part of a program that interacts with the user and uses icons to represent program features.

graphics accelerator An accessory that is built into the video card and can improve Windows' performance by as much as two or three times.

graphics adapter board A graphics board that plugs into an expansion slot inside a computer and has a monitor plugged into the board.

graphics file A file that arranges and stores the information needed to display a graphic.

Graphics Interchange Format (GIF) A bit-mapped color graphics file format for IBM-compatible computers. GIF is used to exchange graphics on bulletin boards because of its efficient compression technique for high-resolution graphics.

graphics software A program used to create charts, graphs, and drawings.

groupware A type of software designed for sharing information and communicating easily among networked PCs and workstations. An example is Lotus Notes, which enables the members of workgroups to present ideas, organize information, and obtain feedback.

hacker A computer enthusiast who pushes computer systems to his or her highest possible level of performance.

hard copy Printed computer output, differing from the data stored on disk or in memory.

hard disk A storage medium that uses several rigid disks (platters) coated with a magnetically sensitive material and housed in a hermetically sealed mechanism.

hard disk interface An electronic standard for the connection of a hard disk to a computer.

hardware The electronic components, boards, peripherals, and equipment that make up a computer.

hashing The process in which the position of a record is determined through the use of a mathematical computation to produce an address where the unique key field is stored.

head-mounted display (HMD) A set of head-mounted goggles that is an integral part of virtual reality systems and enables users to feel as if they are exploring a real world created within a computer system.

hierarchical database A database that links data using a hierarchical relationship. The data element at the top of the hierarchy is known as the parent element, and there may be several child elements beneath the parent element. The structure that is created resembles a pyramid or an organizational chart.

hierarchy chart The design tool that shows the top-down design of a program; also called a structure chart.

high-density disk A floppy disk that can store 1M or more of data.

high-level language A programming language, such as C, that crudely resembles human language.

hit In an on-line search, items that are returned that match your search terms.

home page In a hypertext system (like the World Wide Web), the point of entry to a group of related documents. Also called a welcome page, the home page contains introductory information as well as hyperlinks to related resources.

host computer The computer responsible for managing the network.

host processor A processor responsible for controlling all peripheral devices as well as the mathematical operations of a network.

Human Genome Project A research project seeking to map the genetic plan of a human being.

hypermedia/hypermedia system A hypertext system that enables the user to navigate through graphics, sound, animation, and video to find data related to a topic. In a hypermedia system, such as the World Wide Web, you click underlined words in a document to access other resources on other computers.

hypertext The nonsequential retrieval of a document's text. The reader pursues trails through the document by means of links.

Hypertext Markup Language (HTML) A language designed to transmit documents that can contain different media formats in the same document: text, graphics, movies, sounds, and hypertext links to other documents and resources.

Hypertext Transfer Protocol (HTTP) The rules, or protocol, of the World Wide Web. HTTP is the Internet standard that supports the exchange of information on the Web. HTTP enables Web authors to embed hyperlinks in Web documents.

Hytelnet A tool that helps you access various sites through Telnet.

IBM compatible A microcomputer that uses all or almost all of the software developed for the IBM Personal Computer and accepts the IBM computer's cards, adapters, and peripheral devices.

icon An on-screen symbol that represents a program, a data file, or some other computer entity or function.

Image APB A criminal investigation service that broadcasts images through paging channels. A sketch or photograph of an individual, such as a missing child, can be sent to every officer who has a portable computer and a pager.

imaging device An important diagnostic tool that is able to take a number of images. Examples are the CAT scanner, MRI, and ultrasound imaging.

impact printer A printer that operates by pressing a physical representation of a character against an inked ribbon, forming an impression on the page.

import To bring information from one program into another program.

incremental backup Backing up of only the files in which changes have been made since the last incremental backup.

indexed file A compact file containing information about the physical location of records in a database file that can be accessed directly or sequentially.

Indexed Sequential Access Method (ISAM) A popular method of file organization because of the flexibility of data retrieval. Many on-line information services use ISAM files to maintain huge bibliographic databases.

indexed sequential file A file whose records can be accessed either directly (randomly) or sequentially; also called an indexed file.

information Data that has been made meaningful and useful.

Information Superhighway A high-speed digital transmission system capable of providing high-speed connectivity to homes, schools, and offices.

information system A computer system specifically designed to help a business process data to produce information.

infrastructure A means of transporting goods and information.

inkjet printer A nonimpact printer that forms an image by spraying ink from a matrix of tiny jets.

input The information entered into a computer for processing purposes.

input device Any peripheral that enables a user to enter data into the computer. Examples are the keyboard, mouse, trackball, voice recognition system, and modem.

insert mode A program mode in which the inserted text pushes existing text to the right and down.

Institute of Electrical and Electronic Engineers (IEEE) A professional society for computer engineers.

instruction set A list of the specific instructions that tell the CPU what to do.

integrate To combine programs or systems for a special purpose.

integrated circuit A semiconductor circuit containing more than one transistor and other electronic components; often referred to as a chip.

Integrated Drive Electronics (IDE) A popular hard disk interface standard that offers high performance at a low cost.

integrated package A single program that combines the features of a word processing program, an electronic spreadsheet, a database management system, and graphics.

Integrated Services Digital Network (ISDN) A system for transmitting voice, video, and data over lines with digital transmission (no analog transmission).

intelligent agent A program that uses some levels of artificial intelligence and is based on general directions rather than specific instructions.

Intelligent Transportation System (ITS) A system, partly funded by the U.S. government, to develop smart streets and smart cars. Such a system can warn travelers of congestion and suggest alternative routes.

intelligent tutoring program An educational computer program that can adapt based on a student's responses, with the computer selecting material for the student to review.

interactive processing Processing performed while directly connected with and accessible to a computer (online) and done as soon as the data is entered.

interactive television Technology developed by cable television companies and telephone companies to connect PCs to televisions, which are connected by cable to a mainframe computer with a large database. Such a network enables users to shop, play games, watch movies, and obtain financial news by sending messages to the central computer. See also *on-demand television*.

interlaced monitor A monitor that refreshes every other line.

internal modem A modem designed to fit into the expansion slot of a personal computer.

Internet A system of linked computer networks that facilitates data communication services, often referred to as the "information highway." An international packet-switching network supported mostly by universities, research centers, and government agencies.

Internet protocols The standards that enable computer users to exchange data through the Internet.

interpreter A translator for high-level programming languages that translates and runs the program at the same time.

intranet A network designed to facilitate communications within an organization, as well as with customers and partners.

IPOS cycle The transformation of data into information through input, processing, output, and storage.

iteration A programming construct in which the same set of instructions is executed as many times as necessary to process all the data; also called a loop.

Java A programming language that can be used to add animation, sounds, and interactive programming to a Web page.

job control language (JCL) Another term for the command interpreter or user interface, which is the part of the system software that communicates with the user.

Joint Photographic Experts Group (JPEG) A group that developed a common graphics format used to store digitally encoded pictures.

joystick An alternative pointing device to a keyboard; joysticks are used primarily for games and computer-aided designs.

justification The alignment of text at the left margin, the right margin, or both margins.

just-in-time (JIT) manufacturing A method of monitoring inventory that triggers the manufacturing process only when inventory levels are low.

kerning The adjustment of the spaces between characters and words.

key field A unique field used to identify a record in a database.

kilobyte (K) The basic unit of measurement for computer memory and disk capacity, equal to 1,024 bytes.

knowledge base A database of if-then knowledge.

label A heading or description that helps someone viewing a spreadsheet to understand it.

landscape mode Page orientation in which the page width is greater than its height.

laptop computer A portable computer that is light and small enough to be held on your lap.

laser printer A popular nonimpact, high-resolution printer that uses a version of the electrostatic reproduction technology of copying machines.

last-mile problem The lack of local network systems for high-bandwidth multimedia communications that can accommodate the Information Superhighway.

leading The space between the lines of text.

leased line A dedicated line provided by the telephone company.

light pen An input device that uses a light-sensitive stylus to draw on-screen or on a graphics tablet, or to select items from a menu.

line graph A graph that uses lines to show the variations of data over time or to show the relationship between two numeric variables.

line printer A printer that can produce text but not graphics.

liquid crystal display (LCD) A small, flat-screen monitor used with laptop computers.

local area network (LAN) Computers within a limited area that are linked by high-performance cables so that users can exchange information and share hardware, software, and data resources.

logic construct A type of construct (simple sequence, condition, iteration, or case) on which all programs are based.

logic error An error that is the result of an incorrect algorithm.

logistics The planning and carrying out of a complex plan, usually involving moving material and people from one location to another.

loop A programming construct in which the same set of instructions is executed as many times as necessary to process all the data; also called an iteration.

low-level language A language, such as machine language or programming language, that describes exactly the procedures to be carried out by a computer's central processing unit.

machine language The native binary language recognized and executed by a computer's central processing unit and consisting of 0s and 1s.

macro A series of keystrokes that you define to automate one or more actions.

magnetic disk The most commonly used type of secondary storage for computer programs and data files.

magnetic tape In secondary storage, a sequential, high-capacity mass storage and backup medium.

magneto-optical (MO) disk An erasable disk that combines magnetic particles used on tape and disk with new optical technology.

mail merge A utility that draws information from a database and incorporates that information into a form document to create multiple copies of the document.

mainboard See *motherboard*.

mainframe computer A multiuser computer designed to meet the computing needs of a large corporation.

maintenance Support required to keep a computer system running properly.

management information system (MIS) A computer-based system that supports the information needs of different levels of management.

massively parallel processors In a supercomputer, a processor containing hundreds of processors so that the supercomputer can perform hundreds of tasks simultaneously.

master file A file containing all the current data relevant to an application.

master page A page showing the way you want the final document to look.

MEDLINE A computer database developed by the National Library of Medicine, with a memory bank of references to 6 million articles from 3,500 medical journals worldwide.

megabyte (M) A measurement of storage capacity equal to approximately 1 million bytes.

megaflop One million floating-point arithmetic operations per second.

megahertz A unit of measurement equal to 1 million cycles per second, commonly used to compare the clock speeds of computers.

membrane-switch keyboard A reliable and durable keyboard that is resistant to hazards like liquids or grease because the keyboard is covered by a protective film.

memory Temporary workspace in a computer.

memory chip A chip located on a computer's motherboard.

microcomputer Any single-user computer with its arithmetic-logic unit and control unit contained on one integrated circuit (the microprocessor); often called a personal computer or PC.

microcomputer specialist A computer specialist who often works with end users by helping them purchase, install, and use their microcomputers.

microfiche A sheet of microfilm that stores reduced images of text or graphic material; provides a fast and cost-effective form of storage for computer output.

microfilm A film that stores reduced images of text or graphic material; provides a fast and cost-effective form of storage for computer output.

microprocessor An integrated circuit containing the arithmetic-logic unit (ALU) and control unit of a computer's central processing unit (CPU).

microwave An electromagnetic radio wave that has a very short frequency.

microwave transmission The use of microwaves to transmit data; used by telephone companies and computer networking utilities.

minicomputer A multiuser computer designed to meet the needs of a small organization or a department in a large organization.

MIPS Millions of instructions per second.

mobile data terminal (MDT) The remote terminal that has access to a mainframe computer at the law enforcement agency's headquarters; the mainframe has a database containing vehicle and driver's license information, including outstanding warrants and criminal records.

modem A hardware accessory needed to link two computers through a telephone system.

modular Top-down program design; the programmer starts thinking generally and then works down to specifics.

modulation The conversion of a digital signal to its analog equivalent, especially for the purposes of transmitting signals using telephone lines.

modulation protocol The standards used to govern the speed by which a modem sends and receives information over the telephone lines.

module A box in a structure chart that indicates a major task the program must accomplish.

molecular manufacturing   Research in computer technology based on devices that use atom switches; also called nanotechnology.

monitor   The complete device that produces an on-screen display; a TV-like display showing the resulting data output.

monochrome   A monitor display that shows one color against a black or white background.

monospaced font   A typeface in which the width of every character is the same; produces output similar to typed characters.

morphing   A special animated graphics technique in which one image appears to change and become something entirely different.

motherboard   A large circuit board containing the computer's central processing unit, microprocessor chips, RAM, and expansion slots; also called a mainboard.

Motion Picture Experts Group (MPEG)   A group that developed standards for video compression to improve the quality of the video on a monitor.

mouse   A palm-size input device with a ball built into the bottom; used to move a pointer to draw, select options from a menu, modify or move text, and issue commands.

multimedia   The presentation of information using graphics, video, sound, animation, and text.

multimedia games   Computer games that usually include text, graphics, and sound and that emphasize interactivity.

multimedia system   A computer system that includes specialized audio devices, such as microphones, CD-ROM drives, cassette tape drives, and music keyboards.

multiplex central wiring   A continuous-wire system in which one wire makes a complete circle throughout the machine, with separate addresses for every function.

multiplexor   A device that combines input signals from many computers and sends the combined signal along the communication channel.

multiprocessing   The use of multiple processors so that a computer system, workstation, or network server can execute more than one instruction, or process more than one program, at the same time.

multiprogramming   The capability of processing many programs concurrently for multiple users. Memory is divided and then allocated to the programs being processed concurrently.

multitasking   The capability of operating system of switching between tasks.

multithreading   The capability of running different parts of one program on different processors.

Musical Instrument Digital Interface (MIDI)   A standard for both cabling and communication between computers and digital musical instruments.

nanosecond   One billionth of a second.

nanotechnology   Research in computer technology based on devices that use atom switches; also called molecular manufacturing.

National Information Infrastructure (NII)   An infrastructure capable of delivering text, graphics, video, and sound almost instantaneously.

National Research and Educational Network (NREN)   A network that will enable linked universities to exchange billions of bits of data per second.

native application   A program that is compatible with the microprocessor of a computer.

natural language   A human language, such as English or Japanese.

needs assessment   A list of all the types of tasks that you want a computer to accomplish.

netiquette   A set of unwritten rules governing the use of e-mail and Usenet newsgroups on the Internet.

network browser   An application that enables the user to search locations on the Internet.

network cable   One of the hardware components needed to create a LAN; this cable can be either a twisted-pair cable or a fiber-optic cable.

network database   A database structure that organizes data in a parent-child relationship; all the relationships among the data items must be determined during the design phase. In a network structure, a child can have more than one parent or no parent at all.

network interface card   An adapter that enables a user to connect a network cable to a microcomputer.

network operating system   The software needed to run a network.

network research specialist   A person who conducts research on the Internet and other on-line services and then writes a report on the results.

neural net/neural network   Computer circuitry that does not use the linear IPOS design used by most computers today but mimics the structure of the human brain. Neural nets "learn" by trial and error and are very good at recognizing patterns and dealing with complexity.

newsgroup   An on-line discussion group.

newsreader   A program designed to access Usenet newsgroups.

node   In a LAN, a connection point that can create, receive, or repeat a message.

nonimpact printer   A printer that forms a text or graphic image by spraying or fusing ink to a page.

noninterlaced monitor   A type of monitor that minimizes flicker and reduces eyestrain.

notebook computer   A portable computer small enough to fit into an average-size briefcase.

numeric coprocessor   A microprocessor support chip that performs mathematical computations at speeds up to one hundred times faster than the arithmetic/logic unit; integrated into newer microprocessor chips.

object code   A version of the program that can be understood by the computer.

object linking and embedding (OLE)   A tool used for joining documents in different applications. Changes in either document are reflected in the other document.

object-oriented database   The newest type of database structure, well-suited for multimedia applications, in which the result of a retrieval operation is an object of some kind, such as a document. Within this object are miniprograms that enable the object to perform tasks, such as displaying a graphic. Object-oriented databases can incorporate sound, video, text, and graphics into a single database record.

object-oriented programming (OOP) A programming technique that creates generic building blocks of a program (the objects). The user then assembles different sets of objects as needed to solve specific problems.

odd parity An error-checking protocol in which the parity bit is set to 1 if the number of 1 digits in a byte adds up to an even number.

on-demand television A British system, serving as a prototype in the U.S., that merges cable television and telephone service to enable subscribers to call into a computer database and order movies or shows "on demand." See also *interactive television*.

on-line information service A for-profit firm that makes current news, stock quotes, and other information available to its subscribers over standard telephone lines.

on-line processing Processing performed while directly connected and accessible to a computer.

open bus system A bus system that has expansion slots on the motherboard.

operating mode The current status of a program, usually displayed by a mode indicator at the bottom of the screen. Common modes are Ready and Wait.

operating system A group of programs that help the computer's components function together smoothly.

optical character recognition (OCR) Recognition of a specific typeface developed to be read by early scanners. OCR devices scan written or typed text and transform it into computer-readable form.

optical disk A large-capacity data storage medium for computers, on which information is stored at extremely high density in the form of tiny pits.

optical mark reader (OMR) A reader that senses magnetized marks made by the magnetic particles in lead from a pencil.

optical processors Experimental processors that use light rather than electrons and are several hundred times faster than the electronic circuits used today.

optical recognition system A scanning device that provides another means of minimizing keyed input by capturing data at the source.

optical scanner A scanning device that captures typed documents, pictures, graphics, or even handwriting for use by a computer.

output The results of processing information shown on a monitor or printer.

output file A file that results from data processing.

packet A small unit of data containing an address, telling the communications hardware where the communication should be sent.

packet-switching network A wide area network that achieves high data-transmission speeds with minimal errors by dividing information into packets that are sent by the most efficient route and then reassembled and checked for accuracy at their destination.

painting program A program that enables you to paint the screen by switching on or off the individual dots or pixels that make up a bit-mapped screen display.

palmtop computer A reduced-size computer with reduced capabilities.

paragraph A unit of text that begins and ends with the Enter keystroke.

parallel conversion In a system conversion, the changing of existing data files to a new format by running both systems for a while to check that the new system gives answers at least as good as those of the old system.

parallel port A connection for the high-speed flow of data along parallel lines to a device, usually a parallel printer.

parallel processing Arranging microprocessors in a parallel pattern rather than a serial pattern; parallel processing can greatly increase the speed of supercomputers.

parallel processors Processors arranged in a parallel pattern to increase the MIPS the computer can accomplish.

parent element A data segment that begins a hierarchy.

parity bit An extra bit added to a data word for parity checking.

participatory learning A learning approach supported by different multimedia products incorporating sound and animation to help preschool and kindergarten children learn to read.

Pascal A computer programming language often used to teach programming to beginning computer science majors.

password A unique word that a user types to log on to a system. Passwords should not be obvious and should be changed frequently.

PCI local bus A bus design that directly connects video circuits with the microprocessor and improves performance.

peer-to-peer model A model in which all the computers can access the public files located on other computers within a network.

performance monitor A monitor used to help maximize the computer's performance by keeping track of what is happening with the various hardware devices.

peripheral device A device connected to and controlled by a computer, but external to the computer's central processing unit.

personal computer (PC) A microcomputer; usually used in reference to an IBM computer or an IBM-compatible computer.

personal digital assistant (PDA) A small, handheld computer that accepts input written on-screen with a stylus; designed to keep phone directories and calendars and to provide calculating capabilities.

personal finance program A program, with built-in calculators, that categorizes expenditures and prints checks; used for personal finances.

personal identification number (PIN) A number used by a bank customer to verify identity when a customer uses an ATM.

personal information manager (PIM) A program that provides four essential functions: contact management, calendar and schedule management, task and project management, and mail merge and print.

personal operation The use of computers by individuals within the company to improve personal productivity.

phased conversion   The changing of existing data files to a new format by implementing the new system one part at a time.

photo-editing program   A specialized graphics program that enables the user to create illustrations with the computer and to remove blemishes, add coloring, and resize pictures.

picture element   The dots that combine to form the image you see on a computer screen.

pie graph   A graph that displays a data series as a circle to emphasize the relative contribution of each data item to the whole.

pilot conversion   The changing of existing data files to a new format one part at a time.

pipelining   A design that provides two or more processing pathways that can be used simultaneously.

pixel   The smallest picture element that a device can display and out of which the displayed image is constructed.

Plain Old Telephone Service (POTS)   A term used to describe the standard analog service.

Platform for Internet Content Selection (PICS)   A voluntary ratings system that is widely endorsed by companies contributing to the Internet, used to inform users of cyberporn on the Internet.

platter   One of several disks that make up the hard disk.

plotter   A printer that produces high-quality output by moving ink pens over the surface of the paper.

plug and play   New technology jointly developed by Intel Corporation and Microsoft and designed so that all a user needs to do is plug in a peripheral and it is ready to work.

point   A unit of measurement equal to 1/72 of an inch.

point-of-sale processing   The recording of payments and new charges to update a master file continually.

point-of-sale (POS) terminal   A cash register connected to a computer that finds the product price and updates store inventory at the time of each sale.

Point-to-Point Protocol (PPP)   An Internet standard providing direct connections through telephone lines.

port   An interface that controls the flow of data between the central processing unit and external devices such as printers and monitors.

portrait mode   Page orientation in which the page height is greater than its width.

power user   A computer user who has gone beyond the beginning stages of computer use. A power user uses the advanced features of application programs, such as software command languages and macros.

presentation package   A software package used to make presentations visually attractive and easy to understand.

primary memory (RAM)   The computer's main working memory where program instructions and data are stored so that they can be directly accessed by the central processing unit through the processor's high-speed data bus.

printer driver   A file containing the information that a program needs in order to print your work on a given brand and model of printer.

private line   A dedicated line provided by the telephone company.

procedure   The steps that must be followed to accomplish a specific computer-related task.

processing   Operations performed on data to transform it in some way.

professional responsibility   A professional standard that involves doing the best job possible even though the user may not immediately recognize the difference between the best job and a poor job.

program   A list of instructions telling the computer what to do.

program file   A file containing instructions written in a programming language to tell the computer what to do.

program trading   A software program used to analyze stock market trends and to obtain buy and sell recommendations on a minute-by-minute basis.

programmable   Capable of being controlled through instructions that can be varied to suit the needs of an individual.

Programmable Read-Only Memory (PROM) chip   A read-only memory chip programmed at the factory for use with a given computer.

programmer   A person trained in the use of a programming language who creates, tests, and documents computer programs.

programming   The creation of a list of stored instructions that tell the computer what to do.

programming language   An artificial language composed of a fixed vocabulary and a set of rules used to create instructions for a computer to follow.

PROM (Programmable Read-Only Memory) chip   See *Programmable Read-Only Memory (PROM) chip*.

prompt   A symbol or phrase appearing on-screen to indicate that the computer is ready to accept input.

proportional font   A font that places more characters on a line and requires a different amount of space based on the shape and needs of each character; a proportional font closely resembles printed text.

proprietary file format   A data-storage format used only by the company that makes a specific program.

protocol   A set of standards for exchanging information.

prototype   A small model developed in the process of systems analysis.

pseudocode   Created in the 1970s as an alternative to flowcharts, a stylized form of writing used to describe the logic of a program.

public data network (PDN)   A network that builds its own high-speed data highways using microwaves, satellites, and optical fiber.

public domain   See *public domain software*.

public domain software   Noncopyrighted software that anyone may copy and use without charge or acknowledging the source.

public file   A file that a user has made available for others to access.

public file archive   Directories of computers that have been set aside to provide free public access to programs and files.

punched card A means for inputting data and instructions into a first-generation computer.

query language One of four parts of a database management system (DBMS) that enables users to ask specific questions of the database.

QWERTY keyboard The standard typewriter keyboard layout, used also for computer keyboards.

RAID (Redundant Array of Inexpensive Disks) A new type of hard disk composed of more than one hundred 5.25-inch disks with a controller mounted in a single box.

random-access file A direct-access file; a file in which an individual item can be accessed.

random-access memory (RAM) Another name for the computer's main working memory, where program instructions and data are stored to be easily accessed by the central processing unit through the processor's high-speed data bus. When a computer is turned off, all data in RAM is lost.

random-access storage medium A magnetic disk, coupled with a disk drive that can store and randomly retrieve data on the disk. If you need the 157th item, the drive head can go directly to that item and read it.

range In a spreadsheet, a rectangular group of cells that is treated as a unit for a given operation.

Rapid Application Development (RAD) A methodology for developing new applications for computers that is quicker than the traditional method of developing systems, and with greater user involvement.

read-only A capability of a file of being displayed but not altered or deleted.

read-only memory (ROM) The part of a computer's primary storage that doesn't lose its contents when the power is turned off.

read/write head The disk drive's magnetic head.

real-time processing The processing of data as soon as it is entered.

record A complete unit of related data items stored in named data fields in a database.

record matching The search of dissimilar computer databases in an attempt to match one record with another on the basis of a common name or Social Security number.

redesigning A process in which system professionals apply CASE tools to an existing system and receive computerized records of the system details.

reduced instruction set computer (RISC) A central processing unit in which the number of instructions the processor can execute is reduced to a minimum to increase processing speed.

reengineering The process of taking a broader look at how to redo a system.

refresh rate The rate at which a monitor and video adapter pass the electron guns of a cathode-ray tube from the top of the display to the bottom. The refresh rate determines whether the display appears to flicker.

relational database One of four database structures in which files are linked in some way.

relative file A special type of direct-access file that does not use a mathematical formula to determine the address of the records, but bases the address on location in the field.

remote terminal A terminal located at some distance from the computer to which it is connected.

repetitive stress injury (RSI) Wrist strain resulting from too much time spent keying in data; RSI can also affect the arms, shoulders, or neck.

report file A file holding a copy of a report in computer-accessible form until it is convenient to print it.

report generator One of four parts of a database management system (DBMS) that helps the user design and generate reports and graphs in hard copy form.

resident program The part of an operating system that stays in primary storage at all times.

resolution A measurement, usually expressed in linear dots per inch (dpi) both horizontally and vertically, of the sharpness of an image generated by an output device such as a monitor or printer.

resource discovery software A set of tools used to explore the Internet. Examples of such software are Archie, Gopher, and Veronica.

results ranking In an on-line search, a ranking that puts the resources returned in an order based on each resource's relevance to your query.

ring topology The physical layout of a local network in which all nodes are attached in a circle, without a central host computer.

robot A computer that outputs motion, not information.

ROM BIOS (Basic Input/Output System) chip See *Basic Input/Output System (BIOS) chip.*

root directory The main directory of a disk.

router A connector between LANs that uses identical protocols; packets are received and examined and then sent on.

row A block of cells running horizontally across a spreadsheet.

run-time program A program that comes with a presentation program and enables a presentation to run without the application.

satellite transmission The transmission of data worldwide by means of satellite.

saving The transferring of information to storage to prevent its loss when the computer is turned off.

schema The structure of a database.

scope The extent of a problem, or project, that you can address.

search engine Software that gives you the ability to search for Internet resources. Search engines are usually accessed through Web browser software.

search item In an on-line search, the words that describe your search topic.

secondary storage A nonvolatile storage medium, such as a disk drive, that stores program instructions and data.

sector A pie-shaped wedge of the concentric tracks encoded on the disk during a low-level format.

segment A group of fields.

sequencer A software program used to play MIDI files.

sequential access An information storage and retrieval technique in which the computer must move through a sequence of stored data items to reach the item to be retrieved.

sequential file A file in which the entries are processed in the order in which they were encoded.

Serial Line Internet Protocol (SLIP) Internet standards providing direct connections through telephone lines.

serial port A port that synchronizes and manages asynchronous communication between the computer and devices such as serial printers, modems, and other computers.

server A high-capacity, high-speed computer with a hard disk; the server controls all or some procedures on a network.

shareware Copyrighted software that may be tried without expense but requires the payment of a registration fee if you decide to use it.

shell A utility program designed to provide an improved user interface for a program or operating system usually considered difficult to use.

shortcut In Windows 95, an icon that provides fast access to a program.

simple sequence A programming construct in which the instructions to the computer are executed in the order in which they appear.

simulation A computer game that reflects aspects of the real world.

site license A contract with the software publisher that allows multiple copies of software to be made for use within an organization.

slide A photographic transparency on film arranged for projection.

slide show A predetermined set of charts and graphs displayed one after the other.

Small Computer System Interface (SCSI) An interface that amounts to a complete expansion bus, into which you can plug devices such as hard disk drives, CD-ROM drives, scanners, and laser printers.

smart card A card that resembles a credit card but has a microprocessor and memory chip. Smart cards are used to access information ranging from a medical history to the purchase of goods where the dollar amount is automatically debited.

smart cars Cars with microprocessors that provide for more control and interaction with the environment. Smart cars can diagnose their own internal problems, operate safely, warn the driver of potential problems, and help with navigation.

smart terminal A terminal with processing capabilities and disk drives so that users can download information.

social computing The capability of ordering goods electronically and automatically billing a customer's credit card.

soft copy A temporary form of output, as in a monitor display.

software System, utility, or application programs expressed in a computer-readable language.

software emulator A program that makes one CPU pretend to be another.

software package A computer program delivered to the user in a complete and ready-to-run form, including all the necessary programs and documentation.

software piracy The making of illegal copies of copyrighted software.

software suite A collection of full-featured, standalone programs that usually share a common command structure and have similar interfaces.

sound board An adapter that adds digital sound reproduction capabilities to an IBM-compatible PC; also called a sound card.

sound card Used to process music in a computer; also called a sound board.

sound file A file containing digitized sound that can be played back if a computer is equipped with multimedia.

source code The typed program instructions that people write before the program has been compiled or interpreted into machine instructions that the computer can execute.

source-data automation An automation system in which keyboards and display units are placed in the most convenient spot for data entry.

spacing The spaces not used by the characters in a document.

special-purpose program A program that performs a specific task, usually for a specific profession.

speech synthesis The capability of a computer of "speaking" through synthesized computer-generated voices.

spell checker A program that looks up words in an electronic dictionary to verify spelling.

spreadsheet The two-dimensional matrix of rows and columns where you can enter headings, numbers, and formulas.

spreadsheet file A file containing one or more spreadsheets created in the proprietary file format of a spreadsheet program.

star topology The physical layout of a local network in which a host computer manages the network.

status line A line of an application program's display screen, usually at the bottom, that describes the state of the program.

storage The retention of program instructions and data within the computer so that this information is available for processing purposes.

stored-program concept The idea, which underlies the architecture of all modern computers, that the program should be stored in memory with the data.

structural unemployment Unemployment caused by advancing technology that makes an entire job obsolete.

structure chart The design tool that shows the top-down design of a program; also called a hierarchy chart.

Structured Query Language (SQL) An IBM-developed query language widely used in mainframe and minicomputer systems.

style and grammar checker A program that electronically checks the style and grammar of your document.

style sheet A collection of styles frequently used in a specific type of document.

stylus A pen-shaped instrument used to select menu options on a monitor screen or to draw line art on a graphics tablet.

subdirectory A directory created in another directory. A subdirectory can contain files and additional subdirectories.

subject directories Web search tools that contain resources classified by subjects in broad categories and multiple levels of subcategories.

subnotebook A special-purpose computer that sacrifices some storage and processing capabilities in order to maintain a low weight.

subordinate module In a structure chart, a module that is one level down from the superordinate module and to which control may be temporarily transferred.

subschema An outline of the fields that a user will be able to use in a database.

Super Video Graphics Adapter (SVGA) An enhancement of the VGA display standard that can display as much as 1,280 pixels by 1,024,768 lines with as many as 16.7 million colors.

supercomputer The largest, fastest, and most expensive type of computer made, designed to execute complex calculations rapidly. Supercomputers are used mostly for scientific research.

superordinate module In a structure chart, the module to which control is transferred after all the instructions in a subordinate module have been executed.

superscalar architecture A design that lets the microprocessor take a sequential instruction and send several instructions at a time to separate execution units so that the processor can execute multiple instructions per cycle.

supervisor program A part of the operating system that remains in storage at all times.

support Maintenance required to keep a computer system running.

surge A momentary and sometimes destructive increase in the amount of voltage delivered through a power line.

surge protector An inexpensive electrical device that prevents high-voltage surges from reaching a computer and damaging its circuitry.

switched lines Telephone lines for which the telephone company switching station determines the telephone line to use.

synchronous transmission The transmission of data between computers at timed intervals.

syntax The rules governing the structure of commands, statements, or instructions that are given to a computer.

syntax error The errors detected by the language translator; a mistake in following the rules of the language.

synthesizer A piece of equipment that uses FM (Frequency Modulation), sampling, or waveguiding technology to produce a sound pattern.

system An organized way to accomplish one or more goals. A system can be natural or artificial (made by people).

system clock The CPU processing function regulator that produces a pulse at regular intervals.

system software All the software used to operate and maintain a computer system, including the operating system and utility programs.

system unit The big box that contains the processing circuitry and storage devices of a computer.

systems analysis A phase of systems development in which the systems analyst or the systems development team determine what the new system should accomplish.

systems analyst A person who creates specifications, calculates feasibility and costs, and implements a computer system. The systems analyst looks at the entire scope of a firm's information-processing activities and tries to devise more effective methods.

systems design A phase of systems development in which the general requirements defined in the analysis phase are converted into detailed specifications for the new system.

systems development life cycle (SDLC) An organized way of creating a system.

systems development/acquisitions A phase of systems development in which the systems analyst either writes the programs that make up the system or acquires the software package that will do the job.

systems implementation A phase of systems development in which the organization adopts the new system.

systems model A model describing the relationship between data and information, showing that data goes into a process and information is output.

task management software Software that organizes and presents tasks both graphically and in the form of "to do" lists.

taskbar In Windows 95, the bar at the bottom of the screen, used for launching applications and switching tasks.

tariff A list of communications services and charges submitted to the government by a common carrier.

TCP/IP support The capability of sending and receiving Internet data packets through the use of special software.

telecommunications The linking of two computers through the telephone system.

telecommunications software Software that transforms a computer into a terminal capable of connecting to a multiuser computer system by means of the telephone.

telecommunications specialist An individual who establishes all the capabilities of a computer system within a company.

telecommuting The combination of telecommunications with computing.

teleconference A meeting in which the participants do not physically meet but use telephones and computers to meet.

teleradiology A recent addition to the imaging field in which the imaging signals, in binary form, are sent over fiber optic communication lines to imaging output equipment some distance away for a radiology expert to read and interpret.

Telnet   A service of the Internet that allows a user to access remote computers outside the user's area. Through Telnet, a user can access libraries, databases, and other public services all over the world.

template   A standard format used to create standardized documents.

terminal   An input/output device consisting of a keyboard and video display and commonly used with multiuser systems.

test   The process of finding hidden errors in a program after the visible logic errors have been eliminated.

text file   A file containing nothing but standard characters such as letters, punctuation marks, and numbers.

thread   All the replies to an interesting article on Usenet.

time bomb   A virus program designed to sit harmlessly on a system until a certain event or date causes the program to become active.

time-sharing   A technique for sharing the resources of a multiuser computer in which each user has the illusion that he or she is the only person using the system.

toolbox   A set of programs with icons and buttons that helps programmers develop software without having to create individual routines from scratch.

top-down   A modular program design in which the programmer starts thinking generally and then works down to specifics.

topology   The physical layout of a local area network.

track   One of several concentric circular bands on computer disks where data is recorded.

trackball   An input device, similar to the mouse, that moves the mouse pointer on-screen.

tracking device   Satellite devices used to pick up signals in order to track either a group of animals or an individual animal that has been tagged.

trade show   An annual meeting in which computer product manufacturers, designers, and dealers display their products.

Traffic Alert and Collision Avoidance System (TACS)   A system that helps pilots avoid air collisions; commercial aircraft are now required to have TACS installed and to use and obey it.

transaction   A sale, purchase, order, or return that is tracked by commercial computer systems. On the Web, the connection that a client makes with a server to request a resource; the server sends the requested resource back to the client, and the client breaks the connection.

transaction file   A file used to store input data until it can be processed.

transaction processing system (TPS)   A system that oversees the day-to-day operations of the company; examples are inventory, accounting, personnel, and manufacturing systems.

transient program   The parts of the operating system that are kept on disk and loaded into primary storage only when needed.

transmission mode   A mode that enables a computer to know where one byte ends and the next byte begins on the transmission medium.

transponder   A microchip, containing unique identification information, that is implanted under the skin of an animal and used to prove ownership of the animal; also a transmitter/receiver that communicates with the Air Traffic Control system.

Trojan horse   A virus disguised as a useful program, but containing hidden instruments to perform a malicious task instead.

Turing machine   A hypothetical general-purpose computer machine, described in a paper by the English mathematician Alan Turing in the late 1930s.

Turing test   A test developed by Alan Turing and used to determine whether a computer could be called intelligent.

twisted-pair cable   A simple, inexpensive, and slow wired transmission medium used in telephone systems.

typeover mode   An editing mode in word processing programs by which new material replaces (types over) existing text.

underlining   A special effect used to enhance a document and draw attention to a specific area.

Uniform Resource Locator (URL)   A code developed to identify a resource on the Internet. Like an address, a URL contains strings of characters that determine which server to connect to and which resource on that server to find.

uninterruptible power supply (UPS)   Provides power to a system for several hours if the power fails.

universal identifier number   In the computer industry, a name for a Social Security number. Universal identifier numbers are used to cross-link databases.

universal product code (UPC)   A label with a series of bars that can be either keyed in or read by a scanner to identify an item and determine its cost.

upload   The transfer of a file from your computer to a remote computer.

Usenet   A collection of more than 5,000 newsgroups.

user   A person who uses a computer and its applications to perform tasks and produce results.

user friendly   Easy to work with.

user-friendly program/system   A program or computer system designed so that individuals who lack computer experience or training can use the system without becoming confused or frustrated.

user interface   The part of the system software that communicates with the user.

user name   The name identifying the person who originates or receives electronic mail.

utility program   A program that assists in maintaining and improving the efficiency of a computer system.

V.32 bis   An early modulation protocol standard that established a data exchange rate of 14400bps.

V.34   The most recent modulation protocol, which permits two similarly equipped modems to exchange data at a rate of 28800bps.

vaccine   An antivirus program designed to protect against computer viruses.

value   A numeric cell entry in a spreadsheet.

value-added network   Enhanced services in which a company will lease dedicated lines and add services in order to improve the communications and then sell the enhanced services.

vector graphics   A graphic image composed of distinct objects that can move independently.

very-large-scale integration (VLSI)   A level of technological sophistication in the manufacturing of semiconductor chips that allows the equivalent of more than 100,000—and up to 1 million—transistors to be placed on one chip.

VESA local bus   A bus design that directly connects video circuits with the microprocessor and improves performance.

video card   Video circuitry that is designed to fit into an expansion bus and that determines the quality of the display and resolution of your monitor.

video digitizer   A voice recognition device that can capture input from any type of video device and transform it.

video memory   Memory capability supplied on graphic boards to enable graphics-intensive programs to run smoothly and quickly.

video RAM (VRAM)   A specially designed random-access memory chip that maximizes the performance of video adapters.

videoconferencing   The sending of video signals as well as telephone and computer data signals.

virtual memory   A means of increasing the size of a computer's random-access memory (RAM) by using part of the hard disk as an extension of RAM.

virtual reality (VR)   A computer technology that immerses the user in the illusion of a computer-generated world.

virtual university   A form of distance education that enables students to complete a degree at home on a computer.

voice recognition system   A system in which the computer recognizes human speech and transforms the recorded words into computer-readable digitized text or instruction.

Voice User Interface (VUI)   A microcomputer interface capable of recognizing spoken input from a variety of individuals.

volatile   Susceptible to loss; a way of saying that all the data disappears forever if the power fails.

VRAM   See *video RAM.*

Web browser   The software that enables you to go from one resource to another by following hyperlinks. Popular browsers include Netscape Navigator, Internet Explorer, and Mosaic. The basic capabilities of a browser are of retrieving documents from the Web, jumping to links specified in the retrieved document, and saving and printing the retrieved documents.

Web database   A Web search tool built by software "robots," or intelligent agents, that travel over the Web to look for subjects and information for the database. The quality of a search tool that uses database technology is determined by how comprehensive the database is and how well the search engine finds what you need and presents it to you.

Web page   A document that you create to share with others on the Web. A Web page can include text, graphics, sound, animation, and video.

Web site   A group of related Web pages.

Webmaster   A person responsible for the visual layout of a Web site, its written content, its links to other locations, and often the techniques to follow up on the customer's inquiry.

what-if question   An important form of exploration in a spreadsheet, in which you change the key variables to see the effect on the results of the computation.

wide area network (WAN)   A computer network that directly connects computers separated by long distances.

wireless transmission   Transmission that uses radio waves, generally over short distances.

word   A unit of information, composed of bits and bytes, that can be stored in one memory location.

word processing   A type of program that transforms a computer into a tool for creating, editing, proofreading, formatting, and printing documents.

word processing software   Software that usually has more features and flexibility than a special-purpose word processor and that has been developed for use on general-purpose computers. For example, word processing software can be updated and allows the importing of documents.

word processor   A special-purpose machine or software program designed to perform word processing (to create, edit, proofread, format, and print documents).

word wrap   A word processing feature that automatically moves words down to the beginning of the next line if they extend beyond the right margin.

work area   The on-screen area in which you build a spreadsheet.

workgroup operation   An operation involving individual departments or other workgroups that handle a specific task.

workstation   A powerful desktop computer designed to meet the computing needs of engineers, architects, and other professionals who need detailed graphic displays; in a LAN, a workstation runs application programs and serves as an access point to the network.

World Wide Web (WWW)   A worldwide hypermedia system that uses the Internet as its transport mechanism.

worm   A virus designed to alter data in memory or on disk.

Write Once, Read Many Compact Disc (WORM CD)   An optical disk drive with storage capacities of up to one terabyte. After data is written, it becomes a read-only storage medium.

zip disk   A removable cartridge that can hold more than 125M on a single 3.5-inch disk.

Answers

The answers provided here are for odd-numbered questions only.

Lesson 1A
Answers to Matching
1. e   3. c   5. a   7. h   9. b
Answers to Multiple Choice
1. c   3. a   5. b   7. b   9. b
Answers to Completion
1. cyberphobia   3. Hardware   5. Bit
7. Microcomputers or personal computers   9. general-purpose

Lesson 1B
Answers to Matching
1. c   3. b   5. g   7. h   9. f
Answers to Multiple Choice
1. d   3. d   5. d   7. a   9. d
Answers to Completion
1. punched cards   3. Lady Augusta Ada Byron
5. second   7. unbundled   9. User friendly

Lesson 2A
Answers to Matching
1. h   3. b   5. c   7. e   9. i
Answers to Multiple Choice
1. c   3. a   5. d   7. c   9. d
Answers to Completion
1. RAM   3. downwardly compatible   5. ASCII
7. ROM BIOS   9. motherboard

Lesson 2B
Answers to Matching
1. j   3. a   5. c   7. d   9. f
Answers to Multiple Choice
1. b   3. a   5. d   7. d   9. d
Answers to Completion
1. backup   3. hashing algorithm   5. sequential
7. sequential   9. CD-R drive

Lesson 2C
Answers to Matching
1. d   3. b   5. e   7. a   9. j
Answers to Multiple Choice
1. c   3. c   5. c   7. b   9. b
Answers to Completion
1. picture element or pixel   3. Keying mistakes
5. mouse   7. banking   9. scanner

Lesson 2D
Answers to Matching
1. h   3. j   5. i   7. a   9. f
Answers to Multiple Choice
1. d   3. c   5. d   7. b   9. a
Answers to Completion
1. massively parallel processor   3. gigaflop   5. notebook
7. embedded computer   9. workstation

Lesson 3A
Answers to Matching
1. e   3. c   5. b   7. d   9. j
Answers to Multiple Choice
1. b   3. a   5. b   7. b   9. b
Answers to Completion
1. operating system   3. Multitasking   5. UNIX
7. program or software   9. DOS

Lesson 3B
Answers to Matching
1. g   3. q   5. d   7. a   9. b
11. r   13. o   15. l   17. m
Answers to Multiple Choice
1. c   3. c   5. a   7. c   9. b
11. b   13. c
Answers to Completion
1. Machine Language   3. Spaghetti   5. mnemonic
7. generations   9. HTML   11. Syntax   13. Module

Lesson 4A
Answers to Matching
1. h   3. e   5. g   7. i   9. j
Answers to Multiple Choice
1. a   3. a   5. b   7. e   9. c
Answers to Completion
1. beta   3. prototype   5. documentation
7. BIOS   9. Structured programming

Lesson 4B
Answers to Matching
1. d   3. j   5. e   7. f   9. g
Answers to Multiple Choice
1. c   3. c   5. d   7. e   9. a
Answers to Completion
1. Management Information Systems
3. business operations, objectives of the enterprise
5. Help Desk   7. System   9. information system

Lesson 5A
Answers to Matching
1. c   3. f   5. g   7. j   9. d
Answers to Multiple Choice
1. a   3. c   5. c   7. c   9. d
Answers to Completion
1. typeover   3. Justification   5. landscape
7. proportional   9. macros

Lesson 5B
Answers to Matching
1. e   3. j   5. d   7. h   9. i
Answers to Multiple Choice
1. d   3. d   5. a   7. c   9. c
Answers to Completion
1. @AVG   3. B3   5. block or range   7. active cell   9. productivity

Lesson 5C
Answers to Matching
1. f   3. j   5. h   7. e   9. i
Answers to Multiple Choice
1. d   3. d   5. a   7. a   9. d
Answers to Completion
1. flat   3. query language   5. hierachical
7. hierarchical   9. data sercurity

Lesson 6A
Answers to Matching
1. i   3. c   5. j   7. b   9. f
Answers to Multiple Choice
1. a   3. d   5. d   7. c   9. d
Answers to Completion
1. run-time program   3. video   5. Hypertext
7. information kiosk   9. slides

Lesson 6B
Answers to Matching
1. i   3. c   5. j   7. b   9. f
Answers to Multiple Choice
1. a   3. a   5. d   7. d   9. b
Answers to Completion
1. graphic   3. bundle   5. Task management
7. animation graphics   9. digitizing tablet

Lesson 7A
Answers to Matching
1. j   3. c   5. h   7. d   9. i
Answers to Multiple Choice
1. b   3. a   5. c   7. c   9. b
Answers to Completion
1. Analog signals   3. communication channel   5. telecommuting
7. public domain   9. online information service

Lesson 7B
Answers to Matching
1. f   3. g   5. b   7. h   9. i
11. l   13. o   15. p
Answers to Multiple Choice
1. b   3. c   5. d   7. a
9. c   11. f   13. b   15. a
Answers to Completion
1. local area   3. network interface card   5.   host
7. wide area network or WAN   9.   tariff
11. the World Wide Web   13. Star or ring or bus

Lesson 8A
Answers to Matching
1. i   3. g   5. a   7. b   9. h
Answers to Multiple Choice
1. b   3. d   5. d   7. a   9. a
Answers to Completion
1. Internet   3. Internet   5. Unix
7. school or educational institution   9. Web site

Lesson 8B
Answers to Matching
1. f   3. j   5. i   7. g   9. h
Answers to Multiple Choice
1. a   3. b   5. b   7. c   9. a
Answers to Completion
1. engine   3. Boolean operators   5. Webmaster
7. HTTP or Hypertext Transfer Protocol
9. Uniform Resource Locator or URL

Lesson 9A
Answers to Matching
1. e   3. c   5. j   7. d   9. b
Answers to Multiple Choice
1. b   3. a   5. b   7. b   9. d
Answers to Completion
1. ethics   3. Shareware   5. site license   7. cracker
9. competency

Lesson 9B
Answers to Matching
1. h   3. e   5. g   7. a   9. f
Answers to Multiple Choice
1. d   3. c   5. b   7. c   9. a
Answers to Completion
1. defragmentation   3. Wrist rests, ergonomic keyboards
5. color blindness   7. surge protector   9. monitors

Lesson 9C
Answers to Matching
1. h   3. i   5. a   7. e   9. g
Answers to Multiple Choice
1. b   3. b   5. a   7. c   9. d
Answers to Completion
1. Privacy   3. e-mail   5. Cyberporn   7. virus
9. European Commission

Lesson 9D
Answers to Matching
1. g   3. i   5. j   7. b   9. f
Answers to Multiple Choice
1. d   3. a   5. d   7. c   9. b
Answers to Completion
1. natural   3. robot   5. artificial life or a-life
7. atom   9. glyphs

Lesson 10A
Answers to Matching
1. c   3. d   5. i   7. g   9. b
Answers to Multiple Choice
1. c   3. c   5. c   7. d   9. d
Answers to Completion
1. excellent   3. OCR or optical character recognition
5. trade show   7. disabilities   9. structural unemployment

Lesson 10B
Answers to Matching
1. f   3. b   5. g   7. i   9. j
Answers to Multiple Choice
1. d   3. d   5. c   7. c   9. a
Answers to Completion
1. head-mounted display, sensor gloves   3.   cashless
5. Robots or Robotics   7. personal identification number (PIN)
9. Litigation support

Lesson 10C
Answers to Matching
1. c   3. j   5. a   7. b   9. f
Answers to Multiple Choice
1. b   3. c   5. b   7. b   9. a
Answers to Completion
1. DNA   3. robots   5. teleradiology   7. MEDLINE   9. satellites

Lesson 11A
Answers to Matching
1. h   3. d   5. a   7. b   9. f
Answers to Multiple Choice
1. b   3. c   5. c   7. d
Answers to Completion
1. needs assessment   3. modem   5. graphics accelerator
7. Power Macintosh

Lesson 12A
Answers to Matching
1. c   3. h   5. i   7. f   9. g
Answers to Multiple Choice
1. d   3. d   5. a   7. b   9. d
Answers to Completion
1. Multimedia   3. simulation   5. WORKLINK
7. edutainment   9. Distance learning

Lesson 12B
Answers to Matching
1. h   3. g   5. j   7. d   9. i

Answers to Multiple Choice
1. c   3. d   5. d   7. d   9. a

Answers to Completion
1. smart car   3. global positioning satellites   5. transponder
7. airline reservation system   9. ALVINN or Prometheus

Lesson 12C
Answers to Matching
1. c   3. h   5. j   7. e   9. d

Answers to Multiple Choice
1. d   3. a   5. c   7. d   9. a

Answers to Completion
1. NCIC 3. Software piracy 5. bulletin board systems
7. lock   9. Database

Lesson 12D
Answers to Matching
1. e   3. d   5. j   7. b   9. a

Answers to Multiple Choice
1. a   3. a   5. a   7. b   9. b

Answers to Completion
1. multimedia   3. games   5. gaming
7. sound card   9. digital

INDEX

Symbols

A

B

C

ISPs (Internet service providers), 8:5-8:6
IT (Information Technology), 4:19-4:20
  CIO (Chief Information Officer), 4:21
  CKO (Chief Knowledge Officer), 4:21
  client-server computing, 4:27
  computer architecture, 4:27
  data collection, 4:25
  data warehousing, 4:28
  DBMS applications, 4:27-4:28
  electronic commerce, 4:28
  hierarchical organization, 4:24
  operational managers, 4:21
  organizing, 4:25
  projects, 4:25
  ranking, 4:22-4:23
  staff, 4:22
iteration logic constructs, 3:26

J

Java, 3:39, 8:22-8:23
Java Beans, 3:44
JCL (Job Control Language), 3:6
JIT (Just-In-Time) manufacturing, 10:26
jobs, see career opportunities
joysticks, 2:47
JPEG, 2:30
justifying text, 5:6

K

kerning, 5:11-5:12, 5:19
key fields, 2:35
  relational databases, 5:38
keyboard input, 2:44-2:46
killer applications, 3:33
kilobits, 7:6
kilobytes, 1:11-1:13
knowledge base, 9:50-9:51
knowledge management, see IT

L

labels (spreadsheets), 5:21-5:22
Landscape mode (desktop publishing view), 5:9
languages
  natural, 9:50
  programming, 3:22, 3:31-3:32
    assembly, 3:32
    BASIC, 3:35
    C/C++, 3:35
    COBOL, 3:35
    FORTRAN, 3:35
    high-level, 3:34
    HTML, 3:39-3:40
    Java, 3:39
    machine, 3:32
    OOP (object-oriented programming), 3:42-3:44

Pascal, 3:35
    Web development, 3:39
  translators, 1:42, 3:36-3:37
LANs (local area networks), 1:40, 7:29-7:33
laptop computers, 2:74
laser printers, 2:56
last mile problem, 7:7, 8:3
law enforcement, 12:35-12:41
law firms, 9:23-9:24, 10:23-10:24
LCDs (Liquid Crystal display), 2:52
leading, 5:11
leased lines, WANs (wide area networks), 7:33
libraries (clip art), 6:12
life forms (dance), 12:49-12:50
light pens, 2:48
line graphs (spreadsheets), 5:27
line printers, 2:56
loading, 3:4-3:5
local area networks, see LANs
logic constructs (programs), 3:26
logic errors, debugging, 3:30
logistics (delivery services), 12:25
LOGO, 3:37
loop logic constructs, 3:26
Lotus 1-2-3, 5:20-5:21
  color-coded maps, 5:28
  control panel, 5:20
Lotus SmartSuite, 6:18
low-level languages, 1:12

M

machine language, 1:12, 3:30, 3:32
Macintosh finder, 2:33
Macintosh System 7.5, 3:14
  multitasking, 3:6
Macintosh System 8, 3:15
magnetic disks, 2:24
macros, 5:8
  spreadsheets, 5:28
magnetic tape, 2:23
  R-DATs, 2:23-2:24
  sequential access, 2:23
magneto-optical disks, 2:28
mail merge, 5:8
mail, see e-mail
mainframes, 1:18, 2:68-2:69
maintenance, systems, 4:5
Management information systems (MIS), see IT
manufacturing, 10:24-10:26
master files (data-processing applications), 2:35
master pages, 5:9
MCA bus, 2:8
medicine, 10:36-10:37
megabits, 7:6
megabytes, 1:11-1:13, 2:23
megaflops, 2:68
membrane-switch keyboards, 2:45

memory, 1:11-1:13
  cache memory, 2:16
  chips, 2:13
  future progress, 9:54
  primary, 2:13
  purchasing considerations, 11:8-11:9
  RAM, 2:13, 2:16
  virtual, 2:16
  Windows 95 system requirements, 3:11
merging documents software (PIMs), 6:21
MICR systems, 10:22
microcomputers, 1:18, 1:39, 2:6, 2:65, 2:70, 2:72-2:73
  millenium bug, 4:8
  specialists, 10:7
microfilm/microfiche, 2:56-2:58
microprocessors, 1:39, 2:11-2:12
  cache chips, 2:16
  chips, 2:6
  CISC, see CISC
  CPU view, 2:5
  DEC, 2:12-2:13
  external data bus, 2:7
  internal data bus, 2:7
  internal view, 2:14-2:15
  Motorola chips, 2:12
  Pentium chips, 2:10-2:12
  purchasing, 11:7-11:8
  RISC, see RISC
  ROM BIOS chips, see ROM
Microsoft
  IIS (Internet Information Server), 7:39
  SQL Server, 7:39
  Systems Management Services, 7:39
microwaves
  communication channels, 7:22
  transmissions, 7:6
  WANs (wide area networks), 7:33
MIDI (Musical Instrument Digital Interface), 6:3-6:5, 12:48-12:49
middleware, 7:40
.mil domain name, 8:5
millennium bug, 2:36, 4:7-4:8
Minicomputers, 1:18, 1:38, 2:69-2:70
  motherboards, 2:17
MIPS (Millions of Instructions per Second), 9:56
MIS, see IT
mnemonics (programming), 3:34
mobile data terminals, 12:39
models
  LANs (local area networks), 7:31-7:32
  simulating complex systems, 10:35-10:36
modems, 2:17, 7:4-7:5, 8:12
  purchasing considerations, 11:10
  speeds, 8:27-8:28
modulation, 7:4-7:5

Autonomous Land Vehicle in the Neural Network, 12:27-12:28
cruise ships, 12:28
delivery services, 12:25-12:27
fuels, 12:27
trains, 12:27-12:28
travel guides, 12:27
Trojan Horse (virus), 9:38-9:40
troubleshooting programs, 3:24
TrueBASIC, 3:37
TRW (credit reporting), 9:34
turing machines, 1:31-1:32
Turing test, 1:32, 9:47-9:49
tutoring (education with computers), 12:7-12:8
twisted-pair cables, 7:6, 7:22
typefaces, 5:7
Typeover mode, 5:5

U

underlining text, 5:6
Uniform Resource Locators, *see* **URLs**
United States Privacy legislation, 9:39-9:40
UNIVAC, 1:33
universal identification numbers, 12:38
UNIX, 3:15
C/C++ programming, 3:35
UPCs (universal product code), 10:21
uploading, 7:10
UPS (uninterruptible power supply), 9:21
URLs (Uniform Resource Locators), 8:5-8:6, 8:21-8:22
Usenet (newsgroups), 8:7, 8:11
utility programs, 3:15

V

V.32 bis modem, 7:5
V.34 modem, 7:5
vaccines (viruses), 9:38-9:40
values (spreadsheets), 5:21
VANs (Value-added networks), 7:36
VBA (Visual Basic for Applications), 3:43, 4:12
Office 97, 6:20
VBScript, 3:43
VCL (Visual Component Library), 3:44
vector graphics, 6:23
version numbers (software), 4:5
 high-level programming languages, 3:37-3:40
 cal bus, 11:9
 ferencing, 6:23, 7:12,
 purchasing
 s), 11:9

video digitizers, 2:52
video games, 1:14-1:15
video memory, 2:55
virtual memory, 2:16
virtual reality, 9:53-9:55
manufacturing, 10:26
virtual universities, 12:11
viruses (vaccines), 9:38-9:40
VisiCalc, 1:40, 5:20
Visual Basic, 3:43
Visual Basic for Applications, *see* **VBA**
Visual Component Library, *see* **VCL**
VLSI (very large scale integration), 1:39
voice-grade transmission, 7:24
voice recognition devices, 2:50-2:51
volatile media (RAM), 2:16
volatile storage media, 2:23
VRAM, 2:55, 11:9
VUI (Voice User Interface), 2:51

W

WANs (wide area networks), 1:40, 7:33-7:34
weather analysis, 10:36-10:39
Web browsers, *see* **browsers**
Web databases, 8:23
AltaVista, 8:25-8:26
see also search engines
Web domain name, 8:6
Web sites, 10:16-10:17
WEB-TV, 8:12
Webmasters, 8:27, 10:7
wide area networks, *see* **WANs**
wideband transmission, 7:24
windows, multitasking, 3:6
Windows 95, 3:10-3:11
Explorer directory, 2:33
multithreading, 3:6
Plug and Play feature, 3:11, 11:5
Windows 98, 3:11-3:12
Internet Explorer 4.0, 3:11-3:14
WinZip, 7:23
wiretapping, 9:33
wireless transmission (future progress), 9:57-9:58
wiring
coaxial cables, 7:22
fiber optic, 7:22
LANs (local area networks), 7:30
twisted-pair, 7:22
WANs (wide area networks), 7:33
wizards, 4:12
Excel spreadsheets, 5:24
word processing, 5:3-5:5
boldface, 5:6
checkers, 5:8
compared to desktop publishing, 5:12, 5:19
cutting and pasting, 5:5
editing, 5:5

find and replace, 5:6
fonts, 5:7
formatting, 5:6
Insert mode, 5:5
justifying text, 5:6
macros, 5:8
mail merge, 5:8
paragraphs, 5:5
printing documents, 5:7
saving documents, 5:7
thesaurus, 5:8
Typeover mode, 5:5
underlining, 5:6
word wrap, 5:5
see also text editors
word size, 2:6
word wrap (word processing), 5:5
workgroups (groupware), 3:16
worksheets, *see* **spreadsheets**
workstations, 2:70-2:71
WORM CDs (Write Once, Read Many Compact Disc), 2:28
worms (virus), 9:38-9:40
WWW (World Wide Web), 8:4
browsers, 8:5-8:6, 8:21
client/server architecture, 8:20-8:21
connecting, 8:27-8:28
HTML, 3:39-3:40
hyperlinks, 8:21
hypertext, 8:21
Internet association, 8:20-8:21
Java, 8:22-8:23
pages, 8:25-8:27
programming languages, 3:39
searching, 8:23, 8:25-8:26
Web sites, 8:20-8:22, 8:26-8:27
URLs, 8:21-8:22
Virtual Web Library, 8:25-8:26

X-Z

X.25 networking protocol, 7:24
Y2K, *see* **millenium bug**
Yahoo!, 8:23
Zip disks, 2:26